AF575762

GUSTAV KLIMT

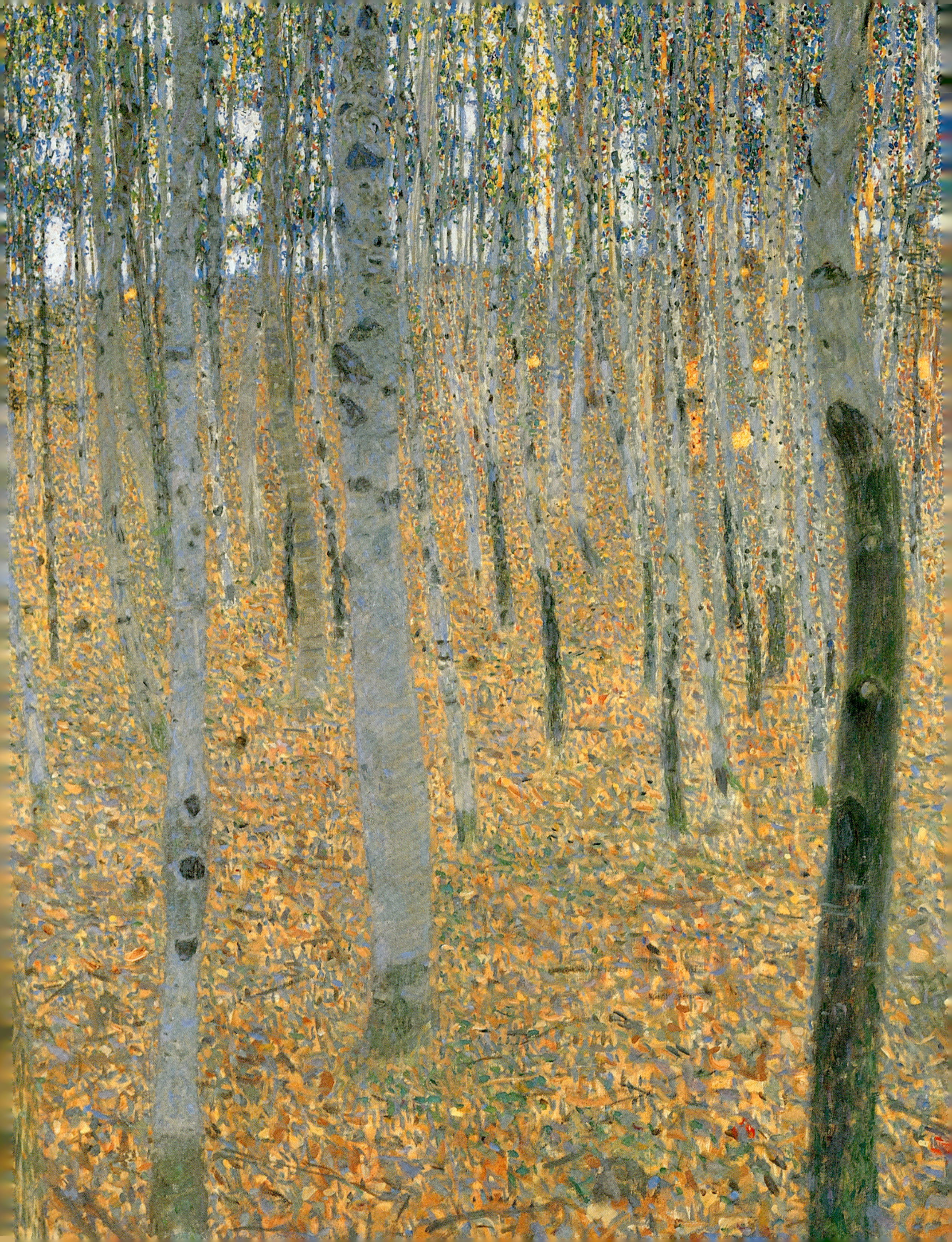

ART MASTER

GUSTAV KLIMT

A N HODGE

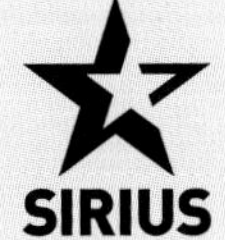

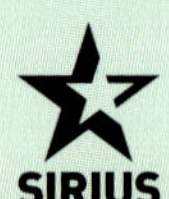

This edition published in 2024 by Sirius Publishing, a division of
Arcturus Publishing Limited,
26/27 Bickels Yard, 151–153 Bermondsey Street,
London SE1 3HA

ISBN: 978-1-3988-5096-5
AD006171UK

Printed in China

CONTENTS

Introduction 6

CHAPTER 1
The Artist as a Young Man 8

CHAPTER 2
The Secession Years 20

CHAPTER 3
Femmes Fatale 42

CHAPTER 4
Landscapes 58

CHAPTER 5
The Later Works 76

Timeline 92

Further information 93

List of illustrations 94

Index 96

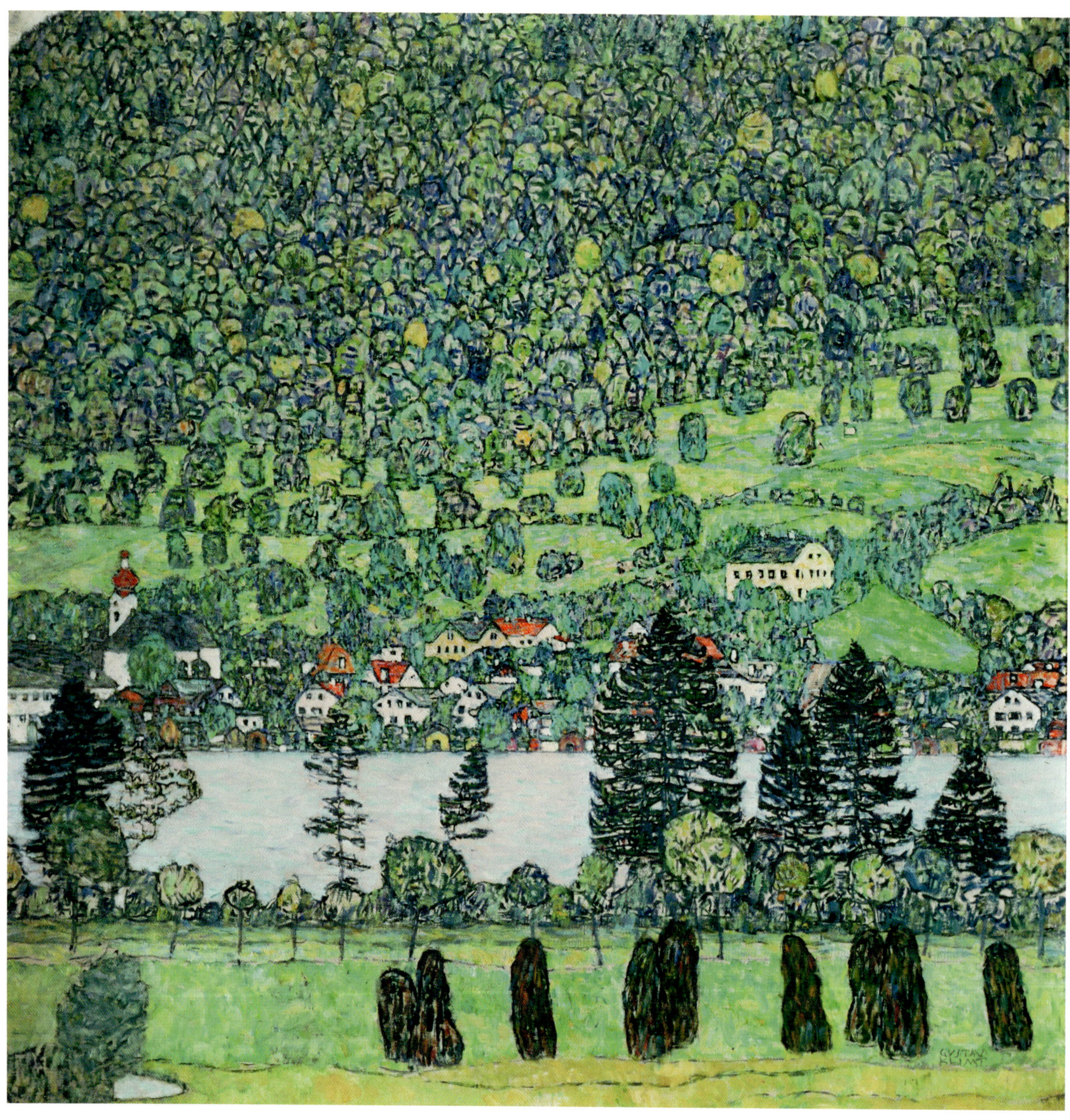
GUSTAV
KLIMT

INTRODUCTION

Gustav Klimt (1862–1918) occupies a unique position in the history of art. Born in Vienna towards the end of the nineteenth century, his art initially reflected the city's academic tradition. Before long, however, his paintings began to look like nothing the world had seen. Putting symbolism at the forefront of his work, Klimt created exotic, sensuous portrayals of women whose otherworldly demeanour recalled the art of ancient civilizations. Over time, he developed an elaborate technique using gold and silver leaf to decorate his paintings, often further ornamenting them with patterns and decorations drawn from an array of sources, including Byzantine mosaics and Egyptian murals.

Although Klimt's paintings became increasingly intricate and mysterious, the artist's own life was relatively straightforward. An introverted character, Klimt valued his privacy and lived modestly, mainly surrounded by family. In 1897, he found himself unwittingly thrust into the limelight as the leader of the Vienna Secession, a radical movement that saw value in all the arts while wanting to free art from the stifling confines of conservative, late nineteenth-century Vienna.

Alongside a desire to live a quiet life, Klimt was a man of few words who wrote very little other than a handful of postcards. The little that he has written has therefore been seized upon and pored over for clues, the obvious danger here being that people can easily read too much into what was intended as a fairly casual remark. Indeed, in one of his rare pronouncements, he talks about keeping his own life separate from his art, while tantalizingly suggesting that there were many pointers to be found in his paintings:

> There is nothing special about me. I am a painter who paints day after day from morning until night. Figures and landscapes, portraits less often.
>
> I have the gift of neither the spoken nor the written word, especially if I have to say something about myself or my work. Even when I have a simple letter to write I am filled with fear and trembling as though on the verge of being sea-sick. For this reason people must do without an artistic or literary self-portrait. And this should not be regretted. Whoever wants to know something about me – as an artist, the only notable thing – ought to look carefully at my pictures and try to see in them what I am and what I want to do. *

This hardworking, straightforward approach to his work is backed up by photographs that show an unremarkable stocky, bearded man dressed in a long robe and sandals. We know too that he loved routine, taking his breakfast at the same place, the Tivoli Café in Schönbrunn, every morning and seldom travelling anywhere, much less abroad. He never married, but had relationships with women who were often his models, and fathered a number of illegitimate children. His affairs were discreet and never appeared to ruffle any feathers. It is also clear that he defended his pictures fiercely when under attack and insisted on getting the price for them he believed he deserved.

It might seem surprising, perhaps even disappointing, that Klimt, given his unexceptional life, became the greatest artist of fin-de-siècle Vienna with an influence that stretches to this day. This book, part of *The Great Artists* series, explores the work of this intriguing and enigmatic Art Nouveau figure and attempts to unravel the many contradictions that lie at the heart of his complex, visionary paintings.

Forest Slope in Unterach on the Attersee, *1916. Working on an easel in the open air, Gustav Klimt painted many landscapes on the calm shores of Lake Attersee while on holiday with his companion Emilie Flöge.*

*from an undated statement, Vienna City Library

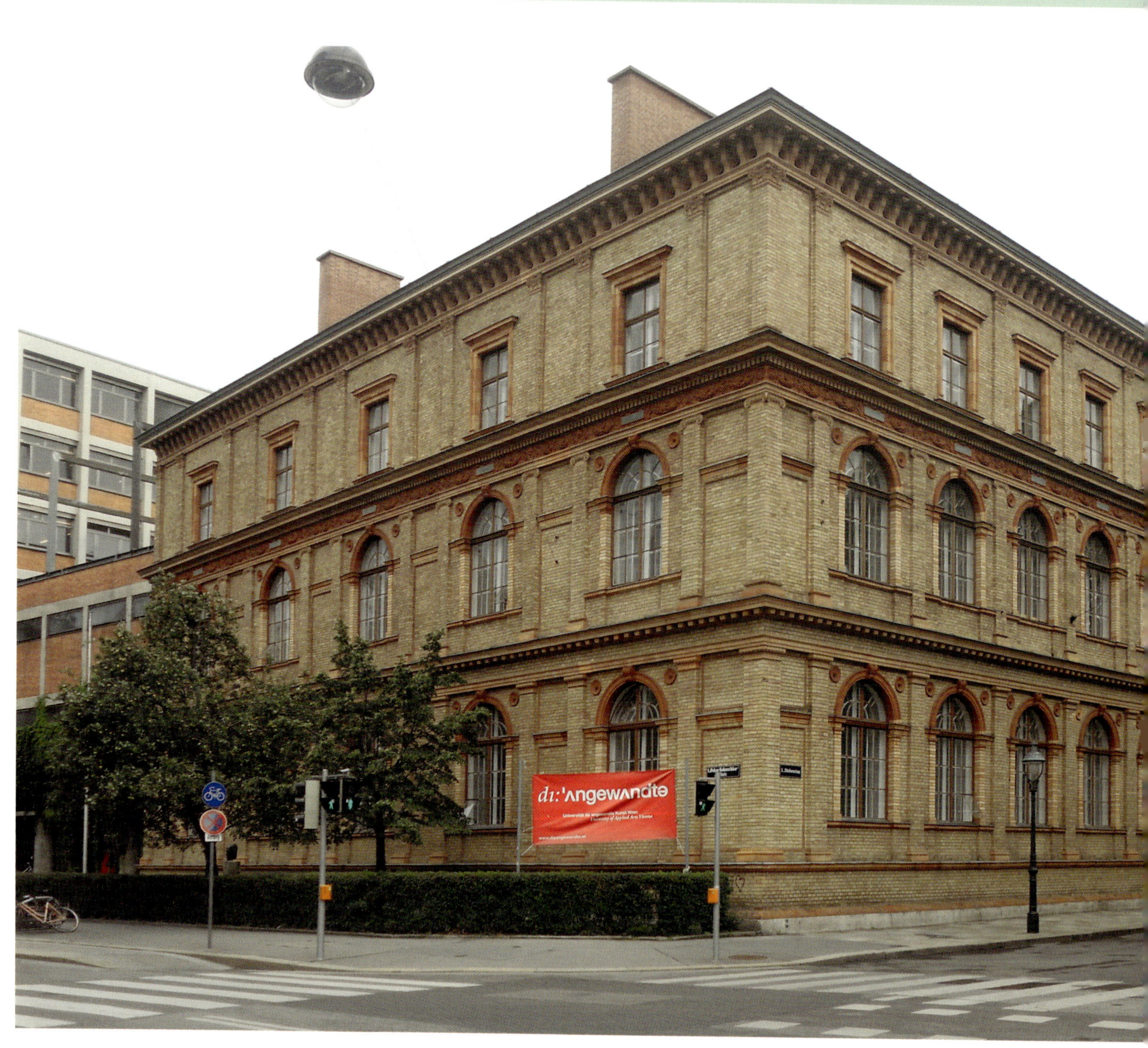

Founded in 1863, the Kunstgewerbeschule (the Vienna School of Arts and Crafts) was set up to provide an advanced education for artists and designers. The building now houses the University of Applied Arts.

CHAPTER 1
The Artist as a Young Man

Gustav Klimt was born in Baumgarten, a rural suburb of Vienna, on 14 July 1862. Although his family was by no means wealthy, they were artistic. His father, Ernst Klimt (1834–92), was a gold engraver by trade. Originally from a peasant family in Bohemia (now part of the Czech Republic), Ernst emigrated to Austria in search of work. Here he met and married a local Viennese girl Anna Finster (1836–1915) and the couple went on to have seven children – three boys and four girls. Anna originally had high hopes of becoming an opera singer, an ambition that stalled once she became a mother.

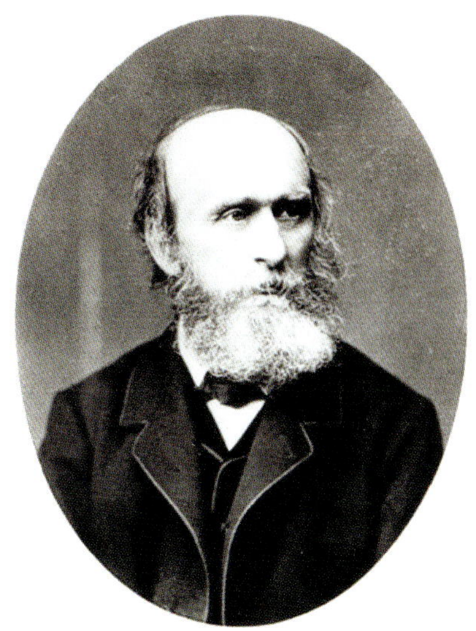

Rudolf Eitelberger von Edelberg (1817–85) who founded the Kunstgewerbeschule.

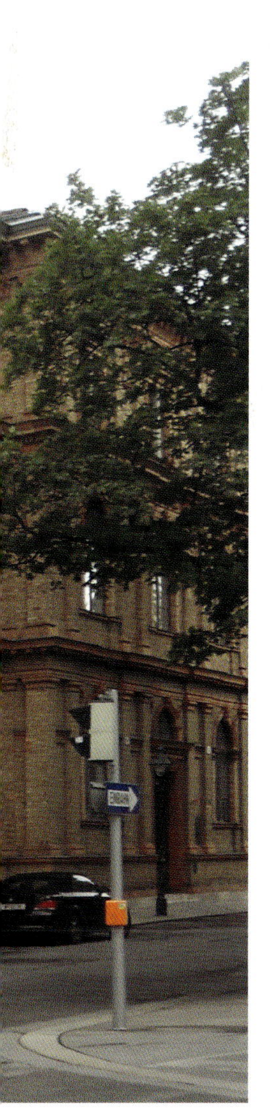

Despite working with rich metals, Ernst struggled to provide for his growing family, particularly after the Panic of 1873, a depression that began when the Vienna Stock Exchange crashed. Further tragedy hit the family a year later: when Klimt was 12, his five-year-old sister Anna died and not long afterwards his sister Klara had a mental breakdown. An hereditary predisposition towards mental illness was something that troubled Klimt throughout his life. For the time being, however, his family's ongoing financial struggle meant that he needed to focus his mind on turning his precocious talent for drawing to good use. He was encouraged to leave school at 14 to enter the Kunstgewerbeschule (the Vienna School of Arts and Crafts), the idea being that he might be able to contribute to the family finances by becoming an art teacher. Klimt was not the only one in the family to demonstrate an early artistic talent. His younger brothers Ernst and Georg Klimt also produced work that showed exceptional skills in art and design, and both would join their elder brother at the School of Arts and Crafts over the next couple of years.

Klimt studied at the Kunstsgewerbeschule for seven years – from 1876 to 1883. Opened in 1864, it was a new institution modelled on London's Metropolitan School of Design, based in South Kensington (which would later become the Royal College of Art). The Principal, Professor Rudolf Eitelberger von Edelberg, was a reformer who looked to the English Arts and Crafts movement for inspiration. He saw all art forms as being of equal importance and believed that there should be no distinction between art and crafts – arguing that all the art forms should be brought together under the umbrella term *Gesamtkunstwerk*, or total artwork.

The education that Gustav received was traditional and thorough: he learnt the techniques of metalwork, mosaic and fresco and was exposed to work from different eras and cultures, including Greek and Egyptian art. Pupils at the School were encouraged to copy the work of other artists, to study perspective and refer to the classical model when constructing their drawings. Klimt was exceptionally talented at drawing and took this and decorative painting as his specialized subjects. Recognized as an exceptionally gifted student, Klimt was singled out to study under the prestigious painter Ferdinand Julius Laufberger (1829–81). The predominate influences on Klimt in these early years were Lawrence Alma-Tadema (1836–1912), the Dutch painter who settled in England and specialized in paintings of classical antiquity and Hans Makart (1840–84), a Viennese contemporary whose huge canvases evoking colourful, decorative historical scenes were much admired by Klimt. At this early stage there was very little to suggest that this model student would radically break free from the traditional, almost entirely academic approach for which he was so skilled – much less that he would be the initiator of a whole new artistic movement.

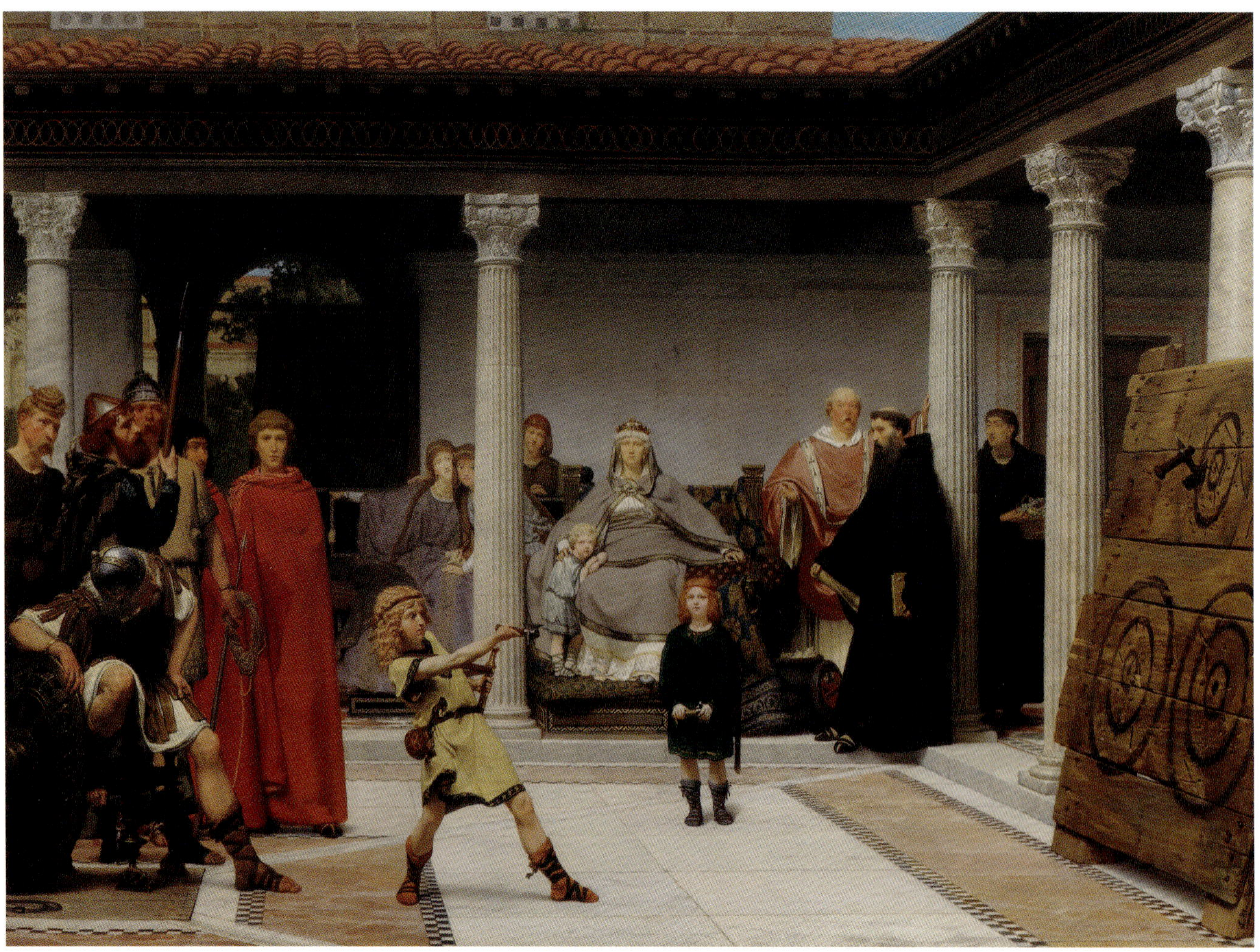

The Education of the Children of Clovis, *Lawrence Alma-Tadema, 1861. Klimt admired the Dutch painter for his draftsmanship and depictions of classical antiquity. In this work, Queen Clotilde, the wife of King Clovis, is shown training her three young children to hurl an axe to avenge the death of her father.*

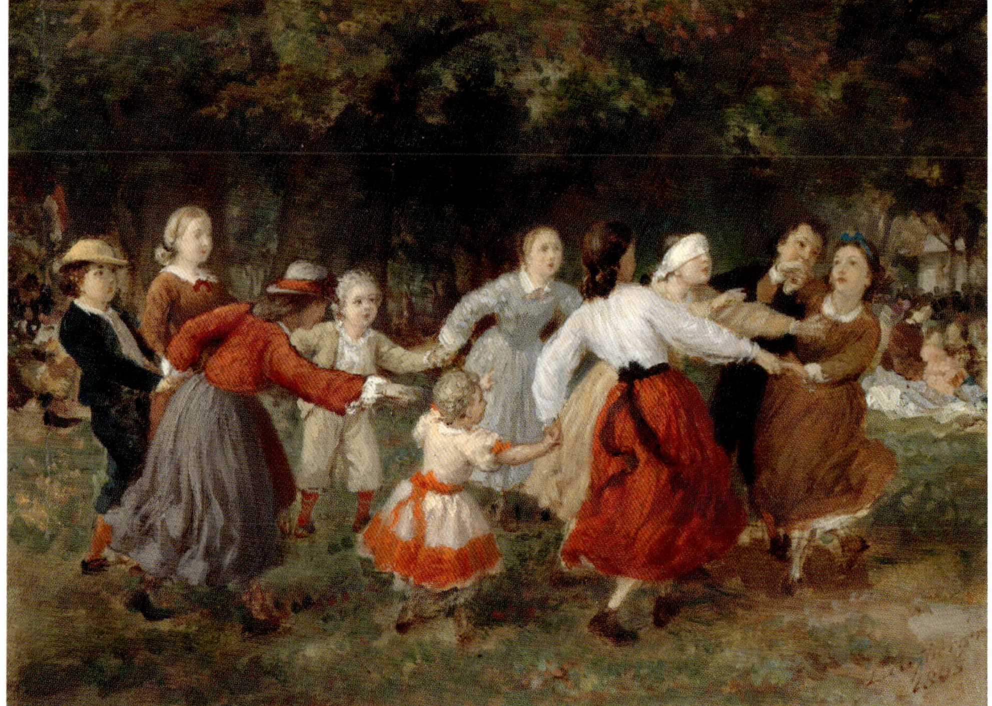

Das Blinde Kuh Spiel, *Ferdinand Laufberger, 1865. Laufberger was appointed professor of figurative drawing and painting at the newly established Kunstgewerbeschule in 1868. In Laufberger's depiction of the children's game, the blind cow stumbles around trying to catch hold of its tormentors.*

In 1877 Gustav's brother, Ernst and their friend Franz von Matsch (1861–1942) also enrolled in the school. The two brothers and their friend shared a studio and began working together, and by 1880 they had started to receive commissions. A strong economy and Vienna's massive building boom, particularly on the Ringstrasse – the new boulevard constructed around the city – helped the three young artists and their fledgling business known as the Painters' Company (Künstler Compagnie) get plenty of paid work.

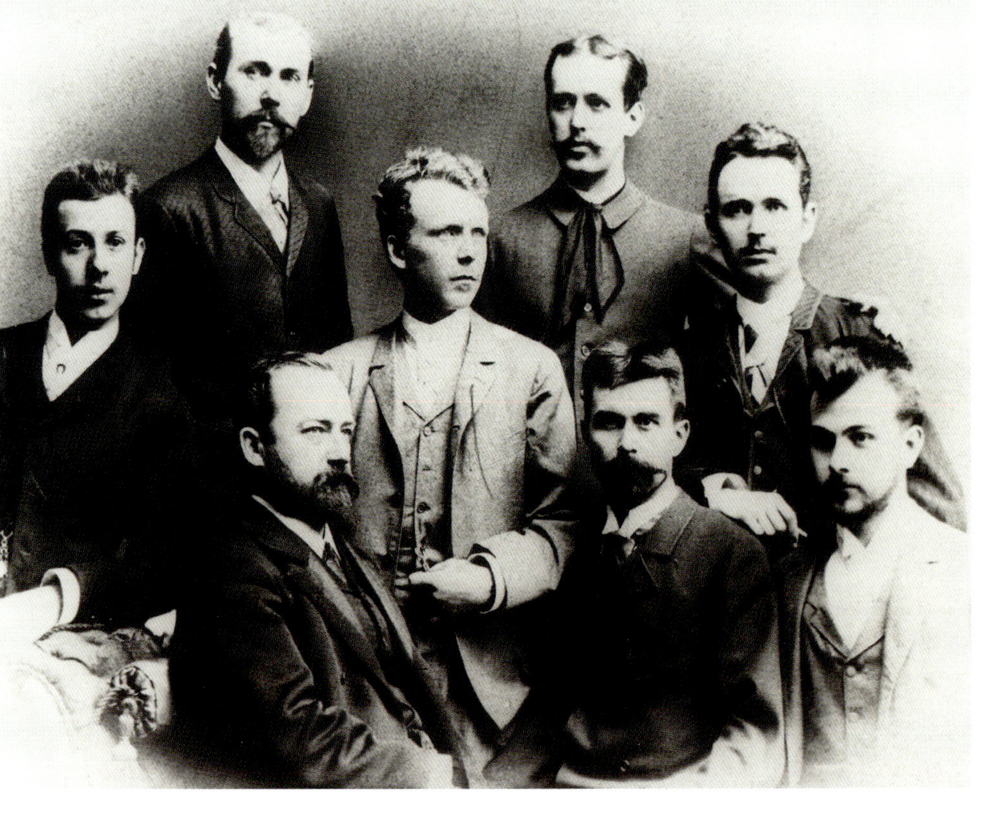

Ferdinand Laufberger's students photographed in 1880. The professor sits to the left of Gustav and Ernst Klimt in the front row, with fellow company member Franz Matsch to the right at the back.

In 1879 the three young artists – along with Klimt's younger brother Georg, who had also by now joined the School of Arts – were recommended by Prof Laufberger to work on decorations for *Festzug*, the pageant to celebrate the silver wedding celebrations of Emperor Franz Joseph to Elisabeth of Bavaria. Hans Makart, the painter most admired by Klimt and who was by now a leading celebrity in Viennese high society, was directing the work on the pageant. Known as the painter prince of Vienna, Makart had forged his own allegorical style based on classical antiquity, combining this with ornamental decoration and the swaggering manner of what came to be known as Late Baroque. Gustav greatly looked up to the older artist. Makart's work, whether as a painter or interior decorator, chiefly celebrated occasions and events in Viennese history. He worked on huge canvases that he treated rather like a stage set, filling them with lots of little people busily engaged in action. A confident and socially adept character, Makart used his studio as a salon, often re-enacting historical moments in costume, while going all out to impress members of Viennese high society.

Apart from admiring and assimilating aspects of Makart's glamorous allegorical style, Klimt particularly revered his use of rich, vibrant colour. Known as 'the magician of colours', Makart used to mix asphalt into his colours to make them more intense – combining this with a skilful use of light and shade to heighten the dramatic impact of his scenes. Klimt was completely overawed by Makart's talent – one story has it that he even bribed a servant to be allowed to sleep on the floor of his idol's studio in the hope that he might absorb some of his greatness.

After their work on the pageant, the three painters were employed in their own right in 1880 to create four decorative ceiling paintings for the Palais Sturany in Vienna – the magnificent residence of a Viennese architect. The two Klimt brothers and Matsch were still working in the Makart style – adapting his particular brand of classical antiquity – but for this commission they also took much inspiration from woodcuts created by the

Entwurf zum Festzug, *Hans Makart, 1879. Klimt's idol, Hans Makart, organized a festive procession to honour the 25th wedding anniversary of Emperor Franz Joseph I and Empress Elisabeth of Austria. This scroll-like painting is a record of the event that took place in Vienna in front of the imperial couple.*

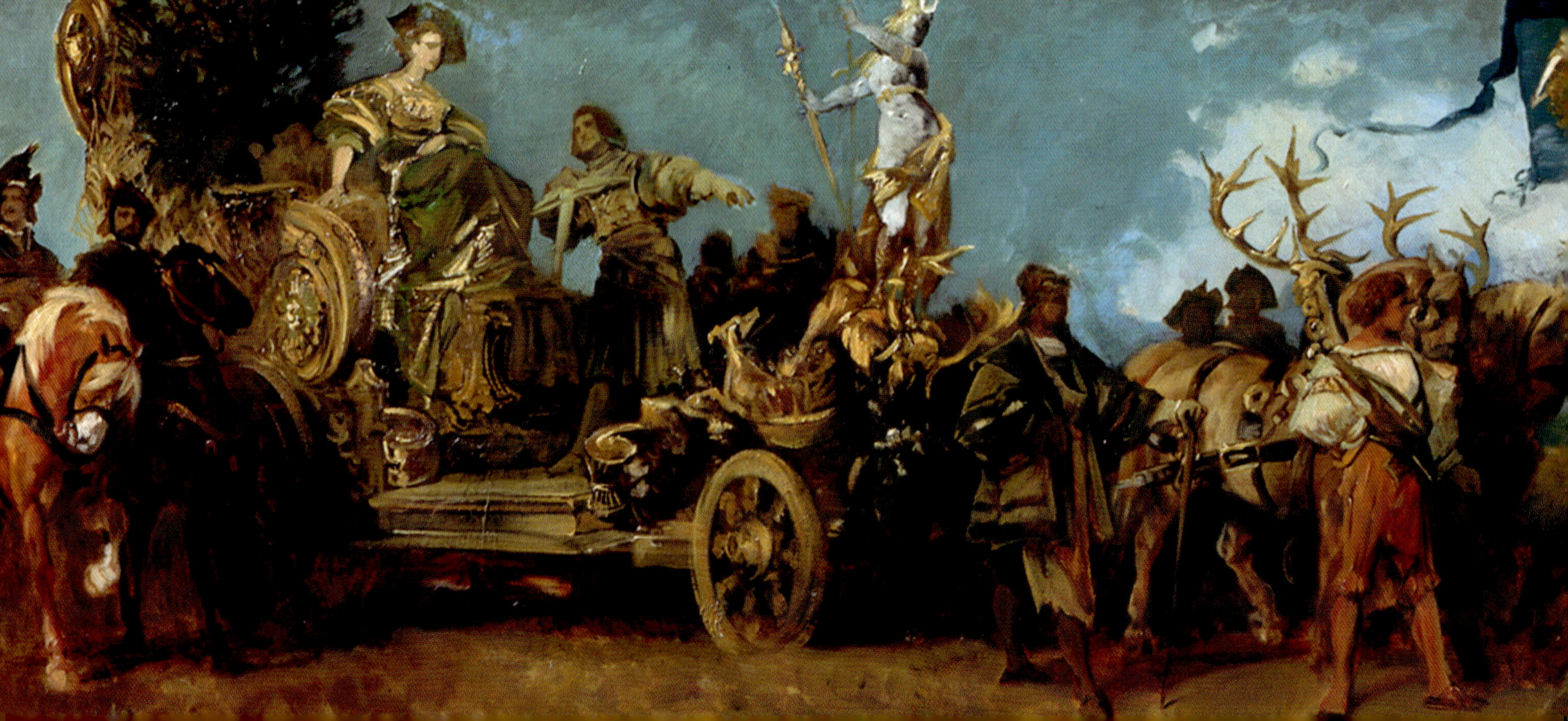

great German fifteenth-century draughtsman Albrecht Dürer. Klimt studied these woodcuts assiduously and drew upon his own facility as an engraver (and what he had learned growing up with a master engraver as a father) to depict animals in his designs with extraordinary faithfulness. The next two years saw further work for the company in and out of Vienna, including commissions in Croatia and Bohemia (now the Czech Republic).

By the time the three artists left the School in 1883, the company was starting to flourish and they accepted further commissions to decorate villas and theatres outside Vienna, this time in Bucharest and Carlsbad. In 1884, Hans Makart died an early death at the age of 44. This must have been a difficult time for Klimt – a huge admirer of Makart's work, he had been literally following in his footsteps for several years. Nonetheless, it is a sign of how established Klimt and his fellow company members were by this time that the commissions continued to come in, and a year later they were working on new designs for the Emperor himself. Based on Shakespeare's *A Midsummer Night's Dream*, the scheme was for the Villa Hermes (known in German as the Hermesvilla), a country residence near Vienna, built by the Emperor Franz Joseph for his wife Sisi. Klimt's designs were well researched and well executed, but the Empress – who was 16 when she married Franz Joseph – became very timid over the years and refused to spend even a night there.

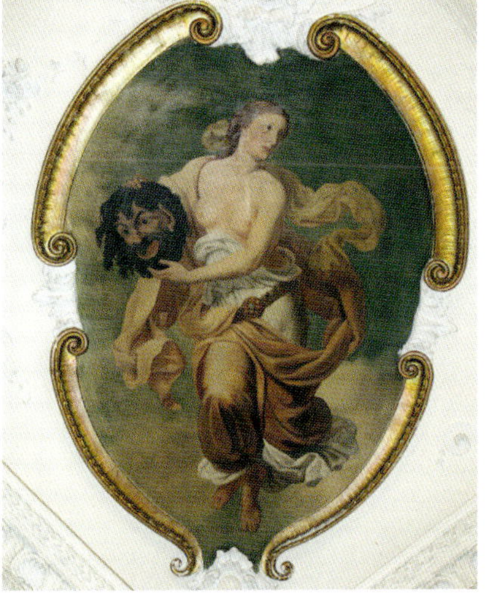

Schottenring 21, Detail in the Beletage, *Gustav Klimt and Franz von Matsch, 1888. In 1880 Klimt and Matsch took on a commission to develop work for the Palais Sturany.*

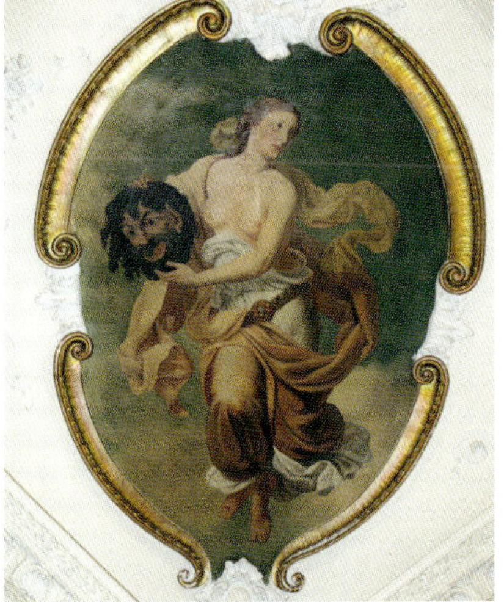

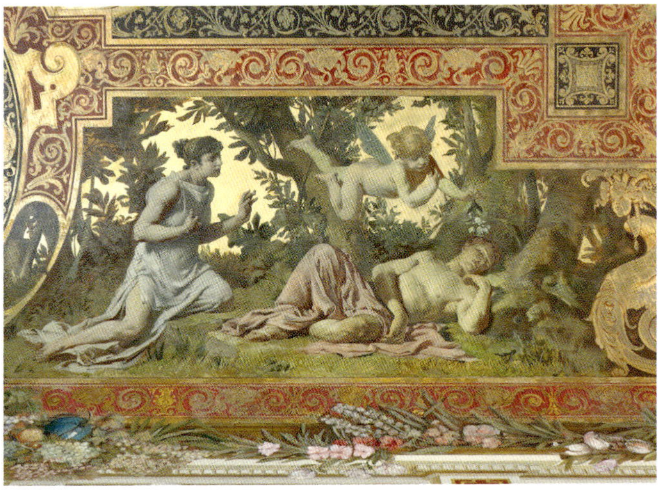

A Midsummer Night's Dream (Puck mistakes Lysander for Demetrius), *Gustav Klimt, Franz von Matsch and Ernst Klimt, 1884–5. From the Villa Hermes.*

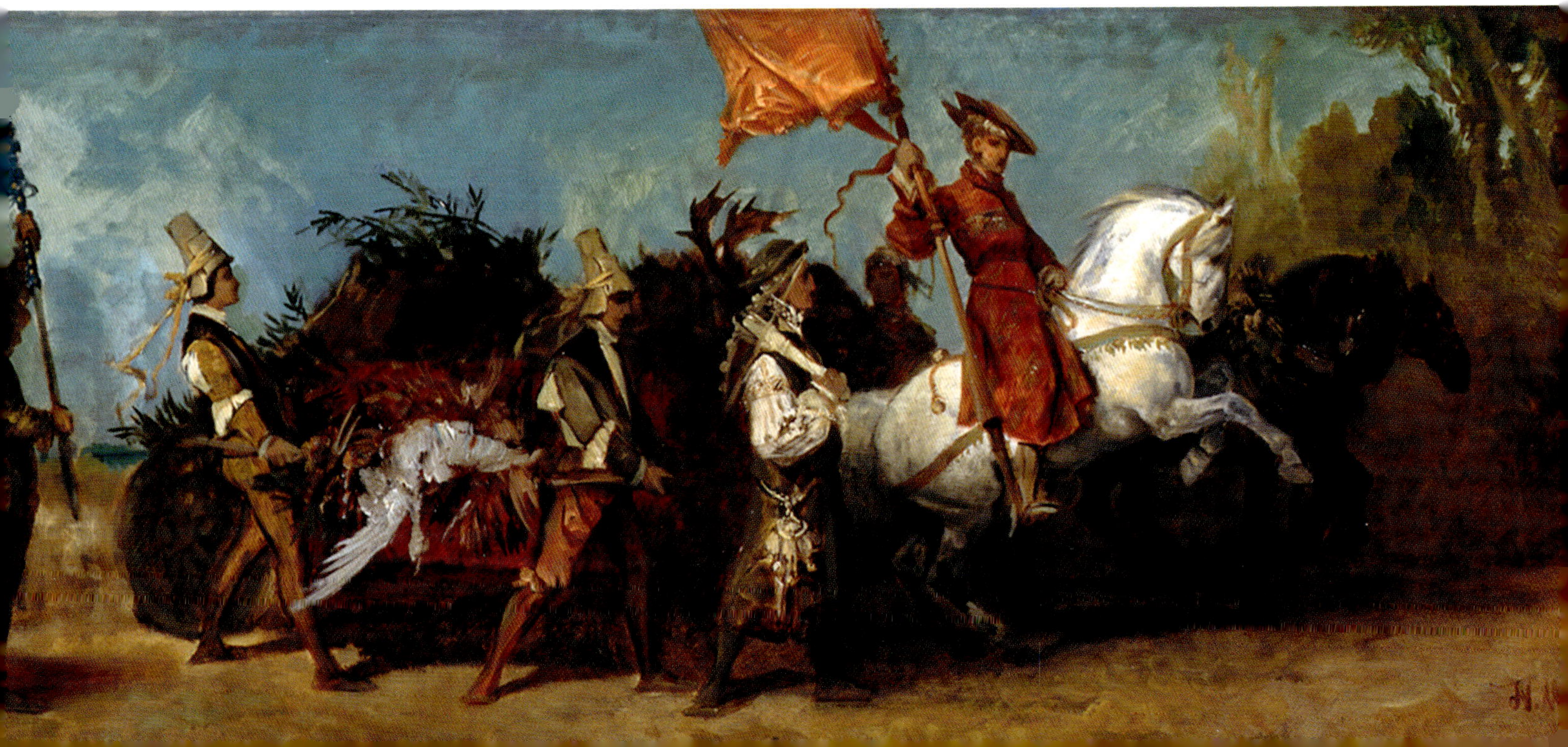

VIENNA AND THE *BELLE ÉPOQUE*

Towards the end of the nineteenth century, Austria was a country of contradictions and compromise. In 1867, after various military defeats and negotiations with Hungary, Emperor Franz Joseph was the figurehead of the Austro-Hungarian Empire. The Emperor ruled his dual monarchy from the magnificent Schönbrunn Palace in Vienna. In spite of a backdrop of military and political manoeuvring, this date marked the beginning of an unparalleled era of wealth and ostentation in Vienna known as the *Belle Époque*. With two million inhabitants between 1867 and World War I, Vienna stood alongside Paris as the impressive and resplendent capital of Europe.

Emperor Franz Joseph made some sweeping changes to the city's geography, including knocking down the city walls in 1857 to make way for the Ringstrasse, a horseshoe-shaped perimeter road. Many public buildings were erected, including a new parliament, museums, the Opera and the Court Theatre. Otto Wagner, an architect known for his modernist sympathies, designed the Stadtbahn, an urban rail network in 1890. Alongside the civic buildings, new private residences sprung up with ornate façades and lavishly decorated interiors. Drinking water was improved, and electric lamps and trams were introduced. This was a new world on the move – with a need to show that it was on the move.

In this febrile and pleasure-loving atmosphere, the dominant haute bourgeoisie flourished – hosting magnificent banquets and packing the theatres and opera houses. The poor, by contrast, remained poor and in inadequate housing.

The most significant impact of the *Belle Époque* was on the cultural life of the city. Amid all the opulence and decadence, the contrasts between old and new, traditional and modern became ever wider, driving the artists and intellectuals who were ensuring that Vienna was right at the heart of Europe's creative map. There was an astonishing array of musical talent centred around Vienna. Mozart, Haydn, Beethoven and Brahms had all lived and composed in the city. Now, Richard and Johann Strauss's waltzes and operettas were adopted with élan by the bourgeoisie for their lavish balls. Gustav Mahler lived in Vienna for 10 years, his work acting as a bridge between the nineteenth-century Austro-German tradition and the modernism of the early twentieth century. Initially, art and sculpture remained pretty much as it always had been – conservative, academic and based on rules and proportions – until Gustav Klimt and the Viennese Secession brought radical change.

The neurologist Sigmund Freud added to the new intellectual life of the city with his *Interpretation of Dreams*, published in 1899. Key to our understanding of psychoanalysis, the text built upon the analysis of Freud's own dreams and the personal crises surrounding the death of his father. His ideas about the power of the unconscious have played a central part in the way we view the self in the modern world, as well as the impact that the past has on the present.

With all the old certainties no longer providing the safe moral backdrop to the Habsburg Empire, Vienna experienced the *Belle Époque* as a golden age – a period of innovation and sheer aesthetic brilliance that Klimt helped to define and in which he was the brightest star. If Klimt's art, with its focus on the beautiful and the erotic, helped to establish the period's obsessions more than anyone else in Vienna at this time, it also helped to sow the seeds of its decay. The elegance and gaiety of Vienna in the late nineteenth century went through a process of turmoil and dissolution, coming to a shuddering end in 1914 with the outbreak of World War I.

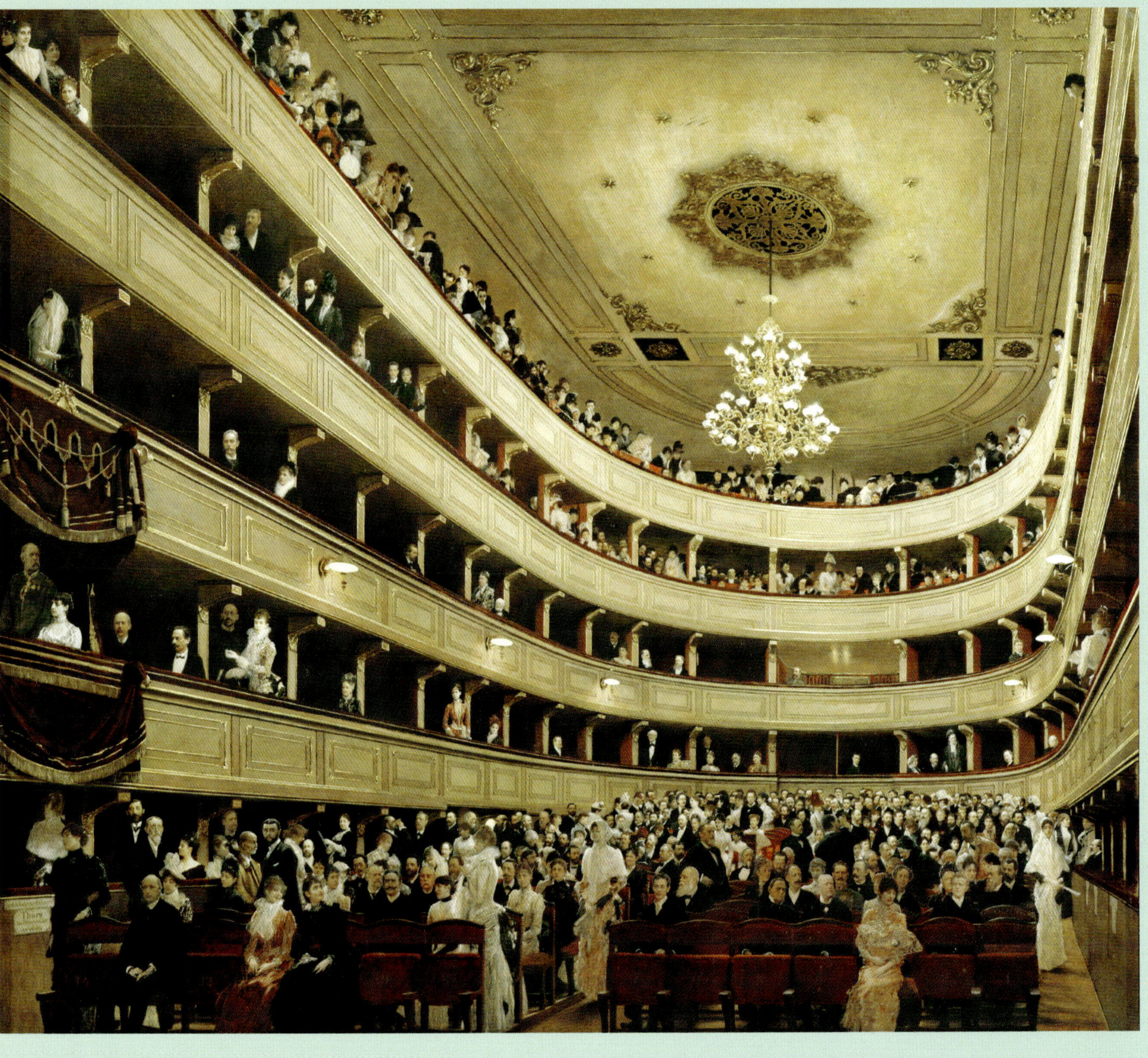

Auditorium in the Old Burgtheater in Vienna, *1888. All the tiny figures in the audience in this gouache painting are actual portraits of Klimt's contemporaries, painted with astounding accuracy. One of Klimt's most celebrated early works, it won the Emperor's Prize in 1890.*

In 1886, the Painters' Company was given their most prestigious commission to date, to work on the interior of the Burgtheater, the replacement for the old theatre in Vienna. Up until this point the three painters had worked as a group, but important distinctions were beginning to emerge and now Klimt suddenly took the lead and found himself propelled into the limelight. The commission was to create 11 allegorical paintings in all. Klimt took on the largest and most demanding space – the vaulted entrance and the central ceiling. Appropriately, the motifs all came from theatrical productions, with Klimt working on scenes from a classical Greek drama, a medieval mystery play and Shakespeare's *Romeo and Juliet*. For this commission, Klimt started to draw upon realistic portraits using photographs as reference and his own family (including himself) as models. In 1888, Klimt received the Golden Cross of Honour from Emperor Franz Joseph for his contributions to the Burgtheater murals.

Some of the extraordinary realism that Klimt was to deploy in this commission can also be seen in *Auditorium in the Old Burgtheater* (see p. 15), a separate painting he made in 1888. This gouache painting of the old Burgtheater before it was destroyed unexpectedly reveals the view of the auditorium as seen from the stage. The audience is represented in astounding detail – all the 200 tiny portraits are faithfully accurate, and individual personalities including the composer Brahms are recognizable, as well as contemporary politicians and dignitaries. This ability to conjure up such an extraordinary illusion through such careful attention to truth – presenting the viewer with a heightened version of reality – is one of the hallmarks of Klimt's later style and one at which he was to prove a supreme master.

Klimt's ambitious painting did not go unnoticed or unrewarded. Indeed, fashionable Viennese society members depicted in it were more than happy to have been modelled and celebrated in this way. *Auditorium in the Old Burgtheater* won the Emperor's Prize in 1890, for which Klimt received 400 guilders.

If Klimt began his professional career painting interior murals and ceilings in large public buildings, he was also pursuing other projects, including several portrait commissions. Most often painted from photographs, these included the portrait of *Joseph Pembaur*, the pianist and piano teacher, 1890, notable for its hyperrealism and decorative broad frame. Klimt had also created designs for a publication entitled *Allegories and Emblems* for the Viennese publisher Martin Gerlach while he was still at art school in 1881. The book was designed to instruct students on how to depict allegorical themes, and Klimt worked on a series of designs that showed his evolving style. One significant device was Klimt's use of a broad frame, sometimes in gold, as a border for his classical figures, with decorative details that echoed the content of the main image.

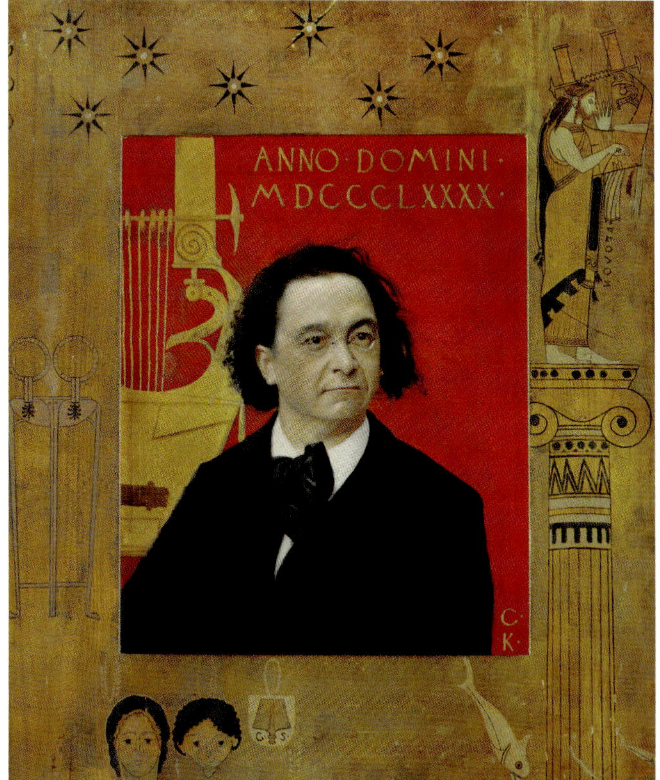

Joseph Pembaur, *1890. Born in Innsbruck in 1875, Pembaur was a piano teacher and concert pianist. Klimt's near photographic portrait shows his great skill as a realist painter.*

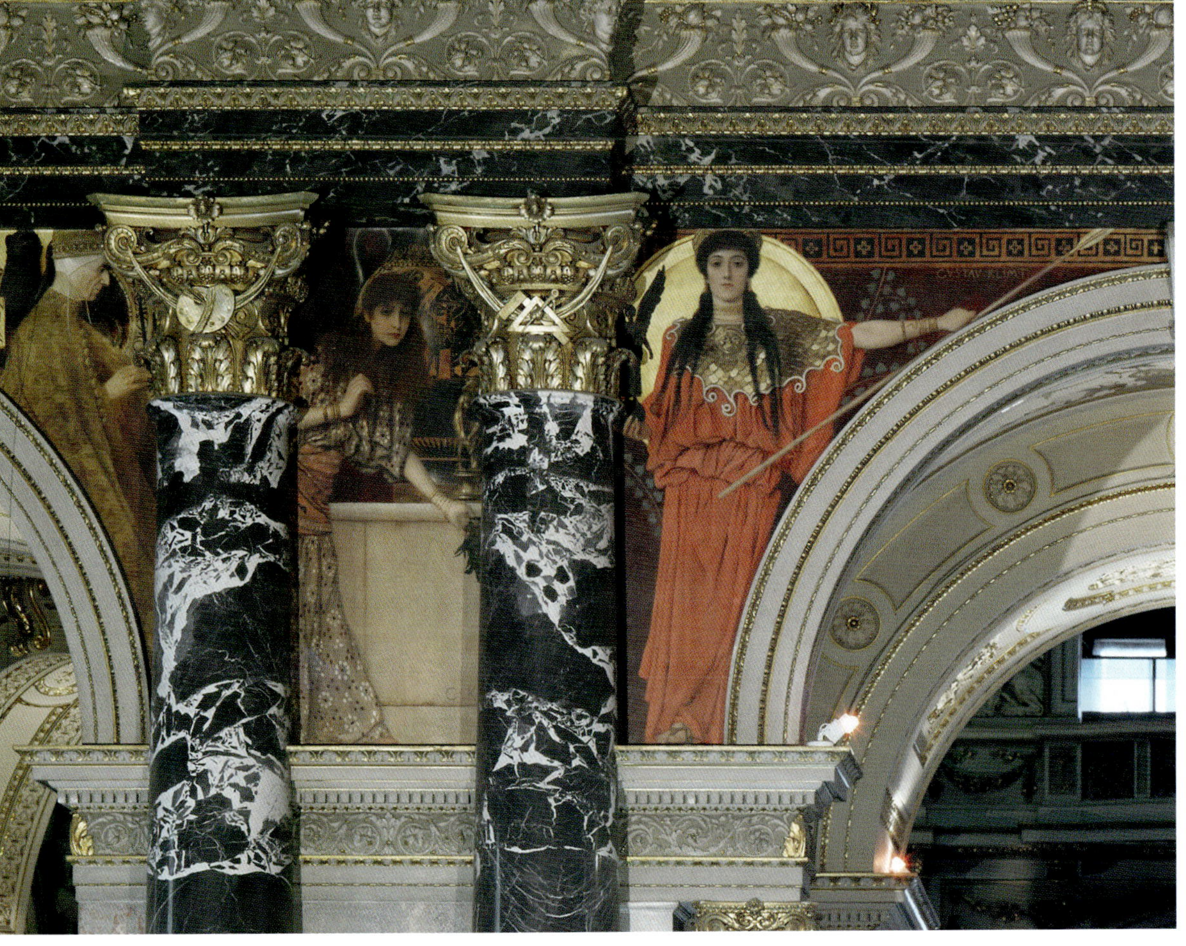

Egyptian Art I and II, Greek Antiquity I and II, *1890–1. The Kunsthistorisches Museum in Vienna opened in 1891 under Emperor Franz Joseph who commissioned a cycle of paintings by Klimt for the main staircase. These early works reveal the beginning of Klimt's Art Nouveau style.*

In 1890 the Painter's Company secured another hugely significant commission, to work on the newly built Kunsthistorisches (Museum of Art History) in Vienna. Hans Makart was originally proposed for the commission, but it was given to Klimt and his company after his death. The building was the home of the Emperor's art collection and was to be open to the public for the first time. Although the artists were informed that their designs had to pay homage to their benefactor and his magnificent patronage of the arts, they produced a comprehensive, eclectic scheme that ranged over many different periods and styles of art history.

On this commission, Klimt began to make innovations that not only made him stand apart from the work of his fellow artists but which surpassed any of his own advances to date. His decorations plucked ideas and inspiration from the ancient civilizations of Greece and Egypt, mixing these with references to the work of the artists of the Italian Renaissance artists, such as Bellini, Botticelli and Donatello. Aside from taking the viewer on a chronological romp through the history of art, Klimt created wondrous illusions – his painted figures on the ceilings and walls look literally like they have been carved out of stone. Among these illusionistic portrayals, *Ancient Greece (The girl from Tanagra)* stood out. This young woman is not merely a representation of that idealized classical beauty already familiar to Viennese society – she has the look of a contemporary woman. She has a pre-Raphaelite head of hair and a languid, sensuous look, foreshadowing the femmes fatales beauties that were to become the trademark of Klimt's mature work.

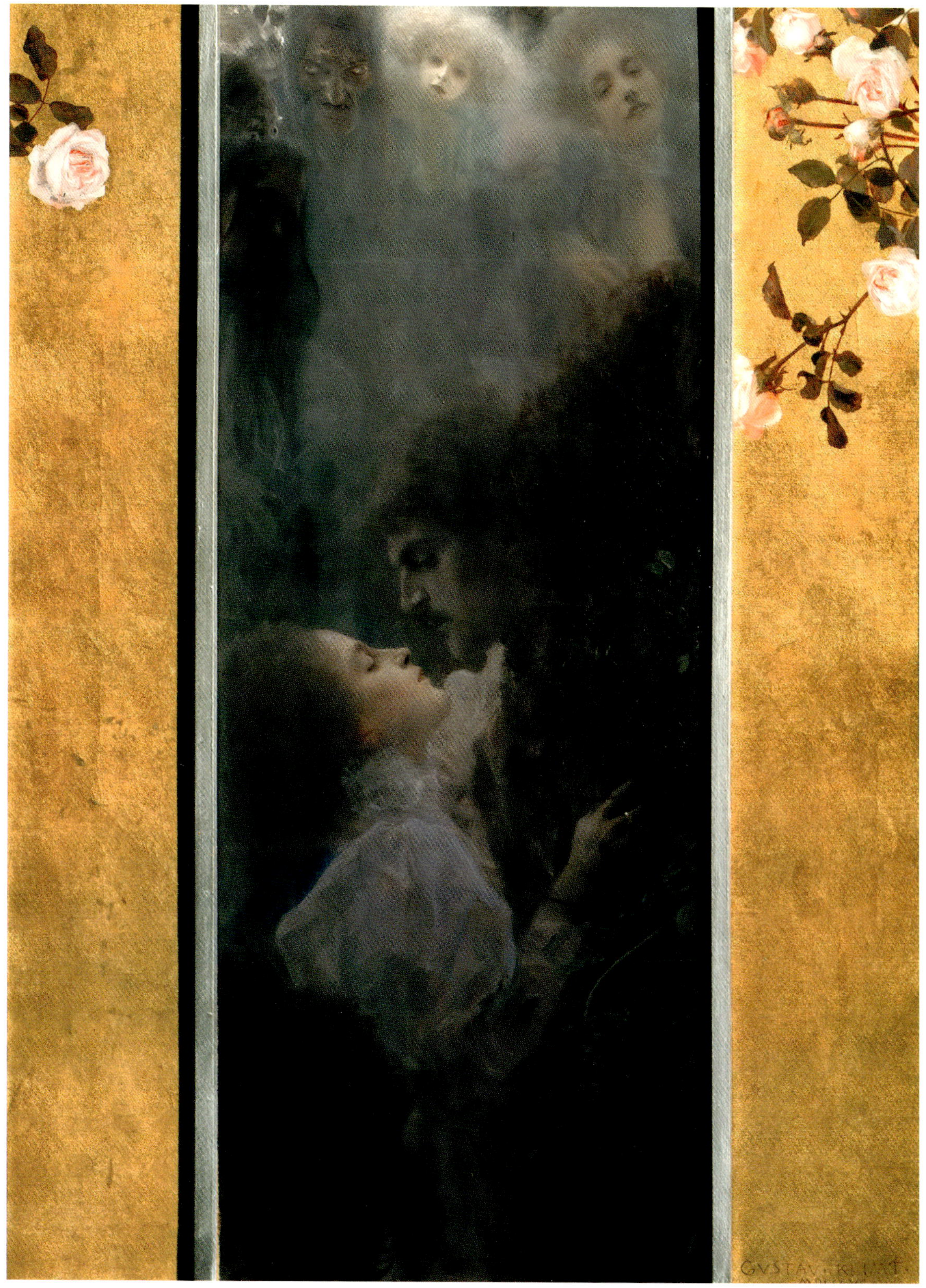

Love, 1895. *In this romantic allegorical image, Klimt depicts a young couple wrapped in each other's arms and shrouded in mist. Above their heads, harbingers of death and sickness hover. The roses on each of the golden panels signify the fragility of youth and beauty.*

In 1891, Klimt became a member of the co-operative Austrian Artists' Society, a powerful and conservative group representing all that was traditional about Viennese art. Success meant that the Painter's Company could move to a larger studio in the Josefstadt area of Vienna; success that was hugely overshadowed by the deaths of his father and his brother Ernst the following year. Gustav took on the financial responsibility for his brother's widow and child as well as his mother and younger siblings. Grief affected Klimt's artistic vision and he painted little for four years. However, he eventually emerged with a new confidence about his evolving personal style, which was to take him even further away from his contemporaries.

Matsch was a conformist when it came to art, wanting to work in a traditional style with appropriate and time-honoured subject matter. He moved out of the Josefstadt studio, though the pair continued to work together on commissions, including one received in 1894, to complete four decorative panels and the large ceiling in the Great Hall of the University of Vienna. The concept for the work was the triumph of light over darkness, the four panels representing Theology, Philosophy, Medicine and Jurisprudence. The paintings took Klimt nine years to complete, during which time he crossed swords with both Matsch and the commissioners on several occasions. Essentially, Klimt's new evolving symbolist style was at variance with the cultural expectations of traditional bourgeois society. His critics objected to the content of the work – the nudity and the lack of moral purpose – as well as what they considered to be the baffling symbolism.

Klimt's evolving allegorical style can also be seen in *Love* and *Music I*, two portfolios of works sent to the publisher Martin Gerlach in 1895. Gerlach approached Klimt for paintings for a book entitled *Allegories and Emblems*, which would provide artists with ideas and models when depicting allegorical themes. In *Love* a man and a woman are clasped in a romantic embrace. It is subject matter that Klimt would return to several times, most notably in *The Kiss*, 1907. Here, it is almost as if time has stopped still. The golden border traps the couple in a cubicle, forcing their bodies closer together. They appear as in a dream, shrouded in mist, with faces representing their tragic destiny hovering above. The surrounding golden, stylized background was to become one of Klimt's trademarks from this point on, the frame picking up on the decorative details on the inner canvas. *Music I* shows a young woman, in a deep blue dress, with a cloud of auburn hair against a backdrop of classical statuary. Lost in thought, she plucks at her golden lute. Again, the excess of rich gold decoration and the stylized, non-naturalistic way Klimt uses it across the canvas, is a harbinger of what was to come.

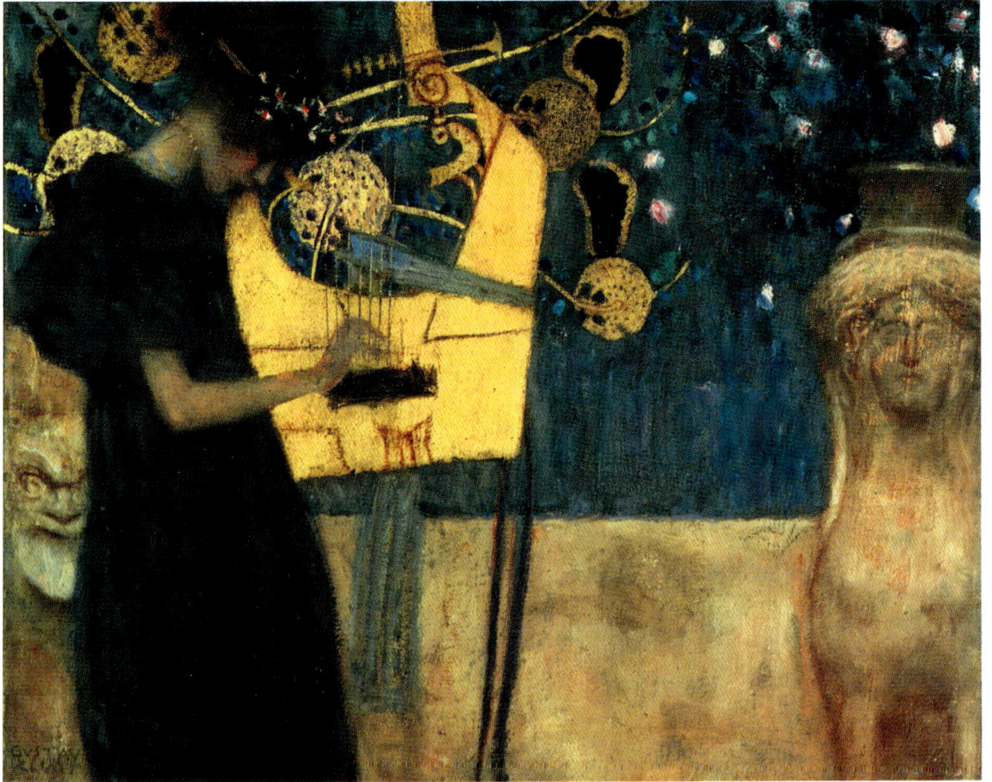

Music I, *1895. A painting that shows Klimt's early ability to draw from different sources to create a harmonious whole. Standing against a classical setting, the young woman herself seems drawn from more modern times.*

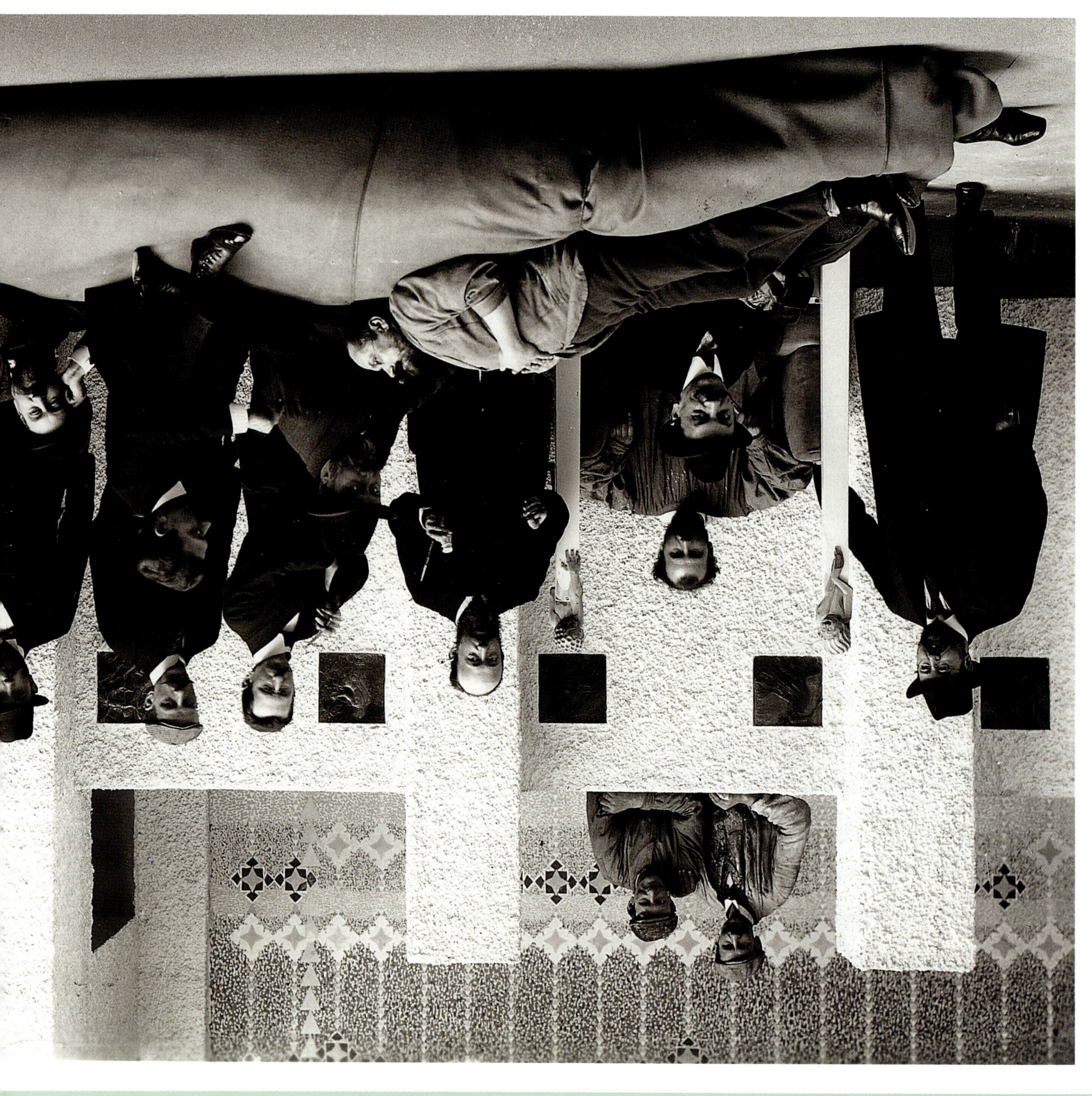

CHAPTER 2
The Secession Years

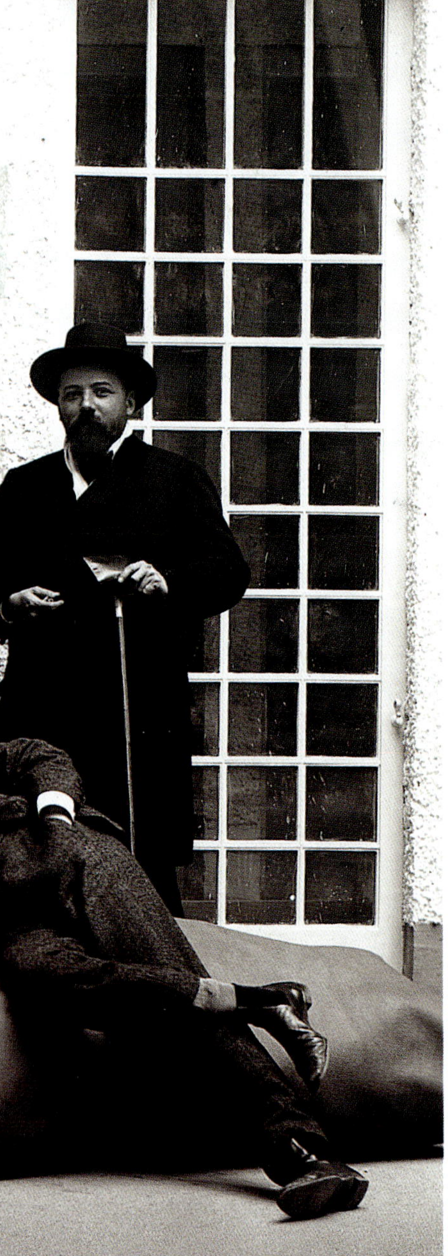

Austria in the 1890s was something of an artistic backwater. There were important changes happening in the arts in the rest of Europe, not least in France, where the entirely original Impressionist paintings of Manet and Degas were starting to find a wider audience. In Vienna, housed in a large mansion off the city's Ringstrasse, the Austrian Artists' Society had been founded in 1861 and represented all that was traditional, bourgeois and inward-looking about the cultural life of the city. Promoting Austrian artists at the expense of all others, the society staged exhibitions that Klimt and others felt were dull, lacking in 'modern' work from abroad and unashamedly commercial. It was against this backdrop that the Viennese Secession was founded in 1897, essentially as a form of protest against the established art of the time in Vienna. (*Secession* is a term most often used when part of a state breaks away and achieves its own autonomy.)

If the impetus behind a new movement was a desire for change and to embrace some of the exciting and progressive developments abroad, this was also fuelled by the success of a counterpart breakaway movement in Munich. Initially seen as a separate group under the wing of the Austrian Artists' Society, it soon became clear to the malcontents that their position within the parent organization was untenable. A formal constitution was drawn up and Klimt was elected the first President of the new Union of Austrian Artists (Secession).

Although by all accounts quite shy and introverted, Klimt suddenly found himself propelled into the spotlight. He was clearly passionate about the need to reinvigorate artistic life in Vienna because he had personally experienced many frustrations and disappointments on commissions. However, his unhappy and at times depressive temperament made him an unlikely spearhead for a revolutionary movement.

In breaking away from the establishment, the artists of the Viennese

A group of artists involved in the 14th Seccession exhibition of 1902. Klimt is seated on a chair in the second row, dressed in his characteristic smock type robe. Koloman Moser, his friend and fellow Secessionist, is in front of him.

Secession did not have a manifesto or even a particular style of art and design that they favoured. From the start they welcomed international artists, inviting leading Czech and German artists to join. The first exhibition staged in the summer of 1898 was predominantly drawn from the work of international artists.

One founding principle of the Secession, and one which was ultimately to play an important part in its demise, was a belief that all the various art forms should be on an equal footing. Architecture and design were seen as sharing centre stage with painting and sculpture – fuelled in part by the fact that architect Josef Hoffman and graphic designer Koloman Moser were leading figures in the new movement.

The Secession also founded their own journal, which set new standards in typography and graphic design. *Ver Sacrum* (*Sacred Spring*) was published in a square format and showcased the new Secessionist style with its lyrical and decorative imagery. Klimt was a regular contributor for two years. In the first issue, his bold line drawing *Nuda Veritas* showed a naked femme fatale staring directly at the viewer – a drawing he was to develop into a painting in 1899, oil and gold on canvas and 2 metres (6½ feet) high.

The two Secession artists who went on to found the Wiener Werkstätte. On the left, Austrian architect and designer Josef Hoffmann (1870–1956) and on the right, artist Koloman Moser (1868–1918).

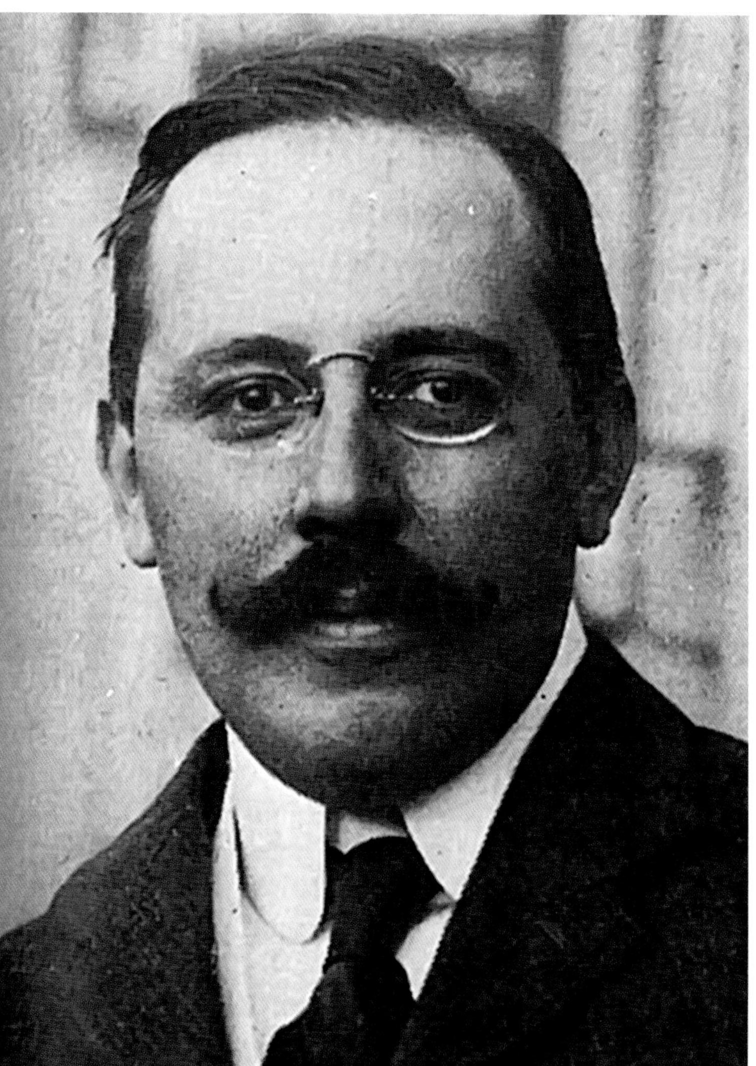

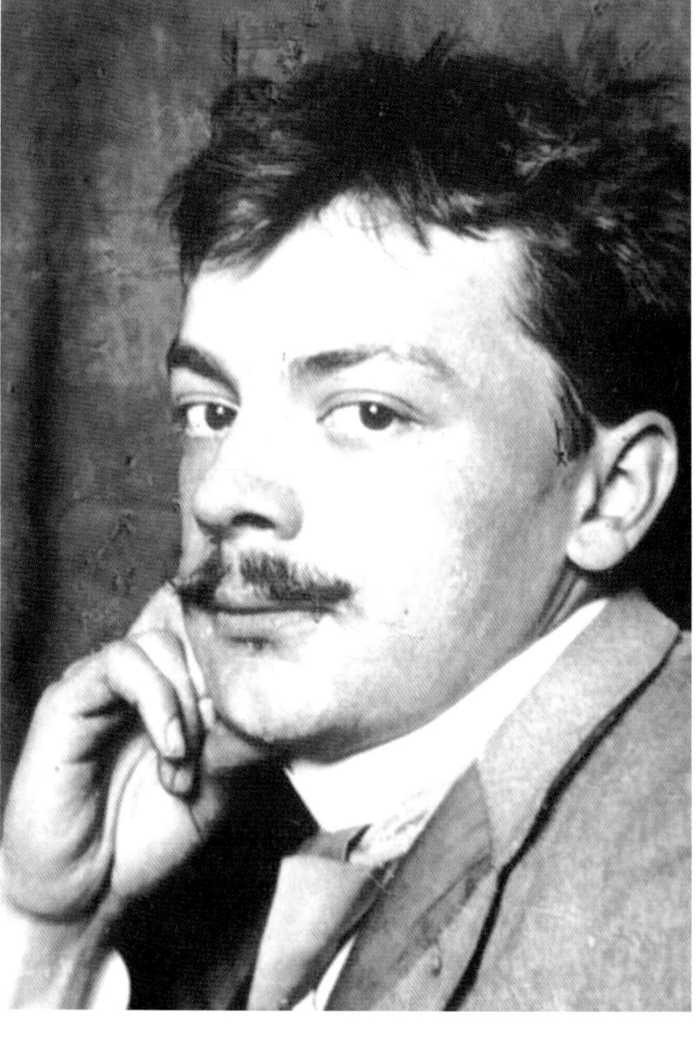

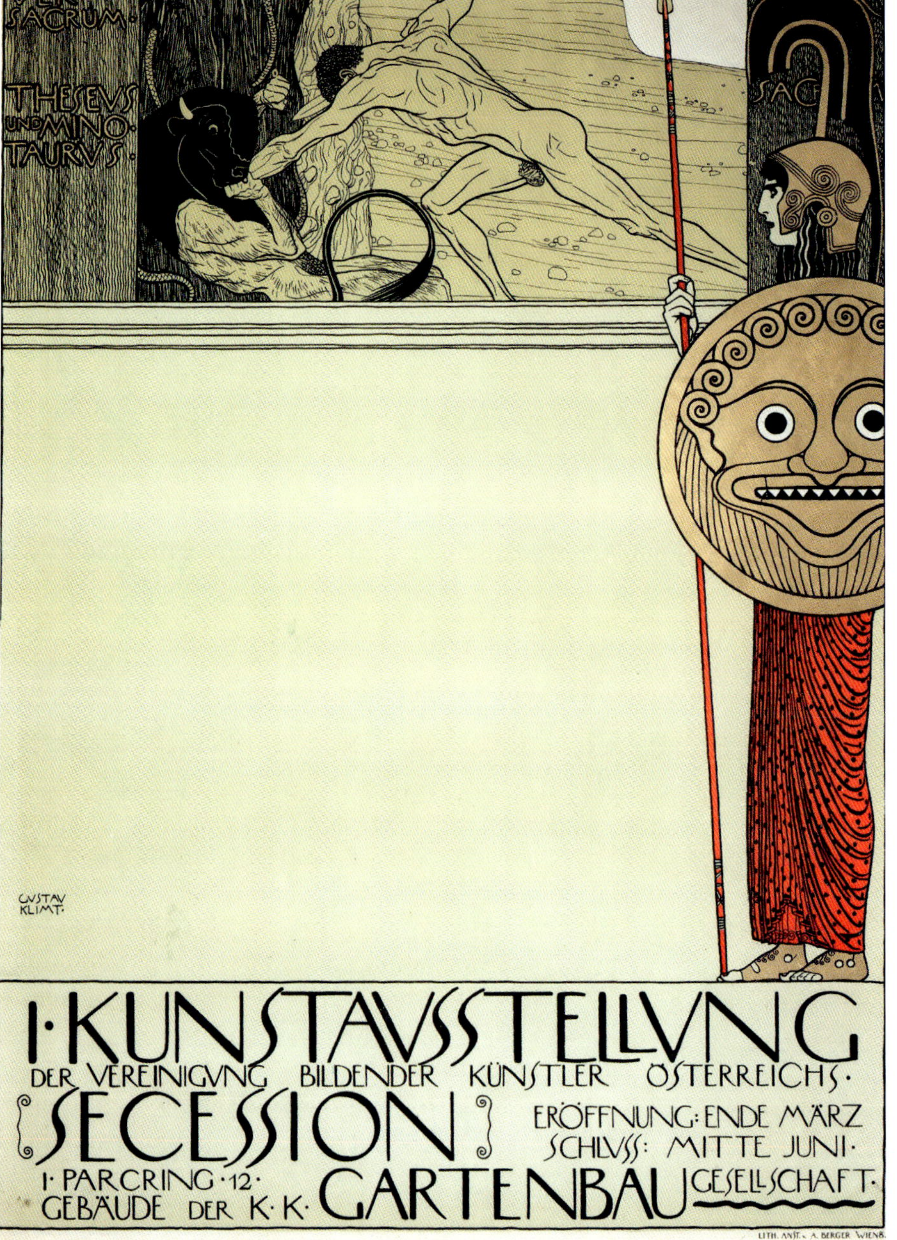

Poster for the First Art Exhibition of the Secession Movement, *1898. The Secessionists were keen to make their exhibitions stand out from everything that had gone before. Klimt's modern design, with its image of Theseus fighting the Minotaur, uses blank space and decorative type to create a distinctive image.*

The journal developed a new harmony between word and image. Writing was an important part of the magazine and the Bohemian-Austrian poet Rainer Maria Rilke and English playwright and poet Charles Swinburne both contributed to it. In the journal, and in their work in general, the Secessionists paid special attention to literature, often quoting from prose and poetry. As for Klimt himself, he was always mindful of his literary heritage, and allegedly used to carry books around with him, texts such as *Faust* by Goethe and *The Divine Comedy* by Dante. He produced several covers for the journal, which quickly became collector's items.

Klimt, with architect Hoffman and fellow painter Carl Moll, were the main drivers behind the Secession's exhibitions. Klimt designed the poster for their first Vienna Secession exhibition in March 1898. Inspired by ancient Greek vases, the top third of the image features Theseus fighting the Minotaur and shows the sinewy body of a young naked man (Theseus appears without the customary fig leaf) driving a sword into the Minotaur. Richly symbolic, Klimt portrays the young man's struggle as a battle between the forces of light and dark. The design has a modern fresh feel with one third of the image left blank and the bottom quarter spelling out the details of the exhibition in an elegant script decorated with spirals and dots.

The Secession's first exhibition opened in a space hired from the government – to great acclaim. It attracted nearly 60,000 visitors, some good reviews and, importantly, sales that meant money could be ploughed back into the project to build a new pavilion for successive exhibitions. Klimt's friend and colleague Hoffman and another architect Joseph Maria Olbrich worked on the new building, which opened in record time for the Second Secessionist exhibition in November 1898. Significantly, the forward-thinking motto over the doorway declared: 'To our time its art, and to art its freedom'.

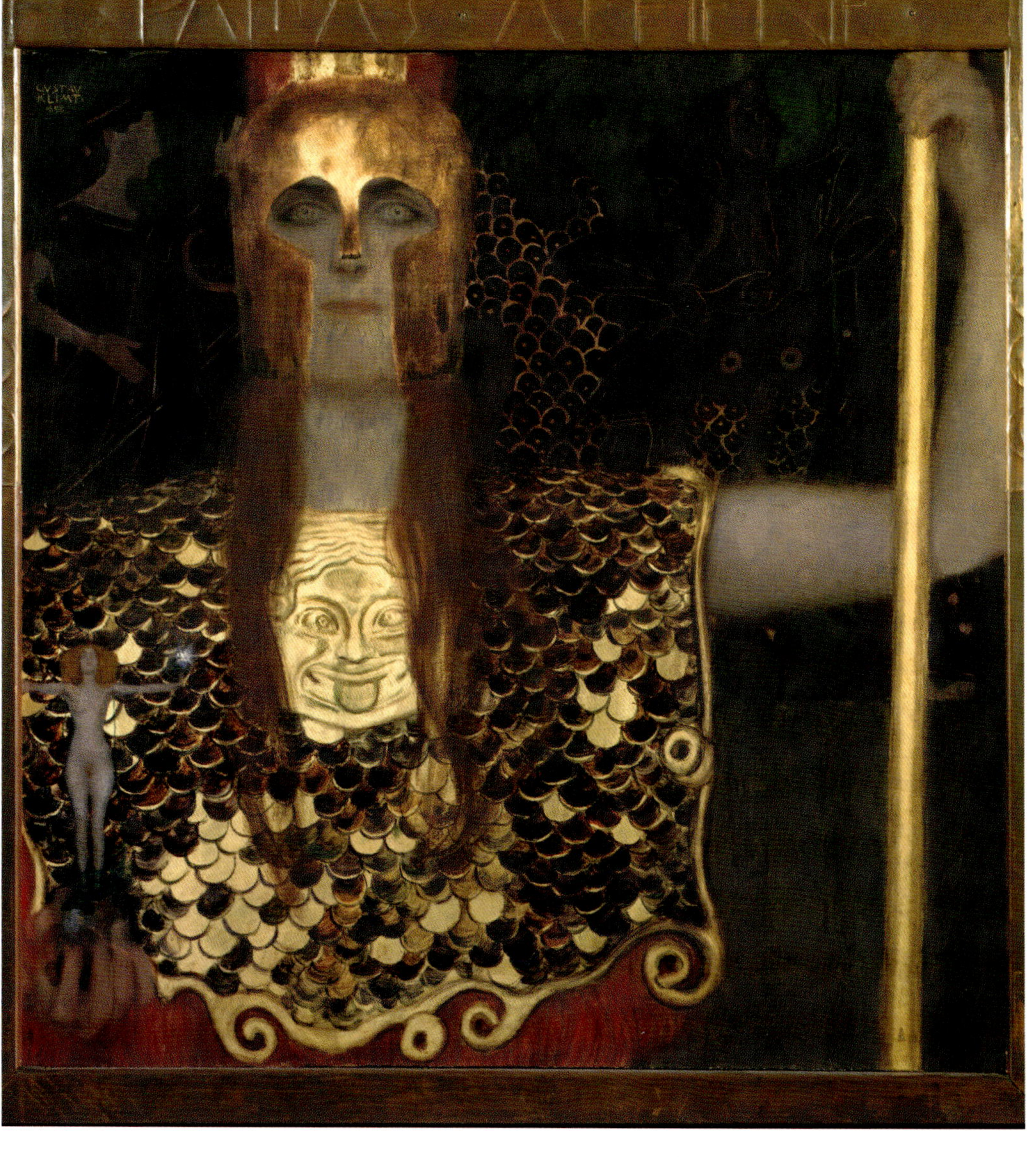

Pallas Athene, *1898. The Secessionists adopted Pallas Athene – the goddess who was the patron of arts and crafts – as their emblem. Her burnished gold armour and helmet point the way forward to Klimt's excessive use of gold in his later portraits.*

The Emperor himself visited the second exhibition, which again attracted record numbers of visitors and substantial sales. Klimt showed seven works this time, including his portrayal of *Pallas Athene*, the Greek goddess of Wisdom, Crafts and War. In this painting, Klimt portrays a woman warrior standing erect with a long gold spear or orb and a magnificent golden headdress and breastplate. Her eyes are glacial, her expression fixed and determined. There is no doubt that she is or will be victorious, her triumph being over her (most likely) male adversaries or perhaps even men in general. In her right hand, Athene holds a tiny figure of a naked woman – frail, fleshy, yet protected by her goddess.

Klimt was following standard themes in tackling the battle of the sexes, but his Athene resembles a more modern and intimidating woman, rather than the standard goddesses seen in classical paintings. The painting is an amalgamation of several styles and influences that Klimt has made all his own. There is a new level of golden embellishment and ornament – his brother Georg made the decorative frame – and this marks the beginning of Klimt's blurring of the boundaries between flesh and gold ornamentation, with flesh becoming gold and gold becoming flesh.

Pallas Athene also marked the beginning of Klimt's love affair with strong women protagonists. Although the female form was crucially important to Art Nouveau, Klimt continued to portray his female heroines as assertive and in charge of their own destinies, which was at odds with traditional representations of women as meek and acquiescent.

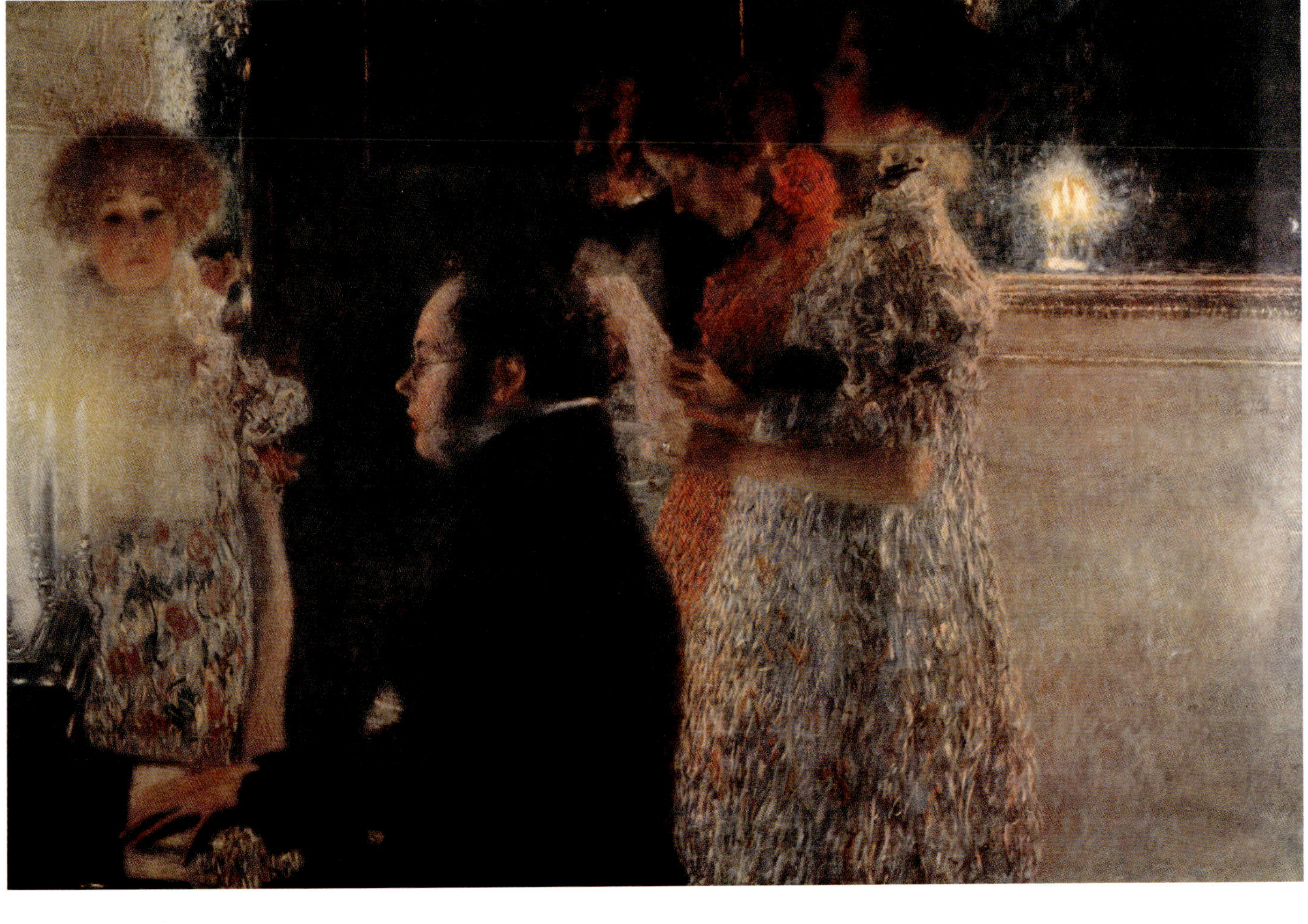

Schubert at the Piano, *1899. Klimt painted this portrait of Schubert for one of his patrons, the Greek industrialist Nikolaus Dumba. The softness and light as well as the stippled brushstrokes lend it an Impressionist quality.*

In 1898, alongside all his Secessionist activity, Klimt also took on another commission – the decorations for the Ringstrasse mansion of Nikolaus Dumba. Klimt researched and executed two works for the music room – *Music II* and *Schubert at the Piano*, which reveal a new softness and approach to light, helping to bridge the gap between his early classical academic style and his later symbolist inspired work. The heroine in *Music II* has all the hallmarks of a later Klimt femme fatale – the bouffant hair, the winsome appearance and the detached languid air. *Schubert at the Piano* is a soft, flattering portrait of the bourgeoisie's favourite musical composer, shown playing to a group of society ladies in a candlelit setting.

In the same year Klimt painted *Sonja Knips*, the first of his portraits of Viennese society wives. Patronage was extremely important to the fledgling Secession movement and most patrons came from the Jewish families of the Viennese bourgeoisie. These included the steel magnate Karl Wittgenstein, the Lederer family and the Knips family, who had made their money in metal industry and banking and had already engaged Josef Hoffman to design their house.

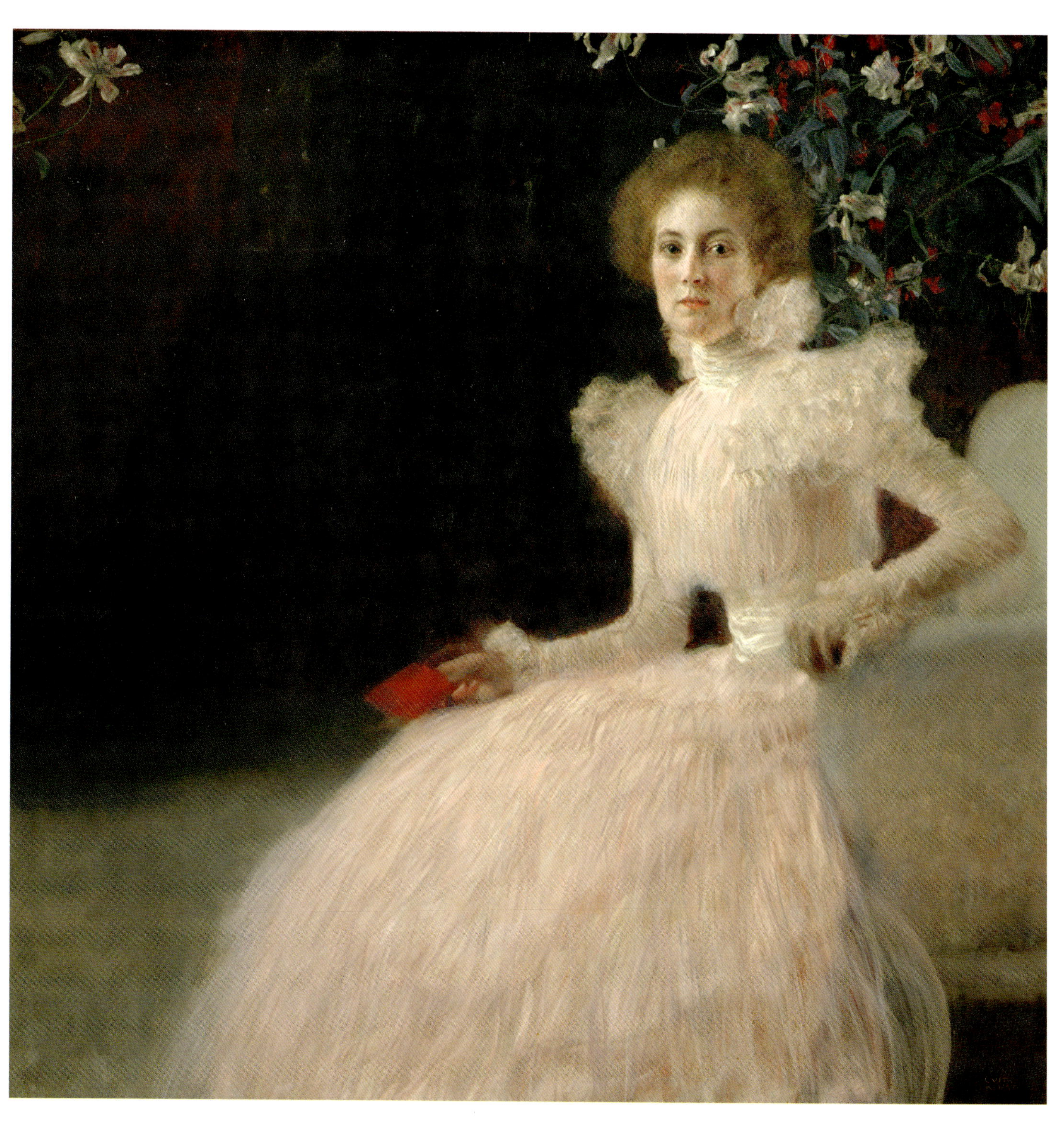

Sonja Knips, *1898. Sonja, the wife of Anton Knips, another of Klimt's patrons, is seated in a gauzy pink dress, and set against a plain dark background. The softness of the portrait recalls some of those by Whistler whom Klimt knew through reproductions of his work.*

Klimt's portrait of Sonja was to grace the Knips' salon. It is a work that shows a number of different influences, including Klimt's old master Makart, in terms of the off-centre, sideways composition, and the American painter J M Whistler in terms of the softness, in particular the feathery pink brushstrokes Klimt has used on her dress. Klimt never met Whistler (who was primarily based in England), but they corresponded and he saw reproductions of Whistler's work in art gazettes such as *The Studio* and *The Art Journal*. Klimt greatly admired Whistler in terms of composition, colouring and technique. In this portrait, Sonja Knips has a poised, proud, perhaps even disdainful expression that Klimt was starting to make his own in his ongoing portraits of femmes fatales.

Rows over the ceiling paintings, commissioned in 1894 by the Ministry of Education for the Great Hall of the University of Vienna, continued to dog Klimt over the next decade. The theme for the work – the victory of the intellect over ignorance – seemed especially ironic since Klimt had to fight prejudice and incomprehension from a multitude of people, including members of the university, academics, the clergy and even Matsch, his fellow artist and business partner.

Unsurprisingly, given all the disagreements, the paintings remained unfinished for many years. However, in 1900, Klimt decided to show the incomplete *Philosophy* to members of the university, who were unanimous in their criticism of it. This was in part due to the inclusion of naked figures and their unexplained links to philosophy as well as to Klimt's inexplicable symbolism. This did not deter Klimt from sending the painting to the 1900 World Exhibition in Paris, where it was awarded a gold medal.

Medicine, *1907. This detail from* Medicine, *one of the notorious University paintings, shows Hygeia, the Greek goddess of health, with a snake wound round her arm and holding a cup. Looking upwards, Klimt's use of perspective emphasizes her extraordinary strength.*

THE BEETHOVEN FRIEZE

Klimt and his fellow Secessionists saw the 14th exhibition at their building in Vienna in 1902 as special and they wanted people to experience a total work of art. They decided to celebrate Beethoven, whose work was greatly admired at the time. An heroic sculpture of Beethoven by Max Klinger, the German symbolist artist, formed the centrepiece. Music was arranged for the occasion – the fourth movement of Beethoven's *Ninth* was performed at the opening with an orchestra conducted by Gustav Mahler. Work by various artists selected in relation to the theme was positioned in the many spaces around the building. Klimt agreed to provide a mural.

Architect Josef Hoffman created a new interior out of bare, concrete – pale walls, forming an ideal backdrop to Klimt's delicate golden visions. Situated for the most part high up on the walls, Klimt painted directly onto the dry plaster, applying a range of decorative materials, including silver and gold leaf, mirror, coloured glass, chalk, graphite and even curtain rings.

Klimt saw his frieze as a symbolic translation of Beethoven's last symphony, in which the central theme was the life cycle. Symbolic figures suggested the passage of time from procreation, pregnancy and birth to disease, old age and death. At 34 metres (112 feet) long, the *Beethoven*

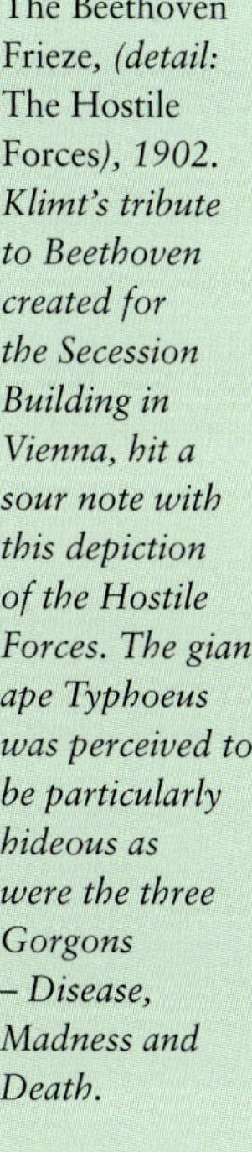

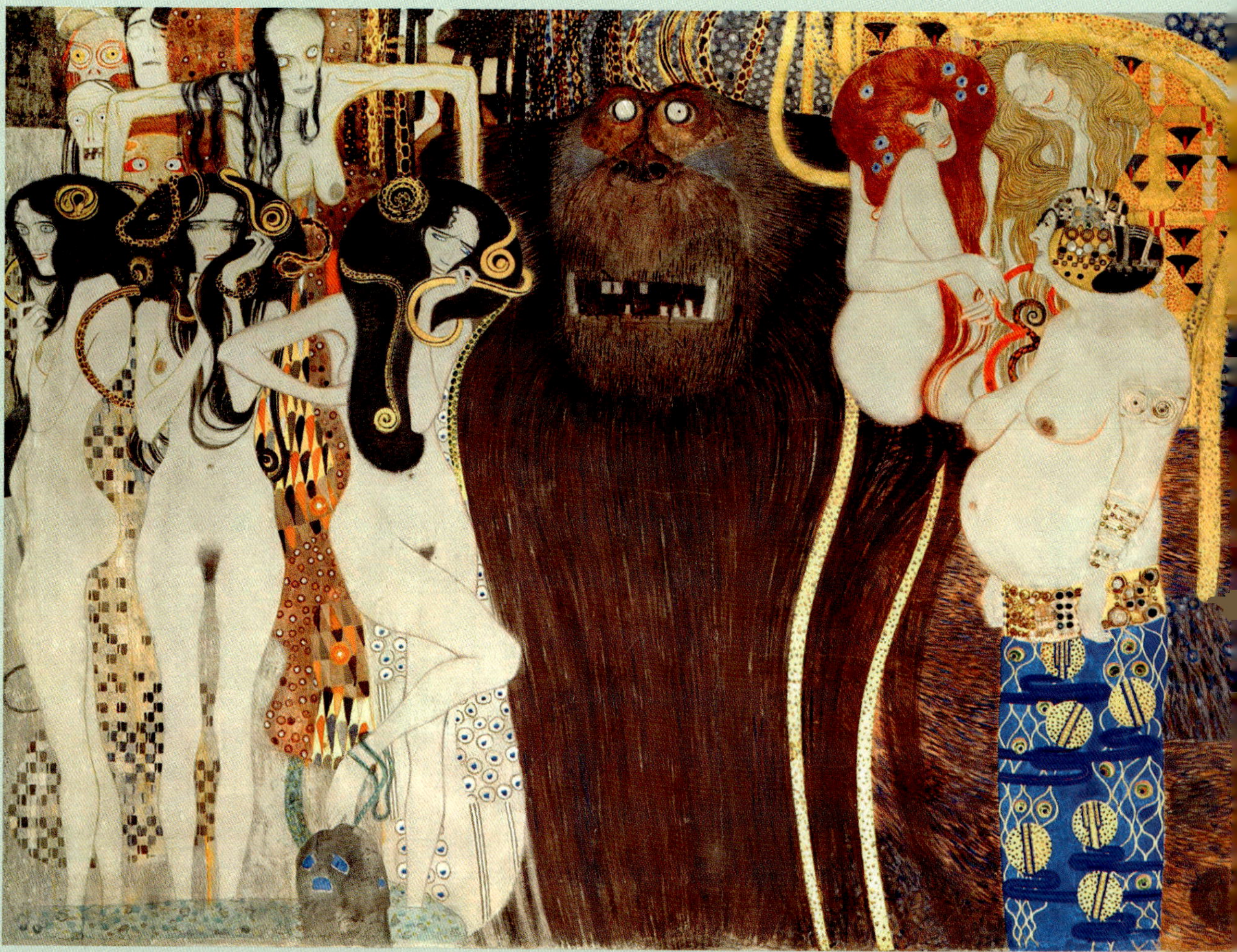

The Beethoven Frieze, *(detail:* The Hostile Forces*), 1902. Klimt's tribute to Beethoven created for the Secession Building in Vienna, hit a sour note with this depiction of the Hostile Forces. The giant ape Typhoeus was perceived to be particularly hideous as were the three Gorgons – Disease, Madness and Death.*

Frieze comprised three painted walls in a sequence. Essentially the three parts depicted firstly the suffering of the weak and a yearning for happiness; secondly hostile forces; and finally, the redemptive power of the arts.

It was the second part of the Frieze dedicated to *Hostile Forces* with its three Gorgons – disease, madness, death – that created the most negative reaction from Klimt's contemporaries. The image of the naked older woman in the foreground with her large breasts and stomach led to charges of ugliness and even obscenity. The frightening apparition of a giant ape, complete with a serpent's tail and wing, visible despite the wealth of ornamental detail, further alienated an audience already uncomfortable with images of skeletal figures with protruding eyes. Aside from the criticism for the rigidity and repulsive nature of his figures, Klimt's contemporary audience was particularly repelled by the male and female nudes. His wide range of erotic vocabulary was just far too challenging for his viewers.

The final section, *The Arts, Chorus of Paradise*, is an altogether more uplifting image, in which a choir of girls sings Beethoven's 'Ode to Joy'. A naked couple in the foreground appears to be enjoying a moment of sexual intimacy. Like so many of Klimt's allegorical works – and despite further explanations in the catalogue that was produced at the time – much of the exact meaning remains unclear. Nevertheless, with its further entanglement of Klimt's erotic and aesthetic sensibilities, the *Beethoven Frieze* was and still is considered an important milestone in his career. Rescued from the walls and kept in storage, the work was preserved and finally put back on show in 1986.

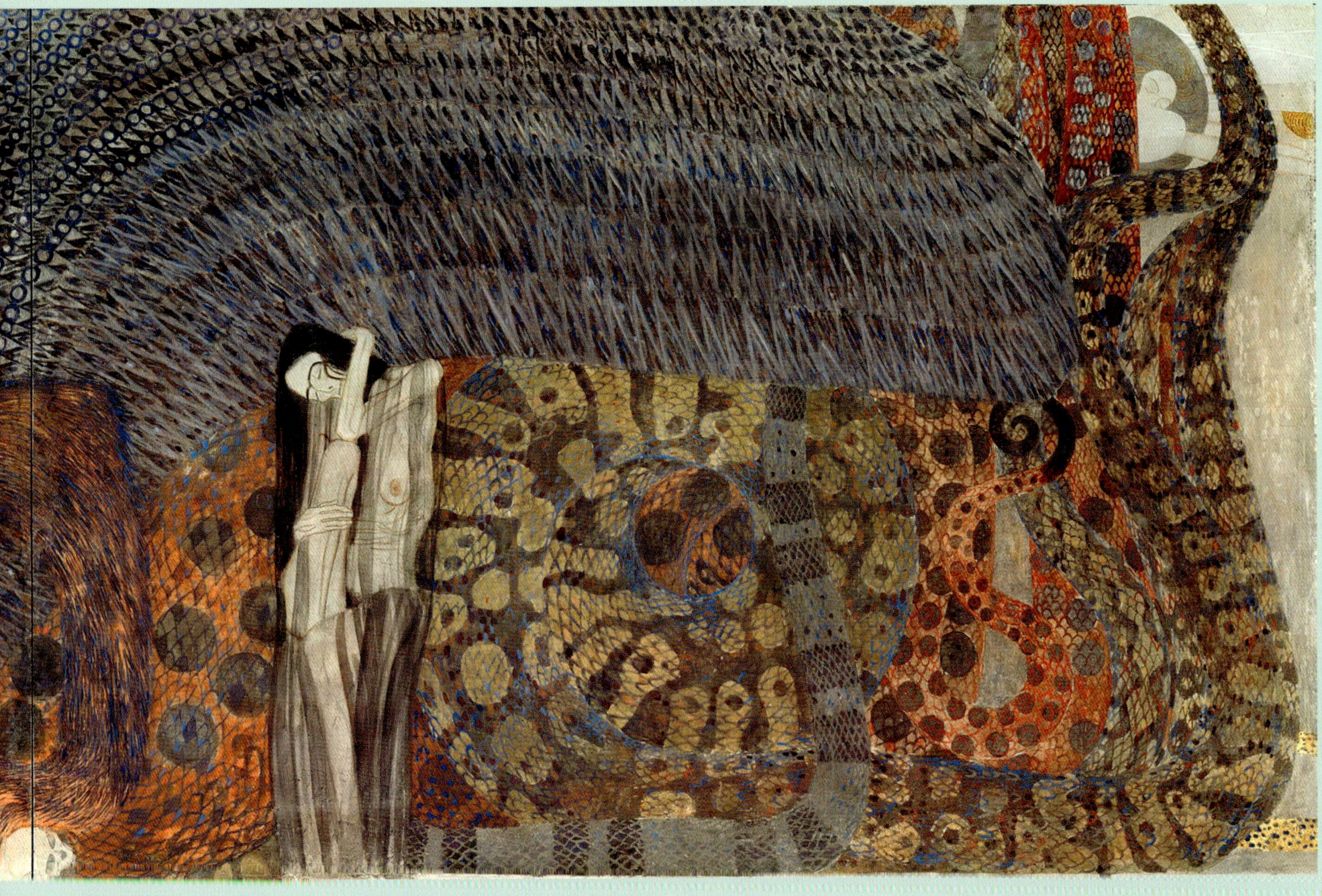

Klimt showed *Medicine* the following year, and again the reaction was nothing short of disastrous. This time it was physicians pitching in to condemn the fact that the work did not do enough to celebrate medical and scientific advances. The central image of Hygeia, the goddess of health, was seen as another of Klimt's femme fatales – with her arms encircled by golden snakes suggestive more of a sorceress than a spiritual being of enlightenment. The work was deemed to be inappropriate, depressing and mocking in equal measure.

Undeterred, Klimt applied for the position of professor at the Academy of Fine Arts (a position he had applied for in 1893) but was turned down. It was his last application for a teaching position. In 1903 he also travelled to Ravenna in Italy and was greatly affected by the Byzantine mosaics that he saw there.

The Secession, meanwhile, continued to stage more than one exhibition a year – between 1898 and 1905 they organized a total of 23 exhibitions. Arnold Böcklin, Edvard Munch, Henri de Toulouse–Lautrec, Auguste Rodin, Alphonse Mucha, Walter Crane and Charles Rennie Mackintosh were among the international artists who showed regularly.

In 1902, Klimt contributed a three-part frieze to the 14th exhibition. Known as the *Beethoven Frieze*, Klimt's work was designed to accompany a special orchestration by Gustav Mahler of the fourth movement of Beethoven's *Ninth Symphony* to be performed at the opening. Klimt applied his utopian vision to three painted walls in sequence. His focus was the optimistic idea of the salvation of mankind through the power of art and love. Rich in ornamentation and suffused with gold, mosaic patterning and brilliant colour, Klimt's complex and powerful work drew upon a range of different styles and references, including Greek vase painting, Egyptian painting, African sculpture and Japanese prints.

The *Beethoven Frieze* divided its audience. Although much admired for its ambitious lyricism, the symbolism of the work continued to baffle some of its viewers, while others were disturbed by its frank, unabashed portrayal of sexuality – in particular the plethora of nude figures, mostly female but some male. Others were more positive in their response, including the artist Auguste Rodin, who exhibited at the first Secessionist exhibition in Vienna and who congratulated Klimt on his 'so tragic and so divine work'.

In 1903, the Secession movement spawned

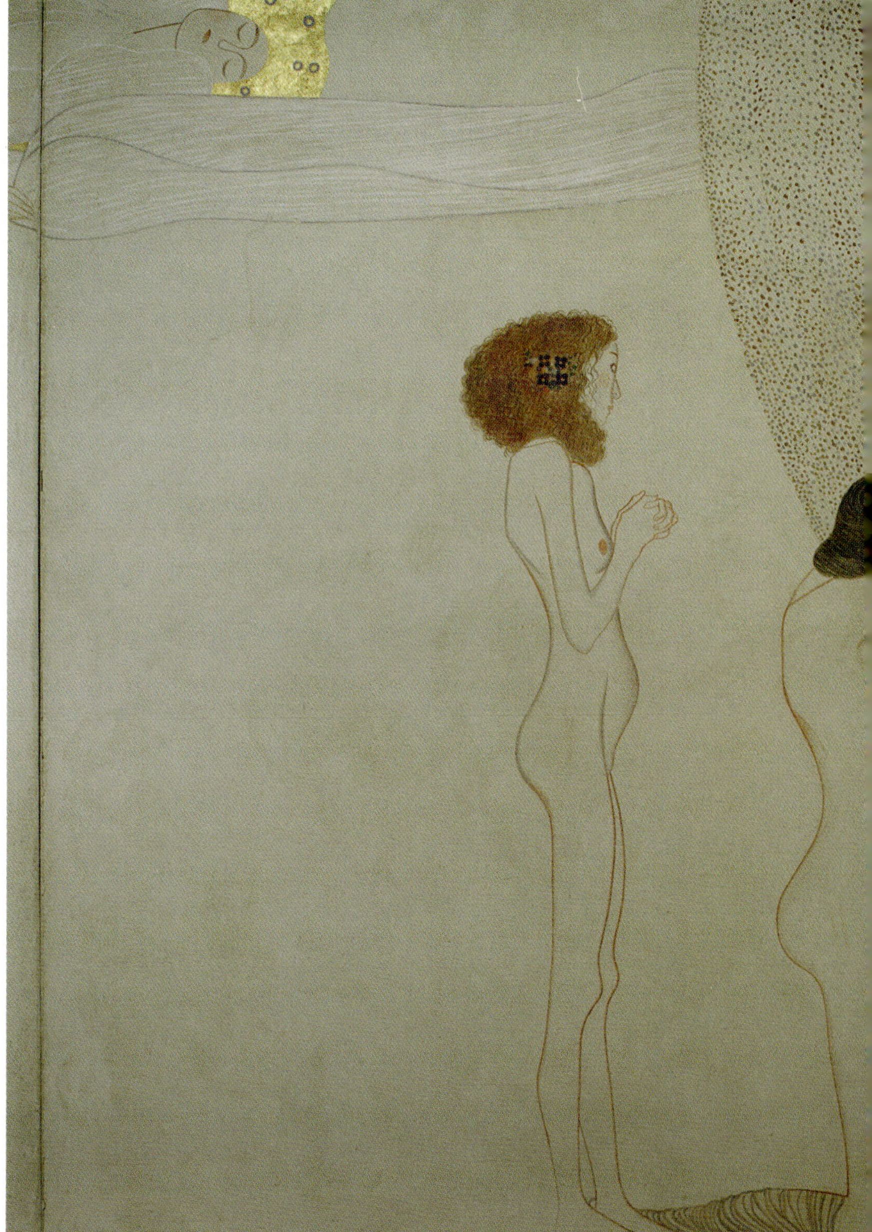

another vital offshoot – namely the Wiener Werkstätte, or Vienna Workshop. Brought together by the architect Josef Hoffman and the designer Koloman Moser, the idea behind this powerful grouping of artists and designers was to create a cooperative that would sell work, train young artists and actively promote the work of all its artist/designer members on an equal footing. Klimt had close ties with the fledgling set-up and designed furniture and textiles for them. It also brought him into closer contact with the woman who was to become his greatest friend and companion, Emilie Flöge.

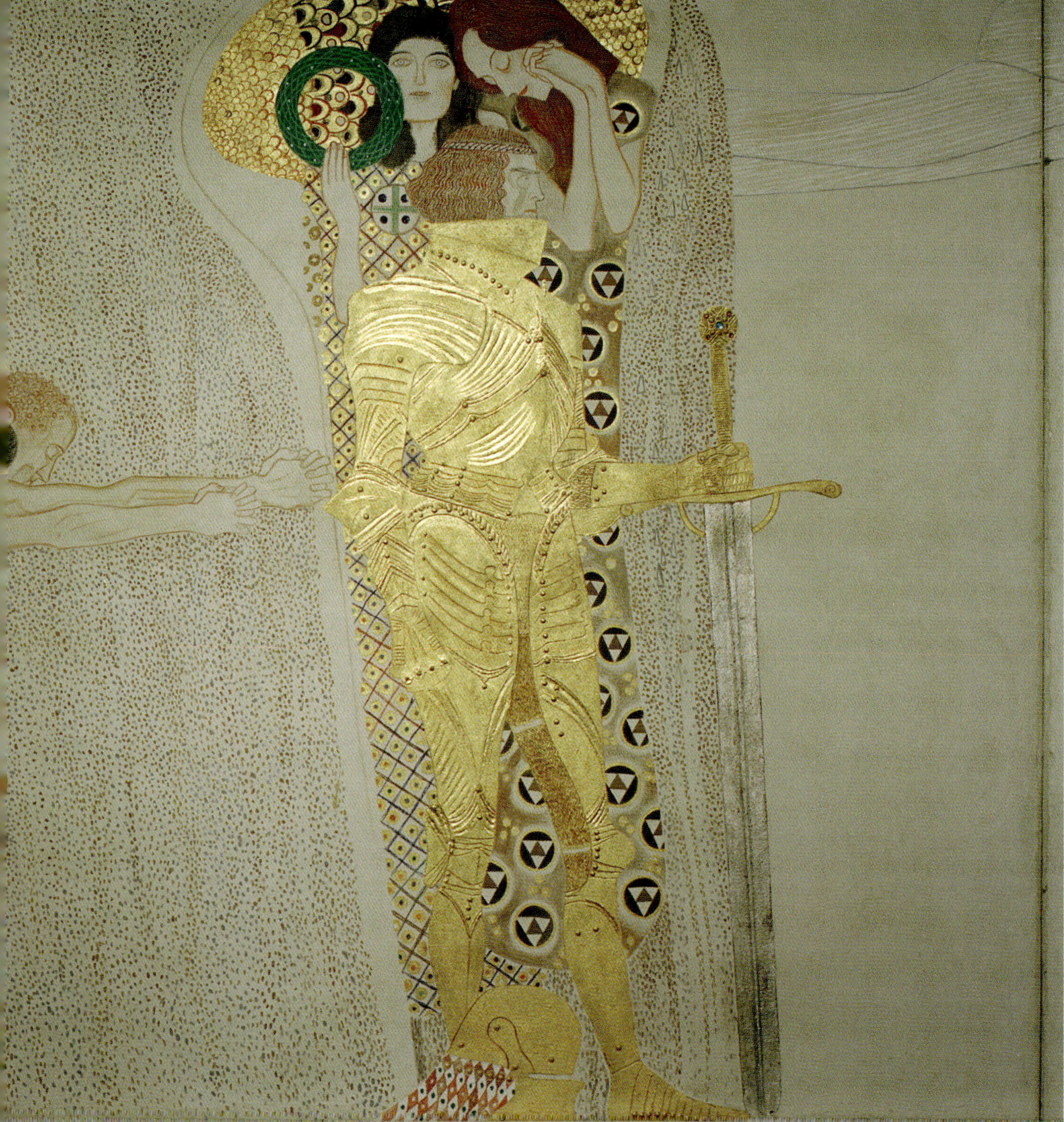

The Beethoven Frieze, *(detail:* Yearning for Happiness*), 1902. In the first part of the* Beethoven Frieze, *Klimt depicted the sufferings of feeble mankind. The well-armed strong one in golden armour is being impelled to take up the struggle for happiness.*

EMILIE FLÖGE

If 1897 denotes the founding of the Viennese Secession, it also marks the year that Gustav Klimt first started spending summers with his companion Emilie Flöge in the Kammer am Attersee region of Upper Austria.

After his father and brother had died in 1892, Gustav Klimt assumed guardianship of Helene Flöge, his brother's widow and baby daughter, and through this became friendly with her younger sister Emilie, who was 12 years his junior (and then aged

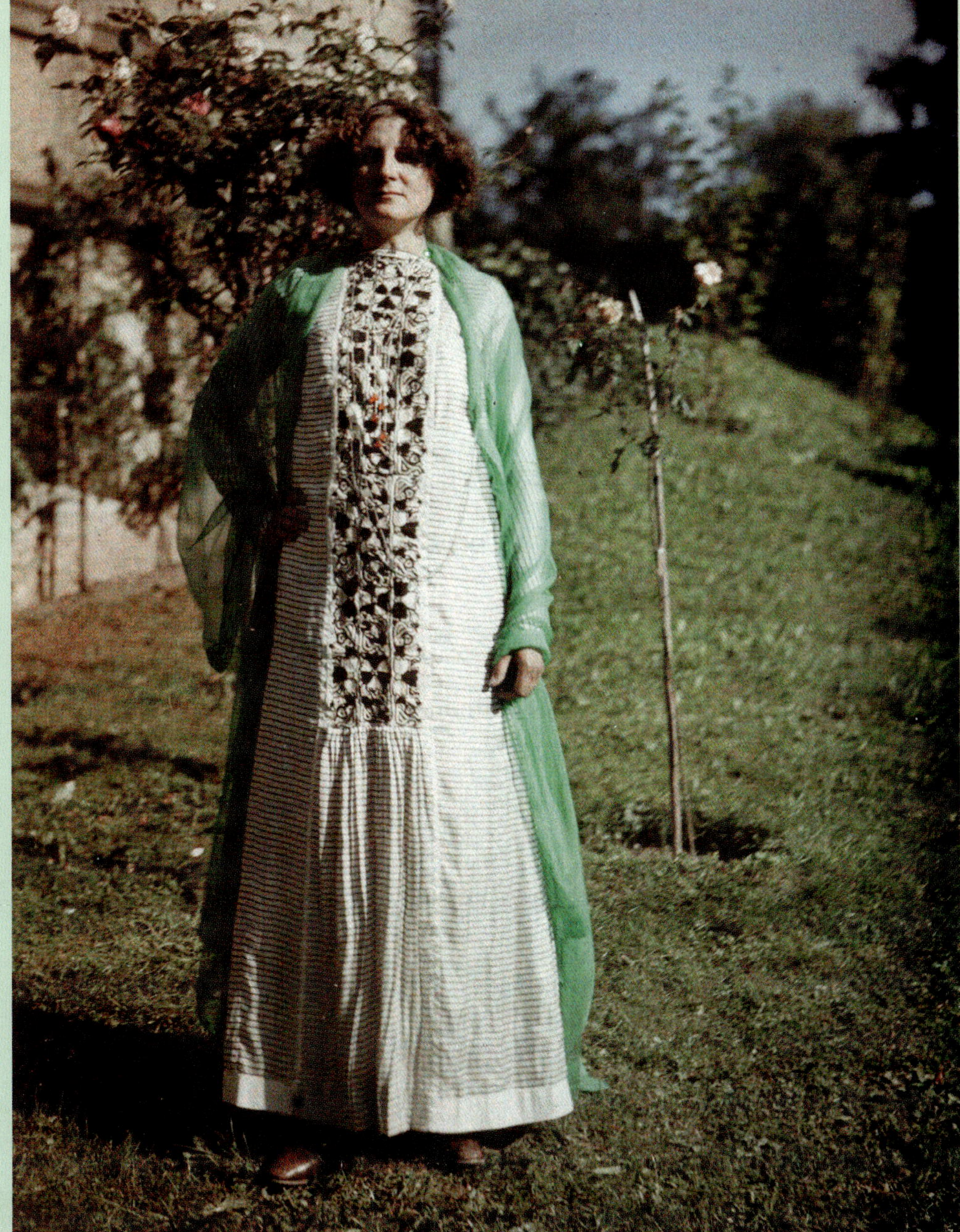

Emilie Flöge on holiday in Lake Attersee c. 1910. She is wearing a white gown with a textured frontispiece designed by Klimt.

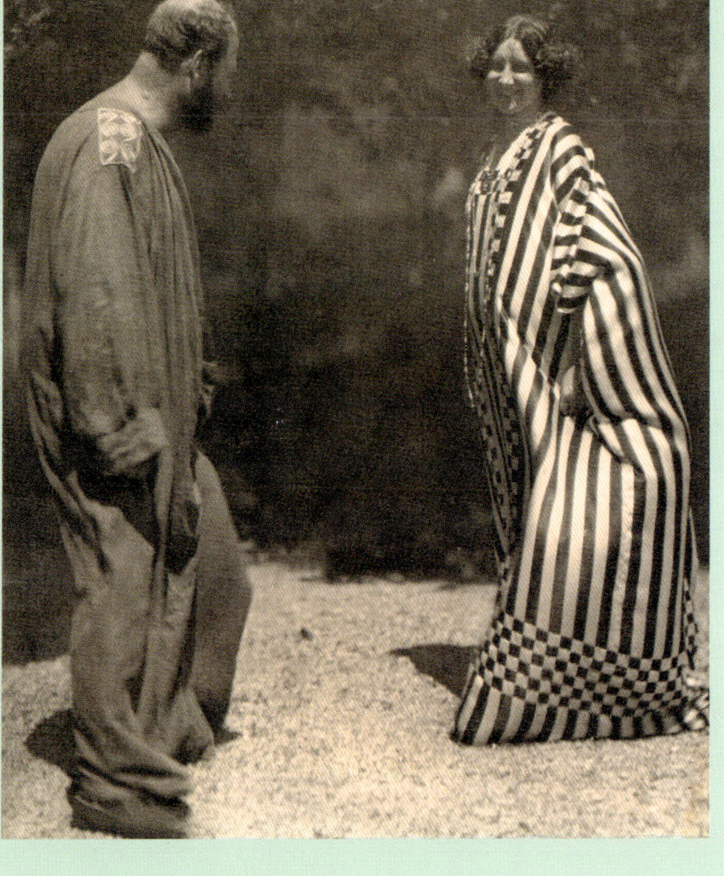

Emilie Flöge wears a dress designed by Klimt for her fashion house – a characteristic Secessionist design with contrasting black and white stripes and incorporating a chequerboard pattern.

only 18). Emilie's father was a master craftsman who manufactured smoking pipes and she was the youngest of four siblings, with two sisters, Pauline and Helene, and a brother, Hermann. In 1895, Pauline opened a dressmaking school, where Emilie gained couture knowledge and skills, paving the way for the opening of a new designer clothing business a decade later with her sister Helene.

In 1903, the Wiener Werkstätte, or Vienna Workshop, was set up as a co-operative for artists and designers. Based on the English Arts and Crafts movement, the aim was to get rid of hierarchical distinctions between art and craft while promoting the specialist nature of all the arts. Both Klimt and Emilie were involved with the Werkstätte, and in 1904 founder members Josef Hoffman and Klaus Moser helped to refit the interior of the Flöge Sisters fashion house in one of Vienna's most prestigious streets. Klimt, meanwhile, designed some new fabrics for the sisters – featuring bold colours and striking patterns. Flöge and the salon were supporters of 'reform clothing' in Vienna, a liberating style of clothing for women based on free-flowing dresses and an end to the tight-fitting corset.

A photograph of Klimt and Flöge shows two people caught in a pose that looks almost like the precursor to a dance. She is smiling at the camera, wearing a voluminous, tent-like dress made of material designed by Klimt and featuring a black and white chessboard pattern and stripes; the artist wears a floor-length painter's smock. There are several similar photos showing the pair in long kaftans, posing in a boat on Lake Attersee where, for three months most summers until 1916, they made regular excursions together.

The relationship between Klimt and Emilie seems mainly to have revolved around a deep and lasting friendship. From the time they met, they were close companions who not only holidayed together but went to the opera and theatre and attempted to learn French. Whether they were ever lovers is a matter of speculation – they never married and Klimt pursued many other sexual affairs while they were seeing each other. Most of his lovers were very different from the smart, independent, talented, middle-class Emilie Flöge – she represented a very pure and sacred kind of love at odds with the many models and working-class women with whom he actually had sexual relations. It has also been speculated that Flöge, who never married and had no other known partners, was a lesbian. This is one explanation for the intense friendship and creative partnership she maintained with Klimt, who happily indulged his avid sexual appetite elsewhere but clearly preferred her company above all others.

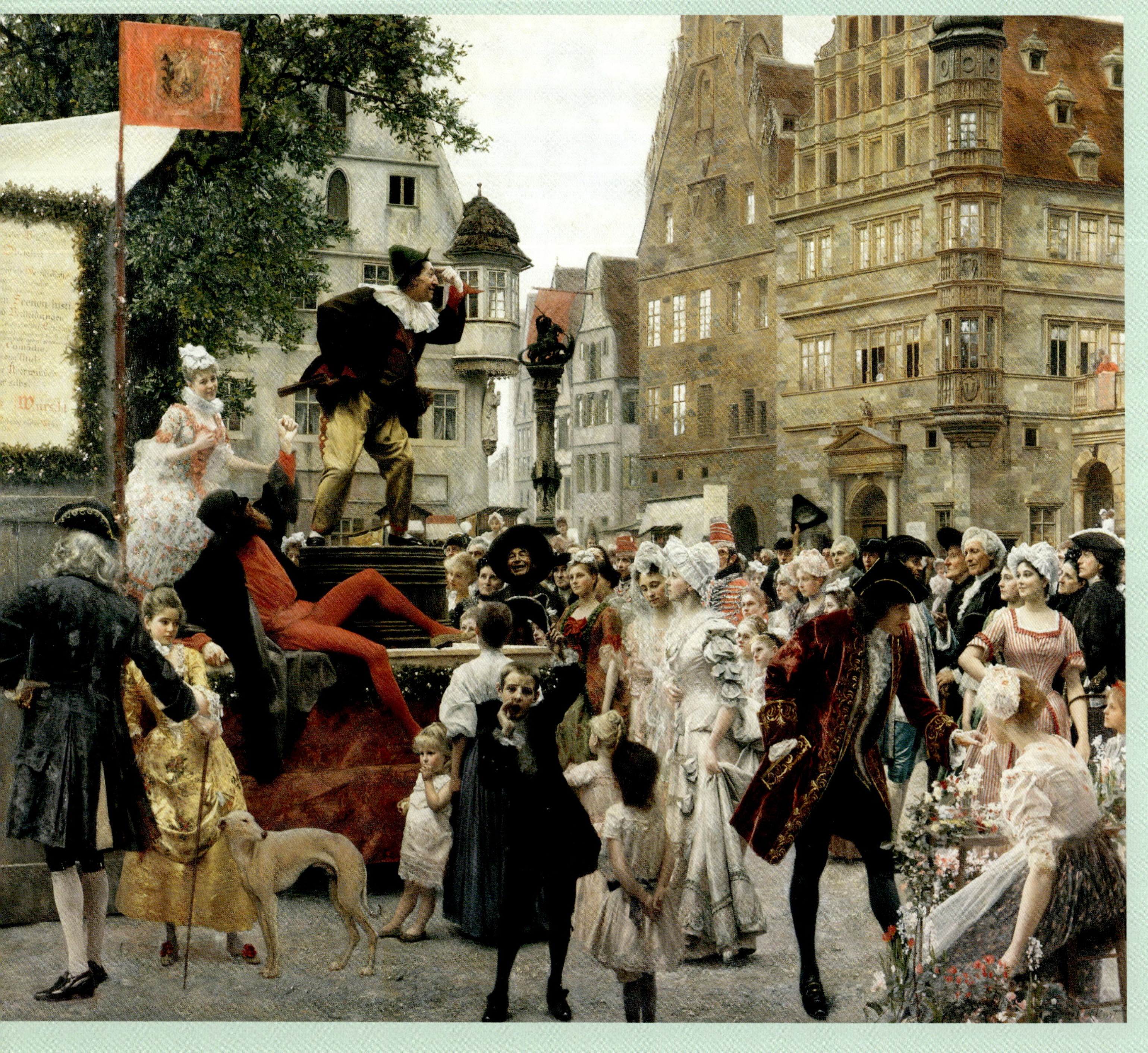

A Theatrical Buffoon on a Makeshift Stage at Rothenburg, *1893. Klimt's brother Ernst originally painted this work on the Burgtheater ceiling in 1893. Klimt finished it after his brother's death, and in the centre added a portrait of a young Emilie Flöge in a red and green gown.*

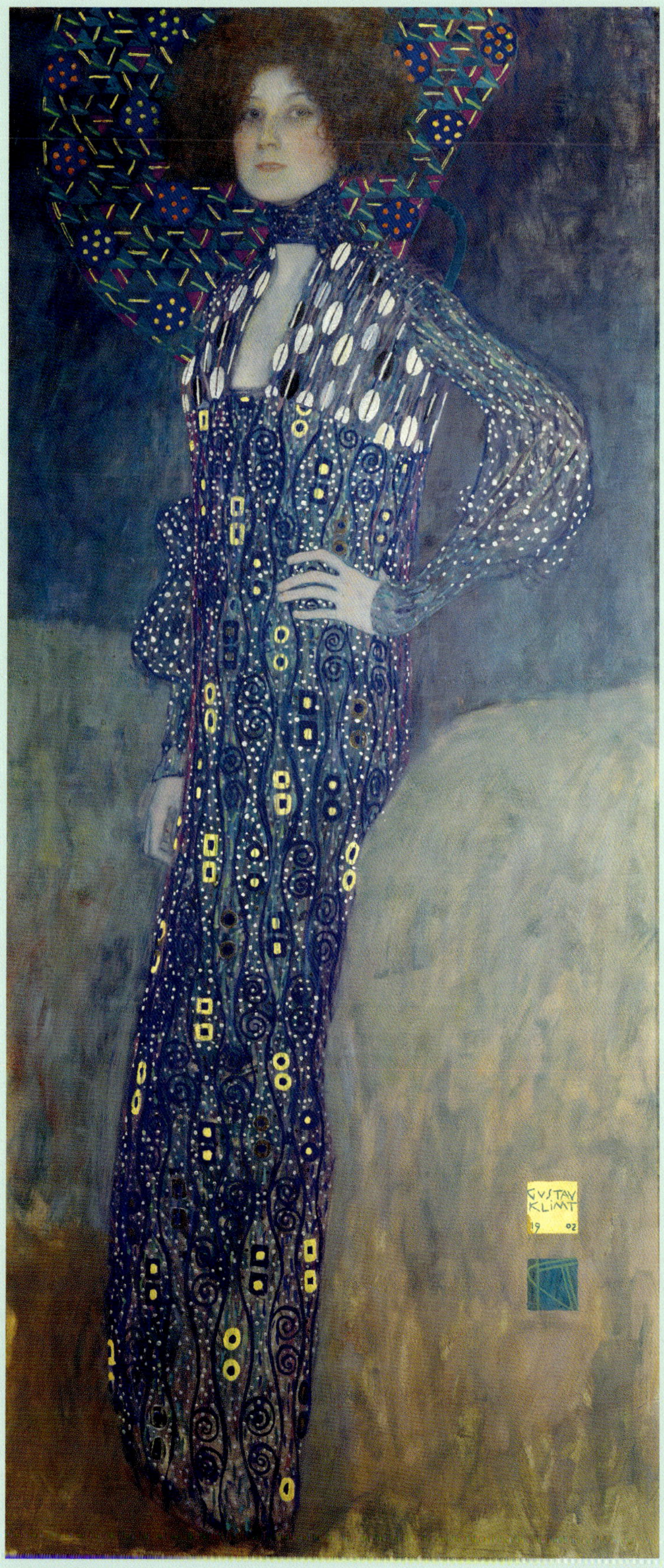

Klimt used Emilie as a model several times. In 1891, when she was only 17, he painted her portrait. Her face is in profile and the painting has an integral gold frame decorated with Japanese style foliage. In this, Flöge's serious expression and determined gaze indicates a strong-willed temperament somewhat at odds with the youthful innocence of her gauzy white gown. A youthful Flöge also appeared in a painting called *A Theatrical Buffoon on a Makeshift Stage at Rothenburg*. This was originally painted on the Burgtheater ceiling in 1893 by his brother Ernst, and Klimt finished the work after his brother's death, adding a portrait of Emilie standing in a red and green gown.

A later portrait from 1902 shows Flöge again, this time wearing one of Klimt's designs for her fashion house – a floor-length blue dress with a large elliptical shape of the same fabric behind her head, framing her face and curly hair. The stunning dress has an all-over pattern of gold and silver circles and bars – Flöge is presented as a bejewelled icon, an idealized portrait in which her goddess-like status and modesty is literally preserved in a golden casing. Hand on hip, Flöge radiates self-possession, her sangfroid seemingly offering a direct challenge to the viewer. Interestingly, this is not a portrait that she, her family or Klimt himself much liked and he sold it a few years later to the City Museum in Vienna.

Some claim that Emilie was the model for the woman depicted in *The Kiss*. The evidence for this is scant, however, and seems to be based on wish fulfillment by those who want to see Flöge and Klimt's relationship as more than platonic.

At the end of World War II, Flöge's possessions, including clothing from her business and gifts from Klimt, were destroyed in a house fire at her home on Ungargasse, where she had been forced to relocate her business following the annexation of Austria into Nazi Germany in 1938. She died aged 78 in 1952 in Vienna.

Fraulein Emilie Flöge, *1902. Klimt's portrait of his companion Emilie Flöge. Klimt borrowed the two signature boxes on the right at the bottom from Japanese art – one of his great passions.*

WIENER WERKSTÄTTE

The Wiener Werkstätte, the cooperative of artists and designers formed in 1903, was the brainchild of two important Secession members – the architect Josef Hoffman and the designer Koloman Moser – and their financial backer, the wealthy textile manufacturer and patron of Klimt, Fritz Waerndorfer. The concept behind the new set-up followed on from the earlier idea of *Gesamtkunstwerk*, or total artwork, espoused by the Secession. Any hierarchy between art forms should be disregarded. Art and design were considered of equal importance. Makers should produce objects that were at once aesthetically pleasing, simple and functional. Harmony was the key word when it came to design. Nothing was considered off-limits or unworthy of a design make over. Grand architectural projects – the complete overhaul of a Viennese mansion, for example – was a project to be tackled alongside the redesign of pots, pans, textiles, clothes and jewellery.

The Werkstätte's egalitarian principles and practical, hands-on emphasis was inspired by the English Arts and Craft movement, following on from William Morris, John Ruskin and the work of Charles Rennie Mackintosh. All three founder members were particularly enthused by Mackintosh, whose work had been shown at the eighth Secession exhibition in 1900. They were drawn to the way his work created a subtle fusion between geometric lines and angles and the sweeping curves of symbolism. They also much admired the fact that Mackintosh and his wife Margaret Macdonald created entire rooms filled with beautiful objects.

The entrance of the Wiener Werkstätte's shop in the inner city of Vienna, c. 1907.

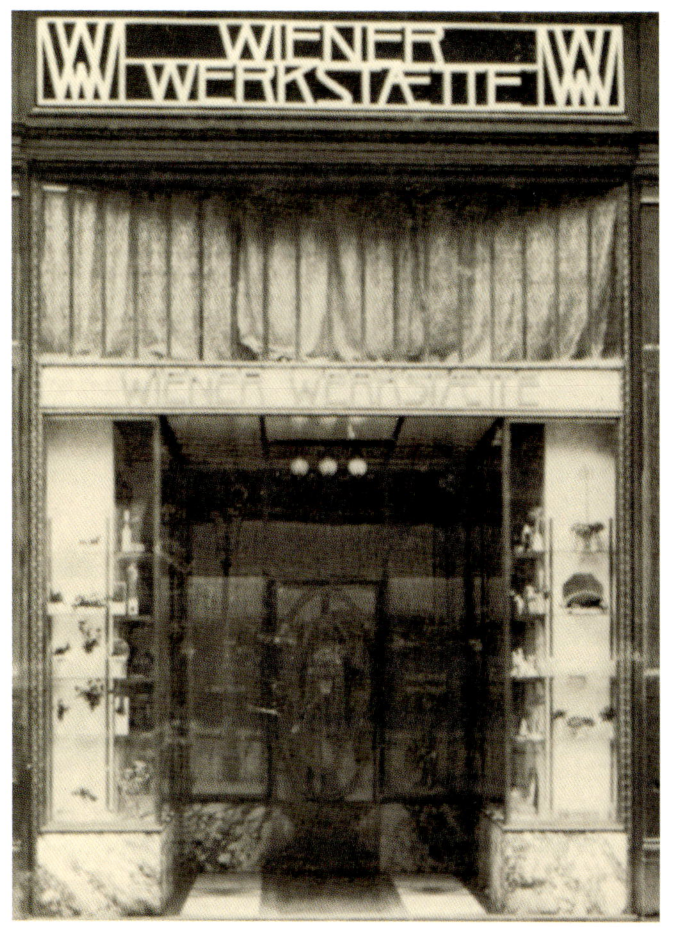

The idea behind the Werkstätte was to create a level playing field for art and design. This depended on investing time and energy into specialist techniques, particularly as it was believed that some of these were threatened by a move towards industrialization. Workshops were set up to train younger artists in metalwork, furniture, bookbinding and glassmaking, for example.

After the success of the workshops, and with about a hundred people working there, Hoffman and Moser felt that the applied arts needed more of a showcase, and set about finding new premises. In 1905, they found a new home in Vienna at 32/34 Neustiftgasse, where a high-ceilinged reception area and exhibition room could display many of the objects made by the Werkstätte members. Aside from producing a wide range of items for sale, many of the members also contributed to the architectural commissions that Hoffman received.

One project that Hoffman worked on was to design a sanatorium at Purkersdorf to the west of Vienna. His sketches for the building show a spare, uncluttered concrete building with little ornamentation, typifying the Werkstätte's pure, restrained yet graceful approach to design. *Fruit Basket*, 1904, made by Hoffman, is another typical 'pure' piece of design: all in silver, the basket consists of a tray standing on thin

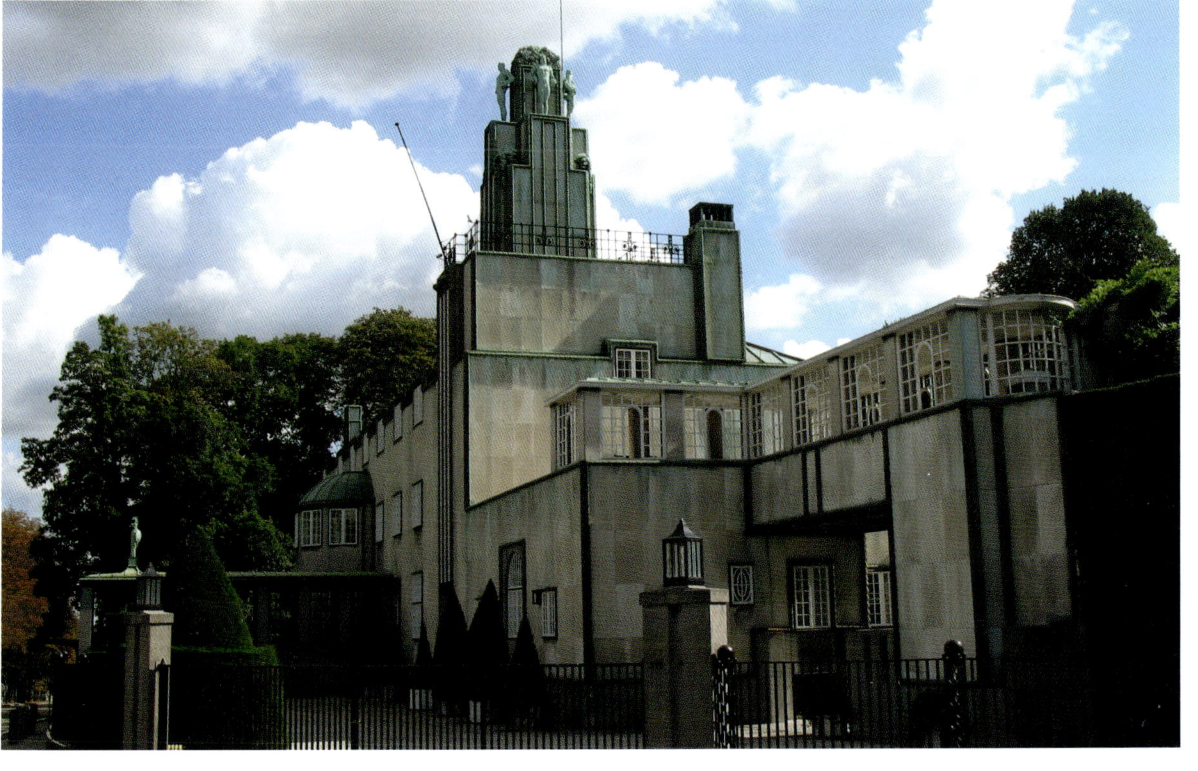

The exterior of Palais Stoclet designed by Josef Hoffman for Belgian industrialist Adolphe Stoclet on the outskirts of Brussels. A great masterpiece of Art Nouveau design.

geometric bars, decorated with tiny beads of silver. Overall it is a very elegant design, that typifies the Wiener Werkstätte's approach to elevating functional objects.

The exact moment that Klimt, a board member and close associate of all three founder members, began to become closely involved with the Wiener Werkstätte is not known. Having once declared that it is 'better to spend one day on one thing than to produce ten things in one day', Klimt recognized that his considered approach to his craft was a natural fit with the group. There were many points of contact. The Wiener Werkstätte often made frames for Klimt's paintings. This was not a simple case of choosing the right frame, since Klimt saw his frames as an extension of the picture itself and integral to the overall effect of the work. Klimt also had his studio redesigned by members of the Werkstätte, early on in the group's existence. Klimt was not initially best pleased with the result as he was away when it was realized, leaving him with several hefty items of furniture, including a Hoffman-designed sideboard that he was forced to navigate around in his studio. Klimt also bought several items from the Werkstätte, including jewellery and ceiling lights.

Klimt's collaborations with the Werkstatte extended to painting pictures for interiors, as well as designing fabrics and clothes. Along with Moser and Hoffman, Klimt helped to redesign the interior of the Flöge Fashion house, creating a new stylish showroom for the Flöge sisters. In return, the three sisters – Helene, Emilie and Pauline – often featured the Werkstätte's stark geometric fabric designs in their shop.

Koloman Moser left the group after disagreements with Waerndorfer in 1907. His departure marked the beginning of a new ornamental phase in the group's development, with Hoffman introducing luxurious materials into his architectural projects. Hoffman designed the grand building Palais Stoclet for Belgian industrialist Adolphe Stoclet on the outskirts of Brussels. Hoffman employed a team of craftsmen from the Werkstätte, working on every last detail in the house, from the doorknobs to the cutlery. Hoffman also asked Klimt to create a mosaic frieze for the ground floor. This frieze drew on a vast array of ornamental items and sumptuous materials, heralding the group's new style, which Waerndorfer did much to encourage. One of Klimt's most important patrons, Waerndorfer was the driving force behind another of the later projects involving Hoffman, Klimt and other Werkstätte members – namely, the design and decoration of Cabaret Fledermaus, a Viennese nightclub.

THE STOCLET FRIEZE

In 1905, the Belgian financier Adolph Stoclet commissioned Josef Hoffman and the Wiener Werkstätte to complete their dream of creating a total of work of art – namely, an entire new house and all its contents. No ceiling was put on the budget. Klimt's role was again to provide a mural – in this case, a frieze that ran along two sides of the rectangular dining room, with an accompanying panel on the short wall.

This commission lasted for four years and Klimt did extensive preliminary work. He drew preparatory cartoons and, in collaboration with the makers in the Wiener Werkstätte who engraved the designs into the marble, reapplied the outlines by hand. His designs draw upon the Byzantine mosaics of Ravenna and Oriental art. The Tree of Life is the work's central motif. The golden branches of the trees spiral over the entire wall and contain a host of tiny elements, including birds, flowers and Egyptian-style eyes. In *The Expectation*, an inlaid panel, a gorgeously bejewelled Egyptian queen wrought out of rich gold triangles waves her arms and sidesteps. In *The Embrace* the tip of a man's

Palais Stoclet's ornate marble dining room showing Klimt's frieze.

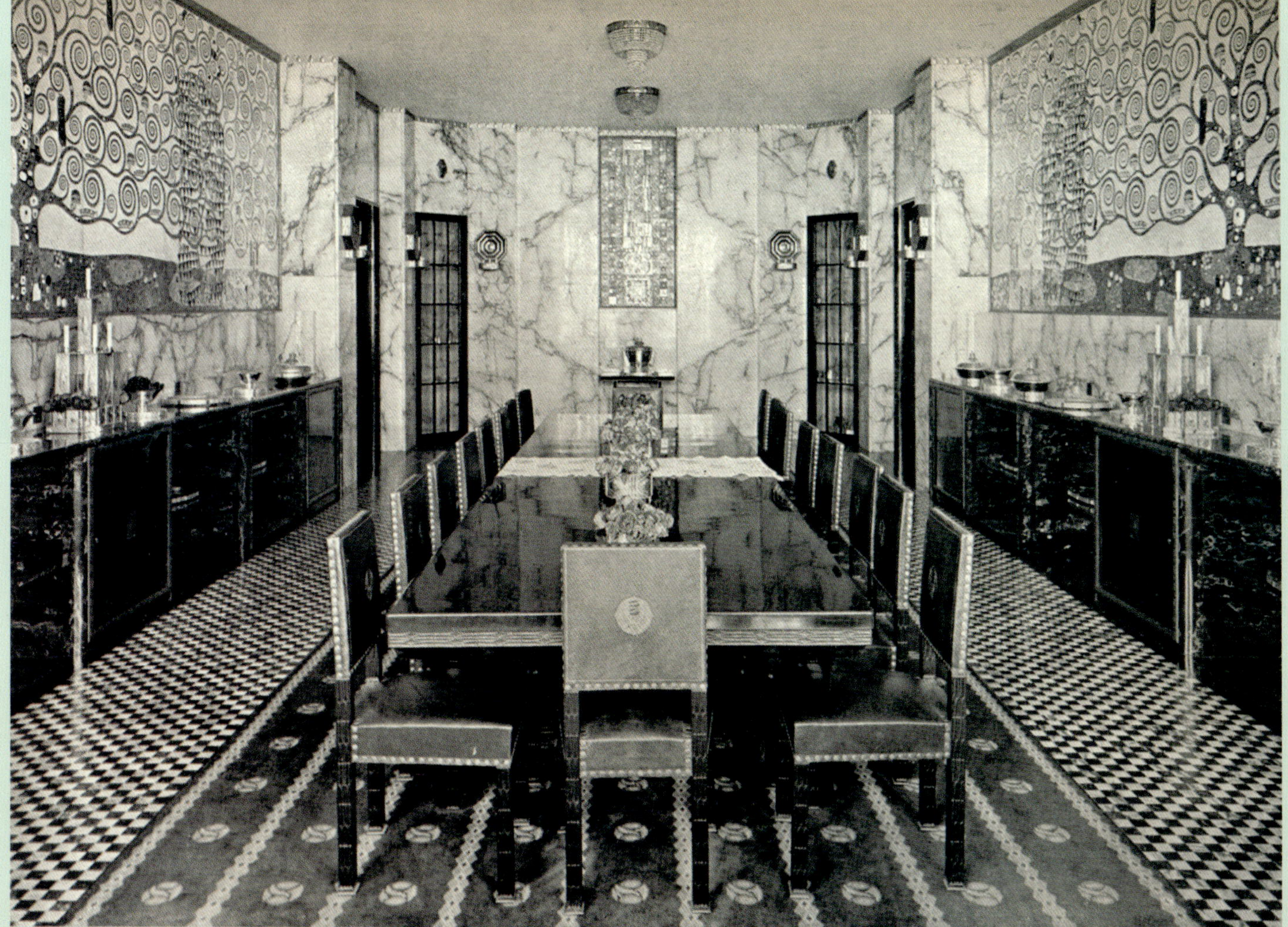

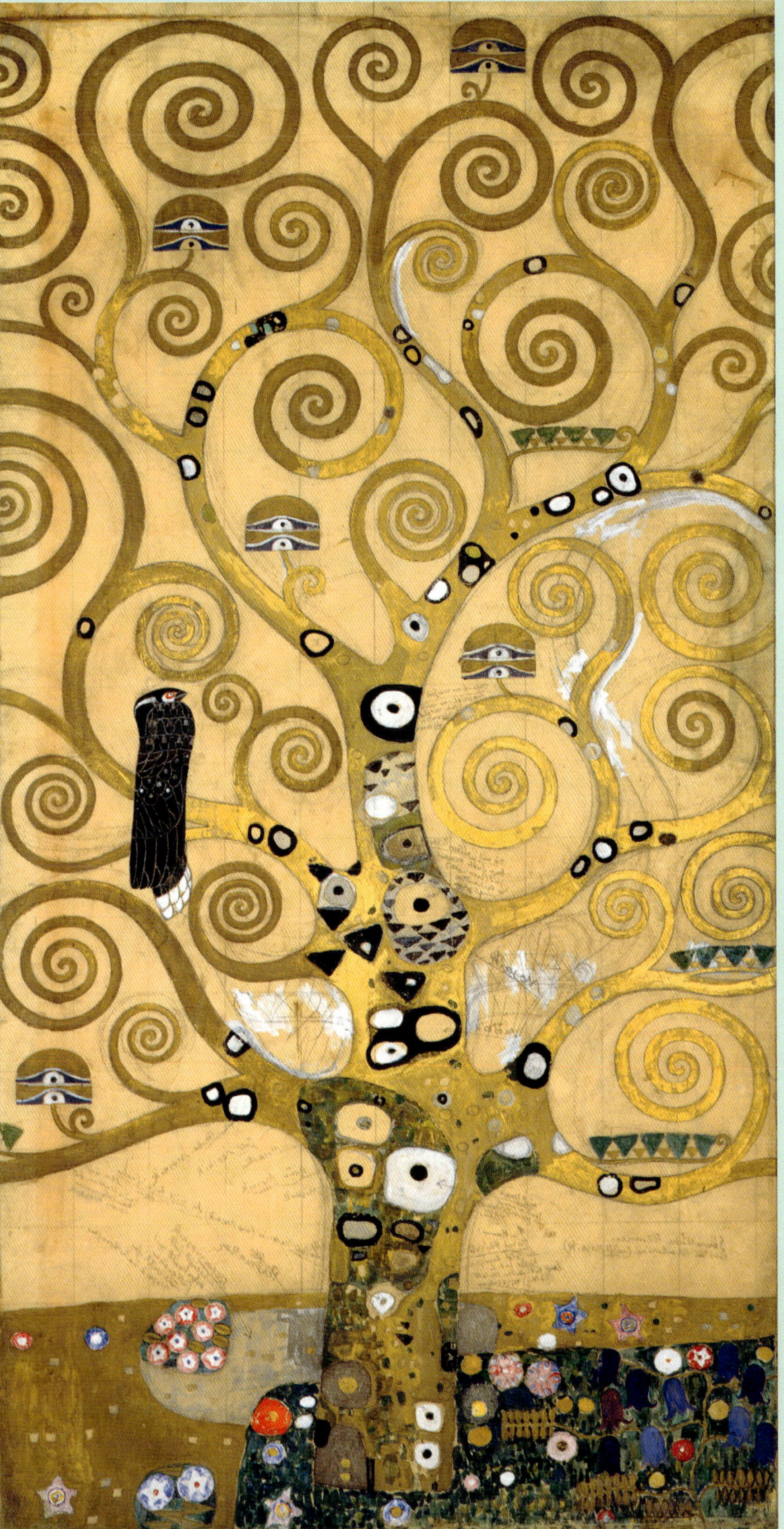

head is barely visible seen from behind as he is swallowed up in an embrace with his lover. Both figures are covered in richly decorated cloaks. The work echoes the placing of the couple in the last section of the *Beethoven Frieze* and prefigures Klimt's celebrated painting *The Kiss*, produced only a couple of years later.

The *Stoclet Frieze* is the most abstract of the two murals. As decoration it is sumptuous and makes the most of its costly materials. As a piece of work designed for a private residence, it was intended to please the eye rather than make a grand allegorical statement. Still hurt by the reception he had received for his earlier mural, Klimt was reluctant to let the Viennese public in to see the work. The Palais Stoclet still exists although nowadays in a different form. The frieze he created for it was the last of Klimt's mural works.

The Tree of Life, Stoclet Frieze, *1905–09. The central image of the Frieze, Klimt's theme is the Garden of Eden with its allusions to nature, the seasons and the abundance of life.*

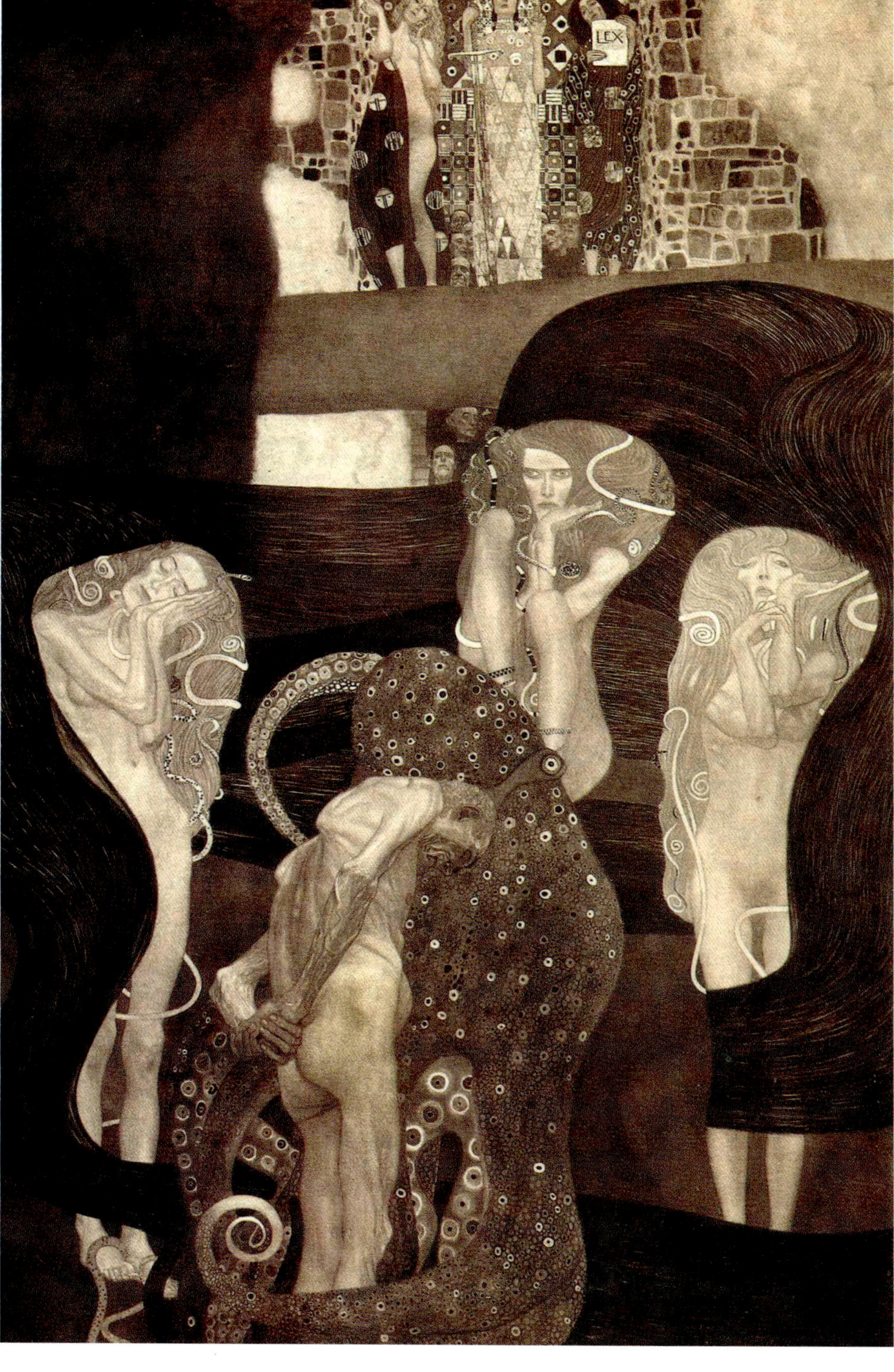

Jurisprudence, *1903. One of the objections Klimt's critics had to this work was that the final painting with its scene of grim torment and misery differed radically from the oil sketch he had submitted.*

The contradiction that became more painfully obvious in the later years of the Werkstätte was that despite its desire to be an egalitarian movement, spreading harmony and beauty to all, the people most able to benefit were the well-off. As the designs got more rarified, fewer people were able to afford them, and by 1932 the group was no longer in existence.

Josef Hoffman, the principal architect behind the Wiener Werkstätte, was commissioned in 1904 by Adolph Stoclet to design a house in Brussels from scratch. Stoclet was a wealthy industrialist and no expense was spared on the project, which involved contributions from a number of artists, including Klimt. Both Oskar Kokoschka and Egon Schiele, two young artists who were still students, contributed designs, though these were eventually rejected in favour of more established artists.

In 1904 Klimt started on his working designs for an ornamental mosaic, using semi-precious stones as well as enamel to cover three walls. It was to display Klimt's mastery of mosaic, a technique that he had intensely studied on his recent visit to Ravenna. He continued to work on the project for the next five years. The idea behind the frieze was the life cycle – with the tree of life as a central motif. A monumental collaboration between art and architecture, the *Stoclet Frieze* is also perhaps the greatest expression to the Secessionist belief in the importance of the interaction of all the art forms.

The final *Faculty Painting – Jurisprudence* – was exhibited alongside *Philosophy* and *Medicine* in 1903. The painting contains three female figures representing Truth, Justice and Law, who stand over the naked figures of men, including one pinned down by an octopus. The imagery was perceived as shocking in its vengefulness while inappropriately revealing the insecurity of man in the modern world. Klimt was accused in Parliament of ‘pornography’ and of ‘perverted excess’.

With financial help from a patron, Klimt eventually decided to buy *Philosophy* back. *Medicine* and *Jurisprudence* were bought by Koloman Moser his good friend in the Wiener Werkstätte. After Moser’s death the works were compulsorily purchased by the Nazis and eventually destroyed by the retreating German army in 1945.

The outcry prompted by the *Faculty Paintings* was like nothing Klimt had faced before. The attack was on many different levels: some questioned the state patronage of the work (the familiar refrain being ‘what a waste of money’); others its philosophical content and inherent pessimism; there were also fundamental questions about aesthetics, including whether this should be regarded as art at all. In the face of such bitterness and hostility, the fragility of Klimt’s temperament was exposed and the insouciant air he had hitherto adopted was no longer in evidence. In spring 1905 he finally gave way. He withdrew from the commission and shortly afterwards, along with his colleagues Hoffman, Moser and Roller, from the Secession itself.

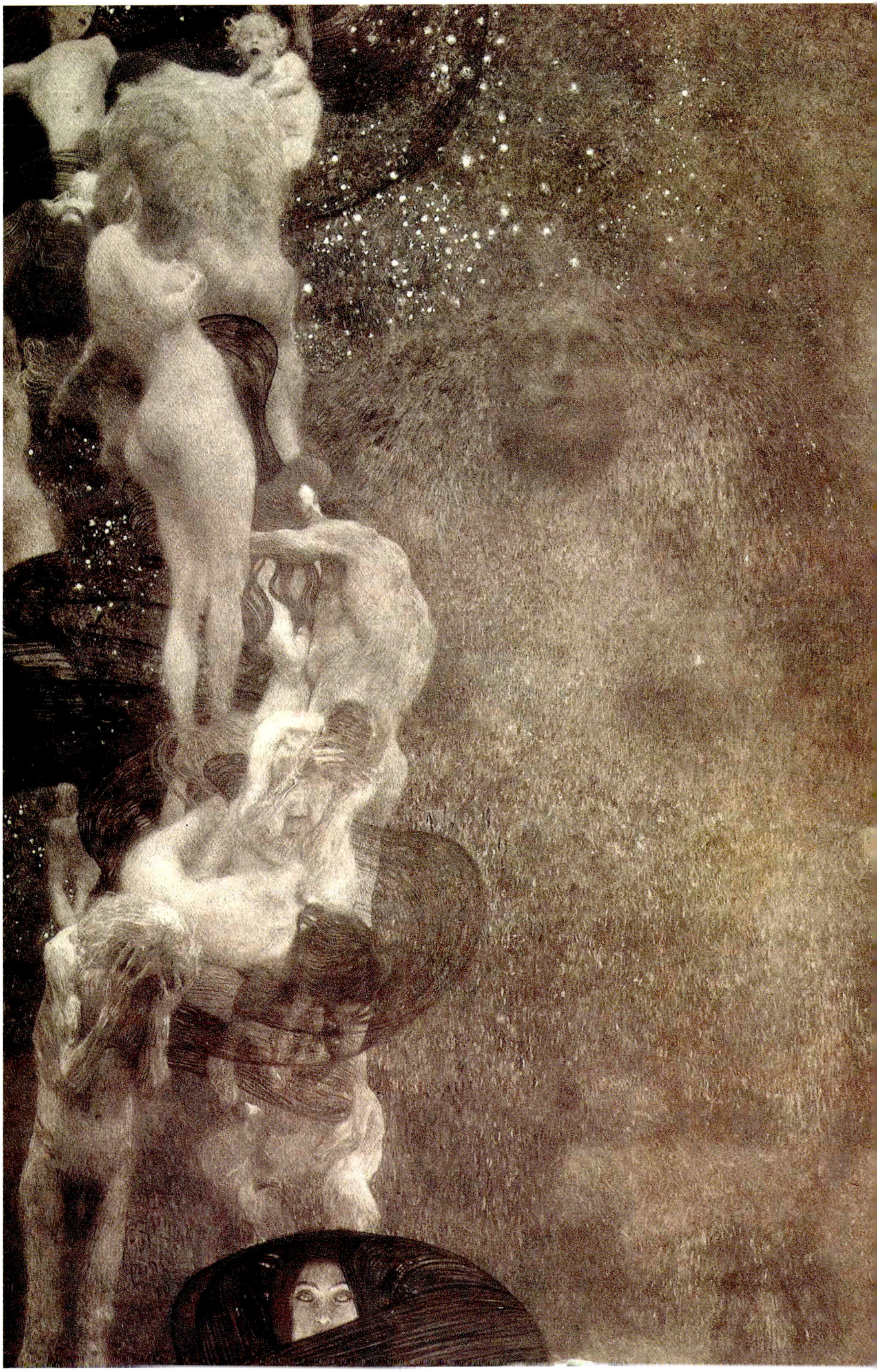

Philosophy, *1899–1907. The first of the three University ceiling paintings to stir up controversy, with Klimt’s detractors baffled by its apparent lack of connection to the realm of Philosophy.*

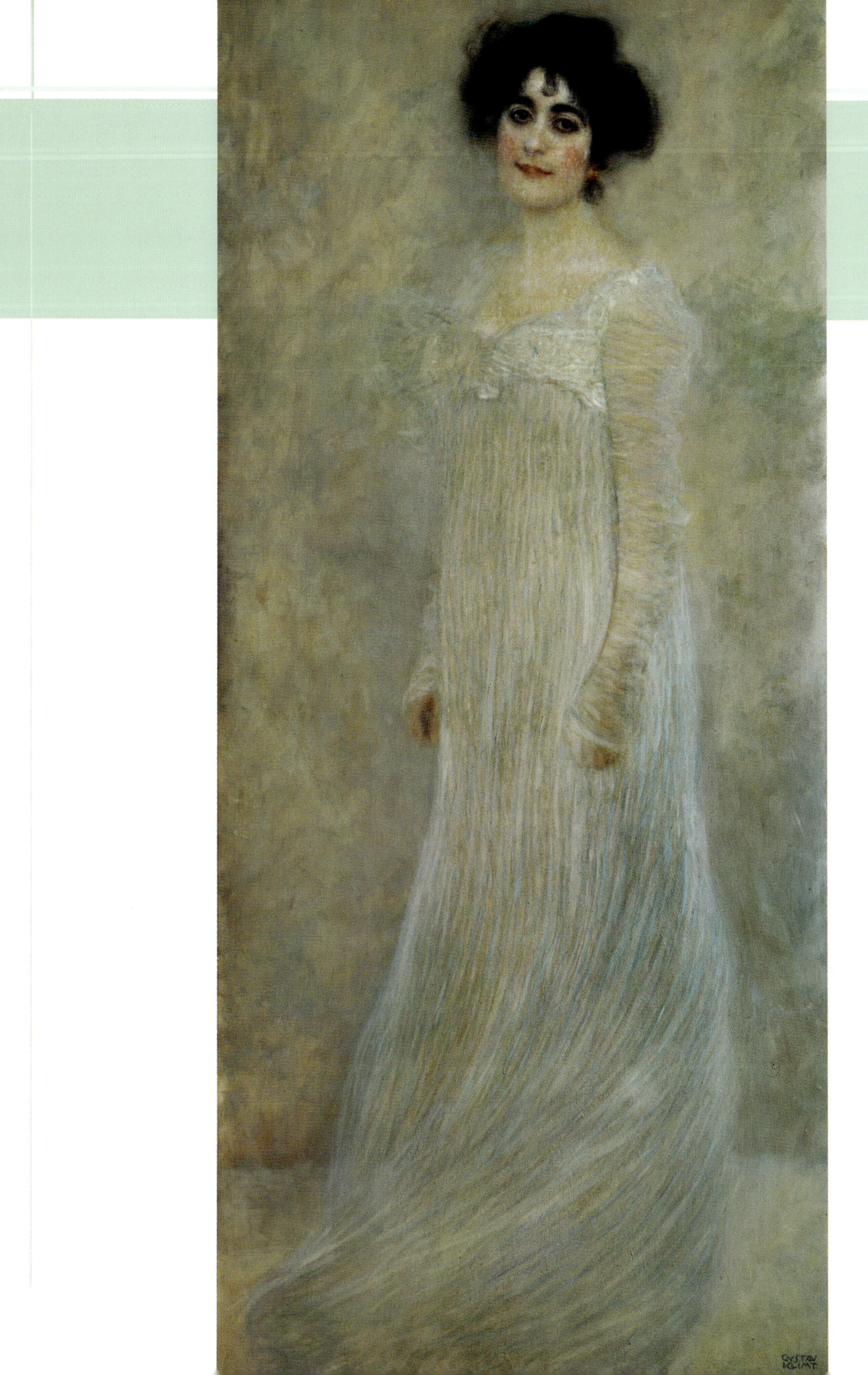
GUSTAV
KLIMT

CHAPTER 3
Femmes Fatales

It is clear that Klimt is one of those artists for whom writing or thinking about art is less important than actually doing it. Klimt rarely wrote about art and therefore those wanting to find extra meaning in his life and work have fallen upon the little that is recorded. In an essay entitled 'Commentary on a non-existent self-portrait', he stated, 'I have never painted a self-portrait. I am less interested in myself as a subject for a painting than I am in other people, above all women ... There is nothing special about me. I am a painter who paints day after day from morning to night... Whoever wants to know something about me... ought to look carefully at my pictures.'

One of Klimt's overriding themes is women and, particularly during his Secessionist period, attractive, powerful and seductive women. The concept of the femme fatale – a woman who is dangerous, even fatally so, having the ability to ensnare her lovers and lead them into compromising or deadly situations – is not new and indeed is an archetype of literature and art. In Western culture of the late nineteenth and early twentieth centuries, the femme fatale became a fashionable trope. The women whom Klimt chose to depict in his paintings were often based on allegorical figures from Bible stories and ancient Greek and Roman mythology. The models who posed for these femmes fatales were mostly women known to Klimt and in some cases, women with whom he enjoyed an intimate, sexual relationship. In addition, a couple of the women were the wives of businessmen and leading figures of Viennese society who had commissioned their portraits, and they were also his lovers. During his lifetime Klimt went to great lengths to ensure that these affairs did not reach the ears of his patrons, a scandal of this sort being almost certain to destroy his career.

It is perhaps unsurprising, therefore, that in his portraits of society wives Klimt depicts the strong powerful women whom he was to return to time and again. *Serena Lederer* (1899) and *Gertha Felsovanyi* (1902) are both almost full-length and are attractive, flattering portraits of women married to prosperous Viennese businessman. The tones are muted and their long pale robes softly tumble to the floor. There is, however, something slightly unnerving and ambivalent about their gaze: both stare at the viewer with the same detached air, their haughtiness perhaps suggestive of the fact they are uncomfortable or unwilling to be seen as subordinate.

Serena Lederer, *1899. In a move clearly designed to flatter and charm, Klimt painted many of his patron's wives including Serena, the wife of industrialist August Lederer. However, in this instance, Serena is thought to have commissioned the portrait herself.*

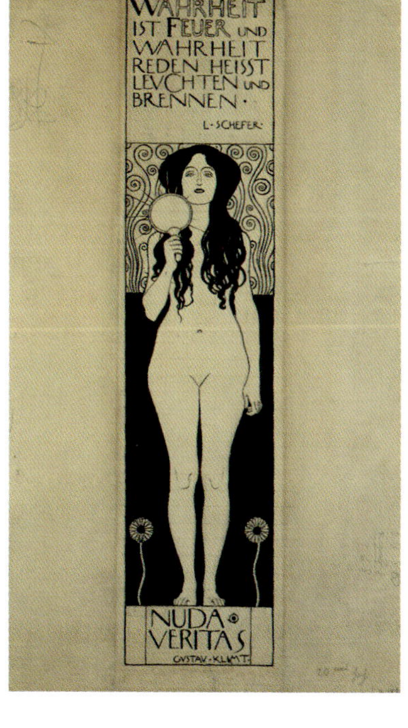

Nuda Veritas, *1898. Klimt's original illustration that appeared in the Secessionist magazine* Ver Sacrum.

Moving Water, *1898. In Klimt's watery world, women are naked and at one with the flowing waves, an erotic image that provoked some criticism.*

Klimt was clearly under some constraint himself when creating these portraits of their wives for his patrons. It was in his allegorical Secessionist paintings where he allowed his central theme – the power of women, and the liberating force of sexuality and eroticism – to predominate. In 1899, he produced a second version of *Nuda Veritas*, originally created as an illustration for the Secessionist journal *Ver Sacrum*. In this large painting, a naked red-haired woman holds up the mirror of truth while a serpent lies dead at her feet. In its painted gold frame a quotation by German dramatist Friedrich Schiller in stylized lettering reads, 'If you cannot please everyone with your deeds and your art, please only a few. To please many is bad.' The quotation from Schiller was an attempt to assuage the Viennese public, which would be affronted, Klimt knew, by such a blatant image of a woman, with her pubic hair completely visible. This real life nude was therefore a gauntlet thrown down as a challenge to the idealized beauties of the past. Alongside *Pallas Athene*, his vision of a Greek goddess as self-possessed warrior, *Nuda Veritas* marked the start of a different type of female heroine – one who could bewitch and seduce while operating on instinct and assuming control.

Central to Klimt's idea of the femme fatale was the idea that feminine eroticism could be seen as self-sufficient and impossible to capture. The association with water is key in this respect and with Art Nouveau in general. The symbolist poets and artists of the Romantic era developed the motif of a water nymph or siren, originally found in Greek mythology. The poet Rainer Maria Rilke, composer Claude Debussy and artists Auguste Rodin, Arnold Böcklin and Edward Burne-Jones were amongst those who saw woman as an elementary being tied to nature, who could seduce and destroy in equal measure. In his paintings of femmes fatales, Klimt built on this idea, presenting an underwater world full of shimmering light and dark, in which fish dart, algae and coral grow on rock and women are shown naked, their pale flowing bodies drifting or succumbing to the tide.

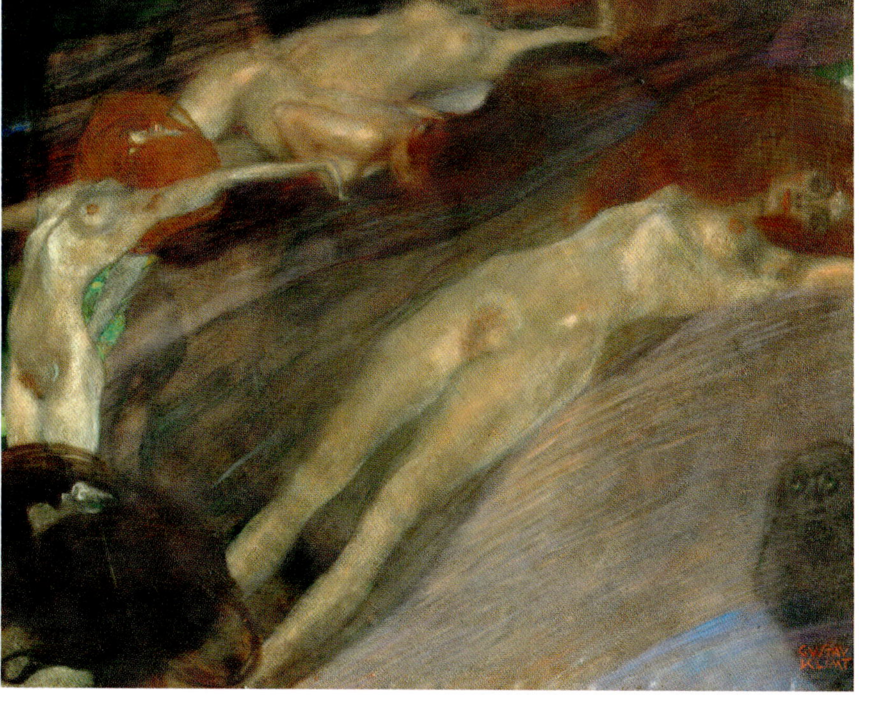

As it was in ancient mythology, water here can be seen as a symbol of the womb and, as such, an emblem of birth, fertility and woman-ness. Consciously or unconsciously, Klimt seems to be making a connection with Sigmund Freud's work about the interpretation of dreams, published in Vienna at the turn of the century. Water here is one of the elements of the unconscious and is associated with intuition and emotion – the supposed realm of the feminine. The ability to see visual echoes between the waves and movement of water and the curves of the female form helped Klimt and others to define the linear, flowing curves of the Art Nouveau graphic style.

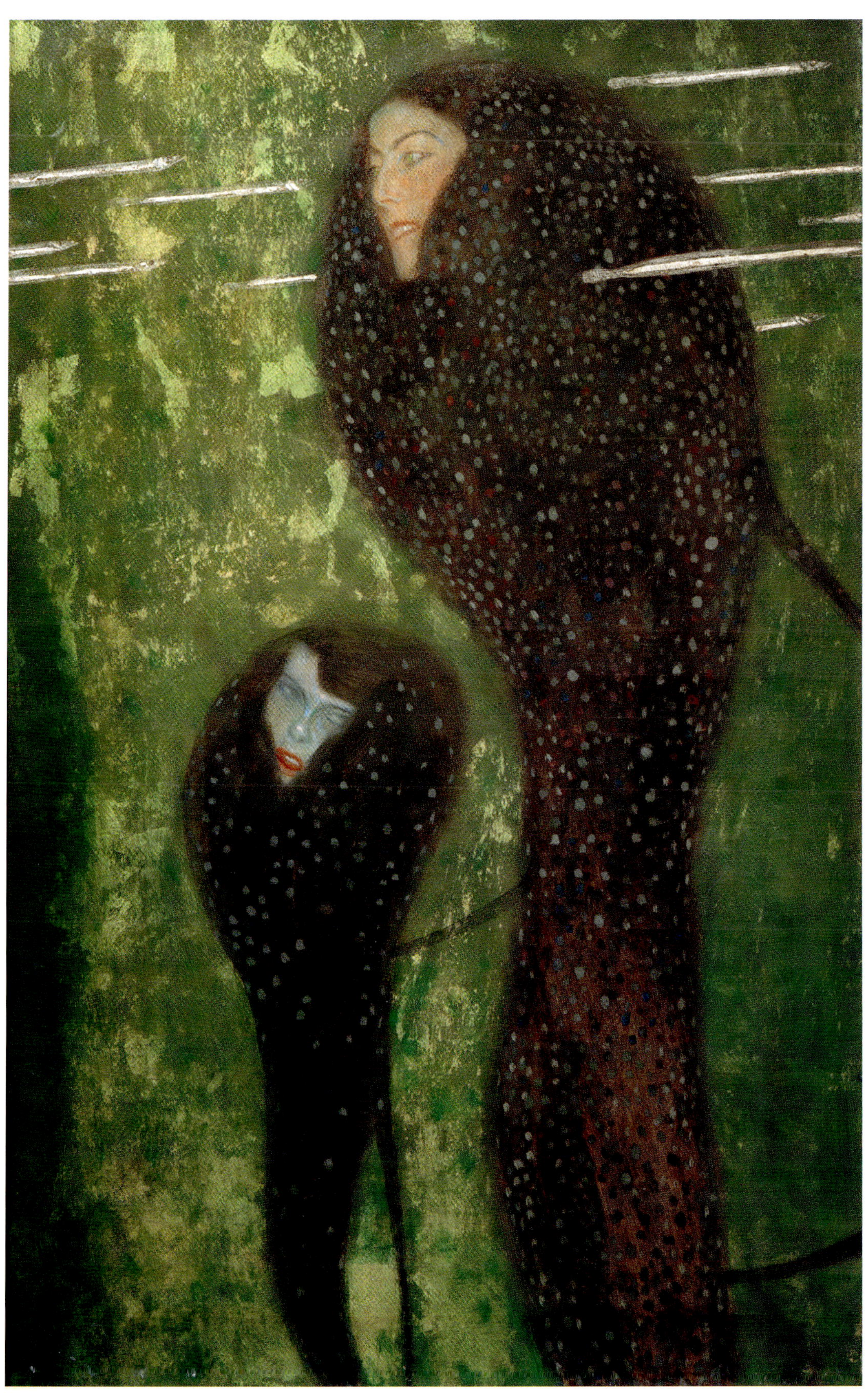

Mermaids, *1899. A curious painting in which Klimt appears to be symbolically linking women and water again, although this time the women are disembodied with their heads wrapped in dark shrouds.*

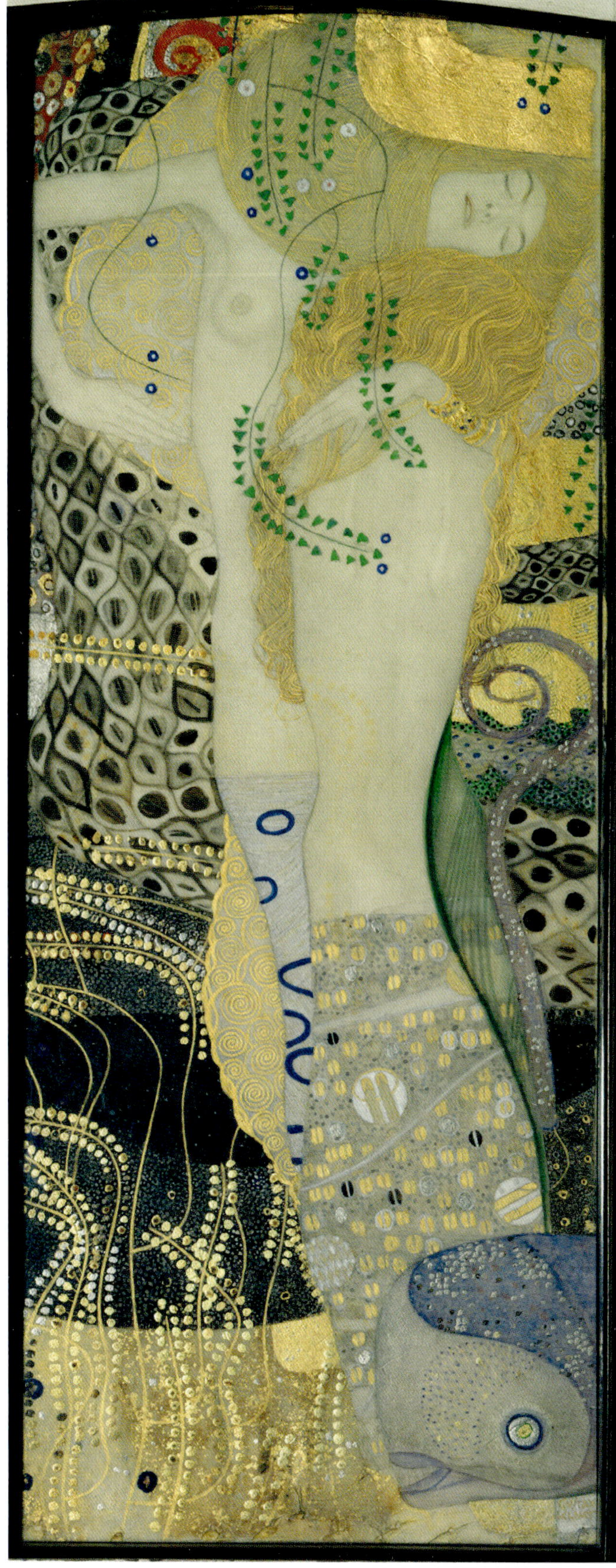

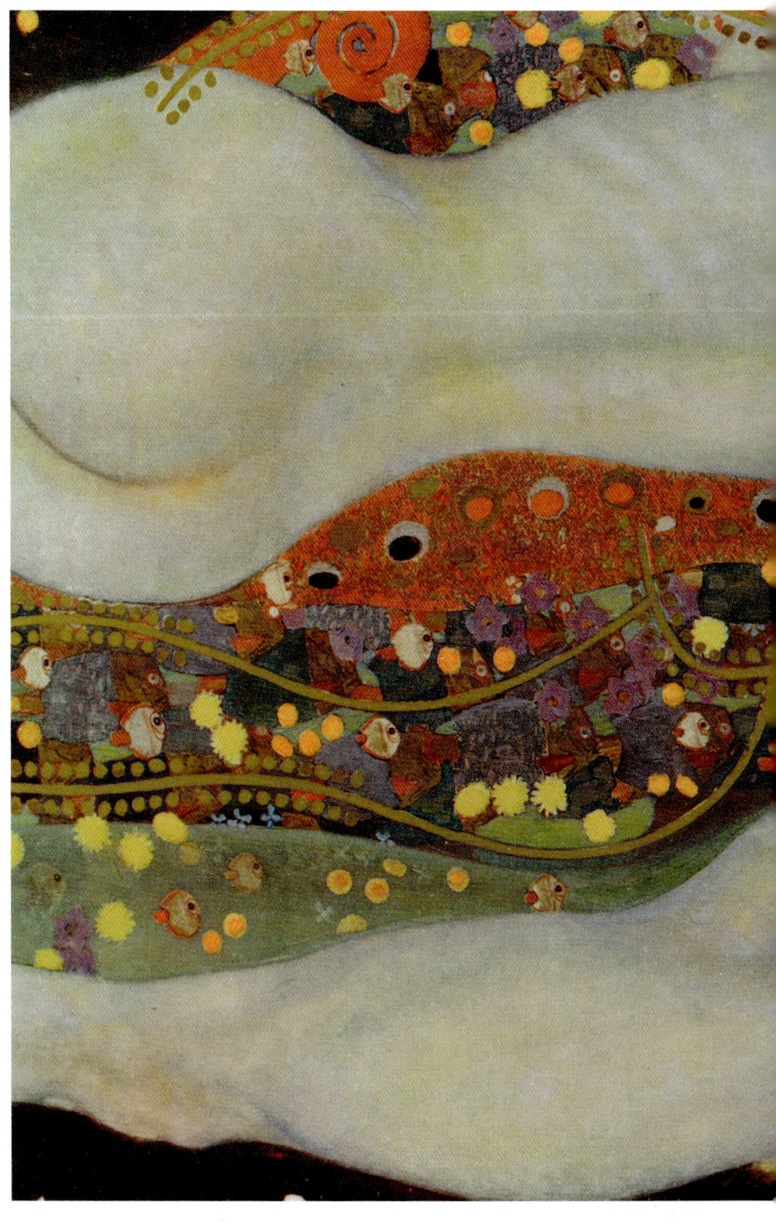

Left: Water Serpents I, *1904–07. Klimt's painting of two women locked together in a lover's embrace, is made more respectable by its seductive gold patterning and exquisite details.*

In these watery visions, women swim as fish and the associations of eroticism and sensuality come into play as their naked bodies float or languidly glide in the water. In *Moving Water* (1898), sensuous, naked female bodies stretch out luxuriously, abandoning themselves to the waves. Stranger still is *Water Nymphs (Silverfish)* (c.1899) in which

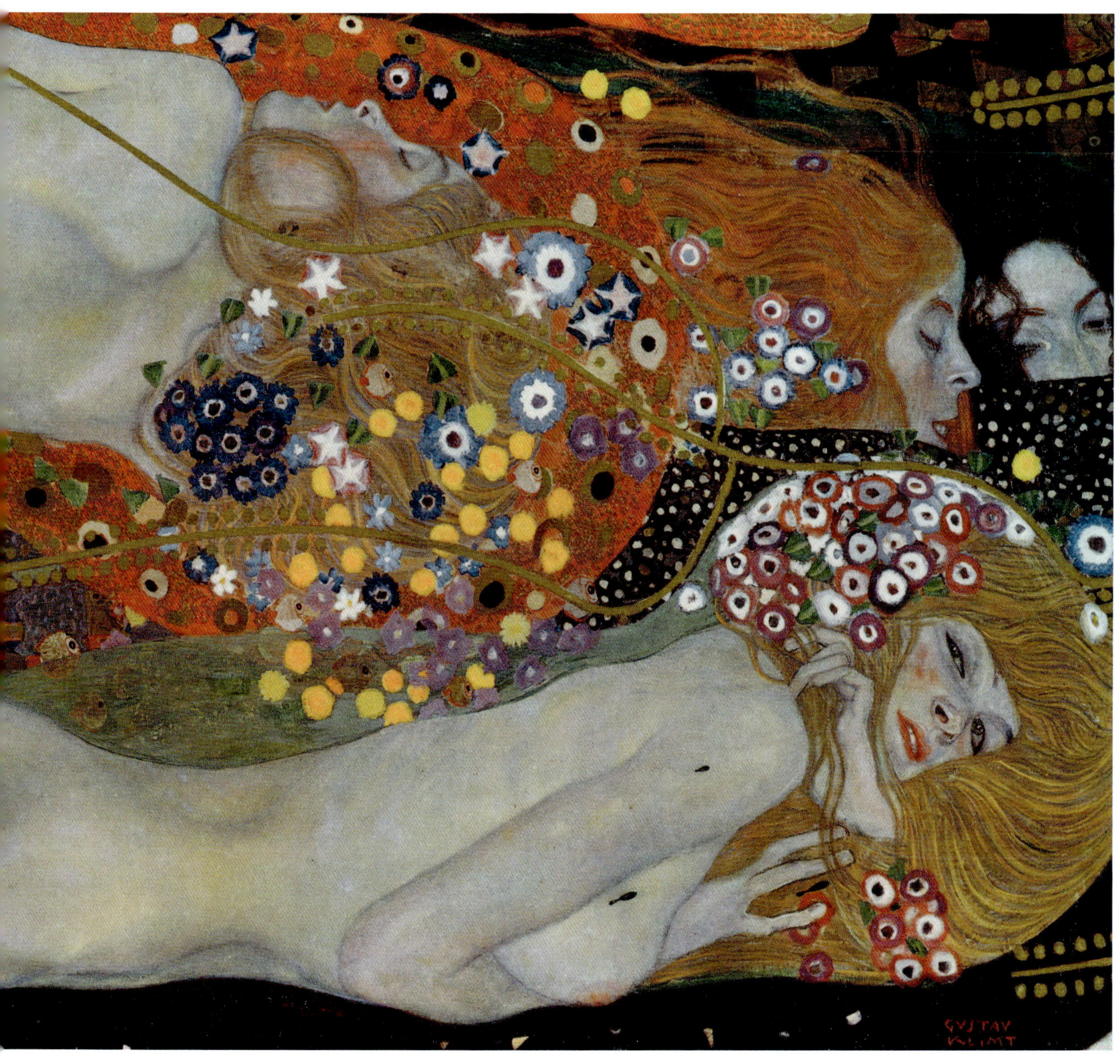

Water Serpents II, *1904–07. The sheer beauty of these women with their pale sinuous bodies and plant-entangled hair again helped to make this painting more palatable to Viennese society.*

the faces of two women with fixed, almost diabolical expressions, appear in the gloam wrapped in a dappled shroud – a cocoon that curiously seems almost sperm-like. In both *Water Serpents I* (1904–07) and *Water Serpents II* (1904–07), Klimt presents a world of women in which men are totally absent. The women themselves seem to take pleasure in their own eroticism. In *Water Serpents I*, a woman merges almost completely into a fish, her hands covering her bare torso, eyes shut and mouth open in ecstasy. In *Water Serpents II*, four female figures swim together as one in a tightly packed shoal, with their hair entangled by hundreds of tiny plants, their enmeshed bodies suggestive of both metamorphosis and an unknowable, inaccessible sexual intimacy.

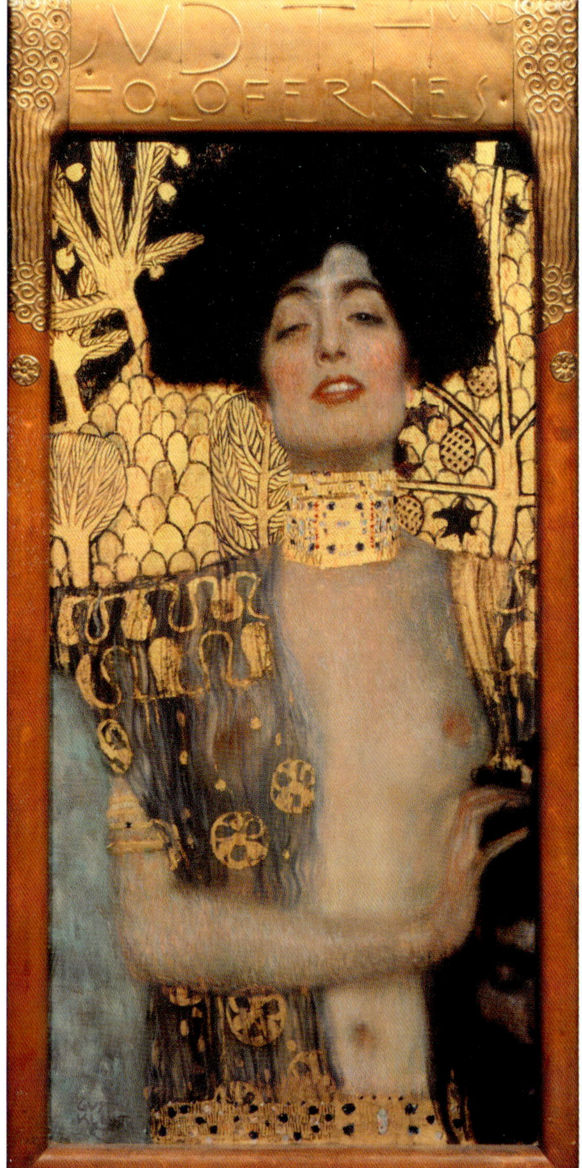

Right: Judith I, *1901. In the first of his interpretations of the biblical story of Judith and Holofernes, Klimt's main focus is in creating a strong and powerful heroine – one of his femmes fatales.*

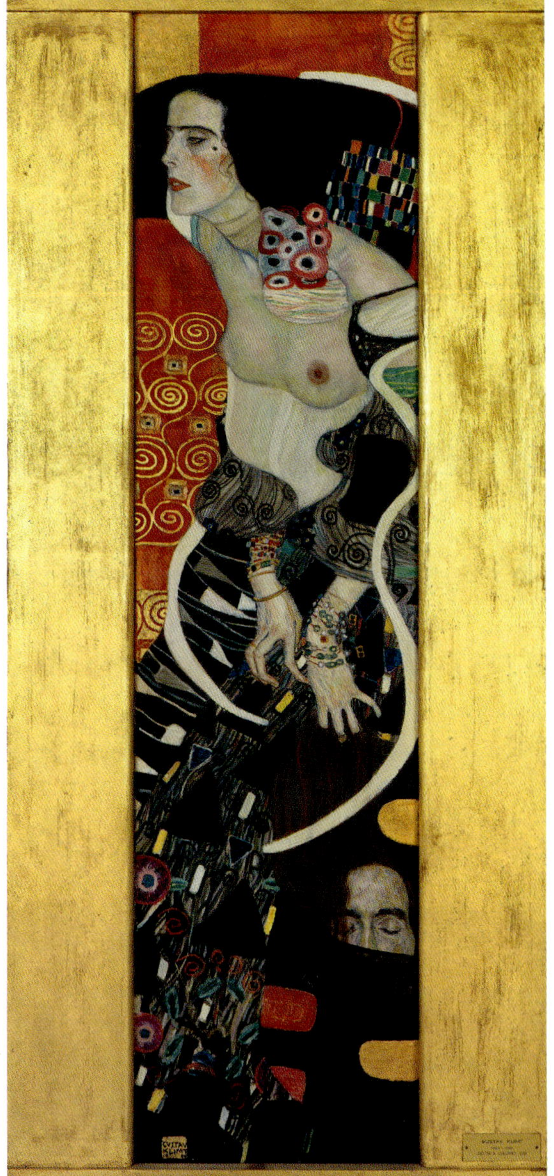

Far right: Judith II *(*Salome*), 1909. In the second version of the Judith and Holofernes story painted some eight years later, Judith is less idealized, her hands are like claws and her face and posture more menacing.*

Judith and the Head of Holofernes, also known as *Judith I* (1901), marks the start of Klimt's golden style and is another of his celebrated femmes fatales. Gold leaf abounds in this painting – the difference between this and earlier works is that the gold becomes the dominant material and is incorporated fully into the structure of the painting. The ornamentation of the painting is lavish and is mirrored in the frame, showing the Byzantine influence picked up by Klimt on his trip to Ravenna in Italy.

In Klimt's interpretation of the Old Testament story, Judith stares challengingly, even triumphantly out at the viewer. She holds the decapitated head of Holofernes, Nebuchadnezzar's general, who was waging war on the town. It is a symbolic image overlaid by the association between sexuality and death, with Judith's head tilted backwards, her eyes half closed and her mouth open, seemingly enjoying a moment of ecstasy. In no sense does Judith resemble the stereotypical portrayal of a biblical heroine

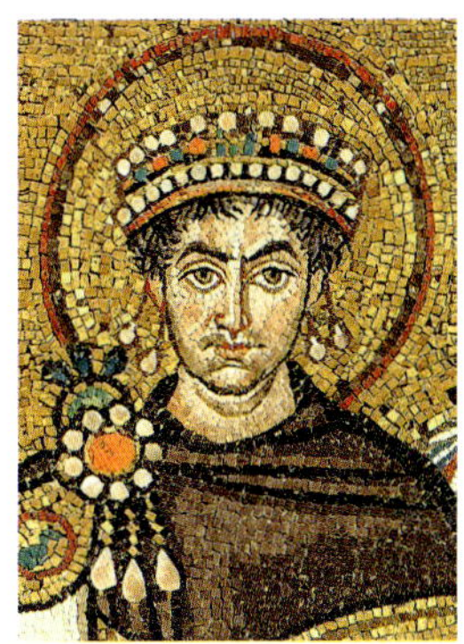

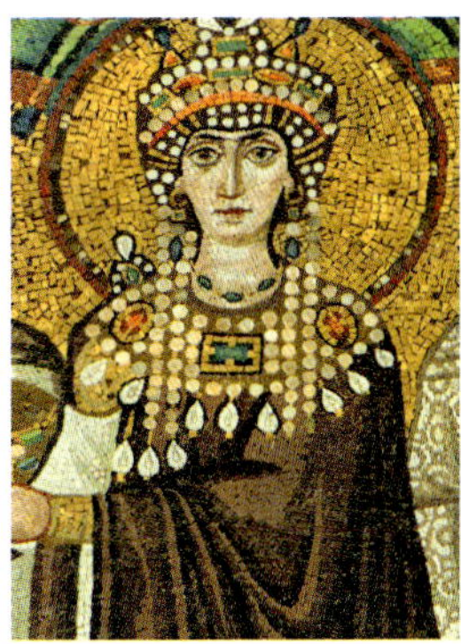

Mosaics of Emperor Justinianus (left) and Empress Theodora (right) in the Basilica of San Vitale in Ravenna.

who has executed such a grim deed. With her heavily lidded eyes, cloud of dark hair, unabashed stare and sumptuous gold collar, she looks as if she would be more at home singing in one of Vienna's fashionable nightclubs. Klimt's Judith therefore scandalized those who set eyes on her: some believed that Klimt had mistaken Judith for Salome and tried to re-appropriate the painting whenever it appeared.

Critics have described how they see Klimt's Judith as a mistress of her own desire and as a representation of both the yearning and fear that was prevalent in the male erotic imagination of the time. Interestingly, in his 1909 version of Judith, Klimt makes some changes that would seem to put a different slant on his intentions second time around. In *Judith II*, the gold and decorative elements are reduced. Judith's body is turned slightly, her hands are twisted above Holofernes' disembodied head and her expression is impassive, if a little more tense. Overall, the charming insouciance of the first portrait has disappeared, to be replaced by a woman who looks indeed like she might have committed a terrible act. The two paintings of Judith seem to sum up Klimt's contradictory and ambivalent feelings towards his femmes fatales and, seemingly, to women in general. On the one hand they completely fascinated him and made him desire them; at the same time, they made him extremely fearful.

The dark-haired, imposing model Klimt used for both his portraits of Judith was Adele Bloch-Bauer, who is believed also to have been his mistress. Bloch-Bauer was the wife of one of his patrons, the sugar magnate and banker Ferdinand Bloch-Bauer, so Klimt was clearly taking a great risk in becoming sexually involved with her. Klimt had numerous affairs, mostly with his models, and was the father to 14 illegitimate children. He avoided scandal and managed to keep these relationships out of the public eye during his lifetime, but several of his models won court cases to establish the legal rights of their offspring once he died.

Despite his unprepossessing appearance – he was a stocky, hirsute

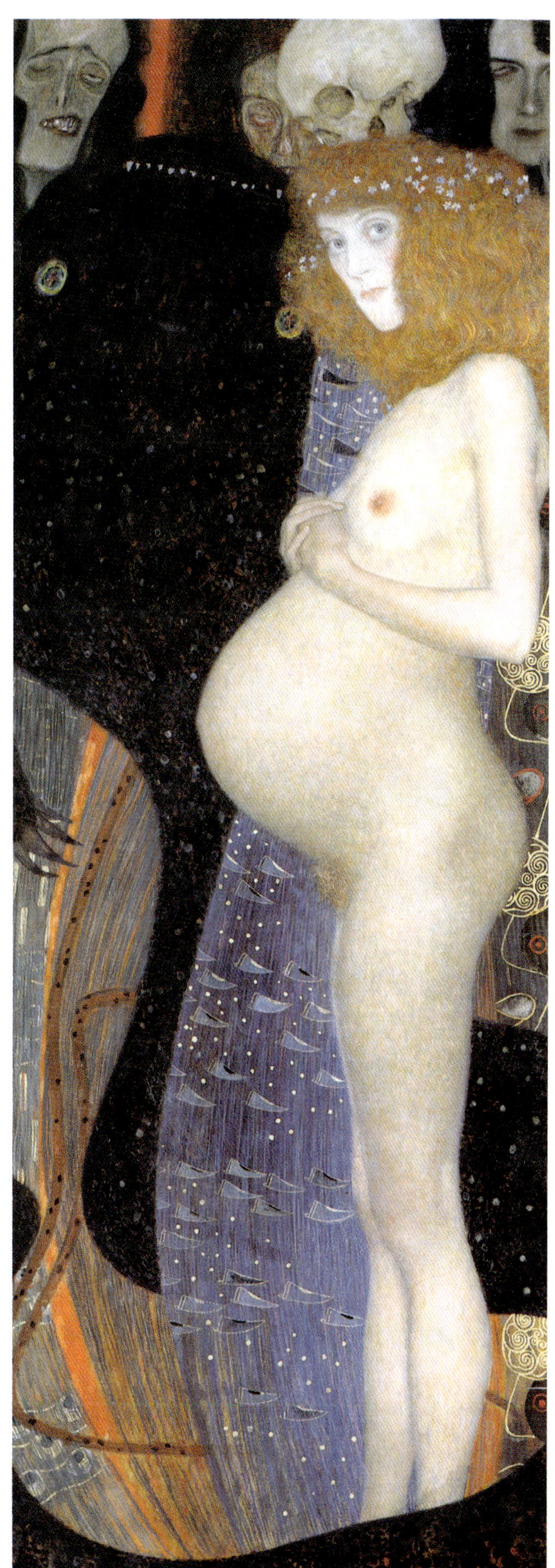

Hope I, *1903. Klimt knew this painting might offend and it was first exhibited three years after it was finished. A special frame was built with closing doors to hide the protruding belly.*

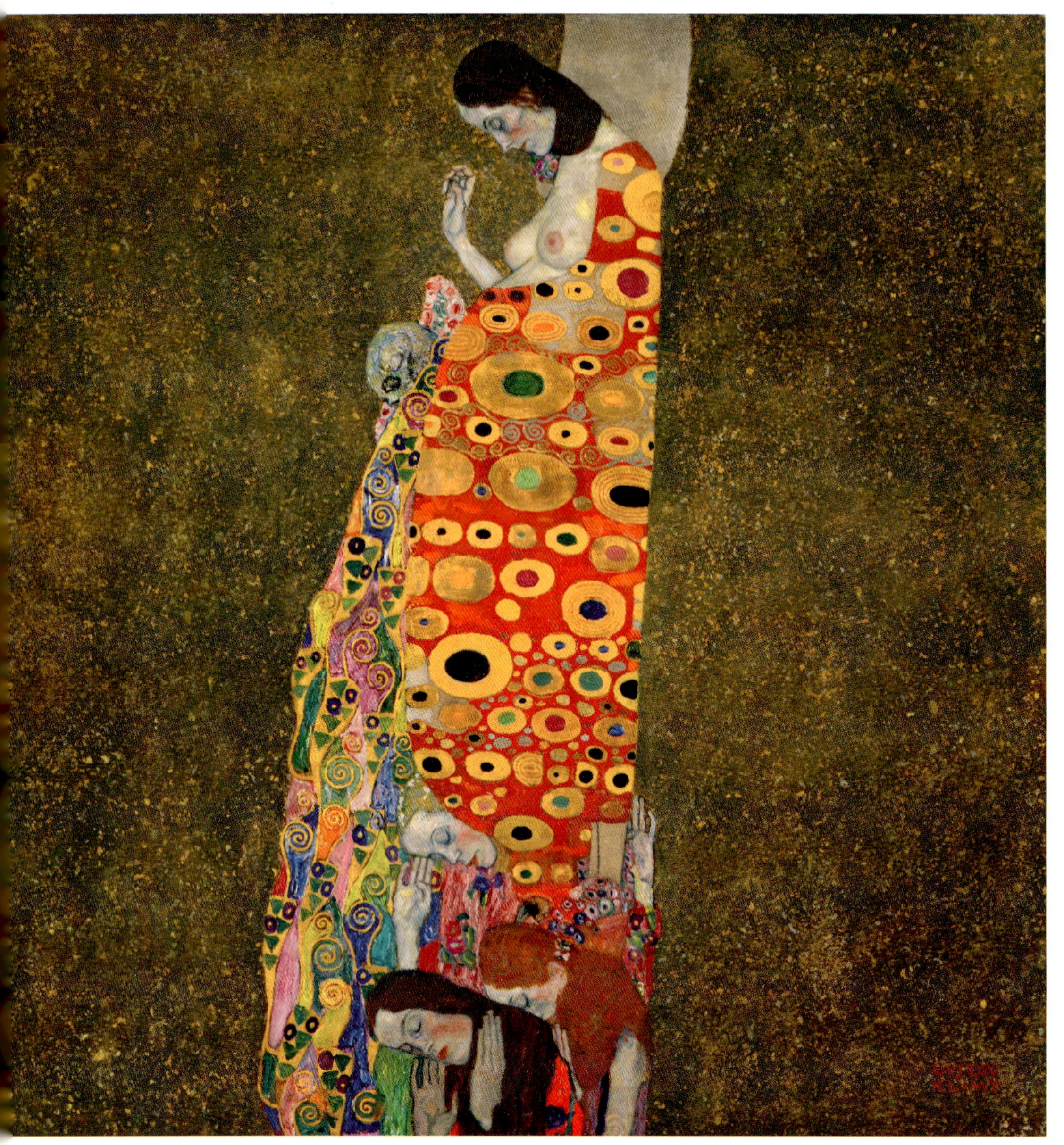

man with a square jaw – Klimt famously loved women and undoubtedly relied on his position as a successful artist to win over the beautiful young models who came to his studio to sit for him. While these women clearly loved the fact that Klimt could make them look so glamorous, there is no evidence that he exploited or abused the women in any way. An unrepentant but ardent suitor, he seems to have chosen affairs with his models over marriage as a way of establishing the central importance of art in his life. Relationships with women, except possibly for his intense association with Emilie Flöge, came second. This meant that he enjoyed the best of both worlds – a ready supply of beautiful women to admire, seduce and paint while remaining free of the complications or daily drudgery that he feared would drag him away from his art.

Hope II, *1907–08. Klimt treats his second Hope painting as an allegory. The expectant woman is covered up with richly decorated robes, her head is bowed and a group of women worship at her feet.*

Marie Zimmerman (known as Mizzi) was another of his regular models and Klimt was the father of two of her sons. She has been identified in his earlier Impressionistic work *Schubert at the Piano* (1899), where she stands to the right of the composer, illuminated by candlelight and pregnant with Klimt's child. She posed again for *Hope I* (1903) although in this instance Klimt altered details of her facial features while leaving her flame red hair true to life. This painting, with Mizzi's unabashed stare, pale naked body and pregnant belly highly visible, was considered highly offensive to Klimt's contemporaries. As with so many depictions of the female and the feminine, Klimt's work is ambiguous. On the one hand, it can be read as a lyrical and joyous celebration of womanhood and new life; on the other, there are various masks, skulls and monsters surrounding the pregnant woman, which are also suggestive of disease and death. Declared obscene when it was exhibited in 1903, *Hope I* was bought by Fritz Waerndorfer, one of Klimt's patrons, who kept it enclosed within a special cabinet at his home.

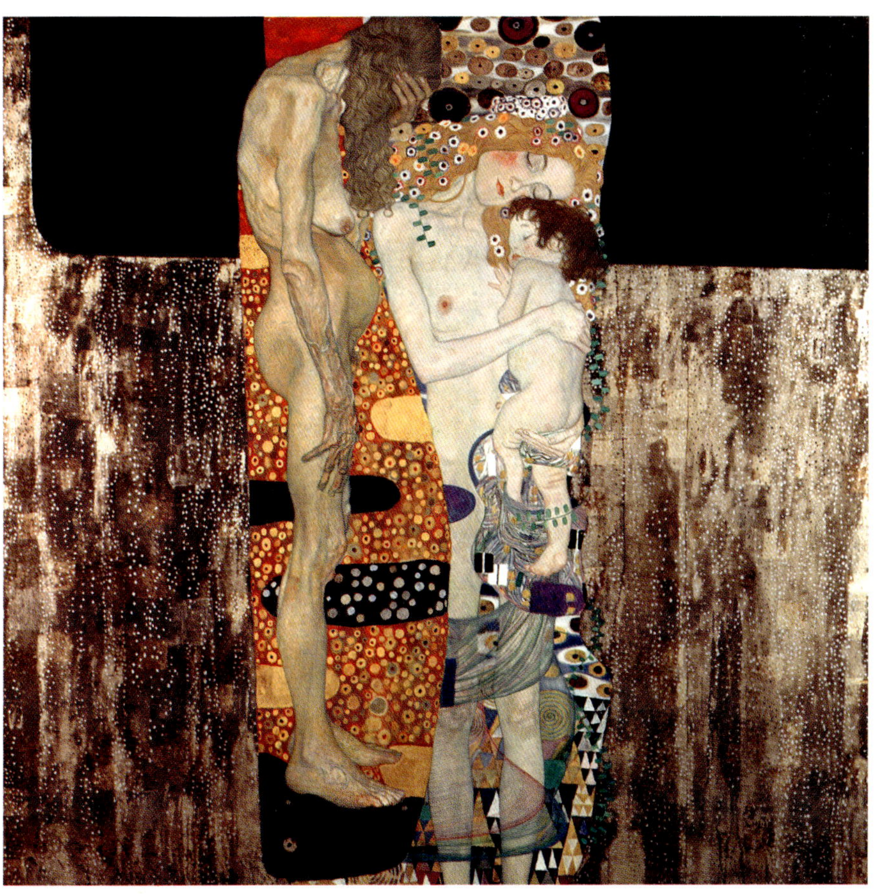

Hope II (1907/08), painted several years later, features a different model and an altogether less ambivalent tone. In the second version, the destructive symbolic elements have withered away and the woman's body is covered up to her bare breasts in a beautifully ornamental sheath-like rich gold robe. At her feet, three women with their eyes closed appear to be praying, relating back to Klimt's allegorical theme of the Madonna and Child.

Klimt's obsession with the feminine and the transience of beauty resurfaces again in the *Three Ages of Woman* (1905). In his allegorical treatment of the life cycle – childhood, maturity and old age – an older woman stands to the left of the painting, with one bony hand by her side and the other holding her long locks in front of her face. Emphasizing the inescapable passage of time, the raw, naturalistic treatment of her flesh seems almost contemporary, as if Klimt had studied Lucien Freud's fleshy nudes. The other two figures – a mother and child – rest on each other's bodies, their studied poses, pink cheeks and rosebud mouths being more typical of Klimt's idealized beauties. Again, striking another contemporary note, the whole painting is divided into different sections, including two black squares, and grey and brown panels with a rain of tiny white specks like tumbling stars. In addition, the figures stand within their own decorative space, richly littered with gold and veils of gauzy material. Here Klimt uses space in a dynamic and challenging way, causing our eye to dart around the work as the movement between the figures and the ground constantly shifts.

The Three Ages of Woman, *1905. The three figures in this work represent childhood, maturity and old age and exemplify one of Klimt's mature themes: the life cycle. Awarded the gold medal at the International Exhibition of Art in Rome in 1911.*

While creating some of his most celebrated allegorical works, Klimt was also busily fulfilling commissions for his patrons, including in 1905 *Portrait of Margarethe Stonborough-Wittgenstein* and a year later *Portrait of Fritza Riedler*. The first of these was a portrait of the daughter of Karl Wittgenstein, one of his most significant patrons, on the eve of her marriage to an American doctor, Thomas Stonborough. As with previous society portraits, Margarethe is tall, imposing, dressed in a long white frock and appears somewhat detached from her surroundings. Behind her head there are various panels, including a central gold embellished panel, a nod to his richly allegorical paintings. It seems that Klimt is more interested in the composition as a whole rather than the sitter, a point borne out by the fact that Margarethe herself disliked the work and removed it from her wall as soon as she could.

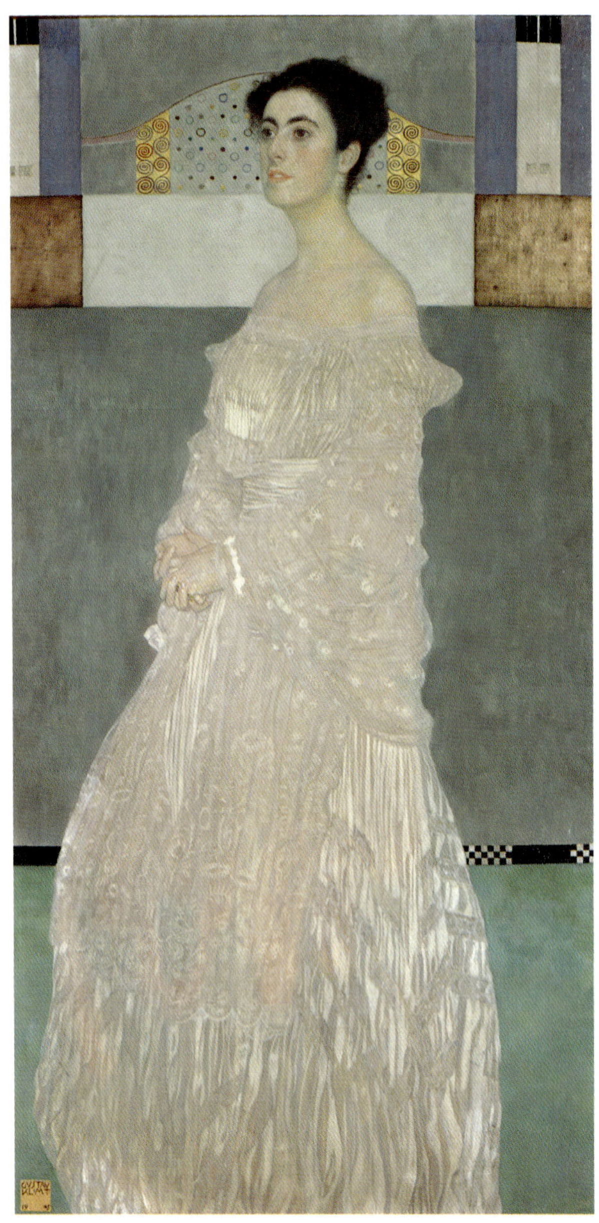

Margarethe Stonborough-Wittgenstein, *1905. This portrait of one of his patron's daughters was painted on the occasion of Margarethe's marriage to an American doctor.*

Portrait of Fritza Riedler takes this sense of cross-pollination between the commissioned portraits and the allegorical paintings a whole stage further. The German-born Fritza Riedler was the wife of a professor of engineering at the University of Vienna and the couple moved in the circles of Viennese high society. Between 1904 and 1905 Riedler visited Klimt's studio, where he made numerous studies of her before embarking on this daring portrait. In it, Klimt takes a series of imaginative risks, creating tension between the abstract and the figurative parts of the painting. The armchair in which she sits has become a two-dimensional outline filled in with gold and silver eye or mouth-shaped motifs. The gold and silver are picked up by the small squares dotted across the background wall. On the carpet beneath her feet, there are a couple of squares that resemble eyes or mouths – motifs that are generally seen as symbols of eroticism.

Riedler's grey dress is insubstantial, almost a washy sketch, and gets swallowed up by the patterning on the armchair. As in the portrait of Margarethe Stonborough-Wittgenstein, Klimt has placed a simplified shape behind Riedler's head, in this case a rough semi-circle. The device serves to frame and draw attention to her face while at the same time recalling ancient decorative Egyptian art and, more particularly, the headdresses used by Diego Velázquez (1599–1660) in his portraits of the Spanish Infanta.

We stare up at Riedler or she looks down on us, depending on the way you look at it. She has, as with so many of Klimt's portraits of women, great poise, but there is also a melancholic air about her that creates a sense of realism in the midst of such an abstract and stylized portrayal. The use of gold and silver leaf in the delicate small rectangles distributed over the surface and the two golden bars to the left show the growing importance that he attached to the decorative qualities of his work as well as their integration into the overall design. This is a development that was to find its full expression a year later in Klimt's magnificent portrait of Adele Bloch-Bauer.

The portrait of Riedler marks the beginning of Klimt's celebrated 'golden phase', generally agreed to be between 1906 and 1908. Within these years, Klimt was a master at the height of his powers, producing gilded depictions of fin-de-siècle women, which manage to be abstract and representational, conservative and modern.

The wife of Ferdinand Bloch-Bauer, an Austrian Jewish banker 17 years her senior, Adele Bloch-Bauer was the model for both of Klimt's portraits of Judith, and some also believe that she was his lover. Undeniably Adele was a beautiful, elegant woman whom Klimt adored and their relationship (whether consummated or not) started in the 1890s. The Bloch-Bauers were connoisseurs of art and part of the Viennese cultural set; Adele ran a salon from their home which attracted leading composers, artists and writers.

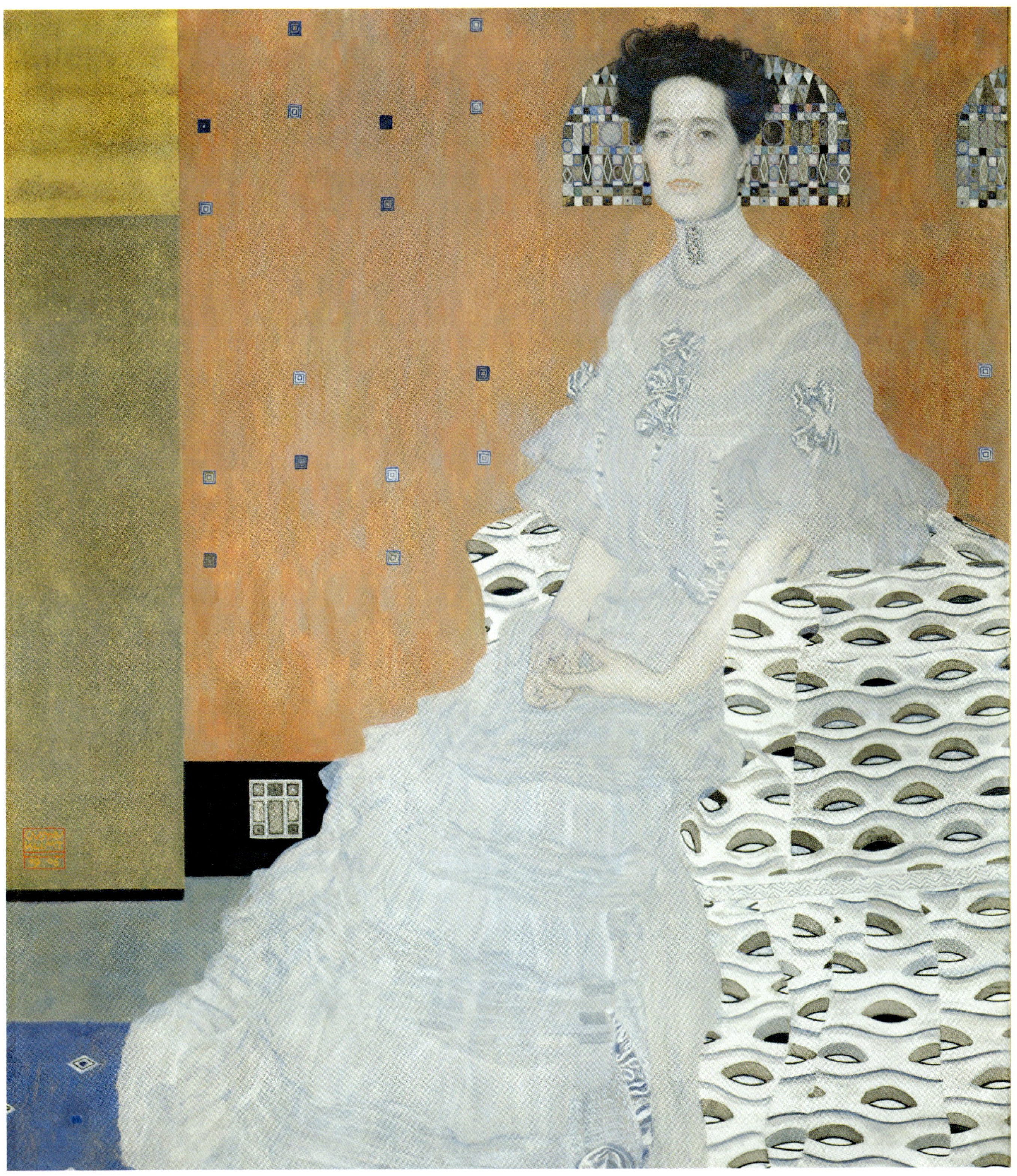

Fritza Riedler, *1906. Klimt's portrait of another wealthy Viennese woman clearly shows the transition of his work away from realism towards a more stylized approach favouring decoration and pattern. It also shows the influence of Velázquez'* Portrait of the Infanta Maria Teresa of Spain.

THE KISS

Along with the *Mona Lisa*, Gustav Klimt's *The Kiss* is one of the most reproduced images in the world. Few people have probably seen the real thing, housed in the Galerie Belvedere museum in the Belvedere Palace, Vienna. Yet countless copies of the work (on everything from posters and greeting cards to mugs and key rings) have made this work one of the most popular and inescapable images of our time.

What gives *The Kiss* its enduring appeal? Painted by Gustav Klimt between 1907 and 1908, at the height of what has become known as his Golden Period, the work is oil on canvas with added silver and gold leaf. A large square painting, it measures 180 × 180cm (71 × 71 inches), and its focus is the two life-size figures – a man and a woman – locked in a sensuous embrace. The lovers are shown kneeling on a carpet of tiny flowers, their bodies entwined by a sinuous outline around their flowing, highly decorated, rich gold robes.

Although he clearly intended the painting to be seen as an allegory, as was also true of many similar paintings drawing upon biblical stories and myths, Klimt was not explicit about his intentions. This has led some to believe that the couple depicted in the work could represent Adam and Eve – Adam with his crown of vines and Eve with her crown of flowers. Others have seen this as a representation of the Ovid narrative, the moment when Apollo kisses Daphne.

Perhaps what is most interesting about this painting are the many and various different interpretations that viewers and critics alike have brought to it. Many see this work as the quintessential expression of one of the deepest passions known to mankind, sensual love. To other observers this depiction of a loving affair between a man and woman is a new development in Klimt's oeuvre, given that many of the male and female relationships he had previously depicted appear much less harmonious. Closer inspection of *The Kiss* reveals that the lovers are not actually kissing, which seems to reflect the fact that people see want they want to see rather than what is actually there. Klimt clearly saw the painting as an allegorical work, and it is this ability to lend an ordinary romantic or even erotic encounter higher spiritual meaning that gives it such charm.

Aside from the passionate subject matter, what distinguishes *The Kiss* is Klimt's unique approach, seen here in all its glory: the curving lines, alluring use of gold and brilliant jewel-like ornamentation. Drawing on elements from Byzantine mosaics, which Klimt had seen at Ravenna in Italy, and from the bold patterning of the English Arts and Craft movement, this is Klimt at the height of his powers. Produced around the turn of the century, when Vienna was going though its own golden period, this painting is one of the most celebrated examples of the Viennese Art Nouveau (or Jugendstil).

Klimt was one of the greatest exponents of Art Nouveau, an ornamental style of art characterized by its use of a sinuous, flowing line and organic forms, but he did not invent it. As a movement, Art Nouveau flourished throughout Europe and the United States between about 1890 and 1910. Its curvy lines and the floral and plant-inspired motifs were employed in many art forms, including painting, architecture, interior design, posters, jewellery and glass design.

Unlike the Faculty Paintings, made for the ceiling of the University of Vienna's Great Hall and deemed pornographic, *The Kiss* was well received when it was first publicly exhibited in 1908. It was bought unfinished by the Austrian government and has resided in the Belvedere Museum ever since. The museum paid 25,000 crowns (about $240,000 today) and if it were ever sold, it would probably reach one of the highest sums ever paid for a painting in the world. By way of comparison, when Klimt's portrait of Adele Bloch-Bauer came up for sale in 2006, it reached a staggering $135 million.

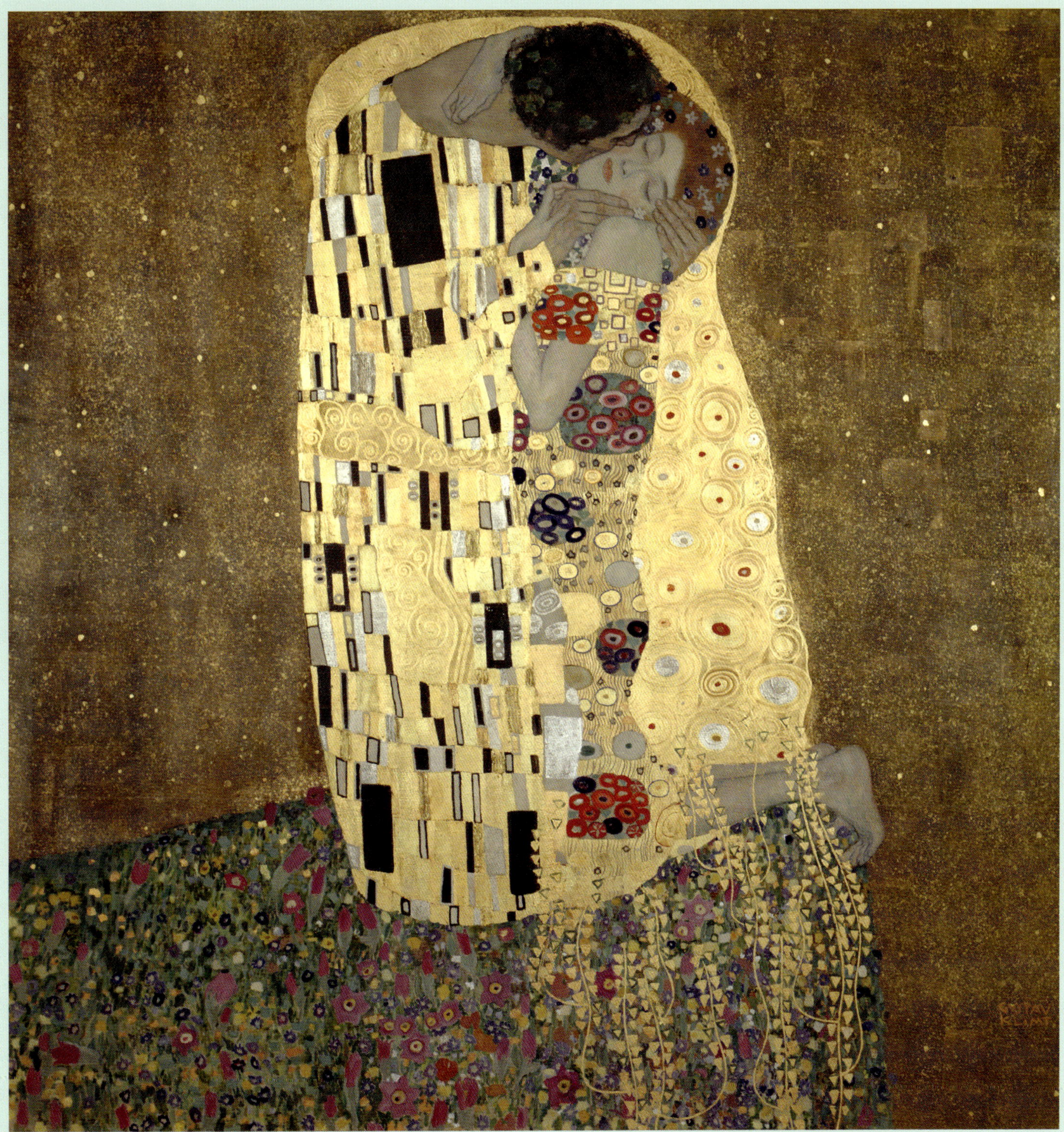

The Kiss, *1907–08. Over the course of his career, Klimt made several paintings of two figures locked in a passionate embrace. Unarguably the most famous one, it is often held up as his greatest work.*

Commissioned by Ferdinand in 1903, Adele's portrait took Klimt nearly four years to complete (and was followed up with a second portrait that he finished in 1912). Painted at the height of his golden period, the naturalistic elements – Adele's thin pale face and hands – are surrounded by rich gold decoration and a swirling mass of ovals, blocks and spirals, drawing upon a range of Byzantine and Egyptian motifs. The sitter – if indeed she is seated; her vaporous body has been dematerialized – hovers in a sea of gold. This excess of gold, the swirling spirals and the multitude of Egyptian eyes lends the portrait connotations of magic and transformation as well as an allure and an exoticism. Klimt has created the perfect balance between the realistic and the abstract elements in this painting. Adele's face, with its sad eyes and slightly mournful expression, is compelling and draws the viewer in, while the flurry of ornamental motifs and sumptuous gold creates an altogether more visionary work.

The use of a choker around Adele's neck has intrigued critics and commentators. The device, which has the effect of separating her head from her body and from the decorative elements, is not new to Klimt: there are chokers in the form of scarves and neckpieces in other portraits, including *Judith I* (Adele again), *Fritza Riedler* and *Emilie Flöge*. Some critics feel that this fractured view of the female body was Klimt's subconscious way of being able to exert control over women. Other psychological interpretations have also concentrated on a more morbid aspect to the portrait, seeing the disembodied head and shoulders of Adele Bloch-Bauer as imprisoned and locked inside a gold metal casing.

As already noted, *The Kiss* (1907) is one of Klimt's greatest and most celebrated works. It did not come from nowhere, for similar figures – a man and a woman locked in a close embrace – exist in his mural work for the *Beethoven Frieze* and the *Stoclet Frieze*. In relation to his femmes fatales, *The Kiss* would seem initially to offer a much more traditional view of woman as yielding to the more dominant male. However, critics have brought a range of opinions and interpretations to the work, which offer, at the very least, some alternative readings of this straightforward narrative.

While hardly the dominant figure (unlike the many dominant female figures in earlier paintings), the woman appears to have more control over the situation than the rather more sexually assertive man. Her face remains impassive and even slightly unyielding – could this indicate some sort of reluctance on her part? Are her tense hands and feet a further indication of this?

The ornamentation on the lovers' clothing in *The Kiss* is also strongly contrasted. The woman's robe is adorned with colourful circles whereas the man's is based on black and white squares. Using emblems to differentiate between male and female is not new; throughout the history of art there are examples of artists using symbolism to signify difference. Men and male attributes are often equated with geometric or angular forms and women with circular motifs, such as the moon. Some have speculated that in this juxtaposition in *The Kiss*, as well as in the woman's self-absorption, Klimt saw some kind of innate disjuncture between the sexes which made fulfillment an impossibility. This theory seems to gain some credibility when you examine the evidence of his own experience, in particular with Emilie Flöge, who may have been the model used here and with whom it is believed he never enjoyed a loving relationship. There is a danger here, of course, that reading personal or biographical meaning into the work reduces it. Ultimately, *The Kiss* remains outside such readings, offering us a powerful symbolic declaration of erotic love that achieves its effect by drawing upon a wealth of gold and rich ornamental detail.

Also in 1907, Klimt painted *Danaë*. The painting is based on the classical myth in which the god Zeus rescues Danaë from her father. He, believing her offspring will kill him, has locked her away in a chamber. Zeus impregnates Danaë in a golden shower and in Klimt's unabashedly erotic painting a torrent of gold pieces are shown cascading between her huge thighs. An explicit image, Danaë's pale naked body is shown curled up in a cocoon of gauzy, contrasting black material. Her soporific expression, parted lips and long red dishevelled hair suggest a woman who is not at the point of orgasm but whose self-absorption is complete. Despite its decorative elements, and the fig leaf of respectability that it gains from being based on a classical myth, Danaë's frank eroticism is something that Klimt would return to in his later portrayals of women, in particular the erotic drawings of lovers and of reclining nudes that he made and exhibited from 1910 onwards.

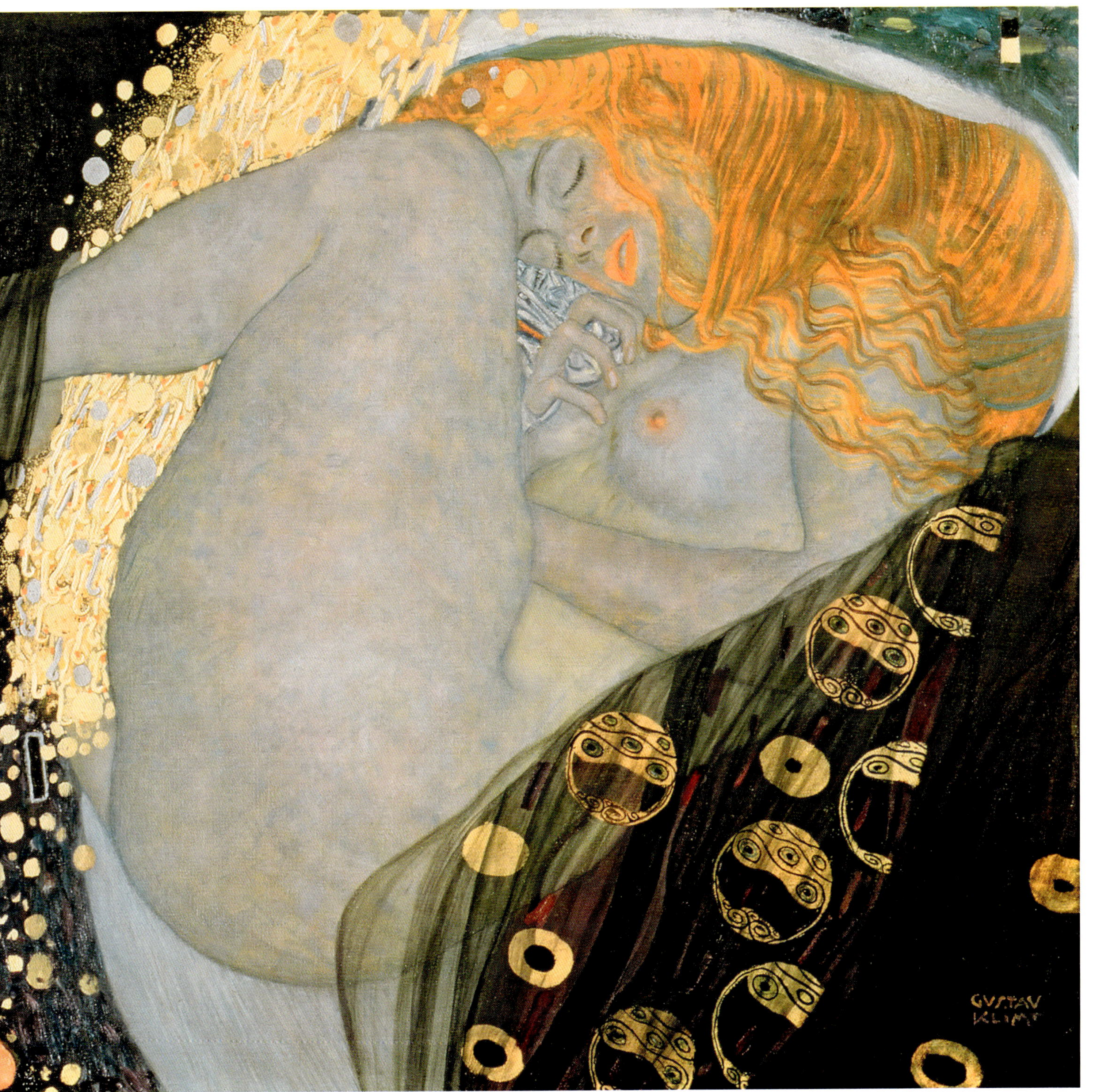

Danaë, 1907. *Based on the myth of Zeus, who visits Danaë when imprisoned by her father the King of Argos, this painting has an erotic charge that supersedes its allegorical significance.*

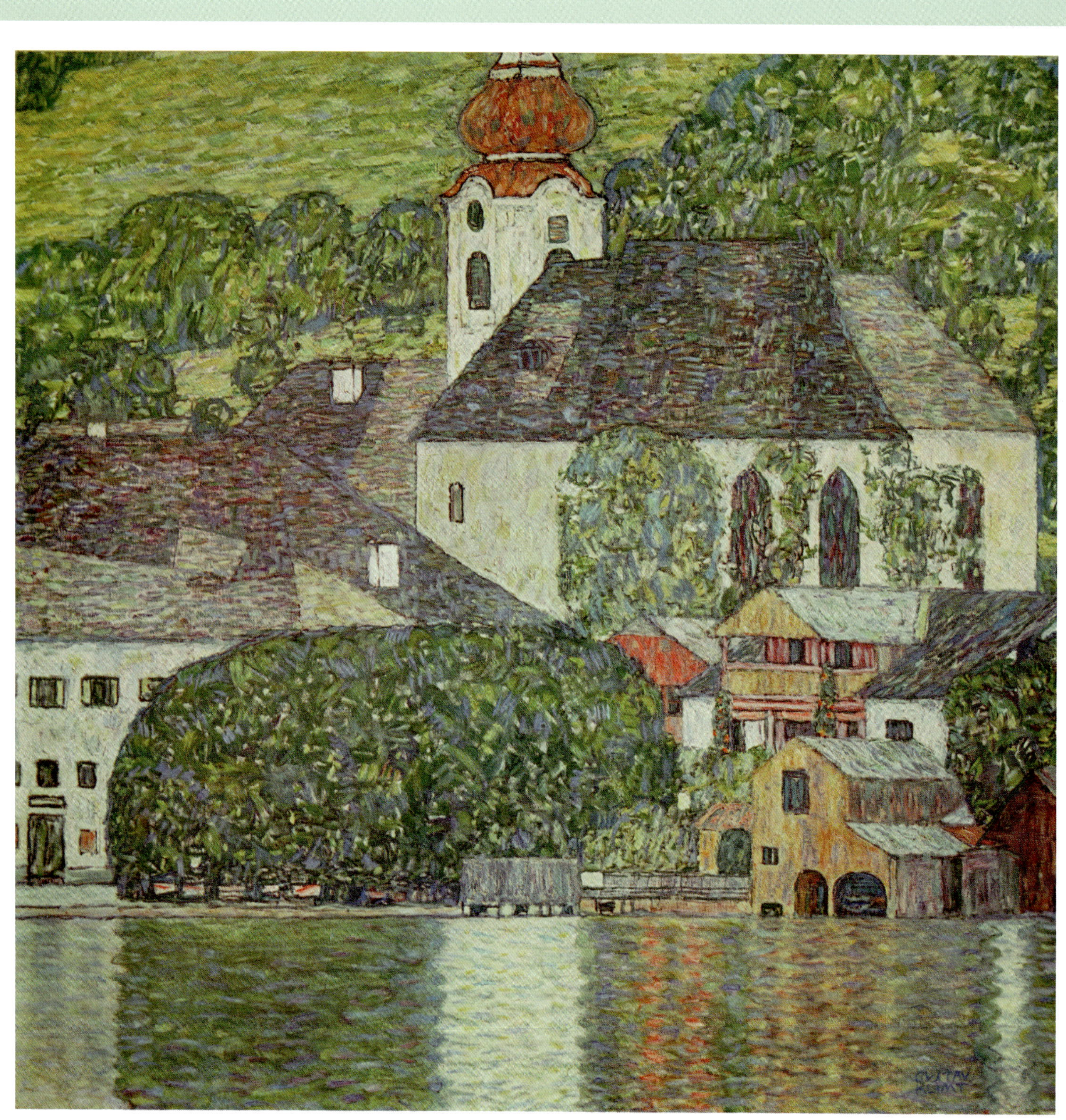

CHAPTER 4
Landscapes

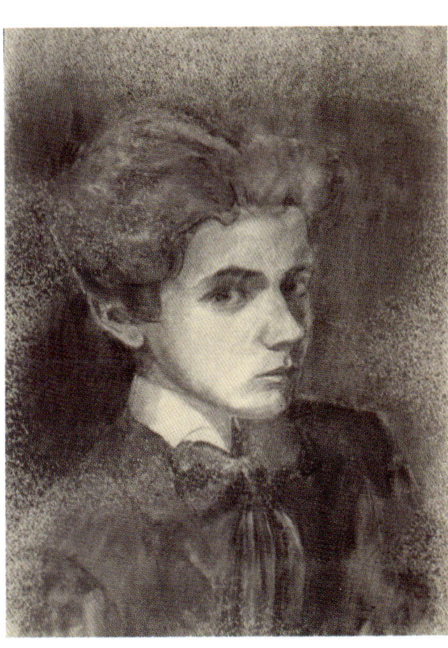

Self-portrait, *Egon Schiele, 1906. A charcoal self-portrait of Egon Schiele, aged 16. Schiele idolized Klimt as a student and the two first met in 1908.*

Around the time that Klimt was creating his golden allegorical paintings, a new generation of artists was starting to make its presence felt in Vienna. Chief among these young artists were Egon Schiele (1890–1918) and Oskar Kokoschka (1886–1980), both of whom revered the older artist and his work. Unlike Klimt, neither of these artists bore the heavy mantle of the classical past on their shoulders. Both were versatile painters who excelled at drawing and who painted figurative subjects, including portraits and landscapes.

Egon Schiele was the son of a stationmaster in the small town of Tulln, Lower Austria. Isolated and reserved at home and school, where he found learning difficult, he spent much of his childhood obsessively drawing trains. In 1906 he applied to study at the Kunstgewerbeschule, the institution where Klimt had studied, and was accepted. Within a year, Schiele was being mentored by Klimt, who was noted for being generous to younger artists and who clearly recognized in Schiele a raw talent as well as similar preoccupations when it came to subject matter.

Although Klimt and his closest associates Hoffman, Moser and Roller had broken with the Secession in 1905, the group continued to exhibit together and in 1908 held what was to be their final exhibition. While Klimt showed 16 works, the focus of the exhibition in 1908 was on the invited artists – including Schiele and Kokoschka – and a range of international artists, including Munch, Bonnard, Matisse, Gauguin and Van Gogh. This meant that Klimt came up close against the dramatic, boldly coloured and highly charged landscapes of both the Fauves and the Expressionists. The experience was decisive for Klimt. Not only did it precipitate his rupture with the Secessionist group altogether, but it also made him feel that his golden style was outdated and inferior to the work of these other artists. Once Klimt decided to break away from what became known as the Klimt Group, he felt isolated and no longer sure of the support of the young artists who had up to this point adored him. He confided to a friend that, 'The young no longer understand me. They go elsewhere. I don't even know whether they appreciate my work any more. It's a bit early for that to happen to me, but it happens to every artist. The young will always want to take everything that's already there by storm and pull it down. I shan't get angry with them over it.'

If Klimt was rattled by the sense that his work might appear overly ornate and decorative when compared with some of his European counterparts, he continued

Church in Unterach on the Attersee, *1916. Standing on the other side of the lake, Klimt used binoculars to capture this view of the church and village of Unterach.*

to pursue an entirely separate body of work – his landscapes. Out of a total of 230 paintings, Klimt produced 54 landscapes. He first began to focus on landscape as a subject matter in its own right in 1897, when he was invited by Emilie Flöge's family to spend his summer holidays on Lake Attersee, a picturesque rural area in Upper Austria. The landscapes reflect the summer weather he enjoyed in the tranquil environs of Attersee: he is not known to have painted any winter landscapes.

Klimt first exhibited landscapes in 1898 at the inaugural exhibition of the Viennese Secession. Over the next decade these were to prove popular and sold well, and today are a much admired and celebrated part of his oeuvre. By and large these landscapes are unadorned – there's almost no gold – they feature no people and they are not designed to tell any specific story. Quite simply, Klimt enjoyed painting the landscapes around the lake, as he found it very relaxing and a change from the pressured life he was leading in Vienna. If he made sketches or preparatory drawings, none of them has survived. He worked *en plein air* – painting directly in the landscape – as the Impressionists did. Sometimes he would set up an easel by the shores of the lake, at other times he would go out in a small boat to paint. He also made use of aids such as a cut-out view finder, binoculars or even a telescope to home in on a particular view. Usually, he finished these paintings back in his Viennese studio.

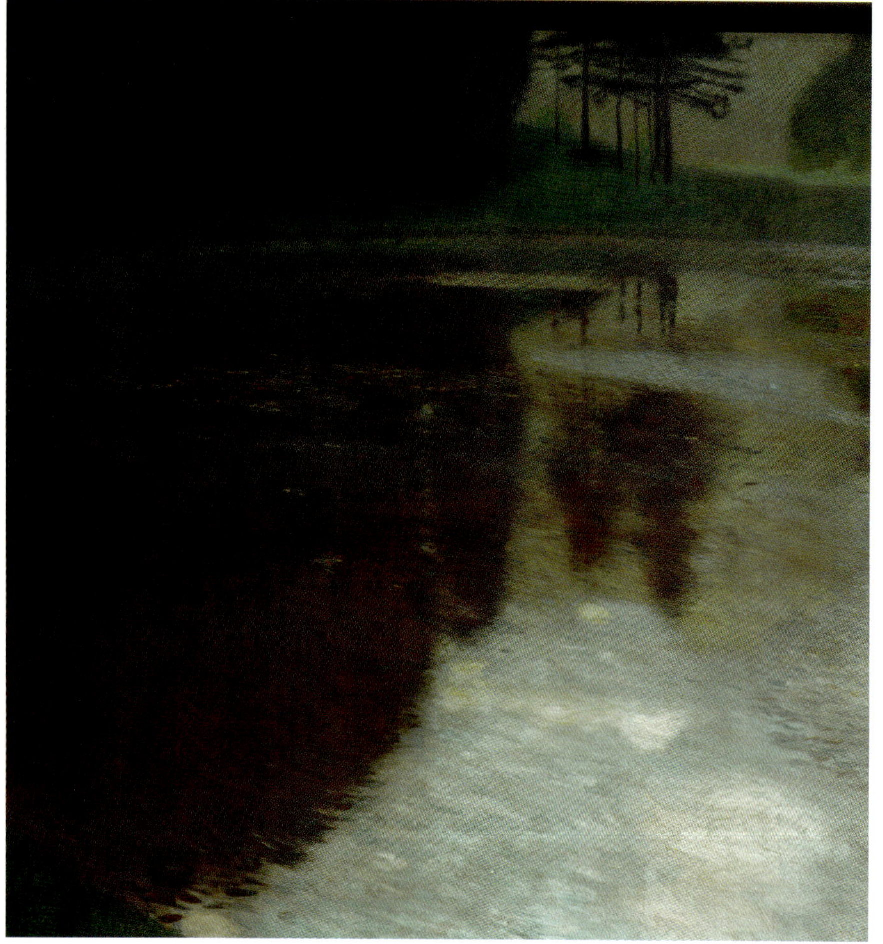

Morning by the Pond, *1899. With its hazy morning light and shimmering reflections, this early landscape recalls the atmospheric work of Impressionist Claude Monet.*

In complete opposition to his allegorical paintings, Klimt's landscapes are devoid of any human presence. Mostly they show us inaccessible places: buildings that are almost completely covered in vegetation or whole expanses of water or fields trapped under a low horizon. As some critics have remarked, it is like looking through a spyhole when suddenly the details come sharply into focus, allowing you to experience a moment that is almost spiritual in its quiet contemplation.

Though Klimt's landscapes do not typically focus on any kind of living being, an early landscape, *After the Rain* (1898–99) does feature animals. The canvas is elongated, which focuses our attention on the chickens wandering randomly in a field beneath trees. It is almost as if we are looking through a narrow doorway onto the scene. The chickens are painted loosely, but their main purpose appears to be to add colour and shape to the overall pattern of this softly painted and serene landscape.

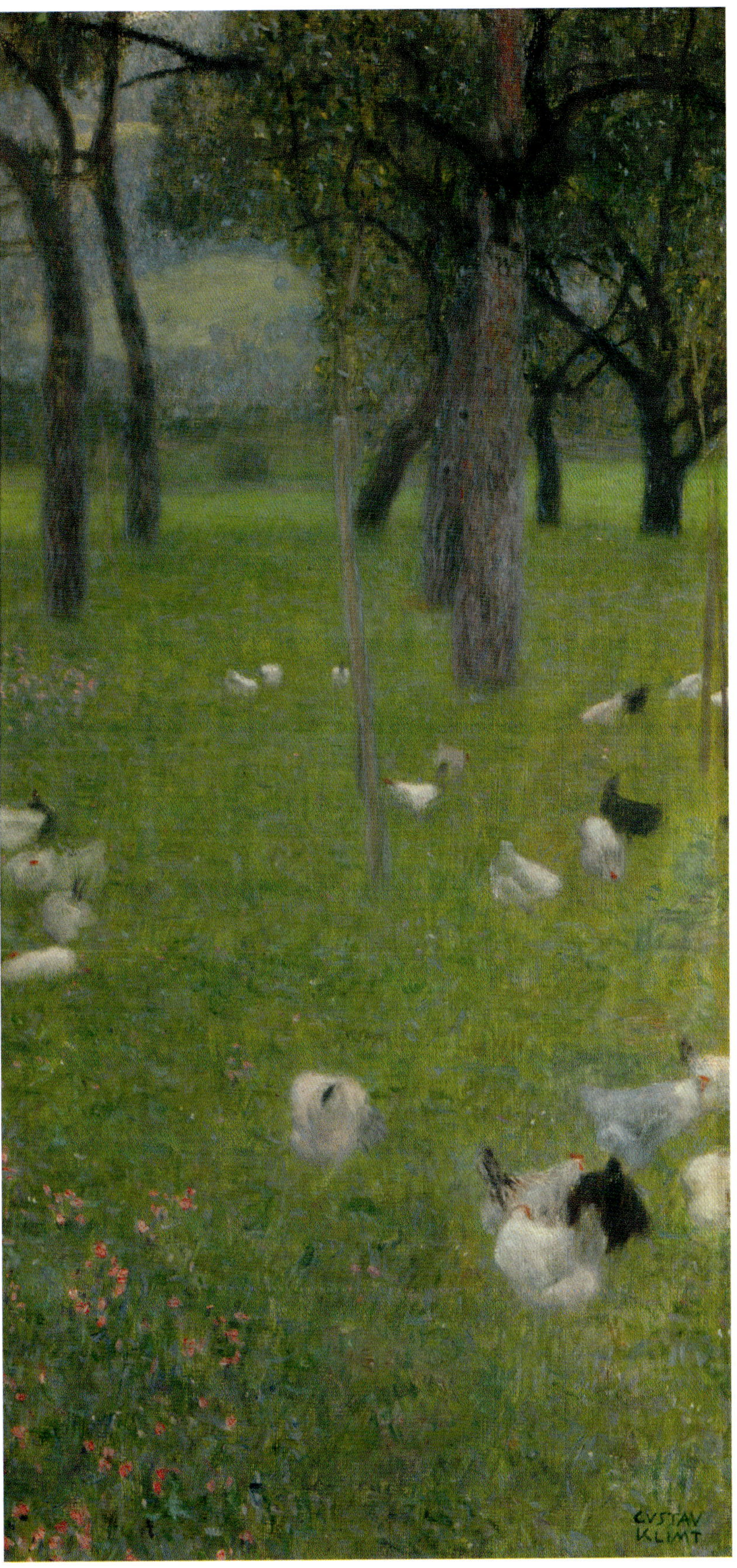

While aware of the artists who were creating Impressionist and Post-Impressionist landscapes, Klimt was less interested in the changing effects of light or weather. His landscapes are at once stylized and detailed – a cross between abstraction and representation. Klimt mostly chose the square format for his landscapes. As he revealed, 'This format makes it possible to bathe the subject in an atmosphere of peace. Through the square the picture becomes part of a universal whole.' Within his squares, a field of tiny marks appears to represent every leaf, tree or stem and the effect is that the overall, undifferentiated plane becomes the subject of the work. In this respect Klimt's landscapes – like his figure paintings – are symbolic, revealing his aim of aspiring to some sort of universal harmony.

Within his square format, Klimt was adventurous in compositional terms with his landscape work. It seems that the uniformity of this repeated format allowed him to experiment. So, for example, he would make the horizon level lower or higher, or crop the view so that trees or other elements would sit to the side or outside of his frame. It is this cropping aspect to his landscape work – the hint at what was going on outside or around the canvas – that makes them seem so modern.

Spending summers on Lake Attersee gave Klimt the opportunity to develop various ways of painting water. *Calm Pond in the Park of Schloss Kammer* (1899) is a beautiful image in which Klimt eschews all detail to allow us to focus solely on the slabs of land and water. The off-centre composition with its left-sided, dark overhanging trees is offset by the subtleties of the surface of the pale water. In its stillness and sense of lyricism, the image recalls the landscapes

After the Rain, *1899. Another early landscape that has a distinctly Impressionist feel with its gentle light and soft daubs of paint.*

of Claude Monet. *Island on the Attersee* (1901) is an early minimal landscape with a modern feel in which the low horizon focuses our attention on the calm expanse of turquoise water. Composed from short, flecked brushstrokes, the water fills up nearly the entire surface, almost engulfing the distant island, an indeterminate dark brooding shape to the top right of the canvas. Compare this to the later work *Church in Unterach on the Attersee* (1916), a dynamic diagonal composition in which the layers of brightly coloured buildings and foliage are reflected in the shimmering lake, striking an altogether more light-filled, positive and harmonious note.

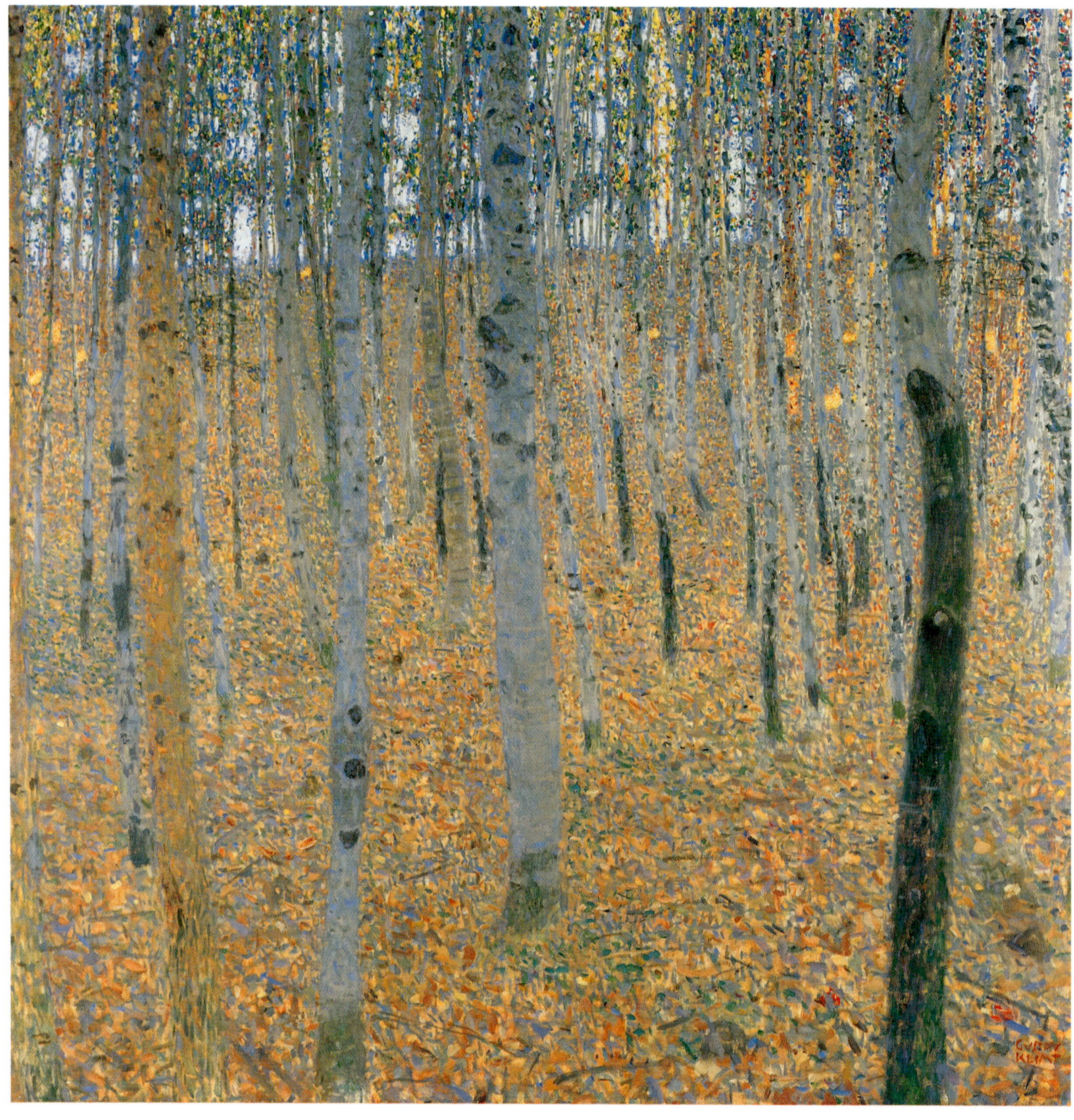

Beechwood Forest, *1903. Klimt made several forest scenes and they all follow the same pattern: row upon row of trees standing on a bed of leaves.*

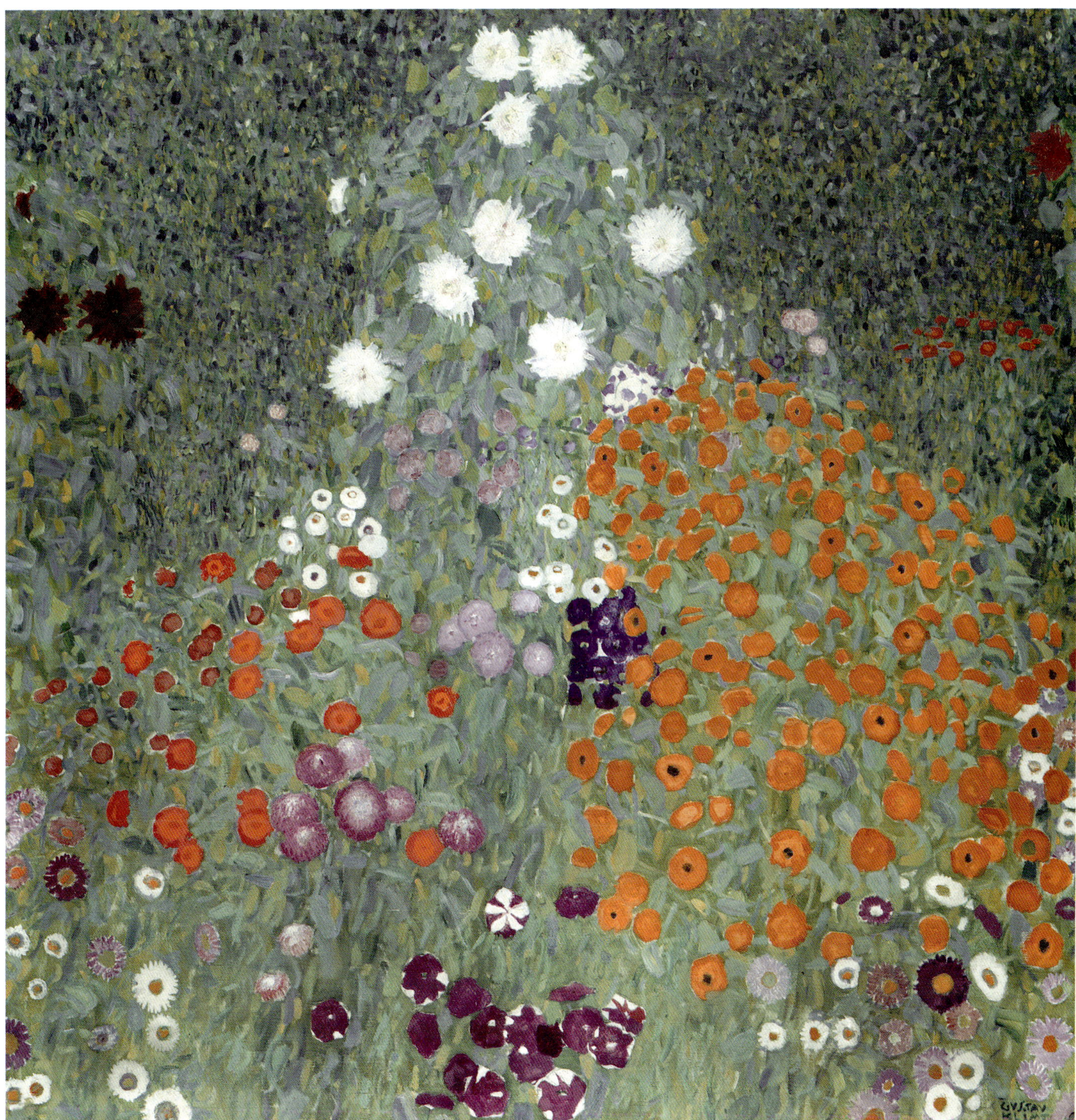

His forest scenes follow a similar pattern. Trees were a recurring motif and in the early 1900s he painted several relatively similar scenes of a network of bare tree trunks upright on a carpet of leaves. Klimt was drawn to these 'empty' forests and walked through the woods at 6.00 a.m. each day while on his summer vacation around Lake Attersee. He noted the fine distinctions between the different trees – fir, pine, birch and beech, for example – and carefully recorded these in his paintings of woods. While relying on

Flower Garden, *1905–07. The fact that Klimt adopted a square format for most of his landscapes allowed him to fill every inch of the canvas, in this case with a field of grass and garden flowers.*

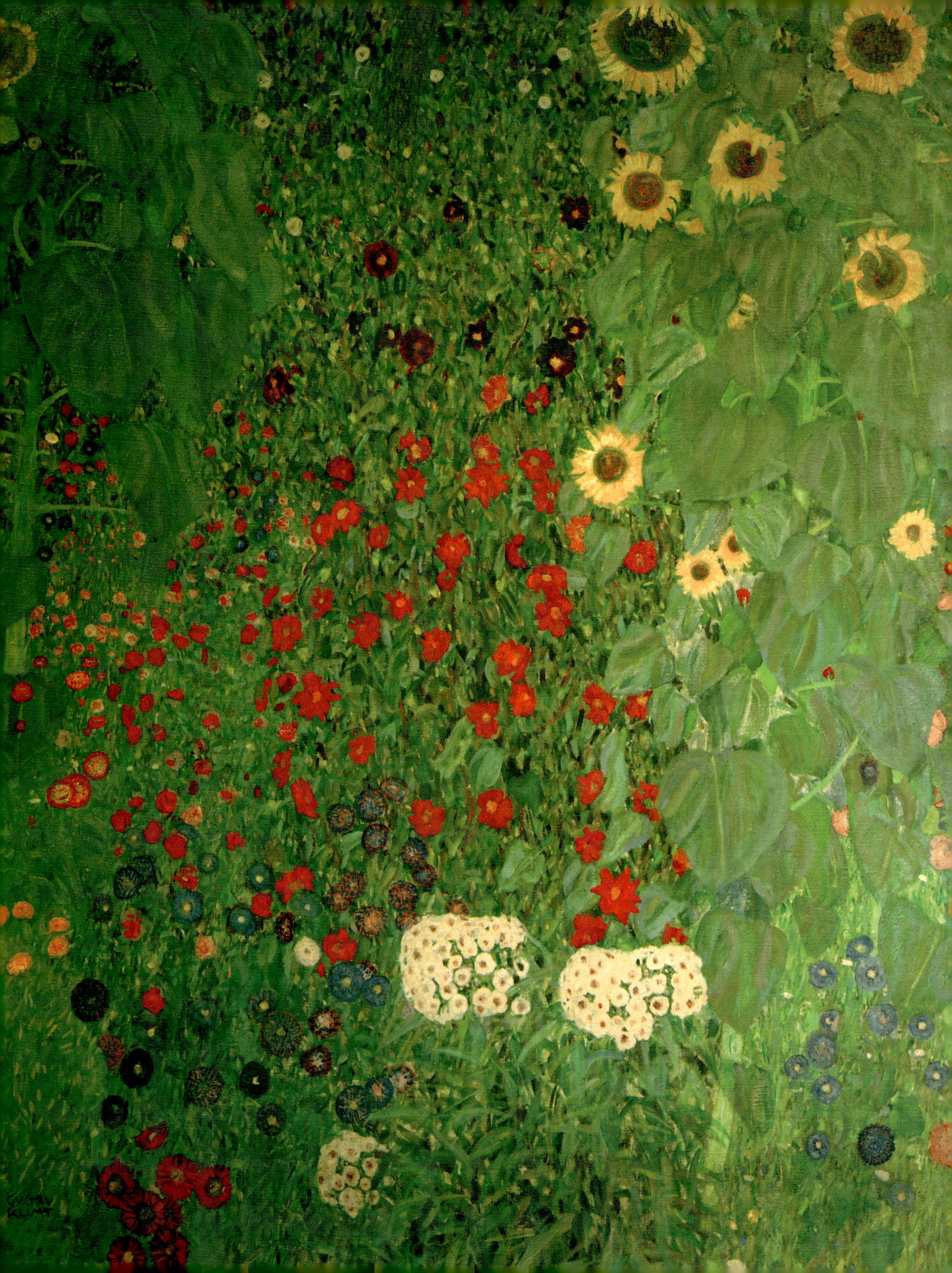

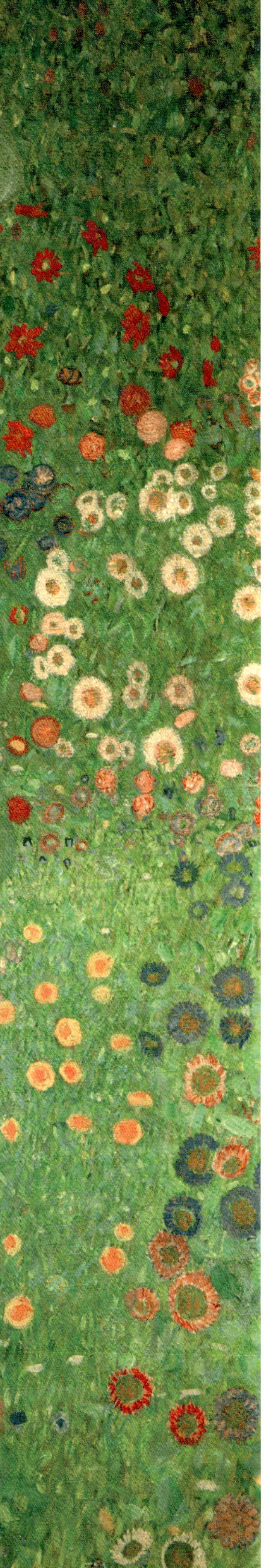

repetition and a sense of pattern, these poetic landscapes also communicate a particularly strong atmosphere of melancholy. In *Beechwood Forest* (1903), row upon row of silver beech trees are depicted on a carpet of orange leaves: there are no figures or creatures, nothing to interrupt the visual rhythm of the whole painting – it is a silent and meditative world.

Many of Klimt's calm landscapes recall Japanese art. Klimt built up his own collection of Oriental art, including Japanese woodblock prints, some Chinese paintings, and other objects including Noh masks, kimonos and porcelain. He sometimes adopted the narrow vertical format from Japanese prints in his work. His use of an overlapping technique to suggest distance, placing some objects in the foreground to partially cover other more distant objects, also came from Japanese painting. The way he played with the level of the horizon to balance it against other elements is another technique he learnt from studying Oriental art.

Clearly Klimt's landscapes provided him with a literal retreat from his world in Vienna, where he had obligations to his patrons as well as to all the other artists with whom he associated. He was also freed up by being able to paint directly from nature and to dispense with the more ostentatious aspects of his better-known golden and ornamental paintings. Klimt loved nature and the natural world and his own garden filled with trees and shrubs was a great source of inspiration for him and also helped to stabilize his mood when he was less than satisfied with his work. *Farm Garden (Flower Garden)* (1905–06) is a square painting filled with flowers and shrubs from his own garden – every inch of the canvas being packed with leaves, stems and blooms. The density of the foliage creates an overall pattern that resembles a piece of fabric. This work, along with a similar painting *Farm Garden with Sunflowers* (1905–06), is faintly reminiscent of Monet's waterlily paintings in the sense that they appear to extend beyond the canvas in a desire to show us the infinite nature of the universe.

Farm Garden with Sunflowers, *1907. Although Klimt has featured sunflowers here, they do not predominate over the rest of the flowers in the garden – his interest appears to be in the effect of the whole rather than the parts.*

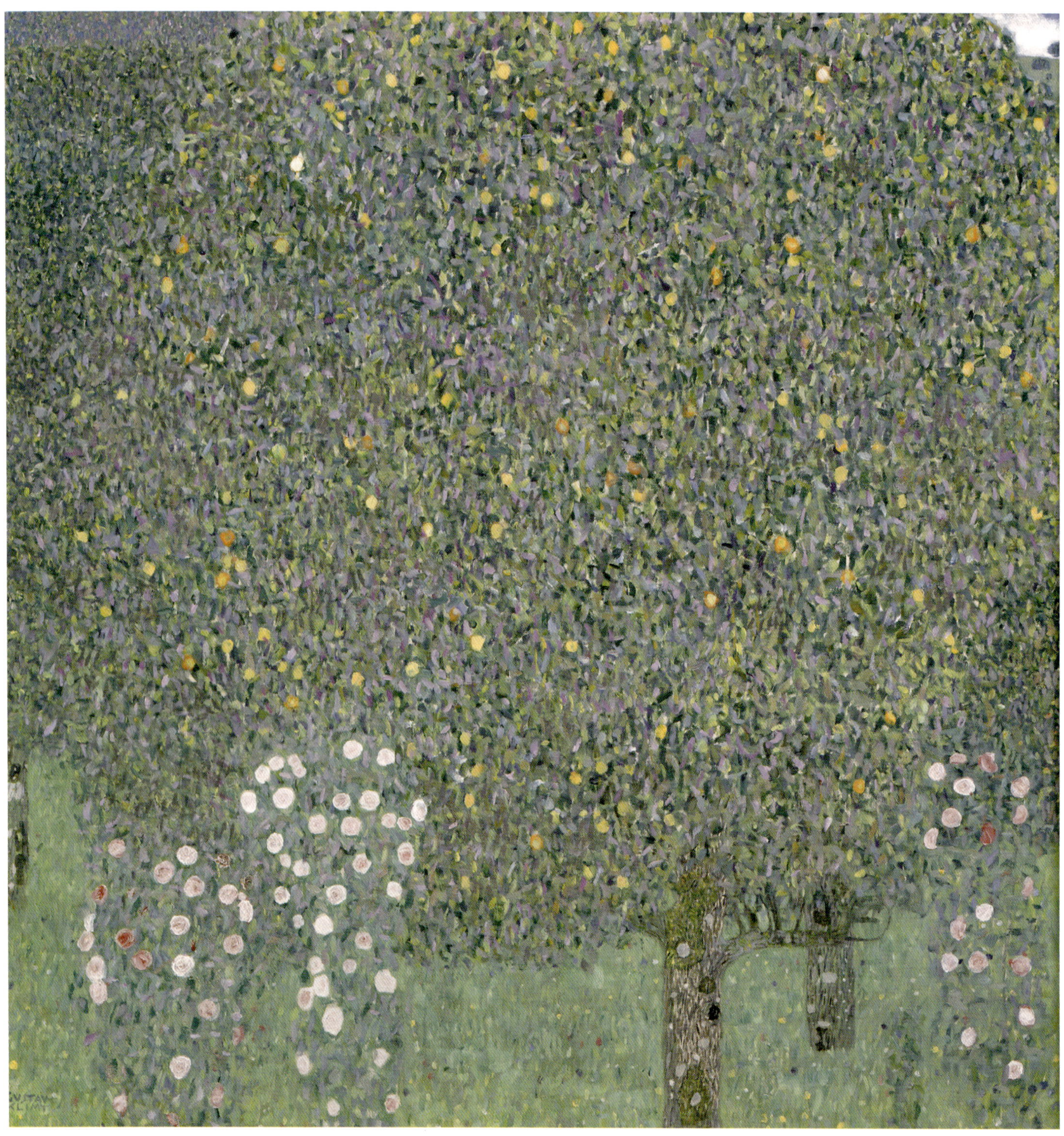

Rose Bushes Under the Trees, *1905. Klimt's approach here – building up the dense layers of vegetation using small daubs of paint – recalls the Impressionists' pointillist technique.*

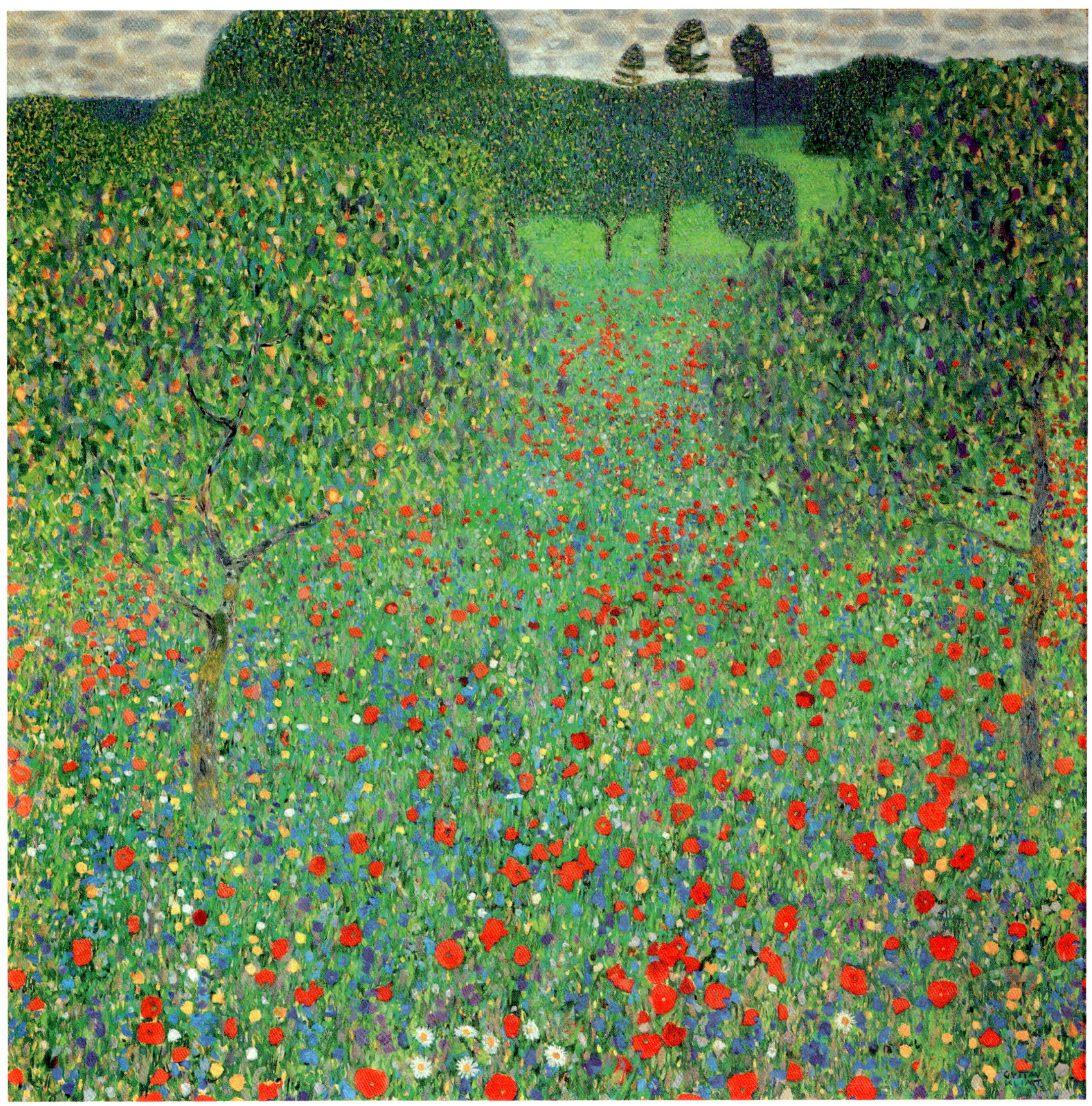

Poppy Field, 1907. *There is a real sense of perspective in this landscape, as the distant hedges and high horizon accentuate the immensity of the poppy field.*

Rosesbushes Under the Trees and *Orchard* (both c. 1905) and *Poppy Field* (1907) extend the idea of repeated pattern even further. Each dizzying landscape is built up using hundreds of tiny dots or slabs of colour, giving the overall effect of a mosaic or even the view offered through a kaleidoscope. *Sunflower* (1907), a giant sunflower appearing out of a mosaic-like flowerbed, is thought to have inspired the composition for *The Kiss*. Emilie Flöge posed for photographs in front of these sunflowers and this resulted in Klimt's celebrated painting a year later.

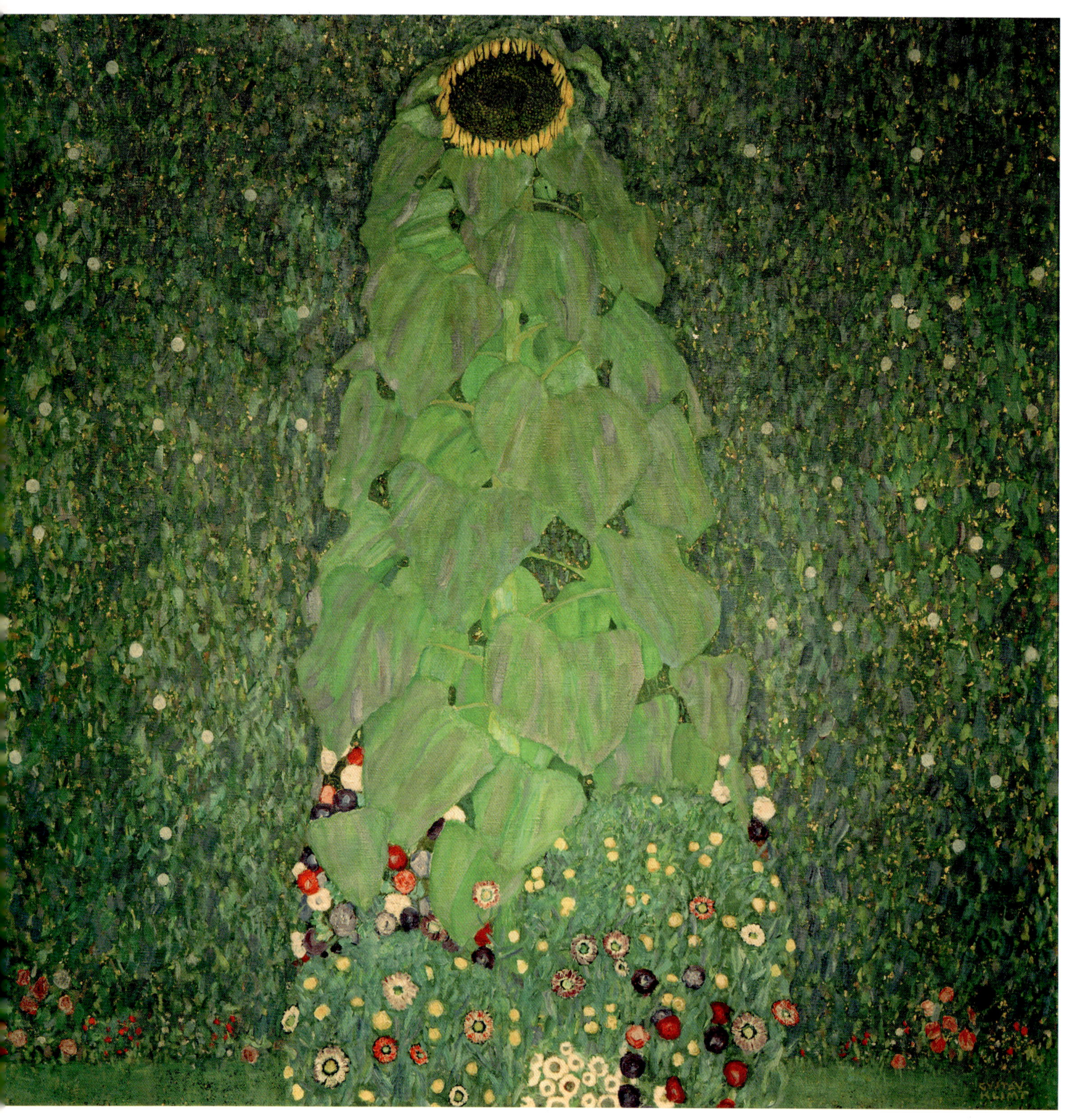

Sunflower, 1907. *Klimt painted sunflowers on several occasions. It is quite likely that he saw Van Gogh's paintings of sunflowers as the Dutch post-impressionist artist showed at the Secession exhibition of 1903.*

Schloss Kammer (an eighteenth-century villa on Lake Attersee) was another subject that Klimt returned to in his landscapes several times. *Schloss Kammer on Lake Attersee I* (1908) is a composition in mainly sludgy browns and olive greens. The villa nestles amongst foliage and the painting's main focus is the muddy reflections in the water. Klimt made two other versions of this scene over the next couple of years, and in the second one the colour has switched to a brighter green with the emphasis on the surrounding vegetation, rather than the water. The third one is altogether more stylized – Klimt painted it from a boat on the lake for his friend and model Adele Bloch-Bauer and the flowers and touches of red give it a jauntier note.

Schloss Kammer on Lake Attersee I, *1908. Klimt painted several versions of* Schloss Kammer, *an eighteenth-century villa rising above the lake.*

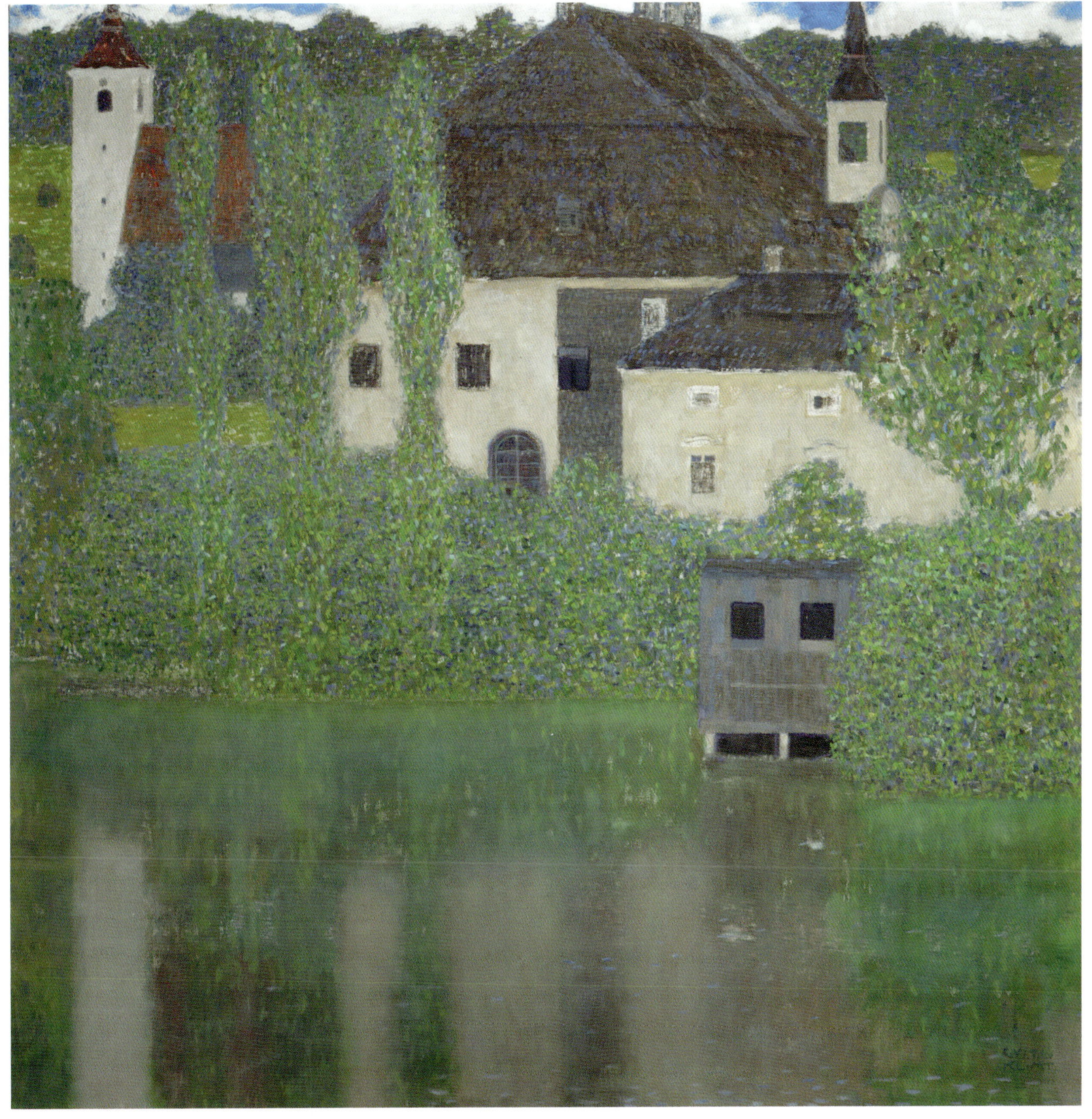

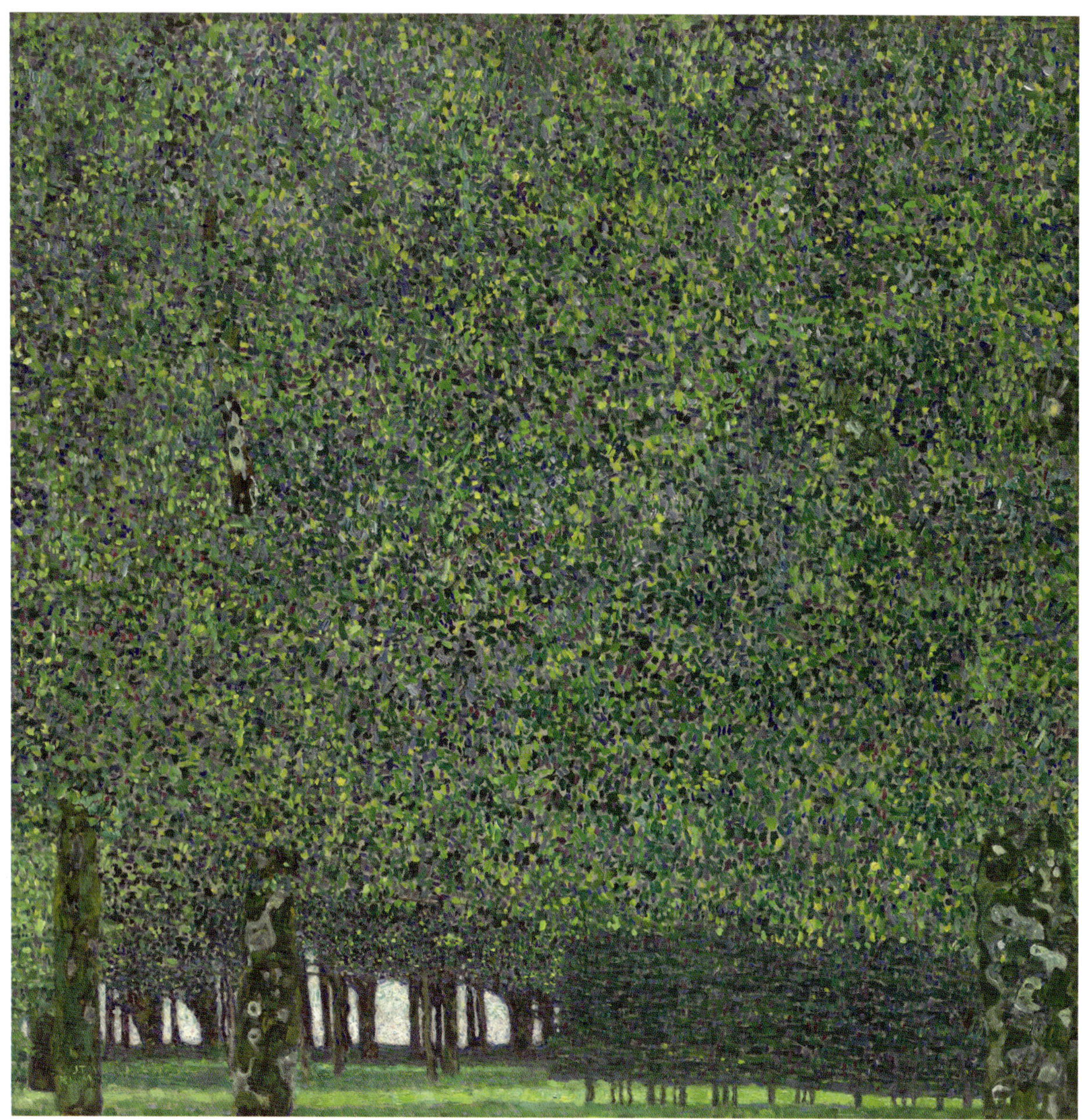

The Park, *1910. With more than two-thirds of the painting occupied by the trees' foliage, Klimt strives to record every single leaf. At the same time, the overall sense of the work is of a tapestry or mosaic.*

Klimt was aware of the new technique of Pointillism developed by the French Impressionist artists Georges Seurat and Paul Signac; the latter had exhibited at the Secession exhibition of 1900 in Vienna. Klimt adapted this technique for his own purposes. He made use of small, distinct dots of colour applied in patterns to form an image but, unlike the Pointillists, he never expressed an interest in utilizing optics in his work or creating illusions of depth. *The Park* (1910) is almost all foliage, apart from some dark vertical lines depicting trunks at the bottom. The great mass of blue, green and yellow dots form a decorative whole, denying the painting any real depth but at the same time creating a real sense of atmosphere and lyricism. Only after a little while do patterns emerge and shift before your eyes, revealing the real impact of the work. One of his most celebrated landscapes, *The Park* initially started life outside but ended up being finished in Klimt's studio.

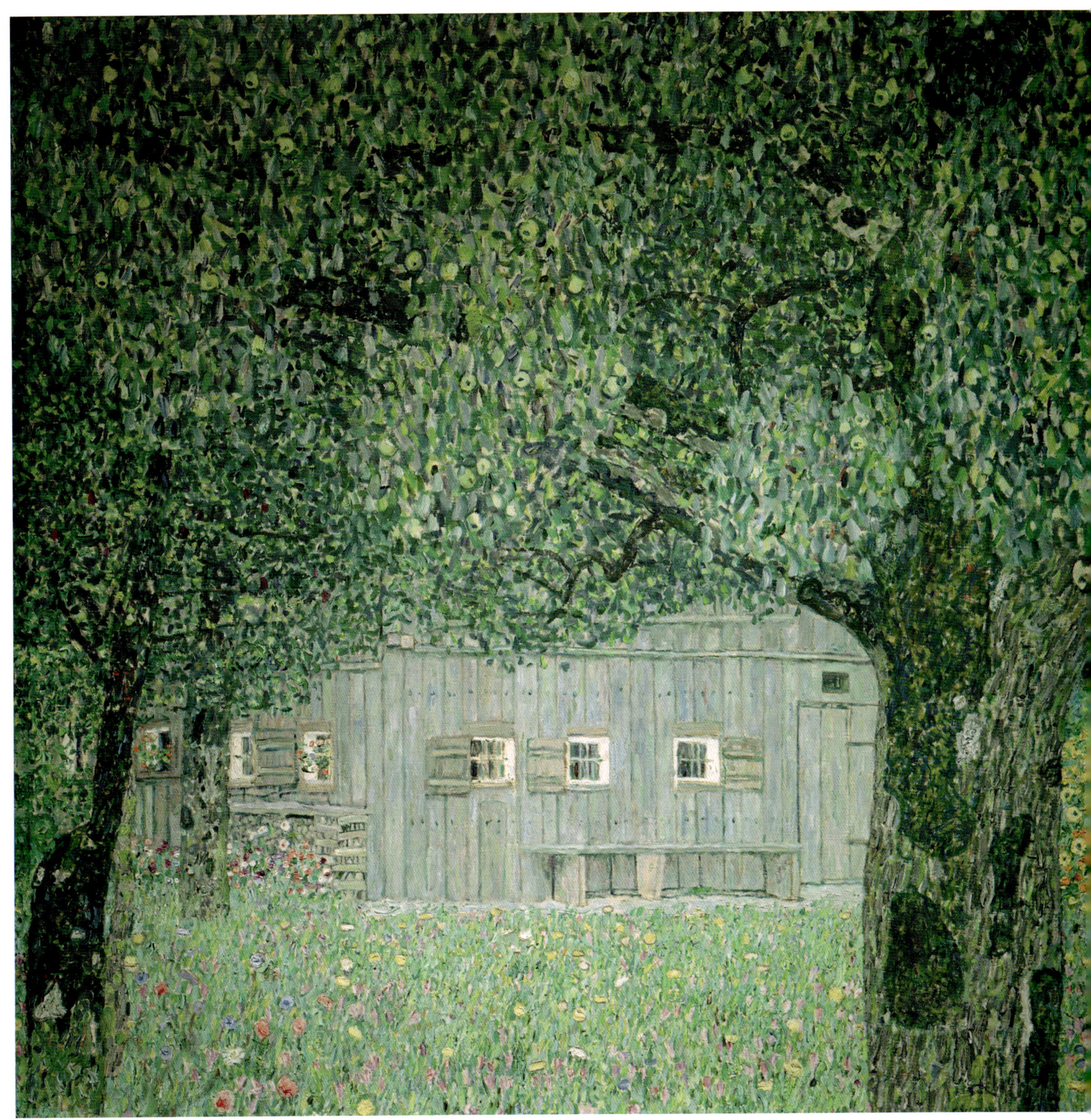

Farm House in Upper Austria, *1911–12. There is a definite shift in this painting towards a looser, more Impressionistic style. The texture of the wooden hut and the greyish purple tones suggest the influence of Van Gogh.*

Other later Klimt landscapes also borrow elements from Post Impressionism – whether the pointillist technique, the undulating brushwork or the muted green, yellow and blue palette. In *Farmhouse in Upper Austria* (1911–12) the brushstrokes appear looser and less tightly packed and the deserted wooden building itself with its grainy mauve planks looks almost like something Van Gogh could have painted. In *Avenue in the Park of Schloss Kammer*, another work from the same year, Klimt depicts an avenue of gnarled trees. The fact that pattern seems less important here than the expressive nature of the work, suggests Klimt is taking a more modern approach akin to that of both Van Gogh and Cézanne. Perhaps the most significant thing about some of Klimt's most mature landscapes is the heightened level of emotional engagement. Not only do they reflect the artist's love of nature, they increase our own understanding and appreciation of the natural world by evoking a range of moods from tranquillity to despair.

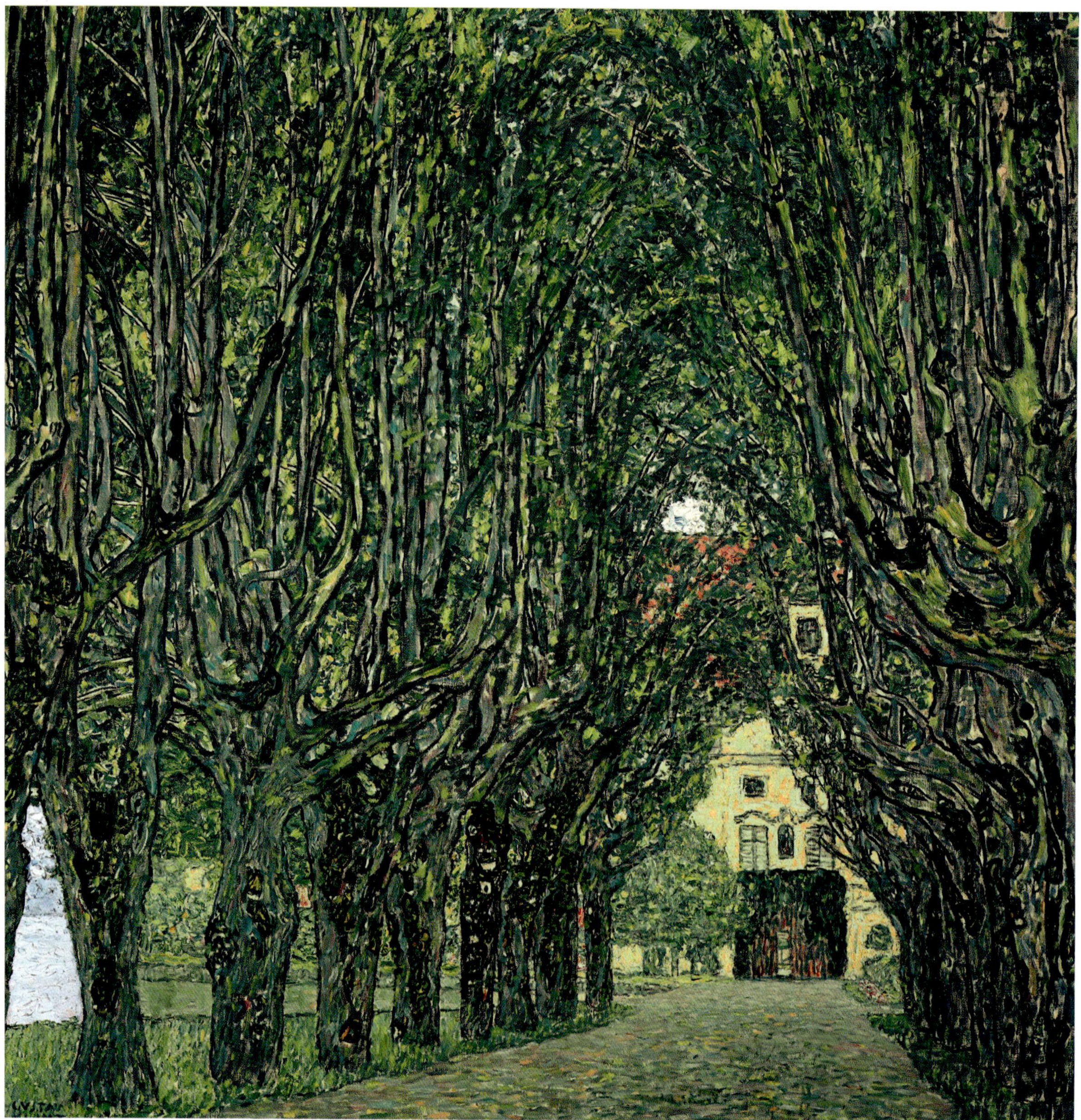

Avenue in the Park of Schloss Kammer, *1912. One of Klimt's most expressive landscapes in which the view through the avenue of gnarled trees is reminiscent of both Van Gogh and Cézanne.*

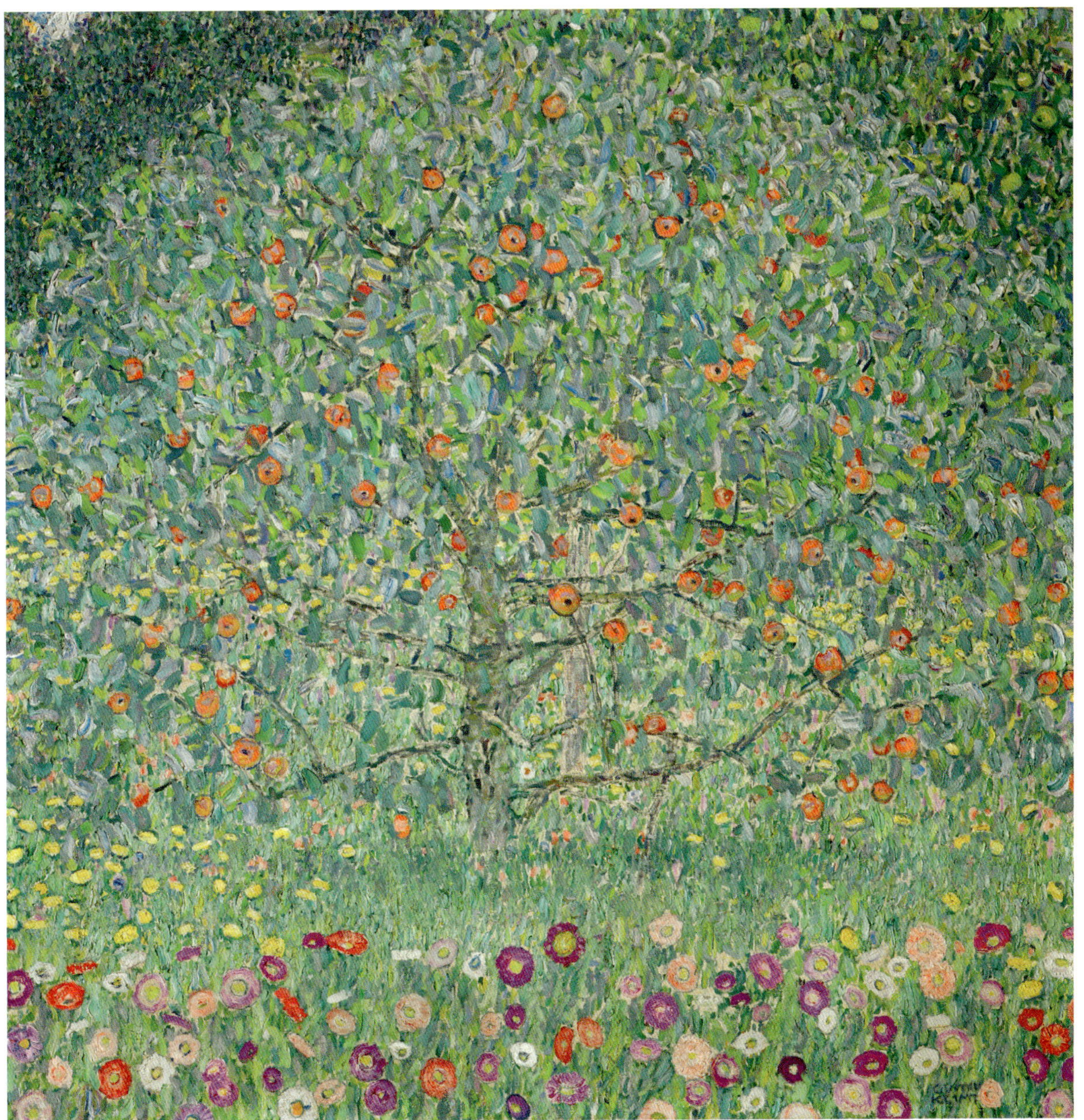

Apple Tree I, *1912. This brightly coloured work with its blooming flowers in the foreground and red apples punctuating the trees appears to be a joyous comment on nature's abundance.*

A darker restless, mood is expressed in *Apple Tree II*, a landscape from 1916. Klimt painted at least three pictures of apple trees, and *Apple Tree II* differs from the all-over patterning and harmonious approach that Klimt adopted for *Apple Tree I* (1912). In both versions Klimt did not attempt to paint the whole tree, but rather presents an off-centre view in which the branches extend to the side and top of the image. In *Apple Tree II* the background is sketchy; the ground a series of hastily applied green brushstrokes with a series of blue and green marks indicating further trees in the distance. The apple tree itself is unrealistic; Klimt depicts the apples as solid dots of colour with a thick outline and this non-naturalistic treatment recalls the work of his younger colleague Egon Schiele.

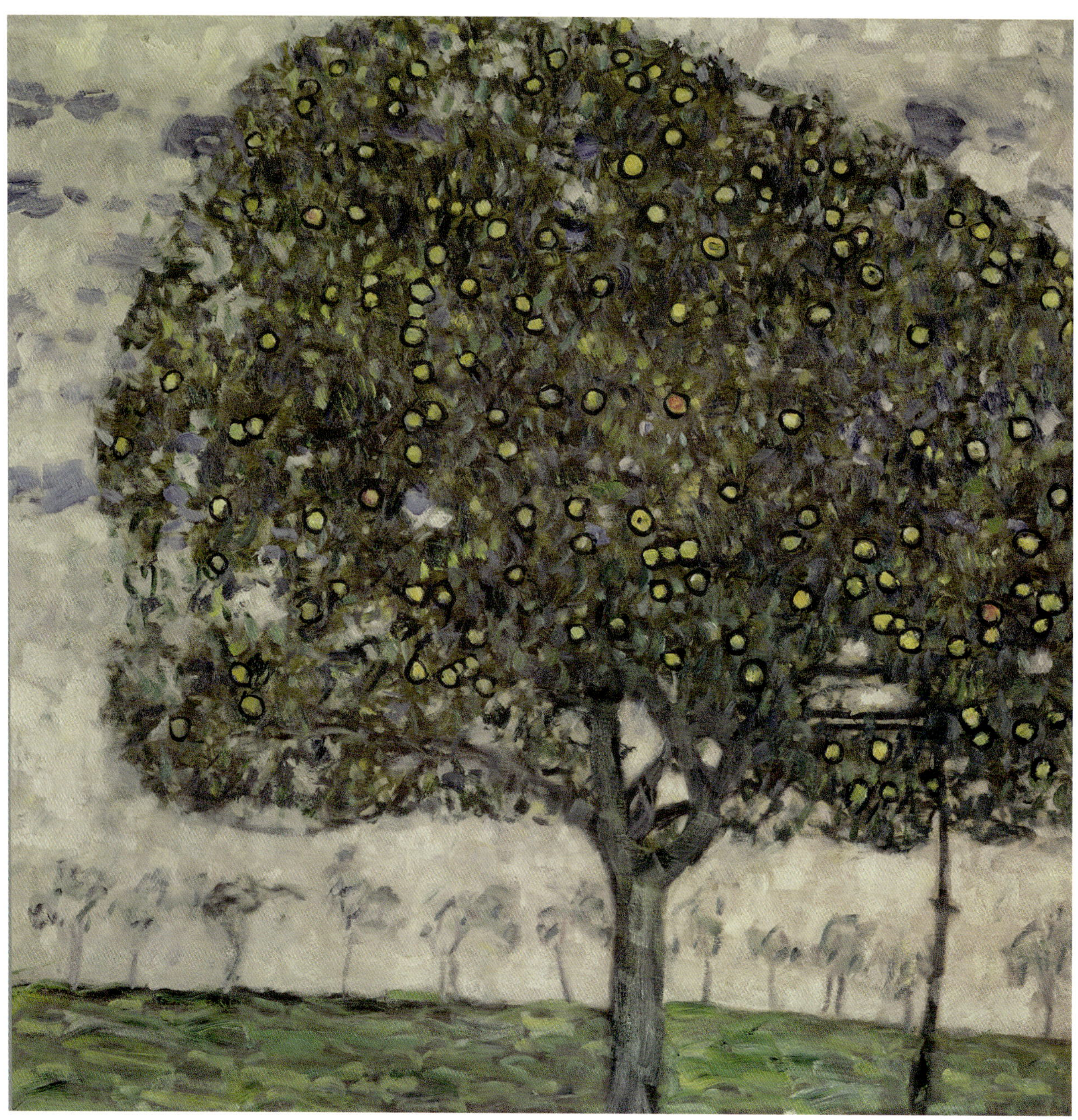

Apple Tree II, *1916. Klimt's second painting of an apple tree with its scudding clouds and darker sky evokes a far less harmonious mood. In 1916 Klimt was well aware of the horrific events unfolding across Europe.*

Klimt's landscapes were well regarded by his contemporaries and were bought by a range of patrons. Industrialist Karl Wittgenstein bought three, including the allegorical *Life is a Struggle (The Golden Knight)* (1903), a gold embellished painting of a knight on a horse in front of a mosaic of flowers. He also bought *Sunflower*, perhaps seeing in both some reflection of his struggle to make it to the top of his own profession. Aside from their painting of Lake Attersee, Ferdinand and Adele Bloch-Bauer acquired *Birch Forest* (1903) and *Apple Tree I* (1912), while the Lederers also acquired several landscapes, some of which were later destroyed by fire. The most significant patron of Klimt as a landscape painter was the industrialist Viktor Zuckerkandl, whose collection included *Rosebushes Under the Trees* (c.1905), *Poppy Field* (1907) and *Apple Tree II* (1916).

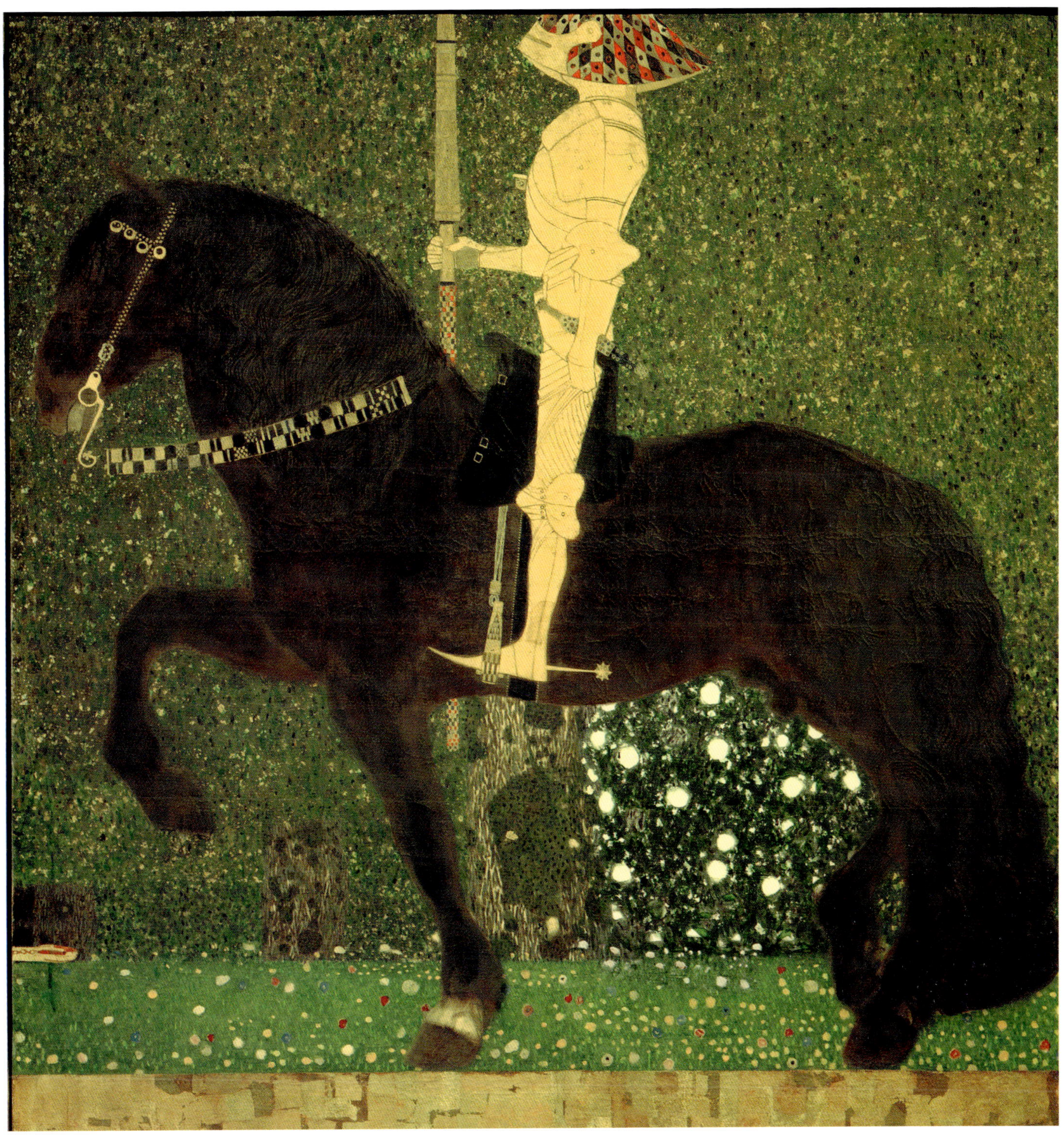

Life is a Struggle *(*The Golden Knight*), 1903. This is a rare instance of an animal appearing in Klimt's work. A golden knight also appears in the* Beethoven Frieze *– psychologically it seems interesting that Klimt was drawn to the motif of a knight in shining armour.*

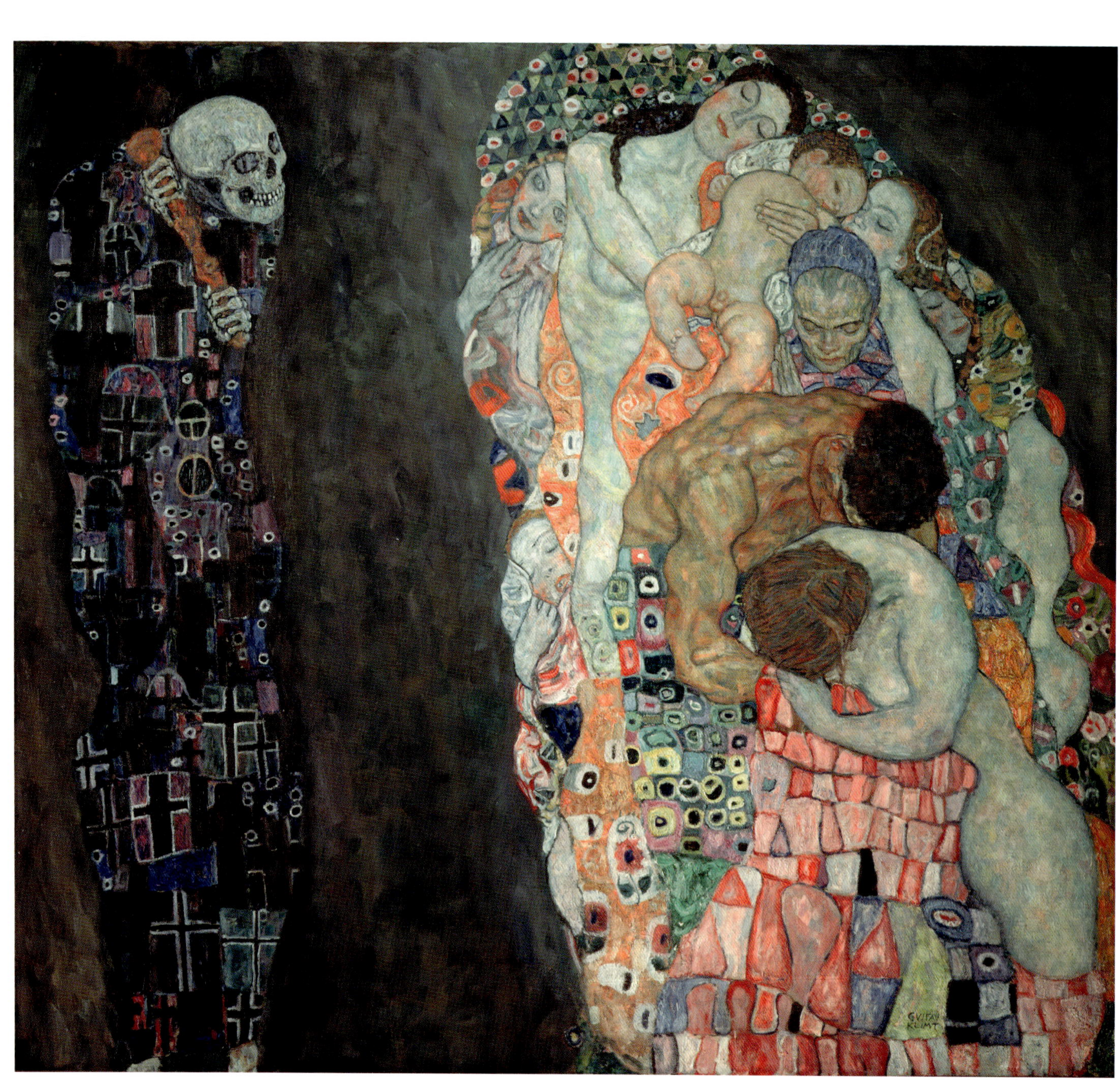

CHAPTER 5
The Later Works

If Klimt's golden phase came to glorious fruition with his 1907 *Portrait of Adele Bloch-Bauer I*, it also marked the beginning of some noticeably different traits in his artistic direction. In 1909, at the breakaway group's second and final exhibition in Vienna, Klimt saw at first hand the work of European artists, including Edvard Munch, Paul Gauguin, Vincent Van Gogh, Henri Matisse and Pierre Bonnard. Klimt was inspired but also a little overwhelmed as their expressive work made him realize his own work by contrast was rigid, stylized and lacked the ability to communicate psychological truths. Later that year, Klimt travelled to Paris, where he not only saw a good deal more of the Fauves' intensely coloured paintings but also discovered the work of Henri de Toulouse-Lautrec. This, combined with the raw emotion that he recognized in younger artists like Schiele and Kokoschka, gave Klimt the impetus to make some important stylistic changes. From 1910 he developed a new freer style that dispensed with the gold and the more excessive decorative elements.

In 1910, Klimt was given an individual exhibition at the 9th Biennale in Venice. His room was designed by the Wiener Werkstätte and was very well received. The city bought *Judith II* – the painting still hangs in the Palazzo di Ca' Pesaro on the Grand Canal. The National Gallery of Modern Art in Rome also acquired *The Three Ages of Woman*. Some Italian critics, however, including some of the Futurist artists, saw Klimt's work as decadent and excessive.

A year later, *Death and Life*, one of his last pictures in his golden allegorical style, won first prize in Rome. The painting shows Death, pictured as the Grim Reaper to the side of the painting, staring at a mass of bodies in repose. These various individuals represent the cycle of life – the different ages of the human race – and in this image Klimt seems to be acknowledging that while death might take individuals, it cannot ever expect to wipe out the whole of humanity. In 1915, in response to his awareness of the work of European artists, and in particular Henri Matisse, Klimt reworked the painting, changing the background from gold to dark blue.

Change was in the air generally as many of Klimt's friends left to live abroad, including, in 1910, Oskar Kokoschka. Klimt stayed in Vienna but became increasingly isolated. Around this time he started to make an annual trip to a spa in Salzburg as a means of counterbalancing his ever-present tendency towards depression. Although it is

Death and Life, *1915. Klimt first painted this work in 1908 and then overpainted the gold background with dark blue seven years later. This was most likely in response to his growing awareness of the work of other European painters whom he much admired.*

true that his work picked up on some of the stylistic changes going on in Europe, he did not fully embrace one particular style or radically depart from his previous subject matter.

Lady with Hat and Feather Boa (1909) and *Woman in Black Feather Hat* (1910) show the strong if temporary influence of Toulouse-Lautrec. Compare both these with Klimt's previous portraits of society ladies, as well as the femmes fatales. The composition is altogether simpler and less fussy. Gone are the white, wispy dresses and the proud but vacant look staring beyond the portrait. In place of the gold there's a preponderance of black – but black used to judicious effect. In *Lady with Hat and Feather Boa*, we can only partly see the unidentified woman's face and hair because they are covered by her hat and coat and further framed by the black-blue tones of the night sky. Behind her head, streaks and daubs of paint provide a hastily composed view of Paris, which Klimt might well have seen for himself on a night out. In the model's costume and pose, *The Black Feather Hat* more directly resembles a painting by Toulouse-Lautrec, while also making use of a restrained palette and pared down composition, which serves to heighten the pensive expression of the red-haired model.

No sooner had Klimt seemingly settled on a new style than he changed it to something else. Perhaps sensing that the femmes fatales had been his strongest suit, or calling card, he looked at ways of transforming this particular style into something less intimidating and something he felt would have a more universal appeal. Through Emilie Flöge, clothes and fashion

Woman in Black Feather Hat, *1910. In this work, influenced by Toulouse-Lautrec, Klimt appears to be turning away from his decorative style in a search for a new level of psychological intensity.*

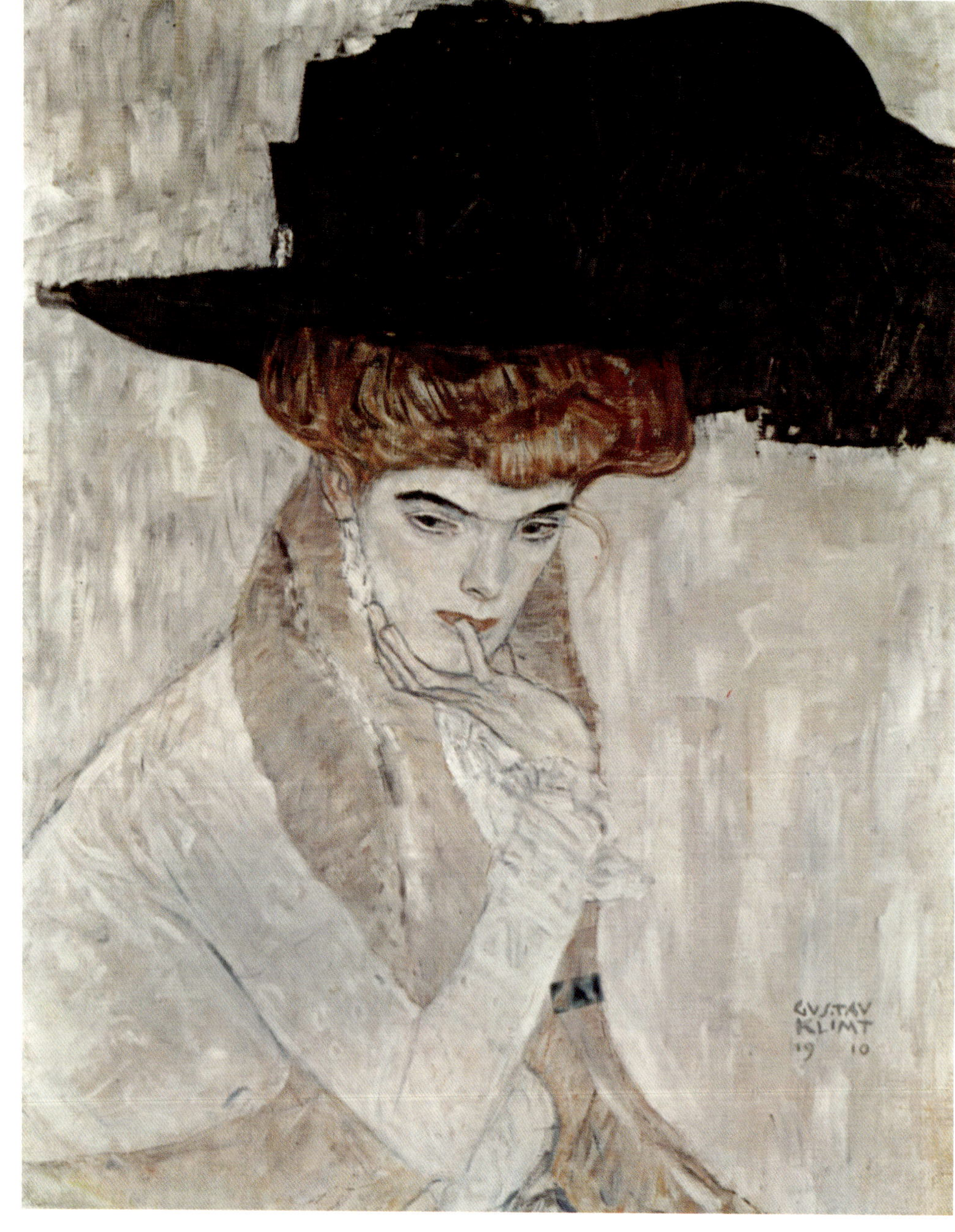

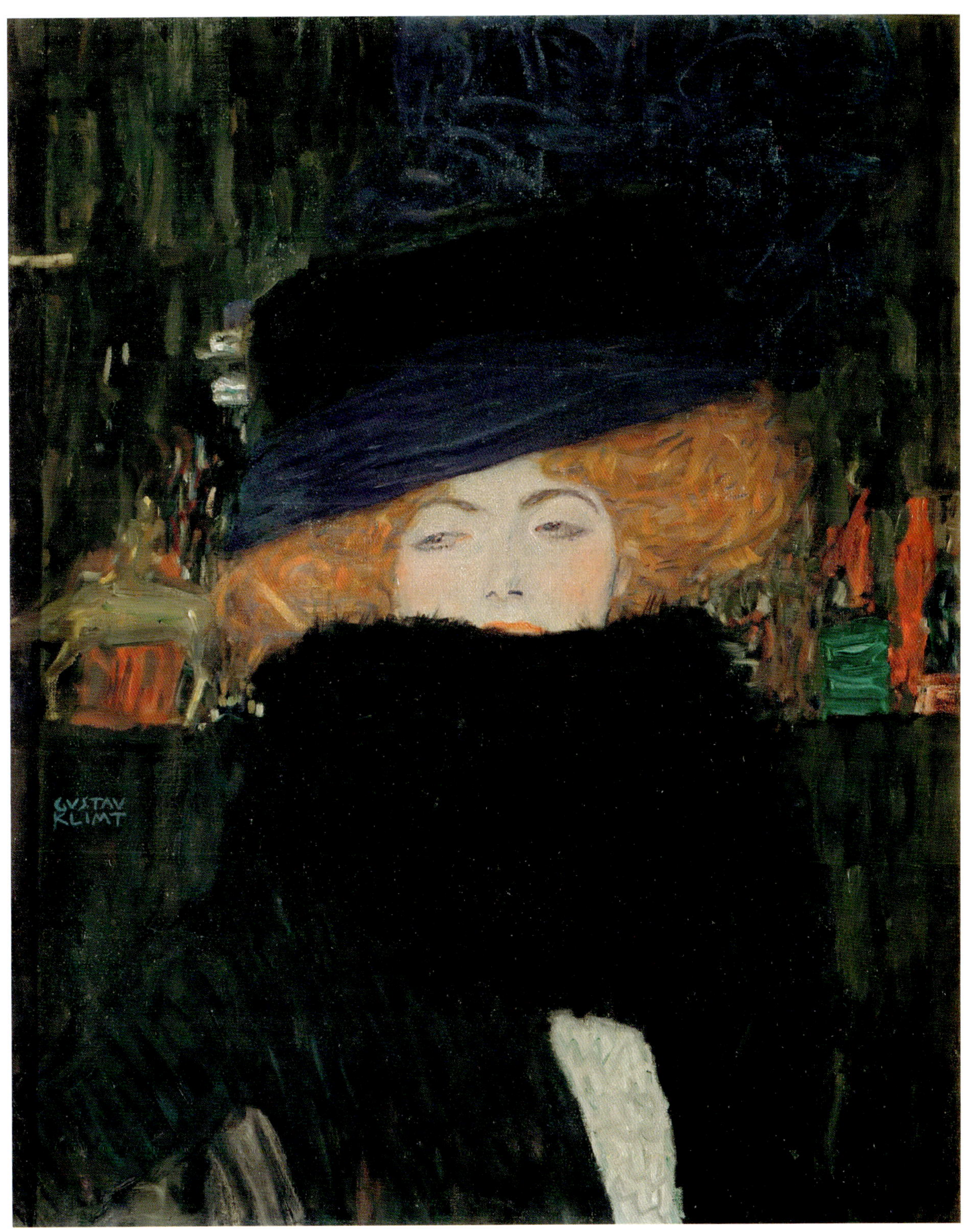

Lady with Hat and Feather Boa, *1909. The redheaded model for this work is thought to be the same as the one for* Woman in Black Feather Hat.

had always played a large part in Klimt's work and, for the later portraits, he brought together a startling and riotous amount of dresses, hats, flowers, fabrics and other decorative accessories to dress his models.

The portrait of *Mäda Primavesi* (1912–13) is an example of this new tendency in Klimt's work. Mäda is the daughter of one of Klimt's wealthiest patrons, the industrialist and banker Otto Primavesi and the actress Eugenia Primavesi. Nine-year-old Mäda stands with feet squarely apart, staring out of the canvas. Her intense, knowing stare makes her look older than her years, but the decorations attached to her hair and dress,

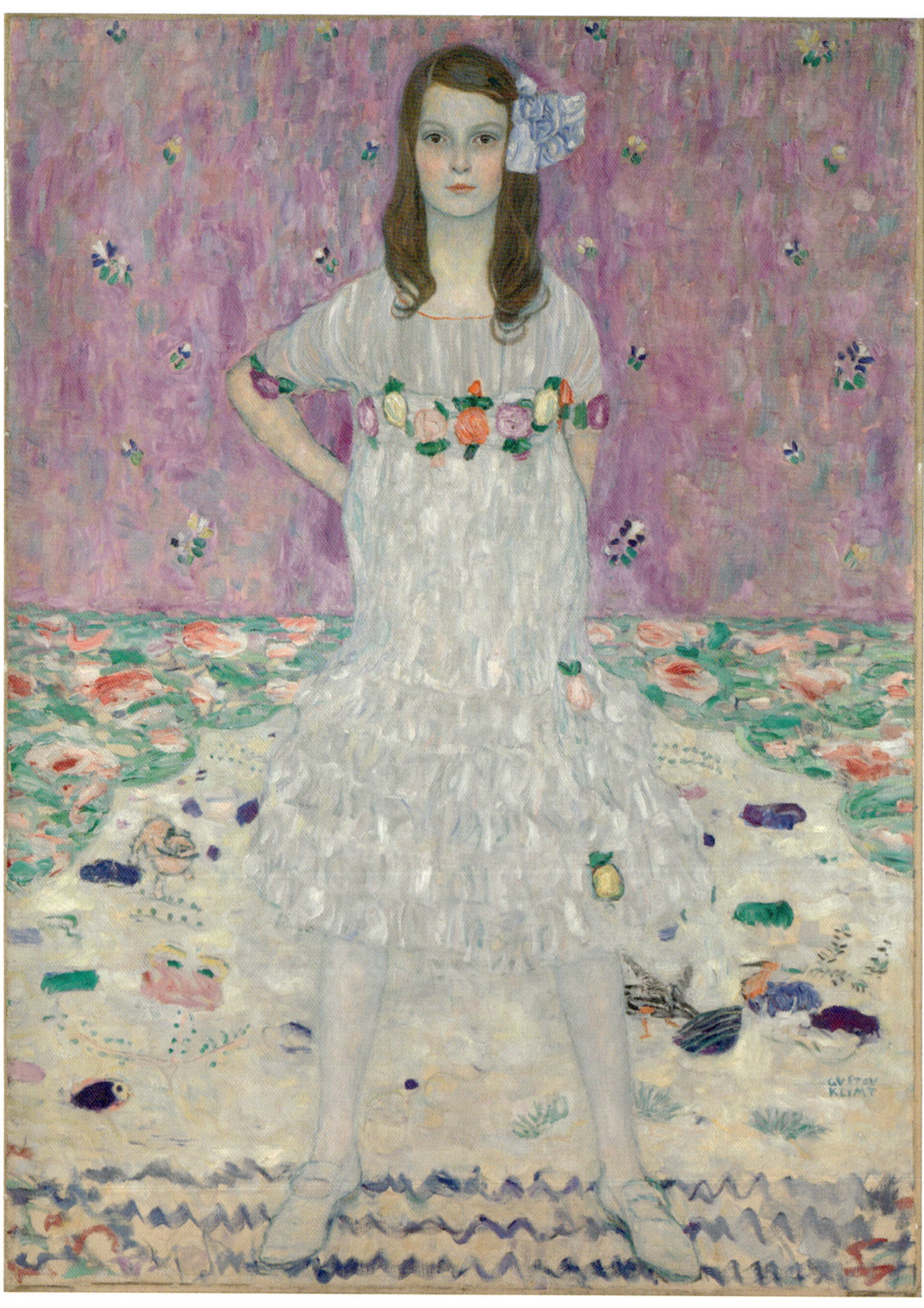

Mäda Primavesi, *1912–13. Mäda was the nine-year-old daughter of Otto Primavesi, one of Klimt's most important patrons. Primavesi's wife, Eugenia, sat for Klimt the following year.*

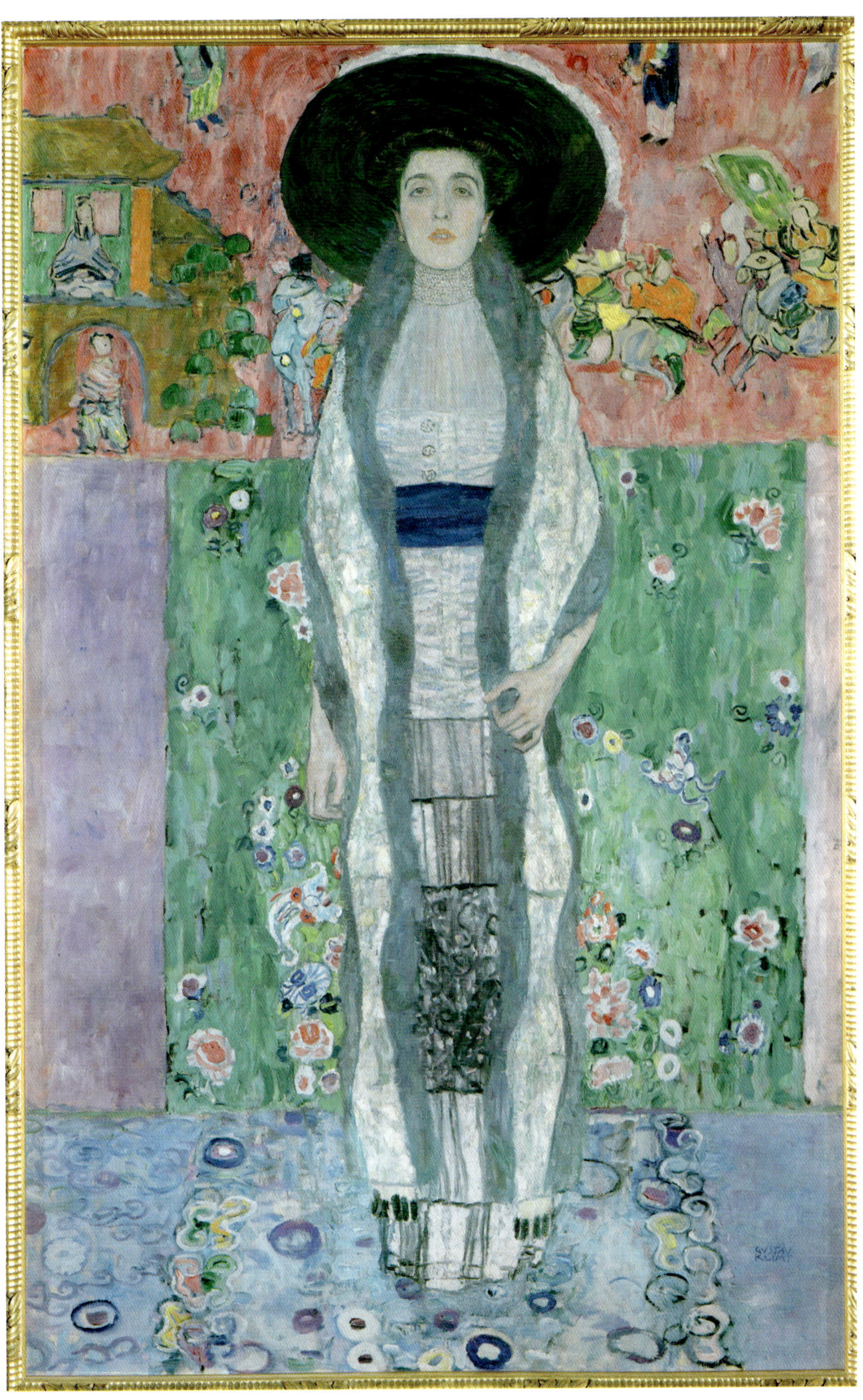

Portrait of Adele Bloch-Bauer II, *1912. The two commissioned portraits of Adele Bloch-Bauer reveal important differences. In this the second one, Adele stands full-frontal – her body merged into the vivid background filled with decorative motifs.*

and festooned around the room, have the effect of making her look younger. The colours in this portrait are a new departure for Klimt – lilac, emerald, lemon and icy blue – while the brushwork is generally freer and the decorative objects often of an indeterminate origin, although no less appealing because of that. Not long after, Klimt also painted Mäda's mother, Eugenia (c.1913), creating another intensely bright and patterned work in which the patchwork of patterns on her dress is almost merged into the mosaic-like background. In 1912, Klimt painted a second portrait of Adele Bloch-Bauer. Adele was only one of a couple of sitters who sat for Klimt twice. In this portrait her face with its faraway eyes and slightly open mouth closely resembles the earlier, infamous portrait of 1907. Klimt had earlier managed to capture the strong face of this tall, dark-haired beauty when he used her as his model for *Judith I* (1901) and *Judith II* (1909). In this decorative second portrait, there is an absence of gold. Adele stands erect, uncompromising, the waves of her gown cascading to the ground. Almost architectural, her dress is divided into sections, and a large circular hat frames her face. The background to the work is highly decorative – divided by colour into further sections that contain a profusion of floral motifs

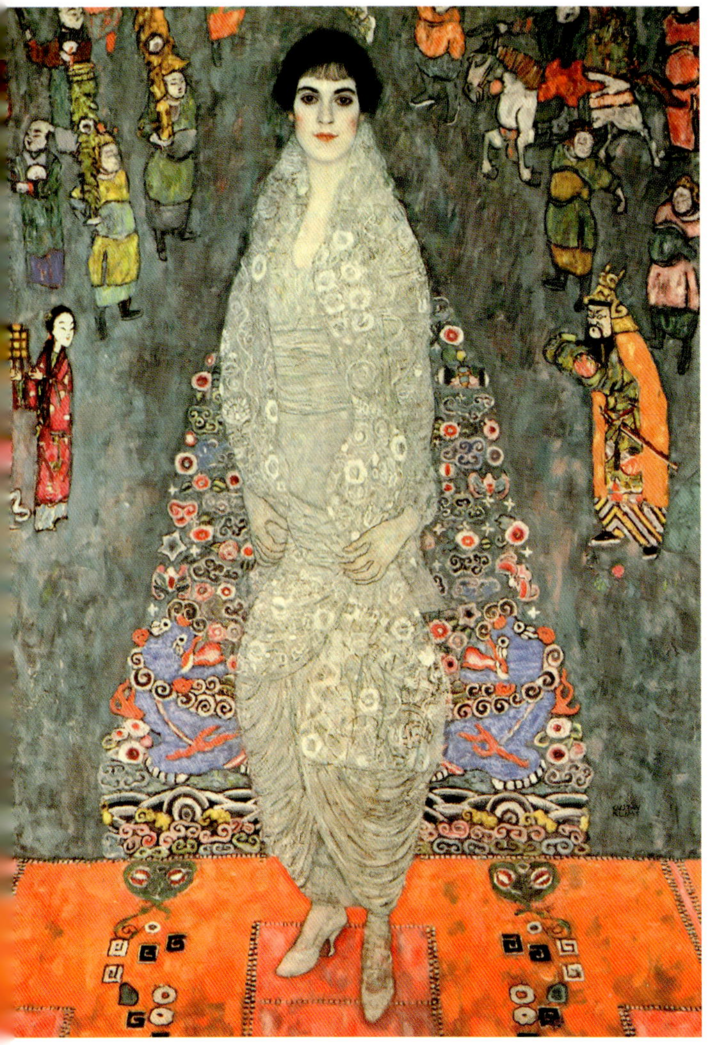

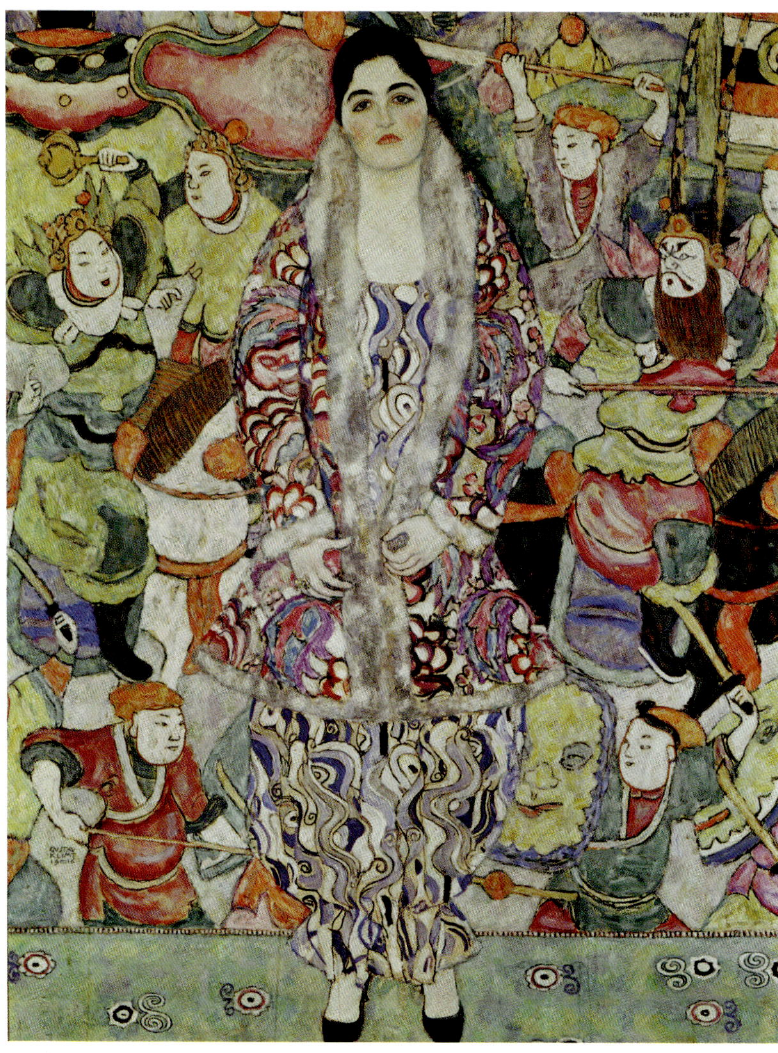

Above left: Portrait of Elisabeth Baroness Bachofen-Echt, *1914. Elisabeth was the daughter of Klimt's patrons the Lederers and this painting was commissioned for her wedding. Her white dress is set against a background of colourful Japanese-inspired motifs.*

Portrait of Friederike Maria Beer, *1916. Friederike Maria Beer commissioned this portrait from Klimt directly. In it she wears a dress that she bought from the Wiener Werkstätte with material that Klimt hand-painted with spiral and eye motifs.*

and a range of ornamental objects. Bright colour and bold pattern suggest the influence of Matisse as well as Japanese woodcuts. Klimt was not alone in his appreciation of Japanese woodcuts. Many of the French Impressionists were also drawn to them and made similar use of 'a bird's-eye view', looking down at their subject from above, when planning the composition of their paintings. The Japanese influence is particularly clear in Klimt's later portraits such as *Portrait of Baroness Elisabeth Bachofen-Echt* (1914) and *Portrait of Friederike Maria Beer* (1916), where figures and objects surround the central figures who are depicted in highly patterned kimono style gowns.*The Virgin* (1912–13) suggests a return to the tangled compositions of earlier allegories. In an exotic pyramid of flowers and patterns, a young virgin dozes amid the writhing pale limbs of other young women. The colour is pure and bright and the brushstrokes thick and loose. The late allegories, like the earlier ones, do not contain a straightforward narrative and some of their meaning was lost on Klimt's contemporaries. What is clear here is Klimt's desire to evoke an entirely female world in which various states of pleasurable being such as desire and contentment are foregrounded. The feminine is consciously evoked through circular symbols, including the moon, the spiral and the shell.

The Virgin, *1912–13. To Klimt this allegorical vision of seven slumbering women entwined with flowers and a riot of patterns seems to represent a state of sexual expectation of awakening.*

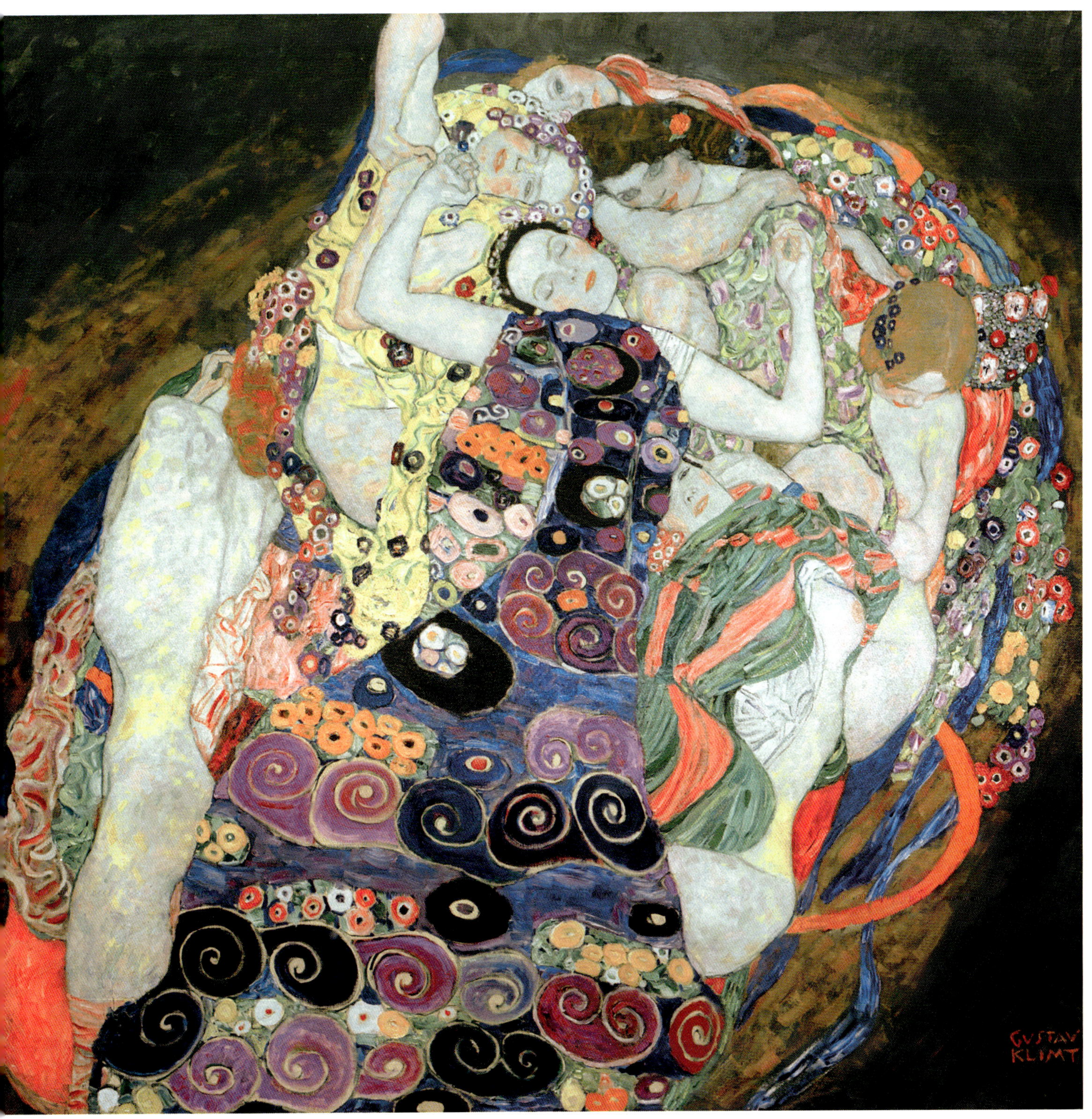

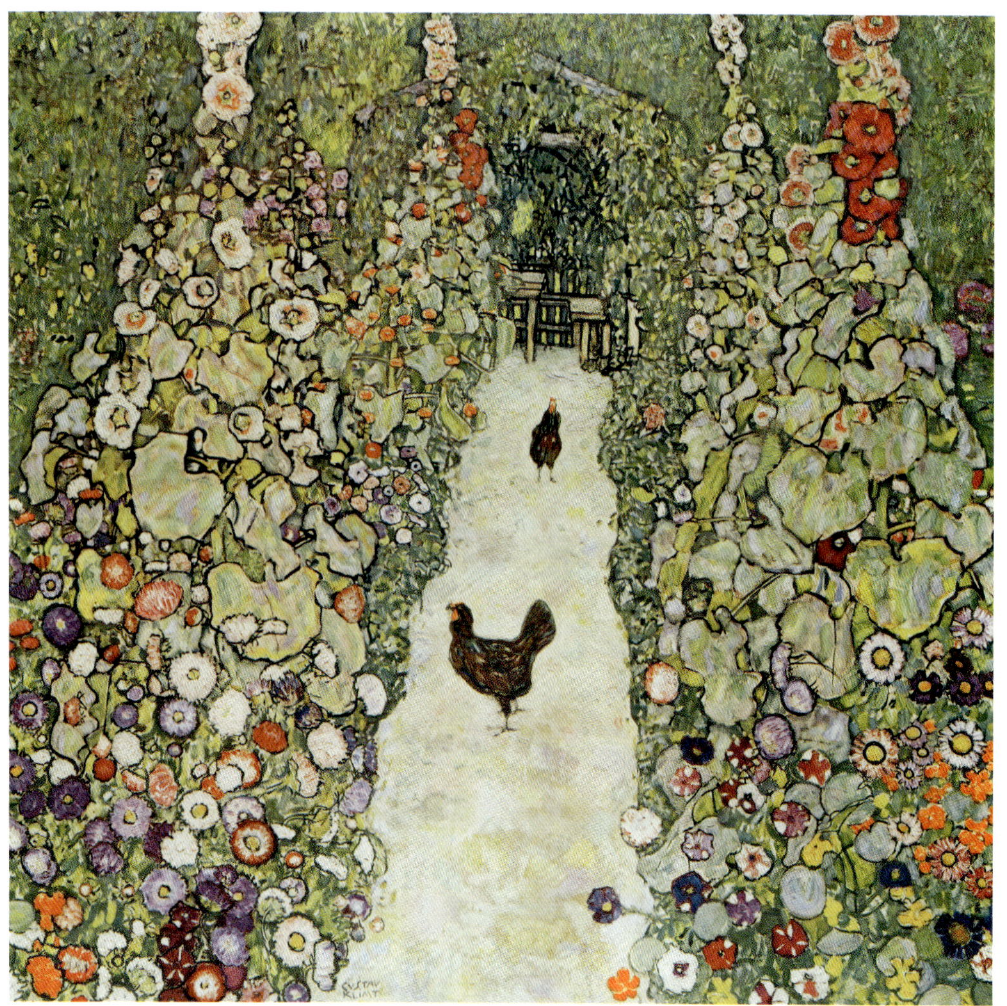

Garden Path with Chickens, 1916. It is interesting to compare this painting with chickens to the earlier After the Rain (see page 61). The soft fluffiness of the earlier work has been replaced by an altogether bleaker, more sombre vision.

This new style of work, with its profusion of floral motifs and Oriental influences, proved highly successful: Klimt was once more a fashionable artist whose work was much in demand. As some critics have identified, however, this development of his femmes fatales portraits, in which the subjects themselves resemble giant dolls trapped, in a box is faintly disturbing. In neutralizing the dangerous vamp or siren, has Klimt started to infantilize his women instead?

In the last part of his life, Klimt retreated to his studio and garden as well as spending holidays on Lake Attersee at the Flöge family home. His wealthy patrons remained loyal to him and he continued to receive commissions. There was generally a waiting list for his portraits. Meanwhile, the Vienna he knew and loved was beginning to crumble around him. Events came to a head when Archduke Franz Ferdinand – Emperor Franz Joseph's heir – and his wife Sophie were shot dead in Serbia in 1914. A month later, Austria-Hungary declared war on Serbia, a move that had the calamitous effect of starting World War I.

The turmoil is reflected in Klimt's later work. Though his portraits show a riot of colour and pattern, the landscapes that he was painting in the corresponding years (between 1915 and 1918) show a move towards a more sombre palette and an altogether darker and more intense mood. In *Garden Path with Chickens* (1916), for example, the fluffy white chickens of the earlier similarly composed *After the Rain* have given way to a sharply delineated pair of black hens. The surrounding landscape is darker and more brooding, the vegetation stands upright by the side of the path, like soldiers forming a guard of honour. These landscapes are probably more reflective of Klimt's inner, private life than the portrait and the figure paintings, and could indicate his depressed state of mind following the grim reality of the outbreak of war in 1914 and the death of his mother in 1915. Klimt had taken on responsibility for his mother as a young man and she was a major influence on him all his life.

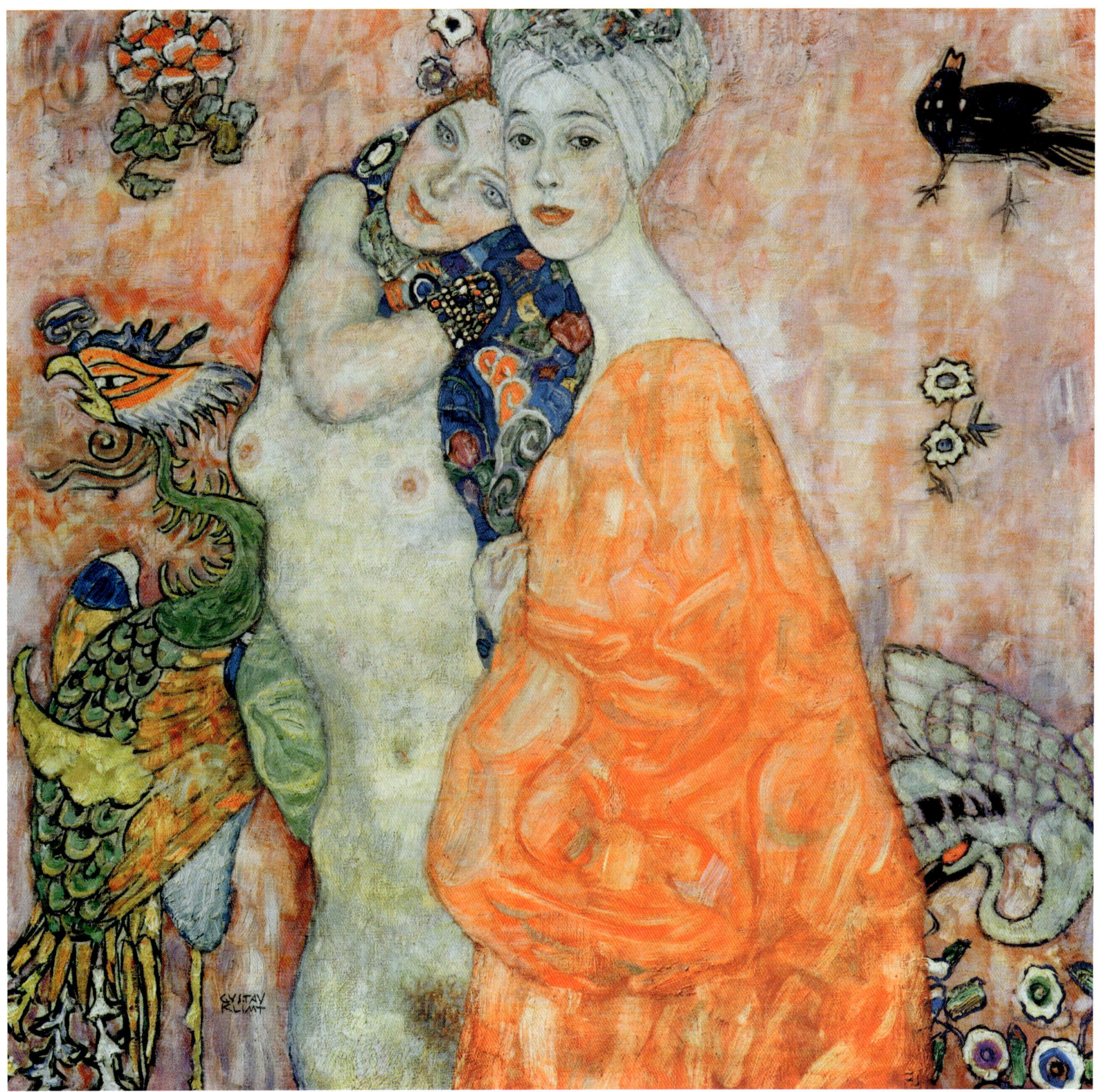

Women and eroticism were Klimt's all-encompassing themes and he continued to develop this aspect of his work right up until his death. *The Girlfriends* (1916–17) with its depiction of two female lovers – one clothed, one naked – is an example of Klimt's interest in depicting acts or moments of great sensuality. Infused with gorgeous red colour and filled with birds and flowers, it is perfectly possible to appreciate this painting on a purely aesthetic level. At the same time, while far from crude or vulgar, Klimt's ready enthusiasm for this type of work can seem a little prurient, even voyeuristic to contemporary eyes.

The Girlfriends, *1916–17. Many of the late works lie somewhere between portrait and allegory. These women appear to be a lesbian couple, but we are not given any further clues to their identity or the story behind the painting.*

KLIMT'S DRAWINGS

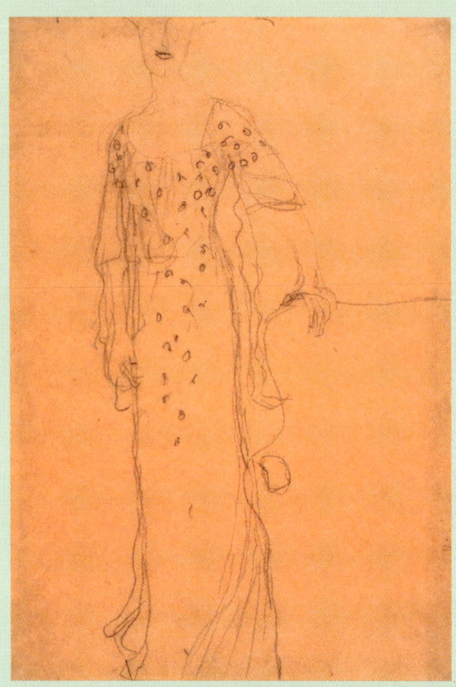

Undeniably Klimt was a great draughtsman and throughout his career he was obsessed with drawing, often building up piles of drawings on his studio floor. He drew not only to make preparatory sketches for paintings, but also because he saw them as an essential part of his daily routine to keep his art practice alive and his hand flowing freely. At first, he worked on cheap materials such as chalk on wrapping paper, but in the later part of his career he worked on Japanese paper in pencil, sometimes introducing colour.

Klimt was a planner and when it came to his portraits and paintings, in particular his commissioned work, he did not leave anything to chance. For his *Portrait of Adele Bloch-Bauer I* alone, he made around 100 drawings. The sketches he made for the *Beethoven Frieze* and the *Stoclet Frieze* reveal some of the compositional experiments he made in advance of executing the work. Some of his later drawings are also preparatory sketches that he made for portraits, including several rapid line drawings of heads, feet and clothes that he made of Baroness Elisabeth Bachofen-Echt, and Friederike Maria Beer in 1916. Klimt did not leave behind any drawings of landscapes – if he did work on sketches for his paintings, which seems reasonable and quite possible, these did not survive,

Study for Portrait of Adele Bloch-Bauer I, *1903. In this study of Adele Bloch-Bauer rapidly composed in charcoal, Klimt notes the intricate details of her dress.*

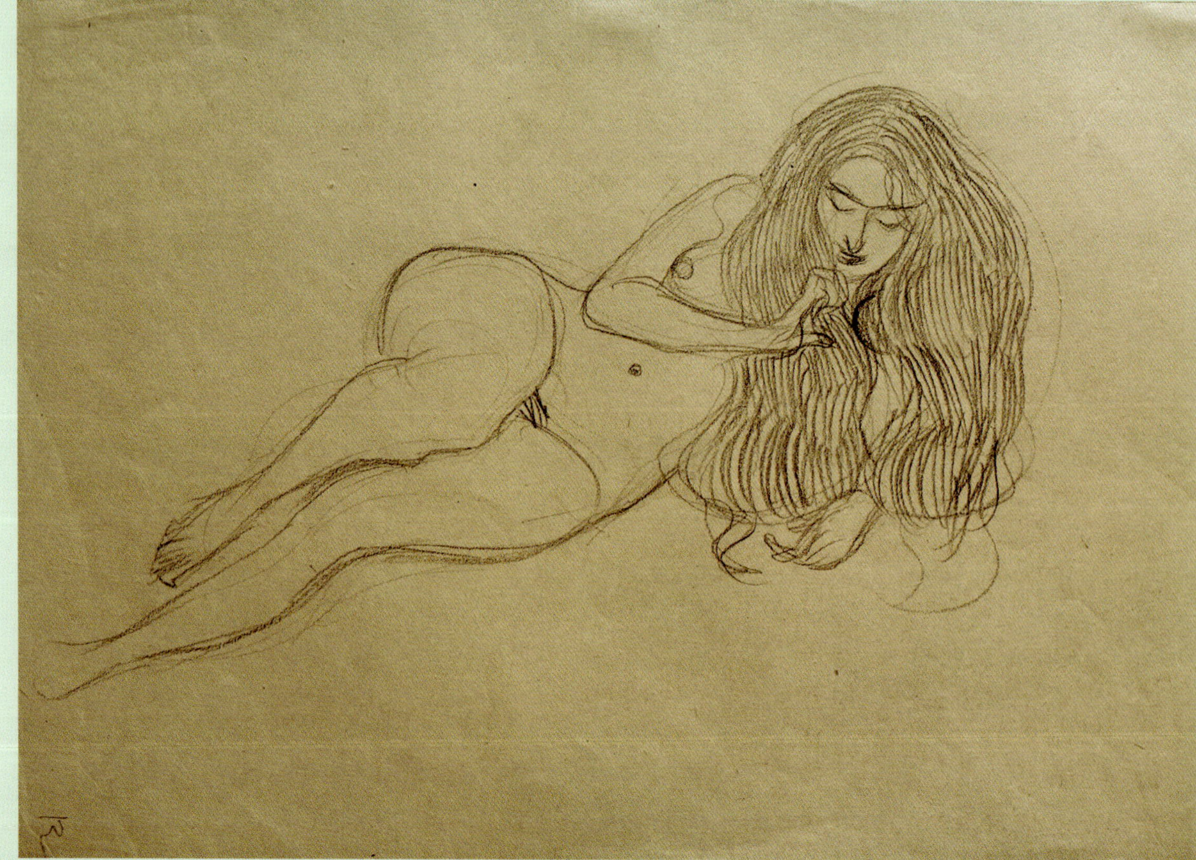

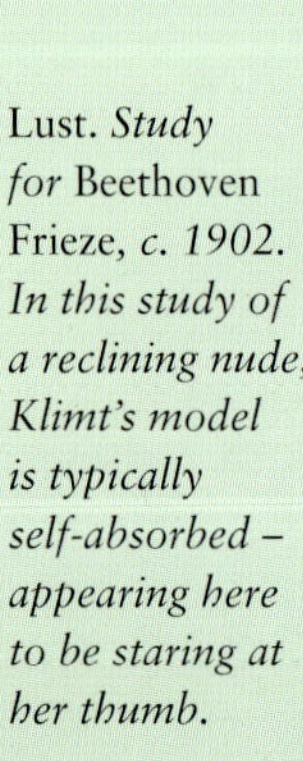

Lust. *Study for* Beethoven Frieze, *c. 1902. In this study of a reclining nude, Klimt's model is typically self-absorbed – appearing here to be staring at her thumb.*

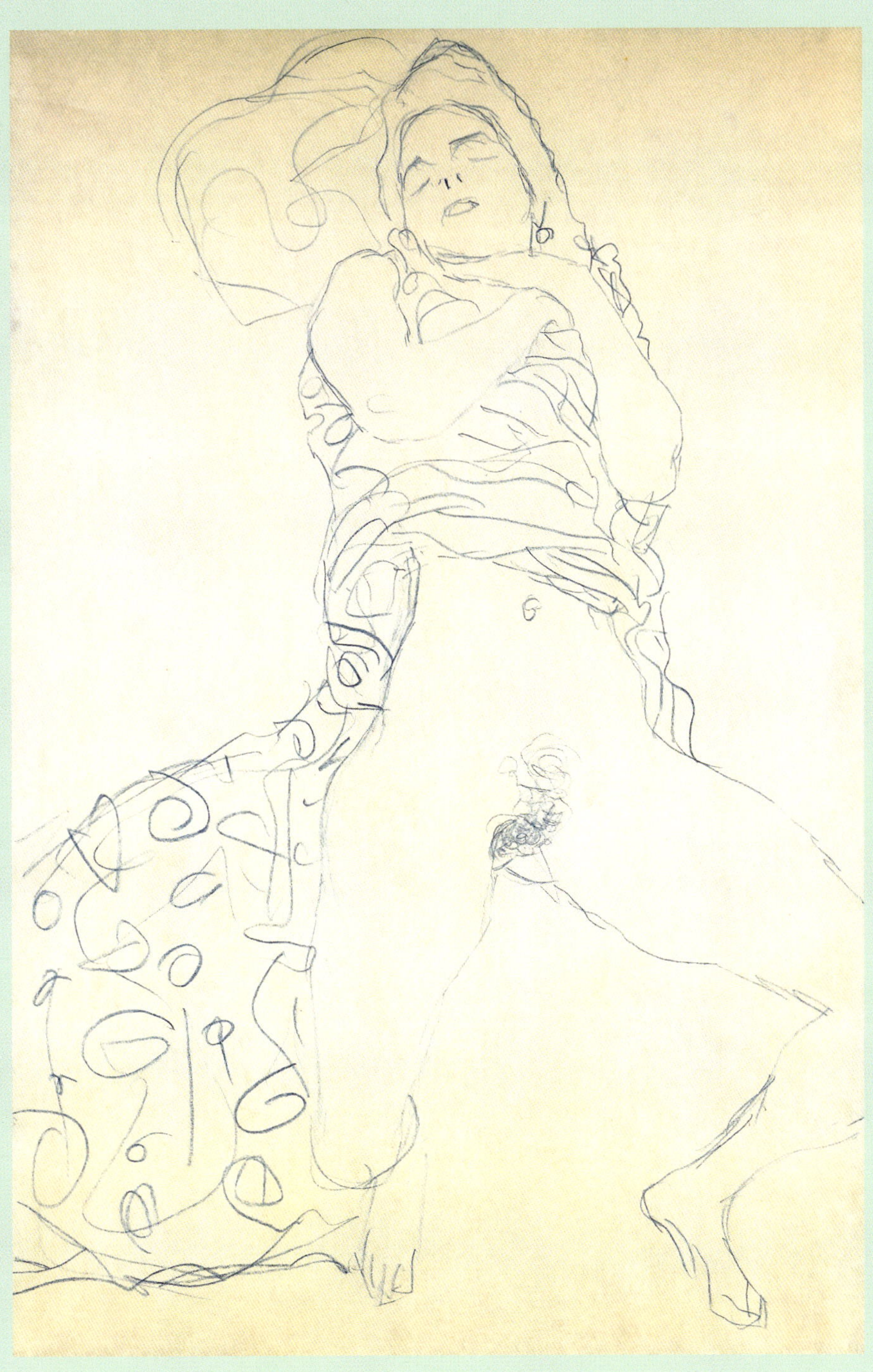

Nude; Halbakt, *1913. In many of Klimt's erotic drawings, his models appear half dressed. The artist is able to conjure up the quality of flesh and the texture of material with a spare, casual use of line.*

Most of his later drawings were of the female nude – mostly of a woman alone, frequently in erotic poses. Sometimes, the models are partially clothed, adding another seductive element to the intimacy of their pose. In most drawings they appear unabashed, curling up or stretching out sleepily as they lounge about. There is a real tension in these drawings between what is revealed and what remains hidden. At times the intimate relationship between the model and the artist is so apparent that the viewer feels compromised and is made to feel like a voyeur. The female subjects are anonymous and passive – we are made aware of the artist's gaze and his manipulation of the situation. Yet the models themselves have the same mixture of haughtiness, distance and sangfroid that we see in the paintings of femmes fatales, which helps to suggest that they are the ones who have real control here.

Aside from their explicitness, however, the drawings themselves are incredible studies of the female form, effortlessly done and beautifully positioned on the page. In some of the later drawings, the scribble of lines just dances across the page. These free, fluid studies of women have a direct quality of line and gesture that make them some of Klimt's best work.

Klimt rarely exhibited his erotic drawings, realizing that they were too much for even *fin-de-siècle* Vienna to handle. In 1918, the year of his death, the art dealer Gustav Nebehay produced an exhibition of some of these works. More than 3000 of Klimt's drawings have survived, although they are rarely put on public display. This is partly down to their frank subject matter and partly because many of them are in the hands of private collectors.

Portrait of Johanna Staude, 1917–18. *This portrait was unfinished at the time of Klimt's death from a stroke in February 1918. How much further would Klimt have been tempted to work on it?*

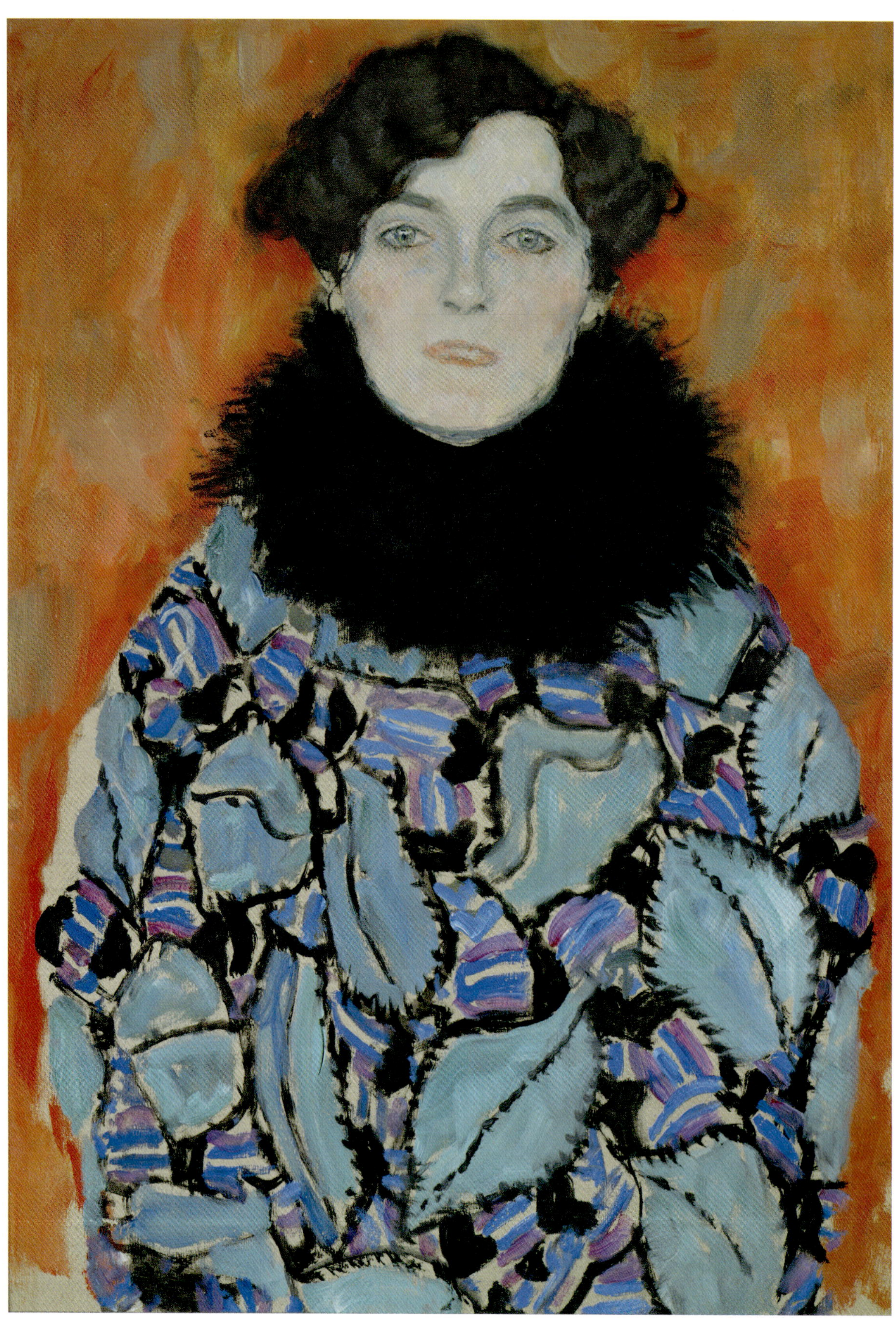

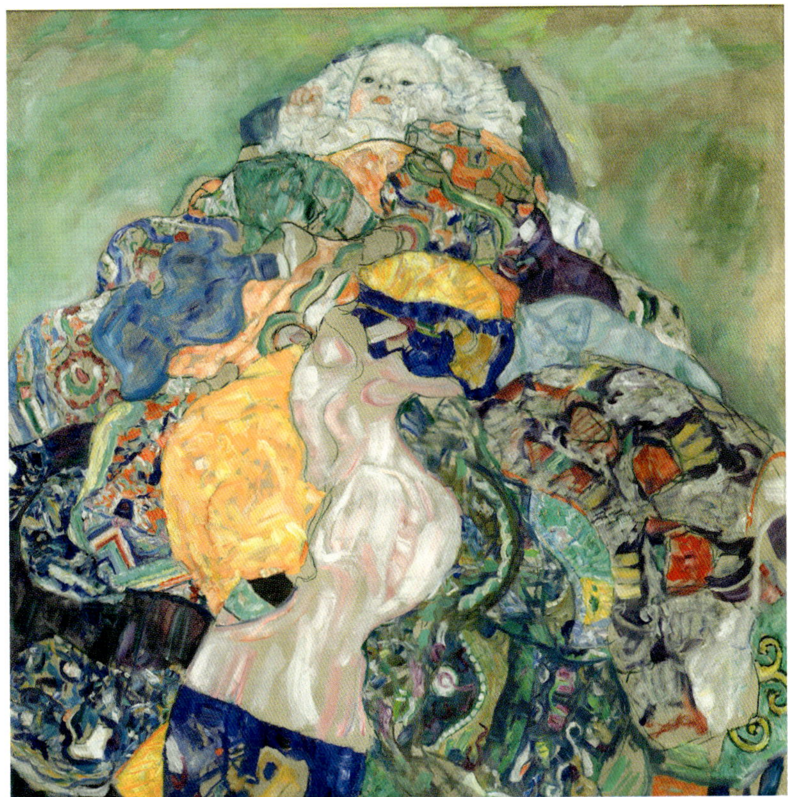

Baby (Cradle), *1917–18. An arresting image because of the dramatic foreshortening, it seems ironic that one of Klimt's last paintings was of a baby in a cradle.*

Pictures of Klimt's studio taken towards the end of his life show some of the unfinished pieces he was working on before he died. These revealed that he worked on several canvases at one time. *Portrait of Johanna Staude* (1917–18) shows a closer head and shoulders view of his model, who wears a patterned blue and purple coat with a black fur collar. Her stare is uncompromising and there is relatively little in the way of decoration. Would Klimt have been tempted to adorn the background had he lived? *The Bride*, another unfinished work from the same period, shows a heap of female bodies representing various erotic states such as desire and ecstasy. As such it forms a narrative companion to Klimt's work *The Virgin* – indeed, two of the faces in this work are very similar to a couple in this earlier work. There is also – unusually in Klimt's allegorical work – a man. It is a bird's-eye view seen from above, inspired by the Japanese art that Klimt was drawn to and collected.

Baby (Cradle) is another extraordinary unfinished image. This is not an allegorical painting but rather a powerful depiction of a baby, whose tiny head appears in foreshortening above its blanket – a technicolour mountain of undulating patterns. Loosely handled and full of movement and life, it seems ironic that this expressive work should be one of Klimt's last.

Just 10 months before the cessation of the war in 1918, Klimt had a stroke that paralyzed him on his right side. He was 55. He asked for Emilie, who came to be with him at his bedside, but he became sick with pneumonia and influenza and died on 6 February.

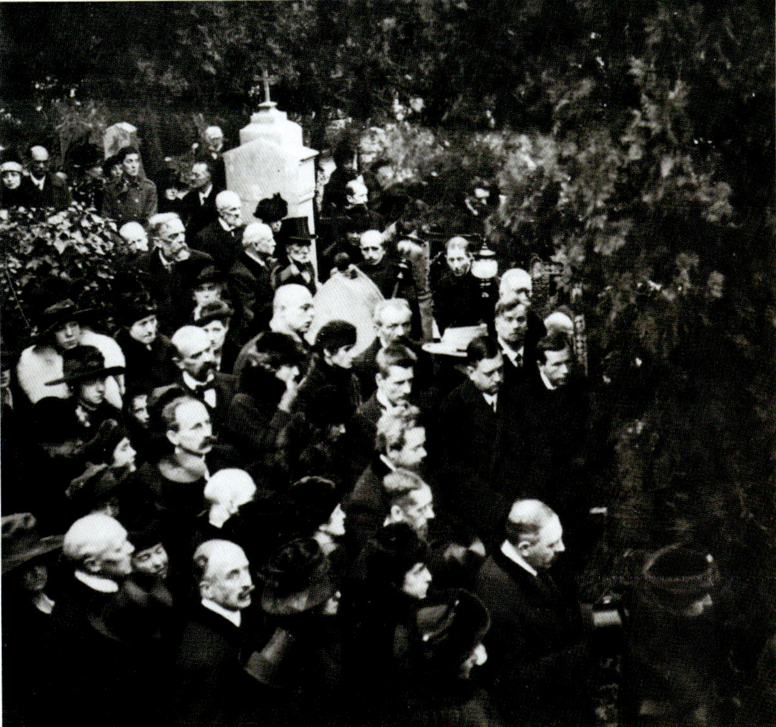

Gustav Klimt's funeral took place on 9 February 1918 at the Hietzing Cemetery in Vienna.

KLIMT'S LEGACY AND INFLUENCE

Klimt is one of the most reproduced artists in the world, so it might seem churlish to say that his influence is limited. But he is a representative of a particular time and place that is now dead and buried. There has been no other artist quite like Klimt. His work – and his golden allegorical paintings in particular – belongs to an era of unimaginable luxury and excess, which we can no longer conjure up, let alone fathom. Overtaken by the horror of World War I, Klimt's art appears outdated and isolated.

Even in his own time Klimt seems out of place. All the great artists who were his contemporaries appear more modern, doing much more to create or further the styles and movements of their particular day, whether that is Expressionists like Munch,

The Cardinal and the Nun *(Caress), Egon Schiele, 1912. In repainting some of Klimt's themes, in this case* The Kiss, *Schiele adopts a much darker even violent approach.*

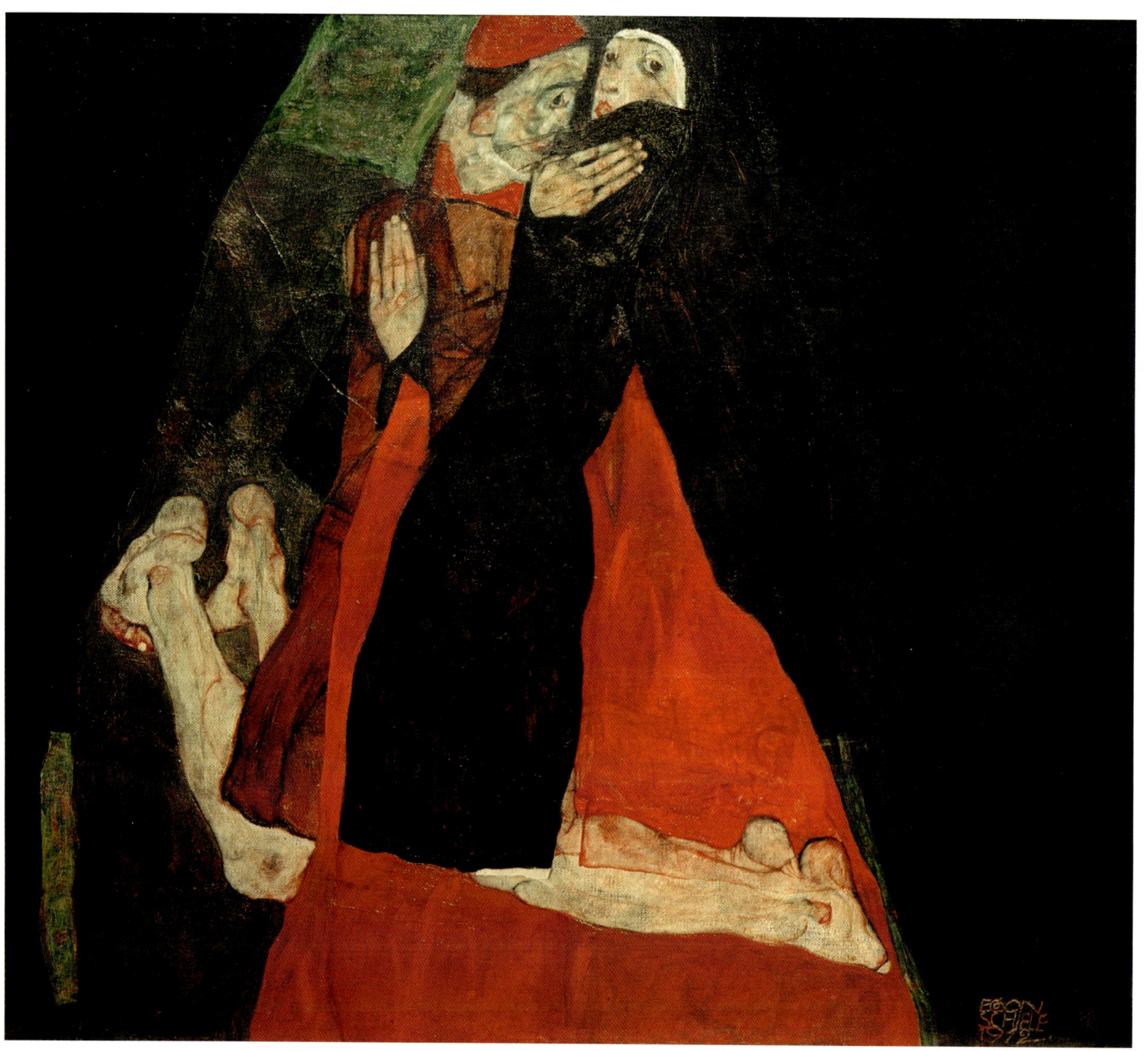

Impressionists like Cézanne, or abstract artists like Kandinsky. In 1907, just as Klimt was working on *Portrait of Adele Bloch-Bauer I*, his golden bejewelled Egyptian queen, Picasso was creating *Les Demoiselles d'Avignon*, his groundbreaking cubist-inspired work with its five working girls.

And yet there is so much to admire about Klimt. His skills as a draughtsman are truly remarkable and his direct, expressive studies of the female form go beyond their sensual or erotic subject matter to reveal an astounding, almost casual ease with line, perspective and mark making.

His landscapes are also unique. Even today it is hard to find an artist whose vision comes close to Klimt's. Despite the extraordinary level of detail – showing us every leaf and every twig – the world that he conjures up is far from naturalistic. It is an hermetically sealed world, and rather than offering us a window onto the world, Klimt puts up a wall through which we cannot enter. This wall is made up of myriad little parts which, like the view through a kaleidoscope, suddenly shift and split into further tiny pieces. The view he offers is singular, untouched by time, yet knowable in a way that recalls dreams which are at once lurid, enchanting and faintly disturbing.

Although no school followed him, he did – for a while, at least – have disciples in Oskar Kokoschka and Egon Schiele. The latter is especially interesting in that it is a case where the pupil, Schiele, overtakes his master in terms of reach and influence.

Around 1911, Schiele began to repaint some of Klimt's themes. With its lovers bound tightly together, *Cardinal and Nun (The Caress)* is clearly based on Klimt's *The Kiss*. The initial intention might have been to pay homage to his master, but Schiele's portrayal of an illicit relationship between two religious figures appears to be both a parody and criticism of his master's work. Furthermore, Schiele appears to be using this subject matter to allude to events and circumstances in his own life.

In Schiele's much darker and intense version, the couple are pitted against each other, in an embrace that looks far from tender and is clearly meant to be seen as a violation of moral codes. Themes of violence and sexual power underscore the image. The triangular composition of the painting seems to suggest a blasphemous reference to the Trinity. The couple's facial expressions display a mix of confusion, fear and secrecy and their naked legs are bent and tense. In a predominantly black painting, the cardinal's bright red cape stands out, a literal red flag.

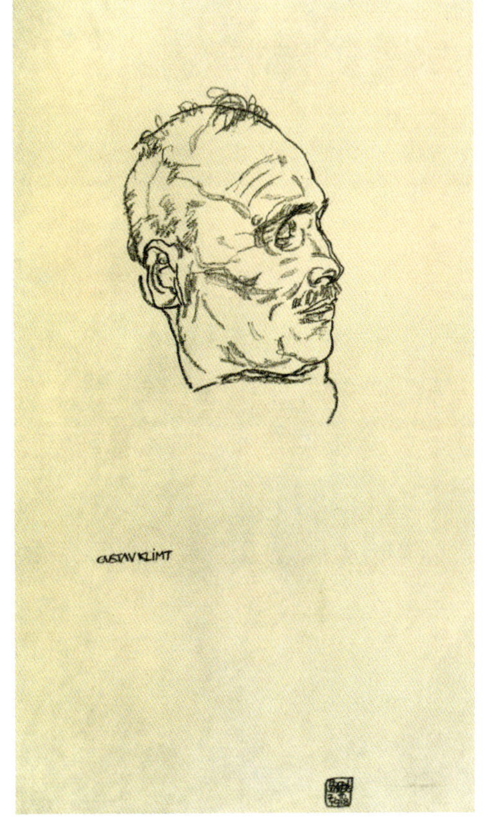

Head of the Dead Gustav Klimt, *Egon Schiele, 1918. Schiele drew this portrait of Klimt in the mortuary of Vienna's General Hospital.*

It appears that Schiele not only wishes to provoke but also hint at issues beyond the picture frame. This painting directly or indirectly relates to events in his own life: during this same year, he was arrested for aiding a 13-year-old girl escape from her father to return to her grandmother.

Schiele made a drawing of Klimt in the morgue of Vienna's General Hospital just after he died. Entitled *The Dead Klimt*, the drawing shows a tiny shrunken head floating in the top half of the paper, with hollowed eyes and no familiar beard. Before the end of the year Schiele would be dead too – also a victim of influenza that swept through Vienna.

Klimt had mentored Schiele in the early part of his career, but by 1912 Schiele was breaking away and finding his own artistic language. Anguish and isolation are the characteristic features of Schiele's style – bodies are often emaciated and vulnerable, a physical fragility and expressiveness that seems far away from the myths and allegories of Klimt's golden world.

TIMELINE

1860s

'62 Gustav Klimt born in Baumgarten.

1870s

'76 Enters the Kunstgewerbeschule (Vienna School of Arts and Crafts), where he studies for seven years.

'77 Gustav's brother, Ernst and their friend Franz Matsch (1861–1942) also enrol in the school.

'79 Work on decorations for *Festzug*, the pageant celebrating Emperor Franz Joseph's silver wedding. Forms Künstler–Compagnie (Painters' Company).

1880s

'80 The Company create four decorative ceiling paintings for the Palais Sturany in Vienna.

'84 Gustav's hero Hans Makart dies an early death aged 44.

'85 The Painters' Company work on a scheme for the Villa Hermes (Hermesvilla), Emperor Franz Joseph's country residence near Vienna.

'86 The Painters' Company work on the interior of the Burgtheater, the replacement for the old theatre in Vienna.

'88 Klimt receives the Emperor's Golden Cross of Honour for his contributions to the Burgtheater murals.

1890s

'90 The Painter's Company work on the newly built Kunsthistorisches (Museum of Art History) in Vienna. A separate painting, *Auditorium in the Old Burgtheater*, 1888, receives the Imperial Award.

'91 Klimt becomes a member of the co-operative Austrian Artists' Society, the traditional Viennese forum for artists.

'92 Klimt's father and brother Ernst die.

'94 Klimt and Matsch commissioned to produce four decorative panels in the great hall of the University of Vienna.

'95 Klimt sends work to the publisher Martin Gerlach for *Allegories and Emblems*.

'97 Klimt founds the Vienna Seccession and is elected its President. Spends summer with companion Emilie Flöge in the region of Kammer on the Attersee.

'98 First Secession exhibition. Founding of journal *Ver Sacrum*. Paints *Portrait of Sonja Knips* and *Pallas Athene*.

'99 Completes decoration of Dumba Palace Music Room. Paints *Music II* and *Schubert at the Piano*.

1900s

'00 Klimt's rejected Secession painting *Philosophy* awarded gold medal in Paris.

'01 Klimt's painting *Medicine* causes further outrage at Seccession exhibition. Paints *Judith* and the *Head of Holofernes*.

'02 Meets Auguste Rodin, who admires Klimt's *Beethoven Frieze* in Secession building.

'03 Visits Ravenna in Italy and sees the Byzantine mosaics. Beginning of the Golden Phase. Paints *Jurisprudence*.

'04 Draws plans for wall mosaics for the Palais Stoclet in Brussels. Paints *Water Serpents*.

'05 Klimt and friends leave the Secession. Paints *The Three Ages of Woman*.

'07 Start of friendship with Egon Schiele. Paints *Danaë* and Adele Bloch-Bauer.

'08 Paints *The Kiss*. Sixteen paintings shown at the Kunstschau, Vienna.

'09 Beginning of work on *Stoclet Frieze*. Paints *Judith II*.

1910s

'10 Success at 9th Venice Biennale.

'11 *Death and Life* painting wins first prize in Rome.

'15 Reworks *Death and Life*, painting over the gold background.

'15 Death of his mother.

'16 Paints *The Girlfriends*. Death of Emperor Franz Joseph.

'17 Starts work on *The Bride*. Begins *Baby* (*Cradle*) (unfinished).

'18 Klimt has a stroke and dies. Numerous unfinished works. End of the Habsburg Empire.

FURTHER INFORMATION

Gill, D. M., *Klimt (Discovering Art: The Life, Times and Work of the World's Greatest Artists series)*, Brockhampton Press, London, 1996

Hodge, Susie, *Gustav Klimt: Masterpieces of Art*, Flame Tree Publishing, London, 2014

Kerrigan, Michael, *Gustav Klimt: Art Nouveau and the Vienna Secessionists*, Flame Tree Publishing, London, 2015

Natter, Tobias G. & Grunenberg, Christoph (ed.), *Gustav Klimt – Painting, Design and Modern Life*, Tate Publishing, London, 2008

Néret, Gilles, *Klimt, 1862–1918*, Taschen, Cologne & London, 2007

di Stefano, Eva, *Gustav Klimt: Art Nouveau Visionary*, Sterling Publishing, New York, 2008

Whitford, Frank, *Klimt*, Thames & Hudson, London, 1990

WEBSITES

Belvedere Museum, Vienna – belvedere.at
Burgtheater – burgtheater.at
klimt.com
Kunsthistoriches Museum – khm.at
Leopold Museum, Vienna – leopoldmuseum.org
Neue Galerie – neuegalerie.org
Secession Building – secession.at
theartstory.org

LIST OF ILLUSTRATIONS

Page 6
Forest Slope in Unterach on the Attersee, 1916, oil on canvas, 110 × 110 cm (43½ × 43½ in), Private Collection. Erich Lessing/ AKG Images.

Page 8
The *Kunstgewerbeschule* (the Vienna School of Arts and Crafts), Wikimedia Commons

Page 9
Photograph of Rudolf Eitelberger von Edelberg. Wikimedia Commons

Page 10
The Education of the Children of Clovis, Lawrence Alma-Tadema, 1861, oil on canvas, 129.5 × 177.8 cm (51 × 70 in), Private Collection. Wikimedia Commons.

Page 11 (top)
Das Blinde Kuh Spiel, Ferdinand Laufberger, 1865, oil on wood, 27 × 37 cm (10½ × 14½ in), Private Collection. Wikimedia Commons.

Page 11 (bottom)
Imagno/Getty Images

Page 12–13
Entwurf zum Festzug, Hans Makart, 1879, oil on canvas, 65 × 279 cm (25½ × 109¾ in), Wien Museum, Vienna, Austria. Wikimedia Commons.

Page 13 (top)
Schottenring 21, Detail in the Beletage, Gustav Klimt and Franz von Matsch, 1888, Palais Sturany, Vienna, Austria.

Page 13 (bottom)
A Midsummer Night's Dream (Puck mistakes Lysander for Demetrius), Gustav Klimt, Franz von Matsch and Ernst Klimt, 1884–85, oil on stucco, Wien Museum, Vienna, Austria.

Page 15
Auditorium in the Old Burgtheater in Vienna, 1888, gouache, 82 × 92 cm (32¼ × 36¼ in), Wien Museum, Vienna, Austria. Erich Lessing/ AKG Images.

Page 16
Joseph Pembaur, 1890, oil on canvas, 69 × 55 cm (27 × 21½ in), Ferdinandeum, Innsbruck, Austria. Erich Lessing/AKG Images.

Page 17
Egyptian Art I and II, Greek Antiquity I and II, 1890–91, oil on stucco, spandrel pictures 230 × 230 cm (90½ × 90½ in) each, pictures between columns 230 × 80 cm (90½ × 31½ in) each, Kunsthistorisches Museum, Vienna, Austria. Erich Lessing/ AKG Images.

Page 18
Love, 1895, oil on canvas, 60 × 44 cm (23½ × 17¼ in), Vienna Museum, Vienna, Austria. Heritage Images/Fine art Images/ AKG Images.

Page 19
Music I, 1895, oil on canvas, 37 × 44.5 cm (14½ × 17½ in), Neue Pinakothek, Munich, Germany. AKG Images.

Page 20
Photograph of artists of the Viennese Secession. Imagno/Getty Images.

Page 22
Photographs of Josef Hoffmann and Koloman Moser. Wikimedia Commons.

Page 23
Poster for the First Art Exhibition of the Secession Movement, 1898, lithograph, 63.5 × 46.9 cm (25 × 18½ in), Private Collection. Heritage Images/Fine Art Images/ AKG Images.

Page 24
Pallas Athene, 1898, oil on canvas, 75 x 75 cm (29½ x 29½ in), Wien Museum, Vienna, Austria. AKG Images.

Page 25
Schubert at the Piano, 1899, oil on canvas, 150 × 200 cm (59 × 78¾ in), destroyed in World War II. AKG Images.

Page 26
Sonja Knips, 1898, oil on canvas, 145 × 146 cm (57 × 57½ in), Galerie im Belvedere, Vienna, Austria. AKG Images.

Page 27
Medicine, 1907, oil on canvas, 430 × 300 cm (169¼ × 118 in), University of Vienna ballroom, destroyed 1945. Erich Lessing/ AKG Images.

Pages 28–9
The Beethoven Frieze, (detail: The Hostile Forces), 1902, 213.4 × 3413.8 cm (84 × 1344 in), Secession Building, Vienna, Austria.

Page 30–1
The Beethoven Frieze (detail: Yearning for Happiness) 1902, 213.4 x 3413.8 cm (84 x 1344 in), Secession Building, Vienna, Austria. k. A./Imagno/AKG Images.

Page 32
Photograph of Emilie Flöge. Moriz Nähr/Imagno/AKG Images.

Page 33
Photograph of Gustav Klimt and Emilie Flöge. Moriz Nähr/Imagno/ AKG Images.

Page 34
A Theatrical Buffoon on a Makeshift Stage in Rothenburg, Ernst Klimt and Gustav Klimt, 1893, fresco, 450 × 100 cm (177 × 39½ in). Fine Art Photographic Library/Corbis/Getty Images.

Page 35
Fraulein Emilie Flöge, 1902, oil on canvas, 181 × 84 cm (71¼ × 33¾ in), Wien Museum, Vienna, Austria. AKG Images.

Page 36
Photograph of Wiener Werkstätte's shop. Josef Hoffmann/Imagno/AKG Images.

Page 37
Photograph of Palais Stoclet. Wikimedia Commons.

Page 38
Photograph of dining room of Palais Stoclet. Heritage Images/Print Collector/AKG Images.

Page 39
The Tree of Life, Stoclet Frieze, 1905–09, oil on canvas, 195 × 102 cm (76¾ × 40 in), Österreichischer Galerie Belvedere, Vienna, Austria. De Agostini Picture Library/AKG Images.

Page 40
Jurisprudence, 1903, ceiling painting, 430 × 300 cm (169¼ × 118 in), destroyed. Wikimedia Commons.

Page 41
Philosophy, 1899–1907, ceiling painting, 430 × 300 cm (169¼ × 118 in), destroyed. Wikimedia Commons.

Page 42
Serena Lederer, 1899, oil on canvas, 188 × 83 cm (75 × 33½ in), Metropolitan Museum of Art, New York, USA. Erich Lessing/ AKG Images.

Page 44 (top)
Nuda Veritas, 1898, black chalk, pencil, pen and ink, 41 × 10 cm (16 × 4 in), Wien Museum, Vienna, Austria. Erich Lessing/AKG Images.

Page 44 (bottom)
Moving Water, 1898, oil on canvas, 53.3 × 66.3 cm (21 × 26 in), Private Collection. Heritage Images/Fine Art Images/AKG Images.

Page 45 (top)
Mermaids, 1899, oil on canvas, 82 × 52 cm (32¼ × 20½ in), Bank Austria Kunstforum, Vienna, Austria. AKG Images.

Page 46
Water Serpents I, 1904–07, oil, gold leaf, mixed media on parchment, 50 × 20 cm (19¾ × 8 in), Belvedere Museum, Vienna, Austria. Erich Lessing/AKG Images.

Page 47
Water Serpents II, 1904–07, oil on canvas, 80 × 145 cm (31½ × 57 in), Private Collection. Erich Lessing, AKG Images.

Page 48 (left)
Judith I, 1901, oil on canvas, 84 × 42 cm (33 × 16½ in), Österreichischer Galerie im Belvedere, Vienna, Austria. De Agostini Picture Library/AKG Images.

Page 48 (right)
Judith II (Salome), 1909, oil on canvas, 178 × 46 cm (70 × 18 in), Cà Pesaro Galleria Internazionale d'Arte Moderna, Musei Civici Veneziani, Venice, Italy. Heritage Images/Fine Art Images/AKG Images.

Page 49 (top left)
Mosaics of Emperor Justinianus and Empress Theodora. Wikimedia Commons.

Page 49 (right)
Hope I, 1903, oil on canvas, 181 × 67 cm (71¼ × 26¼ in), National Gallery of Canada, Ottawa, Canada. Wikimedia Commons.

Page 50 (top)
Hope II, 1907–08, oil, gold and platinum on canvas, 110.5 × 110.5 cm (43½ × 43½ in), Museum of Modern Art, New York, USA. Album/ AKG Images.

Page 51
The Three Ages of Woman, 1905, 180 × 180 cm (71 × 71 in), Galleria Nazionale d'Arte Moderna, Rome, Italy. Canali – Index/Heritage Images/ AKG Images.

Page 52
Margarethe Stonborough-Wittgenstein, 1905, oil on canvas, 179.8 × 90.5 cm (70¾ × 35½ in), Neue Pinakothek, Munich, Germany. AKG Images.

Page 53
Fritza Riedler, 1906, oil on canvas, 153 × 133 cm (60¼ × 52½ in), Österreichischer Galerie im Belvedere, Vienna, Austria. Erich Lessing/AKG Images.

Page 55
The Kiss, 1907–08, oil on canvas, 180 × 180 cm (71 × 71 in), Österreichischer Galerie im Belvedere, Vienna, Austria. AKG Images.

Page 57
Danaë, 1907, oil on canvas, 77 × 83 cm (30 × 33 in), Galerie Würthle, Vienna, Austria. Heritage Images/Fine Art Images/AKG Images.

Page 58
Church in Unterach on the Attersee, 1916, oil on canvas, 110 × 110 cm (43¼ × 43¼ in), Private Collection. Erich Lessing, AKG Images.

Page 59
Self-portrait, Egon Schiele, 1906, charcoal, 45.5 × 34.6 cm (18 × 13½ in), Albertina, Vienna, Austria. Wikimedia Commons.

Page 60
Morning by the Pond, 1899, oil on canvas, 75.1 × 75.1 cm (29½ × 29½ in), Leopold Museum, Vienna, Austria. AKG Images.

Page 61
After the Rain, 1899, oil on canvas, 80 × 40 cm (31½ × 15¾ in) Österreichischer Galerie im Belvedere, Vienna, Austria. Erich Lessing/AKG Images.

Page 62
Beechwood Forest, 1903, oil on canvas, 100 × 100 cm (39½ × 39½ in) Gemäldegalerie Neue Meister, Dresden, Germany. De Agostini Picture Library/AKG Images.

Page 63
Flower Garden, 1905–07, oil on canvas, 110 × 110 cm (43¼ × 43¼ in), Private Collection. Christie's Images/ Bridgeman Images.

Page 64
Farm Garden with Sunflowers, 1907, oil on canvas, 110 × 110 cm (43¼ × 43¼ in) Österreichischer Galerie im Belvedere, Vienna, Austria. AKG Images.

Page 66
Rose Bushes Under the Trees, 1905, oil on canvas, 110 × 110 cm (43¼ × 43¼ in), Musée d'Orsay, Paris, France. Laurent Lecat/AKG Images.

Page 67
Poppy Field, 1907, oil on canvas, 110 × 110 cm (43¼ × 43¼ in), Österreichischer Galerie im Belvedere, Vienna, Austria. Heritage Images/ Fine Art Images/AKG Images.

Page 68
Sunflower, 1907, oil on canvas, 110 × 110 cm (43¼ × 43¼ in), Private Collection. AKG Images.

Page 69
Schloss Kammer on Lake Attersee I, 1908, oil on canvas, 110 × 110 cm (43¼ × 43¼ in), National Gallery, Prague, Czech Republic. Erich Lessing/AKG Images.

Page 70
The Park, 1910, oil on canvas, 110.4 × 110.4 cm (43½ × 43½ in), Museum of Modern Art, New York, USA. DIGITAL IMAGE © 2019, The Museum of Modern Art/Scala, Florence.

Page 71
Farm House in Upper Austria, 1911–12, oil on canvas, 110 × 110 cm (43¼ × 43¼ in), Österreichischer Galerie im Belvedere, Vienna, Austria. AKG Images.

Page 72
Avenue in the Park of Schloss Kammer, 1912, oil on canvas, 110 × 110 cm (43¼ × 43¼ in), Österreichischer Galerie im Belvedere, Vienna, Austria. Erich Lessing/ AKG Images.

Page 73
Apple Tree I, 1912, oil on canvas, 110 × 110 cm (43¼ × 43¼ in), Private Collection. Erich Lessing/AKG Images.

Page 74
Apple Tree II, 1916, oil on canvas, 80 × 80 cm (31½ × 31½ in), Private Collection. Bridgeman Images.

Page 75
Life is a Struggle (The Golden Knight), 1903, oil on canvas, 100 × 100 cm (39½ × 39½ in), Nagoya City Art Museum, Nagoya, Japan. AKG Images.

Page 76
Death and Life, 1915, oil on canvas, 178 × 198 cm (70 × 78 in), Leopold Museum, Vienna, Austria. Erich Lessing/AKG Images.

Page 78
Woman in Black Feather Hat, 1910, oil on canvas, 79 × 63 cm (31 × 24¾ in), Private Collection. Wikimedia Commons.

Page 79
Lady with Hat and Feather Boa, 1909, oil on canvas, 69 × 55 cm (27 × 21½ in), Private Collection. Heritage Images/Fine Art Images/AKG Images.

Page 80
Mäda Primavesi, 1912–13, 149.9 × 110.5 cm (59 × 43½ in), Metropolitan Museum of Art, New York, USA. AKG Images.

Page 81
Portrait of Adele Bloch-Bauer II, 1912, oil on canvas, 190 × 120 cm (74¾ × 47¼ in), Österreichischer Galerie im Belvedere, Vienna, Austria. Erich Lessing/AKG Images.

Page 82 (top left)
Portrait of Elisabeth Baroness Bachofen-Echt, 1914, oil on canvas, 180 × 126 cm (71 × 49½ in), Private Collection. Heritage Images/Fine Art Images/AKG Images.

Page 82 (top right)
Portrait of Friederike Maria Beer, 1916, oil on canvas, 168 × 130 cm (66 × 51¼ in), Mizne-Blumenthal Collection, Art Museum, Tel Aviv, Israel. Erich Lessing/AKG Images.

Page 83
The Virgin, 1912–13, oil on canvas, 190 × 200 cm (74¾ × 78¾ in), National Gallery, Prague, Czech Republic. AKG Images.

Page 84
Garden Path with Chickens, 1916, oil on canvas, 110 × 110 cm, destroyed. Erich Lessing/AKG Images.

Page 85
The Girlfriends, 1916–17, oil on canvas, 99 × 99 cm (39 × 39 in), destroyed. Erich Lessing/AKG Images.

Page 86 (top)
Study for Portrait of Adele Bloch-Bauer I, 1903, charcoal on paper, 45.6 × 31.4 cm (18 × 12½ in). Jewish Museum/AKG Images.

Page 86 (bottom)
Lust. Study for *Beethoven Frieze*, c. 1902, charcoal, 44 × 31.2 cm (17¼ × 12¼ in), Le Claire Kunst, Hamburg, Germany. AKG Images.

Page 87
Nude; Halbakt, 1913, blue crayon on cream paper, 55.9 × 37.2 cm (22 × 14½ in), Private Collection. Christie's Images/Bridgeman Images.

Page 88
Portrait of Johanna Staude, 1917–18, oil on canvas, 70 × 55 cm (27½ × 21½ in), Österreichischer Galerie im Belvedere, Vienna, Austria. Erich Lessing/AKG Images.

Page 89 (top),
Baby (Cradle), 1917–18, oil on canvas, 110.9 × 110.4 cm (43¾ × 43½ in), National Gallery of Art, Washington DC, USA. AKG Images.

Page 89 (bottom)
Photograph of Gustav Klimt's funeral. Ullstein bild/AKG Images.

Page 90
The Cardinal and the Nun (Caress), Egon Schiele, 1912, oil on canvas, 70 × 80.5 cm (27½ × 31¾ in), Leopold Museum, Vienna, Austria. AKG Images.

Page 91
Head of the Dead Gustav Klimt, Egon Schiele, 1918, black chalk, 47.1 × 30 cm (18½ × 11¾ in), Leopold Museum, Vienna. Imagno/AKG Images.

INDEX

Alma-Tadema, Laurens 10
Austrian Artists' Society 19, 21

Bachofen-Echt, Elisabeth 82, 86
Beer, Friederike Maria 82, 86
Beethoven Frieze 28–9, 30, 30–1, 86
Belle Époque 14–15
Bloch-Bauer, Adele 49, 52, 54, 56, 69, 74, 77, 81–2, 86, 91
Bloch-Bauer, Ferdinand 52, 56, 74
Böcklin, Arnold 30
Burgtheater 17

Cabaret Fledermaus 37
Cézanne, Paul 72, 91
Crane, Walter 30

Dumba, Nikolaus 25
Dürer, Albrecht 13

Edelberg, Rudolf Eitelberger von 9
Elisabeth, Princess 12, 13

Felsovanyi, Gertha 43
Flöge, Emilie 32–5, 37, 56, 78, 89
Flöge, Helene 32, 33, 37
Flöge, Hermann 33
Flöge, Pauline 33, 37
Franz Ferdinand, Archduke 84
Franz Joseph, Emperor 12, 13, 14, 24
Freud, Sigmund 14

Gerlach, Martin 16, 19

Hoffman, Josef 22, 23, 25, 28, 31, 33, 36, 38, 40, 41, 59

Kadinsky, Wassily 91
Kiss, The 19, 35, 39, 54–5, 56, 67
Klimt, Anna 9, 19
Klimt, Ernst 9, 11, 12, 19, 34, 35
Klimt, Georg 9, 12, 24
Klimt, Gustave
  death of 89
  description of work 7
  drawings 86–7
  early life and career 9–13, 16–19
  landscapes 58–75
  later works 76–85, 88–9
  legacy and influence 90–1
  Secession period 20–41
  paintings of women 42–57, 85, 86–7
Klinger, Max 28
Kokoschka, Oskar 40, 59, 77, 91
Krips, Sonja 25. 26, 27
Kunstgewerbeschule 8, 9–13
Kunsthistorisches 17

Laufberger, Ferdinand Julius 10, 12
Lederer, Serena 42, 43

Mackintosh, Charles Rennie 30, 36
Mahler, Gustav 14, 28, 30
Makart, Hans 10, 12, 13, 17, 27
Matsch, Franz 11, 12, 19
Moll, Carl 23
Morris, William 36
Moser, Klaus 33
Moser, Koloman 20, 22, 36, 37, 41, 59
Mucha, Alphonse 30
Munch, Edvard 30, 90

Nebehay, Gustav 87

Olbrich, Joseph Maria 23

Painters' Company 11, 16, 17, 19
Palais Stoclet 37, 38–9, 40, 86
Picasso, Pablo 91
Primavesi, Eugenia 80, 81
Primavesi, Mäda 80–1
Primavesi, Otto 80

Riedler, Fritza 51, 52, 53, 56
Rilke, Rainer Maria 23
Ringstrasse mansion 25
Rodin, Auguste 30
Roller, Alfred 59
Ruskin, John 36

Schiele, Egon 40, 59, 77, 90, 91
Schiller, Friedrich 44
Schloss Kammer 69
Secession period 20–41, 59, 60
Seurat, Georges 70
Signac, Paul 70
Staude, Johanna 88, 89
Stoclet, Adolphe 37, 38, 40
Stonborough, Thomas 51
Swinburne, Charles 23

Tivoli Café 7
Toulouse–Lautrec, Henri de 30, 77

Union of Austrian Artists (Secession) 21
University of Vienna 19, 27, 30, 40–1, 54

Van Gogh, Vincent 72
Ver Sacrum 22–3, 44

Waerndorfer, Fritz 36, 37, 50
Wagner, Otto 14
Wiener Werkstätte 31, 33, 36–7, 38, 40–1, 77
Whistler, J M 27
Wittgenstein, Karl 25, 51, 74
Wittgenstein, Margaret Stonborough 51, 52

Zimmerman, Marie 50
Zuckerkandl, Viktor 74

MONACO UNESCO

75 YEARS

This book is published under the auspices of the Permanent Delegation of the Principality of Monaco to UNESCO, as represented by Her Excellency Anne-Marie Boisbouvier, Ambassador Extraordinary and Plenipotentiary, Permanent Delegate

Monaco editorial committee:
Anne-Marie Boisbouvier, Jacques Boisson, Yvette Lambin-Berti, Stéphane Lamotte, Jean Pastorelli, Jean-Philippe Vinci

PREFACES
H.S.H. PRINCE ALBERT II OF MONACO
H.R.H. PRINCESS OF HANOVER

FOREWORD
AUDREY AZOULAY
DIRECTOR-GENERAL OF UNESCO

MONACO UNESCO

75 YEARS

TEXTS STÉPHANE LAMOTTE AND JEAN-PHILIPPE VINCI

ABRAMS I NEW YORK

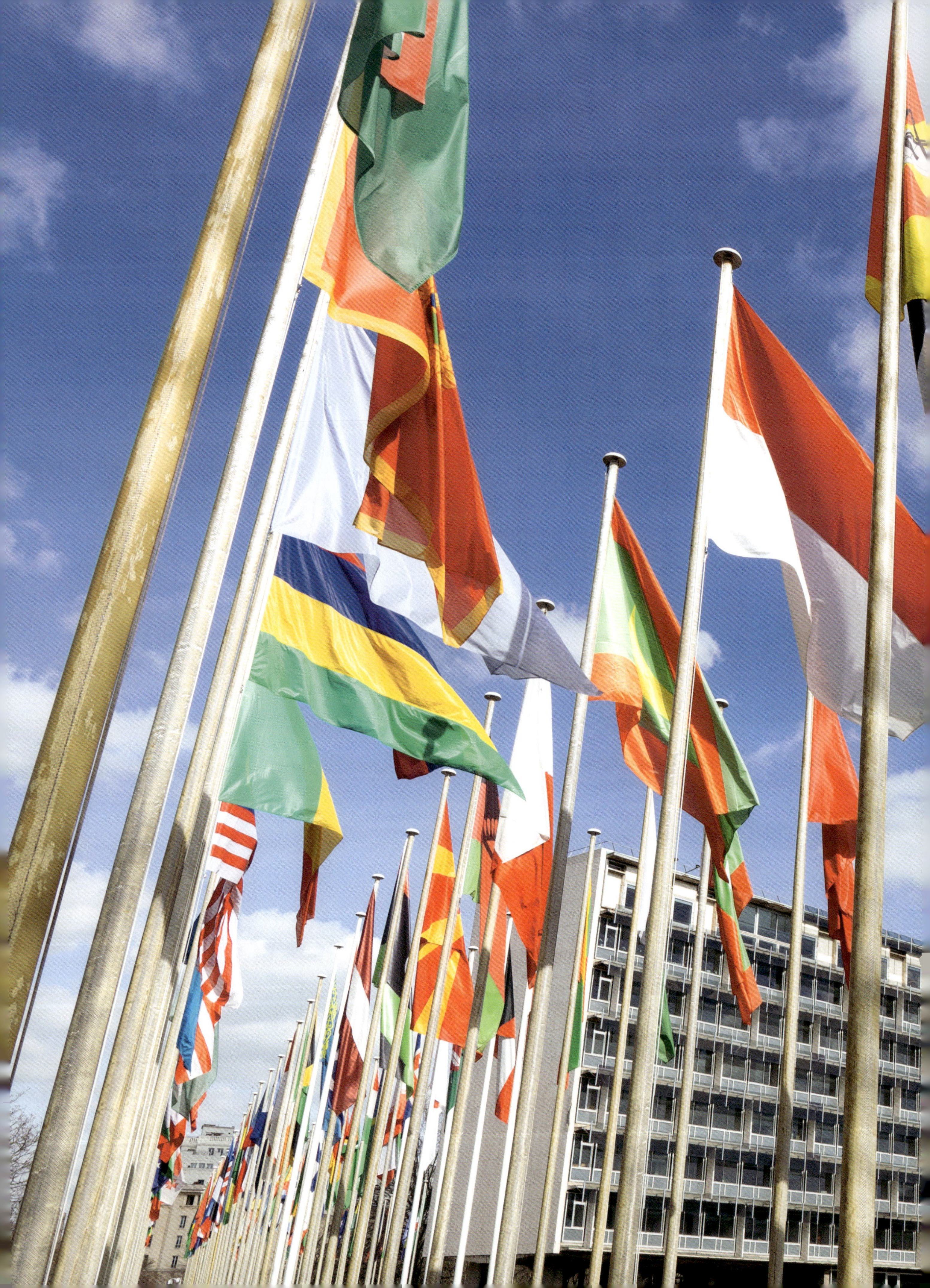

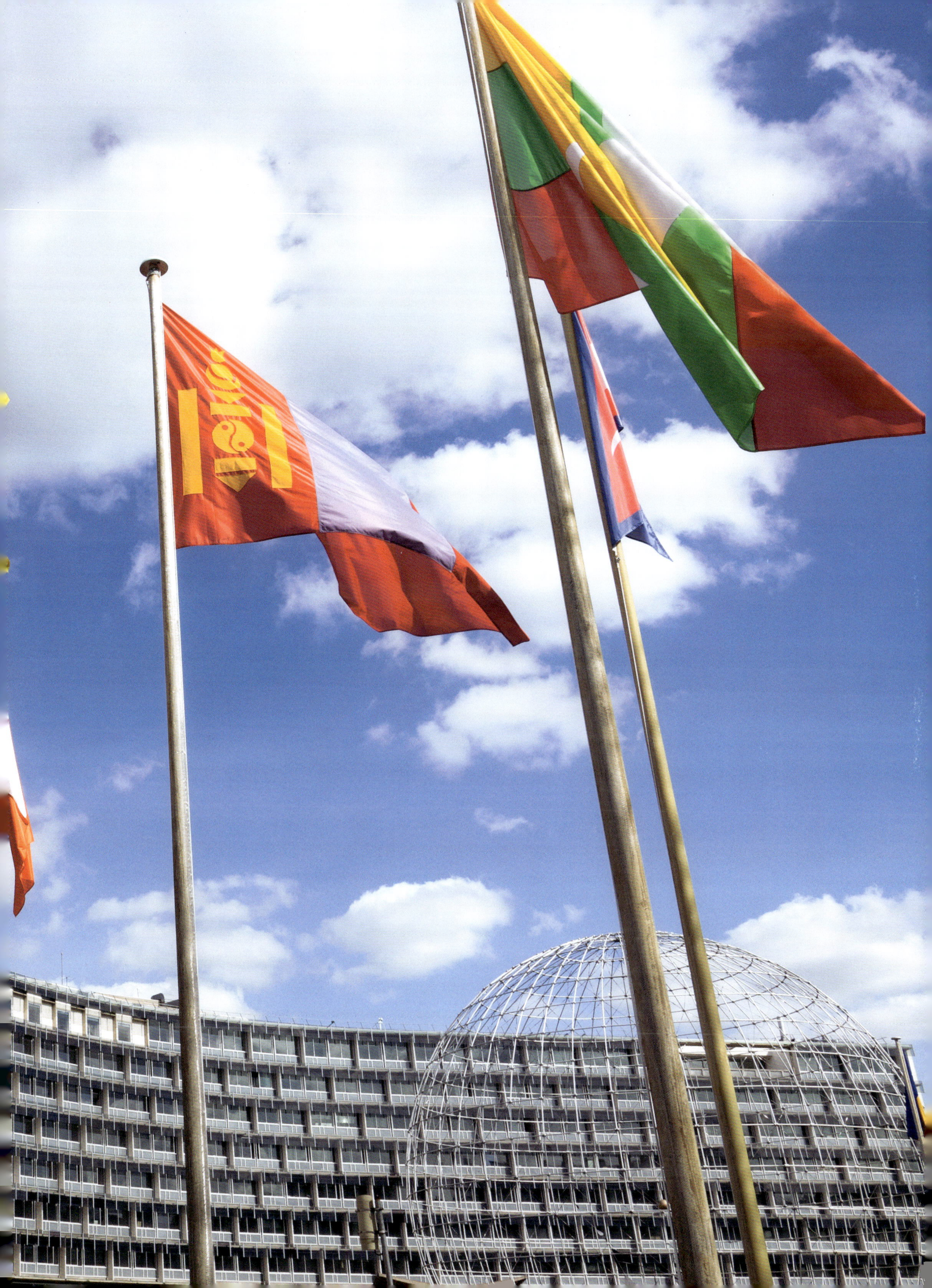

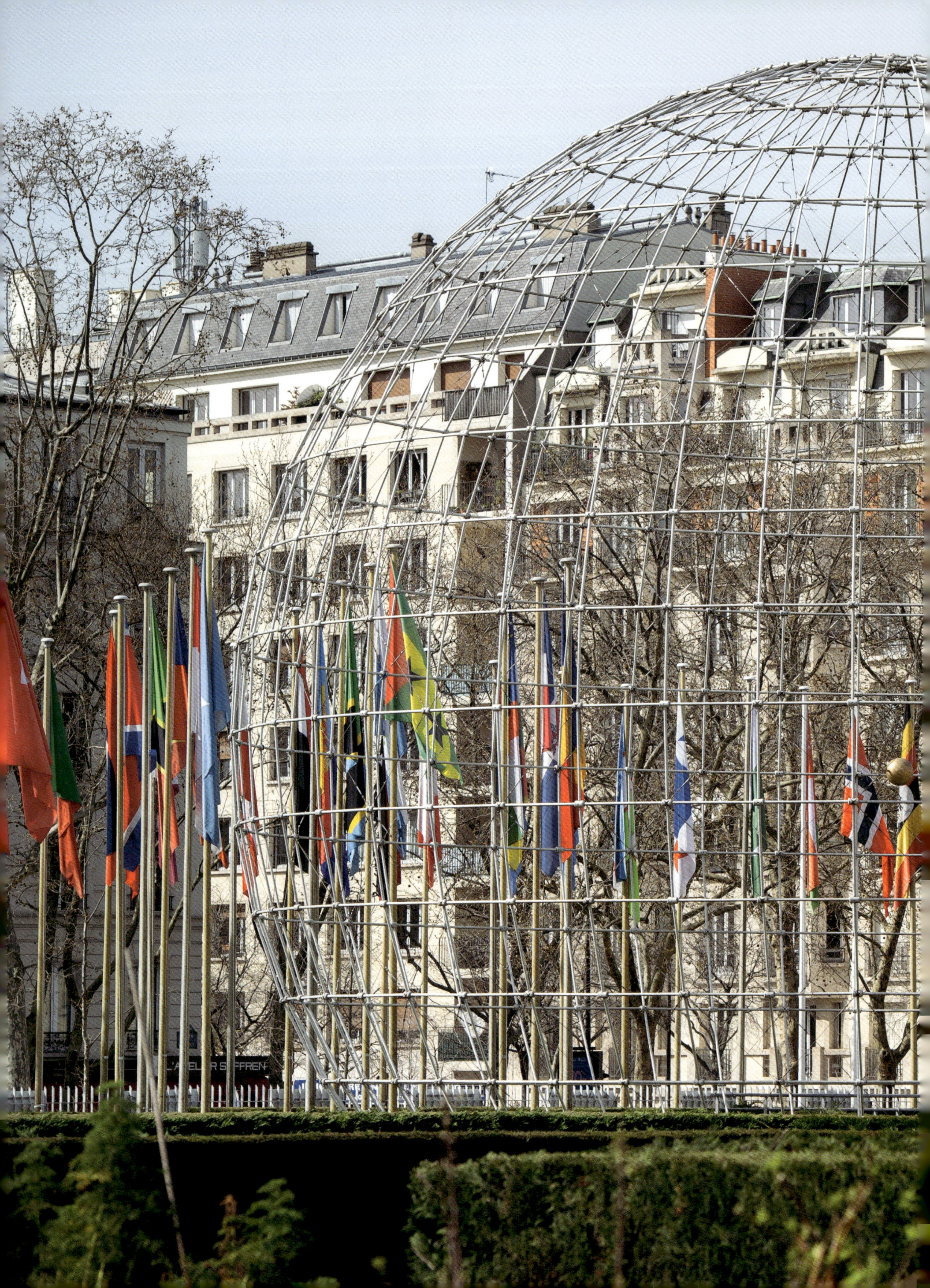

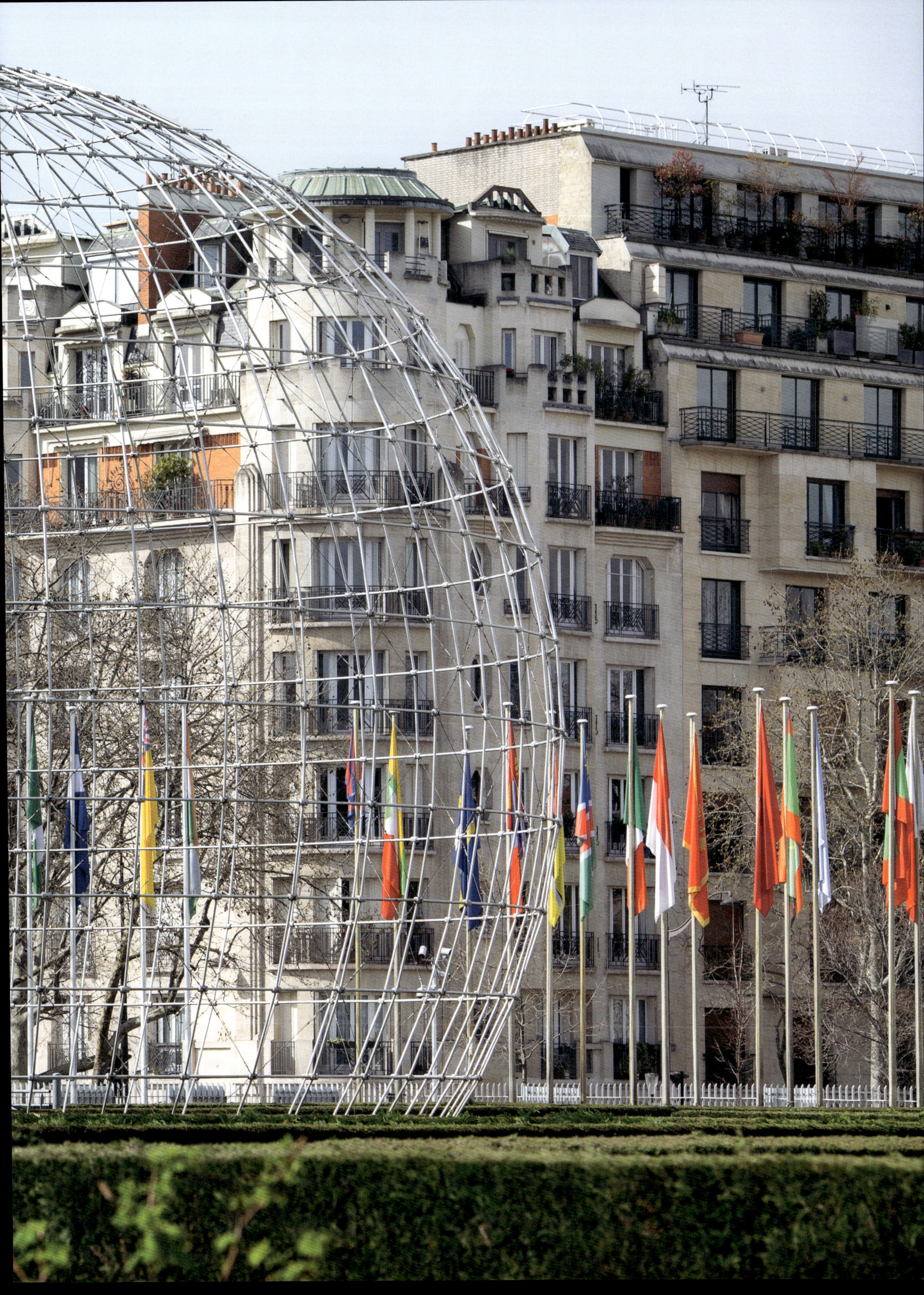

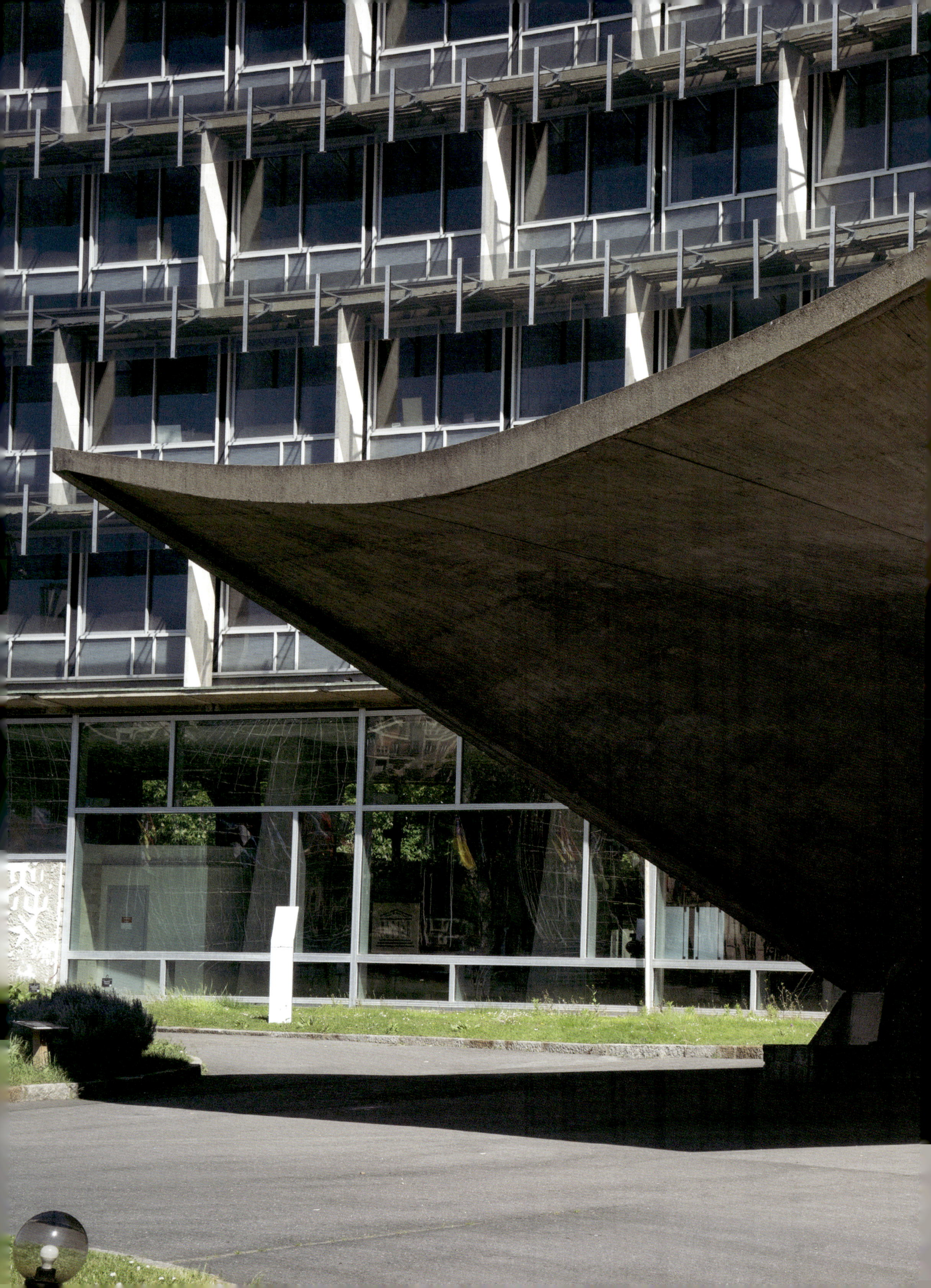

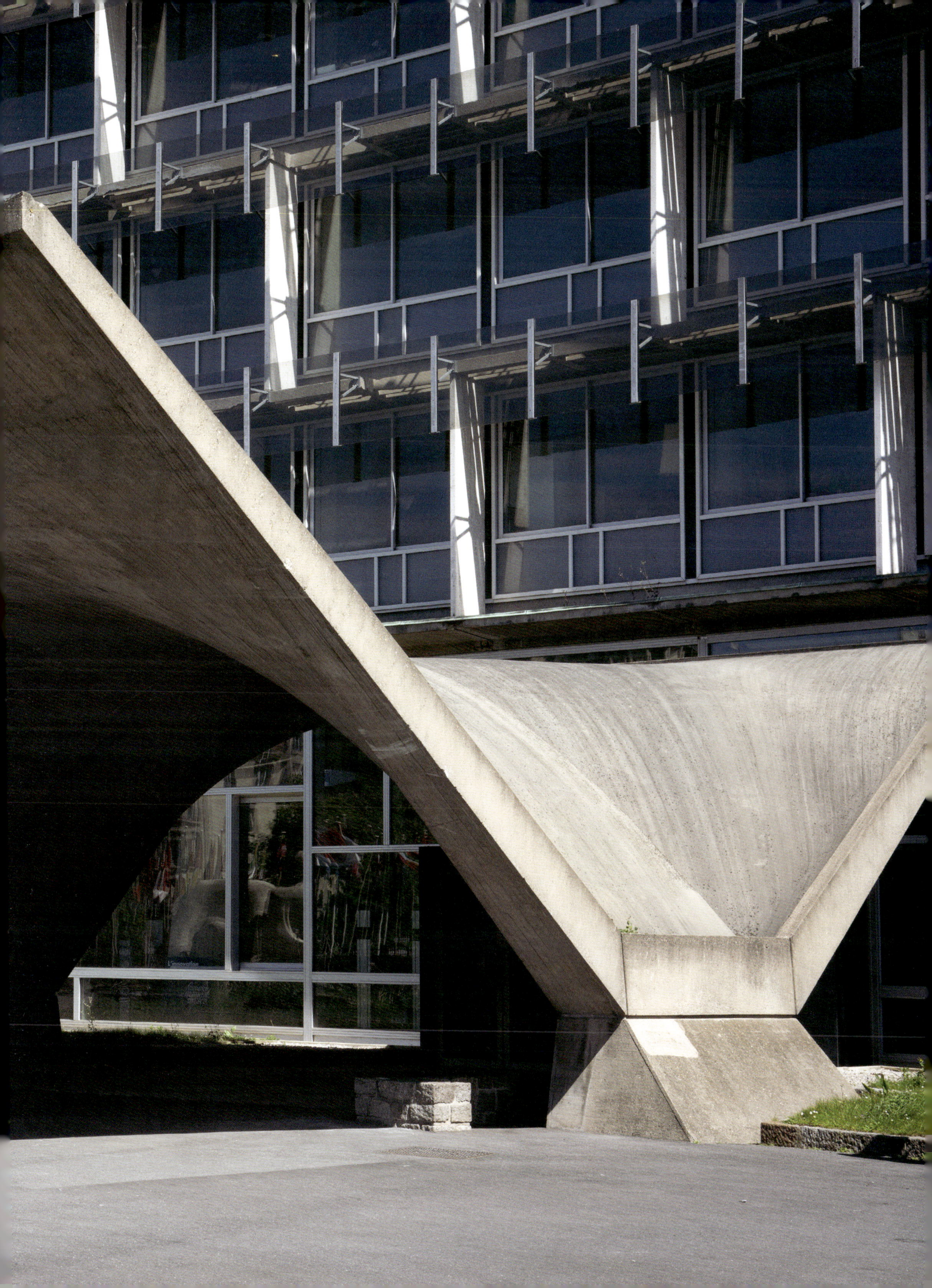

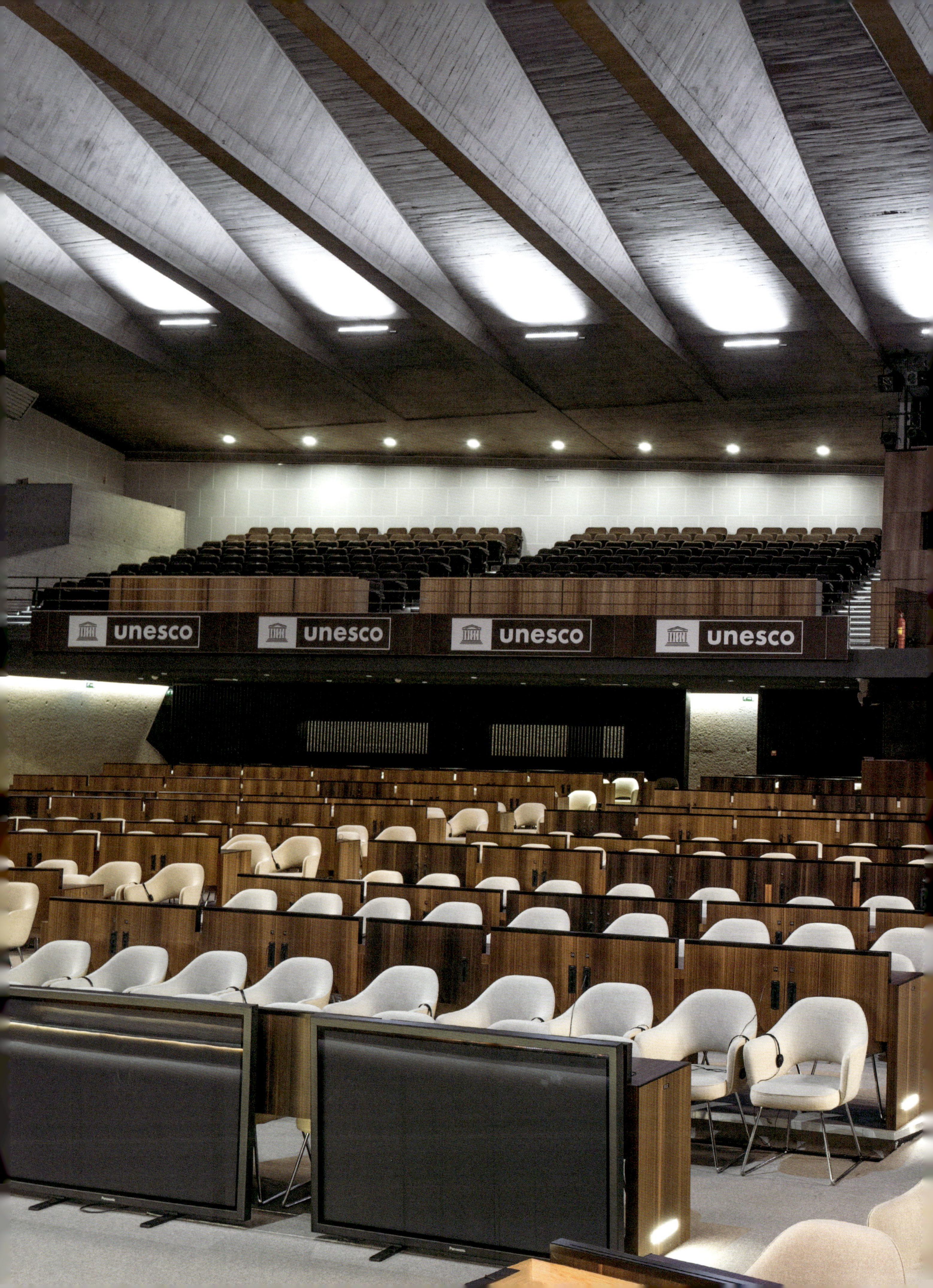

unesco
unesco
unesco
unesco

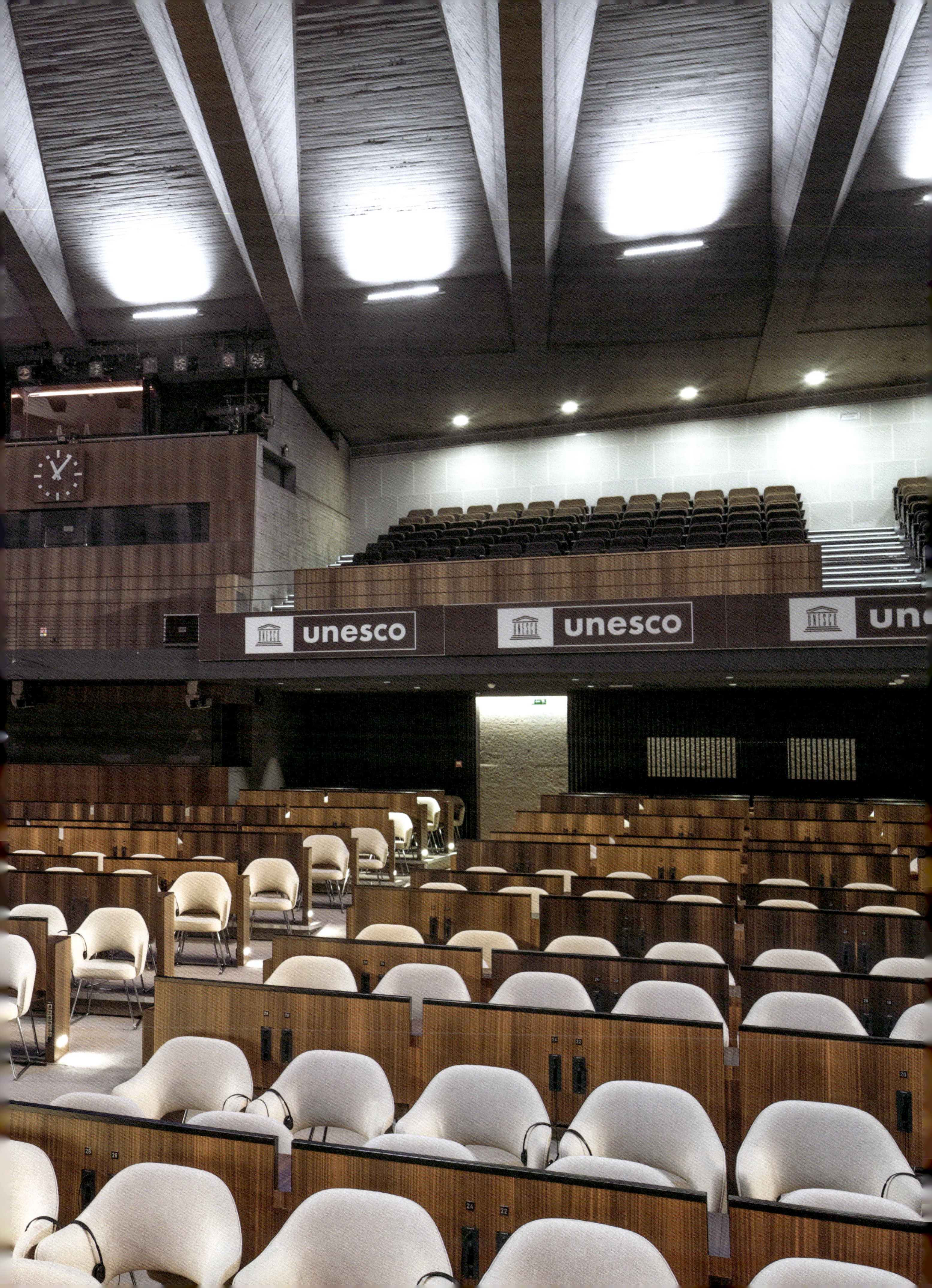
unesco
unesco

July 2024

On July 6, 1949, Monaco officially submitted its instruments of accession to the Director-General of UNESCO. The Principality's admission had been requested slightly less than a year earlier, on July 19, 1947, in the reign of Prince Louis II, and was approved by vote on December 9, 1948, at the General Conference of UNESCO in Beirut.

With the world still reeling from the devastation of World War II and already plunged into a prolonged ideological conflict, that date in early July 1949 marked the beginning of a new era for my country, domestically and also internationally. My father was then a young sovereign of twenty-six, having succeeded his grandfather just a few weeks earlier; admission to UNESCO came as an affirmation of the Principality's global recognition.

That we should join UNESCO was self-evident considering how closely its principles align with those of my predecessors, whose commitment to the arts and sciences, humanism, harmony and equity stretches back across many generations.

Upon my own accession to the Monegasque small throne, I took up most especially the banner of environmental protection and the protection of ocean biodiversity, following in the footsteps of my great-great-grandfather Prince Albert I, and my father Prince Rainier III who argued early for the protection of the Mediterranean. The Principality is therefore especially supportive of the activities undertaken by the Intergovernmental Oceanographic Commission of UNESCO in favor of the United Nations Decade of Ocean Science for Sustainable Development (2021–2030).

The Principality's contribution to UNESCO's programs does not stop there, however, as evidenced by this fine book that retraces our long-standing relationship. Packed with documents, testimonies, and original illustrations from the unerring hand of artist Damien MacDonald, this book gives voice to a shared endeavor that has been going strong for seventy-five years.

Albert II of Monaco

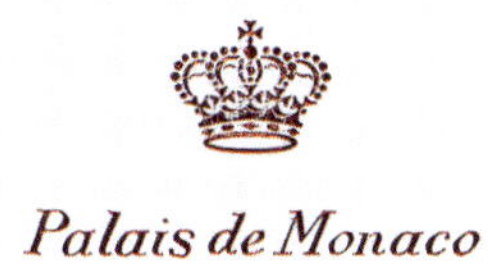

Palais de Monaco

Juillet 2024

Le 6 juillet 1949, Monaco déposait officiellement ses instruments d'adhésion à l'UNESCO. L'admission de la Principauté avait été sollicitée un peu moins d'un an auparavant, le 19 juillet 1947, sous le règne du Prince Louis II, et votée le 9 décembre 1948, lors de la conférence générale de l'organisation, tenue à Beyrouth.

Alors que le monde se relevait à peine d'un conflit mondial destructeur et était déjà plongé dans une longue période de division idéologique, cette date, au début de l'été, marquait le début d'une ère nouvelle pour mon pays, tant sur le plan intérieur qu'international. Mon père, jeune souverain de vingt-six ans, avait succédé à son grand-père quelques semaines auparavant ; et l'entrée à l'UNESCO assoyait la reconnaissance internationale de la Principauté.

Cette adhésion résonnait d'ailleurs comme une évidence, tant les principes de l'organisation font écho à la tradition de protection des arts et des sciences, d'engagement humaniste, d'équilibre et d'arbitrage, portée, au fil des siècles, par mes prédécesseurs.

Dans le sillage de mon trisaïeul le Prince Albert Ier et de mon père le Prince Rainier III, qui a œuvré de manière précoce pour la protection de la Méditerranée, j'ai placé mon règne sous le signe de la sauvegarde de l'environnement et, plus particulièrement, de la préservation de la biodiversité et des océans. La Principauté soutient donc particulièrement l'action de la Commission océanographique intergouvernementale de l'UNESCO, à l'heure de la Décennie des Nations Unies pour les sciences océaniques au service du développement durable (2021-2030).

La contribution de la Principauté aux programmes de l'organisation ne se limite cependant pas à ces domaines, comme en témoigne ce beau livre – foisonnant d'archives et de témoignages, mais aussi d'illustrations originales, dues au trait juste de Damien MacDonald – qui retrace un chemin partagé depuis soixante-quinze ans.

In 2023, AMADE (The World Association of Children's Friends), over which I have the honor to preside, celebrated its sixtieth birthday. Twenty years earlier, Mr Koïchiro Matsuura, then Director-General of UNESCO, appointed me a UNESCO Goodwill Ambassador to promote the education of women and girls. In committing to protect children worldwide and ensure their development, particularly girls and other vulnerable groups, we espoused two core UNESCO principles: the right to education for all (EFA), and culture.

These values lie at the heart of an arts program sponsored by the Principality of Monaco to encourage dialogue and bridge the culture gap, or to quote the words of my grandfather Prince Pierre, a champion of UNESCO: "While our country may not compete with the larger nations in other areas, its contribution to cultural heritage is, at the very least, significant. Monaco, located in the heart of the Mediterranean, has always made its presence felt."

The year 2024 marked another celebration, the commemoration of Monaco's seventy-five years of UNESCO membership. This book recalls the milestones along the way, and seeks to show UNESCO through the lens of the ideals and debates that shape its mission. From the very beginning, the Organization singled out ignorance as the root of human suffering. Conversely, the more we learn about ourselves and other cultures thanks to education, the arts and science, the greater our readiness to engage in dialogue and constantly revisit our assumptions.

Unique and uniquely difficult in terms of implementation, UNESCO's task is the never-ending process of bringing humanity to humankind.

The Princess of Hanover

En 2023, l'AMADE (Association Mondiale des Amis de l'Enfance), dont j'assume la présidence, fêtait son soixantième anniversaire. Monsieur Koïchiro Matsuura, alors Directeur Général de l'UNESCO, me nommait vingt ans plus tôt, Ambassadrice de bonne volonté de l'Organisation en faveur de l'éducation des femmes et des jeunes filles. Cet engagement pour la protection et l'épanouissement de l'enfant à travers le monde, la défense des plus vulnérables, notamment les filles, rejoint deux principes essentiels de l'UNESCO : le droit à l'éducation pour tous (EPT) et la culture.

Ces valeurs, que la Principauté de Monaco encourage, soutiennent une programmation artistique de qualité favorisant le dialogue et le rapprochement entre les cultures car, pour reprendre les mots de mon aïeul le Prince Pierre qui a tant aimé l'UNESCO, « si notre pays ne rivalise pas avec les grandes Nations sur d'autres plans, du moins son activité dans le domaine culturel est-elle tenue pour indiscutable. Au sein du bassin méditerranéen, berceau de la civilisation occidentale, Monaco a toujours manifesté sa présence ».

L'année 2024 est l'occasion d'une nouvelle célébration, la commémoration des 75 ans de l'entrée de Monaco à l'UNESCO. Cet ouvrage en rappelle les principaux jalons et a aussi pour objectif de faire découvrir l'Organisation sous une autre lumière, celle des idées et des débats. Dès le premier jour, l'UNESCO a explicitement considéré l'ignorance comme la source des maux de l'humanité. A rebours, lorsque par l'éducation, les arts et la science, les êtres humains acquièrent un savoir d'eux-mêmes et des autres cultures dans leurs diversités, ils sont alors prêts au dialogue, à l'échange, toujours à recommencer.

Tâche infinie, singulière à cette Organisation dans ses aspects les plus concrets, l'Humanité reste à construire.

La Princesse de Hanovre

Paris, July 10, 2024

The historic partnership between the Principality of Monaco and UNESCO dates back to the creation of our Organization, which the Principality joined in 1949, well before it became a member of the United Nations in 1993. Since then, the Principality has collaborated in many of the areas falling within UNESCO's core remit, with ocean protection at the forefront of our shared efforts.

Commitment to the ocean is a long-standing tradition for the Principality, dating back to the "Prince of the Oceans," HSH Prince Albert I, to whom we owe the General Bathymetric Chart of the Oceans or GEBCO. Since its creation by the Prince in 1903, GEBCO has made it possible to map nearly a quarter of the ocean floor, exemplifying the cooperative strategy at the heart of our shared agenda.

It was this commitment to UNESCO, spearheaded by HSH Prince Albert II in his capacity as "godfather" and founding member of the Ocean Alliance Decade, which led to the May 2022 Agreement on protecting marine areas; to the Ocean Decade, Third Foundations Dialogue, organized by Monaco in June 2023; and to a fellowship program for young scientists under UNESCO's Man and the Biosphere (MAB) program, named the "MAB Young Scientist Awards–Prince Albert I of Monaco," which targets young researchers studying marine, island and coastal issues in biosphere reserves.

I am also thinking here of our joint actions in favor of education, as epitomized by HSH the Princess of Hanover in her capacity as UNESCO Goodwill Ambassador to promote the cause of women and girls, and our cooperation in the realm of sports where we jointly strive to promote respect and inclusivity. Here, I salute the Principality's unflagging support for the International Fund for the Development of Physical Education and Sport and, since its creation, the International Fund for the Elimination of Doping in Sport.

Last but not least, this is a partnership where questions of world heritage receive full attention under the 1972 Convention for the Safeguarding of Marine Protected Areas.

Some places at UNESCO headquarters bear the mark of this privileged relationship, as for instance the *Comptoir Monaco*–a unique space shaped like the half hull of a boat to showcase Monaco's maritime heritage–and the Delegates Lounge featuring the works of Monegasque ceramicist Albert Diato.

May the seventy-five-year cooperative relationship so magnificently celebrated in this book endure in the years to come, so that future decades may find us still hard at work in favor of education, science and culture in defense of peace.

Audrey Azoulay

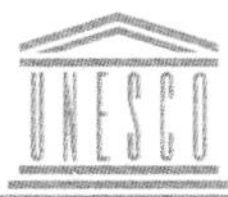

La Directrice générale

Paris, le 10 juillet 2024

La Principauté de Monaco est historiquement un partenaire de premier plan de l'UNESCO – et ce depuis la création de notre Organisation, que la Principauté a rejoint dès 1949, bien avant son adhésion à l'ONU en 1993.

Cette coopération se décline dans de nombreux domaines du mandat de l'UNESCO, au premier rang desquels la protection de l'océan.

Cet engagement de longue date s'inscrit dans la lignée du « prince des Océans », S.A.S. le Prince Albert Ier, à qui l'on doit notamment la fondation dès 1903 de la carte bathymétrique générale de l'océan – un programme de cartographie des fonds marins qui a permis de recenser, plus de 120 ans plus tard, près d'un quart du plancher océanique.

Cette coopération stratégique est aujourd'hui au cœur de notre agenda partagé. Cet engagement, porté au premier chef, par S.A.S. le Prince Albert II en ses qualités de parrain et membre fondateur de l'Alliance de la Décennie de l'Océan, s'est notamment traduit par l'accord de mai 2022 sur la sauvegarde des aires marines, l'organisation par Monaco du Troisième Dialogue des Fondations pour la Décennie de l'Océan en juin 2023, ou encore à travers les prix « Prince Albert Ier de Monaco pour la jeunesse » du programme sur l'Homme et la biosphère, destinés à de jeunes chercheurs pour leurs travaux sur l'océan et les zones côtières dans les réserves de biosphère.

Je pense également à nos actions communes pour l'éducation, qu'incarne de façon exemplaire S.A.R. la Princesse de Hanovre, en sa qualité d'Ambassadrice de bonne volonté de l'UNESCO pour l'éducation des femmes et des jeunes filles, ou à notre coopération dans le domaine du sport, à travers laquelle l'UNESCO et Monaco s'attachent à promouvoir les valeurs de respect et d'inclusion. Je salue à cet égard le soutien constant de la Principauté de Monaco au Fonds international pour le développement de l'éducation physique et du sport et, depuis sa création, au Fonds pour l'élimination du dopage dans le sport.

Enfin, c'est un partenariat qui donne toute sa part aux enjeux du patrimoine mondial, dans le cadre de l'application de la Convention de 1972 pour la protection des aires marines protégées.

Certains espaces, au Siège de l'UNESCO, portent l'empreinte de cette relation privilégiée. C'est le cas en particulier du comptoir Monaco, formé symboliquement d'une demi-carène de bateau, ou des œuvres du céramiste monégasque Albert Diato qui ornent la salle des délégués de l'UNESCO.

Puisse cette coopération de 75 ans, magnifiquement célébrée dans cet ouvrage, se poursuivre dans les décennies à venir et au-delà – pour continuer d'élever ensemble, à travers l'éducation, la science et la culture, les défenses de la paix.

Audrey Azoulay

Audrey Azoulay

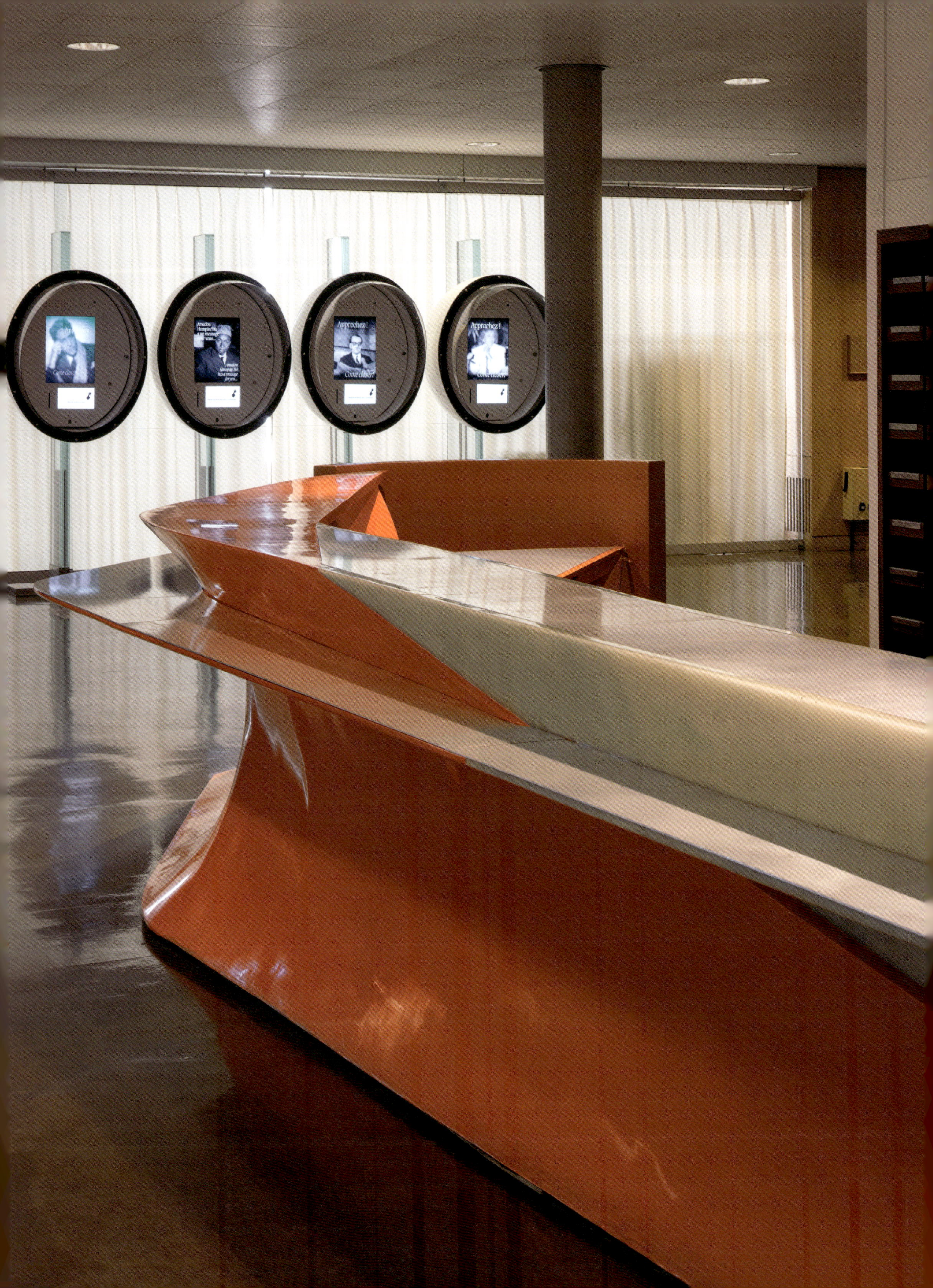
Approchez !
Come closer!

CONTENTS

21 INTRODUCTION

23 MONACO'S ACCESSION TO UNESCO
AFFIRMATION AND RECOGNITION

89 SHARED PRINCIPLES
EDUCATION, SCIENCE, CULTURE

167 A LIVING CONNECTION
THE PRINCELY FAMILY
AND THE UNESCO DIRECTORS-GENERAL

193 MEMORIES OF UNESCO FIGURES

OPPOSITE PAGE The Monaco desk leading to the Delegates Lounge decorated by Monegasque sculptor Albert Diato.

Please see page 220 for a translation of the illustrations featured on pages 22 and 88.

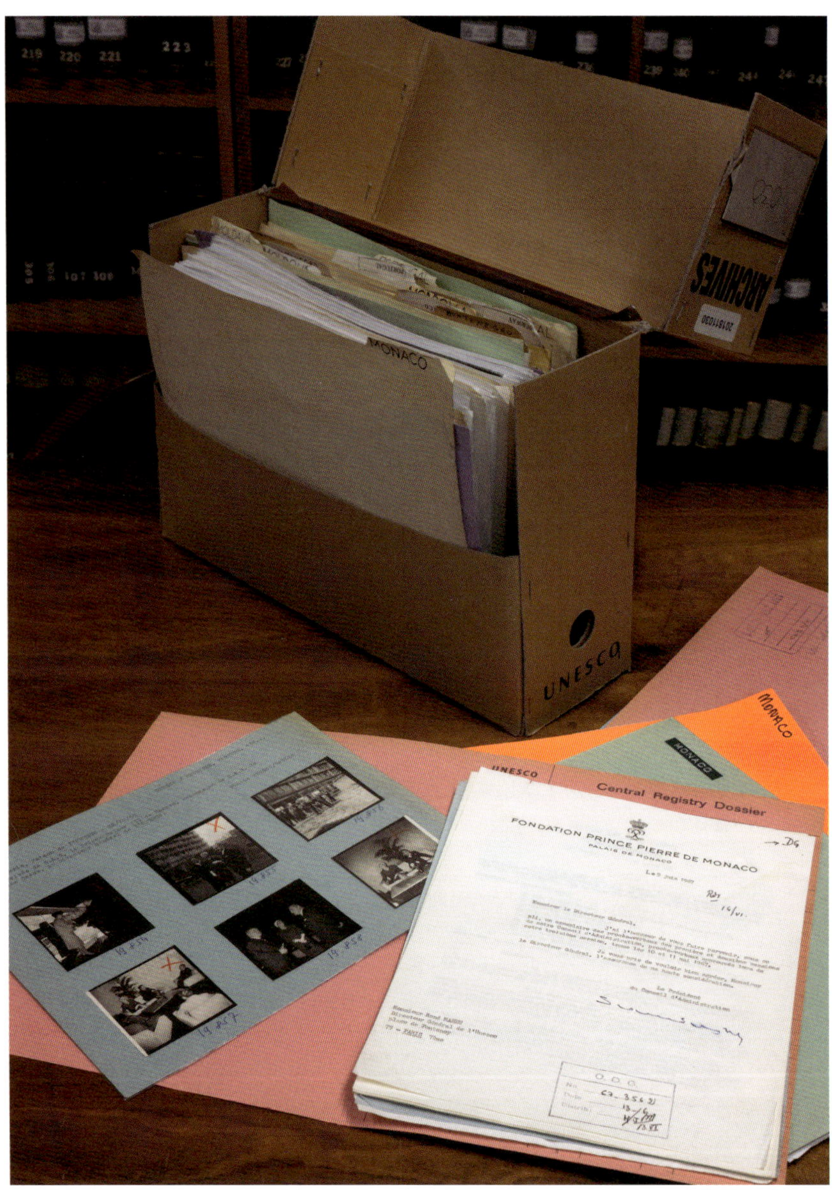

A glimpse of the extensive "Monaco" document collection in the UNESCO archives.
Reading room at the UNESCO library, Place de Fontenoy, Paris.

INTRODUCTION

This book has been written to mark the seventy-fifth anniversary celebrations of Monaco's UNESCO membership. Its primary focus therefore is on memory and historical records, but also on the ideas, values and philosophy that have informed, and continue to inform, the establishment of lasting peace in the world.

UNESCO is committed to equipping itself with the skills required to apply its principles and build on its four pillars: education, science, culture and information.

We have chosen to take a pluralistic approach as a way of connecting with readers in Monaco and UNESCO alike, thus strengthening the already strong bonds between the two partners: on the one hand, the Organization and its different delegations, and on the other hand, the people of the Principality.

It is obviously not possible within the confines of this book to give an exhaustive account of the past seven and a half decades of Monaco's UNESCO membership. Instead, our goal here is to shed light on the areas and events that best illustrate the fruitfulness of that relationship. To that end, we reiterate UNESCO's goals and respective timelines in themed sections focused on Monaco-specific programs: the projects undertaken by the Principality in line with State imperatives, its Monegasque identity and the wishes of the Princely Family. What these represent in essence is a map of collaboration with our apologies in advance for any regions or themes that may have been dealt with too briefly, or not all.

In parallel to this, we also give voice to UNESCO's foremost players at the global level, brought to life in the drawings of Damien MacDonald. Standing alongside their UNESCO counterparts, Monaco's leading figures testify to their commitment to serving their country by increasing UNESCO's visibility. Their inspiration is Prince Pierre of Monaco, a pioneer of modern oceanography whose legacy lives on in the works undertaken by his foundation.

In 2022, H.S.H Prince Albert II took the podium at UNESCO to remind the world that the "works of science, light and peace" championed by his great-great-grandfather Prince Albert I of Monaco, continue to resonate with the principles espoused by UNESCO as set out in Article 1 of its founding constitution: "The purpose of the Organization is to contribute to peace and security by promoting collaboration among the nations through education, science and culture."

The past and the present come together, embodied in a history, an adventure and a steadfast commitment.

Stéphane Lamotte
Jean-Philippe Vinci

L'ENTRÉE DE MONACO S'EST FAITE PROGRESSIVEMENT AU COURS DES QUATRE PREMIÈRES CONFÉRENCES GÉNÉRALES DE L'UNESCO. L'ORGANISATION EST NÉE EN NOVEMBRE 1945 À LONDRES OÙ EST SIGNÉ L'ACTE CONSTITUTIF.

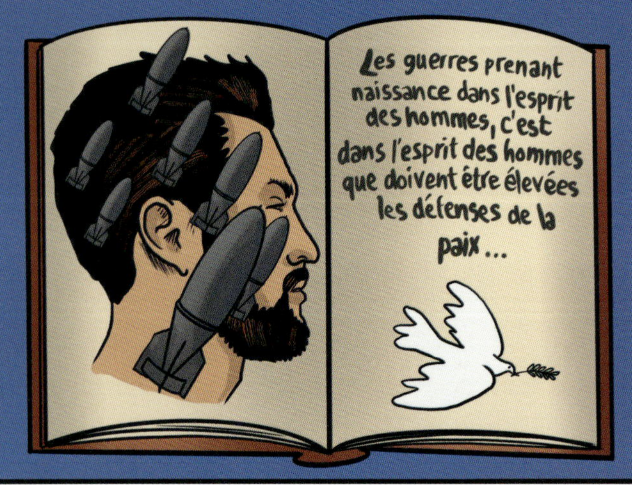

LA PREMIÈRE CONFÉRENCE GÉNÉRALE DE L'UNESCO, DIRIGÉE PAR JULIAN HUXLEY, SE DÉROULE EN NOVEMBRE 1946 À LA SORBONNE À PARIS. RENÉ BOCCA, ÉTUDIANT EN PHILOSOPHIE, INVITÉ DANS LA DÉLÉGATION FRANÇAISE, RÉDIGE UN RAPPORT EXPRIMANT L'INTÉRÊT POUR LA PRINCIPAUTÉ D'ENTRER DANS CETTE NOUVELLE ORGANISATION INTERNATIONALE.

DANS LA PERSPECTIVE DE LA DEUXIÈME CONFÉRENCE GÉNÉRALE, QUI SE TIENT À MEXICO EN NOVEMBRE-DÉCEMBRE 1947, LA CANDIDATURE EST DÉPOSÉE. CEPENDANT, LES DÉLAIS TECHNIQUES SONT TROP COURTS POUR QU'ELLE PUISSE ÊTRE EXAMINÉE ET QUE LE PROCESSUS DE VOTE SOIT ACTIVÉ.

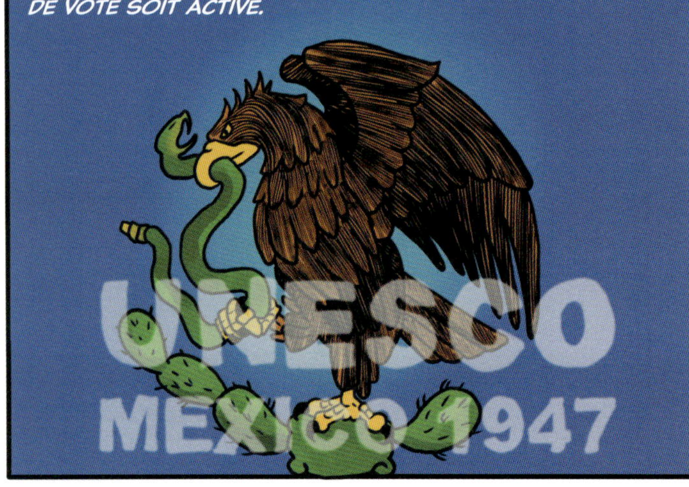

C'EST À BEYROUTH, EN NOVEMBRE-DÉCEMBRE 1948, LORS DE LA TROISIÈME CONFÉRENCE, QUE L'ADHÉSION EST VOTÉE ET VALIDÉE. LE NOUVEAU DIRECTEUR GÉNÉRAL, JAMES TORRES BODET, ENVOIE UN TÉLÉGRAMME DE FÉLICITATIONS AU GOUVERNEMENT PRINCIER.

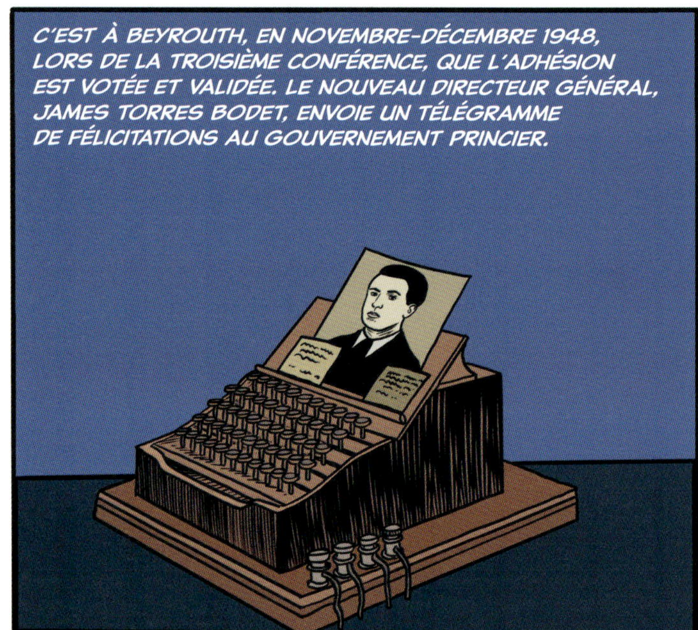

MONACO ENTRE OFFICIELLEMENT À L'UNESCO LE 9 JUILLET 1949, LE PRINCE RAINIER VIENT DE MONTER SUR LE TRÔNE.

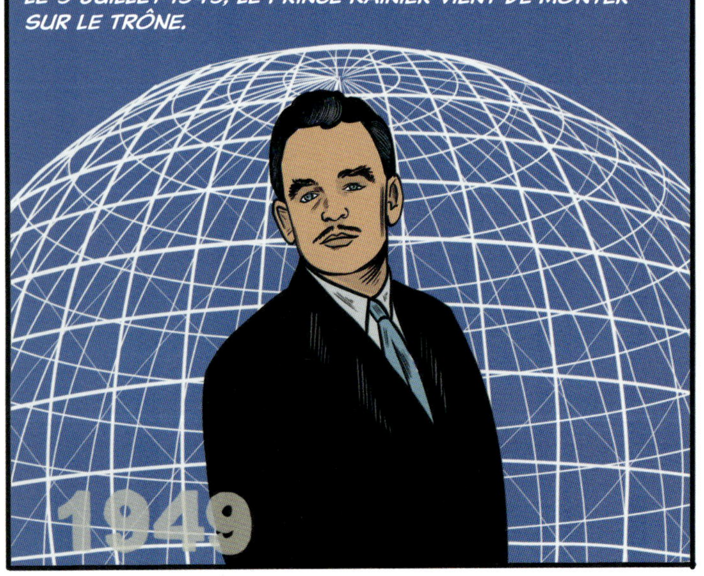

EN NOVEMBRE 1949, MONACO PARTICIPE POUR LA PREMIÈRE FOIS À UNE CONFÉRENCE GÉNÉRALE DE L'UNESCO POUR SA 4[E] SESSION QUI SE TIENT À PARIS. JACQUES RUEFF, MINISTRE D'ÉTAT, EST À LA TÊTE DE LA DÉLÉGATION EN 1949 ET EN 1950. À PARTIR DE 1951, C'EST LE PRINCE PIERRE QUI LA CONDUIT, IL PRÉSIDE ÉGALEMENT LA COMMISSION NATIONALE.

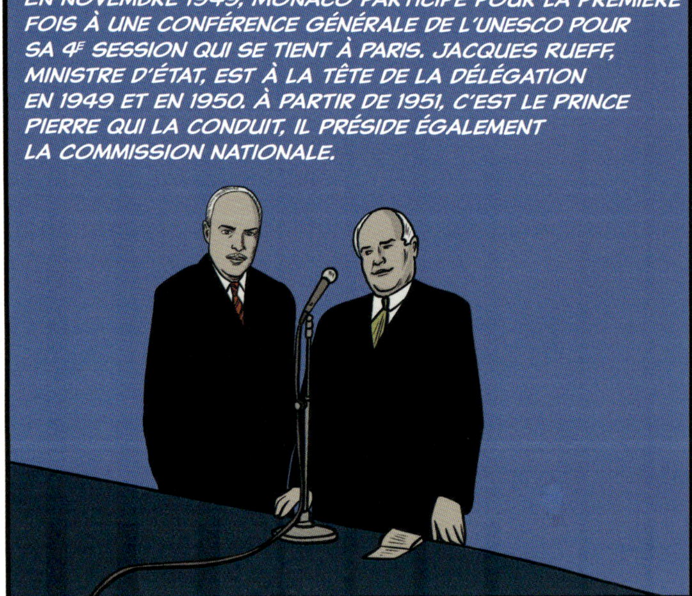

MONACO'S ACCESSION TO UNESCO

AFFIRMATION AND RECOGNITION

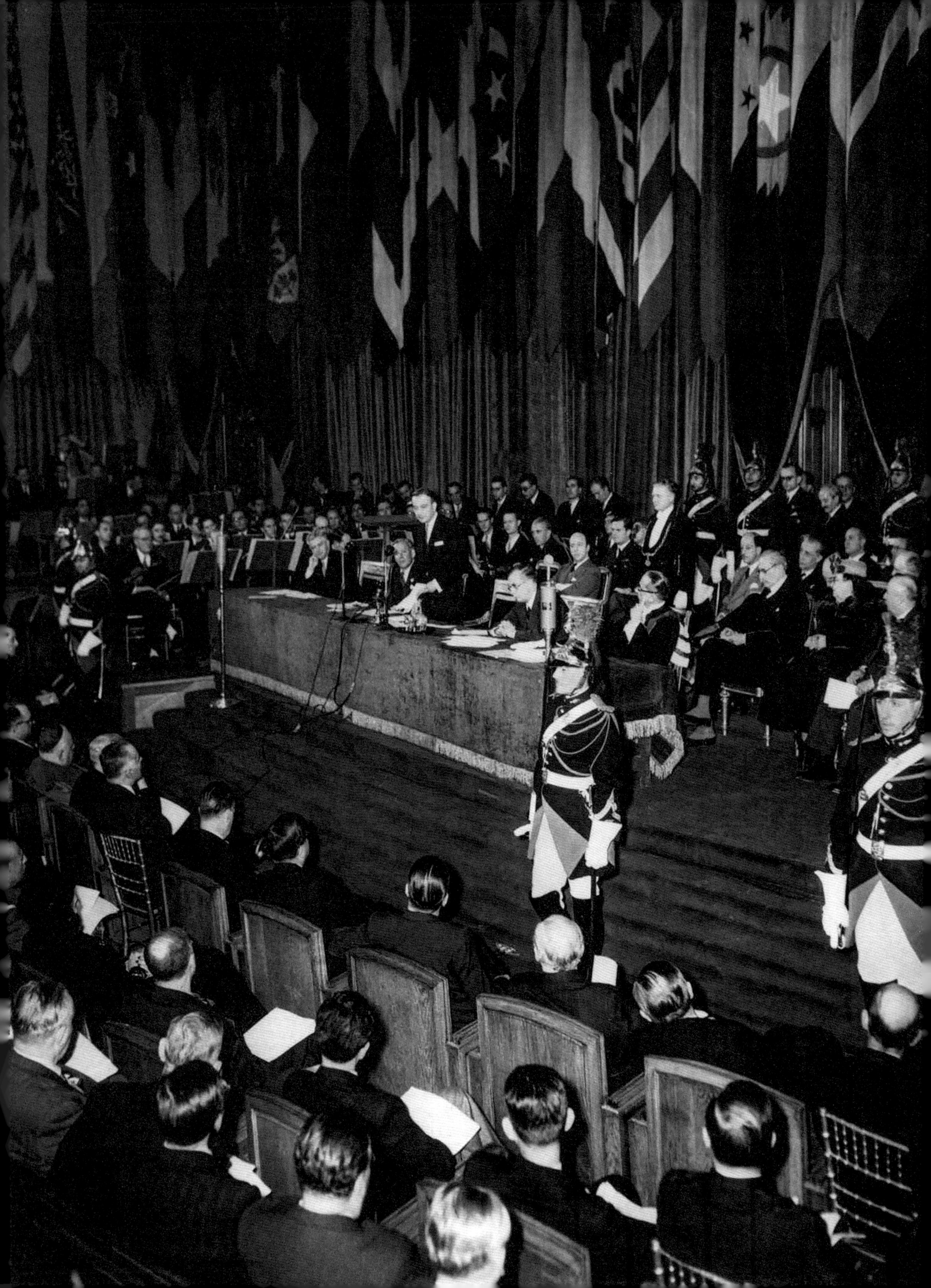

Monaco's accession to UNESCO must be viewed in the context of a political landscape transformed by multilateralism. The end of World War II marked the emergence of a new international scene that favored the active participation of small countries within the world's most enduring organizations. While power struggles continued, the deal worked well for both parties: small countries gained a means of diversifying their security and recognition strategies; global organizations gained legitimacy by upholding principles of equality regardless of their members' characteristics. Monaco's accession to UNESCO also coincided with an important turning-point in history. In the period 1945-1953, before the USSR joined UNESCO, the Organization was the echo chamber of a political polarization pitting the France-centered "Latin clan" against the US-UK-centered "Anglo-Saxon clan," expressed in a linguistic and cultural rift that was not without consequences within UNESCO.

Thus, to understand all the issues at stake in this emblematic case study, we need to examine the internal issues facing the Principality in the light of micro-history and global history, and the challenges posed by multilateralism and global intellectual history.

THE PRINCIPALITY: PRESENT AND ATTENTIVE FROM UNESCO'S EARLIEST DAYS

The United Nations Educational, Scientific and Cultural Organization was founded in London on November 16, 1945 (Document 1), based on the works conducted by the International Committee for Intellectual Cooperation, spearheaded in 1922 by the League of Nations, and the findings of the Conference of Allied Ministers of Education (CAME), held between November 16, 1942 and December 5, 1945. That said, there is no single answer to the origins of UNESCO, but rather a complex, twofold answer that brings together two equally relevant perspectives. Initially, UNESCO may rightly be seen as having resulted from a long-term trend that drew on two sources: the rich legacy of nineteenth-century pacifism which, before World Wars I and II, warned of the dangers of aggressive nationalism; and the interwar intellectual movements centered around figures like Henri Bergson and Paul Valéry, who served on the League of Nations International Committee on Intellectual Cooperation (1922-1946).

November 20, 1946 at the Sorbonne in Paris, opening of the first UNESCO General Conference (November 20-December 10, 1946).

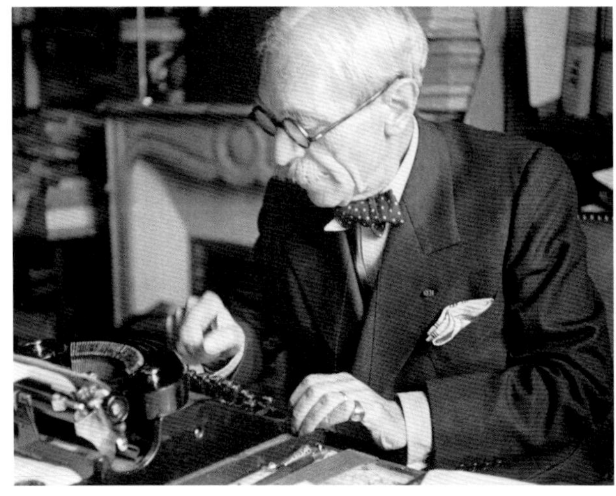

Nowadays however, it is more widely held that UNESCO came into force in response to the horrors of World War II and the discovery of the Holocaust. UNESCO marked a rupture with the past and a longing for a new world order that reflected new international realities. It was born of a deep commitment to lasting peace—a wish for human unity through intercultural dialogue, and a mutual understanding that went beyond economic and political agreements between countries to create "an intellectual and moral solidarity in the mind of humanity." The preamble to the Constitution of UNESCO, nurtured by the convictions of René Cassin (1887-1976), declares that "since wars begin in the minds of men, it is in the minds of men that the defenses of peace must be constructed." It was to put Cassin's universal principles into practice that the fledgling UNESCO gathered its twenty members together for the first General Conference, held at the Sorbonne in Paris from November 19 to December 10, 1946, almost one year to the day after the Organization was founded in London on November 16, 1945. The conference was chaired by Ellen Wilkinson (1891-1947), who presided over the election of UNESCO's first Director-General, British-born Julian Huxley (1887-1975). Léon Blum (1872-1950) headed the French delegation. France's capital hosted the Organization's first headquarters, located in the building of the Hotel Majestic on the Avenue Kléber in Paris—former headquarters of the German military High Command in France. The fact that this was one of the few vacant buildings large enough to accommodate the Organization was not always enough to dispel concerns over the ethics of the move.

DOSSIER | GREAT VOICES PAGES 82-87

The Principality of Monaco was not one of the Founding Member States but sent an observer to the 1946 Conference—a testament to its early interest in the works and values of UNESCO. This was a period of social unrest for Monaco, a country licking its war wounds and crippled by the strikes of 1946, at the end of the reign of Louis II whose twenty-five years on the throne were celebrated in 1947. The time was ripe for a new departure, fueled by a movement that would give the Principality legitimacy on the world stage. A new generation of diplomats and intellectuals committed to make this happen, among them René Bocca (1919-1999), then a young philosophy student in Paris and President of the Comité national des étudiants monégasque (national committee for Monegasque students).

Writer, poet and philosopher Paul Valéry at his desk in December 1937.

A key figure of the new movement, Bocca attended the first General Conference as the distinguished guest of the French delegation. In 1947, at the request of the Monegasque Government, he reported his observations in a working document titled: *L'Unesco ses buts, ses résultats, perspectives monégasques d'avenir* (Document 4, "UNESCO: its goals, achievements, and future prospects for Monaco."). The paper sought as much to provide better insight into the missions of UNESCO as to pave the way for Monaco's candidature. It also underlined their reciprocity of interests: "The Principality is not a member of UNESCO, but it retains the possibility of applying for membership. While there is no denying its small size, Monaco's contribution to the worlds of science and culture is no less significant: the Institut Océanographique et Musée (Oceanographic Institute and Museum); the Institut de la paléontologie humaine (Institute of Human Paleontology); the Musée d'Anthropologie préhistorique (Museum of Prehistoric Anthropology); the Bureau Hydrographique International (International Hydrographic Bureau), and publication of papers and maps; the International Peace Institute, founded by His Serene Highness Prince Albert I; and numerous international scientific symposiums. Then there is the fact that Monaco's geographical position, exceptional climate and financial resources—under normal circumstances, that is—could prove invaluable to the work of UNESCO."

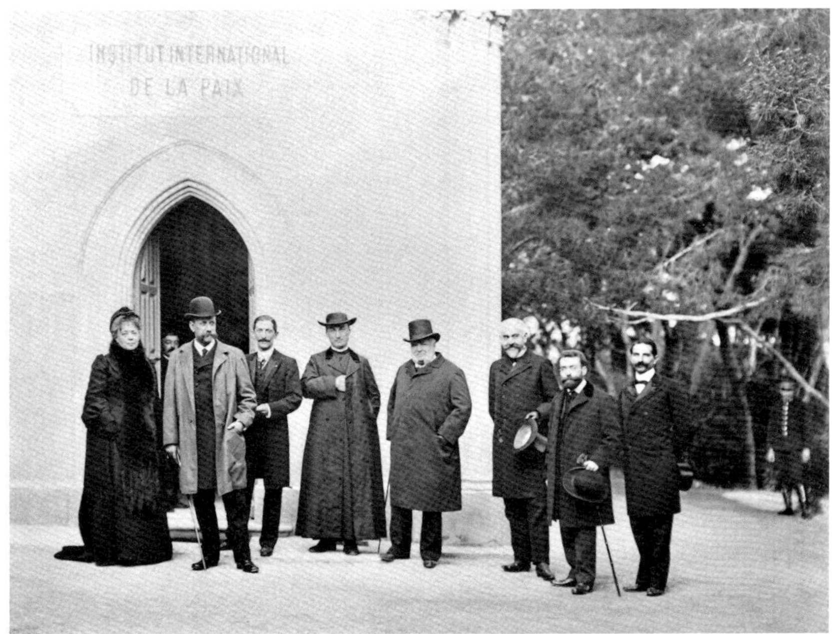

Inauguration of the International Institute for Peace, in Monaco, February 25, 1903. Prince Albert I accompanied by Bertha von Suttner, Gaston Moch, Father Louis Pichot, Gustave Saige, Charles de Monicault, Henri de Maleville and Edmond Izard.

As we will see, for René Bocca, "small state" was a self-designation reflecting an identity imposed from within Monaco itself, not from outside the country. As such, its presence was required at UNESCO, as much to understand the issues at stake and prepare for its forthcoming admission as to demonstrate its commitment and thereby assert itself in the eyes of its future fellow members. Bocca's balanced and comprehensive report laid down guidelines for the future, based on his own detailed understanding of the Organization as an observer who had been privy to its inner workings from the very beginning. Pierre de Witasse (1878-1956), having taken note of Bocca's report, actively supported Monaco's candidature. As the French-born Minister of State of the Principality, he could simultaneously champion the sovereign interests of the Principality and intercede on its behalf with the French authorities. Before arriving in Monaco in 1944, this graduate of Sciences Po (Paris Institute of Political Studies) had for many years worked at the French Ministry of Foreign Affairs. So it was that in March 1947 Maurice Lozé, Minister Plenipotentiary of Monaco to the French legation—what we would now call an ambassador—was unofficially tasked by Witasse with gathering the necessary documents and studying the eligibility requirements. On July 19, 1947, Lozé's findings enabled the Principality to present a formal request for UNESCO membership, in the hope that its candidature would be examined by the Organization at the second General Conference to be held in Mexico City in November-December of that same year. The request was submitted in person by Professor Juan Baime, administrative officer of the Consulate of Monaco in Mexico City, acting in his capacity as an observer to the Princely Government. It would take another few months to bring the project to fruition. The membership process was a lengthy business. Beyond an undertaking to commit to UNESCO's core values, certain administrative requirements had to be met, and political measures put in place that embraced different points of view.

DOSSIER
DOCUMENTS RECORDING 1946-1951 MONACO'S ADMISSION TO UNESCO
PAGES 46-57

A CANDIDATURE WELCOMED BY UNESCO

Having received Monaco's candidature, UNESCO embarked on a multi-stage candidate assessment and validation process. Initially the application was referred to the UNESCO Executive Council, which commissioned a report examining the potential advantages and disadvantages of Monaco's request. Its findings were entirely favorable, with no *a priori* objections being raised. It was clear from the outset

Inauguration of the *Monument Albert Ier*, a work by François Cogné, in the Saint-Martin Gardens in Monaco on April 11, 1951, by Prince Rainier III.

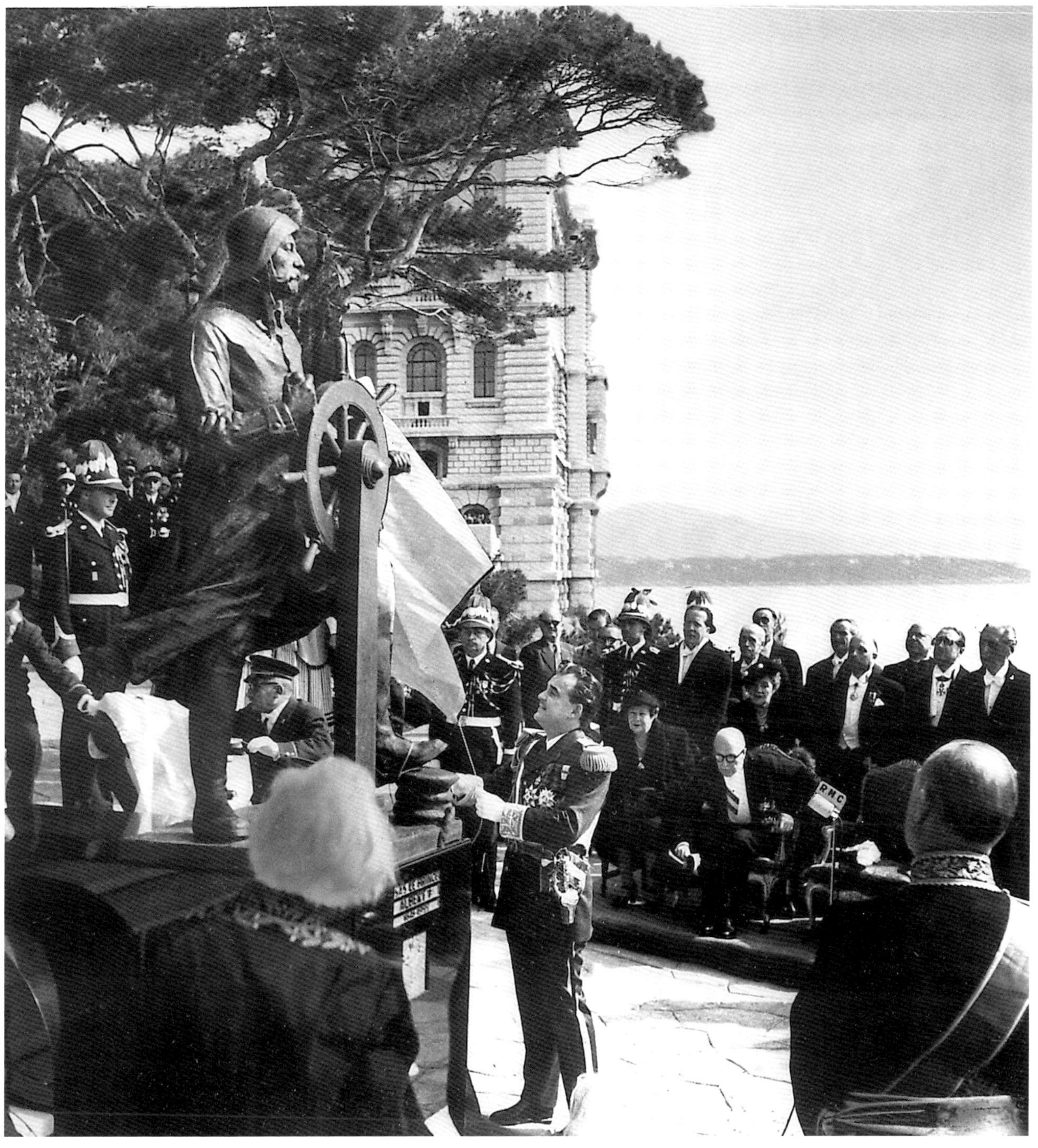
RMC

that the Principality would likely make a significant contribution to the implementation of UNESCO programs, not least through its own scientific and cultural activities. The report laid particular emphasis on the Principality's scientific contribution, especially in terms of oceanography as epitomized by the achievements of Prince Albert I, whose legacy lived on through his involvement in numerous learned societies (the Société de Géographie and the Académie des Sciences in Paris), the activities of his foundations (the Oceanographic Institute and the Institute of Human Paleontology) and the celebration of the centenary of his birth in 1948. UNESCO was meanwhile not insensitive to the international outreach and humanist tradition of the small sovereign state. The report drew attention to the founding in 1903 of the International Peace Institute: a center of expertise for research on multilateral peace operations whose values resonated with those of UNESCO and Albert I alike. A committed pacifist, the Prince took inspiration from his chief of staff Gaston Moch, and his friend Baroness Bertha von Suttner (1843-1914)—in 1905, the first woman to win the Nobel Peace Prize—who strove for a rapprochement between France and Germany right up to the eve of World War I. Mention was also made of the establishment in 1931 of the headquarters of the International Hydrographic Bureau (created under the auspices of the League of Nations); and of the many international symposia hosted by the Principality since 1897, resulting in the signing of an equal number of conventions promoting culture and social welfare. Among these: the Convention relating to the International Telecommunications Union, the Berne Convention for the Protection of Literary and Artistic Property, the Convention establishing the International Hydrographic Organization, and the Agreement on the Creation of an International Office for Epizootics. In the cultural domain, emphasis was placed on the importance of the Monte-Carlo theater (opened in 1879) as a venue for famous performance artists, most notably Diaghilev and the Ballets Russes who took the stage in 1922 at the behest of Prince Pierre. Two years later, the Prince also founded a Society of Conferences, with Paul Valéry as one of its first speakers. While the report acknowledges the Principality's relative weakness at the time in the area of education (no universities or institutes of higher education), it notes that this lacuna might be filled by the Monaco Foundation. Established in 1937 at the Cité Universitaire de Paris, in the aftermath of World War I, the Foundation made it possible for Monegasque students and residents to pursue higher education in the French capital, in line with its objectives of peace building and enabling encounters between young people from all over the world.

The Fondation de Monaco, founded in 1929 by Prince Pierre and inaugurated in 1937, is located in the Cité internationale universitaire de Paris.

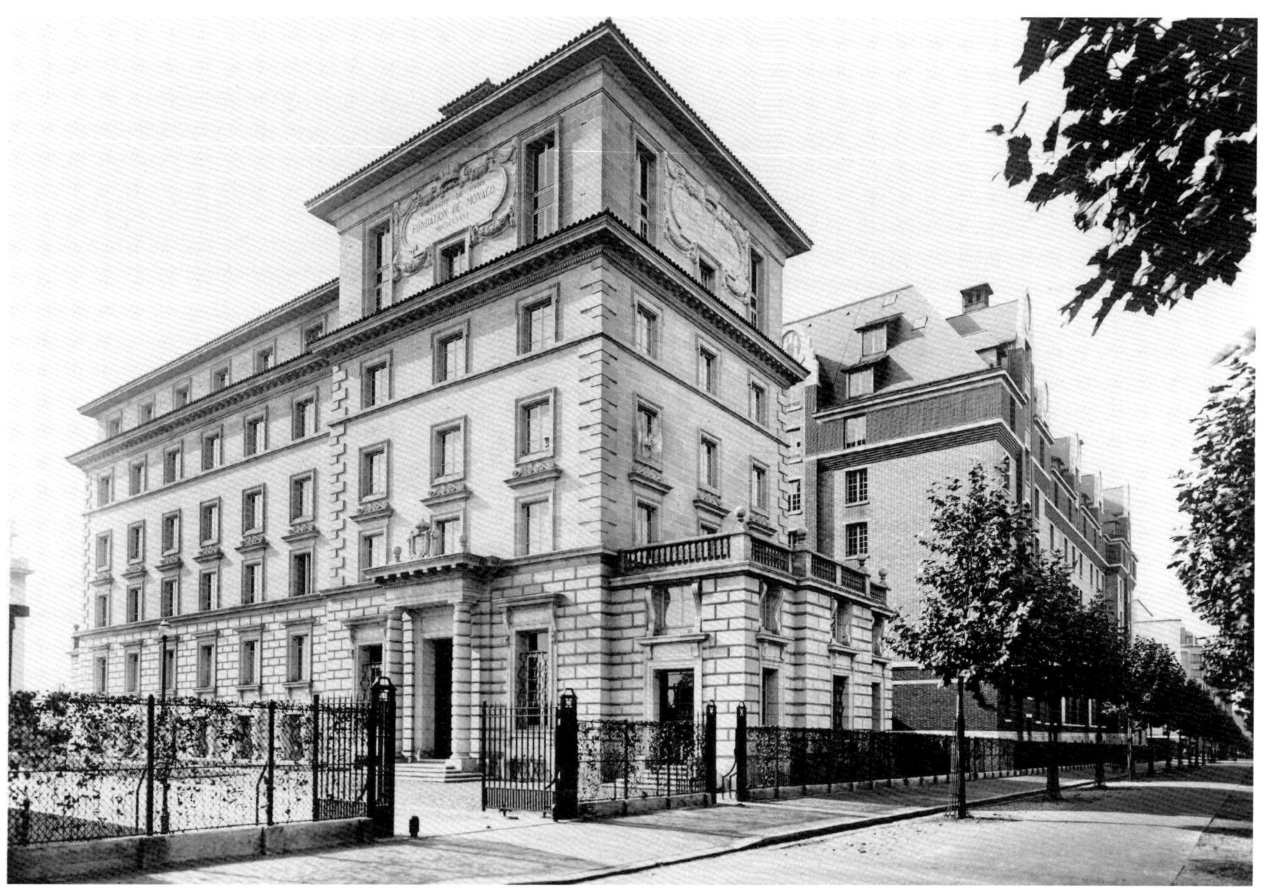
FONDATION DE MONACO

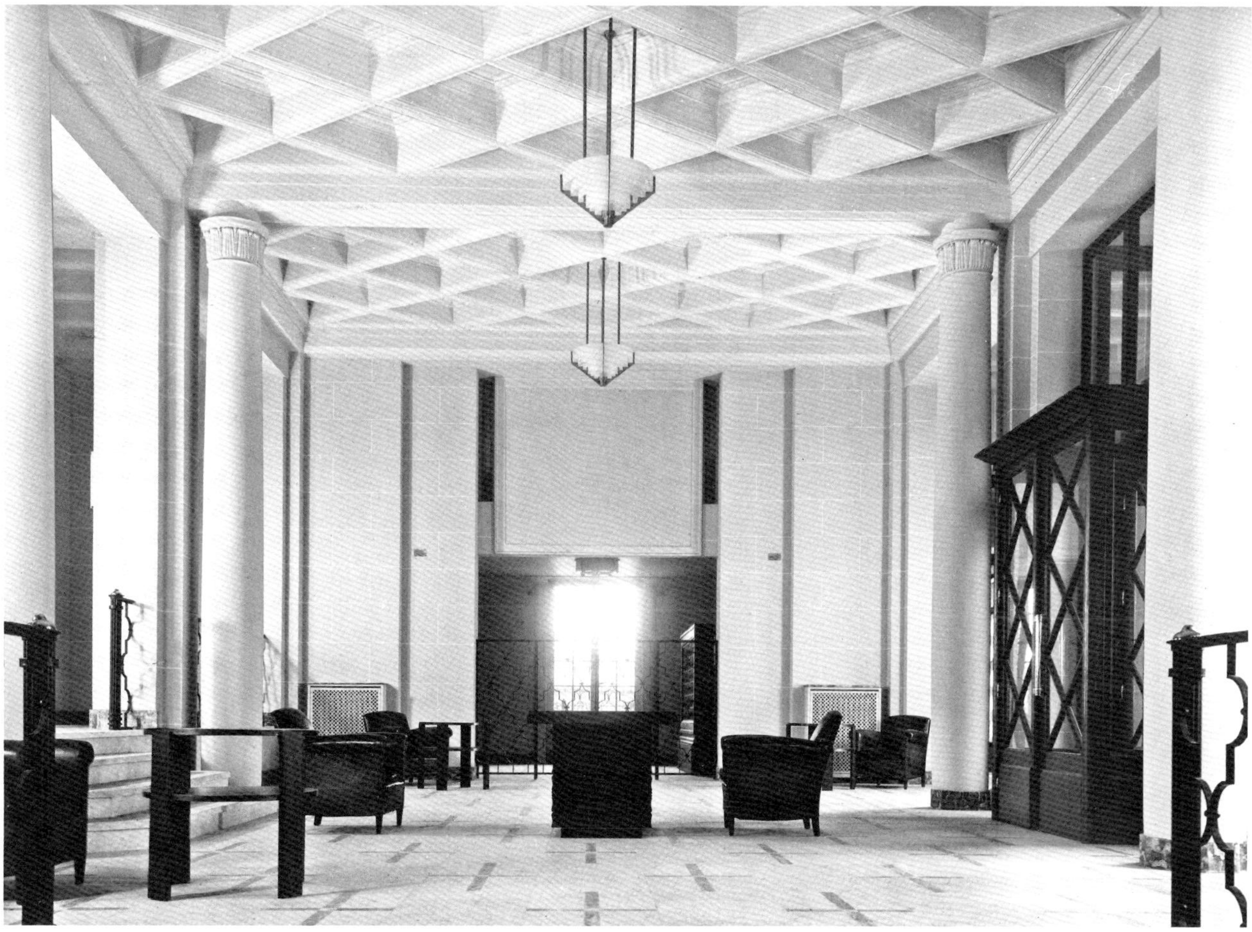

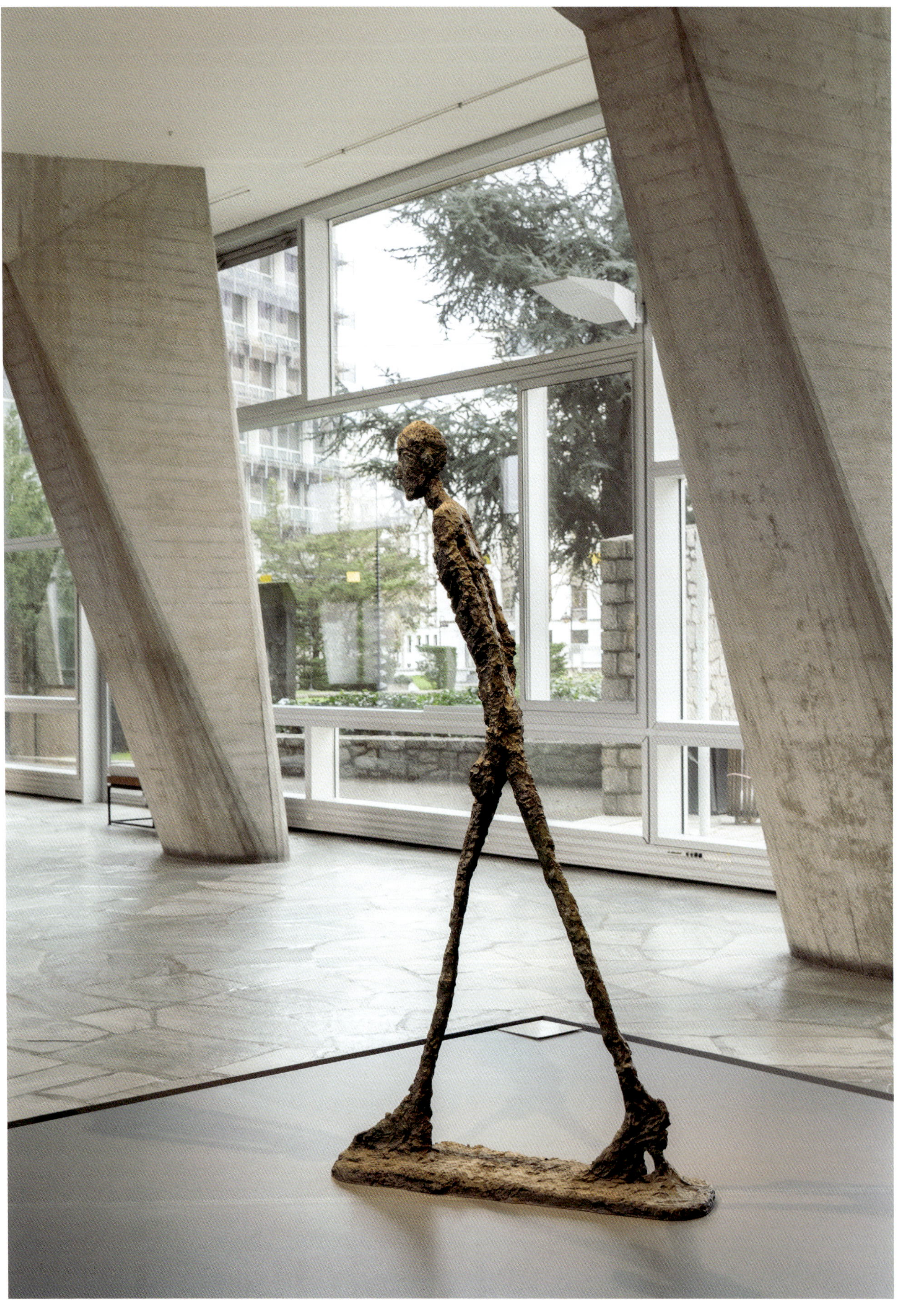

A CONTROVERSIAL STATUS

However, it was not all plain sailing. At the United Nations, Monaco's candidature raised questions to do with the participation of "very small States"—what they could actually bring to the table in terms of financial resources and capabilities, and just how independent they really were. From a legal perspective, the Franco-Monegasque Treaty of 1918 meanwhile raised the issue of the international status of the Principality and the potential limits of its sovereignty. France found itself walking a diplomatic tightrope on the interpretation of the Treaty—an ambivalence that is evident in the reports drafted by French diplomats following Monaco's candidature. While recognizing that the Principality met the admission requirements and putting no legal obstacles in its way, France expressed reservations in principle, likely because Monaco submitted its candidature directly to UNESCO, bypassing French diplomatic channels. Hence the surprise evinced in a letter from Direction Europe at the Princely Government's "attempt to give global clout to nationalist Monegasque tendencies." Concerns were raised that certain members of the National Council of Monaco (the parliament of the Principality) might view UNESCO membership as an opportunity to loosen the bonds with the Princely Government, itself tied to France. Despite the apparent good relations between the two countries, a number of confidential notes testify to the suspicions of the French: "It is therefore essential to curtail the international influence of a territory inhabited by 1,800 people [. . .] Monaco's admission to UNESCO is useless and dangerous [. . .] it is towards America that Monegasque eyes are turned to regain an independence directed against France." On balance however and after giving the matter careful thought, French diplomacy was more inclined to support Monaco's candidature provided the Principality toe the line of its big sister on all major issues. The priority for France was to ensure Monaco's alignment with the "Latin clan"—in which respect, the experts working within the French Ministry of Foreign Affairs took some comfort in the person of Prince Pierre himself, an ardent advocate of UNESCO admission but no less rooted in the classical culture of the Mediterranean. France's fears were also allayed by a draft resolution submitted by the USA and Canada. The American delegation declared its support for Monaco's candidacy, stating that it saw no problem in admitting a State that was not wholly independent. The difficulty, for the Americans, lay not so much in Monaco's sovereignty as in its size

DOSSIER
PRINCE PIERRE
A UNESCO LEADING LIGHT
PAGES 58-65

Walking Man I (1960), bronze sculpture by Alberto Giacometti (1901-1966), UNESCO Art Collection. The architects incorporated the visual arts into their project and the choice of artists was emblematic of the international culture of the time.

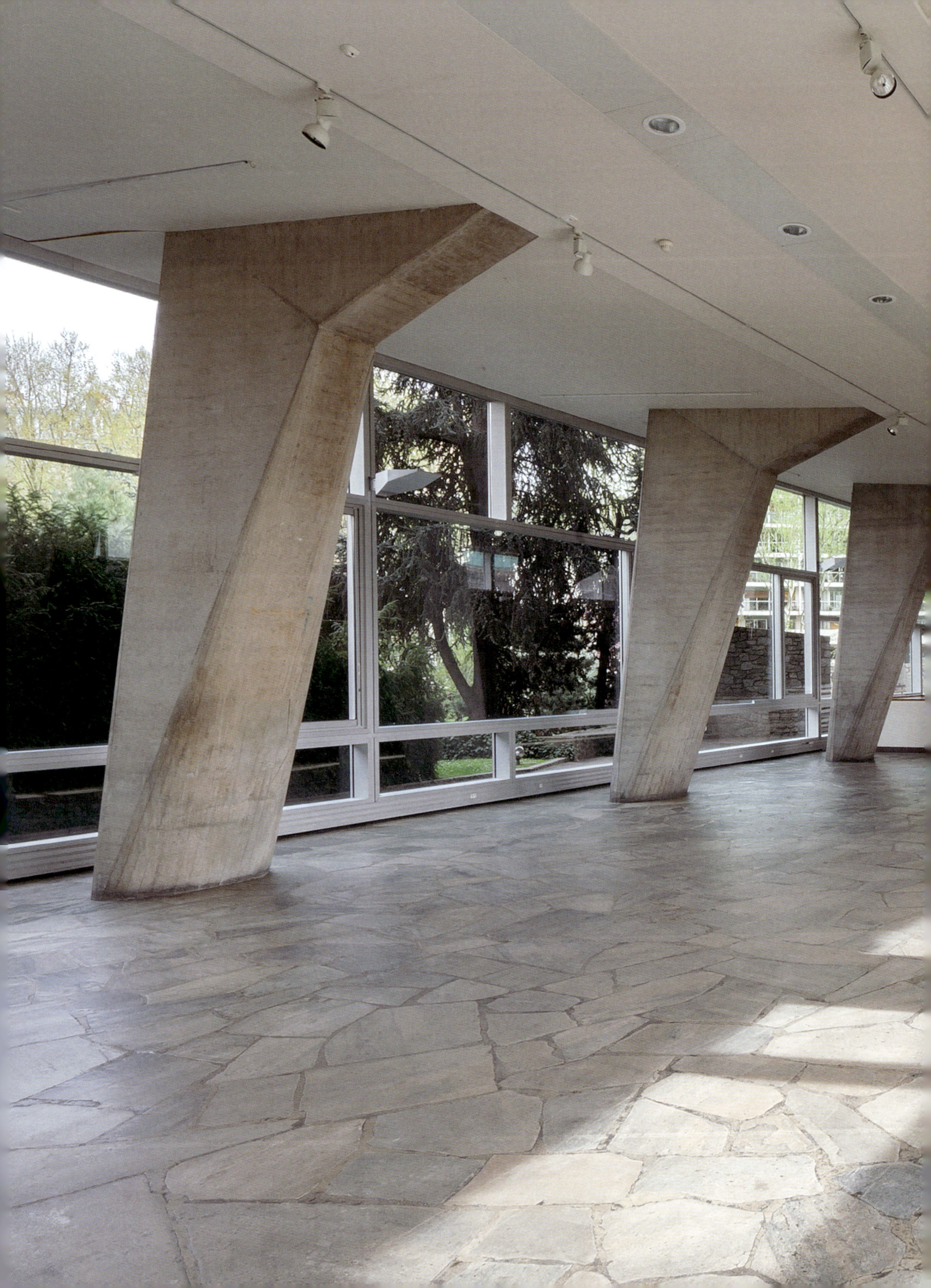

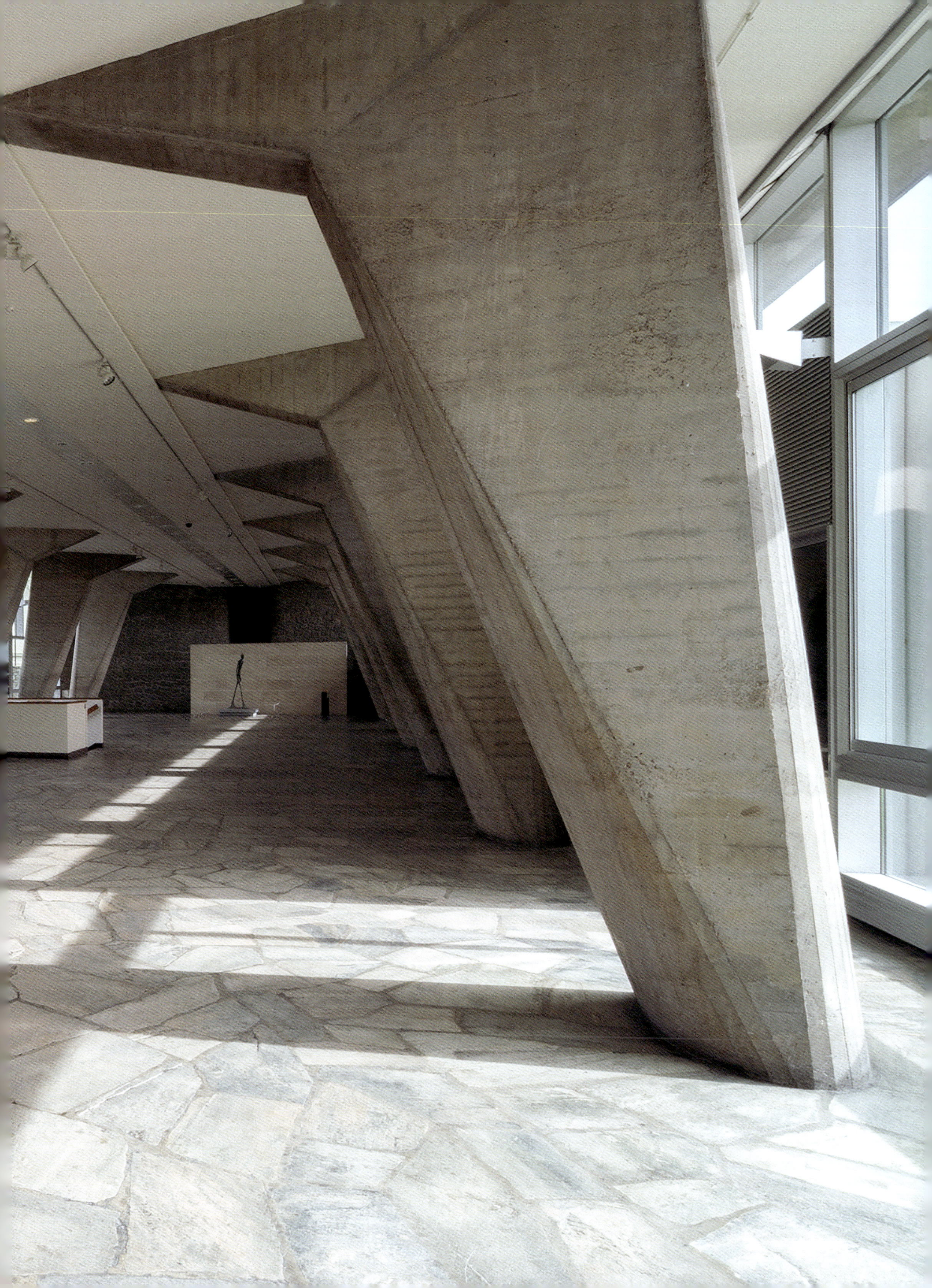

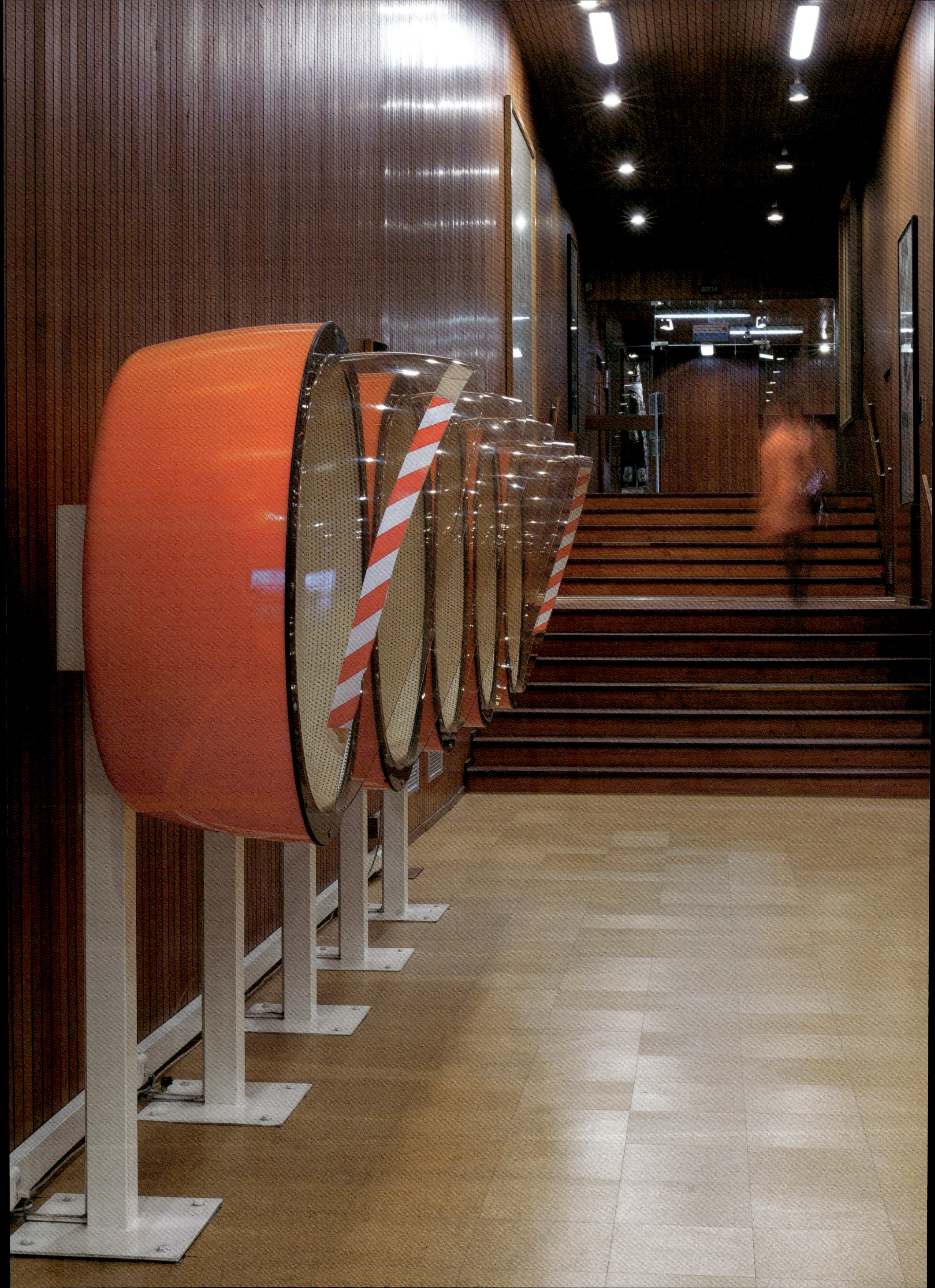

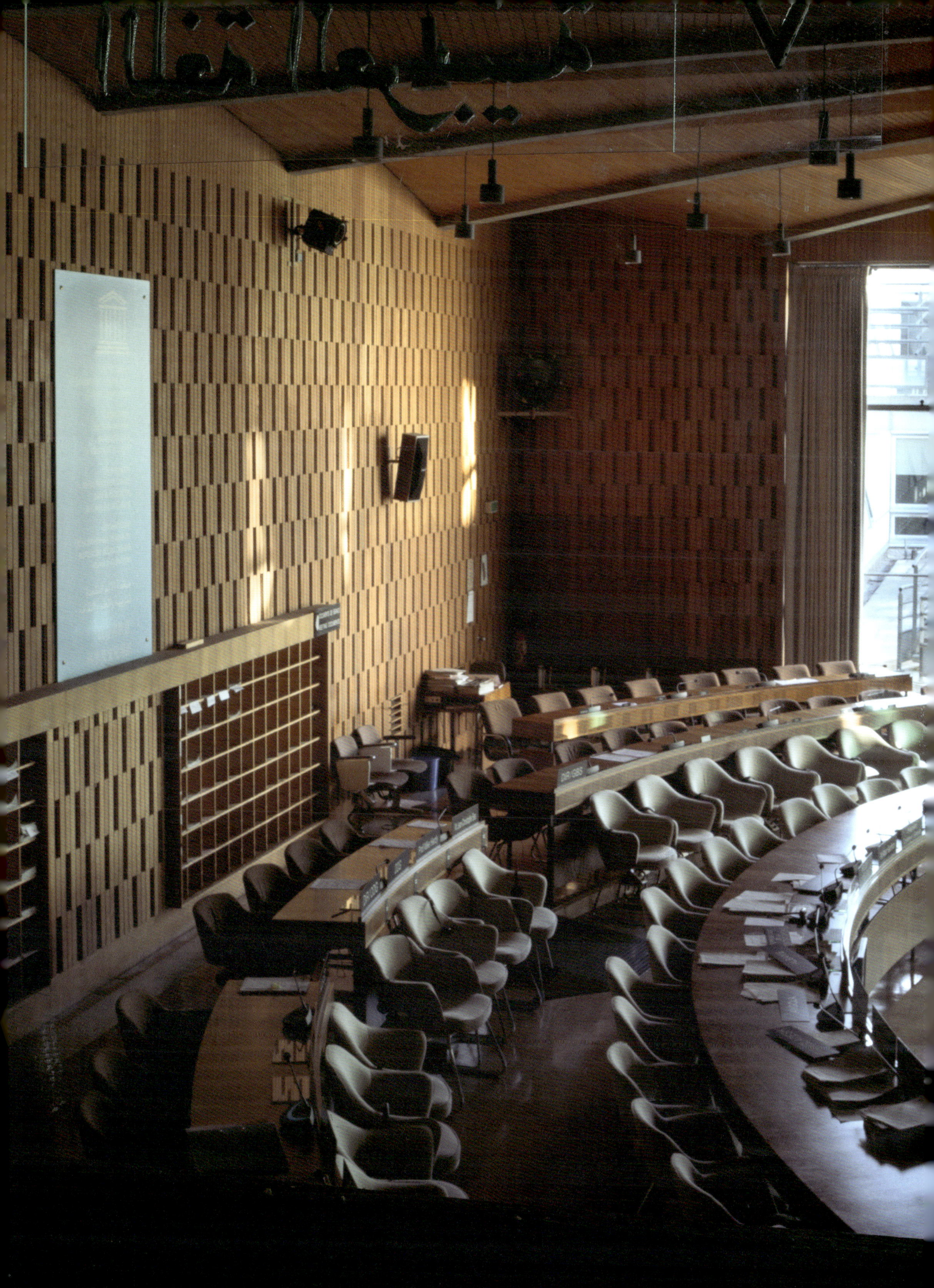

and the admission of "diminutive states" in general, never mind their capabilities and potential contribution. This was France's cue to stop dithering—there could be no question of allowing the USA to assume the role of protector; it was time to demonstrate that Monaco's sovereignty was indeed a reality.

Much discussion and an Executive Summary later, a favorable conclusion was reached: "This treaty establishes close ties between the Principality of Monaco and the French Republic, but it shall not be considered as infringing upon the independence and sovereignty of the former. The Principality enjoys, at international level, the right to conclude treaties with other powers worldwide, the right to fly its flag and the passive and active right of legation. In practice, it fully exercises these rights [. . .] The Principality of Monaco may therefore be characterized as a small independent State that has tied itself to a more powerful neighbor with regard to the exercise of certain powers that do not infringe upon its status as a sovereign State." And with that, the matter was settled by UNESCO to the satisfaction of even the most hesitant and wary of its members.

TOWARD MEMBERSHIP

Agreement having been reached, the next stage in the process required the Executive Board to communicate its recommendations to the United Nations Economic and Social Council, which confirmed the Board's proposal and recommendations and released a favorable opinion in its report of February 5, 1948: "The Economic and Social Council decides to inform the United Nations Educational, Scientific and Cultural Organization that is has no objection to the admission of Monaco to the Organization; recommends that the Organization, in considering the request of Monaco, take into account what contribution Monaco can make in furthering the programme of the Organization." The second General Conference of UNESCO in Mexico City had ended two months earlier, but there was still time to submit the dossier for consideration at the third General Conference, to be held in Beirut from November 17 to December 11, 1948, with delegates from thirty-seven member states in attendance. One of the conference objectives would be to find the right balance between cultural diversity and the need for a common language, hence the decision to hold the proceedings in the cultural melting pot that was Lebanon. Representing the Principality in Beirut in the role of observer was Fernand d'Aillières, secretary of the Monaco Legation, under the auspices of Maurice Lozé, Minister Plenipotentiary to the

PREVIOUS PAGES The building's interior is a manifesto of modern architectural theories, for example the lobby of the secretariat building, which is punctuated by variable-geometry columns that combine poetry and rigor, facilitating circulation and the distribution of departments and light.

Republic of France. D'Aillières played a crucial role, partly as a vocal advocate for Monaco's candidacy in his address to the conference, but also by announcing the vote in its favor. It was on this occasion that the General Conference elected UNESCO's new Director General, James Torres Bodet (1902-1974), Mexico's former Minister of Education and Minister of Foreign Affairs, who took over from Julian Huxley. On December 13, 1948, it was Torres Bodet himself who sent a telegram to Monaco's Minister of State informing him of the vote in favor of the Principality's admission: "Have the honor to inform Your Excellency that third session of the UNESCO General Conference has admitted Principality of Monaco as member of our Organization STOP. Expressing my congratulations to Your Excellency on this occasion, I am confident that the Principality of Monaco will make an effective contribution to the program of our Organization."

DOSSIER
MONACO AT UNESCO 1946-1959
FROM THE SORBONNE TO THE PLACE DE FONTENOY
PAGES 76-81

On July 6, 1949, a few months after the crucial Beirut conference, Monaco officially became the forty-sixth member of UNESCO. The Convention was signed by Maurice Lozé in London, having been approved beforehand by Prince Rainier III. It was a major achievement for this future "Builder Prince" who took power on May 9, 1949, upon the death of his grandfather, and was enthroned on November 19 that same year. On September 6 meanwhile, a draft ordinance was submitted to the sovereign by Monaco's new Minister of State Jacques Rueff (1896-1978), who had taken over from Pierre de Witasse on July 12.

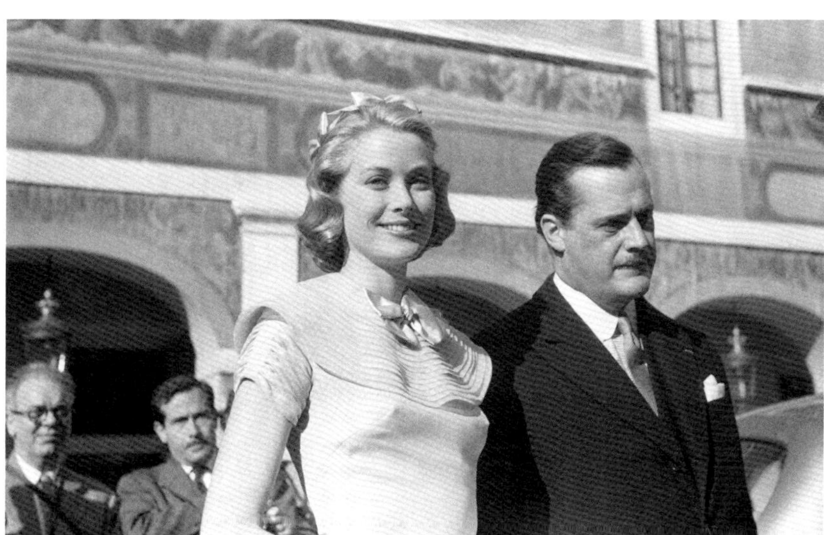

Princess Grace and Fernand d'Aillières, in April 1956, at the royal wedding.
Fernand d'Aillières was Prince Rainier's chamberlain at the time (from 1953).

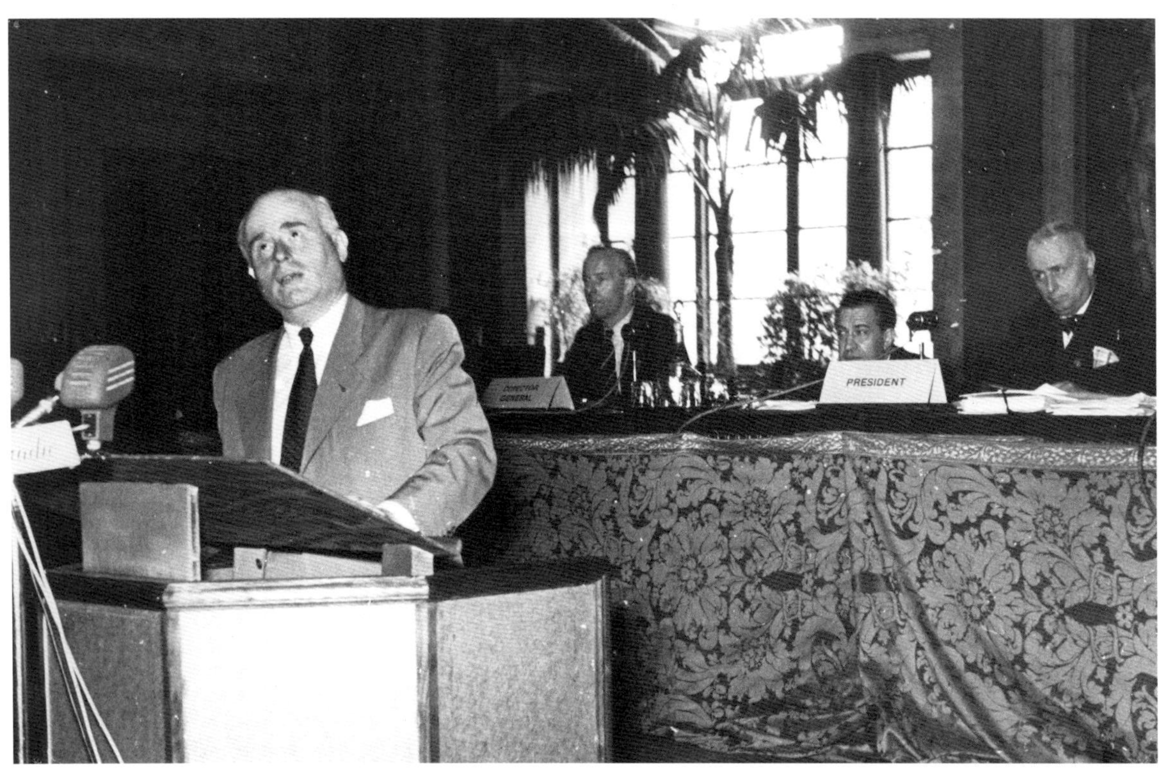
PRESIDENT

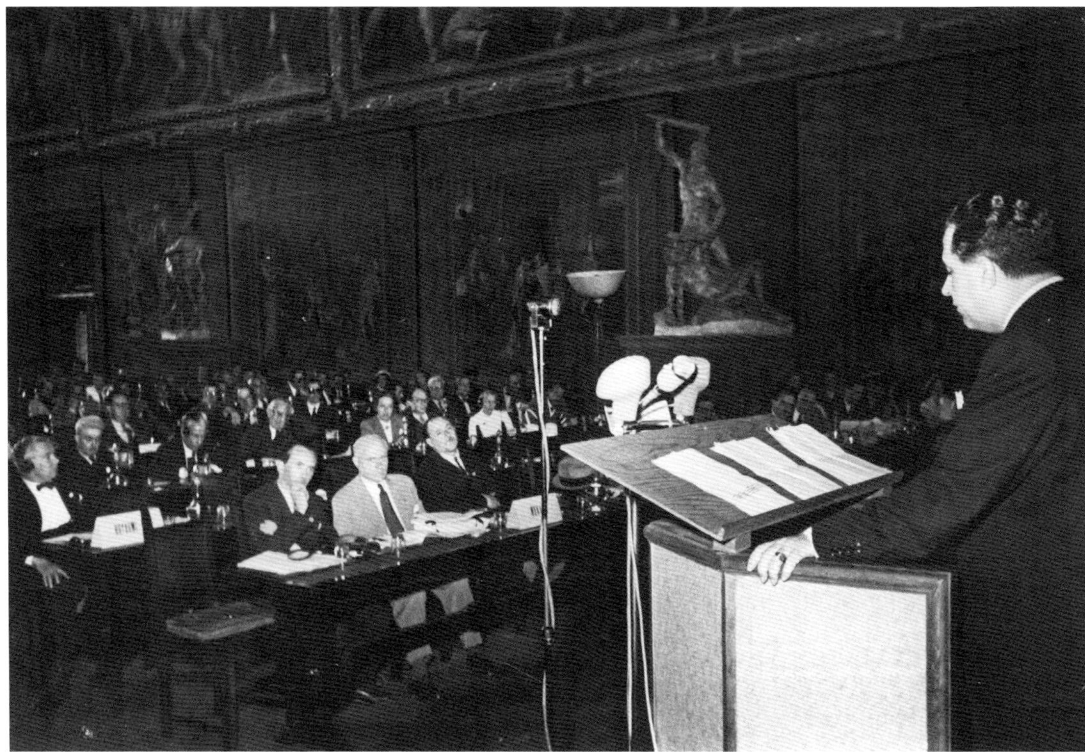

A prominent politician and intellectual, Rueff was a member of the Institut de France, a world-class economist and a leading specialist in financial cooperation. His appointment would prove crucial to the success of Monaco's early years at UNESCO.

In the end, this meeting of the minds and preparatory work produced positive and relatively quick results. The next step was to establish administrative foundations at the national level to reinforce Monaco's admission over the long term. For this, Monaco followed the provisions adopted by France three years earlier at the time of its own UNESCO admission on May 17, 1946, pursuant to the law of May 17, 1946, authorizing the President of the Provisional Government of the French Republic (PGFR) to ratify the convention. This justified Monaco in drafting a sovereign ordinance, issued on September 14, 1949, bringing into force the international convention, signed on November 16, 1945, establishing the United Nations Educational, Scientific and Cultural Organization.

DOSSIER
JACQUES RUEFF AND UNESCO
PAGES 66-69

FULL AND EFFECTIVE MEMBERSHIP

Monaco now had to be given the means to participate fully in the activities of the Organization. There were two available levers. One (recurrent) was through Official State Representation: the Principality sent delegations to the annual sessions of the UNESCO General Conferences. Members were hand-picked by Prince Rainier himself. At the first session following Monaco's admission (UNESCO General Conference fourth session), which took place in Paris in November 1949, the delegation head was Monaco Minister of State Jacques Rueff. Accompanying him were Louis Auréglia, and Fernand d'Aillières who was familiar with the workings of the Organization having played an active part in the previous session leading to Monaco's admission. In February 1950 it was once again Jacques Rueff who headed the delegation to the Florence Conference, the fifth UNESCO General Conference where the quality of Rueff's address captured the attention of the attendees. With him were Louis Auréglia, the newly-appointed President of the National Council, and Paul Noghès, Government Counsellor of the Interior, who were recalled to Monaco before the end of the session and replaced by René Bocca, also present at the conference. In 1951 the Head of Delegation was Prince Pierre (1895-1964), whose Parisian cultural connections contributed behind the scenes to Monaco's UNESCO admission. Prince Pierre remained Head of Delegation until his death in 1964, except on

Jacques Rueff at the fifth UNESCO General Conference in Florence, early June 1950.

two occasions: the Montevideo Conference in 1954 and the Delhi Conference in 1956, both destinations being likely too remote from Monaco and the duties that required his presence.

The second lever was the National Commission for UNESCO: the body that ensures the permanent presence of UNESCO in a country. The National Commissions are part of the overall constitutional architecture of the Organization. They operate on a permanent basis to align the work of their governmental and non-governmental bodies in education, sciences, culture, and communication with the work of the Organization. Acting as consulting, liaison, and information agencies, the National Commissions work to advance UNESCO's objectives through the creation of partnerships with civil society that greatly facilitate the implementation of its programs. Hence the sovereign ordinance of October 16, 1950, establishing the Monegasque National Commission for UNESCO. The Presiding Officer was Minister of State, Pierre Voizard (who held office from 1950-1953), with Louis Auréglia and Paul Noghès as joint vice-presidents. The other members were appointed for a term of three years, in accordance with Article VII of the UNESCO Constitution. Foremost political figures and representatives from the worlds of science and culture, they included oceanographer and naval officer Jules Rouch, who accompanied Prince Albert I on his scientific campaigns; French writer Marcel Pagnol, Director of the Oceanographic Museum and a friend of Prince Rainier; and French writer and philosophy teacher Armand Lunel, winner of the Prix Renaudot Literary Award in 1926. On September 11, 1951, Prince Pierre was appointed President of the National Commission, a position he retained throughout his lifetime, thus serving as both President of the National Commission and Head of Delegation at the UNESCO General Conferences. Upon his death in 1964, UNESCO paid him a moving tribute at its thirteenth General Conference.

DOSSIER
THE BEGINNINGS
OF THE MONEGASQUE NATIONAL COMMISSION FOR UNESCO
PAGES 70-75

OPPOSITE PAGE Paris, UNESCO House, October 22, 1959. Private visit of H.S.H. Prince Rainier III of Monaco, accompanied by H.S.H. Princess Grace, to UNESCO Director-General, Vittorino Veronese.

FOLLOWING PAGES Country signs in the Delegates Lounge, here Monaco.

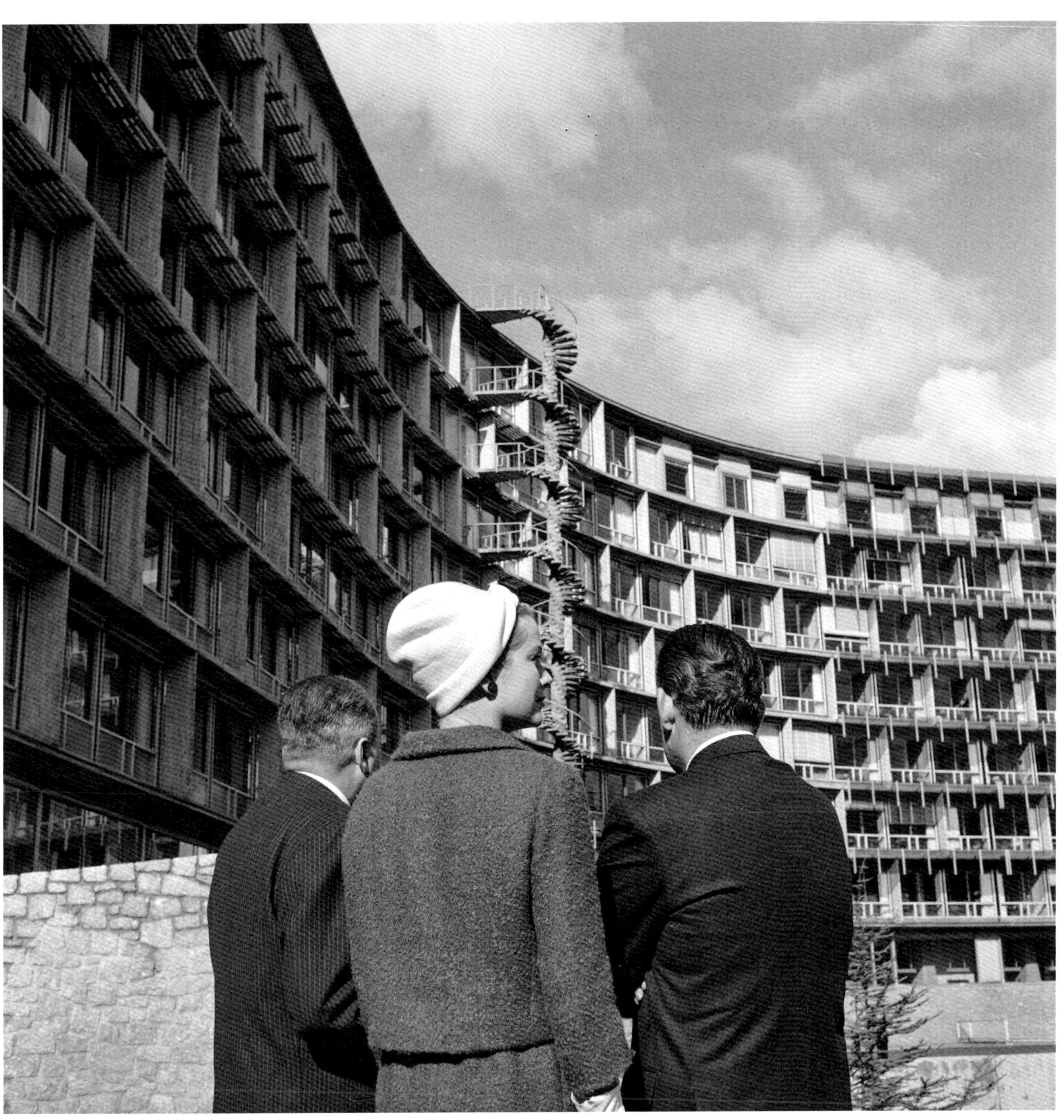

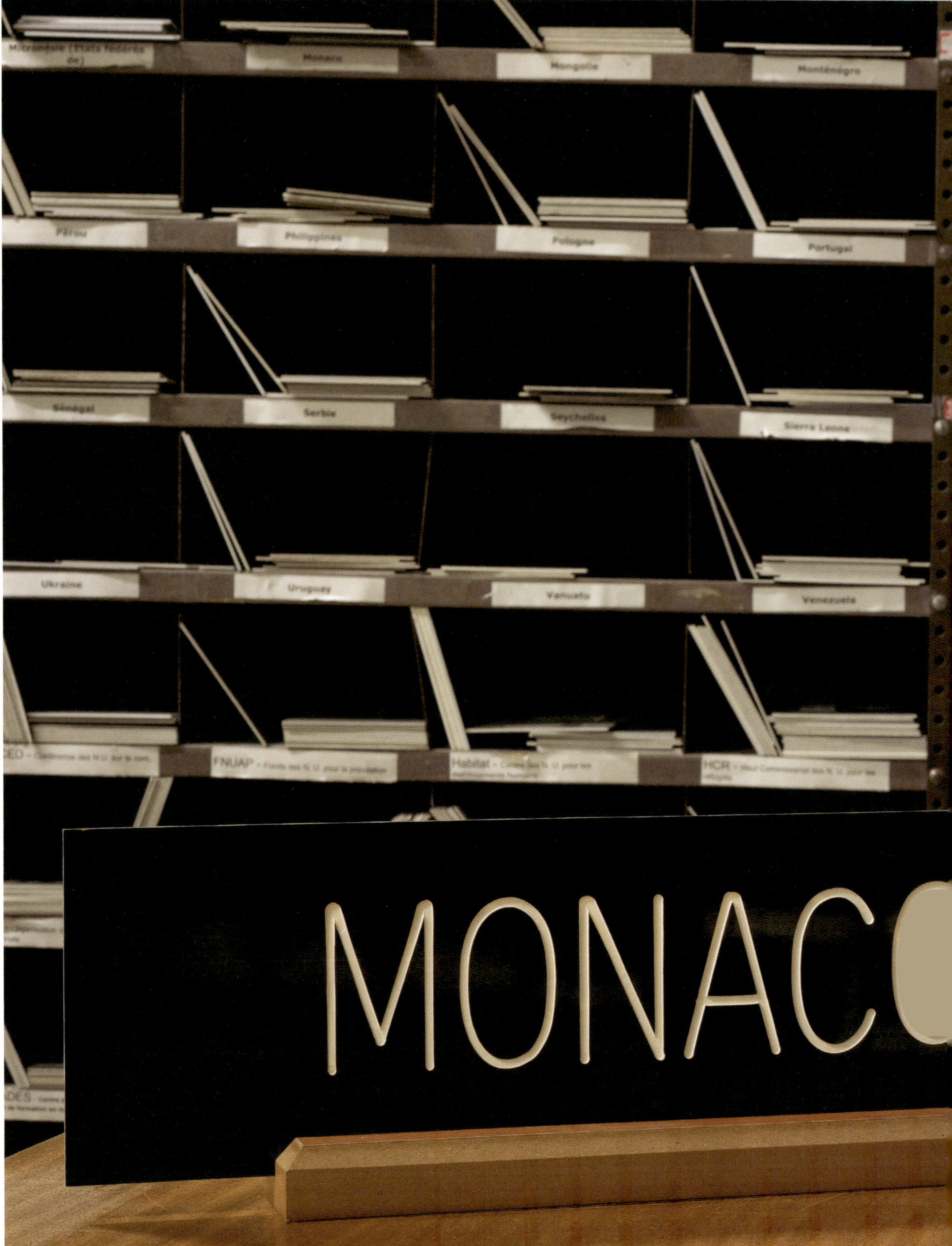
Monaco
Mongolie
Monténégro
Pérou
Philippines
Pologne
Portugal
Sénégal
Serbie
Seychelles
Sierra Leone
Ukraine
Uruguay
Vanuatu
Venezuela
FNUAP
Habitat
HCR
MONAC

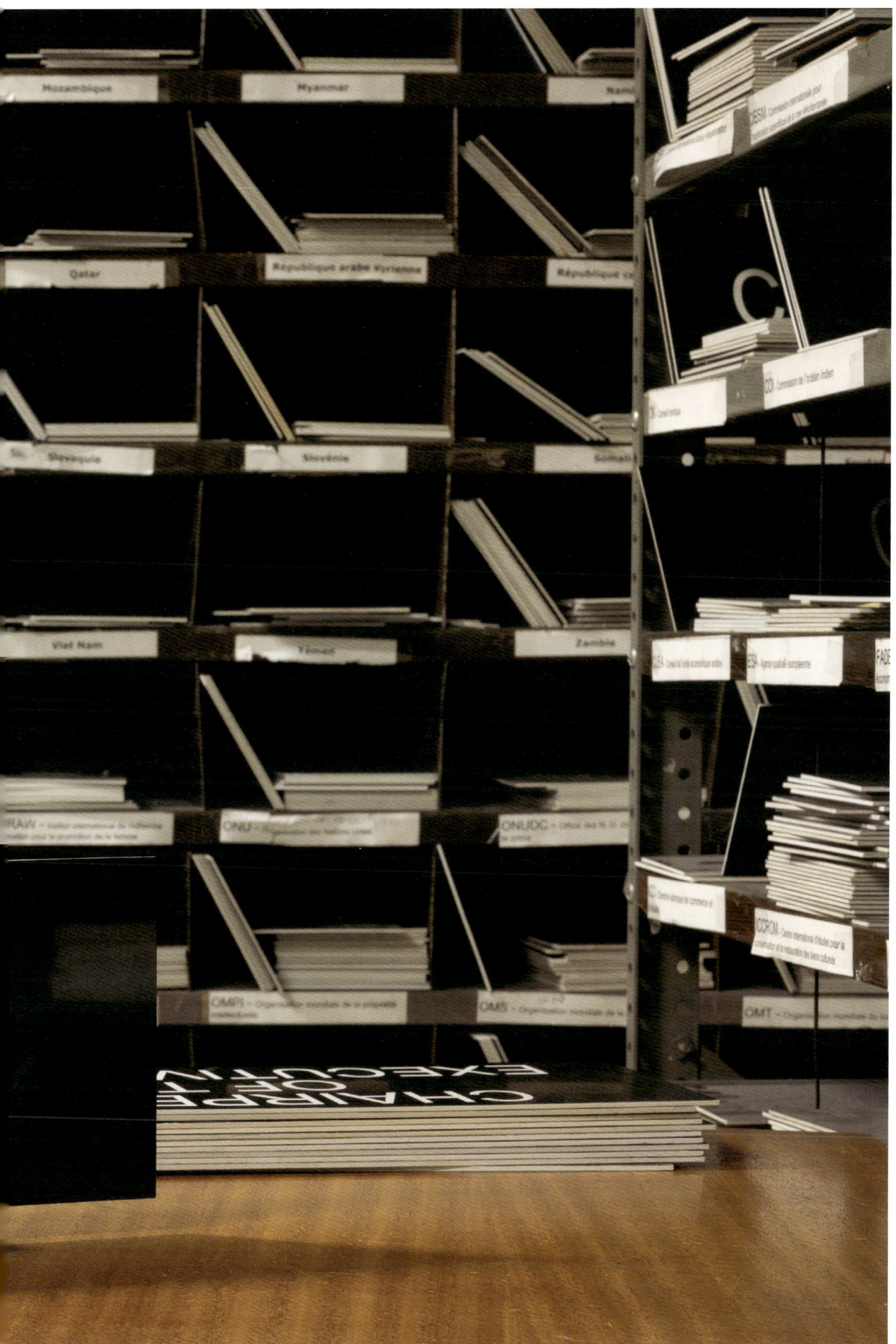
Mozambique
Myanmar
Qatar
République arabe syrienne
Slovaquie
Slovénie
Viet Nam
Yémen
Zambie
ONU
ONUDC
OMPI
OMS
OMT
COI - Commission de l'océan indien
ESA - Agence spatiale européenne

DOSSIER

DOCUMENTS RECORDING 1946-1951 MONACO'S ADMISSION TO UNESCO

Monaco' admission to UNESCO is richly documented, with a wealth of data now stored in various archival repositories, among them the Archives du Palais Princier, Service de la documentation administrative, in Monaco, and the UNESCO Archives in Paris. They consist of correspondence between the two parties (representatives of the Principality and UNESCO), of reports relating to Monaco's candidature, and of official documents endorsing its membership, which are presented here in chronological order detailing each stage of the candidacy process. The archival corpus echoes the events and people featured in the opening pages of this chapter.

PRINCIPAUTÉ DE MONACO

CONSEIL ÉCONOMIQUE

Le Président

Monaco, le 30 Janvier 1947

N° 200

Monsieur A. MELIN

Ministre Plénipotentiaire

de la Principauté de

MONACO

Monsieur le Ministre,

De passage à Paris, pour cause de maladie, j'ai pu obtenir grâce à l'intervention bienveillante de Monsieur le Ministre d'Etat et Monsieur le Ministre Plénipotentiaire de LOZE, qu'un monégasque Monsieur René BOCCA, agrégatif de philosophie, assiste, à un titre quelconque, à la première conférence internationale que l'U.N.E.S.C.O. a tenue à son siège social à Paris, en Novembre dernier.

J'ai l'honneur, par la présente, de vous transmettre, ci-inclus, le rapport rédigé par le seul représentant des monégasques disponible, à Paris.

Veuillez croire, Excellence, à l'expression de ma très haute considération.

Le Président,

[signature]

PRINCIPAUTÉ DE MONACO — CONSEIL ÉCONOMIQUE

L'U.N.E.S.C.O. – Ses Buts ; ses résultats ; perspectives Monégasques d'avenir

—

I – Historique et Buts –

Londres, Novembre 1945

C'est en Novembre 1945 que fut rédigée à Londres par les représentants des Nations Unies la Convention de l'UNESCO [United Nations Educational Scientific and Cultural Organisation : Organisation des Nations Unies pour l'Education la Science et la Culture.] Il fut alors décidé par les Etats Signataires que la Science tout autant que l'Education et la Culture devrait relever de cette Organisation et que l'UNESCO devrait porter un intérêt tout spécial aux « organes d'information des masses » dont les principaux sont la radio, la presse, le cinéma, ainsi qu'à la nécessité de favoriser la connaissance et la compréhension mutuelle des nations

Les Buts

Les deux buts primordiaux assignés à l'UNESCO sont de contribuer « au maintien de la paix et de la sécurité et d'aider à atteindre graduellement à la prospérité commune de l'humanité grâce à l'Education à la Science et à la Culture. En outre on insiste dans le Préambule sur la nécessité de mettre fin à l'incompréhension mutuelle entre les peuples, de combattre les fausses doctrines de l'inégalité des races et des hommes et d'encourager les principes démocratiques de dignité d'égalité et de respect de la personne

OPPOSITE PAGE Letter dated January 30, 1947, reporting on René Bocca's presence as an observer at the first UNESCO General Conference (Paris, November-December 1946).

ABOVE Extract from the preparatory report by René Bocca, then a philosophy student in Paris (undated, most likely January 1947).

Note verbale

EDAC 1-1

NOTE RELATIVE A L'ADHESION DE LA PRINCIPAUTE

DE MONACO A L'U. N. E. S. C. O.

La Principauté de Monaco n'est pas membre de l'Organisation des Nations Unies (O. N. U.), mais elle est membre de diverses organisations internationales avec lesquelles l'Organisation des Nations Unies pour l'Education, la Science et la Culture (U. N. E. S. C. O.) sera nécessairement amenée à collaborer. Le Gouvernement Princier est notamment membre de l'Organisation Internationale de Radiodiffusion (O. I. R.) et de l'Union Internationale pour la protection de la propriété littéraire et artistique.

Malgré l'exiguité de son territoire et la faiblesse numérique de sa population, l'apport de la Principauté dans les domaines scientifique et culturel est appréciable : Institut Océanographique et Musée, Institut de la Paléontologie humaine et Musée d'Anthropologie, Institut de la Paix. Le Bureau Hydrographique International siège à Monaco, de nombreuses conférences internationales y ont tenu leurs assises dans le passé et le prochain mois d'Avril se tiendront le Congrès du Bureau Hydrographique International et la Conférence de l'Organisation Internationale de Radiodiffusion.

Le poste d'émission de Radio Monte-Carlo complète l'outillage de la Principauté et lui permettrait de participer d'une façon effective au réseau mondial de Radiophonie de l'U. N. E. S. C. O.

Ces diverses considérations conduisent le Gouvernement Princier à envisager de solliciter son admission à l'U. N. E. S. C. O.

Undated *note verbale*, issued shortly after René Bocca's report.

OAG

EDA C 1-1

LÉGATION DE MONACO

Paris, le 22 Juillet 1947

DIRECTION DES
RELATIONS EXTÉRIEURES
Reçu le 25/7/47
N° d'Ordre 1643

p.j. 1

Monsieur le Ministre,

J'ai l'honneur de faire savoir à Votre Excellence que je me suis rendu hier, 2I Juillet, à l'Hôtel Majestic au rendez-vous que M. Blonay m'avait donné.

Le Directeur des Affaires Extérieures m'a mené chez M. Jean Thomas, Directeur Général Adjoint à qui j'ai remis la lettre,ci-jointe en copie,par laquelle je faisais part du désir de la Principauté d'être admise parmi les Membres de l'Organisation des Nations Unies pour l'Education, la Science et la Culture.

M. Thomas a accueilli cette demande de la façon la plus aimable et a aussitôt télégraphié à New-York pour en aviser les Services intéressés.

J'ai eu l'occasion dans l'après-midi de rencontrer M. JOXE, Directeur général, chargé des relations culturelles, au Ministère des Affaires Etrangères, que j'ai mis au courant de la démarche que j'avais effectuée.

Veuillez agréer, Monsieur le Ministre, l'assurance de ma haute considération.

M. Lozé

Son Excellence
Monsieur P. de WITASSE
Ministre d'Etat
MONACO

Letter dated July 22, 1947, from Maurice Lozé to Pierre de Witasse, Minister of State, reporting on his dealings with Mr. Blonay, Director of External Affairs, and Jean Thomas, Deputy Director-General of UNESCO.

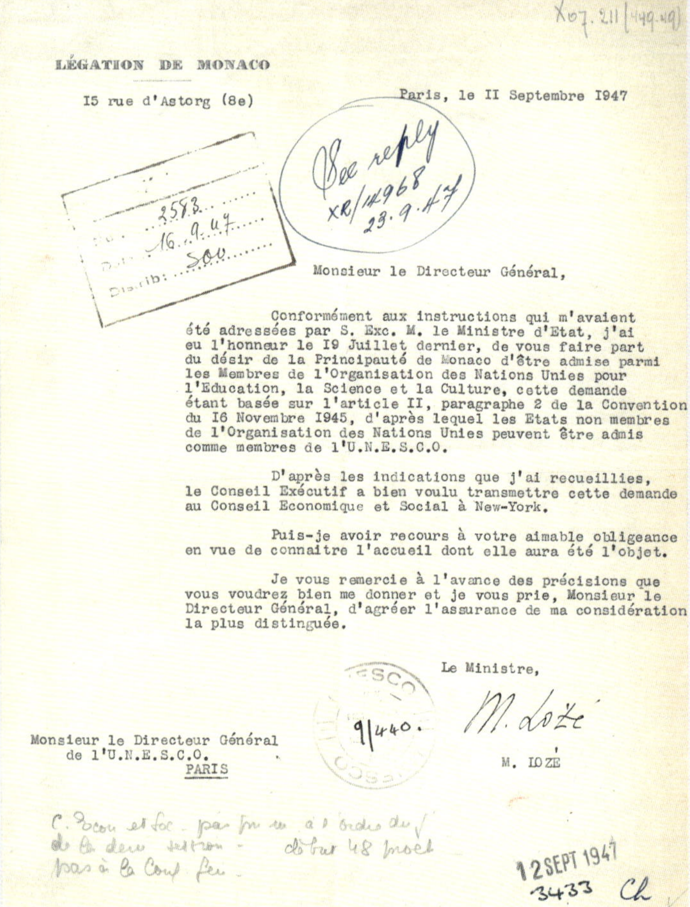

LÉGATION DE MONACO

I5 rue d'Astorg (8e)

Paris, le II Septembre 1947

Monsieur le Directeur Général,

Conformément aux instructions qui m'avaient été adressées par S. Exc. M. le Ministre d'Etat, j'ai eu l'honneur le I9 Juillet dernier, de vous faire part du désir de la Principauté de Monaco d'être admise parmi les Membres de l'Organisation des Nations Unies pour l'Education, la Science et la Culture, cette demande étant basée sur l'article II, paragraphe 2 de la Convention du I6 Novembre 1945, d'après lequel les Etats non membres de l'Organisation des Nations Unies peuvent être admis comme membres de l'U.N.E.S.C.O.

D'après les indications que j'ai recueillies, le Conseil Exécutif a bien voulu transmettre cette demande au Conseil Economique et Social à New-York.

Puis-je avoir recours à votre aimable obligeance en vue de connaitre l'accueil dont elle aura été l'objet.

Je vous remercie à l'avance des précisions que vous voudrez bien me donner et je vous prie, Monsieur le Directeur Général, d'agréer l'assurance de ma considération la plus distinguée.

Le Ministre,

M. Lozé

M. LOZÉ

Monsieur le Directeur Général
de l'U.N.E.S.C.O.
PARIS

XR/14968 — 23 SEPT 1947

Monsieur le Ministre,

J'ai l'honneur d'accuser réception et de vous remercier de votre lettre du 11 septembre 1947.

Le Conseil exécutif de l'Organisation des Nations Unies pour l'Education, la Science et la Culture a en effet transmis votre demande au Conseil Economique et Social, à New York, mais ce dernier n'a pu mettre à l'ordre du jour de sa dernière session la question de l'admission de la Principauté de Monaco parmi les membres de l'Unesco. Cette question a été reportée à la prochaine session du Conseil Economique et Social, qui se tiendra au début de l'année 1948 et, de ce fait, ne pourra être soumise à la Conférence générale de l'Unesco, en novembre prochain.

Je vous prie d'agréer, Monsieur le Ministre, les assurances de ma haute considération.

Julian Huxley,
Directeur général.

E.Monsieur M. Lozé,
inistre de Monaco,
égation de Monaco,
, rue d'Astorg,
aris VIII°

/th

Monaco's candidacy submitted by Maurice Lozé, Minister Plenipotentiary of the Principality of Monaco (1945-1956), and the response from Julian Huxley, first Director-General of UNESCO.

3C/7
PARIS, 17 septembre 1948

ORGANISATION DES NATIONS UNIES
POUR L'EDUCATION, LA SCIENCE ET LA CULTURE

CONFERENCE GENERALE
Troisième Session

Point 7 de l'ordre du jour provisoire

RECOMMANDATIONS DU CONSEIL EXECUTIF CONCERNANT
L'ADMISSION DE NOUVEAUX MEMBRES

Par lettre en date du 19 juillet 1947, le Ministre de la Principauté de Monaco accrédité près le Gouvernement de la République française, agissant sur instructions du Ministre d'Etat de Monaco, a fait connaître au Directeur général que la Principauté de Monaco sollicitait son admission parmi les Membres de l'Organisation des Nations Unies pour l'Education, la Science et la Culture.

Cette requête ayant été soumise au Conseil exécutif lors de sa troisième session, le Conseil a chargé le Directeur général de la transmettre au Conseil économique et social, conformément aux dispositions de l'Article II de l'Accord conclu entre les Nations Unies et l'Unesco.

Après avoir examiné cette requête au cours de sa sixième session, le Conseil économique et social a adopté le 5 février 1948 la résolution suivante :

"Le Conseil économique et social

Après avoir examiné la demande d'admission de la Principauté de Monaco à l'Organisation des Nations Unies pour l'Education, la Science et la Culture, demande communiquée par cette Organisation au Conseil, conformément à l'Article II de l'Accord conclu entre elle et l'Organisation des Nations Unies,

Décide de porter à la connaissance de l'Organisation des Nations Unies pour l'Education, la Science et la Culture qu'il ne fait pas d'objection à l'admission de la Principauté de Monaco comme Membre de l'Organisation ;

Recommande à l'Organisation de tenir compte, en examinant la demande de la Principauté de Monaco, de l'importance de la contribution que la Principauté est susceptible d'apporter à l'exécution du Programme de l'Organisation et,

Preparatory note from UNESCO to study the accession of the Principality, during the third General Conference in Beirut, 1948.

Discours prononcé par M. Fernand d'AILLIERES
Observateur de MONACO
à l'Assemblée Générale de BEYROUTH, lors de l'admission
de la Principauté.

-:-:-

Monsieur le Président,

Mesdames,

Messieurs,

Au nom de mon Gouvernement, j'ai l'honneur de remercier la IIIème Conférence Générale de l'U.N.E.S.C.O. d'avoir bien voulu favoriser l'admission de mon Pays au sein de cette Organisation.

La Principauté de Monaco qui a toujours été à l'avant-garde des réalisations modernes, avait posé sa candidature à l'U.N.E.S.C.O. car elle sentait qu'il y avait là un groupe puissant de pays et d'hommes décidés à tout faire pour améliorer les relations scientifiques, éducatives et culturelles entre les peuples de la terre, et MONACO avait tenu à être à leurs côtés dans cet effort qui a pour but d'atteindre une plus grande compréhension des hommes et des choses - pour leur plus grand bien commun - mais surtout pour celui de la paix du Monde.

C'est avec une réelle joie que je vais pouvoir aviser mon Gouvernement de la décision que vous venez de prendre et lui rendre compte, en même temps, de l'accueil

Speech given by Fernand d'Aillières, Secretary of the Monaco Legation, Monaco's observer at the General Assembly in Beirut, December 6, 1948, on the occasion of the Principality's accession.

II

si chaleureux et si parfaitement organisé qui a été réservé à cette IIIème Conférence Générale de l'U.N.E.S.C.O. par le Gouvernement Libanais et auquel je tiens ici, avec mes remerciements personnels, à rendre hommage.

Je rendrai compte aussi des résultats si fructueux de vos travaux et je suis certain de pouvoir vous dire que la Principauté de MONACO se réjouit d'avance de pouvoir collaborer dorénavant à vos côtés et par tous les moyens en son pouvoir, à votre grande oeuvre de paix et de lumière ...

-:-:-:-:-:-

Le premier nombre qui figure dans les télégrammes après le nom du lieu d'origine est un numéro d'ordre, le second indique le nombre de mots taxés, les autres désignent la date et l'heure du dépôt.

Dans le service intérieur et dans les relations avec certains pays étrangers, l'heure de dépôt est indiquée au moyen des chiffres de 0 à 24.

Voir au dos la signification des principales indications qui peuvent, éventuellement, figurer en tête de l'adresse.

Indications de service.

MONACO-VILLE PRINCIPAUTÉ 14-12 1948

L'État n'est soumis à aucune responsabilité à raison du service de la correspondance privée par la voie télégraphique. (Loi du 29 Nov. 1850, art. 6.)

ORIGINE	NUMÉRO	NOMBRE DE MOTS	DATE	HEURE	MENTIONS DE SERVICE
Cairo	218	64	13	1010	Voie TSF

Ai l'honneur informer Votre Excellence que conférence générale UNESCO a dans sa troisième session admis principauté de Monaco comme membre de notre organisation stop. En exprimant à votre Excellence mes félicitations à cette occasion j'ai toute confiance que principauté Monaco apportera contribution efficace à l'œuvre de notre organisation

TORRES BODET

Directeur général

N° 701 Pour tout renseignement concernant ce télégramme s'adresser au bureau distributeur

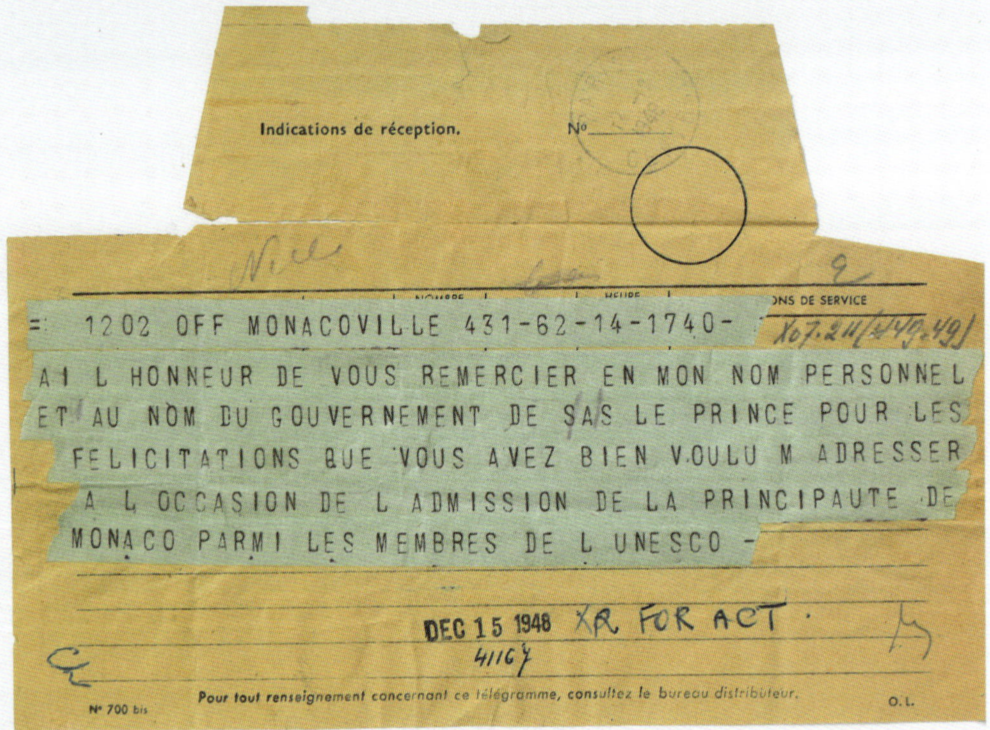

Indications de réception. N°

= 1202 OFF MONACOVILLE 431-62-14-1740-

AI L HONNEUR DE VOUS REMERCIER EN MON NOM PERSONNEL ET AU NOM DU GOUVERNEMENT DE SAS LE PRINCE POUR LES FELICITATIONS QUE VOUS AVEZ BIEN VOULU M ADRESSER A L OCCASION DE L ADMISSION DE LA PRINCIPAUTE DE MONACO PARMI LES MEMBRES DE L UNESCO -

DEC 15 1948 XR FOR ACT

41167

N° 700 bis Pour tout renseignement concernant ce télégramme, consultez le bureau distributeur. O.L.

ABOVE Telegram exchanges between UNESCO Director-General, Jaime Torres Bodet, and Minister of State of the Principality, Pierre de Witasse, following news of the acceptance of the candidacy at the Beirut conference in November-December 1948.

OPPOSITE PAGE AND FOLLOWING PAGE Sovereign order ratifying Monaco's accession to UNESCO, May 24, 1949.

Monaco 1471

Rainier III, par la Grâce de Dieu Prince Souverain de Monaco.

Une Convention créant une Organisation des Nations-Unies pour l'Education, la Science et la Culture en vue d'atteindre graduellement par la coopération des nations du monde dans les domaines de l'éducation, de la science et de la culture, les buts de paix internationale et de prospérité commune de l'humanité en vue desquels l'Organisation des Nations-Unies a été constituée, ayant été signée à Londres le 16 Novembre 1945 par les Représentants dûment autorisés des Etats-Unis d'Amérique du Nord, de la République Argentine, de l'Australie, de la Belgique, de la Bolivie, du Brésil, du Canada, du Chili, de la Chine, de la Colombie, de Cuba, du Danemark, de la République Dominicaine, de l'Equateur, de l'Egypte, du Salvador, de la France, du Royaume-Uni de Grande-Bretagne et de l'Irlande du Nord, de la Grèce, du Guatémala, de Haïti, de l'Inde, de l'Irak, de l'Iran, du Liban, du Libéria, du Luxembourg, du Mexique, du Nicaragua, de la Norvège, de la Nouvelle-Zélande, du Panama, des Pays-Bas, du Pérou, des Philippines, de la Pologne, de l'Arabie Séoudite, de l'Union Sud-Africaine, de la Syrie, de la Tchécoslovaquie, de la Turquie, de l'Uruguay, du Vénézuela, de la Yougoslavie;

Considérant l'article 15 paragraphe 1 de ladite Convention;

Nous déclarons par les Présentes, accepter ladite Convention engageant Notre Parole de Prince et promettant pour Nous et pour Nos successeurs de l'observer et de l'exécuter fidèlement et loyalement.

EN FOI DE QUOI, Nous avons signé cette acceptation de Notre propre Main et y avons fait apposer Notre Sceau.

Donné en Notre Palais à Monaco, le vingt-quatre Mai de l'an mil neuf cent quarante-neuf et de Notre Règne le premier.

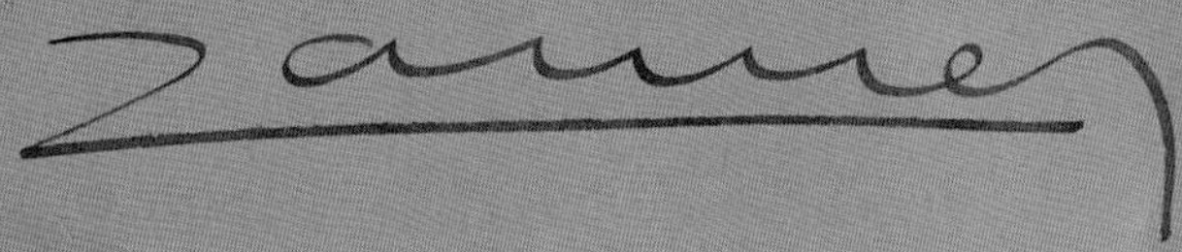

EDAC 1-1

PRINCIPAUTÉ DE MONACO

MONACO LE 14 JUIL 1949

MINISTÈRE D'ÉTAT

RELATIONS EXTÉRIEURES

Nº OAG

prière de rappeler ce numéro

Admission de Monaco à l'UNESCO

P. J.

CABINET DE S. A. S. LE PRINCE DE MONACO 14 JUIL 1949 Nº 4

Vu par S.A.S. le Prince le 18/7/49 Le Chef de Cabinet

Rapport

Le Ministre d'Etat, Directeur du Service des Relations Extérieures, a l'honneur de faire connaître au Cabinet de S.A.S. le Prince que S. Exc. M. Lozé a signé à Londres, le 6 Juillet 1949 à midi, la Convention créant une organisation des Nations Unies pour l'Education, la Science et la Culture et qu'il a remis en même temps l'acceptation de S.A.S. le Prince à la dite Convention.

P. le Ministre d'Etat,
Le Conseiller de Gouvernement,

CABINET DE S.A.S. LE PRINCE

ABOVE Report from the Ministry of State, dated July 14, 1949, to the Princely Cabinet, confirming the signing of the UNESCO Convention in London on July 6, 1949.

DOSSIER

PRINCE PIERRE, A UNESCO LEADING LIGHT

Prince Pierre de Polignac (1895-1964) was without question the prime mover behind Monaco's admission to UNESCO, not least through his enduring commitment to the arts and literature. In 1923, the Prince founded a Society of Conferences in Monaco, with French poet, essayist and philosopher Paul Valéry as one of its first speakers in 1924. The following year Valéry became a member of the Committee on International Intellectual Cooperation, a consultative body of the League of Nations considered a predecessor of UNESCO. The Prince, for his part, was a natural advocate for UNESCO from its earliest hours, partly through his friendship with Jacques Rueff but also as a statesman held in high regard by state authorities worldwide. The Prince was among the first to head Monaco's delegation to UNESCO, and to assume the Presidency of the Monegasque National Commission for UNESCO (1957). In 1951, he spearheaded the creation of the Literary Prize: a highly esteemed award conferred to one outstanding francophone writer every year, beginning with Julien Greene, followed by Henri Troyat and Jean Giono. The prize was a further demonstration of the Prince's personal commitment to culture—one of the three core pillars of UNESCO. In 1964, at the thirteenth session of the General Conference, the Organization rightly paid tribute to the Prince who died as the conference was taking place. In 1966, Prince Rainier III founded the Prince Pierre Foundation in homage to the memory of his father, a great patron of the arts and letters with a passion for literature, music and "all the manifestations of human intelligence."

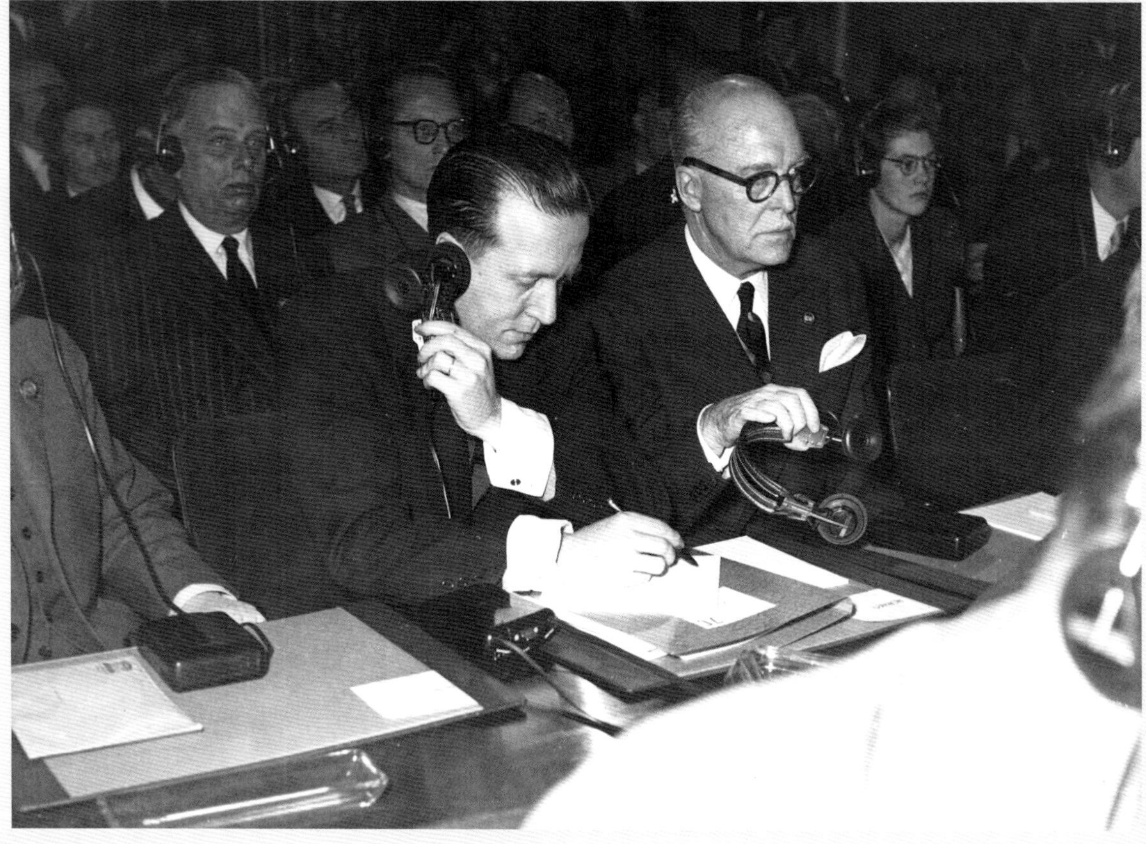

César Solamito and Prince Pierre in Paris in 1952 for the seventh UNESCO General Conference.

om.

X07.717/449.49

OCT 3 1951

XR/GC/264.908

Cher Monsieur,

Je vous remercie bien vivement de votre lettre du 25 septembre 1951 par laquelle vous avez bien voulu me communiquer les derniers changements survenus dans la Commission nationale monégasque.

Bonne note a été prise de la modification de la Constitution de votre Commission nationale et de la nomination de Son Altesse Sérénissime le Prince Pierre de Monaco à la Présidence de la Commission, et je n'ai pas manqué de transmettre ces informations au Service intéressé pour publication de ces informations dans un prochain numéro du Bulletin Officiel.

Veuillez agréer, cher Monsieur, l'expression de mes sentiments très distingués.

Lorna McPhee,
Division des Relations avec les Gouvernements
et les Commissions nationales.

Monsieur Robert Marchisio,
Secrétaire général
de la Commission nationale de l'Unesco,
Ministère d'Etat,
MONACO
(Principauté de Monaco)

PHS/4651

MINISTÈRE D'ÉTAT

COMMISSION NATIONALE
POUR L'ÉDUCATION, LA SCIENCE
ET LA CULTURE

COMMISSION NATIONALE POUR L'UNESCO

PRINCIPAUTÉ DE MONACO

MONACO, LE 19 mai 1961

Monsieur Vittorino VERONESE
Directeur général
U.N.E.S.C.O.
Place de Fontenoy
PARIS - VIIe

Monsieur le Directeur général,

j'aurais souhaité vous parler lors de notre visite Place Fontenoy, de la création à Monaco d'un "Centre International d'Etude des Problèmes Humains" dont la Présidence d'honneur m'a été confiée par le Prince, mon Fils.

Ainsi que la presse vous en a peut-être apporté l'écho, une réunion de Conseil d'administration vient de se tenir à Paris et d'aboutir à l'organisation d'un premier colloque international qui aura lieu du 25 au 30 mai à Monaco, sous le titre "Entretiens de Monaco en Sciences Humaines".

Ne doutant pas de l'intérêt que doit susciter pour notre chère U.N.E.S.C.O. une telle entreprise, je n'ai pas voulu manquer de vous confirmer cette nouvelle.

Les entretiens de cette année n'auront sans doute qu'un caractère exploratoire. Je vous tiendrai au courant de leurs développements et des projets du nouveau Centre.

Je suis toujours, Monsieur le Directeur général, avec les meilleurs souhaits pour vous et tous les vôtres,

votre dévoué

Pierre de Monaco

25 MAI 1961

111027 *23.MAI61 BMS

LEFT Letter from Lorna McPhee, Acting Head of External Relations at UNESCO.

RIGHT Letter from Prince Pierre dated May 19, 1961 to Vittorino Veronese, Director-General, concerning the creation of an International Center for the Study of Human Problems.

S.A.S. PRINCE RAINIER DE MONACO – PRINCIPAUTE DE MONACO 10 NOVEMBRE 1964
C/O Légation de Monaco – 2, rue du Conseiller Collignon – Paris 16e

ORD APPRENDS AVEC PROFONDE EMOTION DECES S.A.S. LE PRINCE PIERRE QUI A ETE SI ETROITEMENT ASSOCIE A L'OEUVRE DE L'UNESCO EN QUALITE DE PRESIDENT DE LA COMMISSION NATIONALE MONEGASQUE ET DE CHEF DE LA DELEGATION DE MONACO A DE NOMBREUSES SESSIONS DE LA CONFERENCE GENERALE stop en lui L'ORGANISATION PERD UN AMI agissant et fidèle respecté et aimé STOP AU NOM DU SECRETARIAT ET EN MON NOM PERSONNEL Votre Altesse je PRIE ACCEPTER MES très sincères CONDOLEANCES

RENE MAHEU
DIRECTEUR GENERAL

12271

S.A.S. le Prince Rainier de Monaco,
Principauté de Monaco
C/O Légation de Monaco – 2, rue du Conseiller Collignon–Paris 16e

S.A.S. PRINCE RAINIER DE MONACO – PRINCIPAUTE DE MONACO 13 NOVEMBRE 1964
C/O Légation de Monaco – 2, rue du Conseiller Collignon
Paris 16e

ORD

AU NOM DE TOUTES LES DELEGATIONS A LA TREIZIEME SESSION DE LA CONFERENCE GENERALE ET EN MON NOM PROPRE VOUS PRIE D'ACCEPTER PROFONDES ET SINCERES CONDOLEANCES A L'OCCASION DE LA DISPARITION DE S.A.S. LE PRINCE PIERRE CHEF DE LA DELEGATION MONEGASQUE DONT L'OEUVRE EN FAVEUR DE L'UNESCO EST UNIVERSELLEMENT CONNUE –

N.M. SISSAKIAN
PRESIDENT CONFERENCE GENERALE ++++

12374

S.A.S. le Prince Rainier de Monaco,
Principauté de Monaco
c/o Légation de Monaco
2, rue du Conseiller Collignon
Paris 16e

ete 5519

TOP Telegram from René Maheu, Director-General of UNESCO from 1962 to 1974, to Prince Rainier III, on the day of Prince Pierre's death, November 10, 1964.

BOTTOM Telegram dated November 13, 1964 from Norair Sissakian, Soviet scientist of Armenian origin, president of the 21st UNESCO General Conference, to Prince Rainier, following Prince Pierre's death (November 10, 1964).

"...As the religious ceremony began in Monaco Cathedral, a requiem mass was celebrated in Paris at the parochial church of Saint-Honoré d'Eylau. In attendance were: Monsignor Ange Pedroni, the Permanent Observer of the Holy See, on behalf of the Apostolic Nuncio; His Excellency Monsieur Jacques Reymond, Minister Plenipotentiary, Chargé d'Affaires for Monaco to the Government of the French Republic, representing His Serene Highness the Sovereign Prince; General Renaud de Corta, Chief of the Military Staff of the President of the Republic, representing French President General de Gaulle; French Prime Minister Georges Pompidou; Maurice Couve de Murville, French Minister for Foreign Affairs; Her Serene Highness Princess Charlotte; Their Excellencies Messrs. Jacques Rueff, Pierre Voizard, Émile Pelletier, Arthur Crovetto, and Madame Pierre de Witasse. Mr. Pierre Coeyteaux represented UNESCO, with Mr. René Novella representing the National Commission for Education, Science, and Culture ..."

Journal de Monaco, November 27, 1964. Funeral of Prince Pierre, Special Edition.

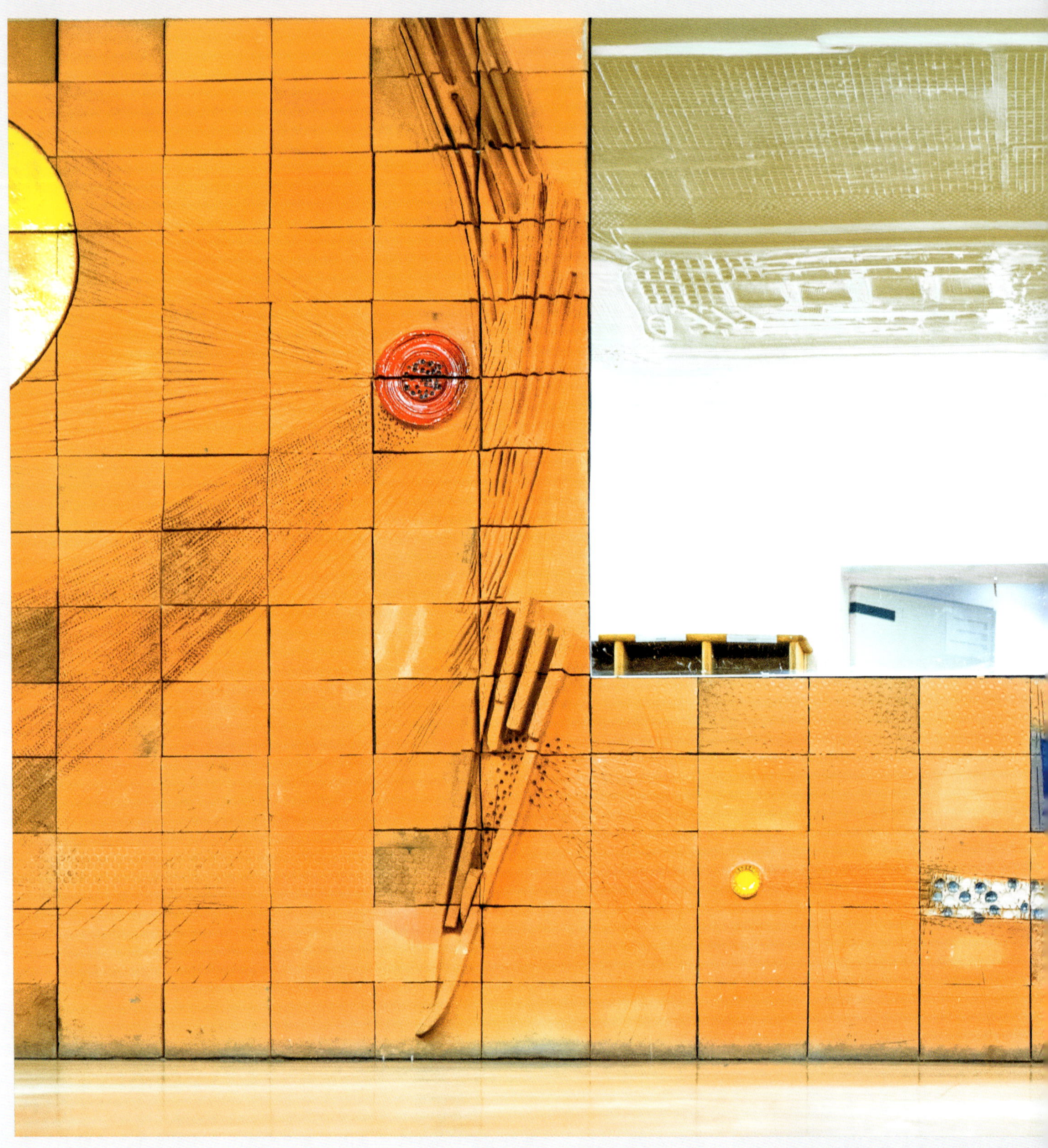

Untitled (1960), Albert Diato (1927-1985). Ceramic mural in sandstone and polychrome glaze. Work commissioned from Albert Diato by the Principality, on the initiative of Prince Pierre, to decorate the "Monaco Lounge", Delegates Lounge, at the UNESCO headquarters.

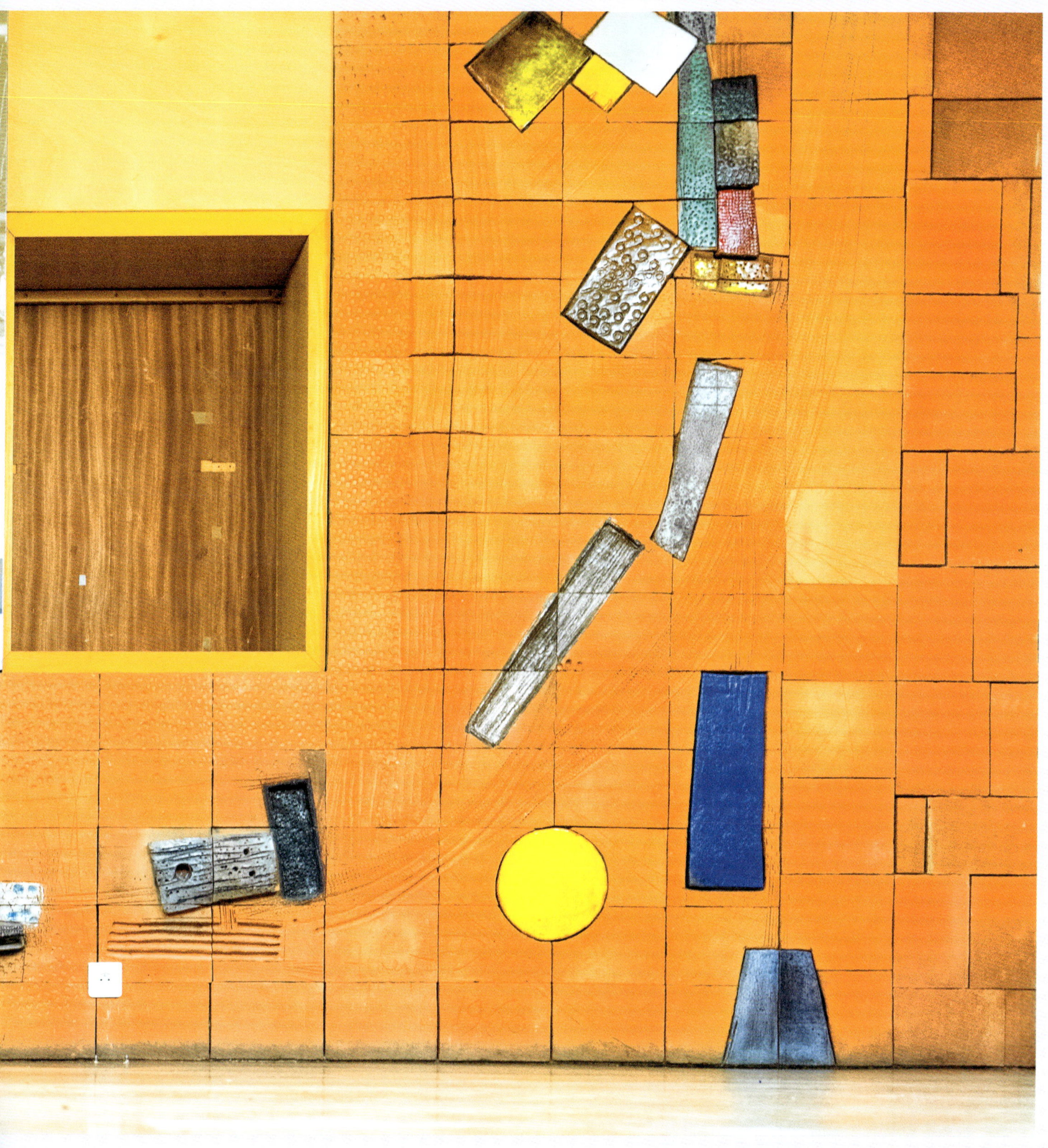

On the tenth anniversary of Monaco's admission to UNESCO on December 9, 1948, at the General Conference of Beirut, and of the adoption of the Universal Declaration of Human Rights, Prince Pierre received Télé Monte-Carlo journalist Mario Beunat at his Monegasque residence of the Villa Clos Saint Pierre. A look back on the Principality's presence within UNESCO, as the Organization took up new headquarters at the Place de Fontenoy in Paris.

"On July 6, 1949, our country became a member of UNESCO. In 1950, a National Commission for UNESCO was established, whose members have always been selected to ensure a harmonious representation of all areas of intellectual activity. Using every means at our disposal, we have striven from the outset to become ever more involved in the noble and generous programe of UNESCO, which primarily aims to generate public interest in international issues [. . .]

As Head of Monaco's delegation to UNESCO, I have taken part in all of its activities. While our country may not compete with the larger nations in other areas, its contribution to cultural heritage is, at the very least, significant. Monaco, located in the heart of the Mediterranean, has always made its presence felt.

'They say the Principality is small!' exclaimed Jean Giono a few years ago on receiving the *Prince Rainier III Literary Prize*. 'I don't think so. A small land maybe, but with big skies.' Perhaps the winds of spirit blow more freely here than elsewhere, but without ever diminishing our luster."

Turning now to the architecture and decoration of UNESCO's new building, "I felt the architects [. . .] came in for some very unfair criticism. People said the building compromised the aesthetic purity of the Ecole Militaire, when in fact the two face away from each other [. . .] Less defensible, to my mind [. . .] is the building on the Place de Fontenoy housing the Ministry of Posts and Telecommunications (PTT) [UNESCO] seems to me to fit perfectly into its allotted site. In terms of living space and gardens alike [. . .] the build does everything

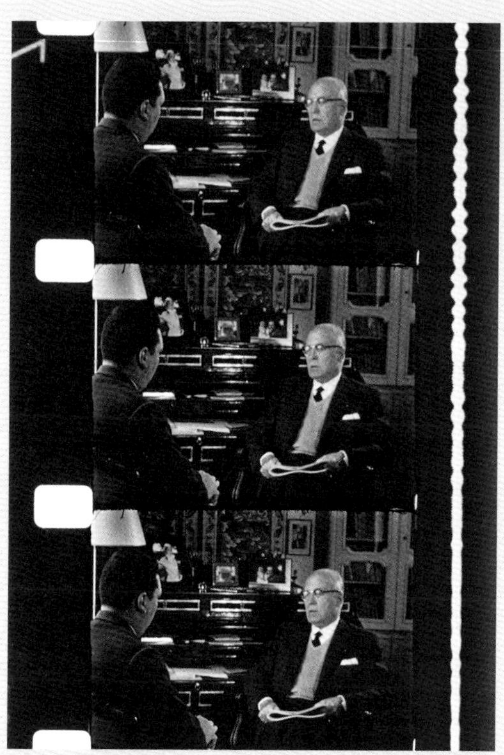

it's supposed to do. Spacious corridors for ease of movement; state-of-the-art media facilities, and rooms reserved for working groups decorated and furnished by the Member States. Monaco will no doubt soon have a little corner of its own to decorate. A great success all things considered—practical, pleasing, more a breath of the contemporary in this part of Paris than a disruptive element [. . .] The artists [. . .] commissioned to create decorative panels in a building with very few walls [. . .] are particularly to be commended, most notably Rufino Tamayo, Roberto Matta, and Afro [Basaldella], who created the lovely decorative panels in the restaurant, on the seventh floor, and on the ground floor. The statues in the garden have proved quite controversial, particularly Henry Moore's sculpture and Alexander Calder's unstable mobile."

Picasso's mural meanwhile, representing the triumph of good over evil, "is difficult to appreciate for want of a good viewing distance. Either you're standing too close, or your view is obstructed by a concrete staircase that tends to blur the distinction between good and evil [. . .] For me, an organization supposed to promote culture has a duty to exhibit artworks that do precisely that."

The Principality's first ten years at UNESCO, as seen by Prince Pierre in an interview with a TMC journalist.

Photograms from the 16 mm sound film (ref. 0000-350-CF5425, Audiovisual Institute of Monaco, TMC collection), broadcast on December 5, 1958 on Télé Monte-Carlo. Adaptation: Thomas Fouilleron and Vincent Vatrican. The first three photographs from the interview appeared on the Monaco page of *Nice-Matin*, on December 6, 1958.

DOSSIER

JACQUES RUEFF AND UNESCO

Jacques Rueff (1896–1978) was a graduate of the Ecole Polytechnique, a member of the Institut de France, an economist of international standing and a foremost specialist in financial cooperation. He would play a crucial role in Monaco's early years at UNESCO: his predecessor, Pierre de Witasse, had laid the ground for Monaco's admission; Jacques Rueff would be the architect of its inclusion. Appointed Minister of State by a sovereign ordinance of Prince Rainier III dated June 30, 1949, and enacted on July 12, just six days after the Principality's official admission to UNESCO, Rueff used his political clout to ease Monaco's passage into UNESCO. He began by drafting a sovereign ordinance of his own, submitted to the Prince and promulgated on September 14, 1949, officially enacting into Monegasque Law the provisions of the UNESCO Constitution signed in London on November 16, 1945. He accordingly served as Head of the Monaco delegation at the UNESCO General Conference, fourth session—the first in which the Principality officially participated—which opened in Paris on September 19, 1949. The address he gave on that occasion was warmly received, not least for the methodological approach taken by the speaker. An intellectual but also a pragmatist, Rueff believed that the fundamental principles of mutual understanding and peace between nations required solid government support to deliver results (Document 1). Before leaving Monaco to take up other functions, he took part in the UNESCO General Conference, fifth session, in Florence (documents 2 and 3) where he restressed the need to consolidate the institutions of an organization still in its infancy: "There is an abyss between the governance of an existing institution with its own traditions, following its own path, and the governance of an organization that has yet to forge a way through an unexplored forest. UNESCO reaches for the summits but, just as the mountaineer must use their ice ax to carve out a trail through the rock face, so UNESCO must chart its own course forward."

In line with his beliefs, Jacques Rueff was eager to make Monaco a center for cultural exchange. Reviving the tradition established by Prince Albert I, on his return from the General Conference in Paris, he organized a study session on the origins of fascism and Nazism (documents 4, 5 and 6). It was held in Monaco in November 1949, under the auspices of the International Council for Philosophy and Humanistic Studies (ICPHS), a non-governmental organization within UNESCO, established in Brussels that same year, with Rueff as its first Chairman (1949-1955). We should also mention his friendship with the then-young Prince Rainier's father, Pierre of Monaco, future President of the National Council of Monaco—a connection that undoubtedly helped to win recognition for the Principality as a valued member of the international community. Some years later, on March 8, 1960, in response to the inaugural appeal of UNESCO Director-General Vittorino Veronese to save the monuments of Nubia, Jacques Rueff accepted a nomination to the international action committee. Among his fellow members was Princess Grace of Monaco, who served on the honorary committee presided over by King Gustave VI of Sweden.

N°73

Rainier III, par la Grâce de Dieu

Prince Souverain de Monaco.

A V O N S O R D O N N E E T O R D O N N O N S :

Article premier.

S. Exc. M. Jacques RUEFF, Notre Ministre d'Etat, est nommé Président de la Délégation de Notre Principauté à la quatrième Session de la Conférence Générale de l'Organisation des Nations-Unies pour l'Education, la Science et la Culture qui s'ouvrira à Paris le I9 Septembre I949.

Article 2.

S. Exc. M. Maurice LOZE, Notre Envoyé Extraordinaire et Ministre Plénipotentiaire en France, et M. Louis AUREGLIA, Docteur en Droit, Lauréat de la Faculté de Droit de Paris, sont désignés en qualité de Délégués à la même Conférence.

Article 3.

M. César SOLAMITO, Ingénieur des Mines, licencié en Droit, est désigné en qualité de Délégué-Adjoint à la même Conférence.

Article 4.

M. Pierre NOTARI, Secrétaire de Légation, Chargé de Mission au Ministère d'Etat, et M. René BOCCA sont désignés respectivement en qualité de Secrétaire et de Secrétaire-Adjoint de Notre Délégation à ladite Conférence.

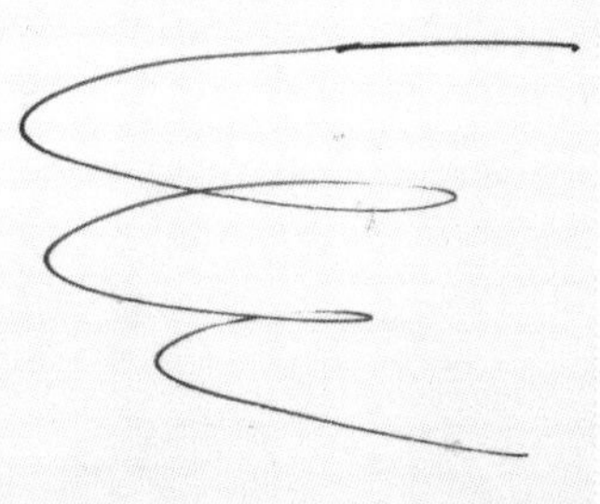

Sovereign order appointing Jacques Rueff chairman of the Monegasque delegation at the fourth UNESCO General Conference in September 1949.

Dans le cadre de l'U.N.E.S.C.O.

LA CONFÉRENCE D'ÉTUDE SUR LES ORIGINES DU FASCISME ET DU NAZISME

s'est ouverte, hier, à Monaco

M. Jacques RUEFF, ministre d'Etat, en a été nommé président

Des professeurs, des docteurs, des personnalités religieuses de tous les pays, se sont donne rendez-vous à Monaco afin de répondre à l'appel lancé par l'U.N.E.S.C.O. au Conseil International de la Philosophie et des Sciences humaines, pour étudier en commun des origines, des méthodes et des techniques du fascisme et du nazisme, d'en déterminer avec toute la précision possible les prodromes, des mouvements politiques et sociaux qui ont contribué à troubler si profondément le monde depuis une vingtaine d'années.

Cette conférence d'experts a été invitée dans la Principauté par M. Jacques Rueff, membre de l'Institut de France, ministre d'Etat de la Principauté et président du Comité International de la Philosophie et des Sciences humaines.

Hier à 15 h. 30, dans la salle du Conseil d'Etat située au palais du Gouvernement, le ministre d'Etat procéda à la séance inaugurale de ce congrès, qui va siéger durant quatre jours à Monaco et qui réunit de nombreuses personnalités internationales.

De même, quelques personnalités monégasques étaient invitées à cette séance : M. Pierre Blanchy, conseiller de Gouvernement pour les Travaux publics et Affaires diverses ; Me Louis Auréglia, délégué de la Principauté de Monaco à l'U.N.E.S.C.O ; M. Charles Palmaro, maire de Monaco ; M. J.-M. Notari, du secrétariat particulier du Prince ; M. Georges Blanchy, vice-président du Conseil national ; M. Gabriel Ollivier, commissaire général au Tourisme ; M. Marcel Michel, secrétaire général du ministère d'Etat ; Mgr Rivière, évêque de Monaco ; les journalistes de la presse parlée et écrite.

M. Rueff prit la parole pour souhaiter la bienvenue aux représentants des diverses puissances assistant à ce congrès. Il rappela l'importance de ces discussions et des travaux qui doivent en découler. Rappelant que malgré la date limite imposée au 31 décembre 1950 pour la clôture de ces travaux, il engageait l'assemblée à les poursuivre, même s'il fallait dépasser cette date, afin d'atteindre les buts proposés à cette assemblée. « Il faut terminer cette mission si importante pour l'avenir et l'évolution de la société humaine ». C'est par ces paroles que le ministre d'Etat a terminé son improvisation

Le professeur Sommerfelt, délégué de la Norvège, vice-président du Conseil International de la Philosophie et des Sciences humaines, au nom de ce Conseil, souhaita bonne chance et surtout réussite dans les travaux à ce Congrès. Il souligna également l'accueil reçu et les heureux auspices qui s'ouvraient devant cette assemblée.

Le professeur Klineberg (Etats-Unis), de la Columbia University de New-York, rappela les efforts déjà accomplis dans le monde afin de remonter aux origines du fascisme et du nazisme, et déclara associer ces travaux comme continuation et peut-être réussite de ceux déjà entrepris.

Le professeur K. Hoeg, Danois, proposa la personnalité de M. Jacques Rueff pour la présidence de ce Congrès. Un vote fut procédé à main levée et M. Jacques Rueff, à l'unanimité, a été élu président.

M. J. Rueff, malgré ses réticences à occuper ce poste, a été obligé de l'accepter.

L'assemblée a déterminé ensuite ses modes de travail.

Elle se réunira tous les jours dans les salons du Nouvel Hôtel de Paris, par commissions.

Le Congrès se terminera vendredi, par une séance plénière et publique où il sera donné un aperçu de l'état des travaux.

Au nom des hospitalisés

Le Syndicat de l'hôpital réclame le chauffage des salles

Se faisant l'interprète des hospitalisés de l'Hôpital de Monaco le Syndicat ouvrier réclame le chauffage des salles et chambres des malades. Le froid ayant soudainement fait son apparition, les hospitalisés en ont éprouvé les premières rigueurs. Plusieurs malades ont fait même appel à leur famille qui leur ont apporté un appareil de chauffage individuel.

Pour la santé et le bien-être de nos malades, un peu de chaleur s.v.p.

Convocations Syndicales

Bâtiment. — Vendredi 18 courant, à 18 h., réunion du bureau et des délégués à la Bourse du Travail. Très important.

Mécaniciens-dentistes. — Réunion de tous les mécaniciens-dentistes et assistantes dentaires demain jeudi, à 21 h., à la Bourse du Travail Prière d'apporter les bulletins de paye. Très important.

Métaux. — Demain jeudi, à 20 h. 30,

Report about the UNESCO conference for the study of the origins of fascism and national socialism, in Monaco, in *Le Patriote de Nice et du Sud-Est*, November 16, 1949.

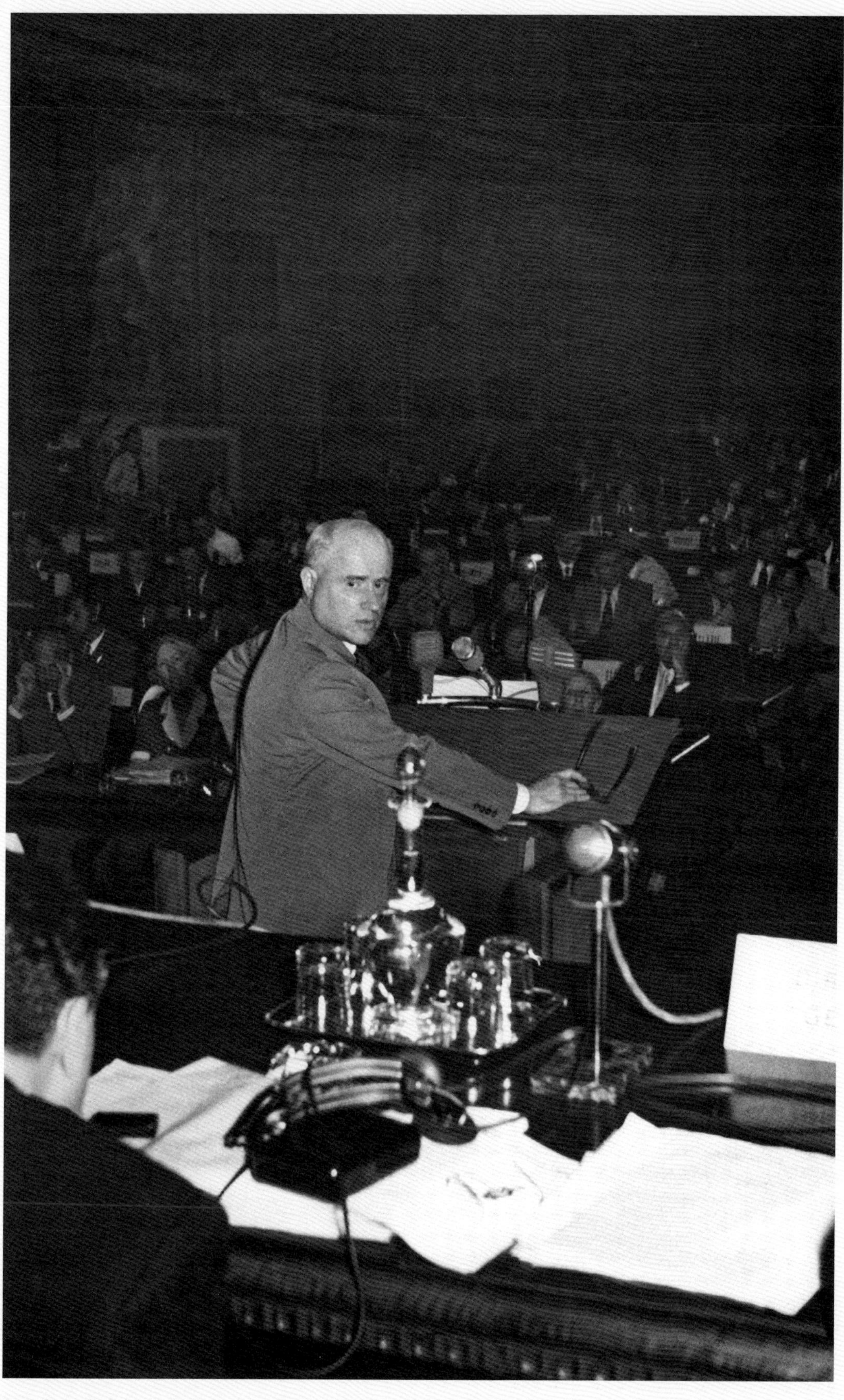

Jacques Rueff at the fifth UNESCO General Conference in Florence, June 1950.

DOSSIER

THE BEGINNINGS OF THE MONEGASQUE NATIONAL COMMISSION FOR UNESCO

The Monegasque National Commission for UNESCO was established by a sovereign ordinance of Prince Rainier III on October 16, 1950, in accordance with Article VII of the UNESCO Constitution. This states that commissions shall comprise representatives of their respective countries and contribute "in an effective way to make UNESCO's objectives better known, broaden its range of influence and promote the execution of its programme by involving the intellectual and scientific communities of their respective countries." All these conditions were met by the first Monegasque National Commission, which was composed of an even mix of French writers, administrators and senior officials, among them: Armand Lunel, writer, winner of the very first Prix Renaudot, and a philosophy teacher at the Lycée de Monaco; writer Marcel Pagnol, a close friend of Prince Rainier III and resident at the time in the Principality; René Bocca and other people instrumental in Monaco's accession to UNESCO; and political representatives such as Paul Noghès, Government Counsellor for the Interior, and Louis Auréglia, President of the National Council.

The first session of the Commission opened on April 19, 1951, with Minister of State, Pierre Voizard presiding. On September 11 that same year, Mr. Voizard stepped down in favor of Prince Pierre, who was not as is often assumed the Commission's first president but retained the position until his death in 1964, leaving his mark on the Organization and enhancing its reputation. His successors were Arthur Crovetto, René Novella, Roger Passeron, Anne Willings-Grinda and Mme Geneviève Vatrican (in office since 2012).

The work of the committee in those early years was essential to establish a framework for its long-term governance. Of particular note were the campaign to raise awareness of UNESCO principles via the *Courrier de l'Unesco* sent out to the various Monegasque entities; the organization of events such as *La semaine de l'Unesco* in 1958, featuring concerts and painting exhibitions commemorating the tenth anniversary of the Universal Declaration of Human Rights; and the creation of the *Club des amis de l'Unesco* (UNESCO club) in 1959.

624 JOURNAL DE MONACO Lundi 30 Octobre 1950

ART. 6.

Notre Secrétaire d'État, Notre Directeur des Services Judiciaires et Notre Ministre d'État sont chargés, chacun en ce qui le concerne, de la promulgation et de l'exécution de la présente Ordonnance.

Donné en Notre Palais à Monaco, le seize octobre mil neuf cent cinquante.

RAINIER.

Par le Prince :
Le Secrétaire d'État,
A. CROVETTO.

Ordonnance Souveraine n° 292 du 16 octobre 1950 portant nomination des Membres de la Commission Nationale de l'UNESCO.

RAINIER III,
PAR LA GRACE DE DIEU
PRINCE SOUVERAIN DE MONACO

Vu l'Ordonnance Souveraine n° 75 du 14 septembre 1949 rendant exécutoire la Convention Internationale signée le 16 novembre 1945 créant l'Organisation des Nations-Unies pour l'Éducation, la Science et la Culture;

Vu l'article 7 de la Convention susvisée qui recommande aux États-Membres de constituer une Commission Nationale où seront représentés le Gouvernement et les différents groupes qui s'intéressent aux problèmes d'éducation, de recherche scientifique et de culture;

Vu l'article 21 de l'Ordonnance Constitutionnelle du 5 janvier 1911 modifiée par l'Ordonnance Souveraine du 18 novembre 1917;

Vu Notre Ordonnance n° 292 du 16 octobre 1950 portant création d'une Commission Nationale de l'UNESCO;

Avons Ordonné et Ordonnons :

ARTICLE PREMIER.

Sont nommés pour trois ans Membres de la Commission Nationale de l'UNESCO :

MM. Aureglia Louis,
Barral Louis,
Barriera Constant,
Bergonzi Raymond,
Besnard Maurice,
Bocca René,
Boisson Robert,
Louys Edouard,
Lunel Armand,
Mlle Malard Suzanne,
MM. Marchisio Robert,
Médecin Auguste,
Amiral Nichols,
Noghès Paul,
Notari Pierre,
Ollivier Gabriel,
Pagnol Marcel,
Commandant Rouch,
Scotto Marc-César,
Solamito César,
Vellay Charles.

ART. 2.

M. Louis Aureglia, Président du Conseil National et M. Paul Noghès, Conseiller de Gouvernement pour l'Intérieur, sont nommés Vice-Présidents de la Commission susvisée.

ART. 3.

Notre Secrétaire d'État, Notre Directeur des Services Judiciaires et Notre Ministre d'État sont chargés, chacun en ce qui le concerne, de la promulgation et de l'exécution de la présente Ordonnance.

Donné en Notre Palais à Monaco, le seize octobre mil neuf cent cinquante.

RAINIER.

Par le Prince :
Le Secrétaire d'État,
A. CROVETTO.

Ordonnance Souveraine n° 293 du 16 octobre 1950 constituant le Statut des Fonctionnaires et agents de la Sûreté Publique.

RAINIER III,
PAR LA GRACE DE DIEU
PRINCE SOUVERAIN DE MONACO

Vu l'Ordonnance Souveraine n° 2514 du 10 juillet 1941 modifiée par les Ordonnances Souveraines nos 2674 et 2967 des 29 septembre 1942 et 26 janvier 1945;

Avons Ordonné et Ordonnons :

TITRE I.
DISPOSITIONS GÉNÉRALES

ARTICLE PREMIER.

Le présent Statut s'applique aux personnes qui, nommées dans un emploi permanent des cadres de la Sûreté Publique, tels qu'ils sont fixés par la Loi, ont été titularisées par Arrêté Ministériel.

Il ne s'applique pas :

1° au Directeur de la Sûreté Publique;
2° aux Commissaires de Police;

"Be it ordained by our Minister of State that there shall be a National Commission for the United Nations Educational, Scientific and Cultural Organization. Considering that Article 7 of the aforementioned convention [constitution] recommends that Member States shall establish a National Commission representing the Government and the various groups concerned with issues of education, scientific research and culture. There shall be appointed for three years as members of the National Commission for UNESCO: Messrs. Aureglia Louis, Barral Louis, Barriera Constant, Bergonzi Raymond, Besnard Maurice, Bocca René, Boisson Robert, Louys Édouard, Lunel Armand, Miss Malard Suzanne, Marchisio Robert, Médecin Auguste, Amiral Nichols, Noghès Paul, Notari Pierre, Ollivier Gabriel, Pagnol Marcel, Commandant Rouch, Scotto Marc-César, Solamito César, Vellay Charles."

Transcription of Ordinance No. 291 of October 16, 1950, establishing a National Commission for UNESCO.

Extract from the *Journal de Monaco* on October 30, 1950, composition of the first National Commission.

INFORMATIONS DIVERSES

Remerciements du Prince Souverain à la Municipalité.

Au lendemain de la Fête Nationale, S.A.S. le Prince Souverain a fait parvenir à M. Charles Palmaro, Maire de Monaco, la lettre suivante :

« Monsieur le Maire,

« A l'occasion de la Fête Nationale, vous m'avez exprimé, au nom du Conseil Communal, des vœux et des sentiments auxquels j'ai été, comme toujours, profondément sensible.

« Les magnifiques fleurs dont vous avez accompagné cet hommage m'ont été extrêmement agréables, et je vous en remercie très sincèrement, en vous demandant d'être mon interprète auprès de vos collègues du Conseil Communal.

« Veuillez croire, Monsieur le Maire, à mes sentiments les meilleurs.

« RAINIER, Prince de Monaco ».

Érection d'une Statue à la mémoire de S.A.S. le Prince Albert Ier. (suite de la 22me liste).

M. et Mme Sainclivier, 500 ; M. et Mme Paul Bouvier, 500 ; M. Claude Pécheral, 1.000 ; M. Paul Lomazzi, 500 ; M. Quitadamo, 100 ; M. Marcel Brivio, 500 ; M. et Mme Robellaz, 200 ; MM. Jean et Georges Médecin, 1.000 ; Capitaine et Mme Goiran, 500 ; M. Jules Persenda, 1.000 ; Mlle Jeanne André, 1.000 ; MM. Edouard-Hemery et Fils, 2.000 ; M. Pierre Isaia, 200 ; Anonyme, 2.000 ; Abbé Jeanjean, Curé de la Paroisse Saint-Martin, 1.000 ; Mme Vve Charles Chopard, 300 ; M. Louis Ghiglion, 500 ; M. Juan Balme, à Mexico 2.000 ; M. Armand Roux, 200 ; M. Alex Del Traglia, 300 ; Comité National des Étudiants Monégasques, 3.000 ; M. René Clérissi, 300 ; M. Albert Grasso, 200 ; Mme Dufresnoy, 200 ; M. Emmanuel Grandi, 500 ; M. Auguste Gaziello, 200.

(23me liste).

M. de Bruyn, Consul de Monaco à Anvers, 2.500 ; M. Joseph Fissore, Consul de Norvège, 3.000 ; M. Coolen, Consul Général de Belgique, 3.000 ; M. Francis Poggio, 300.

Séance inaugurale de la Commission Nationale de l'UNESCO.

Le 19 avril, au Palais du Gouvernement, la séance inaugurale de la Commission Nationale Monégasque de l'Unesco s'est tenue sous la présidence de S. Exc. M. Pierre Voizard, Ministre d'État, entouré de ses deux Vice-Présidents : Me Louis Aureglia, Président du Conseil National et M. Paul Noghès, Conseiller de Gouvernement pour l'Intérieur.

Le Ministre d'État a prononcé l'allocution d'ouverture que voici :

« En déclarant ouverte la première Session de la Commission Nationale Monégasque pour l'U.N.E.S.C.O., je vous remercie, Mademoiselle et Messieurs, au nom du Gouvernement Princier, d'avoir bien voulu, malgré les multiples occupations qui vous incombent, répondre à notre invitation.

« Retenus par les devoirs de leur charge — ou empêchés par la maladie — MM. l'Amiral Nichols, Marcel Pagnol, de l'Académie Française, Gabriel Ollivier, René Bocca, Robert Boisson et César Solamito, me prient de vouloir bien les excuser auprès de vous de ne pouvoir participer à notre réunion d'aujourd'hui.

De tout temps, grâce à la sollicitude agissante de ses Princes et malgré l'exiguïté de son territoire, la Principauté de Monaco s'est fait un honneur de figurer au premier rang des Patries, petites ou grandes, des Lettres, des Sciences et des Arts. Il est inutile, je pense, de rappeler devant vous l'œuvre accomplie dans ce domaine par des Souverains aux noms prestigieux tels qu'Honoré II, Antoine Ier, Honoré III, Albert Ier et Louis II de Monaco.

« Renouant avec la tradition de Ses grands ancêtres, S.A.S. le Prince Rainier Se préoccupe à Son tour d'assurer à la Principauté un rayonnement spirituel digne de Son passé. Nous venons d'être les témoins heureux de l'accueil si sympathiquement flatteur fait par le monde cultivé à l'initiative de notre jeune Souverain, fondant un grand prix littéraire attribué, sur la proposition d'un Jury composé d'éminentes personnalités, à un écrivain de langue française.

« La Principauté de Monaco se devait donc tout naturellement d'apporter sa contribution à l'Unesco, institution spécialisée de l'organisation des Nations Unies, dont l'objet est, vous le savez, de susciter ou de renforcer par l'éducation, la science et la culture, la paix internationale et la solidarité morale et matérielle de l'humanité.

« C'est le 6 juillet 1949, à la suite de la Conférence de Beyrouth, au cours de laquelle les représentants des États Membres de l'Unesco donnèrent un avis favorable à l'admission de la Principauté, que fut ratifiée par le Gouvernement Princier, la Convention qui faisait de notre pays un État Membre de l'Unesco, au même titre et avec les mêmes prérogatives que les autres États Membres, actuellement au nombre de 59.

« Depuis son adhésion, le Gouvernement Princier n'a cessé de coopérer, à la mesure de ses moyens, à l'Institution. En particulier, des délégations présidées par le Ministre d'État ont assisté et activement participé aux Conférences de Paris en 1949 et de Florence en 1950. Dans deux mois, nous enverrons encore une fois nos représentants à la Conférence de Paris, à l'ordre du jour de laquelle sont inscrites des questions du plus haut intérêt. Nous avions même envisagé un instant d'inviter la 7me Conférence Générale de l'Unesco qui se tiendra en 1952, à se réunir à Monaco. Ce projet est encore à l'étude, mais l'ampleur des problèmes surtout financiers que pose l'accueil d'une telle assemblée de plus de mille personnes n'est pas faite pour en faciliter la réalisation.

« Quoi qu'il advienne de ces vues d'avenir, l'étude du programme que s'est assigné l'Unesco, programme des plus étendus, comme vous avez pu le constater à la lecture des documents que nous vous avons fait adresser, ne saurait être l'œuvre des seuls Gouvernements. Cette étude appelle des organismes spécialement créés à cet effet. D'où le recours à des Commissions Nationales qu'institue l'article 7 de l'Acte Constitutif de l'Unesco ainsi conçu :

« Chaque État Membre prendra les dispositions appropriées à sa situation particulière pour associer aux travaux de l'organisation les principaux groupes nationaux qui s'intéressent aux problèmes d'éducation, de recherche scientifique et de culture, de préférence en constituant une Commission Nationale où seront représentés le Gouvernement et ses différents groupes ».

« Ce même article 7 ajoute :

« Dans les pays où il en existe, les Commissions Nationales remplissent un *rôle consultatif* auprès de leur délégation nationale à la Conférence Générale et auprès de leur Gouvernement pour tous les problèmes se rapportant à l'Organisation. Elles

Extract from the *Journal de Monaco* on April 23, 1951, speech by Pierre Voizard, first Chairman of the National Commission.

X07.217(449.49)

MINISTÈRE D'ÉTAT

Service des Relations Extérieures

N° OGD

Commission Nationale de l'UNESCO

PRINCIPAUTÉ DE MONACO

MONACO LE 21 Septembre 1951

Monsieur le Directeur Général,

J'ai l'honneur de vous faire connaître que, sur ma proposition, Son Altesse Sérénissime le Prince a nommé, par Ordonnance Souveraine n°451 en date du 11 Septembre 1951, Son Altesse Sérénissime le Prince Pierre aux fonctions de Président de la Commission Nationale monégasque.

Les rapports entre l'UNESCO et le Gouvernement Princier continueront à être assurés par l'intermédiaire du Service des Relations Extérieures que je dirige personnellement.

Je vous prie d'agréer, Monsieur le Directeur Général, les assurances de ma haute considération.

Le Ministre d'Etat,

Voizard

P. VOIZARD

Monsieur le Directeur Général de l'UNESCO

Letter from Pierre Voizard, Minister of State, first Chairman of the Monegasque National Commission, to UNESCO Director-General Jaime Torres Bodet, September 21, 1951.

X07.217.091

MINISTÈRE D'ÉTAT

Commission Nationale de l'U.N.E.S.C.O.

Le Président

PRINCIPAUTÉ DE MONACO

MONACO, LE 1er Avril 1952

X7.A.(449.49)04

Monsieur le Directeur Général,

Notre Commission Nationale vient de tenir séance, et je suis heureux de vous exprimer la vive reconnaissance de ses Membres, en répondant à l'invitation que nous a portée votre aimable lettre (XR/GC/280.634). M. Marcisio partira pour Paris le 9 Mai. Son adresse y sera: Légation de Monaco, 2, rue du Conseiller Collignon (XVI°).

Je me félicite des occasions qui seront offertes à notre Secrétaire Général pendant ces trois semaines de stage de s'initier, et de se préparer à rendre la coopération de la Principauté aux nobles tâches de l'U.N.E.S.C.O. aussi complète et aussi dévouée que je le souhaite.

Veuillez agréer, Monsieur le Directeur Général, les assurances de ma haute considération.

votre dévoué

Pierre de Monaco

PIERRE DE MONACO.

Monsieur le Directeur Général de l'Organisation des Nations-Unies pour l'Education, la Science et la Culture

19, Avenue Kléber, 19

PARIS

APR 4 1952

XR

170091

Letter from Prince Pierre, new Chairman of the Monegasque National Commission for UNESCO, to the organization's Director-General, Jaime Torres Bodet, April 1, 1952.

« NICE-MATIN » — Samedi 6 Décembre 1958

MONACO

Rédaction, Publicité, Abonnements : Agence, 1, rue Grimaldi MONACO · Téléphone : 024-17

« Cette semaine U.N.E.S.C.O. établirait, s'il en était besoin, les aspirations humanistes de notre Principauté », a déclaré S.A.S. le prince Pierre, président de la Commission Nationale Monégasque pour l'Education, la Science et la Culture

Le dixième anniversaire de la proclamation de la Déclaration Universelle des Droits de l'Homme par l'Organisation des Nations Unies est célébré avec éclat, cette année, en Principauté de Monaco.

Une « Semaine U.N.E.S.C.O. » est organisée par la Commission nationale monégasque pour l'Education, la Science et la Culture, que préside S.A.S. le Prince Pierre.

Voici la déclaration qu'a faite, à l'intention de nos lecteurs, S.A.S. le Prince Pierre, à l'occasion de l'ouverture de la « Semaine U.N.E.S.C.O. » :

Dans quelques jours, le dixième anniversaire de la Déclaration Universelle des Droits de l'Homme, adoptée par l'assemblée des Nations Unies, le 10 décembre 1948, sera célébré partout en ce monde. Chaque année, la Principauté de Monaco organise une « Journée des Droits de l'Homme ». Cette fois, nous avons une « Semaine U.N.E.S.C.O. » pour mieux appeler, à cette occasion, l'attention et l'affection des hommes de bonne volonté sur les tâches de l'U.N.E.S.C.O.

La convention créant l'Organisation des Nations Unies pour l'Education, la Science et la Culture débute par ces mots : « Les guerres prenant naissance dans l'esprit des hommes, c'est dans l'esprit des hommes que doivent être élevées les défenses de la paix. » La Principauté de Monaco, havre de paix et de joie de vivre dans un monde dérouté et parfois déroutant, se devait d'adhérer à une organisation dont les buts correspondent si bien aux idéaux qui, de tout temps, ont inspiré ses souverains.

Le 6 juillet 1949, notre pays devenait membre de l'U.N.E.S.C.O. En 1950 était créée une commission nationale dont les membres ont toujours été choisis de manière à assurer une représentation harmonieuse des différents secteurs des activités intellectuelles. Dans la mesure de nos moyens, nous nous sommes efforcés, dès lors, de participer de façon toujours plus intense au noble et généreux programme de l'U.N.E.S.C.O., qui est principalement de stimuler l'intérêt général pour les problèmes internationaux.

La Principauté a été partie à toutes les grandes conventions qui pouvaient présenter pour elle un intérêt quelconque : convention du droit d'auteur, accord pour l'importation d'objets de caractère éducatif, scientifique et culturel, et, tout récemment, convention sur la protection des biens culturels en cas de conflit armé.

D'autre part, des contacts permanents avec l'organisation centrale [...] *nationale, le gage touchant de sa foi inébranlable en l'avenir du monde.*

Le programme d'aujourd'hui

Dans le cadre de la « Semaine U.N.E.S.C.O. », aujourd'hui, à 13 h., S. Exc. M. Pierre Blanchy, ministre plénipotentiaire, conseiller de gouvernement pour l'Intérieur, chargé de l'Education nationale et vice-président de la Commission nationale monégasque de l'U.N.E.S.C.O., fera une déclaration au micro de Radio-Monte-Carlo.

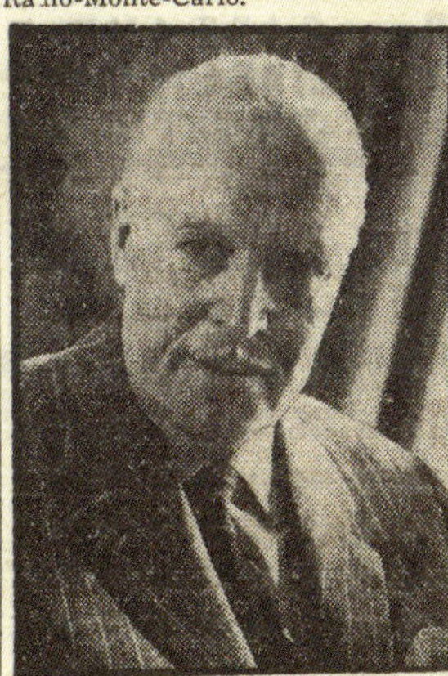

S.A.S. le Prince Pierre de Monaco, président de la Commission Nationale Monégasque pour l'Education, la Science et la Culture (Photo Maestri)

Cet après-midi, à 17 heures, aux Beaux-Arts, aura lieu le vernissage de l'exposition des dessins d'enfants du concours « La Fraternité Humaine », organisé par l'Association Nationale Monégasque des Arts Plastiques.

Avant l'inauguration, présidée par S.A.S. le Prince Pierre, le jury proclamera le palmarès de cette compétition artistique et décernera de beaux prix.

Rappelons que l'entrée de l'exposition sera entièrement libre. Parents et amis des jeunes exposants sont cordialement invités.

Demain dimanche, à 21 heures, salle Garnier, sous la direction du maître Louis Frémaux, l'Orchestre national de l'Opéra de Monte-Carlo, avec le concours du [...]

Les nouveaux décorés de l'A.S. Monaco fêtés au cours d'une manifestation de sympathie très cordiale

A l'hôtel de Genève, avant-hier soir, s'est déroulée une belle manifestation de sympathie en l'honneur des membres de l'Association Sportive de Monaco décorés à l'occasion de la fête nationale.

Cette fête très cordiale était organisée par le Conseil d'administration de l'actif club, en l'honneur de MM. Antoine Romagnan, inspecteur principal de l'Education physique et des Sports, directeur sportif du Comit éde gestion de l'équipe « pro », ancien secrétaire général de l'A.S.M., et Pierre-Martin Robin, président fondateur de l'A.S. Monaco, nommés chevaliers de l'ordre de Saint-Charles ;

M. Joseph Asso, délégué pour le Sud-Est de la Fédération Française de Boxe, vice-président du Comité de Provence, vice-président de la section haltérophilie de l'A. S. M., conseiller technique de la section de boxe, qui a reçu la médaille en argent de l'Education physique et des Sports ;

MM. Ange Vaccarezza, membre du Comité olympique, trésorier général de l'A.S.M., président de la section volley-ball, vice-président de la section natation ; Joseph Franco, président de la Commission technique de la section basket-ball de l'A.S.M.; Laurent Scaglia, membre du Conseil d'administration de la section football de l'A.S.M.; Albert Richelmi, membre du bureau directeur de la section football de l'A.S. Monaco ; Emmanuel Conte, ancien champion, conseiller technique de la section boxe de l'A.S.M.; Jean Giusto, dirigeant, animateur de l'équipe des cadets de la section football de l'A.S.M.

Autour du docteur Charles Bernasconi, président honoraire, nous avons noté la présence de M. André Bronfort, président du Conseil d'administration provisoire de l'A.S. Monaco, chargé du secrétariat général ; MM. le docteur Georges Médecin, Melchior Marchisio, Casimir Miglioretti, vice-présidents ; Laurent Ravera, Edmond Laforest de Minotty, Claude Pécheral, conseillers, et M. Rudy Seggiaro.

Dans une belle allocution, le docteur Charles Bernasconi a chaleureu-sement félicité les nouveaux décorés de l'A.S. Monaco et, portant un toast déférent à S.A.S. le prince souverain, a souligné le plaisir éprouvé au sein du club de voir les mérites de nombreux dirigeants récompensés.

Puis M. Robin, en sa qualité de président fondateur, après avoir remercié les organisateurs de cette manifestation de sympathie, mit l'accent sur le travail effectué au bénéfice du sport par l'A.S. Monaco depuis sa fondation, en 1924, en rappelant les beaux résultats obtenus.

Représentant le commissaire aux Sports, M. Antoine Romagnan a adressé des félicitations à l'A.S.M. [...]

MM. Malchior Marchisio et André Bronfort se sont associés aux paroles du président Bernasconi envers leurs camarades à l'honneur. M. Bronfort fit état des besoins actuels et impératifs de l'A.S.M.

L'on trinqua ensuite à la santé des nouveaux médaillés, à qui nous renouvelons toutes nos sincères félicitations.

NOUVELLES RELIGIEUSES

Au sujet de la procession aux flambeaux du 8 décembre. — Certaines personnes désireuses de participer à la procession qui se déroulera le 8 décembre à Monaco-Ville, se demandent s'il est exact qu'un autobus sera là pour les ramener chez elles.

Nous pouvons les rassurer complètement : à l'issue de la cérémonie, un car de la Compagnie des Autobus se trouvera sur la place de la Visitation. Il se dirigera vers Monte-Carlo, la place des Moulins, Saint-Roman (s'il y a des pèlerins qui en viennent) et repartira jusqu'aux Moneghetti.

Il n'y aura pas de tarif spécial pour cet autobus. On paiera avec les tickets comme pour les parcours ordinaires.

Avec cette facilité qui est donnée aux gens les plus éloignés, on espère que la fête du 8 décembre verra cette année (qui est celle du centenaire de Lourdes) une très importante participation de fidèles venant de tous les coins de la Principauté prier Notre-Dame Immaculée, patronne de notre cathédrale.

SPECTACLES DE MONACO

GAUMONT. — A 15 h. et 21 h. : **La Fille de Hambourg,** une histoire extraordinaire dans les bas-fonds du port, réalisée par Yves Allegret avec Daniel Gélin, Hildegarde Neff, Jean Lefebvre et Daniel Sorano.

PRINCE, 3, rue des Princes, Monaco. — 21 h. : **La Mousson,** Lana Turner, Robert Burton, Fred Mac Murray. CinémaScope. Couleurs.

ROYAL, 9, bd Albert-Ier, Monaco. — 15-21 h. : **Casino de Paris,** superproduc[...]

"UNESCO Week" organized by the Monegasque National Commission, *Nice-Matin*, December 6, 1958.

DOSSIER

MONACO AT UNESCO 1946-1959
FROM THE SORBONNE TO THE PLACE DE FONTENOY

Monaco's admission to UNESCO was marked by very specific locations. The Principality was represented at the first two General Conferences of UNESCO, in Paris at the Sorbonne in 1946, and then in Mexico City in 1947; but it was the Beirut Conference in 1948 that secured Monaco's admission to UNESCO, a membership effective as of 1949. The delegation representing the new Member State of Monaco convened at the Hôtel Majestic, in Paris, which served as UNESCO's temporary home until it moved to its current headquarters on the Place de Fontenoy in Paris. Inaugurated on November 3, 1958, the new building matched the Organization's ambitions in terms of scale and aesthetics alike. A few months later, in 1959, Prince Rainier III and Princess Grace were given a guided tour of the new premises by Director-General Vittorino Veronese (1958-1961).

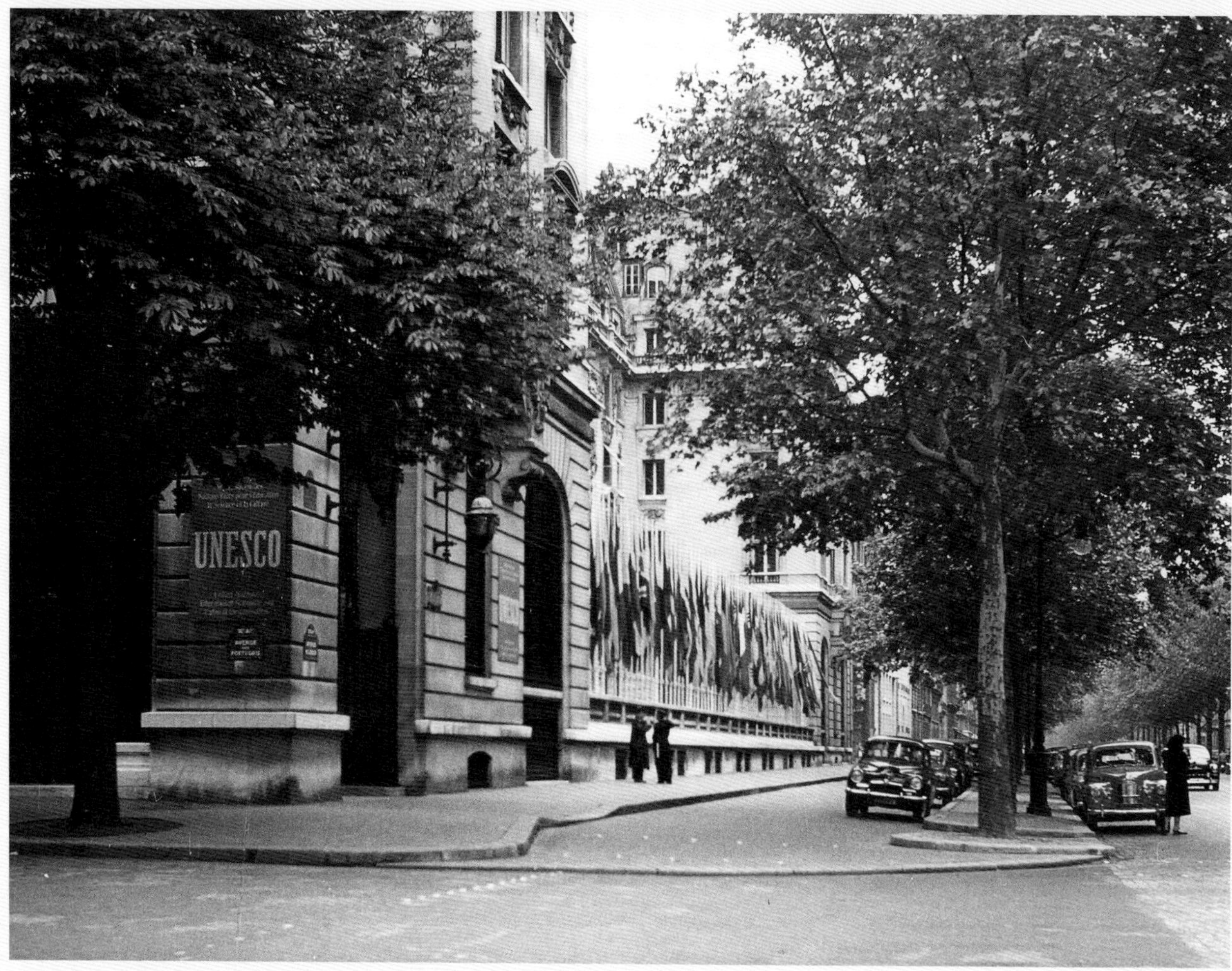

ABOVE Former UNESCO headquarters, from 1946 to 1958, Hôtel Majestic, Avenue Kléber, Paris.

OPPOSITE PAGE Top: second session of the UNESCO General Conference in Mexico (1947). Bottom: opening of the seventh session of the UNESCO General Conference, chaired by Jaime Torres Bodet, Director-General, Avenue Kléber, Paris, November 12, 1952.

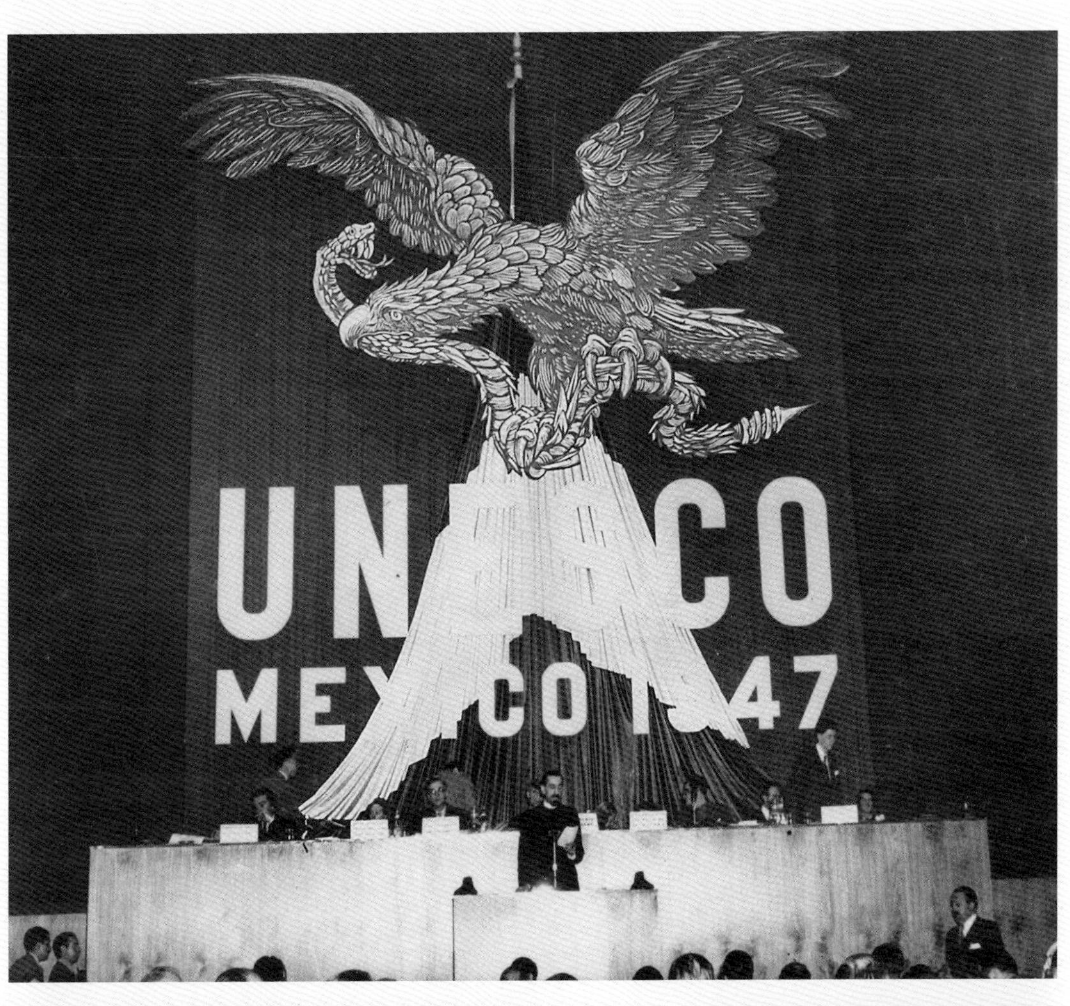
UN CO
ME CO 47

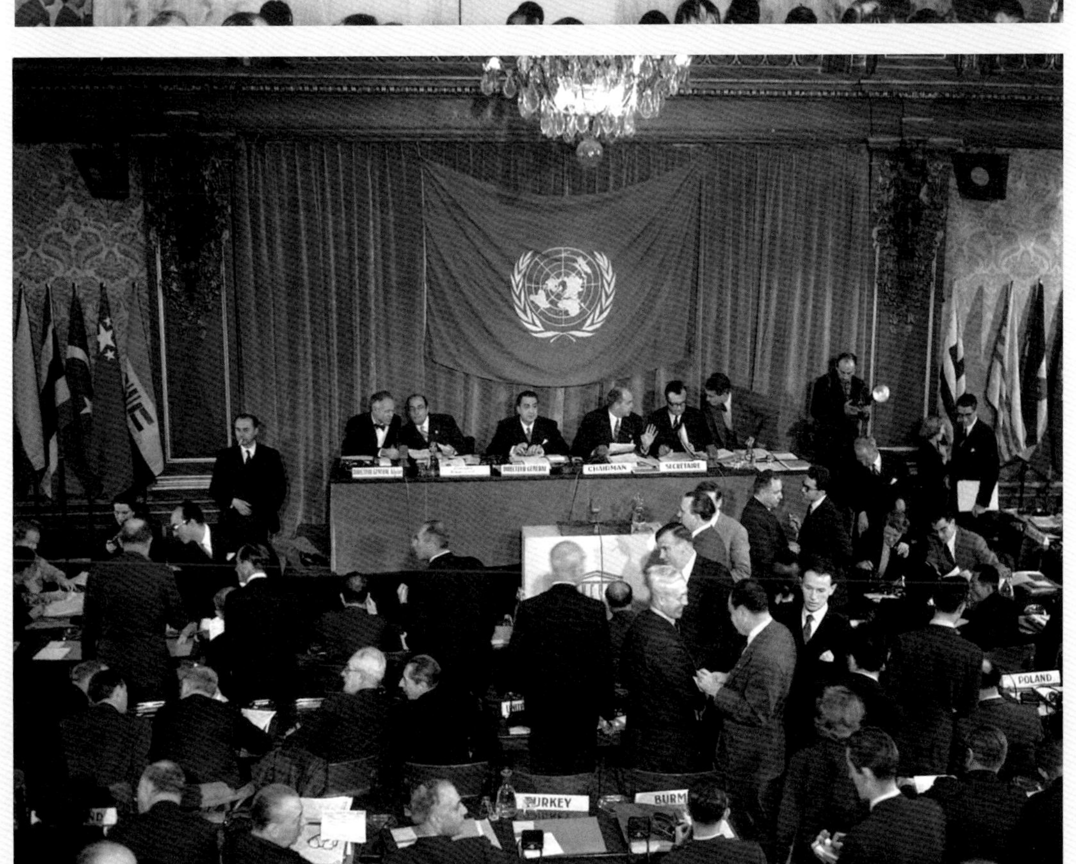
CHAIRMAN
SECRETAIRE
POLAND

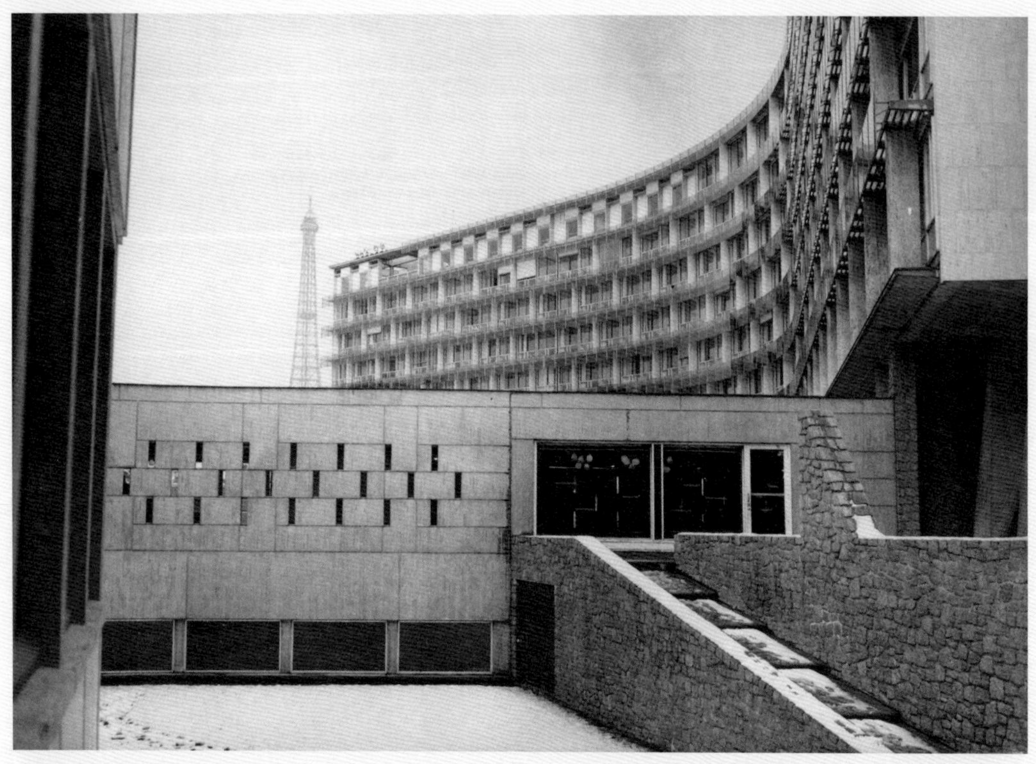

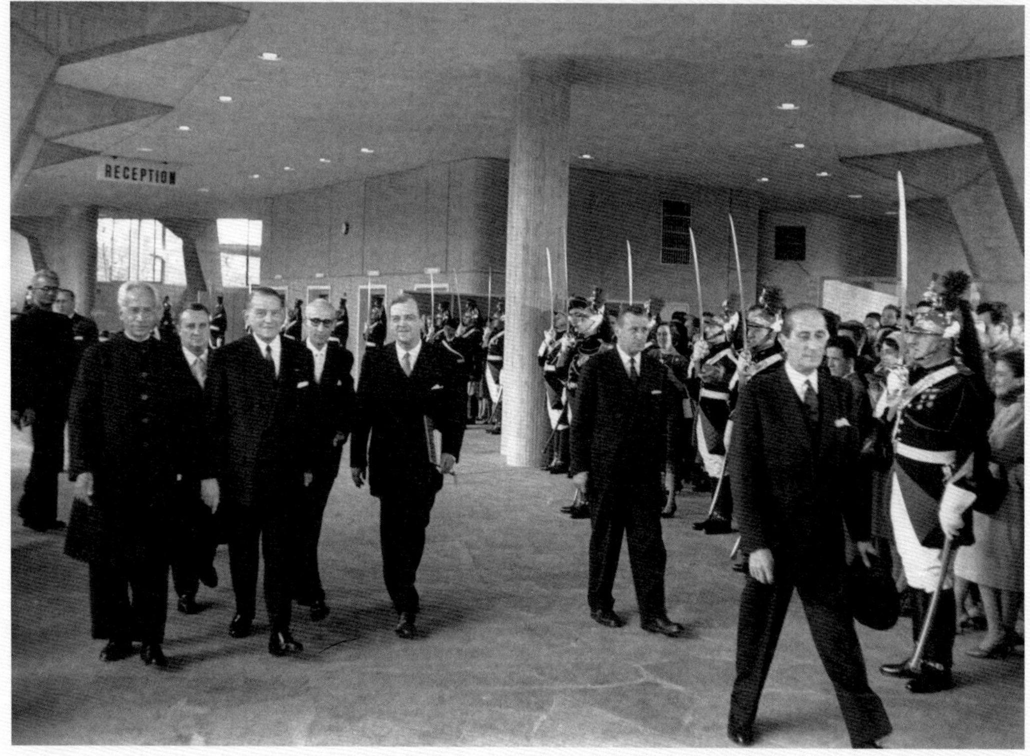

TOP UNESCO House, built in 1955-1958 by architects Breuer, Nervi and Zehrfuss. Current UNESCO headquarters, Place de Fontenoy.

BOTTOM Inauguration ceremony for the new UNESCO headquarters, November 3, 1958.

OPPOSITE PAGE Paris, UNESCO House, October 22, 1959. Private visit by Prince Rainier III of Monaco, accompanied by H.S.H. Princess Grace. The princely couple are received by Vittorino Veronese, UNESCO Director-General. In the background, *Wall of the Sun* (1958), an enameled ceramic mural by Joan Miró (1893-1983, created with Josep Llorens Artigas, 1892-1980).

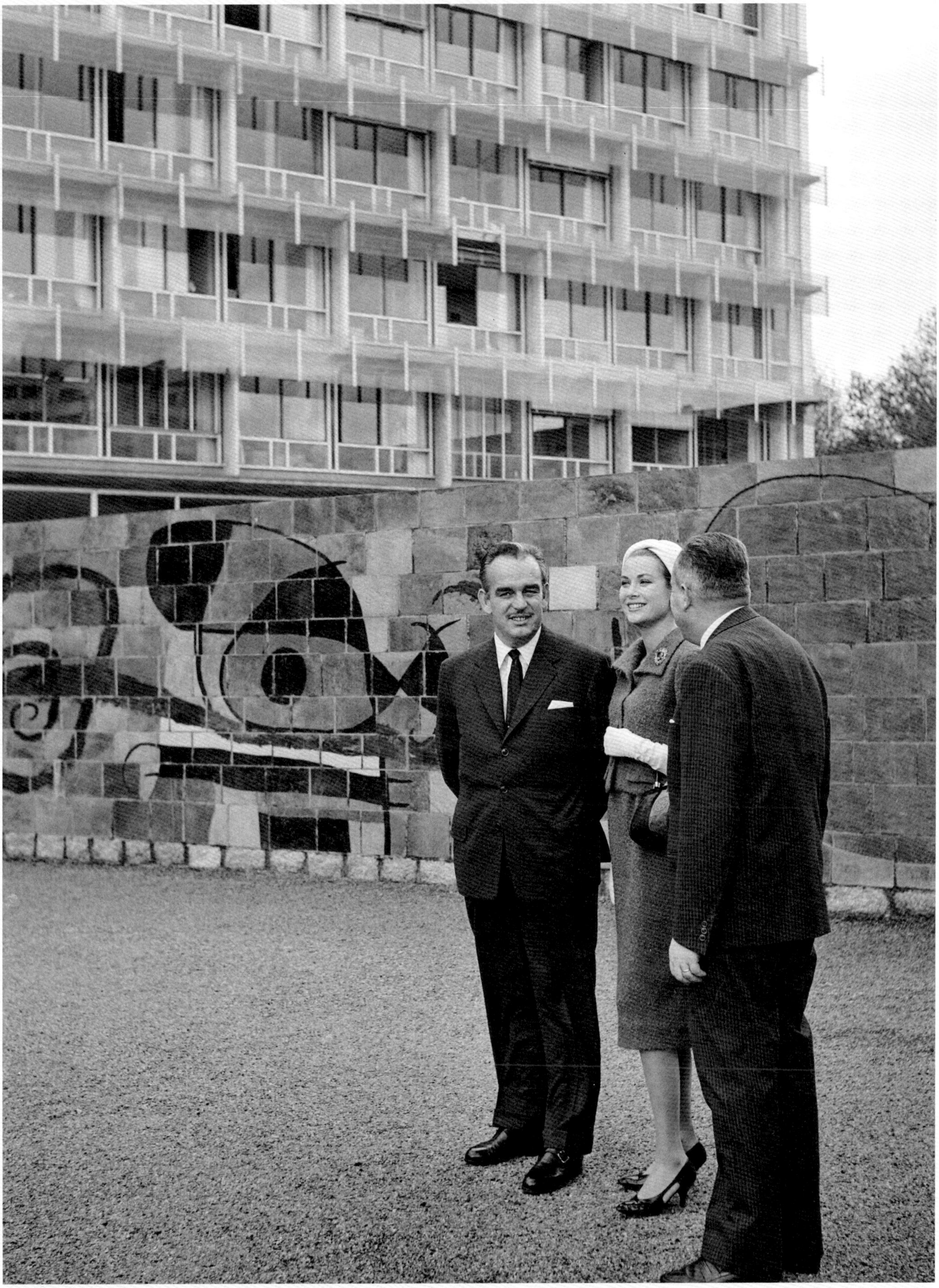

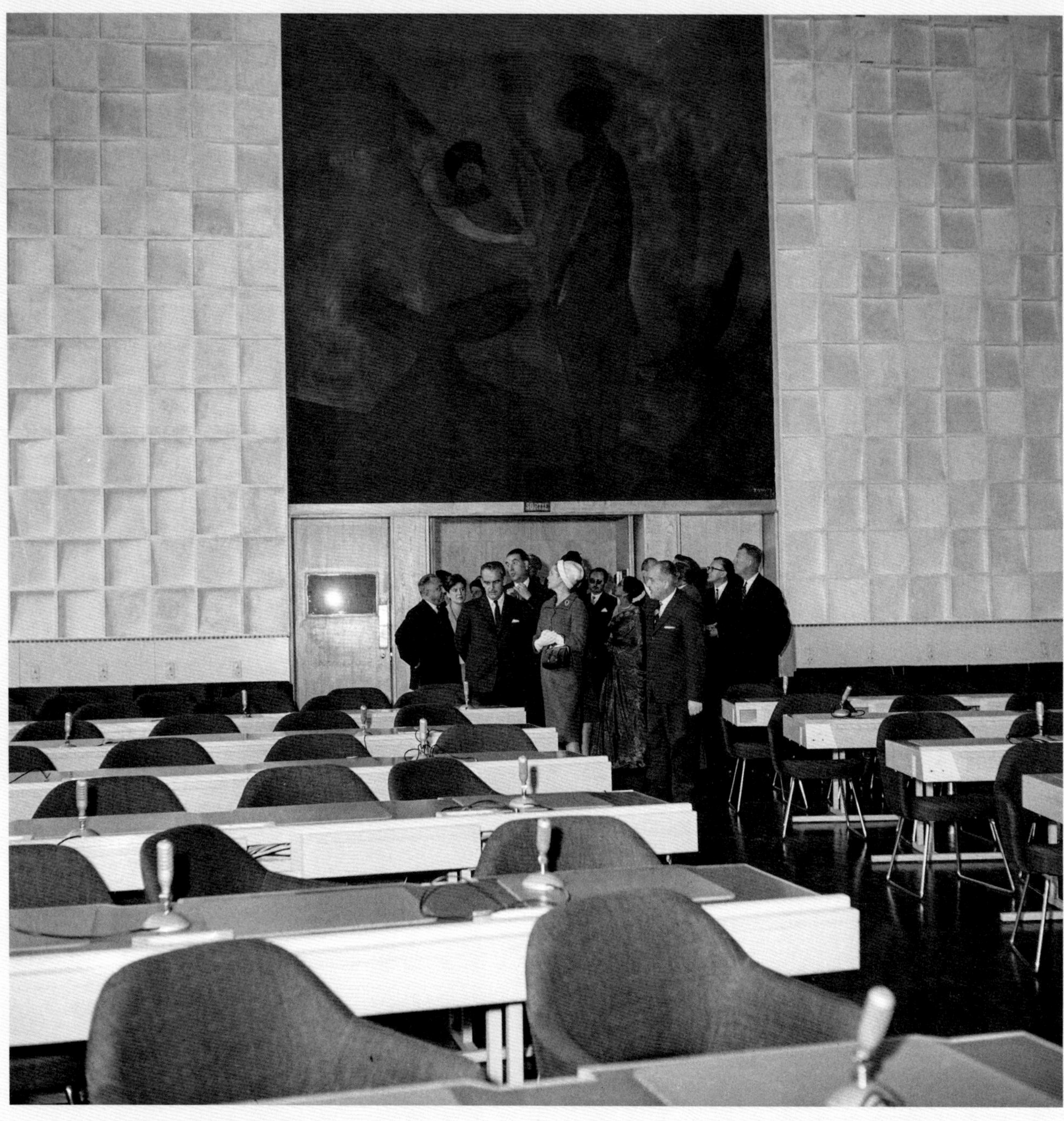

Paris, UNESCO House, October 22, 1959. The Prince and Princess stop in front of the work by Rufino Tamayo (Mexico, 1899-1991), *Prometheus Bringing Fire to Mankind* (1958), decorating Room II, conference building.

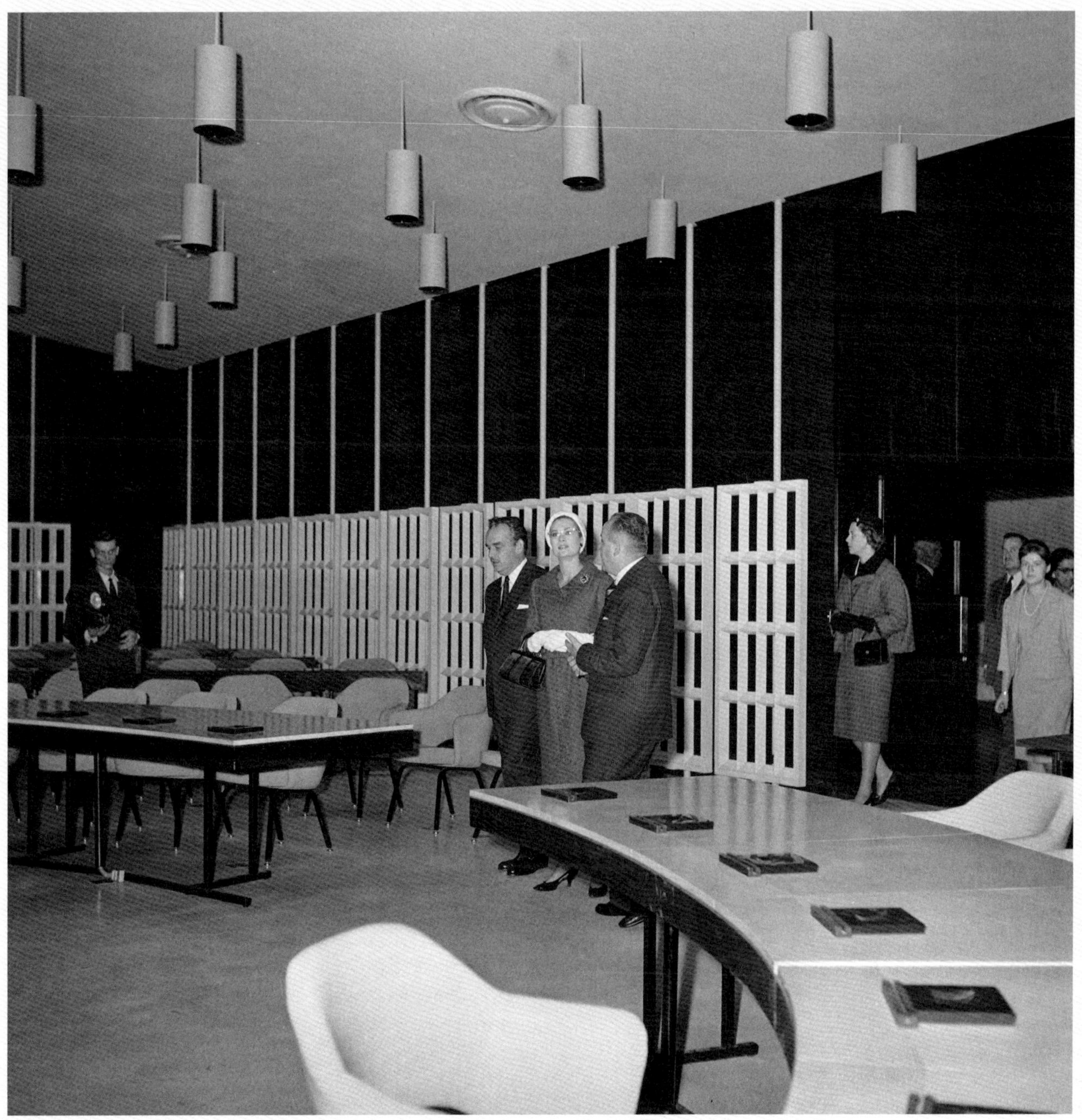

GREAT VOICES

Many are the eminent persons who have expressed themselves at UNESCO—foremost thinkers whose written and spoken legacy is the subject of a collection of podcasts produced by UNESCO in partnership with France Médias Monde. In this section we present contributions that adumbrate UNESCO, works by prominent intellectuals linked to UNESCO, and testimonies from UNESCO Directors-General. Together these articles illustrate the core values of UNESCO: peace, human unity, the safeguarding of cultural diversity, the quest for universal human values, the protection of human rights and the fight against racism.

"Those who want peace will have to attack the evil of war at its roots, that is, in individual minds."

Aldous Huxley (1894-1963), "Mind, Ethics and War", *Correspondence, International Institute of Intellectual Cooperation Bulletin*, No. 3, 1934.

THE INTELLECTUAL FOUNDATIONS OF UNESCO

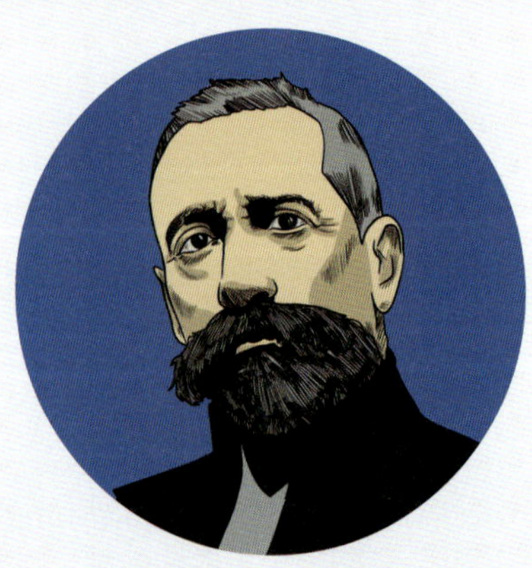

ALBERT I

"What I present here are the emotions of a navigator nurtured by a culture of truth. This book is the fruit of an unwavering determination; it is a work guided by a spirit of honesty and science that unites all people engaged in a righteous struggle for wellbeing and morality. The enlightened mind of the sage is visited by an ideal that is shaped by the notion of future progress, coming upon him like the promise of true civilization in a distant tomorrow. So glorious is this ideal that particularism is put to rout, dispelling the shadows that divide the children of the human family blinded by pride or cupidity, or misled by the cruel lies of military glory [. . .] One may question how such a noble ideal can reign over the customs of mankind while the spirit of conquest continues to drive advanced countries to commit momentous errors; while fanaticism brings ignorance in its wake and begets crimes under the eyes of Europe; while politics, with its armed forces, guns and warships, pose a threat to the entire planet. And yet, from progress is born the force that unites all consciences to become one public conscience, which asserts itself and condemns the abuse of power, whether to crush the individual or despoil an entire people; such is the uncertain dawn that is rising on the horizon to guide the continuing evolution of humanity."

Albert I of Monaco (1848-1922), preface to *La Carrière d'un Navigateur*, March 1901, Paris, Plon, 1902.

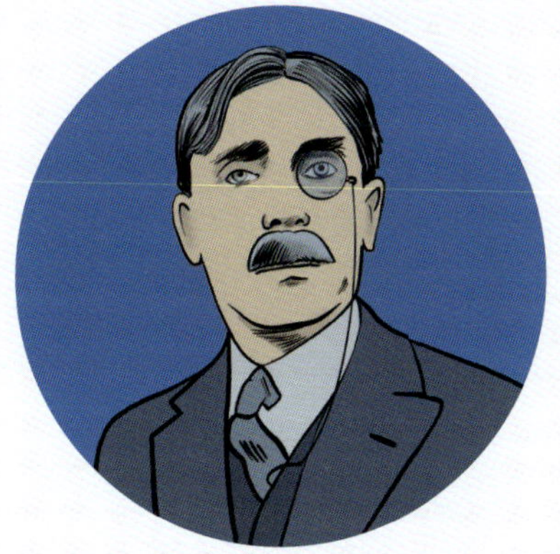

PAUL VALÉRY

" [. . .] Our cooperation exists as yet on paper alone and will have but an administrative existence in the mortal form of paper, as long as the persons concerned are not interested, as long as their minds have not been won over to the idea of cooperation organized as a response to the essential desire of minds to understand and be understood—to the fundamental need of intelligences to complement one another in what they lack and to confirm one another in what they possess."

Paul Valéry (1871-1945), "What a League of Nations Implies", International Committee on Intellectual Cooperation, Geneva, 1930. Cited in Roger-Pol Droit, *Humanity in the making: overview of the intellectual history of* UNESCO, 1945-2005, p. 32.

"Our world requires us to solve infinitely complicated problems in an extremely short space of time... Consider how everything today instantly begets its opposite, and how nothing distinct can survive at this fantastic temperature. War exists in the midst of peace and penury is born of abundance. The astonishing progress of communication is immediately accompanied by the strengthening and tightening of customs barriers. The same man in the same laboratory can conduct research into what kills and what saves, cultivate the good and the bad. In the realm of intelligence itself, we find that applying logic to the nature of things leads to the principle of uncertainty. It must also be admitted that the proliferation of books and instruments of thought produces types of ignorance hitherto unknown. Modern man, with little but newspapers to nourish his spirit, finds nothing but that which must flee from any notion of self-respect [. . .] The transformation of the human universe renders violent solutions unquantifiable and therefore senseless. This is what, perhaps, it would be good to make clear, without in the least appealing to the sentiments."

Paul Valéry, *Lettre sur la société des esprits, Variétés.* In *Œuvres de Paul Valéry*, vol. 1, tome 4, pp. 175-185. Paris: Éditions de la N.R.F., 1934.

PAUL M.G. LÉVY

"'Conflicts are becoming shapeless, without beginning or end or any specific territory' (Freund). What remains, then, of those efforts put in place to prevent international conflicts since the fall of Napoleon? What of the International Peace Movement, which began in 1816 with the creation of the New York Peace Society, closely followed by the British Society for the Promotion of Permanent and Universal Peace (1816)? What of the International Peace Congresses, first held in London in 1843 then restaged at intervals in different European cities, most notably Rome in 1892, which saw the foundation of the International Peace Bureau (IPB)? Out of all these nineteenth-century efforts to defy fate, only the IPB is still in place today. Mention should also be made of the Monaco International Institute for Peace, established in 1903 by Prince Albert I.

"This organization represents the first institutional effort to resolve differences between nations by means of arbitration, and to foster an approach based on intercultural understanding. Need we remind the reader of the construction of the Peace Palace at The Hague in the early twentieth century? [. . .] While none of this was entirely in vain, none of this succeeded in terms of achieving the primary goal: the maintenance of peace. That objective having proved beyond the capabilities of men, were we not obliged to look even more closely at the origins, development and evolution of conflicts, and to call on science to help us establish the possibilities and conditions of lasting peace?"

Paul M.G. Lévy, *Polémologie, recherche sur la paix, irénologie.* In *Cahier du Crésup* no. 1 (Louvain-la-Neuve, 1977), p. 19. A UNESCO research project.

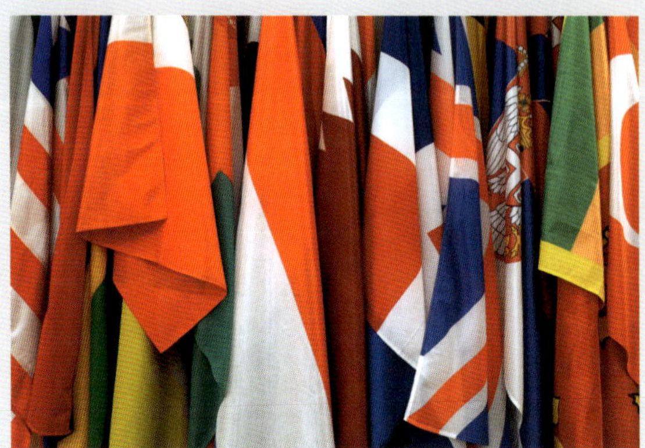

"The Governments of the States Parties to this Constitution on behalf of their peoples declare:

"That since wars begin in the minds of men, it is in the minds of men that the defenses of peace must be constructed;

"That ignorance of each other's ways and lives has been a common cause, throughout the history of mankind, of that suspicion and mistrust between the peoples of the world through which their differences have all too often broken into war;

"That the great and terrible war which has now ended was a war made possible by the denial of the democratic principles of the dignity, equality and mutual respect of men, and by the propagation, in their place, through ignorance and prejudice, of the doctrine of the inequality of men and races;

"That the wide diffusion of culture, and the education of humanity for justice and liberty and peace are indispensable to the dignity of man and constitute a sacred duty which all the nations must fulfil in a spirit of mutual assistance and concern;

"That a peace based exclusively upon the political and economic arrangements of governments would not be a peace which could secure the unanimous, lasting and sincere support of the peoples of the world, and that the peace must therefore be founded, if it is not to fail, upon the intellectual and moral solidarity of mankind."

Preamble to the Constitution of UNESCO adopted in London on November 16, 1945.

THE FIRST DEBATE ON RACE ORGANIZED BY UNESCO

The expert meeting was held in Paris on December 12-14, 1949. Attendees included sociologists Franklin Frazier (U.S.), Morris Ginsberg (U.K.), and Luiz de Aguiar Costa Pinto (Brazil); anthropologists Ernest Beaglehole (New Zealand), Juan Comas (Mexico), Ashley Montagu (U.S.), and Claude Lévi-Strauss (France); and philosopher, educator, and politician Humayan Kabir (India). Two years earlier UNESCO had embarked on emergency talks on human rights, which led to the Universal Declaration on Human Rights in 1948. Questions of "race" and racism being closely connected with human rights, debunking racial categories was a major priority for a postwar world desperate for peace. This meant providing scientific evidence that there was no such thing as "race", referring to human beings, and consequently no basis for a racial hierarchy based on the inherent superiority of one race over another. By first demonstrating and then confirming the existence of a single human "race", UNESCO, spearheaded by Director-General Julian Huxley, aimed to eliminate racism through a public information campaign based on the findings of scientific research.

"The necessity to preserve the diversity of cultures in a world which is threatened by monotony and uniformity has surely not escaped our international institutions. They must also be aware that it is not enough to nurture local traditions and to save the past for a short period thereafter. It is diversity itself which must be saved, not the outward and visible form in which each period has clothed that diversity, and which can never be preserved beyond the period which gave it birth.... By refusing to consider as human those who seem to us to be the most 'savage' or 'barbarous' of their representatives, we merely adopt one of their own characteristic attitudes. The barbarian is, first and foremost, the man who believes in barbarism."

Extract from Claude Lévi-Strauss (1908-2009), Race and History, 1958. Published in conjunction with "racial" studies conducted by other anthropologists and geneticists, as part of a series supporting UNESCO's anti-racist campaign.

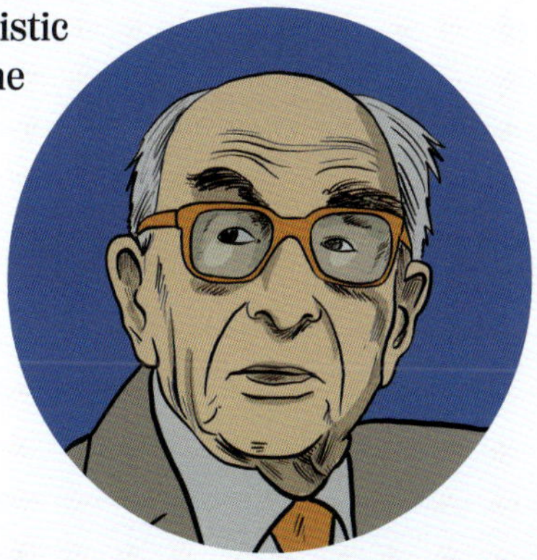

THE NECESSARY AND DELICATE BALANCE BETWEEN THE UNIVERSAL AND THE PARTICULAR

JACQUES MARITAIN (1882-1973)

In 1947, French philosopher and theologian Jacques Maritain was already speaking of the "babelism of modern thinking."

"We have spoken, not without reason, of the babelism of modern thinking. Never have spirits been so cruelly divided. The more we compartmentalize human thought into narrower, ever more specialized boxes, the harder it becomes to grasp those implicit ideologies to which each of us, like it or not, is effectively committed. Mystical doctrines, spiritual traditions, and schools of thought come crashing into each other, as we fail to understand the signs used by others to express themselves. The opinions proffered by our fellow travelers are just so much noise to each of us personally. There is no longer any common ground for speculative thinking, however deep you dig to find it. Speculative thinking has lost its common language."

Jacques Maritain, address to the General Conference of UNESCO, Second Session, on behalf of the French delegation, Mexico City, November 6, 1947.

"There are two ways to lose oneself: walled segregation in the particular, or dilution in the "universal." My conception of the universal is that of a universal enriched by all that is particular; a universal enriched by every particular: the deepening and coexistence of all particulars."

Aimé Césaire (1908-2008), extracted from *Letter to Maurice Thorez*, dated October 24, 1956.

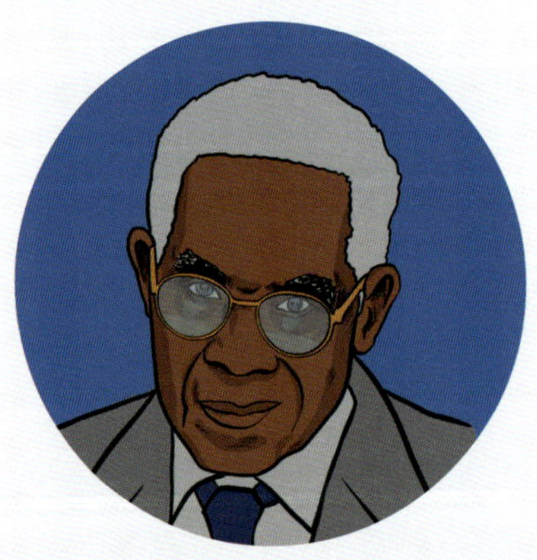

TESTIMONIES FROM UNESCO DIRECTORS-GENERAL

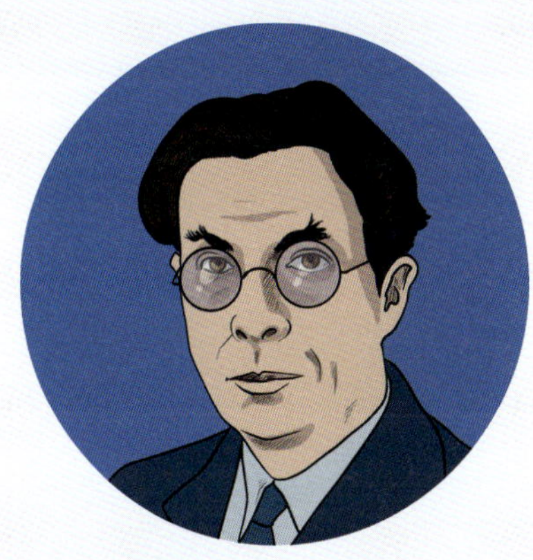

JULIAN HUXLEY (1887-1975),

British biologist, brother of Aldous Huxley and first General-Director of UNESCO (1946-1948). In this farewell address as Director-General of UNESCO, Julian Huxley develops the visionary ideas dear to his heart as a scientist, positive thinker and humanist. For example, the idea of using science to solve socio-economic problems, protect heritage and the natural environment, and preserve the popular traditions of different peoples around the world.

"In relinquishing my office, I would like to thank all Member States for all that they have done to make it possible for us on the Secretariat to get on with the execution of UNESCO's programme. But I would also like to ask them to do something more, namely to examine critically and dispassionately what they themselves are doing in education, science and culture, as measured by the yardstick of the aims and purposes laid down in our Constitution, and the directives set forth in our programme, and also as [a] measure against the achievements of other nations.

"I will give a few examples of what I mean:

" [. . .] ARE YOU ATTEMPTING TO USE NATURAL SCIENCE TO THE FULL—WHETHER IN EDUCATION, to give to your citizens a proper understanding of the method and the actual and potential achievements of science, or in practice, in the actual solution of concrete problems?

" [. . .] ARE YOU TAKING STEPS TO PRESERVE THE POPULAR TRADITIONS OF YOUR COUNTRY IN BALLADS AND SONGS, in costume, in art and craftmanship, and to adapt them to the changed conditions of modern life, so that these rich sources of cultural achievement, in all their diversity, shall not perish from the face of the Earth?

"HAVE YOU TAKEN ADEQUATE STEPS TOWARDS THE CONSERVATION OF NATURE IN YOUR COUNTRY—whether for economic, or social, or aesthetic reasons, a question one asks oneself with added force in this region where mountain sides that we know in biblical times were covered with forests are now largely bare, where great regions of once fertile land which helped to nourish Rome are now barren or even desert, and where birds and beasts have decreased to such an alarming extent.

"WHAT HAVE YOU DONE TO PRESERVE AND MAKE KNOWN YOUR CULTURAL HERITAGE? Have you taken steps to preserve your historical and ancient monuments, to unearth further remains of your past history, to exhibit its treasures and make them known to the world at large—another question one asks here, in this region of ancient history and incomparable cultural diversity, still too little known by the peoples of other lands.

" [. . .] HAVE YOU ENCOURAGED THE CREATIVE ARTIST, whether in painting or music, in literature or drama, to express the spirit of his country and to make life more interesting and more worthwhile for its people?

"And so I might continue with questions in respect of the various fields of UNESCO's work. However, I will merely ask one final but overriding question.

"HAVE YOU LOOKED AT YOUR PROBLEMS FROM A UNESCO ANGLE, that is to say not merely as national problems but as part of a single world problem, where the several nations must learn to make adjustments in the interest of the whole body of nations? I think of such problems as over-population, facilities for study abroad, the utilization and conservation of natural resources, the making available to the world the treasures of national art and history, the removal of those sources of social discontent which are too often the seeds of war. In this regard as well as in measuring your own achievements against those of other nations, UNESCO's Secretariat, through their clearing-house functions, can be of real service."

Julian Huxley, address delivered at the UNESCO General Conference, Third Session, Beirut, December 10, 1948.

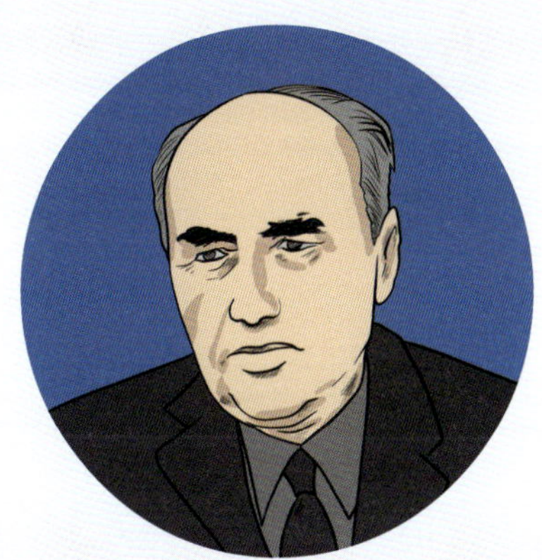

RENÉ MAHEU (1905-1975),

French philosopher and senior official, sixth UNESCO Director-General (1961-1974).

"The demand for human rights is so long-standing and so profound, the violation of human rights has been so ruthless and so widespread in recent times and is still so prevalent today, that we are not entitled to rest on our laurels. [. . .]

"It is, in any case, a fact that we have seen precious words impoverished over the years through being uttered mechanically, without reference to their spiritual roots. And now, today, we find that human rights are in danger of losing their prestige and their power of inspiration, even before they have been completely assimilated and made a reality.

"In certain countries and some circles, there are people who say that human rights have become meaningless, lifeless, in a revolutionary age where it seems normal to sacrifice the justice and happiness of today to the virtue and prosperity of tomorrow. Others aver that human rights are devoid of substance in a technological civilization, where productivity is the supreme value and where the two crucial problems are increased production and distribution of goods. Others, again the apocalyptic or the indifferent simply proclaim the end of the human race, even its non-existence, and in any case the end of humanism. Let us take heed; man is no longer much in fashion among the leaders of the nations, the technocrats and the know-it-alls of our planet."

René Maheu, International Conference on Human Rights, Tehran, April 23, 1968.

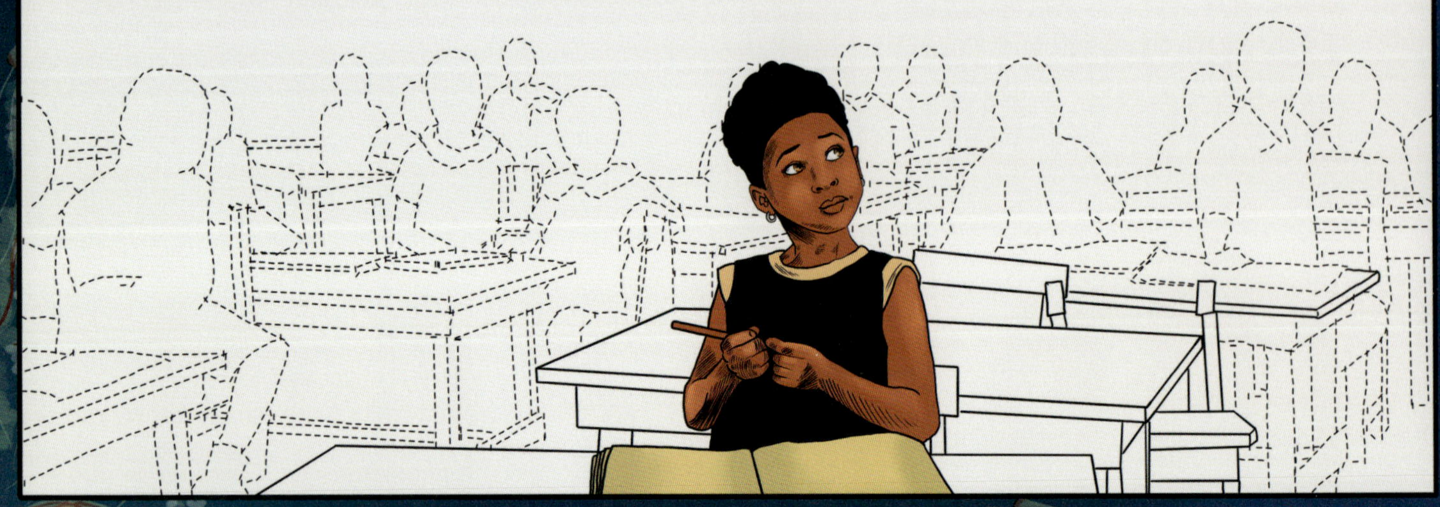
LA PROTECTION ET L'ÉPANOUISSEMENT DES ENFANTS EST AU CŒUR DES ENGAGEMENTS DE S.A.R. LA PRINCESSE DE HANOVRE ET DE L'ASSOCIATION QU'ELLE PRÉSIDE, L'AMADE, NOTAMMENT EN AFRIQUE, EN LIEN AVEC LES OBJECTIFS DE DÉVELOPPEMENT ET D'ÉDUCATION DE L'UNESCO.

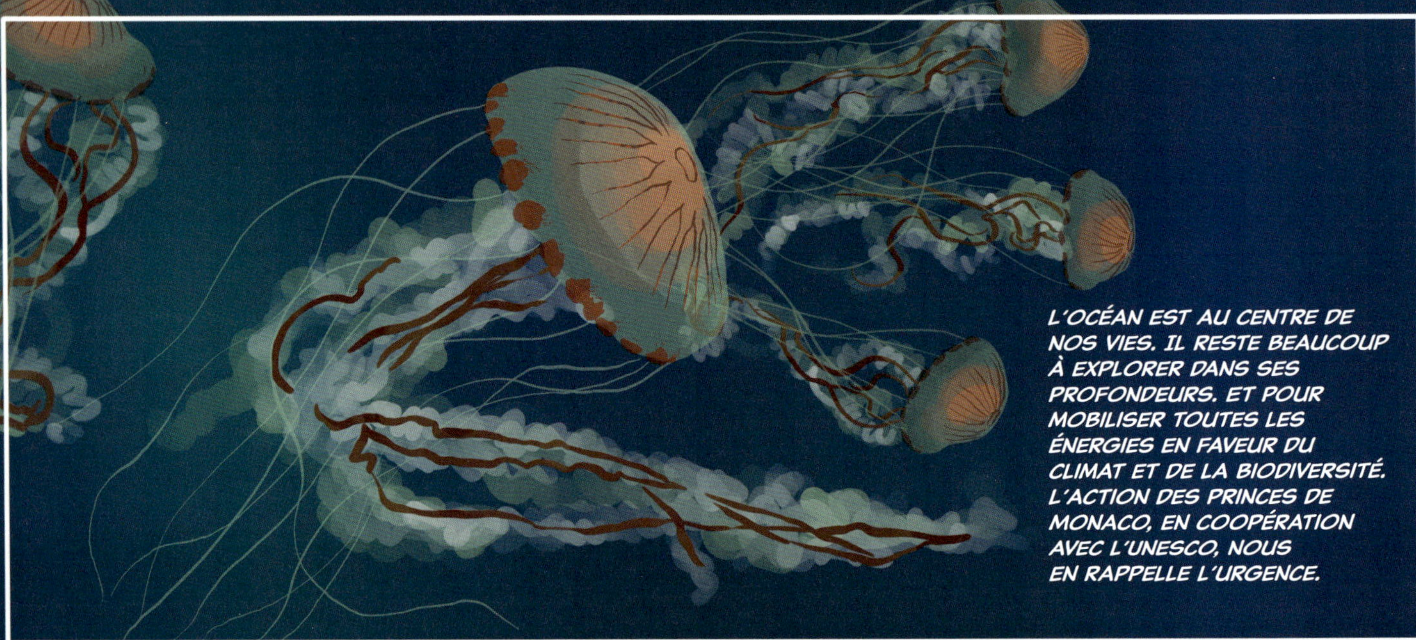
L'OCÉAN EST AU CENTRE DE NOS VIES. IL RESTE BEAUCOUP À EXPLORER DANS SES PROFONDEURS. ET POUR MOBILISER TOUTES LES ÉNERGIES EN FAVEUR DU CLIMAT ET DE LA BIODIVERSITÉ. L'ACTION DES PRINCES DE MONACO, EN COOPÉRATION AVEC L'UNESCO, NOUS EN RAPPELLE L'URGENCE.

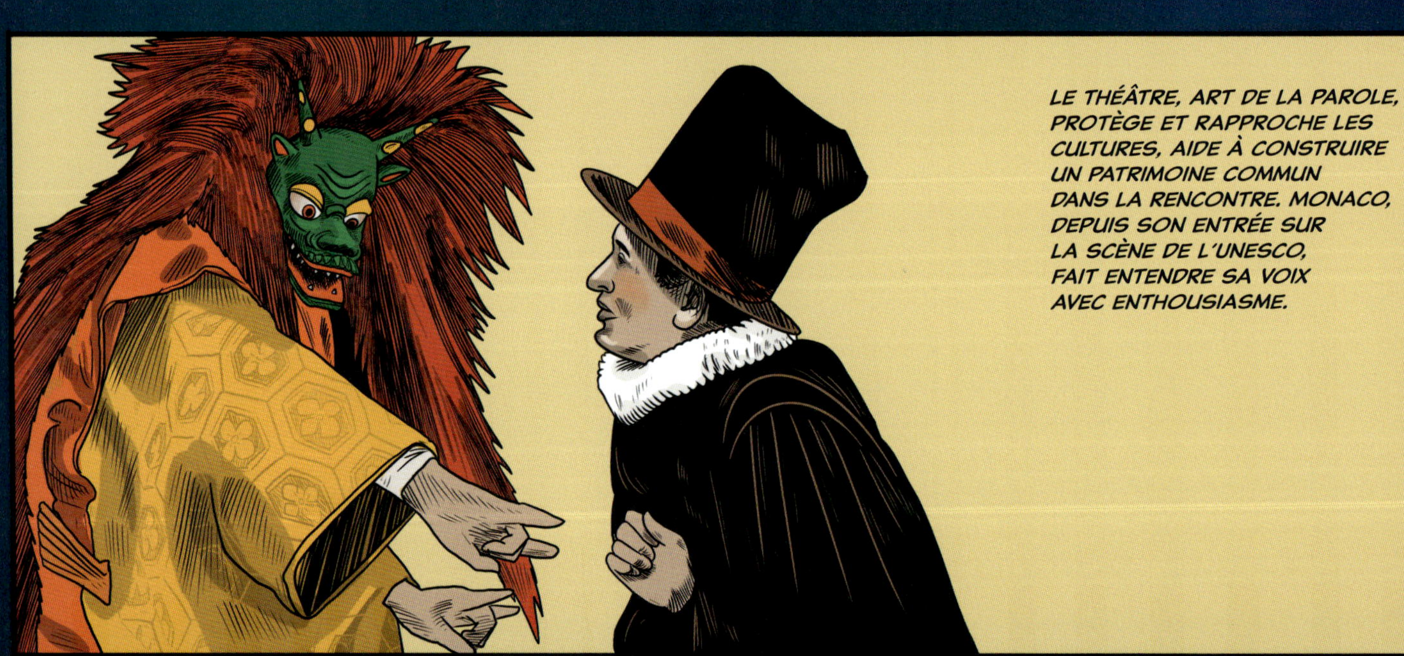
LE THÉÂTRE, ART DE LA PAROLE, PROTÈGE ET RAPPROCHE LES CULTURES, AIDE À CONSTRUIRE UN PATRIMOINE COMMUN DANS LA RENCONTRE. MONACO, DEPUIS SON ENTRÉE SUR LA SCÈNE DE L'UNESCO, FAIT ENTENDRE SA VOIX AVEC ENTHOUSIASME.

SHARED PRINCIPLES

EDUCATION
SCIENCE
CULTURE

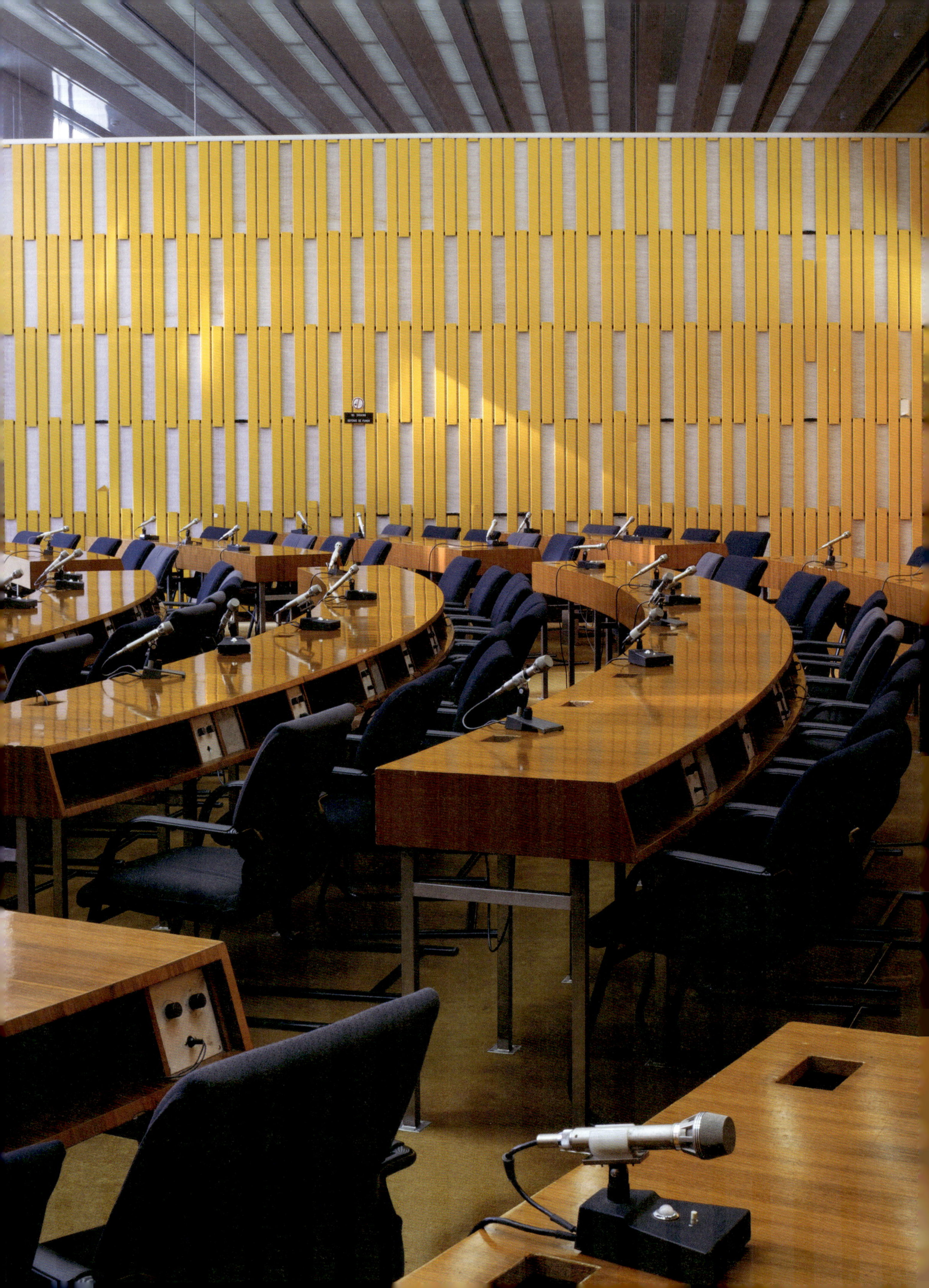

First, a question: how does one summarize the founding principles of an institution that enjoys international renown but whose breadth of activities is so little known that for many people they are reduced to the mere listing of World Heritage sites? How, in short, does one map the immensity of UNESCO's principles and activities? The question is that much more complex when one considers that ever since its creation this now mature Organization has constantly broadened its field of action and adapted in the face of disruption. We do, however, have one guiding thread at our disposal, and that is the originality of UNESCO. The only international organization to promote ethical values and abstract principles, UNESCO, to quote French philosopher Roger-Pol Droit, is a "philosophical" organization. In explicitly undertaking to build peace among people through education, science and culture, UNESCO rekindled the oldest of all human intentions. It gambled that the human spirit had the capacity to bridge the differences between people and committed to eradicate the ignorance at the root of conflict. UNESCO "calls for a new Humanism" said its Director General Irina Bokova (in office, 2009-2017), a collective imperative forged in a common culture and intellectual and moral cooperation on a worldwide scale. For those who founded UNESCO in the ashes of war, as for those steering it through troubled waters today, "there is no greater folly than to accept the inevitability of catastrophe" (Jacques Maritain).

"It is the mission of UNESCO to promote and reinforce the solidarity of consciences. However noble the fruits of its efforts, education, science, culture and information are not ends in themselves but only the means to a spirituality of action in the service of peace."

René Maheu, UNESCO Director General, 1973.

OPPOSITE PAGE AND FOLLOWING PAGES Conference room and corridors of the UNESCO building.

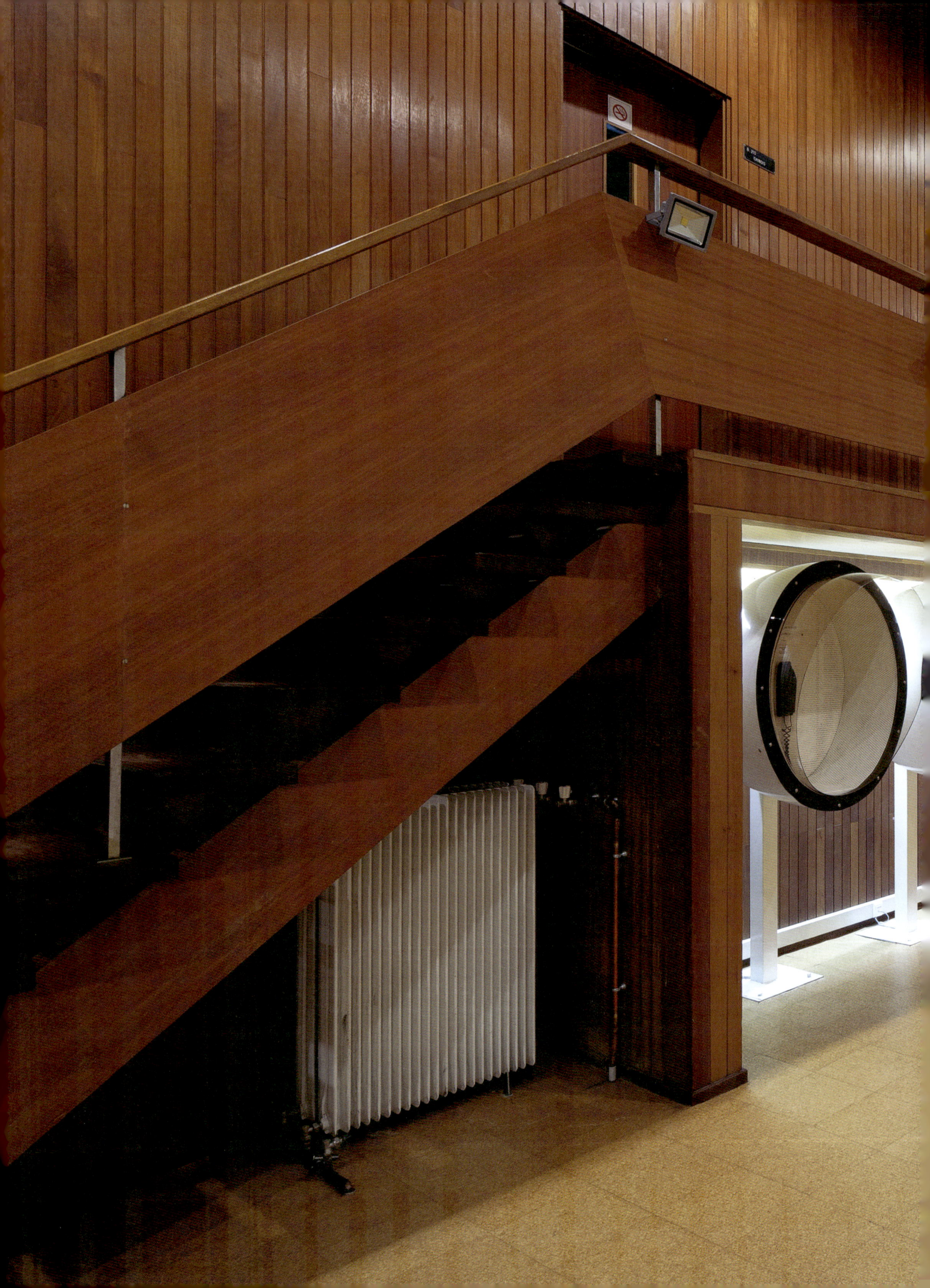

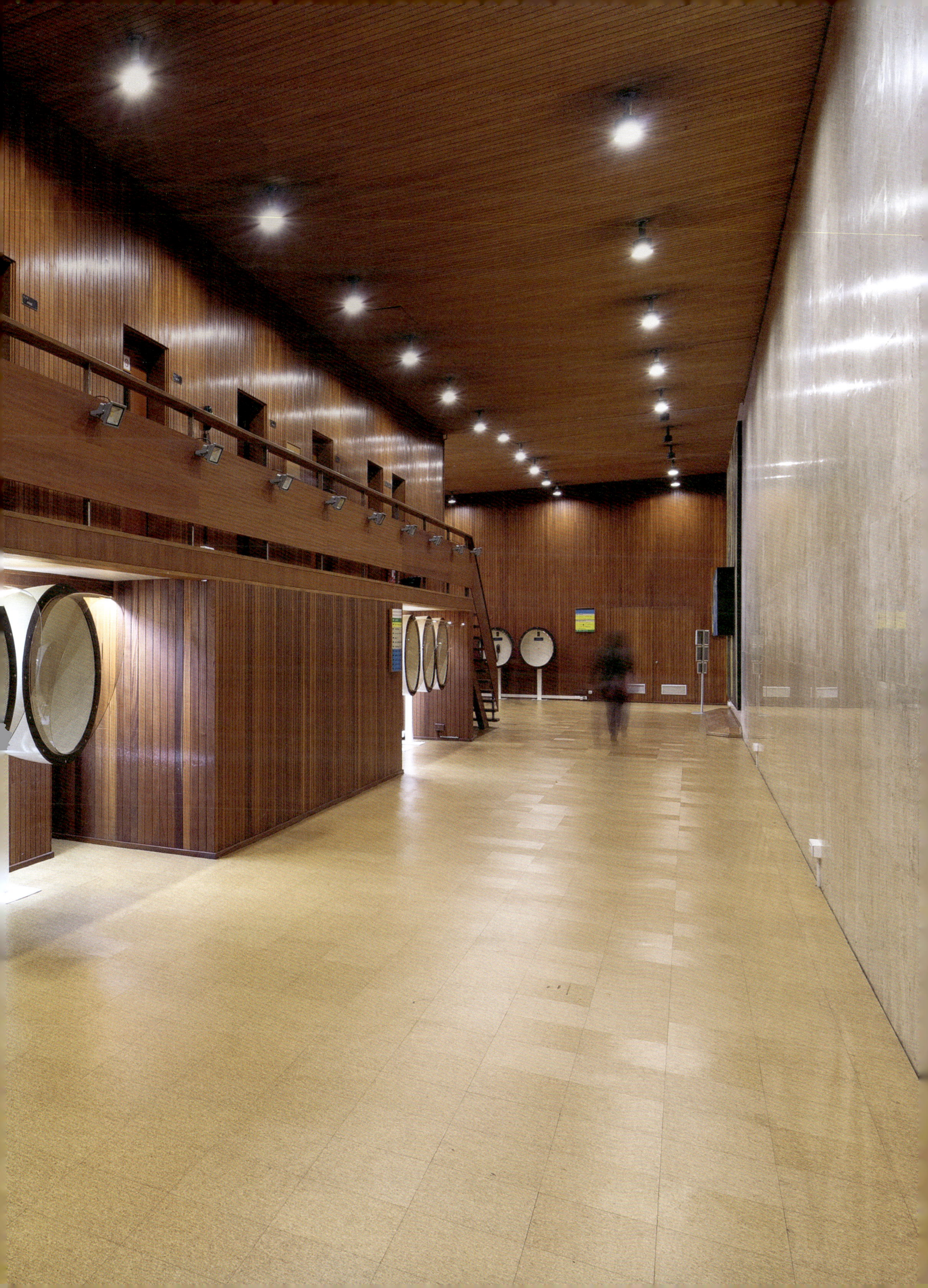

FROM THE WORLD OF IDEAS TO THE APPLICATION OF PRINCIPLES

From the very outset, UNESCO assumed a spiritual duty to defend the rationalism of the Enlightenment without at the same time renouncing the legacy and values of religion—a search for balance with which the Principality could fully identify. All well-intentioned efforts are therefore welcome to build the foundations of a new cooperation, so that from the ruins might come "escapes to other worlds" (Michel de Certeau). To foster that cooperation, the Organization rose to the challenge of listening to the voices of the intellect and technology alike, welcoming members from both sides as the instruments required to convey any value, however insignificant, with the power to turn ideas into action. In 1950 the words of Jacques Rueff resounded like a clarion call at the fifth General Conference of UNESCO in Florence, birthplace of humanism: "UNESCO reaches for the summits but, just as the mountaineer must use their ice ax to carve out a trail through the rock face, so UNESCO must chart its own course forward."

Beckoning it forward are three words, three pillars that frame its endeavors: education, science, and culture. Education leads the way for without equal access to knowledge, there can be no understanding of this world and no understanding of our neighbors. Only collective, ambitious learning can do that—learning without borders, something which is by no means self-evident but essential to lay the groundwork for a culture of peace. Science provides the right tools for the job. Tools for the acquisition and sharing of transparent, solid learning, based on principles, demonstrations and a common fund of knowledge. Science lies at the heart of education—a culture of science at the service of humanity, capable of bridging the gulf between the educated and the uneducated that grows ever deeper as society becomes more specialized. And then there is culture, something "that is not inherited but conquered" said French cultural figure André Malraux, a manifestation of human diversity as polymorphous as society itself. Culture completes our triptych. Eventually a fourth word would add itself to our list, and that is information, a key element in our increasingly connected world.

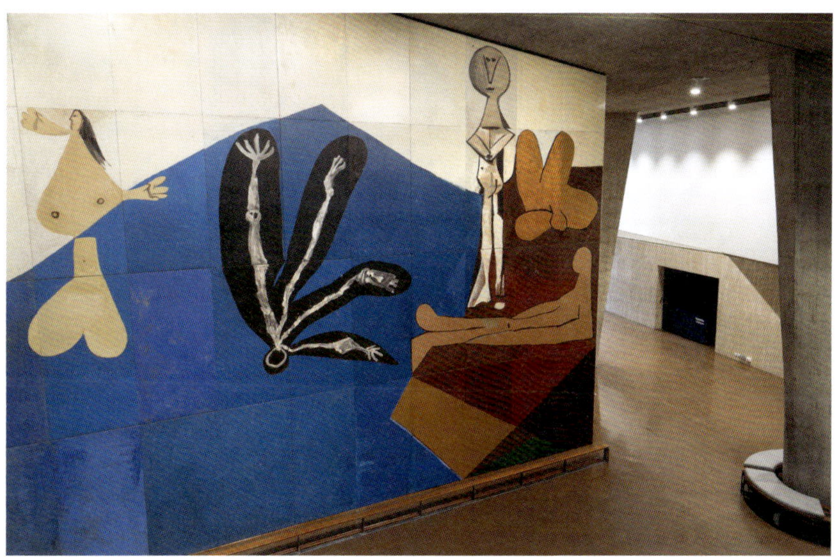

CONSTANTLY ADAPTING TO AN EVER-CHANGING WORLD

As these concepts have been disseminated, enriched and reimagined with time, unsettled too by the vicissitudes of evolving geopolitics, the ideal of peace has often found itself teetering on the edge of an abyss, most notably in the latter half of the twentieth century with its cohort of conflicts connected to the Cold War and decolonization. In 2005, with the specter of September 11, 2001, still looming large, UNESCO Director-General Koïchiro Matsuura in his address on the occasion of UNESCO's sixtieth anniversary, reminded the world that peace and prosperity had yet to be achieved—a lucidity that far from a discouragement, served as a spur to greater commitment and an ever-renewed pledge to uphold the founding spirit of UNESCO.

The thinking has broadened and gained structure in the face of new challenges, but the priorities remain the same. In the case of education, basic education as a human right has expanded to include the right to education without discrimination—protecting children and girls—and the right to education throughout life. The year 1967 marked the launch of UNESCO International Literacy Day; 1970 was International Education Year; and 1990 marked the World Declaration on Education for All, in Jomtien, Thailand. Every new achievement is another

The Fall of Icarus (1958), Pablo Picasso (1881-1953), UNESCO Art Collection. Mural consisting of forty wood veneer panels painted with acrylic, covering a surface of almost 100 m^2. Originally entitled *The Forces of Life and the Spirit Triumphing over Evil*, the composition lost this title in 1958.

step on the yet-tangled road to learning. As regards science, in the aftermath of World War II the priority was to deconstruct racial narratives and demonstrate the absurdity of the pseudo-science of race and ethnicity, as so vociferously condemned by Claude Lévi-Strauss. The focus then shifted to incentives to cooperation, the promotion of research and the implementation of standard-setting instruments. By the nineteen sixties, UNESCO was increasingly preoccupied by the state of the environment, a concern that was confirmed by the Club of Rome report of 1972. The seventies then ushered in a time of vigilance, the development of new fields of application prompting consideration of the misuse of science for destructive ends, and caution in the face of potentially dangerous technologies. This led, in 1986, to the Venice Declaration emphasizing the importance of ethical considerations in scientific research. Last but not least, with the early voices of culture ringing out in praise of great texts and the merits of universal values, we see the concept of cultural identity taking shape with the emergence of new states in the developing world—a concept entirely familiar to small countries like Monaco. Faced with the risk of cultural uniformity, and without relinquishing those universal human values first among which is a new culture of peace, cultural diversity and the preservation of endangered cultures gained ever greater momentum in the service of humanized globalization. In an unstable world imperiled by war, the relationship between culture and democracy became ever more meaningful.

From these major and still current undertakings has come a growing awareness of other essential questions. The relationship between the sexes and the discrimination perpetrated against women was thus the focus of the first United Nations conference on women, convened in Mexico City to coincide with the 1975 International Women's Year, with Monegasque Government official Jacques Boisson in attendance. Other key issues have included: world heritage conservation; the human/Nature relationship; solidarity and tolerance (cf. the Declaration of Principles of Tolerance, 1995); the potential misuse of information technology, particularly the spread of disinformation online; reflections on the human genome and most recently, artificial intelligence. Faced with such a proliferation of rhizomes, it was only natural that the three core pillars of UNESCO—four with the addition of information/communication—should coalesce to form one. Henceforth, what drove UNESCO was the ideal of a public domain of knowledge—a monumental challenge, dizzying in its complexity but no less thrilling.

MONACO IN UNISON WITH UNESCO

The question that now arises is how a UNESCO Member State fits into this framework. Let us not forget that the principle of state primacy is enshrined in the UNESCO constitution: while inspired by universalism, UNESCO derives its international legitimacy from the national sovereignty and actions of its Member States. How then, does a small State anxious to preserve its independence within a multilateral cooperation framework add its stone to the edifice? Monaco for instance, which plays its part but cannot aim to do everything, acts in accordance with its history, capabilities and specificities, fully aware of its many strengths but also of the limits to its achievements—as so often pointed out in the annual reports of the National Commission for UNESCO. Objectively speaking, where does the Principality of Monaco stand within UNESCO? How can we measure the originality of its contribution to that community of minds and nations that UNESCO aspires to create? At risk of stating the obvious, let us remember that Monaco is as indivisible as the rock upon which it stands. Formed from the multilayered legacy of princes and visiting statesmen, Monaco cannot be separated into its parts. As such, it is a test bed for UNESCO'S ambitions. That there is an abiding culture of mutual understanding in Monaco is evident from the cosmopolitanism of its population, foreign residents and nationals rubbing shoulders and cross-border workers flowing into the Principality on a day-to-day basis. In this country whose "borders are made of flowers", to quote French writer Colette, education, science and culture are so intertwined as to be inseparable.

That said, it is science that plays the pivotal role for the Principality, serving as the compass that guides its quest for new horizons of thought. And by science, we primarily mean oceanography, as embodied in the works of Prince Albert I, and in institutions that have established Monaco as a center for marine science. Examples include the Oceanographic Institute (1911, in Monaco and Paris alike), and the International Hydrographic Bureau (1921, renamed the International Hydrographic Organization in 1967).

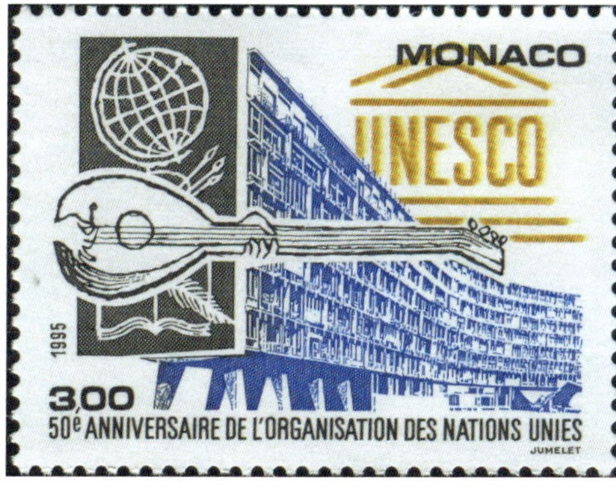

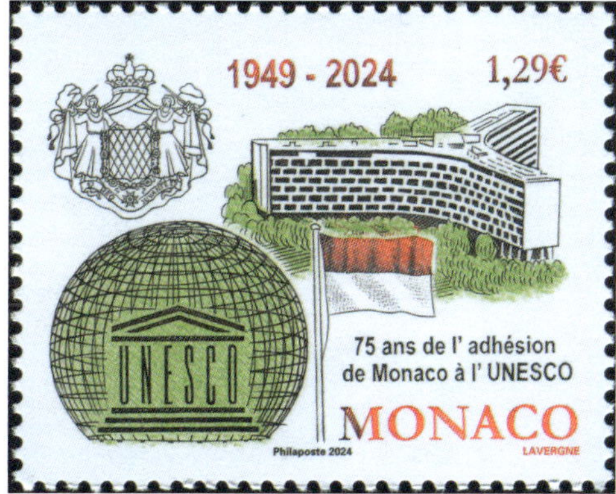

Commemorative stamps illustrating the ties between Monaco and UNESCO: in 1995, for the 50th anniversary of the creation of the UN, and in 2024 for the 75th anniversary of Monaco's accession to UNESCO.

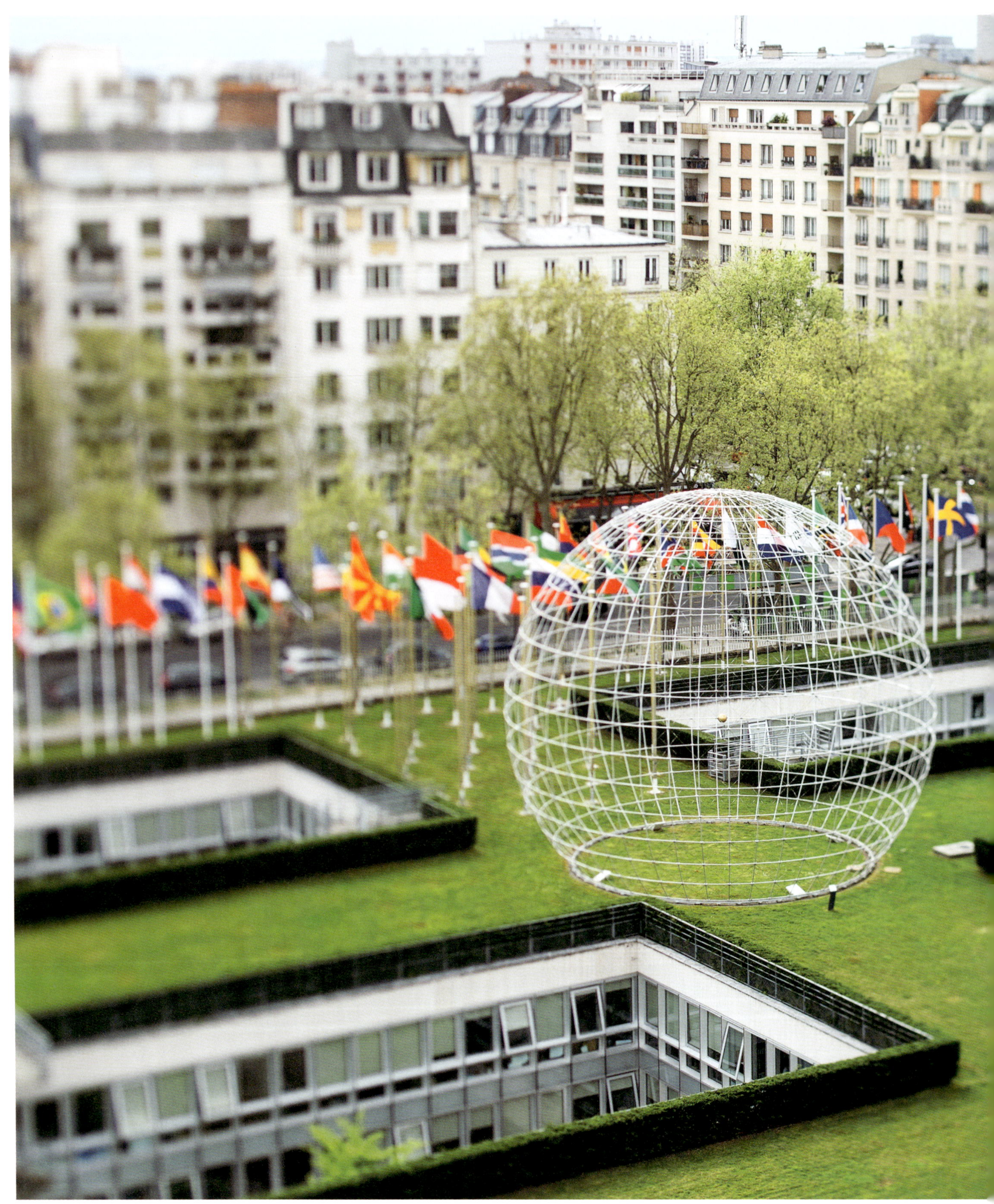

The Symbolic Globe, on the grassy piazza of building IV, a metal structure by Danish engineer Erik Reitzel evoking the logo of the United Nations. View from the École Militaire district, on the corner of Rue de Suffren and Avenue de Lowendal.

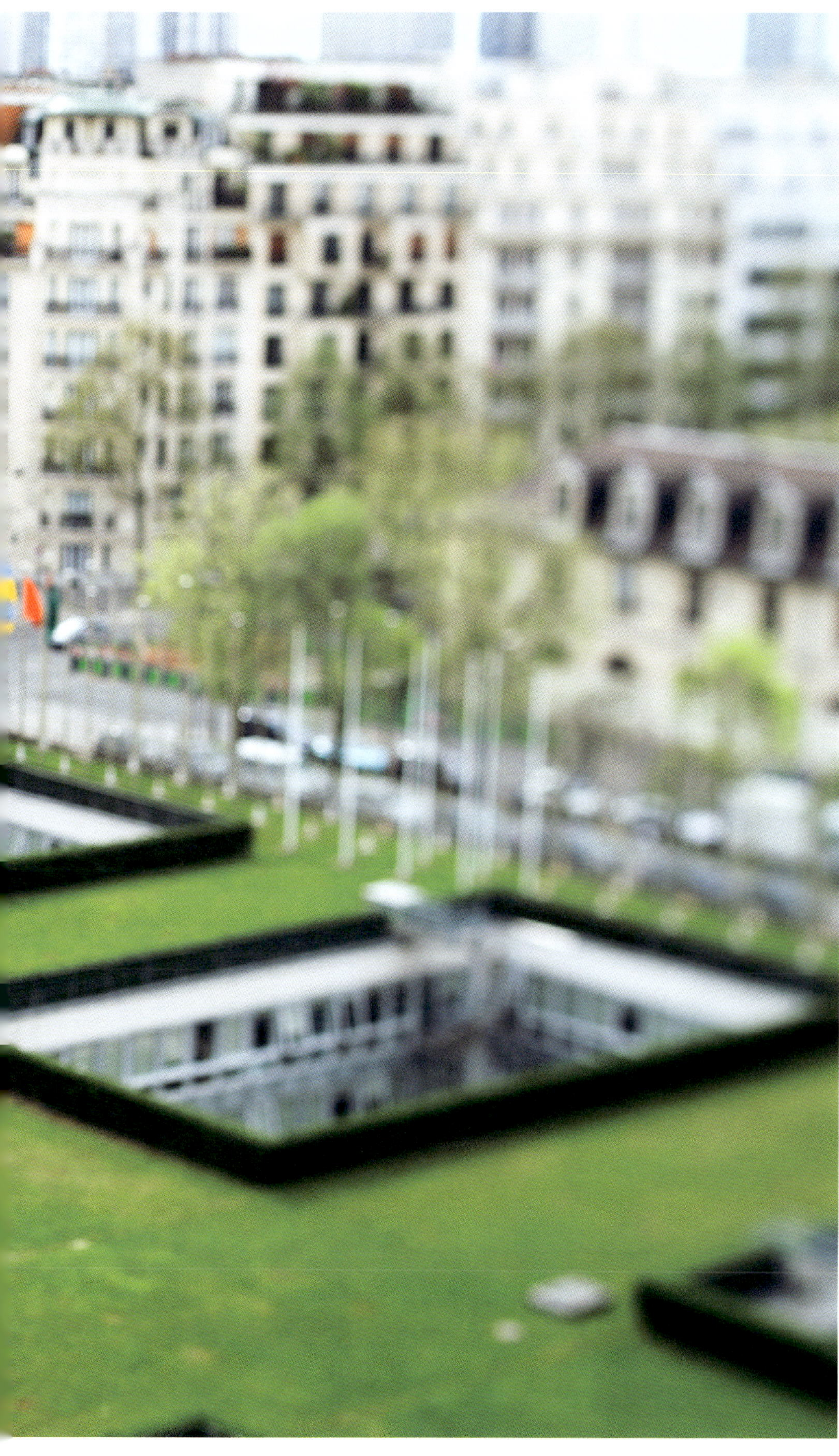

On November 16, 1959, Prince Rainier, following his visit to UNESCO's new headquarters on the Place de Fontenoy a few weeks earlier, addressed the opening of the first scientific conference of the International Atomic Energy Agency (IAEA) on the disposal of radioactive waste, which was held in Monaco, under the auspices of UNESCO. He reminded his audience that throughout its long history, Monaco's deft diplomatic footwork had defused the rival ambitions of its neighbors and shown his country to be "nobody's enemy." He also emphasized that the present conference echoed the philosophy of his great-grandfather Prince Albert I, for whom the scientific domain was "a platform for harmony and global peace." In line with this tradition, in 1960 the Prince created the Centre scientifique de Monaco (CSM, Monaco Scientific Center), equipping the Principality with the means to conduct scientific research and support the work of governmental and international organizations charged with protecting and conserving marine life. The same year, Monaco took part in the preparatory work leading to the creation of UNESCO's Intergovernmental Oceanographic Commission, whose mission was to encourage international cooperation in the realm of marine sciences. Given its expertise, in 1970 the Monaco Scientific Center was naturally designated as the focal point of the Commission. Maintaining the integrity of the ocean was a growing concern, heightened by the issues raised by the climate challenge—in 1973, UNESCO initiated a "world study of pollution in the marine environment." In 1992, Prince Rainier attended the United Nations Conference on Environment and Development in Rio, accompanied by Commandant Cousteau, former director of the Oceanographic Museum. A year before his country's admission to the UN, the Prince launched a vibrant appeal to "turn our blue planet around in a sustainable way, and thus enable our children and future generations to evolve in a healthier, more equitable world.".

DOSSIER | SCIENCES
ONE PLANET, ONE OCEAN, ONE STATE
PAGES 142-148

For Prince Albert II, who succeeded his father in 2005 amid mounting threats to the environment, marine conservation is the focus of his international activities. His foundation, established in 2006, is entrusted with the mission of rallying scientists, political leaders, and economic civil society stakeholders to the cause of conservation. In 2011, the Oceanographic Institute in Paris celebrated one hundred years of existence by renaming itself the Maison des Océans ("Ocean Hub") and expanding its purview to cover various entities involved with environmental and ocean protection, among them the Plateforme Océan Climat, CRIOBE, the French Foundation for Biodiversity

Research (FRB), and the Mediterranean Science Commission. In 2015, the Prince was at UNESCO for Ocean Day; in 2017 he spearheaded the Principality's flagship project, Explorations of Monaco. So it is that Monaco constantly reinvents its scientific quest, as might be expected of the little-known home of IAEA's Marine Environment Laboratories. Originally housed in the Oceanographic Museum, the laboratories then moved to Port Fontvieille to take up residence at 1 Quai Antoine in 1998. As part of the Department of Nuclear Science and Applications, the laboratories use nuclear and isotopic techniques to propose strategies and tools to mitigate the environmental impacts of radionuclides, trace elements and organic pollutants, as well as the effects of climate change.

Alongside marine science, drawing on the legacy of its pioneering princes and numerous archaeological sites worthy of excavation, Monaco is a hub for research into human origins: Anthropology, paleontology and prehistory are studied at the Institute of Human Paleontology in Paris and the Museum of Prehistoric Anthropology in Monaco, attracting an interest that extends well beyond the Principality's borders. In 1960 Princess Grace featured among the members of an honorary committee for the protection of Nubian monuments, an initiative spearheaded by UNESCO Director General Vittorino Veronese. Whatever the place, we find foremost scientists championing the cause closest to their heart—famous names such as Jacques-Yves Cousteau, director of the Oceanographic Museum from 1957 to 1988, and the recently deceased Professor Yves Coppens, to whom the Monaco delegation to UNESCO and Museum of Prehistoric Anthropology paid tribute at UNESCO headquarters in December 2023. Research continues unabated today, showcased by Monegasque scientists and their foreign colleagues, whose media presence reinforces Monaco's influence. We should point out the growing presence of women in the research centers, a welcome development that chimes with "International Day for Women and Girls in Science," a joint UNESCO/UN-Women initiative to promote gender equality in science, celebrated on February 11 every year since 2015. For the general public, in October 2022, to mark the centenary of the death of Prince Albert I of Monaco, the Principality organized its first *Festa d'a Sciença*: a scientific mediation event to promote science to lay people, young and old alike (held a month before UNESCO's World Science Day for Peace and Development on November 10). Also in 2022, Monaco decided to fund a fellowship program for young scientists (YSA) under UNESCO's Man and the Biosphere (MAB) program.

DOSSIER
SCIENCES
MONACO, UNESCO AND THE HUMAN SCIENCES
PAGES 139-141

In July 2024, the MAB Coordinating Council voted to name these grants the “MAB Young Scientists Awards-Prince Albert I of Monaco” in honor of the latter’s contribution to ocean exploration and science.

It is this plurality of science that matters for the Principality—a multichord progression in the realm of scientific creativity, described by Audrey Azoulay in December 2022 as “a language akin to music, part of the intangible heritage of humanity, that touches the heart of each and every one of us.” As such, science is inseparable from education and culture. Fully aware of its advantages in this respect, the Principality leverages those assets to advance science-driven educational programs that promote the right to basic education, gender equality in education and education for all. And there is no shortage of participants, whether among Government members or organizations inspired by the activities of H.R.H. the Princess of Hanover who, as Chairwoman of AMADE and UNESCO Goodwill Ambassador since 2003, spearheads the vision “of a world where every child, whatever their social, religious or cultural origins, can live with dignity, in security, and in the respect of their fundamental rights. A world where every child has the opportunity to express their full potential.” In 1969, to mark the third edition of International Literacy Day, Prince Rainier called on the world “to bridge the immense gap between needs and resources.” And children, of course, are very much part of the equation. Whether privately or publicly educated, Monegasque children receive a quality education that equips them to navigate their increasingly complex world, complete with two courses sponsored by the Government: a module on the history of Monaco to make them aware of their rich heritage; and instruction in the Monegasque language. European and international languages receive special emphasis to help children open up to the world, with the accent on digital education to raise awareness from an early age of global issues and how to address them. In addition, the Department of National Education, Youth and Sports pays special attention to public commemorations and civic reflection to mark significant moments in history. Cases in point are Children’s Rights Day, and the Day of Remembrance of Genocide and the Prevention of Crimes against Humanity, punctuated by meetings and educational projects as

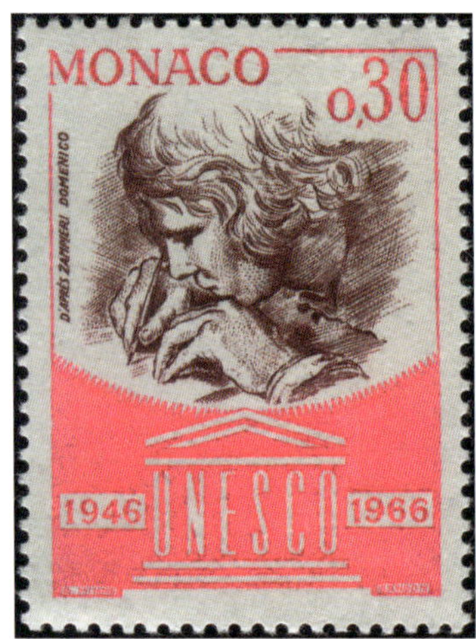

DOSSIER
EDUCATION
L’ASSOCIATION MONDIALE DES AMIS DE L’ENFANCE (WORLD ASSOCIATION OF CHILDREN’S FRIENDS)
PAGES 129-133

ABOVE Commemorative stamp for the 20th anniversary of UNESCO, based on a work by Domenico Zampieri, known as Domenichino (1581-1641), 1966.

OPPOSITE PAGE Letter from Prince Rainier for the third Literacy Day, 1969.

FOLLOWING PAGES Room X, reserved for the Executive Board, building IV of the UNESCO headquarters. It is characterized by its ceiling formed by twenty radiating beams supported by a star-shaped core.

The functional architecture contributes to the work of the delegates and ambassadors, promoting communication and understanding.

Depuis le jour où S. M. I. le Shainshah d'Iran a solennellement annoncé le lancement d'une croisade mondiale contre l'analphabétisme, tous les Etats membres de l'U. N. E. S. C. O., toutes les organisations non gouvernementales spécialisées ont rivalisé d'imagination et de dévouement pour susciter l'enthousiasme général en faveur d'une telle entreprise de solidarité, la plus vaste de tous les temps par le nombre des hommes concernés.

Plusieurs millénaires après l'invention de l'écriture, plusieurs millénaires après l'épanouissement, puis la disparition de civilisations brillantes, et alors que vient d'être donné à la machine le pouvoir de penser et de s'exprimer, des êtres humains, par centaines de millions, demeurent encore dans l'ignorance des quelques signes graphiques indispensables à tout échange fructueux sur le plan intellectuel et à tout progrès.

Pour vaincre l'analphabétisme dans le monde, pour combler rapidement l'immense vide qui sépare les besoins et les ressources, il est indispensable que tous les Etats membres soutiennent le magnifique effort déployé par l'U. N. E. S. C. O. dans cette lutte salutaire et mobilisent à cet effet tous leurs moyens. Aussi la Principauté de Monaco tient-elle à honneur de prendre part à cette noble croisade.

Au seuil de "l'Année Internationale de l'Education", cette "3ème Journée Internationale de l'Alphabétisation" trouvera sa signification la plus complète en retenant l'attention de tous les hommes et en les appelant à réfléchir sur l'un des plus grands objectifs de la famille humaine.

Rainier Prince de Monaco

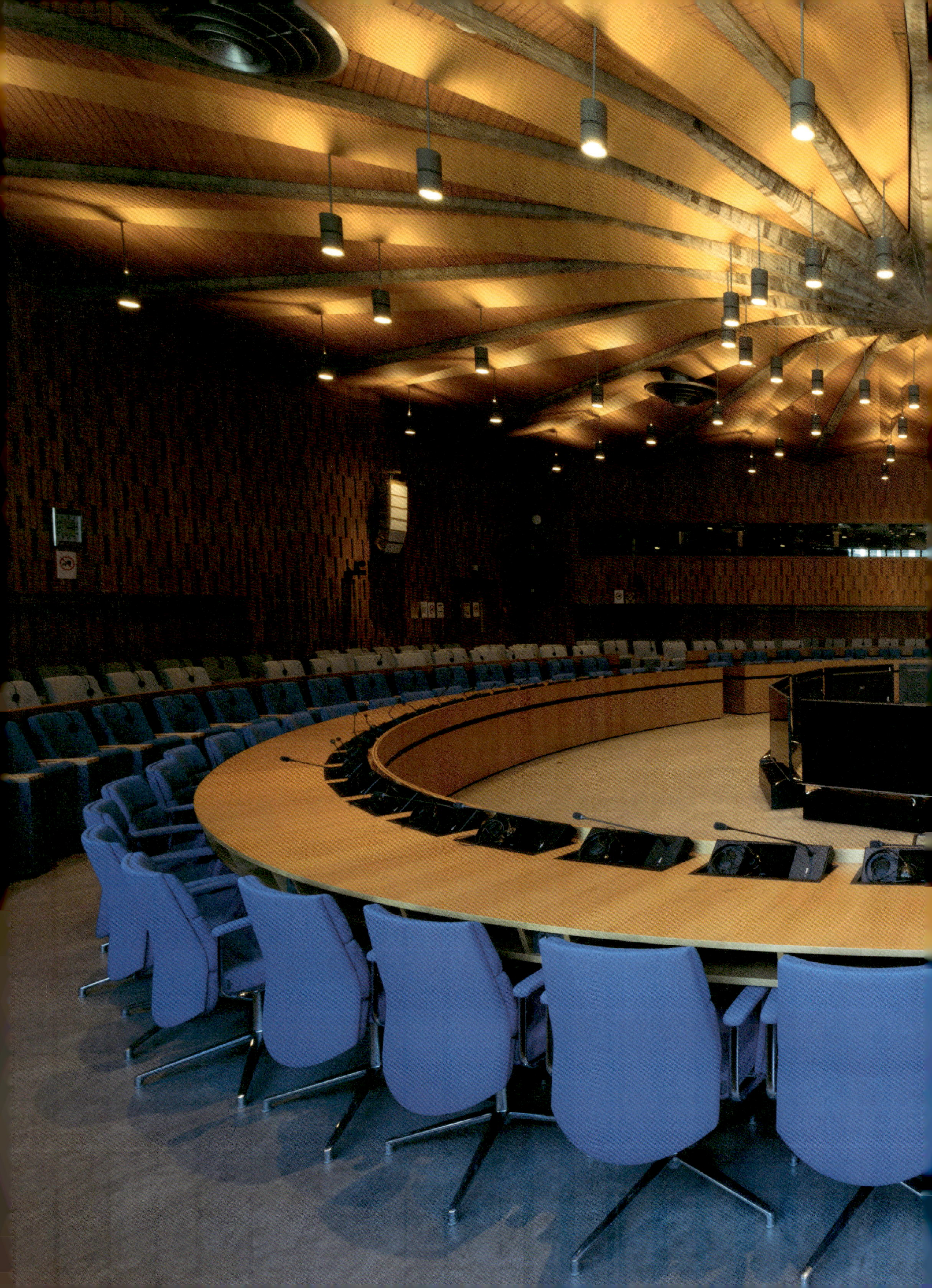

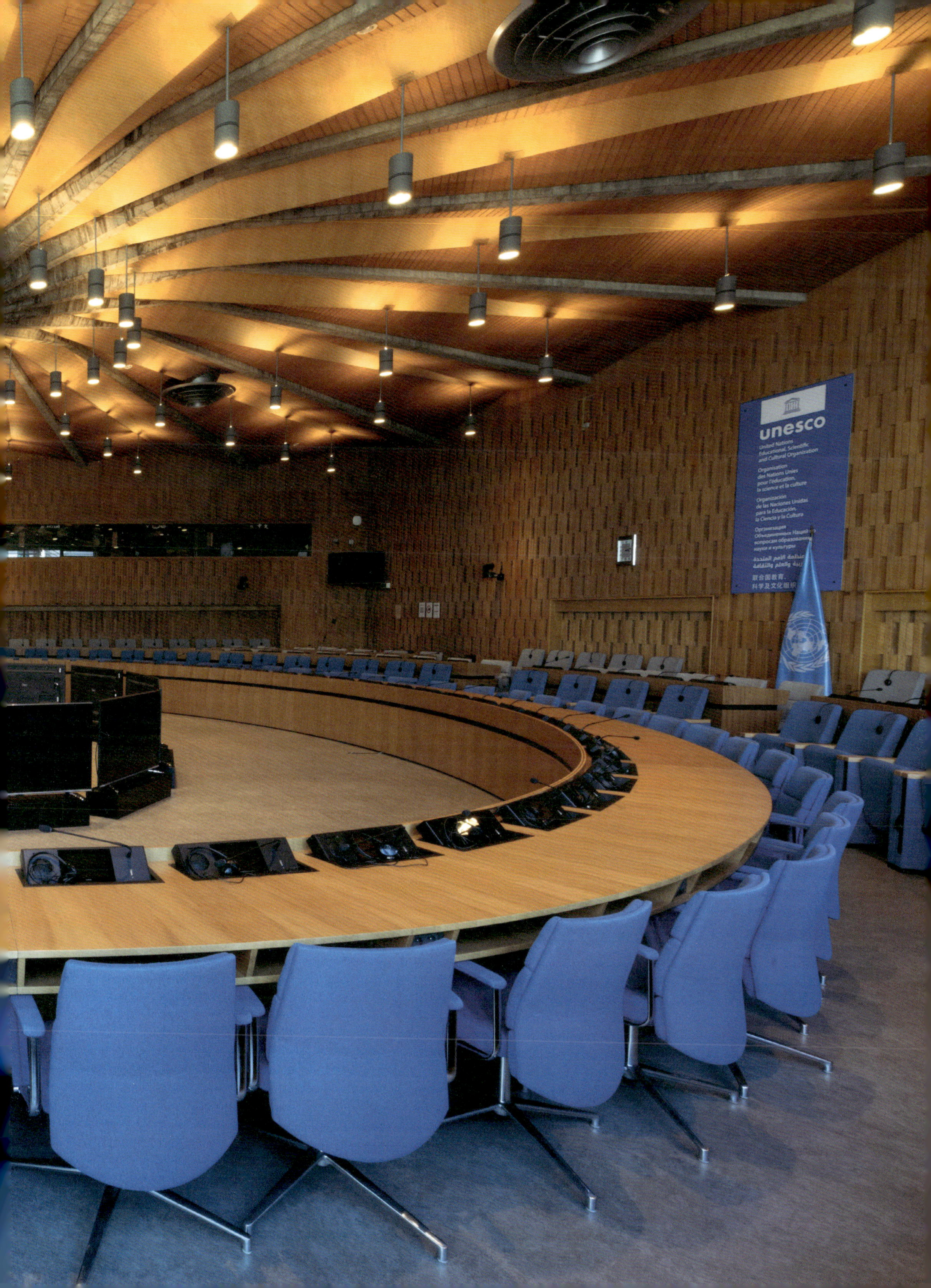
unesco
United Nations
Educational, Scientific
and Cultural Organization
Organisation
des Nations Unies
pour l'éducation,
la science et la culture
Organización
de las Naciones Unidas
para la Educación,
la Ciencia y la Cultura

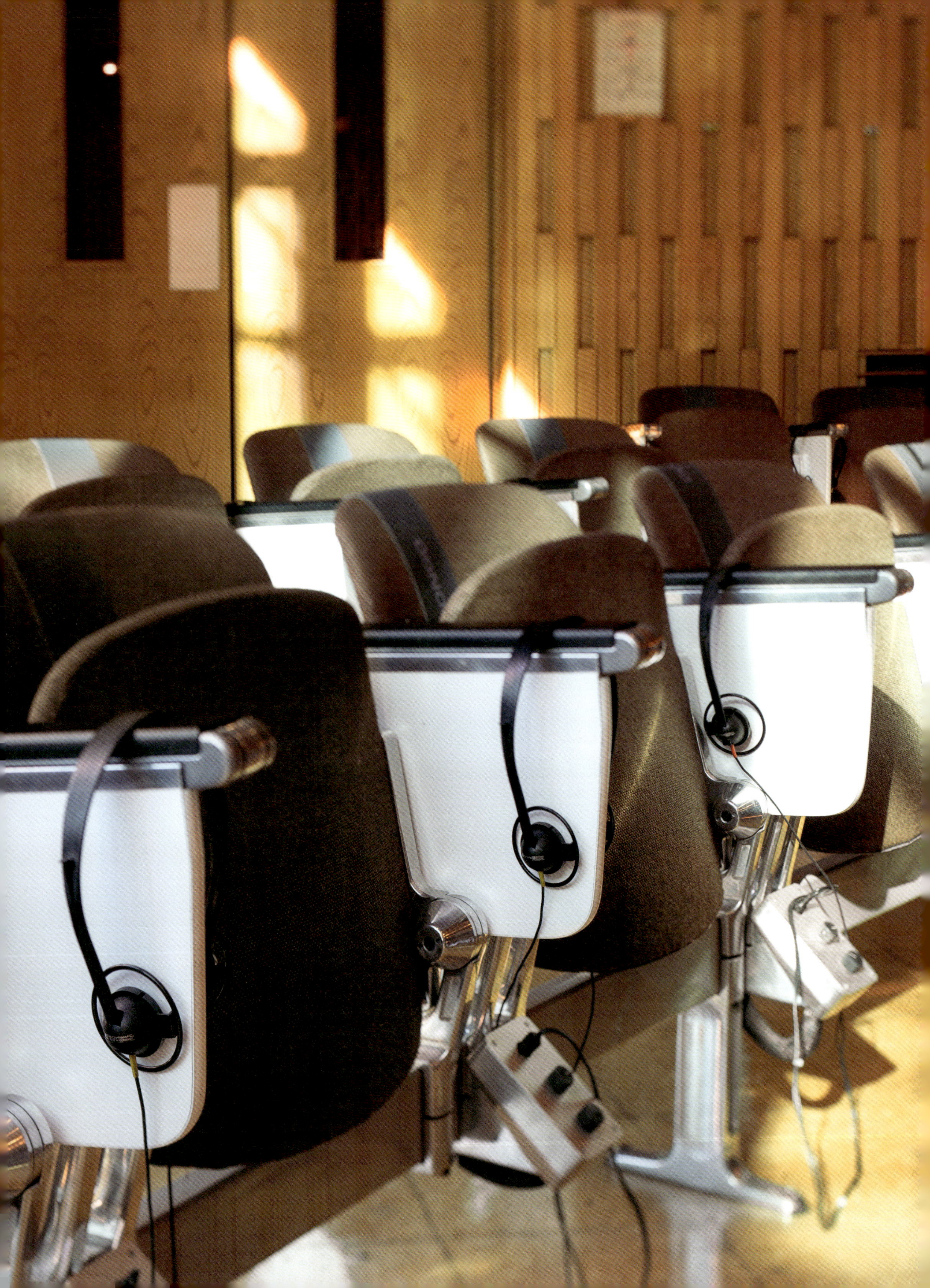

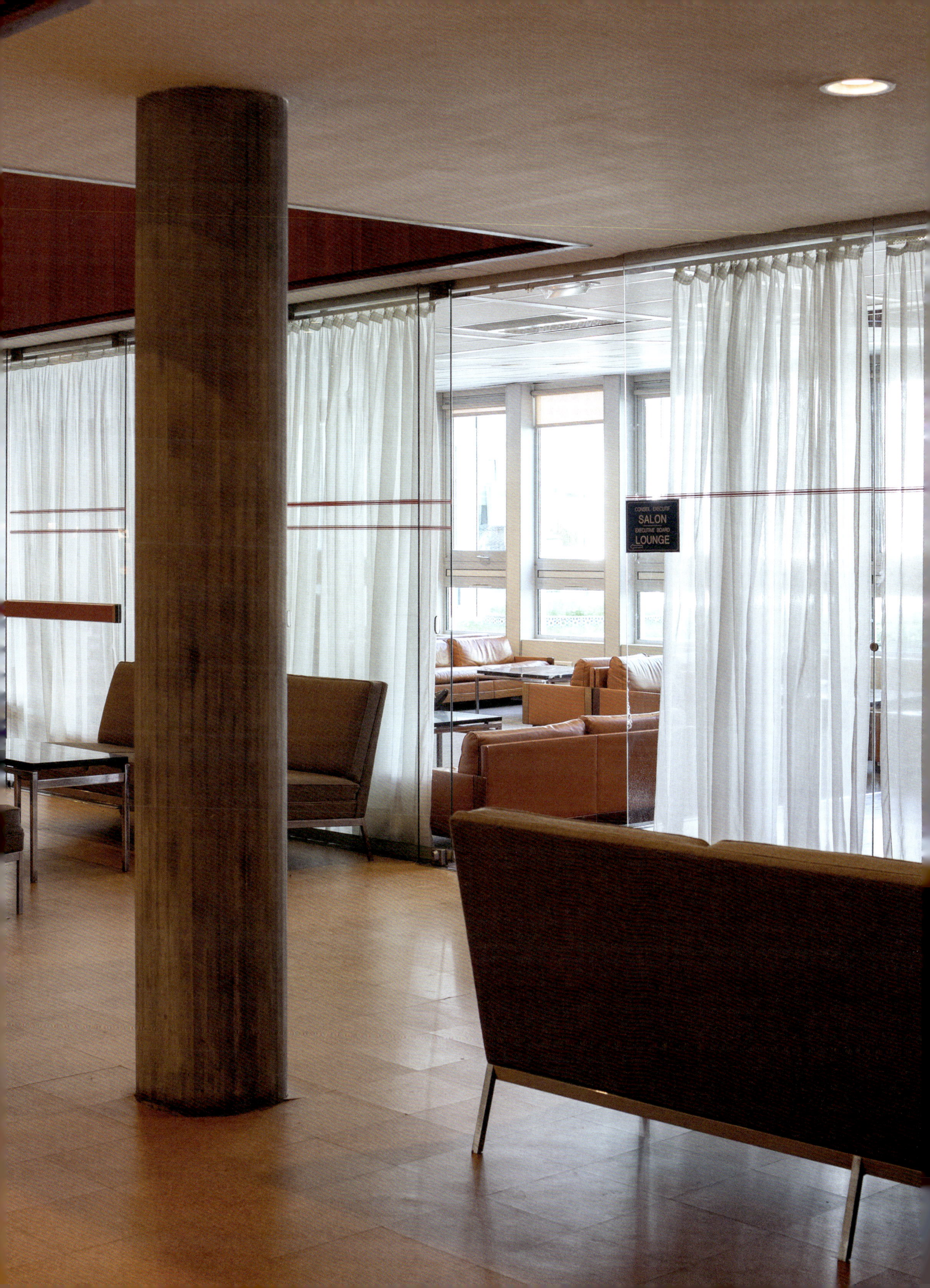
SALON
LOUNGE

requested by the international community, UNESCO and the Council of Europe. The virtues of physical education are meanwhile celebrated on Olympic Day and most especially as part of the initiatives launched by the Princess Charlene of Monaco Foundation to mark World Drowning Prevention Day on July 25. Monegasque pupils who go on to higher education are therefore fully equipped to explore different fields of study, whether at home or in France. They can pursue a degree at the University of Monaco (IUM), a private institution founded in 1986, or train as stage designers at the Pavillon Bosio, École Supérieure d'Arts Plastiques, named after neo-classical sculptor and native of Monaco François-Joseph Bosio. Across the border, there is the Université Côte d'Azur and the preparatory classes for the Grandes Ecoles (*classes préparatoires aux grandes écoles*) of the Lycée Masséna in Nice. Students who opt for a French University or a Parisian *Grande Ecole* can stay at the Fondation de Monaco in Paris, established in 1929 on the initiative of Prince Pierre.

In the realm of culture, the Principality is ever aware of the need to balance insularity with openness. Just as culture itself has expanded over time to include not just literary and artistic production but also lifestyle, sport, and heritage in all its forms—technological, media, and artefactual—so the Principality adapts to new realities, extending its outreach through events that give voice to its small-state identity. There can be no better example of this than the concert held at UNESCO on October 26, 1999, to mark the opening of the Thirtieth General Conference and Monaco's fiftieth membership anniversary. The performers were Les Petits Chanteurs de Monaco of the Monaco Cathedral Choir, whose international tours are a showcase for the art and soul of their tiny nation. Of the three core pillars of UNESCO, culture is without a doubt the oldest and the most visible within the Principality. Steeped in history, Monaco's cultural wealth is the legacy of a policy that has been reaping the fruits of patronage ever since Honoré II first took the title of Prince in 1612. Foremost among its cultural assets are the Prince's Palace, the Oceanographic Museum, the Monte-Carlo Casino, not forgetting the Fontvieille Sculpture Park with its collection of classical and contemporary statues, and the Jardins Saint-Martin. Culture in the reign of Charles III was a lever of state recognition—it was the culture of the Belle Epoque, of Raoul Gunsbourg, Enrico Caruso and Feodor Chaliapin. Subsequently, writers like Cocteau, Colette and Pagnol became friends of the Principality, also Armand Lunel (1892-1977), winner of the Prix Renaudot in 1926 and philosophy teacher at the Monaco lycée, who in 1951 wrote the report for the National

Council on cultural relations between East and West. This is of course the work of the Prince Pierre Foundation, established in 1966 in tribute to a great patron of the arts and letters and a pioneering UNESCO figure. Presided over today by H.R.H. the Princess of Hanover, the Foundation pursues its mission to foster contemporary creativity through the presentation of three annual awards, one each for literature, music and art, and the dissemination of culture via a season of conferences featuring writers, artists and intellectuals. Timeless and ubiquitous, Monegasque culture draws on the achievements of yesterday to meet the concepts of today. The words of Marcel Pagnol, a member of the first Monegasque Commission for UNESCO, still resonate: "Here, the arts can still live in the shade of the olive tree, on the shores of the Latin Sea, where the authority of one guards the freedom of all." These days, a wealth of cultural activities take place under the patronage of H.S.H. Prince Albert II, with H.R.H. the Princess of Hanover, as chairman of the Prince Pierre Foundation, paying special attention to the world of the arts, literature and live performance. Few countries these days stage so many events capable of stimulating the imagination of so many different people, nationals and residents alike. There is the Festival du Fort Antoine, the quadrennial Mondial du Théâtre, concerts at the Prince's Palace, film programming at the Institut Audiovisuel, and the Rencontres des Sites Historiques Grimaldi de Monaco (meetings of the historical sites of the Grimaldis of Monaco), which invites former French and Italian "fiefs" of Monaco for two days of friendship and openness. And few countries are home to so many distinguished performance venues. The Ballets de Monte-Carlo, for example, brings together under one roof the Ballets de Monte-Carlo company, the Monaco Dance Forum, the Princess Grace Academy, the Opera, the Philharmonic Orchestra, and the Prince Rainier III Academy. Theaters include the Théâtre Princesse Grace, the Théâtre des Variétés, the Théâtre des Muses, and the Théâtre Fort Antoine. In the realm of the arts, the new National Museum of Monaco explores contemporary art forms, and the exhibitions held at the Grimaldi Forum and the Oceanographic Museum enhance the Principality's cultural outreach.

DOSSIER
CULTURE
UNESCO, THE PERFORMING ARTS AND LE MONDIAL DU THÉÂTRE FESTIVAL OF AMATEUR THEATER IN MONACO
PAGES 156-159

Also noteworthy is the Monegasque National Committee of the UNESCO Association of Art (AIAP), established in 1955 by Étienne Clérissi (1888-1971) to promote the plastic arts in the Principality and foster collaboration between artists from all countries. All artistic fields are thus well represented in Monaco, including the circus arts as celebrated by the International Circus Festival of Monte-Carlo, launched

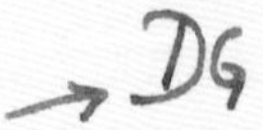

FONDATION PRINCE PIERRE DE MONACO

PALAIS DE MONACO

Le 9 juin 1967

Monsieur le Directeur Général,

j'ai l'honneur de vous faire parvenir, sous ce pli, un exemplaire des procès-verbaux des première et deuxième sessions de notre Conseil d'Administration, procès-verbaux approuvés lors de notre troisième session, tenue les 10 et 11 mai 1967.

Je vous prie de vouloir bien agréer, Monsieur le Directeur Général, l'assurance de ma haute considération.

Le Président
du Conseil d'Administration

Monsieur René MAHEU
Directeur Général de l'Unesco
place de Fontenoy
75 - PARIS 7ème

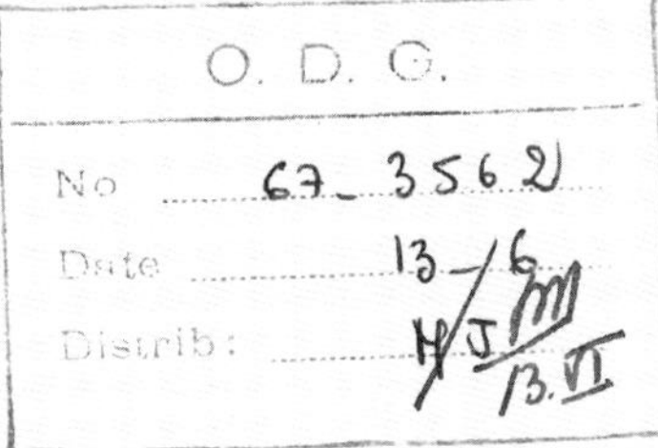
O. D. G.
No 67_3562
Date 13-6
Distrib:

Letter dated June 9, 1967 addressed to René Maheu, UNESCO Director-General, with the minutes of the first sessions of the Prince Pierre Foundation, 1966-1967.

FONDATION PRINCE PIERRE DE MONACO

Conseil d'Administration

1ère Session : 28 et 29 avril 1966

Le jeudi 28 avril 1966, à 11 heures, le Conseil d'Administration de la Fondation Prince Pierre de Monaco a tenu sa première séance de travail au Palais Princier, Salon Matignon, sous la Haute Présidence de S.A.S. le Prince Rainier III.

Assistaient à cette réunion :

S. Exc. M. Paul Noghès, Président du Conseil d'Administration
le Prince Louis de Polignac
le Comte Guy du Boisrouvray
S. Exc. M. François Valéry
M. André Maurois, Président du Conseil Littéraire
M. Emmanuel Bondeville, membre du Conseil Musical, représentant
M. Georges Auric, Président de ce Conseil.
M. René Novella, Secrétaire Général du Conseil d'Administration, assurait le Secrétariat.

Après avoir ouvert la séance, Son Altesse Sérénissime déclara :

Messieurs,

"Je suis extrêmement heureux et ému, en vous accueillant dans ce Palais, de pouvoir procéder à l'installation officielle du Conseil d'Administration de la Fondation qui porte le nom de mon bien-aimé Père.

"Mais avant tout, je voudrais remercier très affectueusement chacun de vous d'avoir accepté de faire partie de ce Conseil, et d'être présent aujourd'hui. Vous me donnez ainsi la preuve que l'idée, que j'avais eue de créer cette Fondation portant le nom du Prince Pierre de Monaco, était bonne. Elle doit donc son existence, non seulement à ma volonté, mais aussi à vos adhésions spontanées.

"Les prix littéraire et de composition musicale portent, tous deux, désormais le nom de Celui qui s'est tant passionné pour les lettres, la musique et pour toutes les manifestations de l'intelligence humaine. Ainsi, le grand souvenir de mon cher Père restera plus vivant encore, puisque chaque année deux prix récompenseront des talents exceptionnels dans les lettres et la musique.

.../...

by Prince Rainier III in 1974. Pursuing his legacy today, his daughter Princess Stéphanie is chairwoman of the Festival as well as honorary chairwoman of the World Circus Federation, with which discussions are underway with a view to inscribing the circus arts on the UNESCO World Heritage List. Cultural events receive government support through the Department of Cultural Affairs, with an astonishing five percent of the state budget going to subsidize cultural entities, artists and writers, mount heritage projects, fund cultural facilities, and promote artistic and cultural education in schools. In fact, Monaco's cultural policy has three objectives: to offer a world-class program of events worthy of a cultural metropolis; to promote cultural participation through exhibitions, conferences and shows, together with quality programs and workshops that celebrate associative thinking; and, in line with UNESCO's Memory of the World program (1992), to protect and enhance the value of the Principality's cultural heritage. Numerous entities play their part, among them: the Archives et la Bibliothèque du Palais Princier, the Institut Audiovisuel, the Mission de Préfiguration des Archives Nationales, the Fonds Régional, the Institut du Patrimoine, the Archives de la Société des Bains de Mer (SBM), and the Comité National des Traditions Monégasques. In response, a decision was adopted at the 219th session of the UNESCO Executive Board, in spring 2024, to preserve the Organization's archives, their value as a source of documentary heritage having been amply demonstrated by research. The Principality was among the decision-makers and, as stated by its delegation, volunteered to donate funds in favor of UNESCO archives for the year 2024, as part of its celebrations to mark seventy-five years of UNESCO membership as well as the hundredth anniversary of the establishment of the International Institute of Intellectual Cooperation.

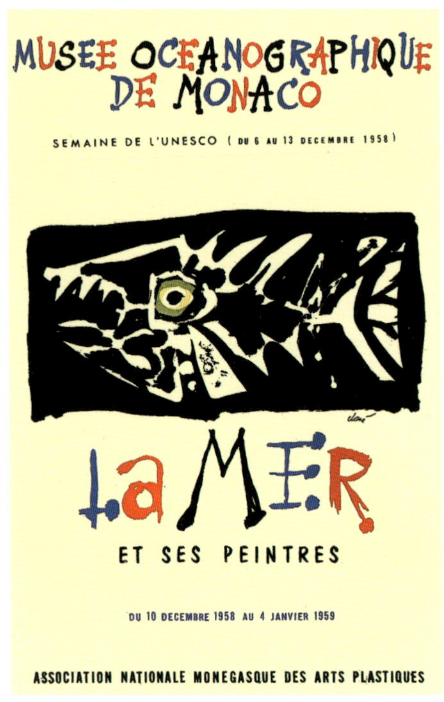

DOSSIER
CULTURE
HERITAGE, MONACO AND UNESCOO
PAGES 160-163

ABOVE Poster for the exhibition *La Mer et ses peintres* (the sea and its painters), held by the Monegasque National Association of Visual Arts, as part of UNESCO Week in December 1958 (with the participation of artists from the Committee and César, Jean Carzou, Bernard Buffet, etc.)

OPPOSITE PAGE Hereditary Prince Albert, honorary President of the Monegasque National Association of Visual Arts since 1995, and Jean-Michel Folon, guest of honor at the Salon, in 1997. The poster is an original creation by the artist.

FOLLOWING PAGES *Earth Sends the Fluids of Life and Blossoming to the Worlds of the Universe (1987),* Liudmila Meshkova (Ukraine, 1938), ceramic mural behind the conference bar, UNESCO Art Collection (added in 1987).

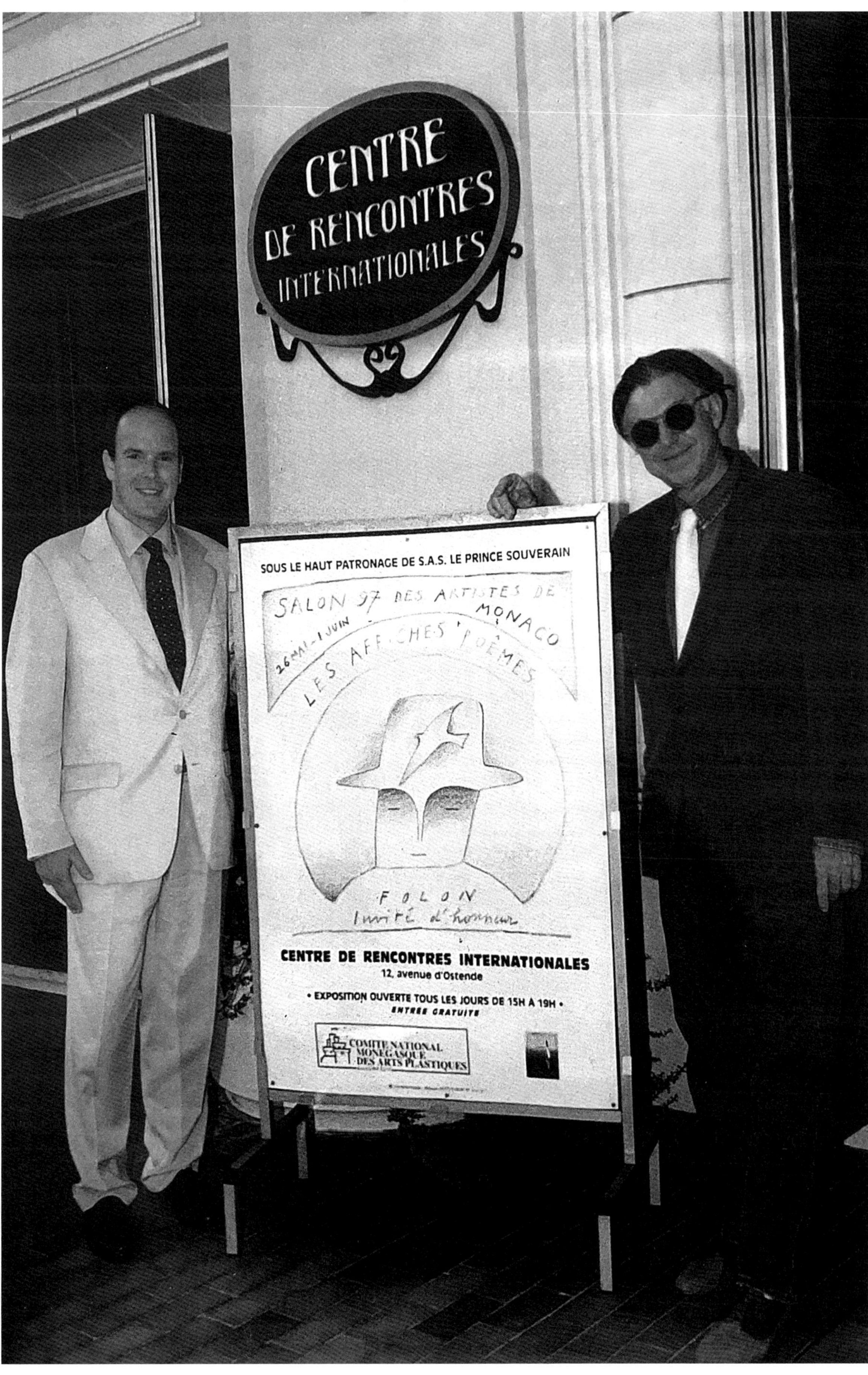
CENTRE
DE RENCONTRES
INTERNATIONALES
SOUS LE HAUT PATRONAGE DE S.A.S. LE PRINCE SOUVERAIN
SALON 97 DES ARTISTES DE MONACO
26 MAI - 1 JUIN
LES AFFICHES POÈMES
FOLON
Invité d'honneur
CENTRE DE RENCONTRES INTERNATIONALES
12, avenue d'Ostende
• EXPOSITION OUVERTE TOUS LES JOURS DE 15H A 19H •
ENTRÉE GRATUITE
COMITE NATIONAL
MONEGASQUE
DES ARTS PLASTIQUES

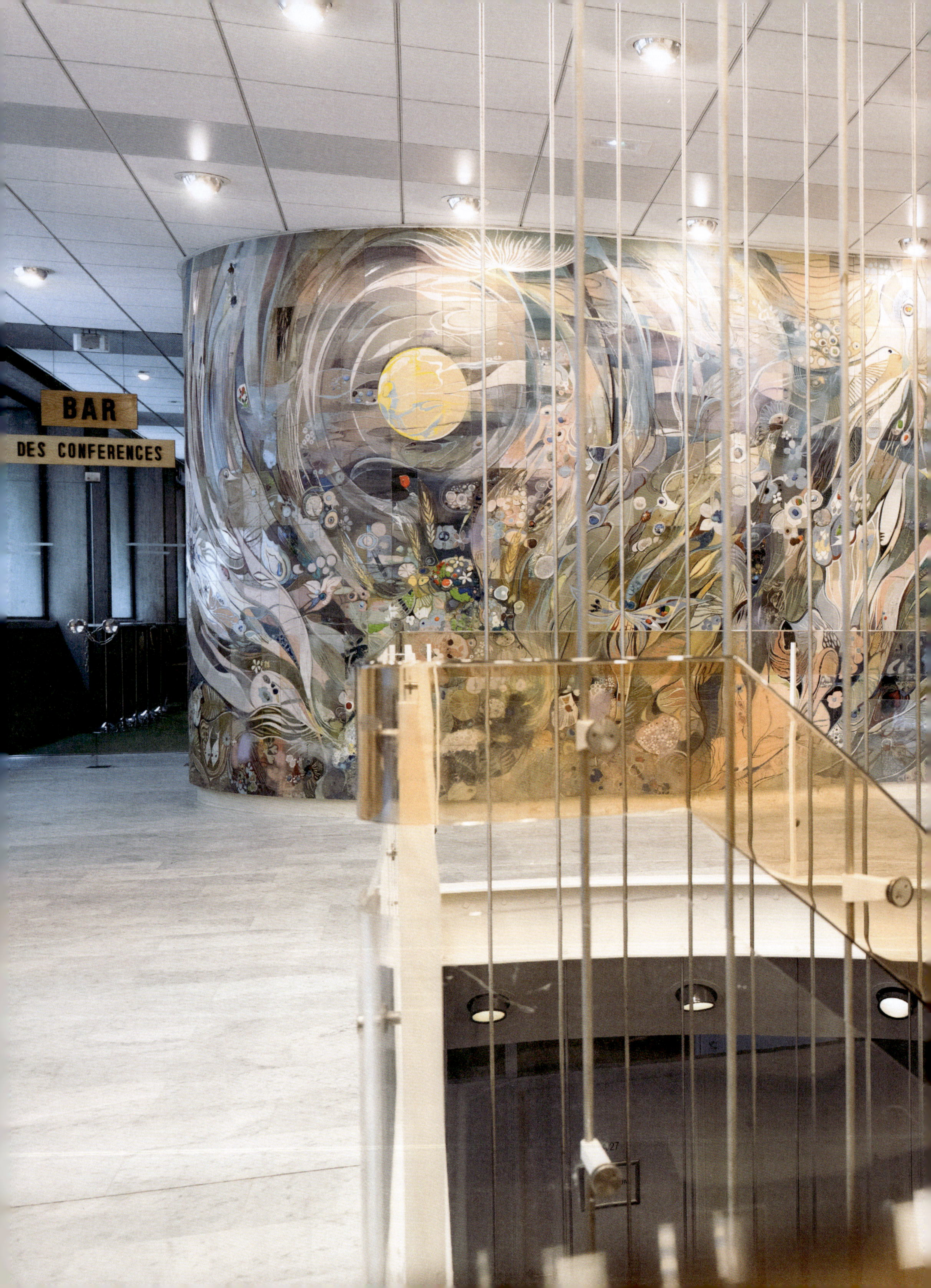

BAR
DES CONFERENCES

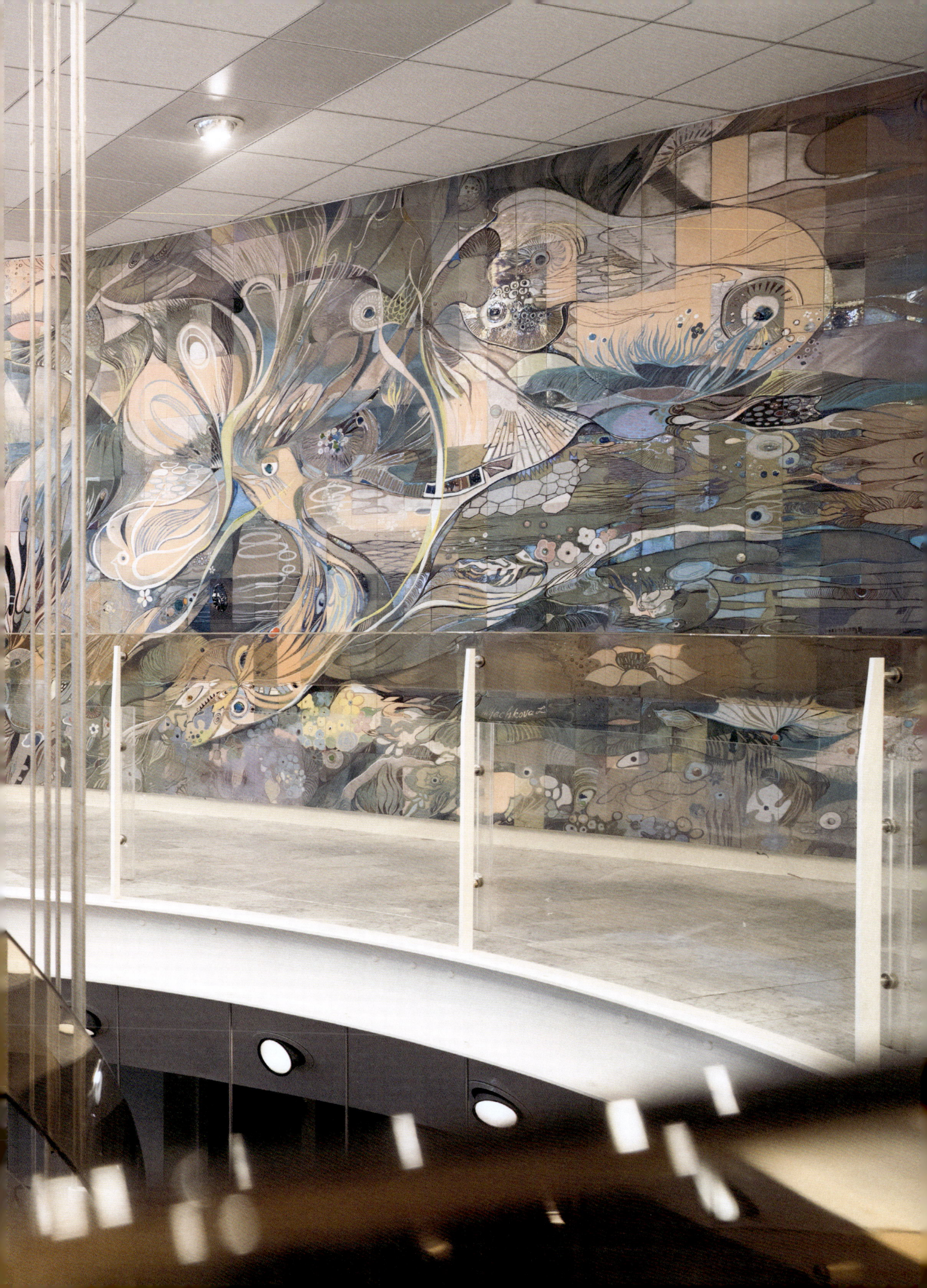

MONACO AND UNESCO, A CONSTANTLY RENEWED DIALOGUE

Science has its shore; education has its rock; culture has its gardens: Monaco is small in size alone. René Maheu was not mistaken when on a visit to the country in 1968, he saluted "this welcoming Principality" with its "eminently positive working conditions." Shortly after him, Senegalese poet Léopold Sédar Senghor came to Monaco in 1977 to receive the Prince Pierre of Monaco Literary Prize for his collected works. In his acceptance speech, he called for more cross-fertilization between the two shores of the Mediterranean, hailing Monaco as "a twentieth-century Greece"—a well-deserved accolade for this country whose acclaimed Rencontres Philosophiques de Monaco make philosophy accessible to all the residents of the city-state. Created in 2015 on the initiative of Mme Charlotte Casiraghi, Monaco's Philosophical Encounters are held in conjunction with the UNESCO Chair "Practice of Philosophy with Children"—a further demonstration of the Principality's close ties with UNESCO.

DOSSIER

EDUCATION

LES RENCONTRES PHILOSOPHIQUES DE MONACO (THE PHILOSOPHICAL ENCOUNTERS OF MONACO)

PAGES 134-135

Monaco feels quite at home at Place de Fontenoy, and most especially in the "Monaco Room": the delegates room, decorated in 1960 by Albert Diato (1927-1985) at the initiative of Prince Pierre. Monaco-born painter and ceramicist Albert Diato embodied the values of UNESCO. Introduced to ceramics through Picasso in Vallauris, he went on to exhibit across the world, producing artworks that now feature alongside those of other famous artists in the UNESCO art collection, among them Pablo Picasso, Joan Miró, Jean Arp, Karel Appel, Afro Basaldella, Alexander Calder, Roberto Matta, Henry Moore, and Rufino Tamayo.

Monaco has also made its presence felt through the efforts of its foreign officials, at times when the development of universal programs required them to put aside their identity. Jacques Boisson, for instance, deserves particular mention for his work with adult literacy units in the period 1968-1982, and his efforts in publicizing human rights research.

Then there is Monaco's presence at UNESCO headquarters—through the day-to-day efforts of its delegations, General Conferences, and its tenures on the Executive Board. The circular seating arrangement of the Executive Board Room is echoed by the ceiling design, symbolizing the equal dignity and collaborative spirit of the board members.

OPPOSITE PAGE *Prometheus Bringing Fire to Mankind* (1958), Rufino Tamayo (1899-1991), acquired by UNESCO to decorate Room II of the conference building in 1958, UNESCO Art Collection.

FOLLOWING PAGES *Bird*, ceramic decoration by Albert Diato commissioned by Prince Pierre for the ceiling of the Princesse Caroline Library, inaugurated on May 3, 1960, on the site of the Place d'Armes police station in Monaco. The work was recently rediscovered, restored and installed at the Lycée Rainier III in 2015, in the entrance hall to the auditorium.

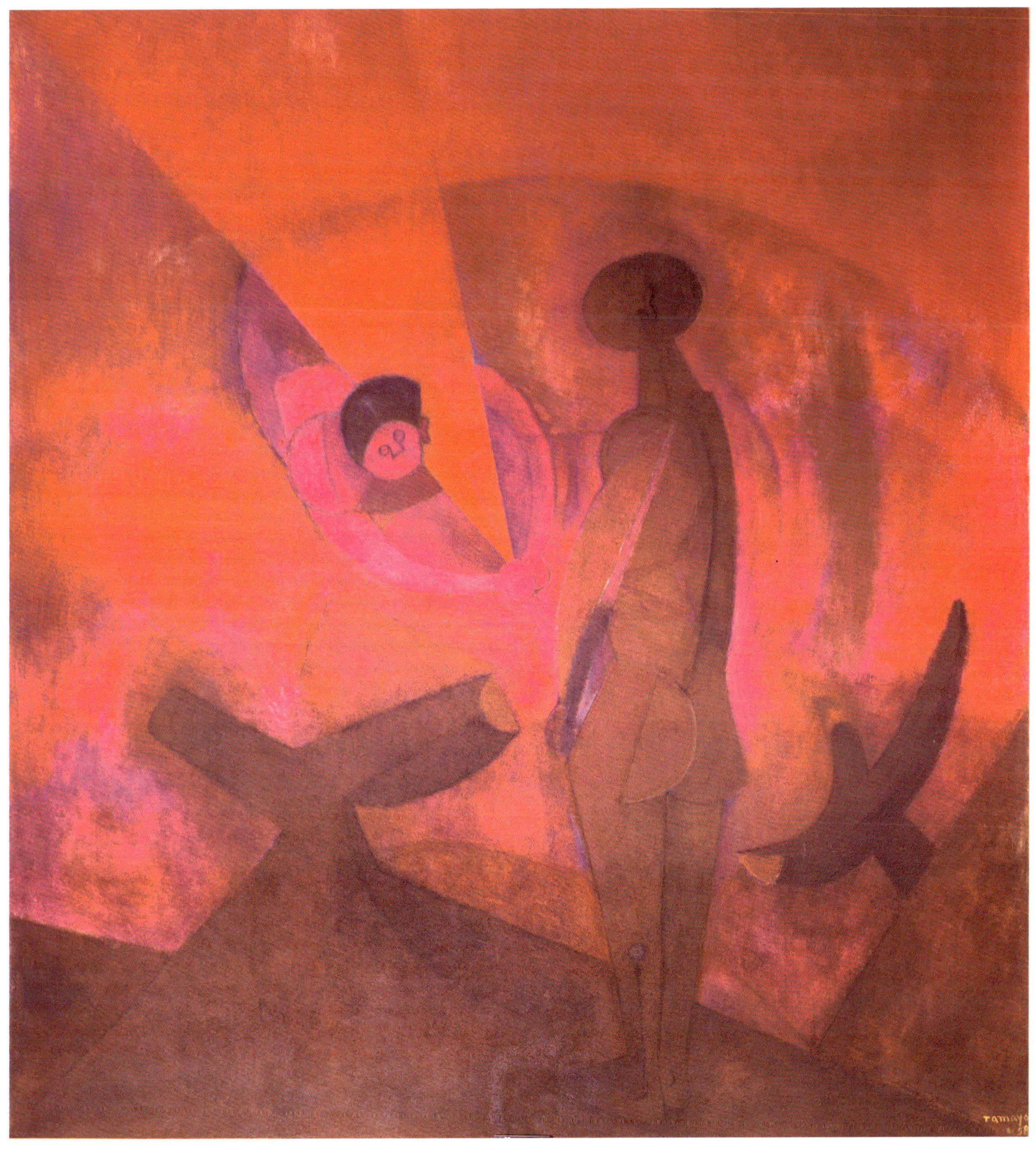
Tamayo

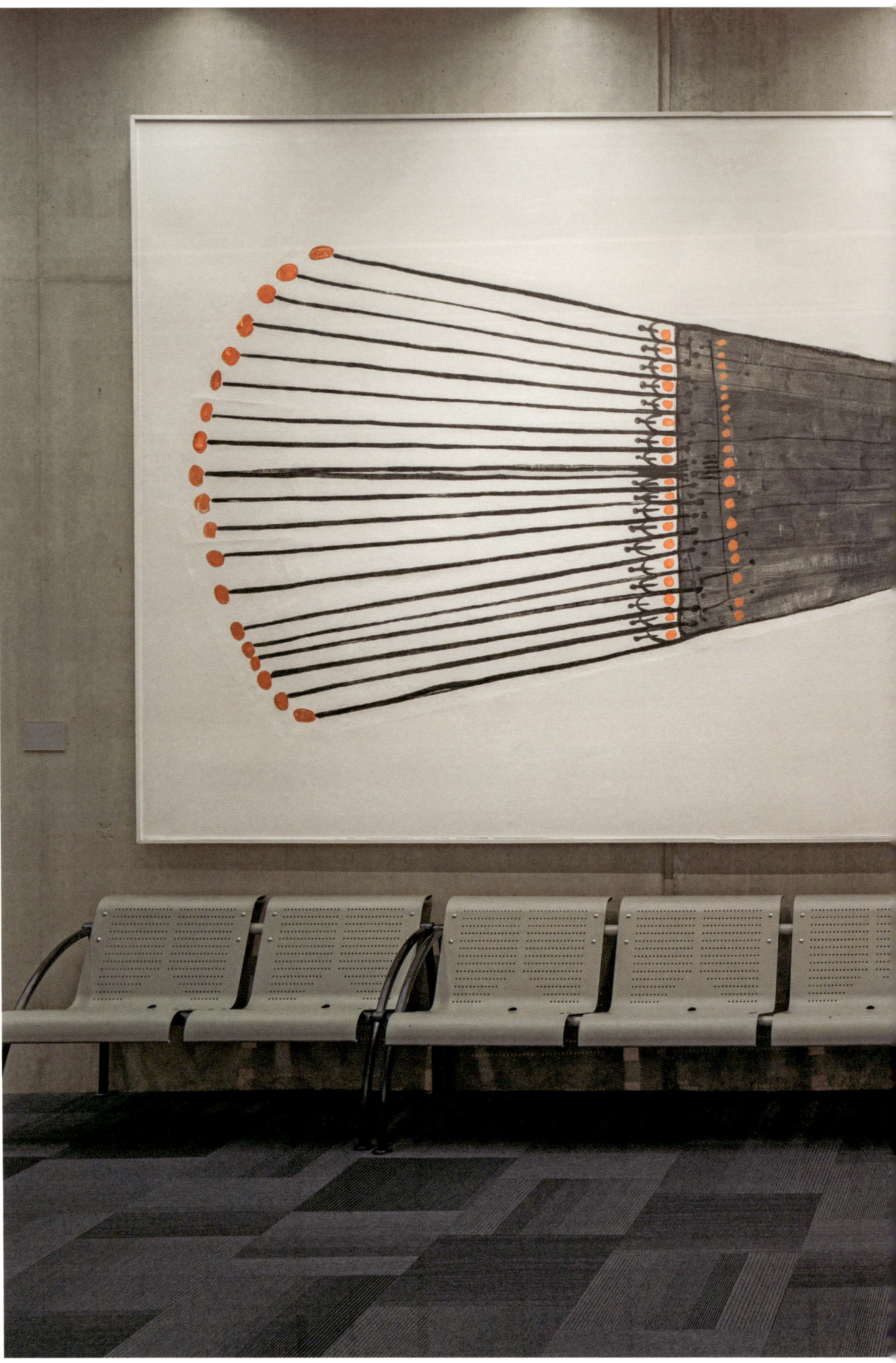

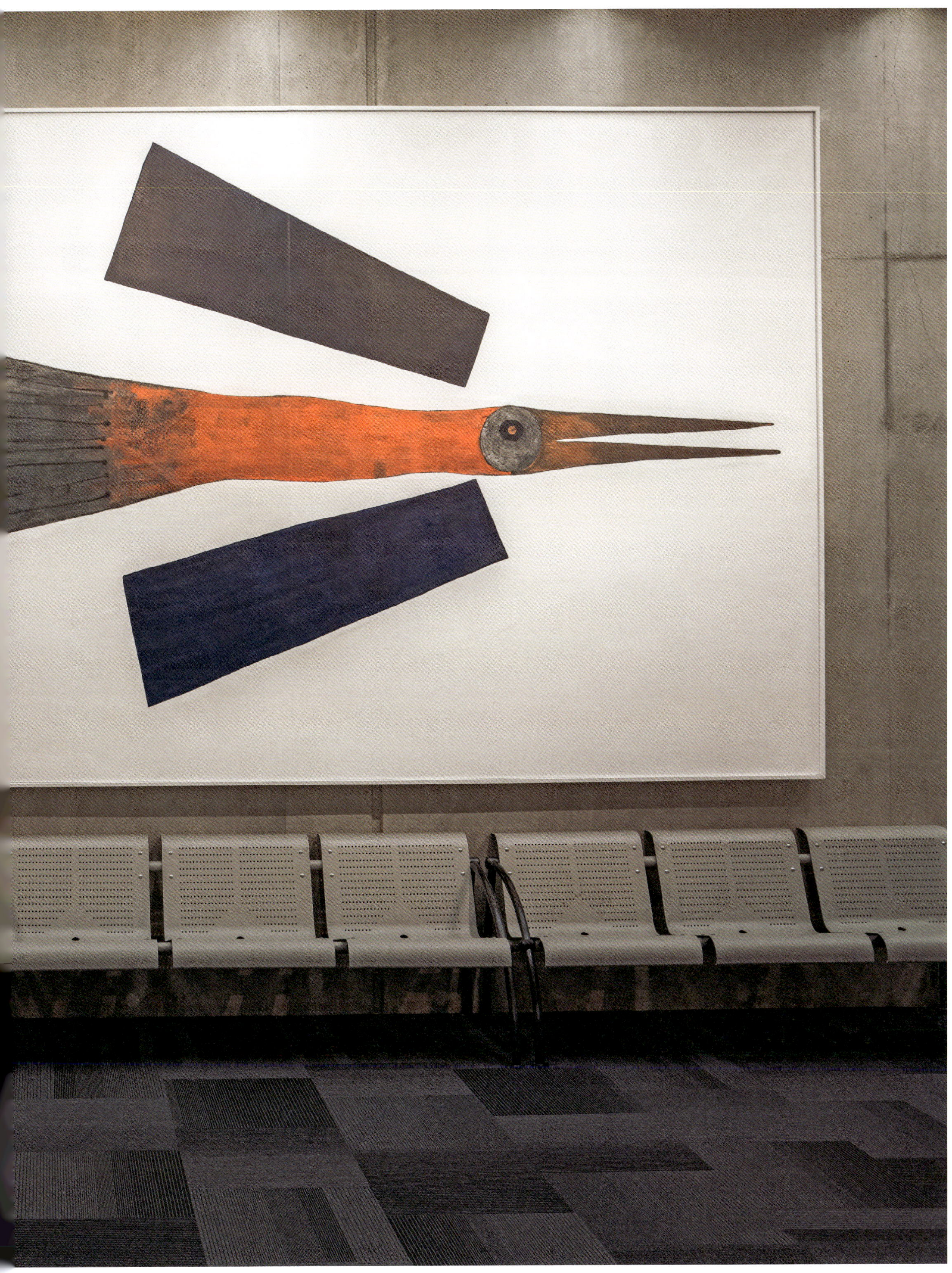

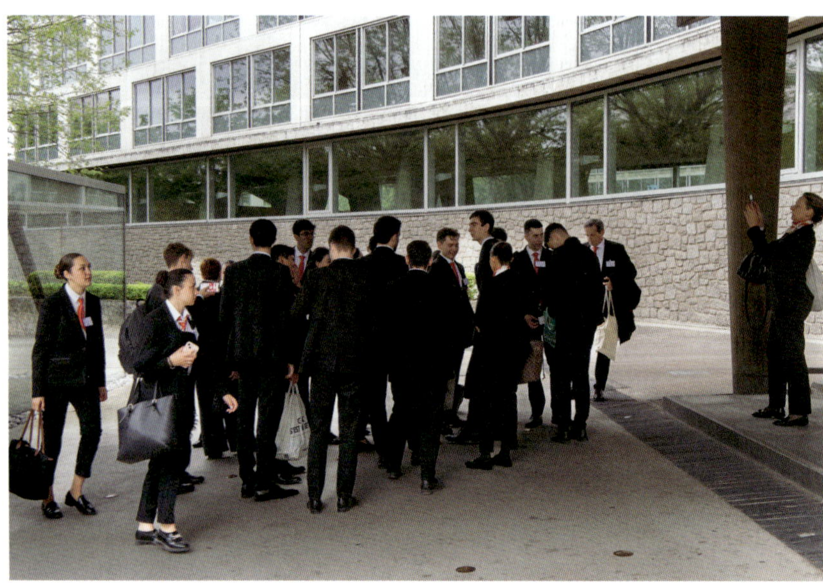

Regular visits by the Monegasque Royal Family, starting with Prince Rainier and Princess Grace in 1959 and most recently, Princess Caroline and Prince Albert II, serve to "deepen the already close ties established over the years between the Principality and UNESCO" (Koïchiro Matsuura). In February 2024, to celebrate seventy-five years of togetherness, the Monte-Carlo Philharmonic Orchestra, under the baton of Mexican conductor Alondra de la Parra, gave a concert for UNESCO ambassadors. In April that year, the students of the Lycée Rainier III Hotel School catered a gala dinner held at UNESCO by the delegation in the presence of H.S.H. Prince Albert II. In June, it was the turn of mezzo-soprano Cécilia Bartoli to perform at the Versailles Royal Opera with the Monte-Carlo Opera Choir, the Musiciens du Prince, and also the actor John Malkovich. In October, photographs of the Prince Albert II of Monaco Foundation will be presented to UNESCO, followed in December by an exhibition of the International Association of Plastic Arts (IAPA) to be held in Monaco.

UNESCO, then, naturally feels quite at home in Monaco. Its presence there is embodied in the day-to-day activities of the National Commission and partner entities, and not least in the warm welcome extended to the Directors-General on their official visits to the Principality, starting with Deputy Director-General Jean Thomas (in office 1946 to 1950) in 1957. It is a presence that is seen and felt in places like the UNESCO Garden, palpable in a marriage of art and Nature that symbolizes

Pupils from Monaco's Lycée Rainier III hotel school arrive at the gala dinner held at the UNESCO headquarters on April 11, 2024 to mark the 75th anniversary of the Principality's accession.

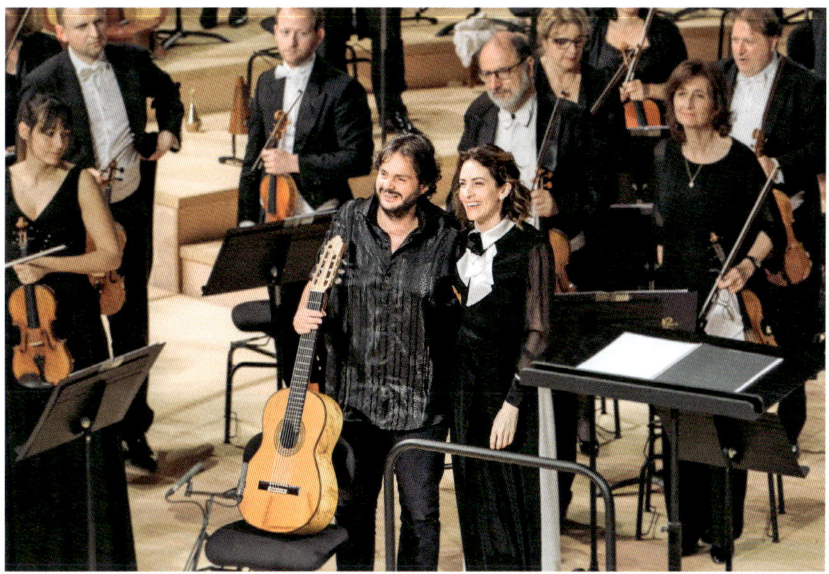

the vibrancy of the relationship. And it is a presence that expresses itself through events such as the Rencontres Internationales Monaco et la Méditerranée (RIMM, International Monaco and the Mediterranean Meetings), which capture the essence of UNESCO's philosophy. In 2020, Audrey Azoulay, speaking at the inauguration of the tenth edition of the Rencontres, spoke for the Organization in expressing her gratitude to the Principality of Monaco "for its loyal support certainly, but I would also add its increasingly active role in every cause that we defend."

DOSSIER
CULTURE
LES RENCONTRES INTERNATIONALES MONACO ET LA MÉDITERRANÉE
PAGES 151-155

To conclude, with the Olympics upon us at the time of writing, there can be no finer example of this connection between Monaco and UNESCO than sport—as a cultural phenomenon, vector of personal achievement, and "bridge between people" to quote René Maheu. This was evidenced in 2016 when Monaco played host to the meeting of the Comité Intergouvernemental pour l'Education Physique et Sportive (CIGEPS, International Governmental Committee for Physical Education and Sport); also in 2024 by *Athletes: Game On for Peace*, a UNESCO Peace and Sport International Dialogue, held at UNESCO headquarters on April 4, in conjunction with the Monegasque Organization, Peace and Sport chaired by Joël Bouzou, to mark the International Day of Sport for Development and Peace on April 6.

On February 16, 2024, to celebrate the 75th anniversary of the Principality's accession, the Philharmonic Orchestra of Monte Carlo, directed by Mexican conductor Alondra de la Parra, gave a concert for the UNESCO ambassadors.

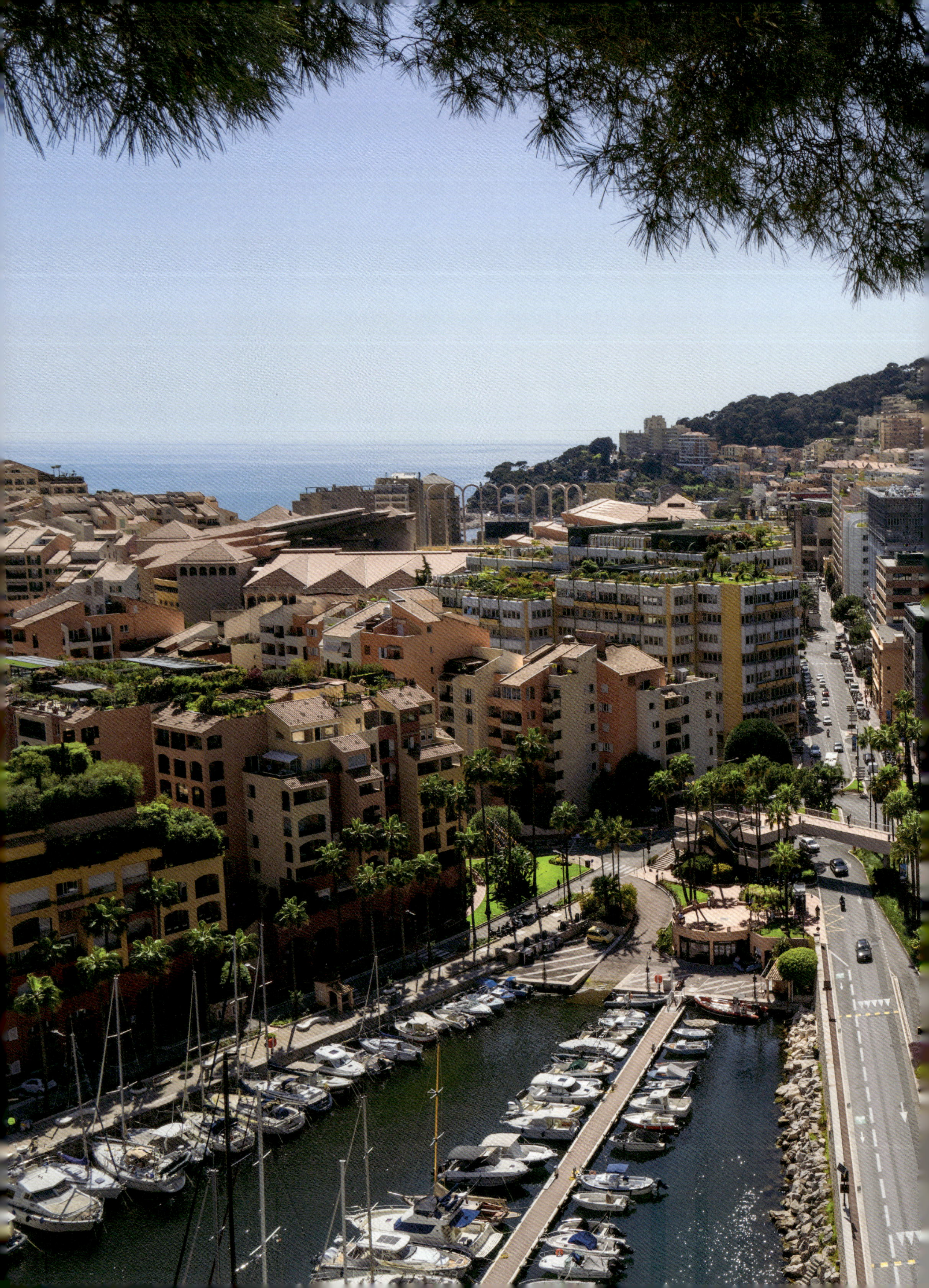

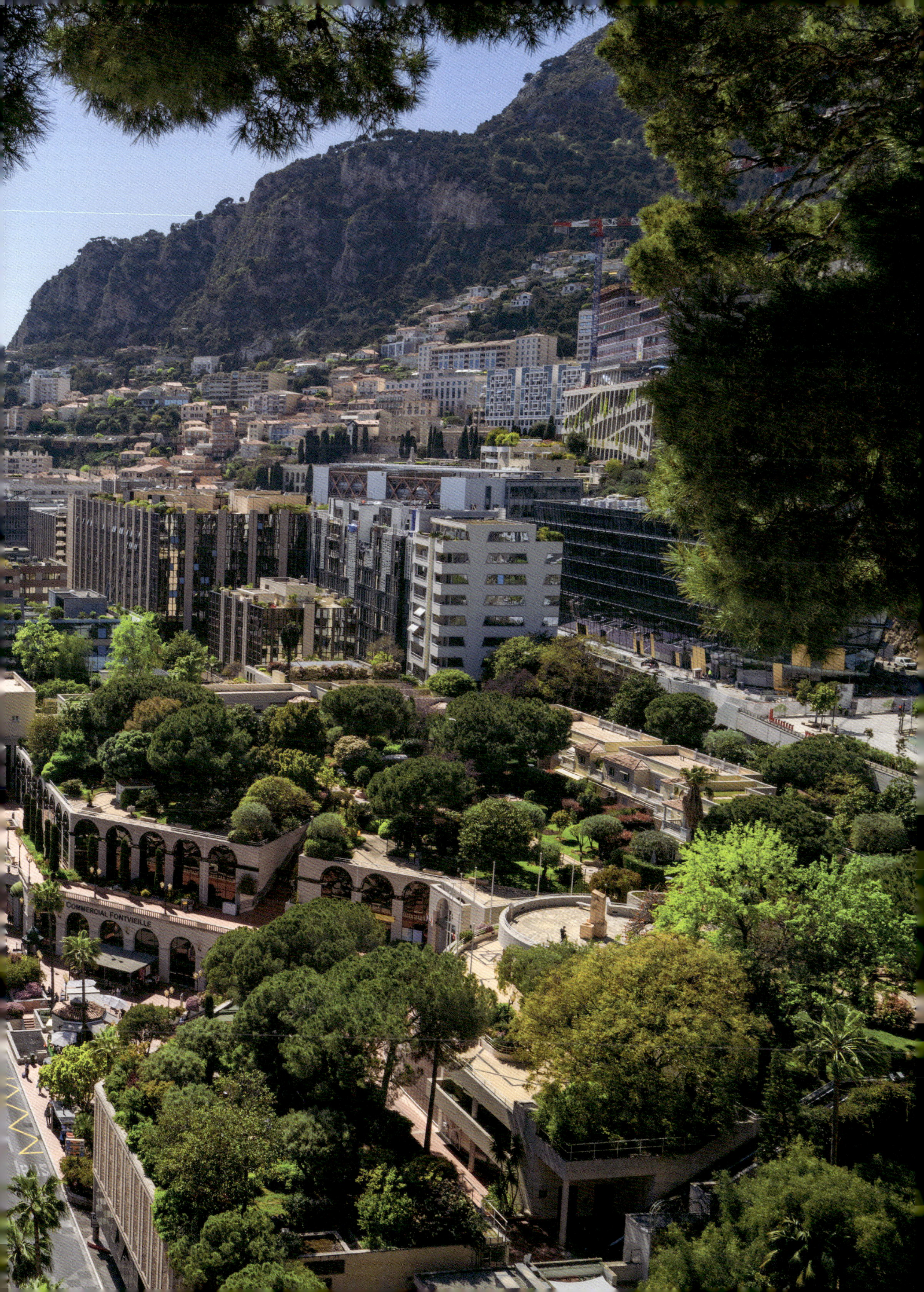
COMMERCIAL FONTVIEILLE

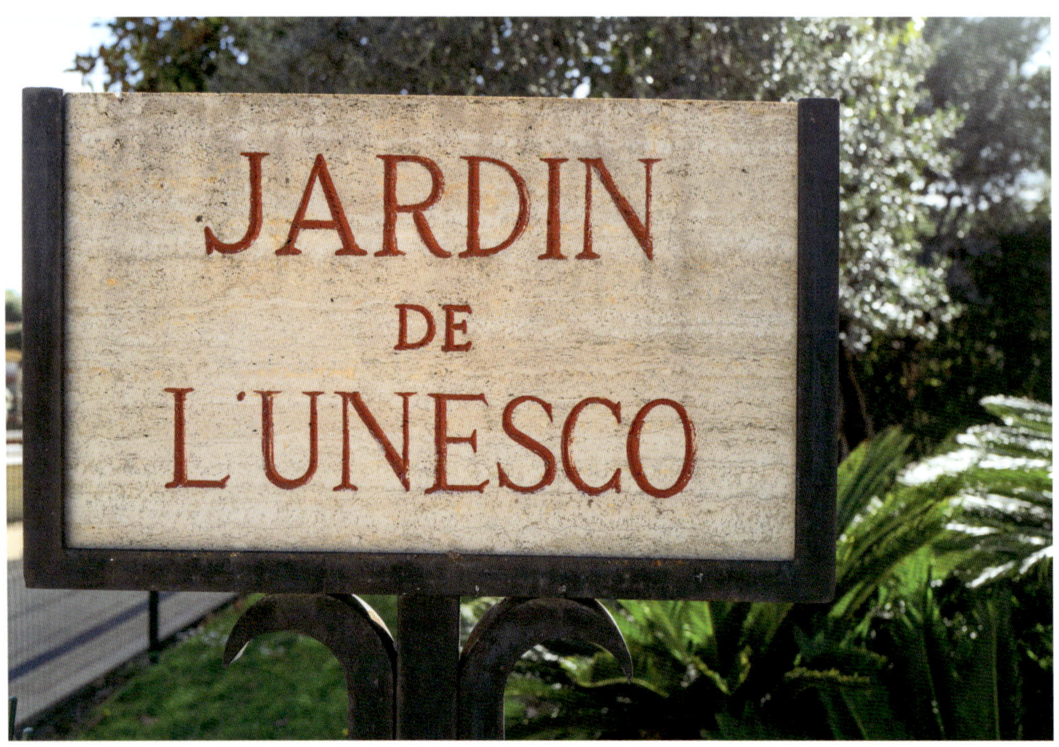

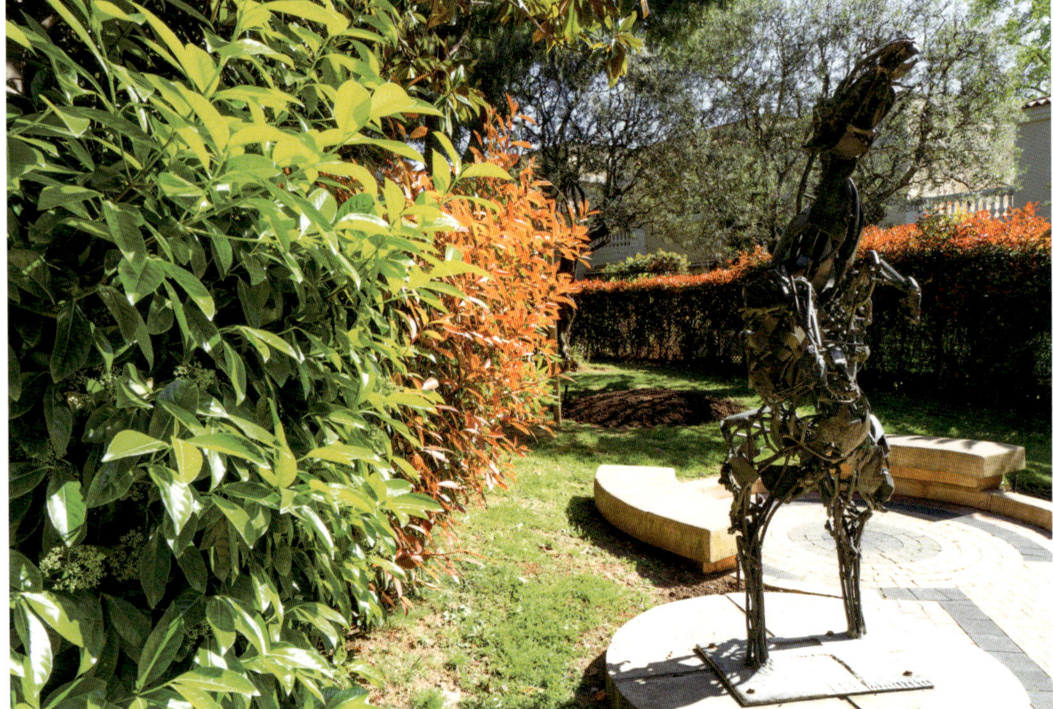

PREVIOUS PAGES View of the UNESCO Garden from the Rock of Monaco. Situated on the terraces of Fontvieille, the garden was created in 1993 and named in 1999 in honor of the organization for the 50th anniversary of the Principality's accession.

ABOVE *And the Seventh Day* (1994), Alessandro Montalbano (born 1962), welded bronze with green patina, UNESCO Garden, NMNM collections. The sculpture depicts a prancing horse driven by a powerful life force.

OPPOSITE PAGE *The Fist (1980)*, César (1921-1998), bronze with brown patina, UNESCO Garden, NMNM collections. The clenched fist could just as easily be an expression of rage or determination. Cast in 1980, the exhibited work is an artist's proof from a series of six.

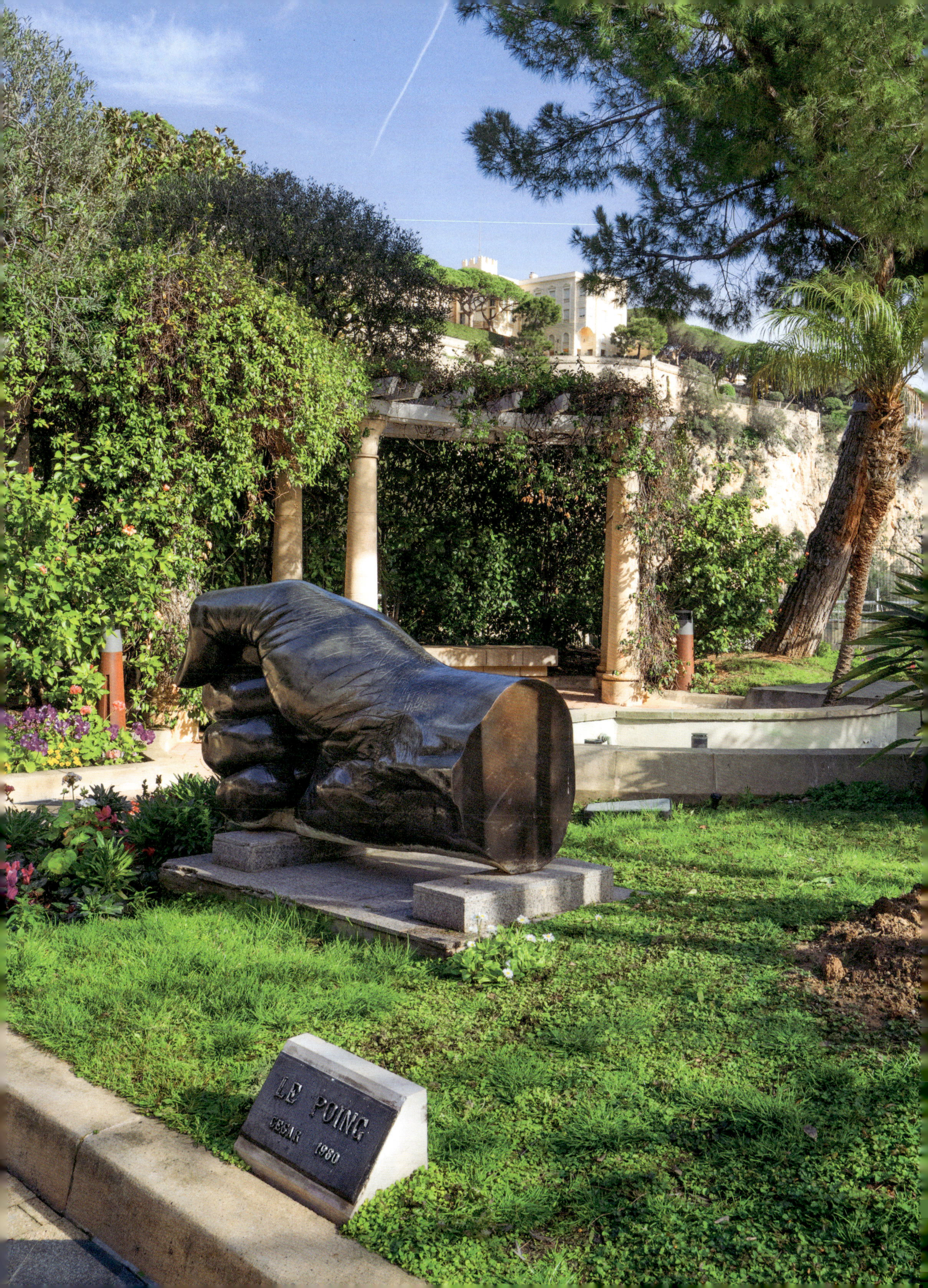
LE POING
CESAR 1980

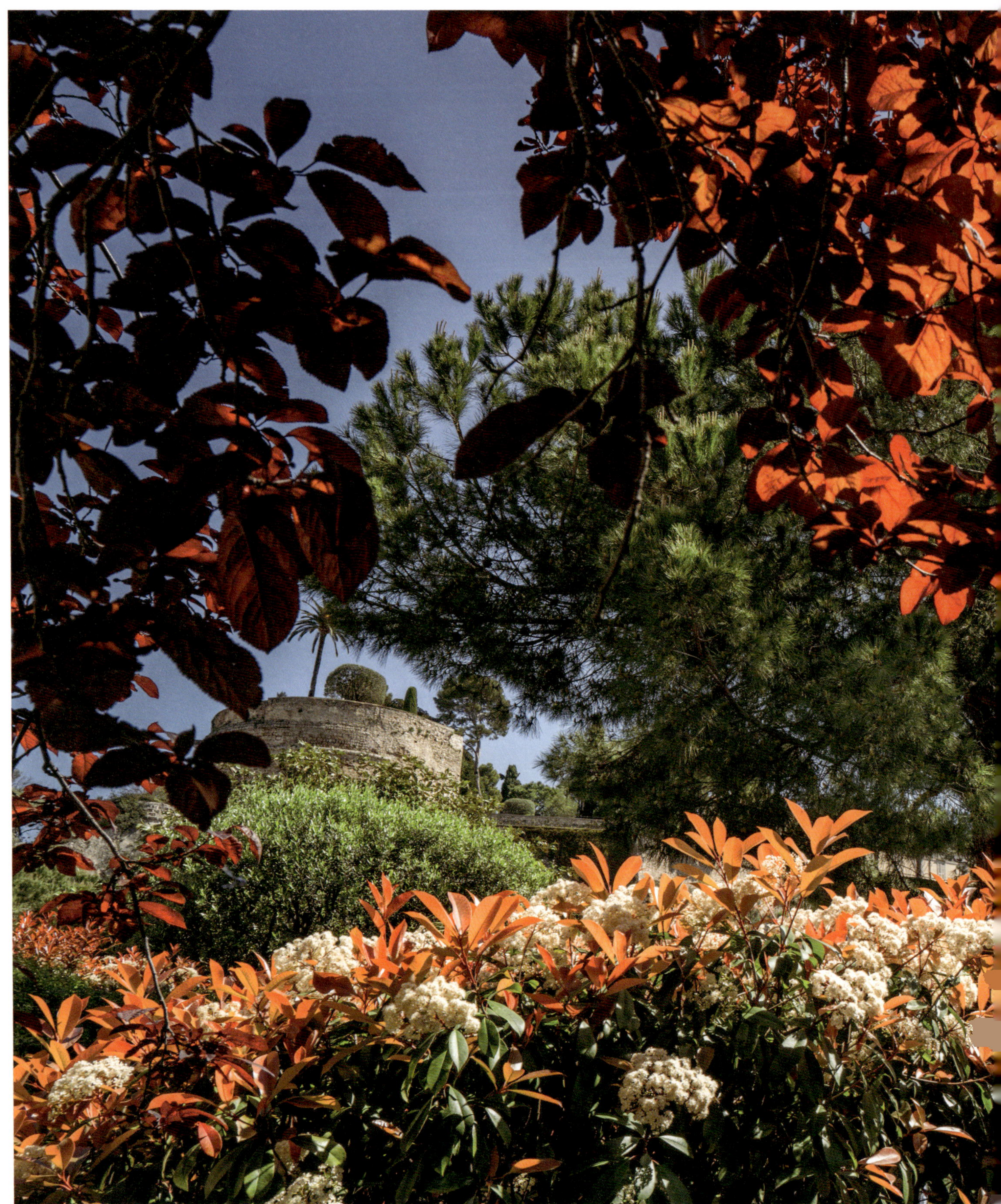

View of the Rock of Monaco from the UNESCO Garden on the terraces of Fontvieille.

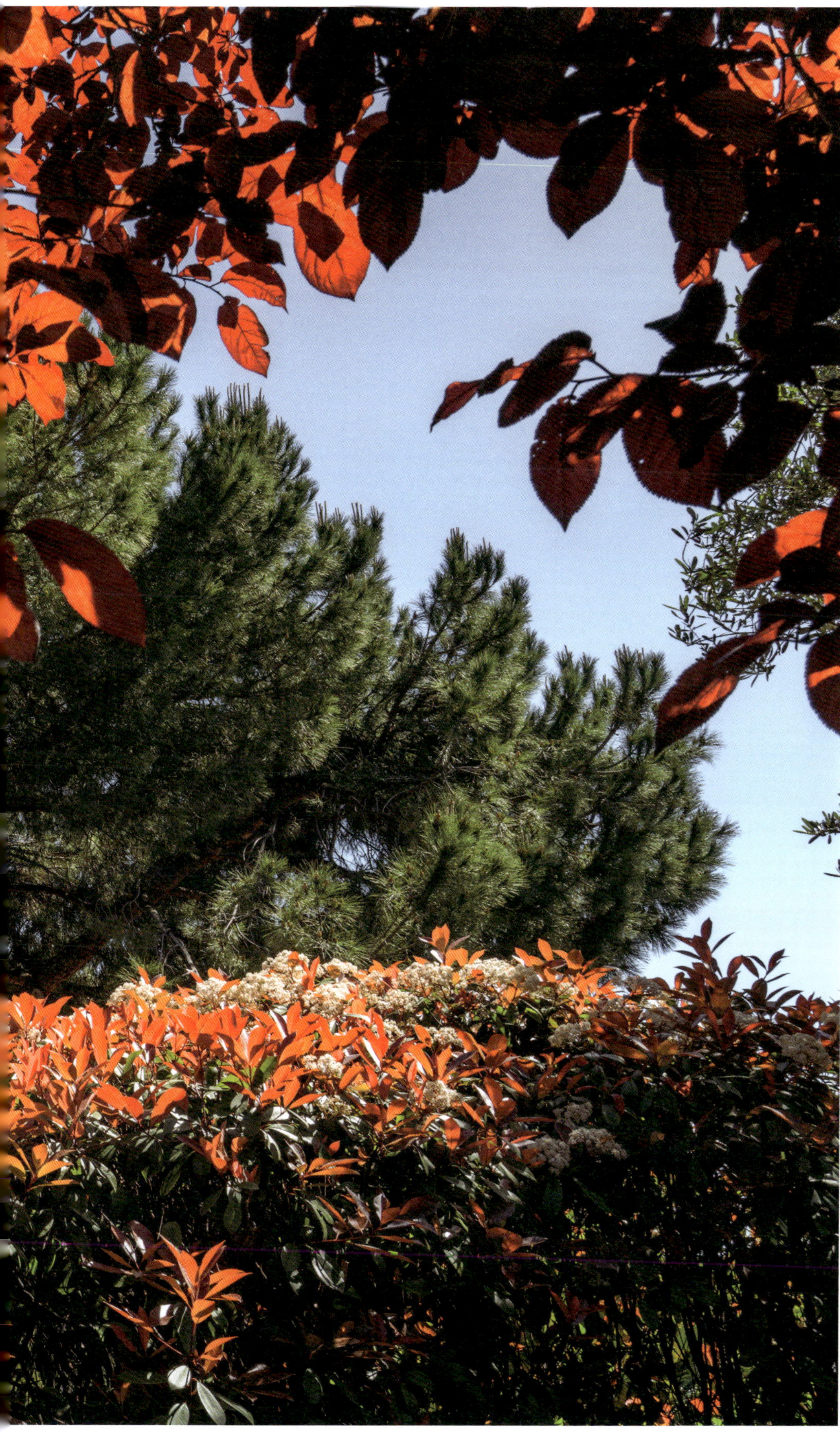

EDUCATION

"You Sirs, who wield such influence and set such store by the influence of science on the education of young people, thus will you fill the hearts of men with an energy that will dispel the specters of ignorance shrouding their cradle."

Albert I of Monaco, inaugural address at the Oceanographic Institute, Paris, January 23, 1911.

"Ignorance was our first and greatest enemy ... To overcome mutual misunderstanding through the dissemination of knowledge was and remains our only battle."

James Torre Bodet, UNESCO Director-General, Decembre, 1950.

AMADE, WORLD ASSOCIATION OF CHILDREN'S FRIENDS

AMADE-Mondiale was established on June 6, 1963, by Princess Grace of Monaco, with herself as honorary president of the Board of Directors and Archduke Otto von Habsburg as president. AMADE-Monaco came into being three years later on July 5, 1966. The World Association of Children's Friends is a Monegasque non-governmental organization focused on charitable activities and the philanthropic support of children. It is committed to protecting small children and helping them develop their full potential, and is built on a vision of a world where every child, regardless of their social, religious or cultural origins, can live safely and with dignity and respect for their fundamental rights. Its activities revolve around projects focused on protection (most notably against abuse), education, health, emergency relief (particularly sanitation) and awareness-raising. Together these projects comprise five programs, implemented at regional and international level alike: Dignity for Women, Capoeira for Peace, Civil Status for All, The Energy of Hope and Unaccompanied Minors. In Africa, for example, one objective is to regularize the civil status of 10,000 "ghost children," under the age of fifteen, within the national digital register of Burkina Faso, to give them access to their rights, particularly education. At regional level, mentoring in education seeks to discourage pupils from dropping out, and provide high-quality tutoring to French children from modest backgrounds, particularly in the Sud-Paca region (Provence-Alpes-Côte d'Azur). The association's vast operational remit also extends to the organization of conferences and seminars inviting discussion of ethical and legal matters. In 2002 AMADE spearheaded a program and declaration on the theme of "Crimes against children, crimes against humanity," which called on the international community to recognize that gross crimes against children shall be regarded as imprescriptible, and the perpetrators brought to justice under the principle of universal jurisdiction.

Presiding over AMADE today is Her Serene Highness Caroline Princess of Hanover, who assumed office in 1993, ten years before her appointment as a UNESCO Goodwill Ambassador in 2003. There can be no finer embodiment of AMADE's mission to protect children worldwide and nurture their development, not least through the provision of high-quality education for all.

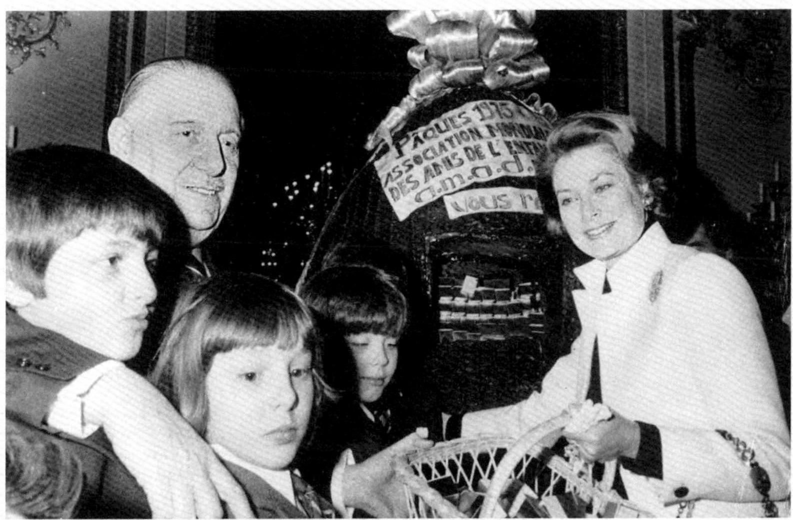

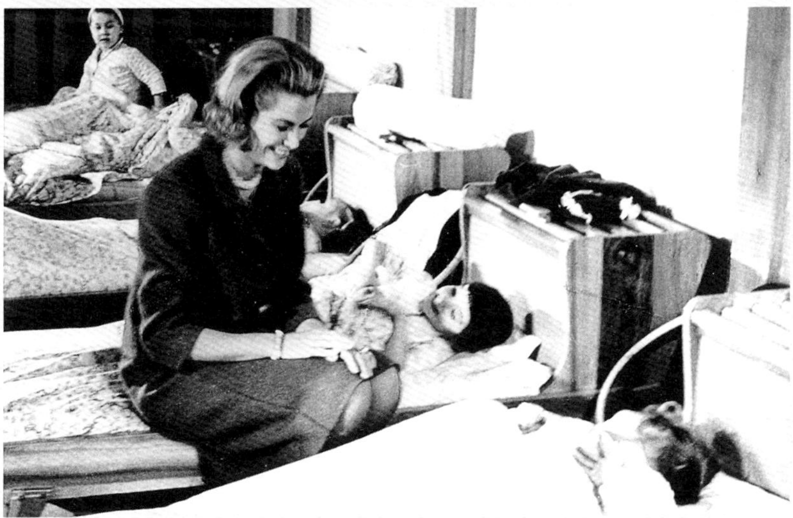

Princess Grace of Monaco, working with AMADE to protect and empower children.

Du 29 juin au 7 juillet à Paris

Colloque international organisé par l'U.N.E.S.C.O. sur l'impact de la violence à travers l'information

L'idée de ces débats est née d'une résolution votée à Monaco par l'A.M.A.D.E.

Du 29 juin au 7 juillet, à Paris, se déroulera un colloque international organisé par l'UNESCO, qui a invité une trentaine d'experts à discuter de l'impact de la violence dans les moyens d'information. Parmi ces experts, des sociologues, des criminologues qui s'entretiendront avec les représentants des moyens d'information, ainsi qu'avec des jeunes.

L'origine de ce colloque se rattache directement à une idée qui a été exprimée par l'A.M.A.D.E. (Association mondiale des amis de l'enfance) qui a été fondée, en 1966, sous la présidence d'honneur de S.A.S. la princesse Grace de Monaco.

L'A.M.A.D.E. est née pour aider et servir l'enfance malheureuse et pour améliorer les conditions de vie de tous les enfants du monde. Sans se désintéresser des besoins purement matériels de l'enfance, cette grande association, qui s'est donnée pour mission d'œuvrer sur le plan international, se propose d'agir, afin que soient offertes aux jeunes les plus larges possibilités d'épanouissement : physique, intellectuel et spirituel.

Aussi a-t-elle voulu s'atteler au problème de la violence qui « traumatise » véritablement les enfants. Dans cette généreuse initiative, elle a tout d'abord voulu limiter son action dans un domaine déterminé : celui de la télévision.

Du Festival international de T.V. à l'U.N.E.S.C.O.

Dans son étude de cette question, l'A.M.A.D.E. a estimé qu'il était, en premier lieu, indispensable d'étudier l'influence de la violence sur les mineurs (de l'enfant qui commence à comprendre jusqu'à l'adolescent ayant presque atteint l'âge de la puberté), de constater que la télévision est le moyen de communication le plus à leur portée pour leur transmettre des scènes de violence et, enfin, de reconnaître que dans le critère de violence, il fallait tout d'abord attaquer le front la représentation du meurtre.

Une résolution, conrétisant ce point de vue, fut votée, en 1967, par l'A.M.A.D.E. qui la présenta l'année suivante aux membres du jury du VIIIe Festival international de télévision de Monte-Carlo, lesquels, à l'unanimité, l'adoptèrent.

A la suite de ce succès, l'A.M.A.D.E. eut quelque temps plus tard une autre satisfaction : celle de bénéficier de la bienveillante compréhension du directeur général de l'U.N.E.S.C.O. qui demanda à la Commission nationale monégasque de reprendre à son compte ce vœu. Ce qui fut fait. Et c'est ainsi qu'à la conférence générale de l'U.N.E.S.C.O., de l'automne 1968, grâce à l'appui de M. René Maheu, directeur général de l'U.N.E.S.C.O., favorable à ce problème, il fut décidé d'organiser un colloque et de voter les crédits nécessaires.

C'est donc ce colloque qui va avoir pour cadre la capitale française.

Atténuer les effets de la violence

M. Pierre L. Cannat, secrétaire général de l'A.M.A.D.E., spécialiste de criminologie, se trouvera parmi les trente experts venus du monde entier pour participer au colloque de Paris.

Nous lui avons demandé de nous faire part de l'objet de cette réunion.

« Il s'agira, nous a-t-il déclaré, de déterminer le rôle des moyens d'information et la manière d'atténuer les effets de la violence afin de dégager des conclusions et des suggestions d'actions futures.

« Le programme est donc extrêmement large. Il va de la définition de la violence et de l'analyse des inquiétudes nées de certains écrits et de certains spectacles à l'examen des responsabilités des moyens de communication de masse et aux aspects pratiques des solutions envisageables. »

Il a souligné que, prenant comme base de départ l'idée de l'A.M.A.D.E., trois points ont été élargis : l'étude de l'U.N.E.S.C.O. ne concernera pas uniquement les enfants mais aussi les adultes ; elle passera en revue tous les moyens de communications de masse, et enfin, elle analysera toutes les manifestations de la violence.

A symposium at UNESCO, from June 29 to July 7, 1970, on the impact of violence in the mass media, based on an AMADE resolution, *Nice-Matin*, June 17, 1970.

"Children are now true subjects of law, but they are also particularly vulnerable and need guidance from their earliest years. Since this is something our society has largely forgotten, AMADE made it the focus of a resolution that was recently approved at the UNESCO General Conference [. . .] In consultation with parents and teachers, we came up with the idea of a 'code for life,' setting out the educational responsibilities of adults. Because let us never forget that the rights of children begin with the responsibilities of their elders."

AMADE, Lettre de l'enfance, 1994, *A Message from the President*—H.S.H. Caroline of Monaco, Princess of Hanover echoes the views of UNESCO Director-General, Federico Mayor.

"My role as a UNESCO Goodwill Ambassador is to spread the message about the importance of education, especially for women and girls.

"Getting children into school is essential to break the cycle of poverty, foster economic and social development, and to prepare future generations to meet the challenges ahead.

"Education should be a priority for governments and the international community—a goal that UNESCO has long been striving to achieve.

"As part of its objectives, AMADE protects the most vulnerable children against violence, exploitation and abuse; promotes their development by contributing to their access to education and health; and supports change through advocacy.

"Over the past ten years, AMADE has supported more than sixty projects in twenty-four countries, for the protection and development of children, totaling almost 6 million euros and impacting 280,000 beneficiaries.

"And I would add that if the human race is to have a bright future, the answer lies in their education! Education is the fertile ground in which human genius can flourish. It provides individuals with the tools, knowledge and opportunities they need to develop their creative, innovative and constructive potential, and so contribute to improving the human condition. Education also gives meaning to our lives."

Interview at UNESCO with H.S.H. the Princess of Hanover, to mark the sixtieth anniversary of AMADE, December 7, 2023.

"CAPOEIRA FOR PEACE"

is an integration program launched in 2014 to rehabilitate former child soldiers in the Zongo refugee camp in the DRC. It supports social reintegration through sport, specifically Capoeira: a traditional Afro-Brazilian cultural tradition granted cultural heritage status by UNESCO in 2014. For these children who are at once the victims and the agents of violence, reviving Capoeira helps them to reconnect, and see themselves in others, which is vital for peace building. Supported by UNICEF, UNFPA and UNHCR, "Capoeira for Peace" lies at the heart of UNESCO's core mission.

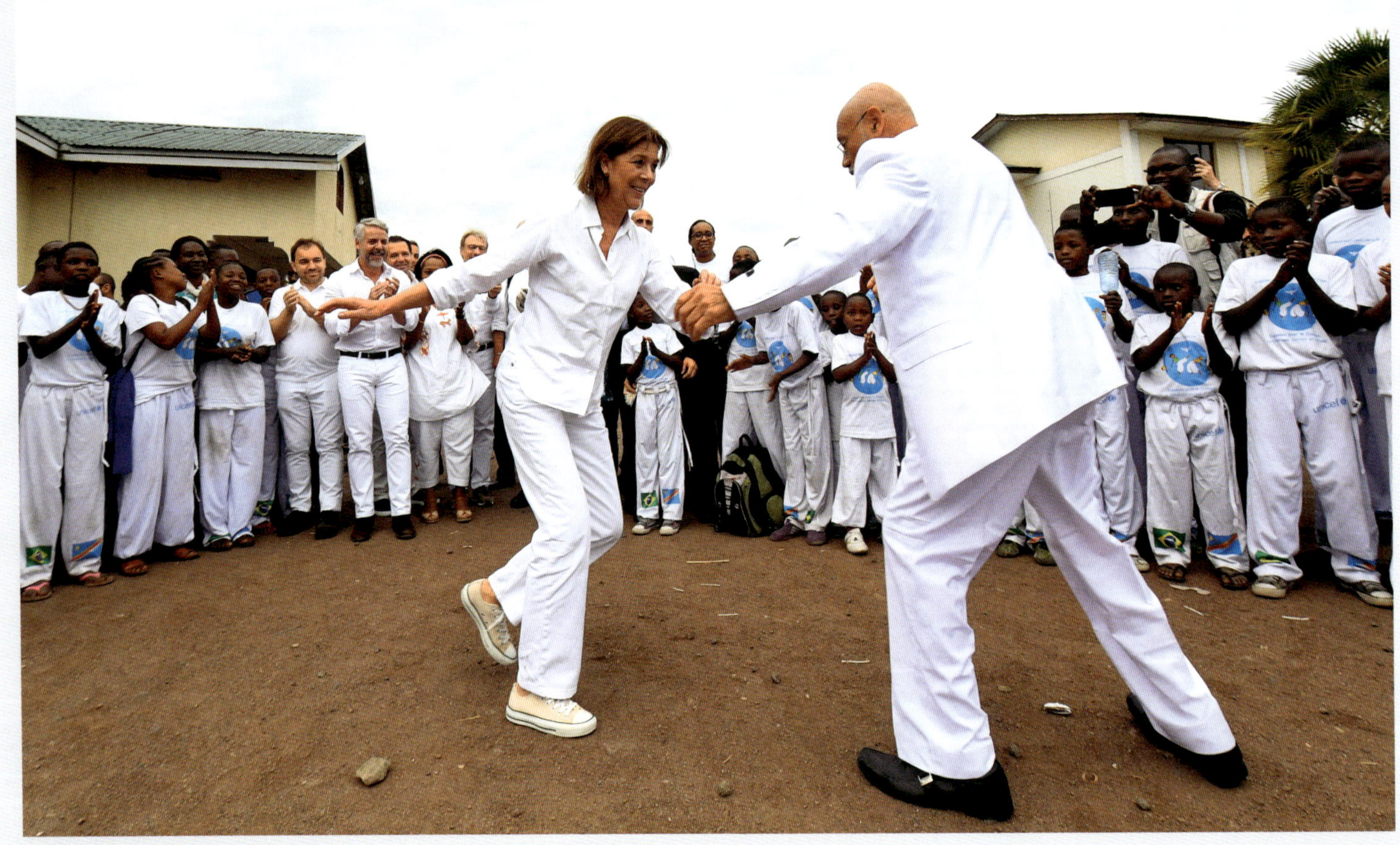

Presence of H.R.H. Princess of Hanover in Goma, Democratic Republic of Congo, in 2016 and 2017 for the AMADE "Capoiera for Peace" program.

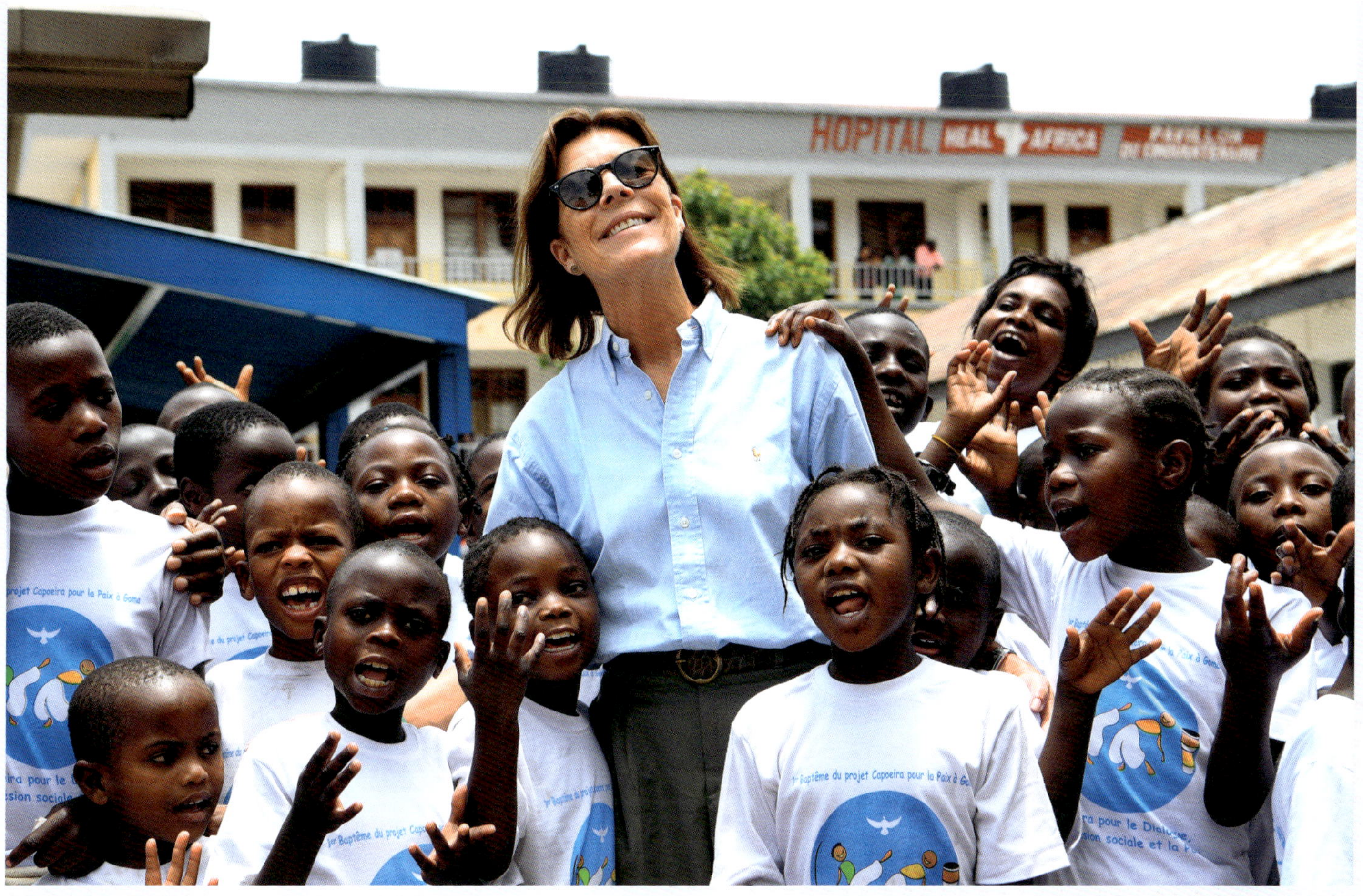

"DIGNITY FOR WOMEN"
is a program dedicated to providing medical and psychological care to girls and women who have been the victims of sexual violence.

H.R.H. Princess of Hanover visits the Heal Africa hospital in Goma, Democratic Republic of Congo, as part of the launch of the AMADE "Dignity for Women" program.

DOSSIER

LES RENCONTRES PHILOSOPHIQUES DE MONACO (THE PHILOSOPHICAL ENCOUNTERS OF MONACO)

In 2015 Charlotte Casiraghi, Joseph Cohen, Robert Maggiori and Raphael Zagury-Orly co-founded the Rencontres philosophiques de Monaco to share philosophy more widely and create a "unique, House of Philosophy" (Robert Maggiori).

Education is of key importance for the *Rencontres*, informing its lectures, seminars, and the selection of its annual prize-winner. Activities organized in partnership with the Department of Education, Youth and Sport-MONACO are open to elementary and high school students alike. Children may attend the monthly seminars and workshops; listen to talks given at their schools by the most eminent figures in contemporary philosophy; contribute papers; participate in contests; and even explore the idea of philosophy as performance. In line with UNESCO's recommendations on education, a range of activities specially designed to appeal to the creative imagination of children has been developed in consultation with Edwige Chirouter, holder of the UNESCO chair "The Practice of philosophy with children: a basis for intercultural dialogue and social transformation." A cross-curricular training program is also available to teachers wishing to enhance their classroom skills.

LES RENCONTRES
PHILOSOPHIQUES
DE MONACO
Sous la présidence de Mademoiselle Charlotte Casiraghi
MERCREDI
8 FEVRIER
2017
18H30 – 20H30
LYCÉE TECHNIQUE ET HÔTELIER
7 ALLÉE LAZARE SAUVAIGO
MONACO
CONFÉRENCE
LES
JEUNES
PHILOSOPHENT
Comment et pourquoi ?
Présentée par Madame Bonnal
Directrice de l'Éducation Nationale,
de la Jeunesse et des Sports
Dialogue avec
Edwige Chirouter, philosophe
Joseph Cohen, philosophe
Robert Maggiori, philosophe
Jean-Philippe Vinci, professeur de philosophie
Avec la participation de Cilvy Aupin
Productrice du film *Ce n'est qu'un début !*

Poster for the conference on Wednesday February 8, 2017.

"Over and above any media support for a new vogue, the importance of philosophy for children is one of UNESCO's core preoccupations. In the context of promoting a culture of peace, the fight against violence and a system of education aimed at eradicating poverty and favoring sustainable development, fostering a critical approach and independent thinking in very young children enables them to judge for themselves, safe from manipulation, and free to choose their own destiny."

UNESCO Chair, "The practice of philosophy with children: a basis for intercultural dialogue and social transformation."

"Above all, philosophy depends on the marshalling of knowledge in the service of intellectual rigor. It therefore naturally belongs in the classroom, and the Rencontres Philosophiques de Monaco is determined to see that it does. Encouraging the teaching of philosophy in local schools is a key objective of the *Rencontres*, which works with Monaco's Department of Education to develop new approaches aimed at making philosophy as much a part of the school curriculum as the Three A's. A good example was an event titled *Les Jeunes Philosophent* [young people philosophize], which gave teachers a unique opportunity to acquire the tools necessary to engage their classes in discussions about philosophy. *Les Jeunes Philosophent* magazine was produced by schoolchildren following the training of volunteer teachers from seven classes, from first grade to fifth grade."

Charlotte Casiraghi, The demands of philosophy.

DOSSIER

ASSOCIATIONS AND CLUBS FOR UNESCO

UNESCO clubs and associations work at local level to promote peace and intercultural dialogue, drawing on the expertise of each community to advance UNESCO's goals. The first ever club came into being in 1947 at Sendai (Japan)—four years before Japan joined UNESCO—in response to the need for solidarity and civic cohesion in the aftermath of World War II. Since then, at least 4,000 clubs and associations have been formed in more than seventy-five countries around the world. In France UNESCO clubs are predominantly found in schools. The first mention of a Monegasque UNESCO club in the records of the National Commission and UNESCO Archives dates back to 1959. The impetus behind it was Jacques Freu, a history teacher at the Monaco Lycée who wanted to bring home UNESCO's values to his students, particularly civil rights as enshrined ten years earlier in the Universal Declaration of Human Rights. In 2004 his efforts ultimately bore fruit with the creation of the UNESCO Club at the Collège Charles III as part of a schools-based effort to build peace and justice. Five more clubs followed, grouped under the Monegasque Federation of Clubs and Friends of UNESCO (established 2007), with their president Milène Escarras providing the momentum. The same period saw young people throughout the Principality launch actions related to education, science, culture, the environment and solidarity. The H_2O Club at the Lycée Albert I, in association with Monaco Aide et Présence (MAP), organized a collection for the Food Bank, the French "Restaurants du Cœur" charity, and the Monegasque Red Cross. In the decade 2004 to 2013, on December 10 every year, young people from mainland France and Overseas France would gather at UNESCO Headquarters to celebrate the Universal Declaration of Human Rights. The year 2008—sixtieth anniversary of the Declaration—marked a milestone: on December 13, students present in Paris for the occasion were able to exchange views with Stéphane Hessel, a witness, like René Cassin and John Peters Humphrey, to the adoption of the Declaration on December 10, 1948.

GREAT VOICES

EDUCATION

"Education should no longer be seen as a preparation for life but rather as a dimension of life."

René Maheu, address of UNESCO Director-General, calling on Member States to make 1970 a turning-point in UNESCO's work in education.

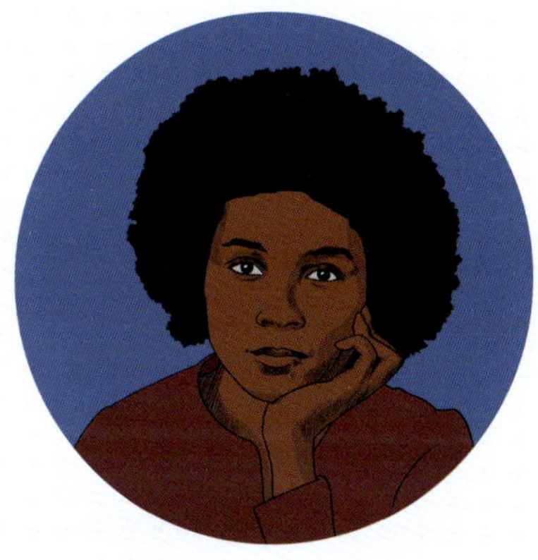

BELL HOOKS

"Home was the place where I was forced to conform to someone else's image of who and what I should be. School was the place where I could forget that self and, through ideas, reinvent myself [...] The classroom, with all its limitations, remains a location of possibility. In that field of possibility we have the opportunity to labor for freedom, to demand of ourselves and our comrades, an openness of mind and heart that allows us to face reality even as we collectively imagine ways to move beyond boundaries, to transgress."

Bell Hooks, *Teaching to Transgress: Education as the Practice of Freedom.* New York: Routledge, Taylor and Francis, 1994.

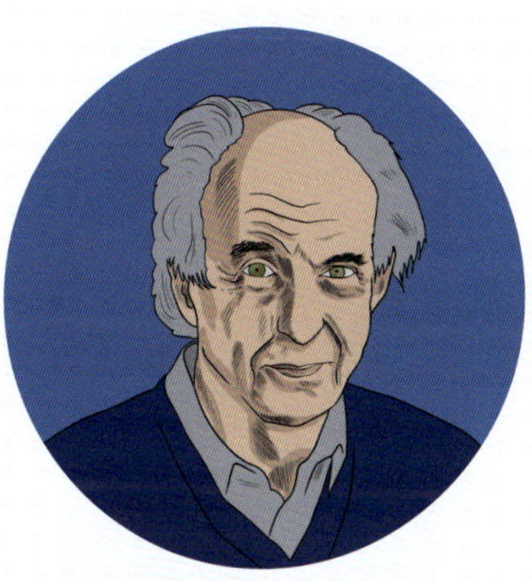

ROGER-POL DROIT

"Education comes first in the acronym UNESCO [. . .] Science and culture follow. This is not by chance. The order may be taken literally: education comes before all the rest. In a sense it represents the unique task. It is involved in everything, and everything flows from it [. . .] Education is now conceived as the totality of resources on which each individual should be able to draw to realize his or her humanity as fully as possible."

Roger-Pol Droit, *Humanity in the Making*, UNESCO, 2005.

SCIENCES

"Gentlemen, in opening the Musée Océanographique de Monaco today I entrust it to the servants of scientific truth. May they find here the peace, the independence and the emulation that nurtures the brain."

Prince Albert I of Monaco, speech at the opening of the Oceanographic Museum, March 1910.

"We live in a world where scientific discovery poses an ever-greater challenge to our moral and philosophical convictions. A world where the increasing imperative for international collaboration in science compels us to confront our values and compare them with those of others. Last but not least, we live in a world where the pace of scientific and technological progress greatly outstrips the pace of ethical thinking, the while making it more necessary than ever."

Koichiro Matsuura, Director-General, Paris, June 20, 2005.

DOSSIER

MONACO, UNESCO AND THE HUMAN SCIENCES

"If our race has concentrated on one task, and one alone—that of building a society in which Man can live—then the sources of strength on which our remote ancestors drew are present also in ourselves. All the stakes are still on the board, and we can take them up at any time we please. Whatever was done, and done badly, can be begun all over again: The golden age which blind superstition situated behind or ahead of us is in us. Human brotherhood acquires a palpable significance when we find our image of it confirmed in the poorest of tribes, and when that tribe offers us an experience which, when joined with many hundreds of others, has a lesson to teach us."

Claude Lévi-Strauss, a leading voice in the early days of UNESCO, author of *A World on the Wane*, Criterion Books, 1961.

The traces of Early Man are everywhere to be found in and around the Principality. Examples include the Grotte du Vallonnet near Roquebrune, Cap-Martin, and the Grotte du Lazaret; the Terra Armata site in Nice; the ancient Grotte du Prince in the Balzi Rossi caves in the hamlet of Grimaldi, Municipality of Ventimiglia; the Grotte l'Observatoire in the Jardin Exotique de Monaco, and the rock engravings of Mount Bégo in the Vallée des Merveilles (Valley of Wonders). This profusion of archaeological remains explains why the Human Sciences have always held the attention of the Princes of Monaco. Albert I, for instance, pursued the excavations launched by his grandfather Florestan I and supported the works, further afield, of archaeologists Léonce de Villeneuve and Marcellin Boule, and l'Abbé Breuil. The findings tell us a lot about the first people to inhabit this region and are carefully preserved in the collections of two major institutions founded for research purposes: the Museum of Prehistoric Anthropology in Monaco (founded 1902) and the Institute of Human Paleontology in Paris (founded 1910). Since then, other prominent archaeologists have taken up the baton, with the prehistorian Louis Barral leading the way. By the time of UNESCO's establishment, Louis Barral (1910-1999) had been Director of the Museum of Prehistoric Anthropology for seven years (in office 1938 to 1971), a position that led to his inclusion on the Monegasque National Commission for UNESCO in 1950 and participation in the Organization's meetings of experts. These days rigorous research in the field of human sciences is the focus of Elena Rossoni-Notter's activities as Director of the Museum of Prehistoric Anthropology since 2018, and those of Professor Henry de Lumley, President of the Board of Directors of the Institute of Human Paleontology (having served as its director from 1980 to 2019).

That the world has opened-up over the years is evidenced by the sixteen years of archaeological and anthropological research carried out in Upper Asia by a joint Monaco-Mongolia team, leading, in April 2013, to the *First Nomads of Upper Asia. Journey into the Heart of the Steppes* exhibition, held in the Salle Miró at UNESCO Headquarters, Place de Fontenoy, Paris. In 2004, meanwhile, to give the project maximum visibility, the International Scientific Committee of the Museum of Prehistoric Anthropology had been established under the presidency of leading paleontologist and co-discoverer of Australopithecus "Lucy," Yves Coppens (1934-2022). His presence "helped to tighten the bonds between the Principality of Monaco and the scientific community," said H.S.H. Prince Albert II, speaking on December 12, 2023, at the UNESCO tribute to Yves Coppens following his death on June 22, 2022. The event was co-organized by the Monaco delegation to UNESCO and the Museum of Prehistoric Anthropology of Monaco; in attendance were H.S.H. Prince Albert II and UNESCO Deputy Director-General, Mr. Xing Qu.

PRINCIPAUTÉ DE MONACO

SERVICE DES RELATIONS EXTÉRIEURES

le 21 Avril 1956

Fouilles Archéologiques

Monsieur,

J'ai l'honneur de vous faire connaître que vous avez été désigné par le Gouvernement Princier pour le représenter à la Réunion d'experts gouvernementaux sur les principes internationaux relatifs au régime des fouilles archéologiques, organisée par l'UNESCO, qui se tiendra à Palerme du 4 au 19 Mai 1956.

Vous voudrez bien m'adresser un compte-rendu sur les travaux de cette conférence.

Je vous prie d'agréer, Monsieur, l'assurance de ma haute considération.

P. le Ministre d'Etat,
Le Chargé de Mission,

Monsieur Louis BARRAL
Conservateur
du Musée d'Anthropologie
Préhistorique
MONACO

Letter dated April 21, 1956 from the External Relations Department to Louis Barral, UNESCO expert.

"Located on the slopes of the Khangai Ridge in central Mongolia, these deer stones were used for ceremonial and funerary practices. Dating from about 1200 to 600 BCE, they stand up to four metres tall and are set directly in the ground as single standing stones or in groups, and are almost always located in complexes that include large burial mounds called *khirgisüürs* and sacrificial altars. Covered with highly stylized or representational engravings of stags, deer stones are the most important surviving structures belonging to the culture of Eurasian Bronze Age nomads that evolved and then slowly disappeared between the 2nd and 1st millennia BCE."

Deer stone monuments and associated Bronze Age sites, inscribed on the UNESCO World Heritage List in 2023.

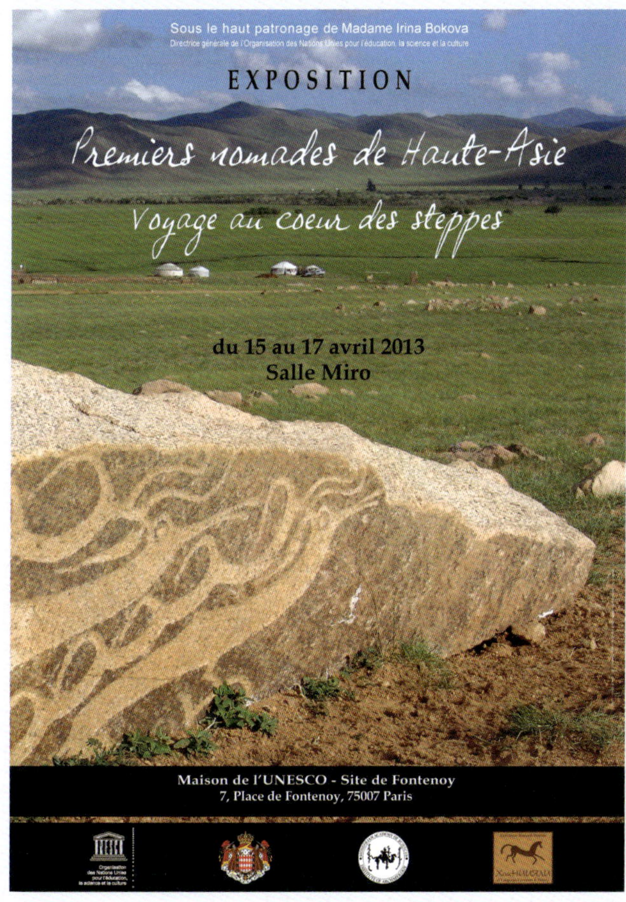

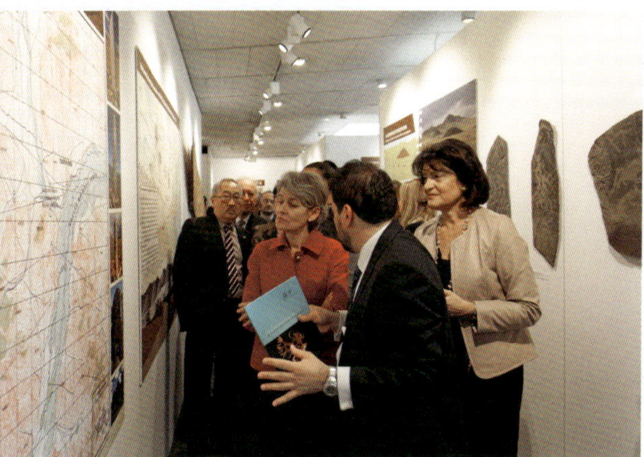

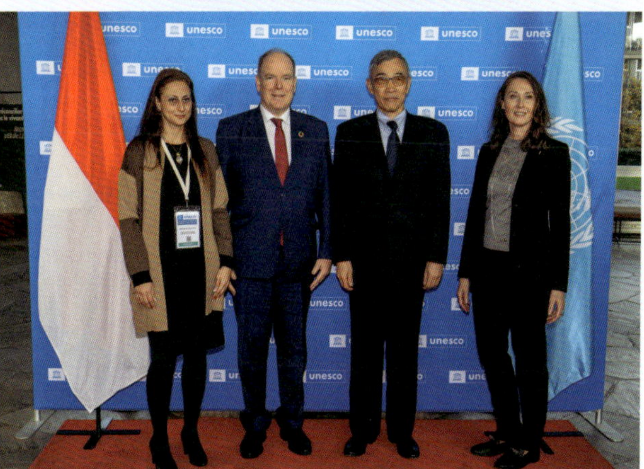

ABOVE Poster from the "First Nomads of Upper Asia" exhibition, UNESCO, April 2013, under the patronage of Irina Bokova, Director-General of UNESCO, and H.S.H. Prince Albert II, coordinated by Jérôme Magail, anthropologist, Project Leader at the Museum of Prehistoric Anthropology, in collaboration with the Archaeology Institute of the Mongolian Academy of Sciences.

TOP On April 12, 2013, to coincide with the 191st session of the Executive Board, attended by Irina Bokova, UNESCO Director-General, and Her Excellency Yvette Lambin-Berti, inauguration of the exhibition "First Nomads of Upper Asia", which shared the results of seven scientific campaigns conducted by the Monaco-Mongolia mission, the fruit of the collaboration between the Principality of Monaco, the Republic of Mongolia and the Russian Federation.

BOTTOM Homage to Prof. Yves Coppens at UNESCO, December 12, 2023. From left to right: Elena Rossoni-Notter, director of the Museum of Prehistoric Anthropology; H.S.H. Prince Albert II; Xing Qu, Deputy Director-General of UNESCO; and Her Excellency Anne-Marie Boisbouvier.

DOSSIER

“ONE PLANET, ONE OCEAN, ONE STATE”

“And I went as far as I could into Oceanography where I felt the solution to major issues in biology was sleeping; where I saw the strongest domain of physical and chemical phenomena from which emerged the birth, propagation and evolution of beings.”

Prince Albert I, Speech on the ocean, April 25, 1921, at the National Academy of Sciences, Washington.

“I would like to begin by thanking the Principality of Monaco, His Serene Highness Prince Albert II of Monaco and the Foundation—dear Olivier Wenden—for bringing us together in this exceptional setting. A setting that commands our attention, through its beauty, historical depth and the life it sustains, reminding us of the central place occupied by the ocean in our lives. How paradoxical then that this ocean that occupies such a central place in our lives should remain such a mystery for humanity and sometimes indeed, though not here in the Principality of Monaco, largely forgotten by climate and environmental campaigners. We must get to know the ocean better, and it is precisely this challenge that is addressed by the United Nations Ocean Decade 2021-2030, with UNESCO proudly leading the way. Because without the ocean, humanity cannot survive.

Address by UNESCO Director-General Audrey Azoulay at the Ocean Decade, Third Foundations Dialogue, June 14, 2023.

Ocean protection is a family tradition for the House of Grimaldi. It all began with the scientific expeditions led by pioneering oceanographer and trailblazer, Prince Albert I, founder of the International Commission for the Scientific Exploration of the Mediterranean, followed by the Oceanographic Institute in 1906. Prince Rainier, always at the vanguard of environmental issues, built on the achievements of his great-grandfather, particularly as an advocate for the protection of the Mediterranean Sea. In 1976 he created the Larvotto Marine Protected Area, and was also instrumental in setting up the intergovernmental cooperation environmental instrument known as the Ramoge Agreement, a name composed of the first syllables of St. Raphael, Monaco and Genova. In 1985 he established INDEMER, the Institute of Economic Law of the Sea, which deals with the legal, economic, social and environmental issues arising from the use of maritime and marine areas. Denis Allemand presides over the Board of Directors, with Philippe Weckel as chair of the scientific council and Tidiani Couma as INDEMER secretary-general. The year 1999 then saw the creation of the Pelagos Sanctuary for Mediterranean Marine Mammals, subject to an agreement between Italy, Monaco and France. Meanwhile, driven by his love for the seas and the oceans, Prince Rainier had made a week-long trip to Spitzbergen from August 2 to 10, 1982, accompanied by the young Crown Prince, now Prince Albert II of Monaco. The memories of those days never left His Serene Highness who, on his accession to the throne in 2005, immediately launched an ambitious environmental policy. In 2006, following in the footsteps of his great-great-grandfather a century earlier, he traveled by dog sled to the North Pole to raise awareness about global warming. Later that year, he established the Prince Albert II of Monaco Foundation as a vehicle for the promotion of ocean protection. Notable campaigns include the 2008 call to end consumption of Mediterranean bluefin tuna, then a threatened species; and the signing in 2009 of the Monaco Declaration on ocean acidification, which was taken up by 150 major names in marine science from twenty-six countries. In 2011, the message from Monaco, echoing the importance placed on the oceans in the Rio+20 outcome document, was an urgent call for the adoption of a sustainable development goal focused on the oceans. Since then, the Prince has been moving forward on two fronts: an ambitious environmental policy for local action; and awareness-raising at United Nations forums, taking into account geothermal resources and medicine from the sea.

Monaco naturally aligns itself with UNESCO's own guidelines for ocean conservation. In March 1960 the Principality was one of the thirty-eight founding states of the UNESCO Intergovernmental Oceanographic Commission (IOC), which works to promote international cooperation in marine sciences to improve management of the ocean, coasts and marine resources. Monaco, as an early member, took an active role in determining the directions taken by UNESCO. The IOC provides a collaborative framework for its now 150 Member States, channeling the efforts of its experts to coordinate programs aimed at strengthening ocean observation capacities, marine research and services, tsunami warning systems, and ocean literacy. Among the IOC experts are Monaco scientists Dr. Michel Boisson, Professor Denis Allemand, and Stéphanie Reynaud, currently a researcher at the Monaco Scientific Center (CSM). In 1982, the first marine site was added to the UNESCO World Heritage list. UNESCO, most notably through the IOC, is currently at the forefront of the United Nations Decade of Ocean Science for Sustainable Development (2021-2030) to support efforts to reverse the cycle of decline in ocean health.

Constantly reinforced over the years, the Principality's commitment to UNESCO's ocean policy has never been stronger than it is today. The entities involved are all quite different but united in their drive for synergy and a common vision aimed at building an "ocean mechanism" (a *mécano de la mer* to quote Denis Allemand and Philippe Mondielli). Chief among them is the Monaco Blue Initiative (MBI), launched in 2010 by H.S.H. Prince Albert II of Monaco and co-organized by the Oceanographic Institute and the Prince Albert II Foundation. MBI is a week-long event, held every year as part of Monaco Week to raise awareness of the pressing challenges facing our oceans and the need for immediate action to save them. It serves as a pivotal platform for scientists, decision-makers, and representatives from the private sector, multinationals and civil society to come together to explore and encourage the potential synergies between Marine Protected Areas and the development of a truly sustainable blue economy.

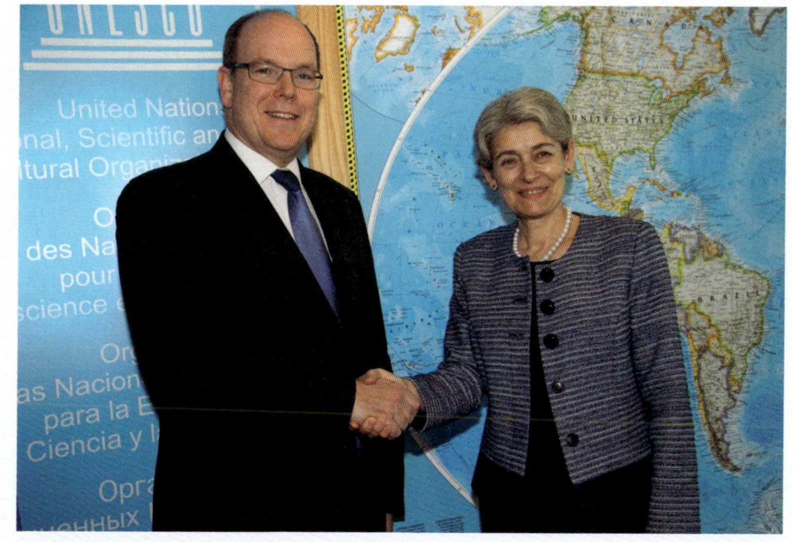

H.S.H. Prince Albert II and Irina Bokova, UNESCO Director-General, at UNESCO for World Oceans Day, in 2015 (World Oceans Day was announced on June 8, 1992 in Rio).

THE PRINCE ALBERT II OF MONACO FOUNDATION

Since its creation in 2006, the Prince Albert II of Monaco Foundation has worked hand in hand with UNESCO, most especially within the framework of the IOC.

The Foundation is primarily committed to concrete actions to conserve the Arctic Marine Environment, such as the expansion of Marine Protected Areas (MAPs) to safeguard marine biodiversity; and the nomination and inclusion of Arctic Marine sites on the UNESCO World Heritage List. In 2018, experts convened in Monaco to discuss the legal and technical aspects of managing and protecting sites of potential outstanding universal value in the high seas through the mechanism of the 1972 World Heritage Convention.

The Principality is also represented in global multi-stakeholder bodies, such as the Ocean and Climate Platform (2014) and the Ice Memory Project (2016), which studies glacial ice cores in Antarctica. With a deep commitment on several fronts, the Principality is likewise a champion of education, one of UNESCO's four pillars. A range of meetings and other activities are available to Monegasque students throughout the year as part of the cultural program run by the Department of Education. In partnership with the Office for Climate Education (established 2018), the Principality provides means to facilitate international cooperation on climate change education. It also supports the Malizia Ocean Challenge (spearheaded since 2018 by Boris Hermann), an educational and sports project that "brings the ocean into schools." Mediatization and awareness-raising are at the heart of the Foundation's missions, as testified by the launch in 2021 of the Environmental Photography Award, followed in 2023 by the Green Shift Festival aimed at coaxing new ecological imaginaries through art and culture.

The partnership with IOC-UNESCO has been reinforced in recent years by the Decade of Ocean Science for Sustainable Development (2021-2030), most notably by the officializing of the Prince Albert Foundation's strategic contribution, subject to the Agreement signed on November 17, 2021. The Agreement complements the Foundation's role as a founding member of the Ocean Decade Alliance, which supports resource mobilization and networking to fulfill the Ocean Decade challenges. In addition, the IOC and the Foundation work together within the context of the Conferences of the Parties (COPs), the decision-making body of the United Nations Framework Convention on Climate Change (UNFCCC) and the Convention on Biodiversity (CBD). In 2023, the Foundation underscored its cultural identity by making Monaco the venue of the "Ocean Decade: Third Foundations Dialogue," an annual event bringing together philanthropic institutions from around the world with a view to finding the best way to generate partnerships and finance mechanisms in support of the Ocean Decade. The Foundation was also present at the United Nations Ocean Conference in Lisbon in 2022, which coincided with Albert I's centenary, and will, of course, attend the third edition scheduled for Nice in 2025.

"Foundations, perhaps because they are more adaptive and flexible, are better positioned to foster innovation and develop solutions, both in terms of technology and approach. They can bring stakeholders together, facilitate dialogue, and encourage effective communication. Such is the basis on which the Prince Albert II of Monaco Foundation aims to contribute to the global impact of the Ocean Decade. Partnering with IOC-UNESCO will help draw attention to the challenges facing the ocean, and we are delighted to have this opportunity to work together."

Olivier Wenden, Vice-President and Chief Executive Office of the Prince Albert II of Monaco Foundation.

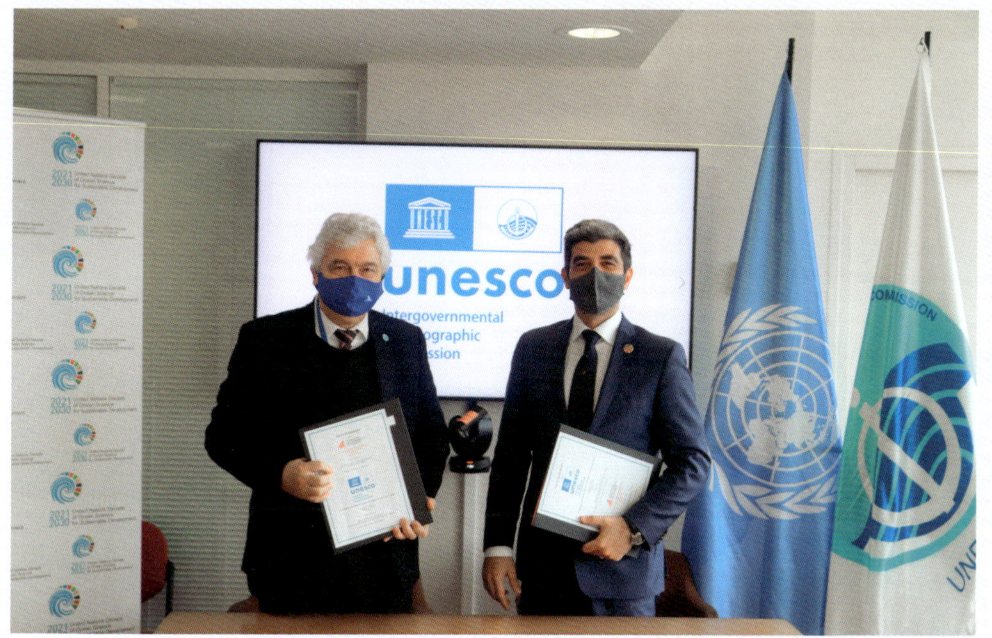

IOC-UNESCO IN PARTNERSHIP WITH THE PRINCE ALBERT II OF MONACO FOUNDATION FOR THE DECADE OF OCEAN SCIENCE

Working together, the two parties agreed on several avenues for collaboration over the three years to come, such as the polar symposium (Monaco, February 2022), the conference on coastal resilience (Monaco, March 2022) and the annual events organized by the Foundation for Monaco Ocean Week and the Monaco Blue Initiative.

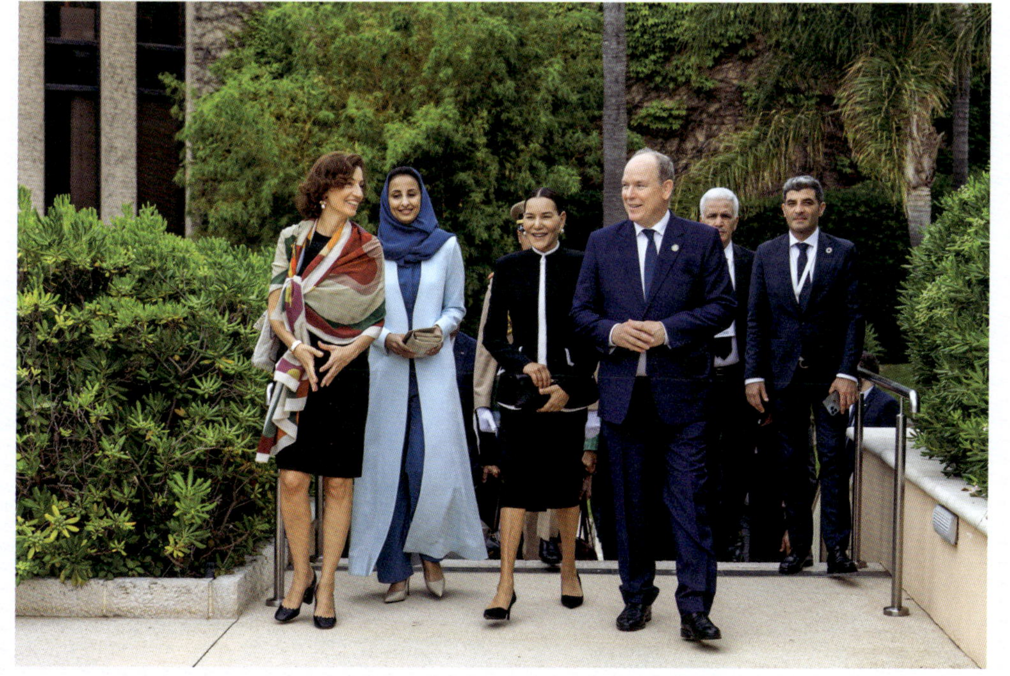

THE THIRD FOUNDATIONS DIALOGUE

In June 2023, the Principality hosted the Third Foundations Dialogue, which was co-organized by UNESCO and the Prince Albert II Foundation. Established in February 2020 by the IOC, the Dialogue serves as an annual forum for the heads of philanthropic organizations from around the world to exchange views on ways to promote the impact of the United Nations Decade of Ocean Science.

TOP Vladimir Ryabinin, Executive Secretary of IOC-UNESCO, who oversees the coordination of Ocean Decade, and Olivier Wenden, Vice President and CEO of the Prince Albert II of Monaco Foundation, November 17, 2021 at UNESCO.

BOTTOM Third Foundations Dialogue, June 13, 2023 in Monaco: with H.S.H. Prince Albert II; Audrey Azoulay, UNESCO Director-General; Princess Hasnaa of Morocco; Princess Hala bint Khaled bin Sultan Al-Saud; and Olivier Wenden, Vice President of the Foundation Prince Albert II.

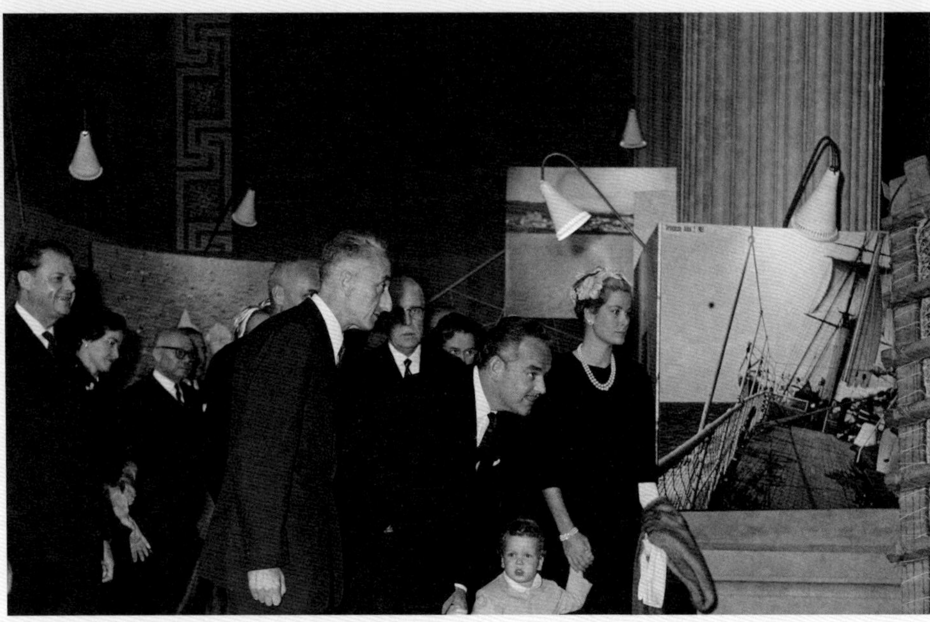

OCEANOGRAPHIC INSTITUTE OF MONACO

The Oceanographic Institute of Monaco was the realization of Prince Albert I's ambition "to protect the oceans but also to make them known and loved." It was founded in two stages and two places, beginning in 1906 with the opening of the Oceanographic Museum in Monaco, followed a year later by the opening of the Oceanographic Institute in Paris (renamed the Maison de l'Océan in 2020). This "dual genesis," as it were, marked a milestone in the cultural and scientific life of the Principality. As Monaco was being considered for admission to UNESCO in 1949, the legacy of the "navigator prince" born a hundred years earlier and whose centenary had just been celebrated, weighed heavily in favor of its accession. That same year, UNESCO's new member was granted a subsidy by the International Council of Scientific Unions of UNESCO (ICSU), repeated in 1950, to set up facilities for research into physical oceanography at the museum.

In 1966, the museum hosted the first international Congress on the history of oceanography. The proceedings were published two years later in the *Bulletin de l'Institut océanographique* (newsletter of the Oceanographic Institute), with the support of UNESCO. Mindful of the Organization's valuable role, oceanographer Jacques-Yves Cousteau (1910-1997) forged strong bonds with UNESCO in his thirty years (1957-1988) as director of the "Temple de la Mer," as the museum became known. In 1992 he was invited to Rio for the United Nations Conference on the Environment and Development (UNCED). Two years later he largely spearheaded the launch of the Cousteau-UNESCO Ecotechnie Program: an international initiative to promote interdisciplinary education, research and policymaking in the field of the environment and development. At the helm of the Oceanographic Institute today is Robert Calcagno, a vocal advocate for UNESCO like Cousteau before him. This is particularly apparent in the world-renowned symposiums and congresses held in the conference hall. In September 2019, for example, the fifty-first session of the Intergovernmental Panel on Climate Change (IPCC) convened at the museum to examine the "Special Report on The Ocean and the Cryosphere in a Changing Climate" (SROCC)—a report compiled at Monaco's instigation five years earlier. This emphasis on the mediatization of culture also led to the Polar Mission exhibition held at the museum in June 2022, followed eighteen months later by a new permanent exhibition, *The Prince and the Mediterranean*, which was inaugurated in December 2023 as part of the centennial celebrations of the birth of Prince Rainier III.

Scientific research was, meanwhile, anything but an afterthought for the Institute, which had its own faculty and laboratories but ceased its research activities in the 1980s. The Oceanographic Museum, for its part, housed two research institutes: the Monaco Scientific Center until it relocated in 2013, and the International Atomic Energy Agency until it too moved to new premises. Then there is the Maison de l'Océan in Paris: an "ocean hub" dedicated to publicizing the latest scientific advances. Last but not least, the Institute partners with various research centers, among them the Institut de Recherches Arctiques at the Université de Versailles Saint-Quentin-en-Yvelines. In 2021, French geographer, explorer and UNESCO Goodwill Ambassador, Jean Malaurie (1922-2024) donated his entire collection of Inuit objects and records of his Polar expeditions to the Oceanographic Institute. In recognition of his generous contribution, in 2023, the Museum hosted an exhibition of his pastel sketches from his Arctic missions titled *Crépuscules Arctiques* ("Arctic twilight"). The same exhibition was held at Institut Océanographique Headquarters in January 2024 a few months before Jean Malaurie passed away.

Prince Albert of Monaco with his parents, Prince Rainier and Princess Grace, Tuesday March 29, 1960, at the private viewing of the exhibition *La Mer profonde* (deep sea), for the 50th anniversary of the Oceanographic Museum founded by Prince Albert I. Center: Prince Pierre and Jacques-Yves Cousteau, Director of the Oceanographic Museum.

THE EXPLORATIONS OF MONACO

Inspired by the great expeditionary spirit of Prince Albert I, the Explorations of Monaco serve as a platform for H.S.H. Prince Albert II to demonstrate his commitment to the discovery, sustainable management and protection of the ocean. The Monaco Exploration Society, established in 2017, brings together the Prince Albert II of Monaco Foundation, the Oceanographic Institute, the Monaco Scientific Center, and the Monaco Yacht Club. It supports these institutions and coordinates international collaborative missions involving partners both within and outside the Principality.

From October 19 to 25, 2022, the Monaco Exploration Society conducted a series of scientific operations around Aldabra Atoll (Seychelles) to determine how best to protect the coral reefs of this UNESCO World Marine Heritage Site, and get young people involved. H.S.H Prince Albert II of Monaco made a personal, two-day visit to the atoll on October 24-25

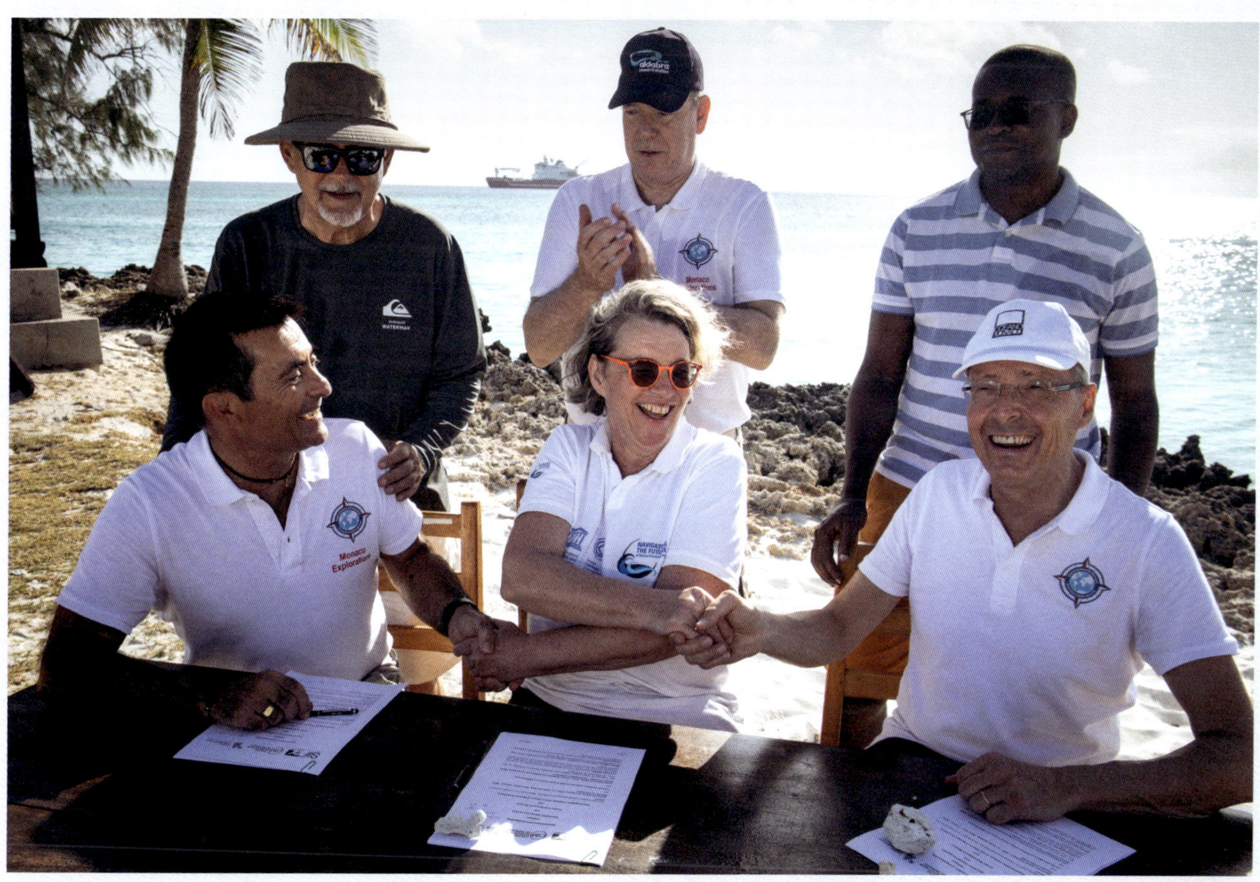

In the presence of H.S.H. Prince Albert II, a memorandum of understanding between the Seychelles Island Foundation, the Scientific Center of Monaco and the Oceanographic Institute of Monaco is signed on October 25, 2022 with the aim of advancing knowledge on the resilience of coral reefs in the Aldabra Atoll World Heritage Site.

MONACO SCIENTIFIC CENTER

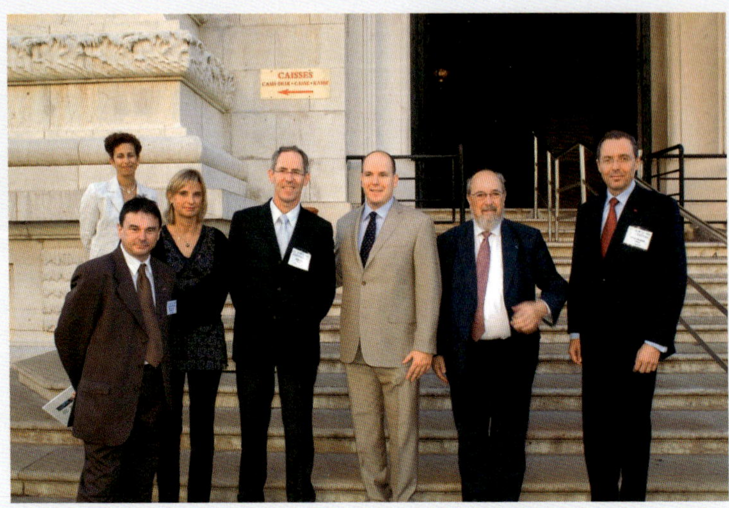

The birth of the Monaco Scientific Center (MSC) was directly linked to the Principality's commitment to UNESCO, following on from the First Scientific Conference of the International Atomic Energy Agency on Radioactive Waste Management, held in Monaco in November 1959 under the auspices of UNESCO. Prince Rainier III, speaking at the opening of the conference, expressed his wish to provide the Principality with the means to conduct observations and research, focusing on science as "a field of international understanding and peace." In creating a new research center and laboratories he would be pursuing his great-grandfather's legacy as an institution builder. The Monaco Scientific Center opened the following year, charged with working with governmental and international organizations to further research into marine conservation. It was initially housed in the Oceanographic Museum, in a low-level radioactivity laboratory run by scientists on secondment from the Commissariat à l'Energie Atomique (CEA, French atomic energy commission). The MSC also took charge of the Meteorology Observatory established by Prince Albert I, and set up two new laboratories, one specializing in neurobiology, the other in the study of marine pollution.

The first president of the MSC was Arthur Crovetto, head of the Monegasque National Commission for UNESCO and founder of a weekly news program, *Le Magazine de l'Océanographie*, broadcast by Radio Monte-Carlo from 1972 to 1977. In line with UNESCO's fourth pillar, information, the program gave a comprehensive overview of all the great oceanographic issues of the time through interviews with leading biological and physical oceanographers.

The MSC these days can be found at Number 8 Quai Antoine I, where it moved in 2013 under the presidency of Professor Patrick Rampal (in office since 2010), with Professor Denis Allemand as scientific director. Its activities revolve around three research departments, each one a major contributor in its field: the departments of marine biology and polar biology, and the department of medical biology that explores the human health benefits supplied by marine biodiversity. Since 2019, the MSC has been gaining visibility as a hub for research into the biology of precious red coral reefs, and the development of innovative solutions to save them. One such innovation is the World Coral Center, co-established with the Oceanographic Institute. Here again, the Center takes its lead from UNESCO, which is committed to the protection of our underwater heritage. The MSC also works hand in hand with the UNESCO Oceanographic Commission, organizing scientific events such as the second international symposium on *The Ocean in a High CO_2 World*, held at the Oceanographic Museum in 2008. The meeting brought together 220 scientists from around the world to explore the latest findings in ocean acidification. Sponsors included SCOR, IOC-UNESCO, ICES and IAEA, with financial support coming from the Prince Albert II Foundation and the Oceanographic Institute. On the strength of this symposium, in 2009 Monaco issued a declaration calling for a reduction in CO_2 emissions.

The MSC naturally enjoys extensive media coverage, in scientific journals and through the papers published by its many researchers and partner laboratories. Of particular note is its role as the organizer of the SCAR coral reef workshops and, most particularly, the SCAR workshops on the implementation of a strategic plan for biodiversity in Antarctica and the advancement of polar research. An MSC researcher was also selected as the lead author of the "Special Report on The Ocean and the Cryosphere in a Changing Climate" (SROCC), and the latest IPCC report (AR6).

THE INTERNATIONAL HYDROGRAPHIC ORGANIZATION

The mission of the International Hydrographic Organization is to foster cooperation between countries equipped to perform hydrographic surveys and chart the world's seas. Established by a convention signed in Monaco in 1967, the IHO began life as the International Hydrographic Bureau, which was inaugurated in June 1921 by Prince Albert I. In 2023, the Prince's pioneering role as an oceanographer was commemorated by UNESCO at the thirty-second General Assembly of the IOC, which celebrated the 120th anniversary of the GEBCO project (General Bathymetric Chart of the Oceans). Present at the event were Her Excellency Anne-Marie Boisbouvier; executive-secretary of the IOC, Vladimir Ryabinin; and IHO Director Mr. Luigi Sinapi.

Second symposium on the ocean in a high-CO2 world, with IOC-UNESCO, Monaco, December 6-9, 2008.
From left to right: Denis Allemand; Nadia Ounaïs; James Orr – AIEA; H.S.H. Prince Albert II; Michel Petit (1935-2019), President of the board of directors of the Oceanographic Institute; and Robert Calcagno.

GREAT VOICES

SCIENCES

"Of all the social and natural crises we humans face, the water crisis is the one that lies at the heart of our survival and that of our planet Earth."

Koïchiro Matsuura, World Water Development Report, 2003.

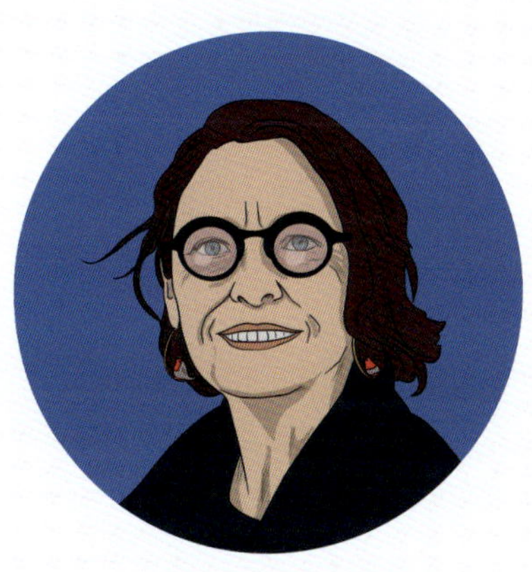

VINCIANE DESPRET

"It is extremely useful to talk about extinctions in terms of numbers [. . .] but it is not enough, because the figures do not move us. [. . .] Emotions are what the new ecological class lacks, according to the French philosopher and sociologist Bruno Latour. Historically, the left has relied on the emotions of emancipation, justice, and progress, which have all been vectors of mobilization. The right has also been able to cultivate emotions linked to the ideas of values and grandeur. But what are the emotions of the ecological class, the class that has to fight against the Anthropocene?

"A number of researchers are now working to answer this question. The Australian environmental philosopher Glenn Albrecht, for example, has coined the concept of *solastalgia* to describe the pain of no longer recognizing the place where one has lived because it has been too damaged. It is a powerful emotion. Art historian Estelle Zhong and philosopher Baptiste Morizot are young French researchers exploring how emotional tool-kits help us attune to the state of the world. The difficulty is that we have to go beyond gloomy passions, which are paralyzing, and be able to identify joyful passions too.

"In her book *Hope in the Dark*, American writer Rebecca Solnit encourages us to remember past struggles to avoid becoming discouraged. We tend to forget that many victories have been achieved through struggle. Rekindling the memory of these struggles is also a source of joyful passions."

Vinciane Despret, *La lutte contre le recul du vivant doit mobiliser des passions joyeuses* ("To combat species decline we need passions of joy"). Interviewed by Agnès Bardon (UNESCO) for the *UNESCO Courier*, December 2022.

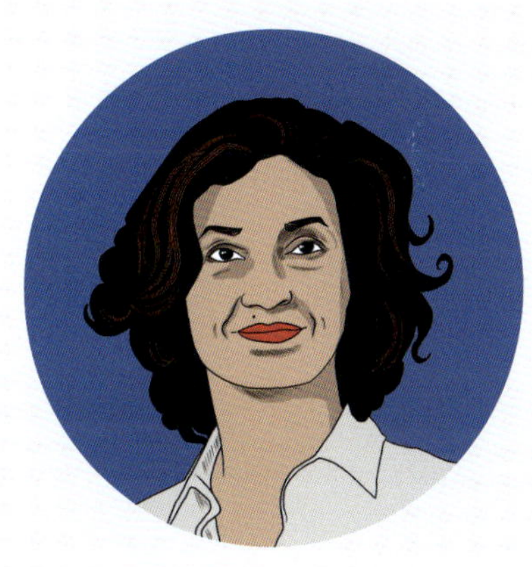

AUDREY AZOULAY

"The world needs stronger ethical rules for artificial intelligence: this is the challenge of our time. UNESCO's Recommendation on the ethics of AI sets the appropriate normative framework. Our Member States all endorsed this Recommendation in November 2021. It is high time to implement the strategies and regulations at national level. We have to walk the talk and ensure we deliver on the Recommendation's objectives."

Audrey Azoulay, UNESCO Director-General.

CULTURE

“There are two ways to lose oneself: walled segregation in the particular, or dilution in the “universal.” My conception of the universal is that of a universal enriched by all that is particular; a universal enriched by every particular: the deepening and coexistence of all particulars.”

Aimé Césaire, extracted from *Letter to Maurice Thorez*, dated October 24, 1956.

“Our vitality and resilience are at stake, at a time when what we need most is a little light relief to keep us from discouragement. We must meet each new onslaught of the epidemic with renewed zest for life [. . .] The arts are another major source of emotion. Through exhibitions and shows, a great many institutions help awaken our consciousness by uniting art and science around the pressing issues of the day.”

H.S.H. Prince Albert II of Monaco,
Lettre ouverte de trente-trois personnalités, Journal du Dimanche, December 13, 2020.

DOSSIER

LES RENCONTRES INTERNATIONALES MONACO ET LA MÉDITERRANÉE (RIMM INTERNATIONAL MONACO AND THE MEDITERRANEAN MEETINGS)

"UNESCO is deeply committed to the fight against the scourges that ravage or threaten the Mediterranean, and refuses to see it as a zone of strife, doomed to violence, conflict, and decline [. . .] Because the Mediterranean is also a space of hope, potential and virtualities, of fabrics yet to be woven and bridges yet to be built [. . .] UNESCO is banking on the Mediterranean because peace is our mission and the future our supreme challenge."

Federico Mayor, UNESCO Director-General, *La Méditerranée, laboratoire de la culture et de la paix* (the Mediterranean, a laboratory for culture and peace), UNESCO Mediterranean Programme, 1995.

The International Monaco and the Mediterranean Meetings (RIMM) were spearheaded by art historian Élisabeth Bréaud in 2001 and placed under the High Patronage of H.S.H. Prince Albert II. The symposia bring together specialists from all walks of life for an exchange of knowledge and expertise on the cultural and natural heritage of the Mediterranean Basin, the major issues currently facing the region, and how to solve them sustainably. The multidisciplinary nature of the event squares perfectly with the cultural principles and values of UNESCO, a connection embodied by Mr. Mounir Bouchenaki, honorary president of the Meetings and advisor to the Organization's current Director-General. Mr. Bouchenaki has served successively as Director of the World Heritage Centre (1999-2000), Assistant Director-General for Culture at UNESCO (2000-2006) and Director-General of ICCROM (2006-2011).

The meetings take place biennially, with each session highlighting the different cultures that fuse and connect in the Mediterranean area; there have been twelve meetings to date, all held at the Oceanographic Museum. Three editions merit particular mention: the 2013 "Myth of Prometheus Meeting", which was graced by the presence of the then Director-General Irina Bokova; the 2020 "Action for Heritage Meeting;" and the 2024 "Mediterranean Gardens Meeting." The inaugural ceremony of the 2020 meeting was addressed by UNESCO Director-General Audrey Azoulay (in office since 2018), who expressed her thanks to the Principality for its loyalty and increasing efforts in support of the causes championed by UNESCO and His Excellency Mr. Laurent Stefanini, then Ambassador of the French Republic to Monaco and former Ambassador, Permanent Representative to UNESCO (2016-2019). At the close of the opening ceremony of this tenth edition, the 2020 RIMMA Award was bestowed upon Mme Azoulay by H.S.H. Prince Albert II. The 2024 Meeting, full title *Jardins en Méditerranée. Le Temps de l'Abondance, le Temps des Vertus, le Temps du Merveilleux* (Mediterranean gardens, a time of plenty, a time of virtue, a time of marvels) resonated with the cultural and environmental challenges of our time. H.S.H. in his opening speech reminded the assembled company of "the Principality's centuries-old vocation [. . .] as a force for cultural concord, and a shared Mediterranean culture free of all nationalism", the while inviting guests to continue to cultivate their garden 'as Voltaire put it, a garden of peace wherein Mediterranean countries may find refuge, today more than ever.'"

"I feel enormously privileged to have been selected by the Principality of Monaco as honorary president of the International Monaco and the Mediterranean Meetings, under the High Patronage of H.S.H. Prince Albert of Monaco [. . .] I am deeply honored to participate in the RIMM and immensely grateful to Your Highness for your presence. It is no accident that the Principality was chosen to host these meetings. Looking back at the history of the Princes of Monaco, one notices that you are descended from a Polar explorer and have yourself led an expedition to the North Pole. As an art lover, you have also demonstrated your concern for sustainable development and the protection of life on Earth. We arrive in the Principality with the fire from the sun—light of Monaco, light of the Mediterranean, so oft evoked by Albert Camus. It now falls to you, Your Highness, to say a few words about these Meetings that we pursue today around the theme of fire."

Address by Mr. Mounir Bouchenaki, Assistant Director-General for Culture at UNESCO, at the Seventh RIMM, 2013.

"Sire,

Allow me to express my gratitude and pleasure in participating in this distinguished event to which UNESCO is honored to grant its patronage.

I extend my special thanks to the organizers of these meetings, and to H.S.H. Prince Albert II for this opportunity to express myself on a theme I hold dear, and which lies at the heart of Mediterranean identity: culture and sustainable development. There can be no better confirmation of the ties binding Monaco to UNESCO, most notably through the commitment shown by the Principality and the Prince Albert II of Monaco Foundation to our scientific programs and the World Heritage Marine Program. This museum illustrates that commitment perfectly. Allow me also to salute my dear friend Mr. Mounir Bouchenaki, honorary president of the RIMM, and Professor Yves Coppens, a steadfast UNESCO supporter with a particular dedication to the protection of archaeological heritage [. . .] The valorization of culture and cultural diversity is essential to reinforce social connectedness and collective development, especially in a pluralistic society such as ours [. . .] I am delighted to bring this message here, to Monaco, to this Mediterranean space that is a school for diversity, whose history trumpets the power that comes from mixing cultures—a power that can move mountains, make us more inventive, more innovative, keep driving us forward [. . .] We can all see the potential in cultural exchange between artists and creators on both sides of the Mediterranean and I view this forum, on the theme of Prometheus who stole fire from the gods to give knowledge to mankind, as an encouragement to push back the boundaries of culture and share its illimitable power."

Address by UNESCO Director-General, Irina Bokova, at the Seventh RIMM, 2013.

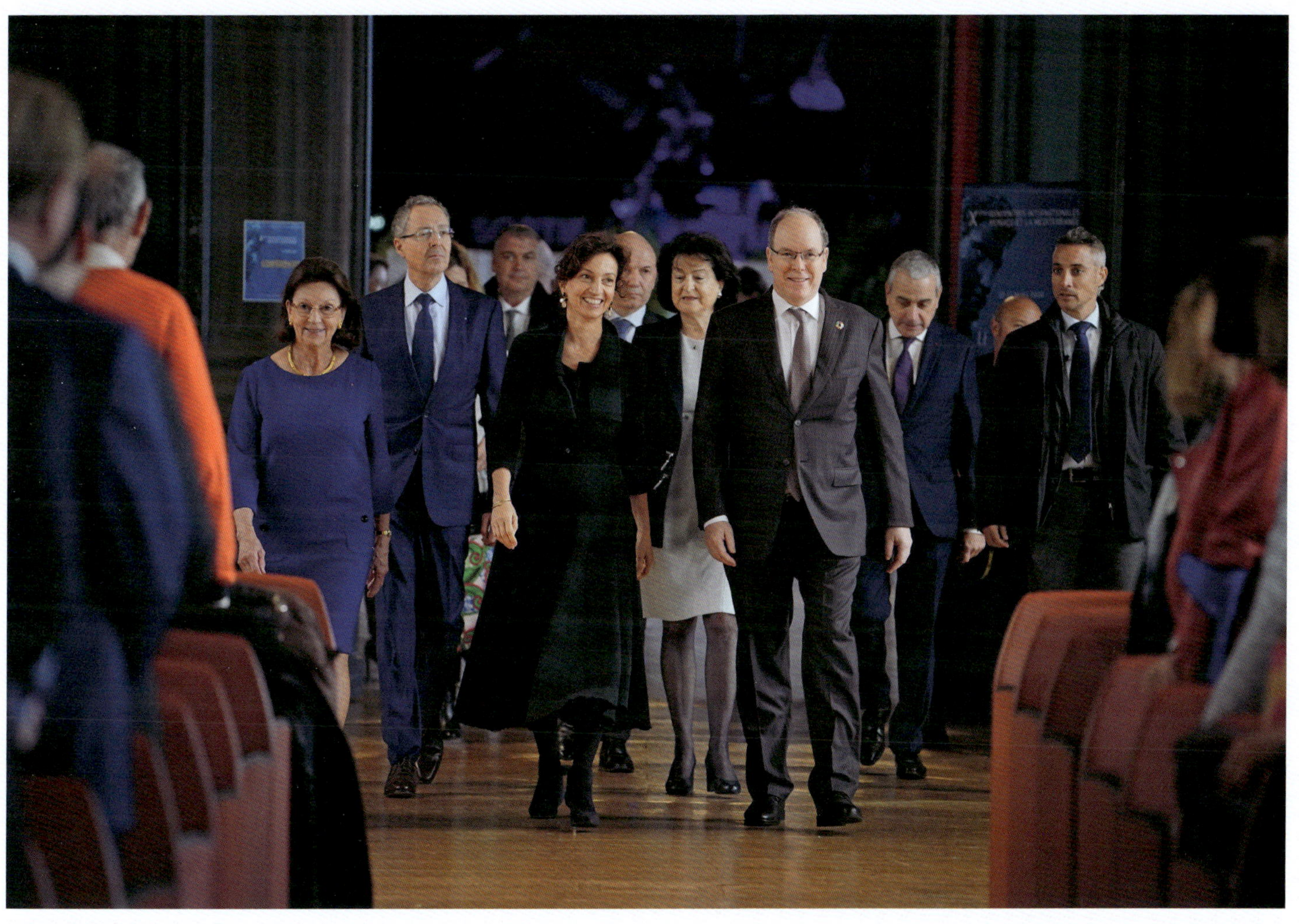

Opening of the tenth International Monaco and the Mediterranean Symposium, March 12, 2020.
From left to right: Elisabeth Bréaud, Director and President of RIMM; Robert Calcagno; Audrey Azoulay;
Her Excellency Yvette Lambin-Berti; H.S.H. Prince Albert II; His Excellency Laurent Stefanini.

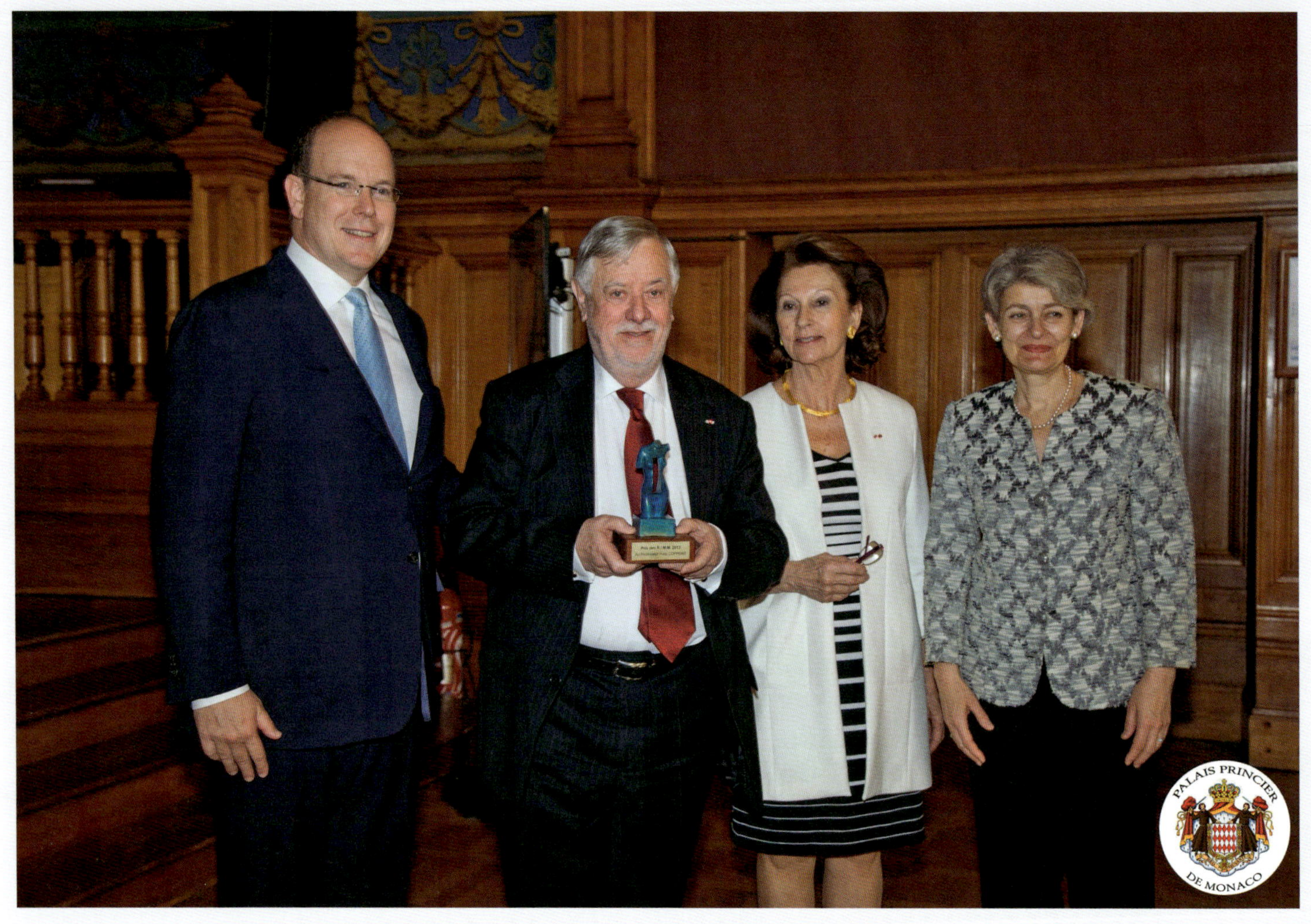

RIMM award ceremony honoring Yves Coppens, March 21, 2013. From L to R: H.S.H. Prince Albert II; Prof. Yves Coppens; Elisabeth Bréaud; Irina Bokova, UNESCO Director-General.

"Sire,

May I begin by saying how happy I am to be here and why I insisted on being here despite the uncertain climate in which we find ourselves. I insisted on standing before you first and foremost to testify, in my capacity as UNESCO Director-General, to our gratitude toward the Principality of Monaco for its steadfast support—and I would add its ever-increasing efforts on behalf of the causes championed by UNESCO, natural and cultural heritage alike—its steadfast support not only of the unbreakable bond between us but also, less well known, education, most notably the education of girls. We have, and for this I wish to thank your Government, an ally at our side, and for this, we are thankful.

I also insisted on being here to voice UNESCO's commitment to *Les Rencontres*. Because I believe they stand as an example of the deep connections between civil societies, and also of the enduring bonds forged through a fruitful exchange of expertise that persists whatever the political uncertainties of the time. I believe, indeed, that there can be no more useful endeavor than this, and none so inherently consistent with the ambitions and ideals of UNESCO. I also came here because this is about the Mediterranean, a region to which I am particularly attached, both personally and in my capacity as UNESCO Director-General. It is this Mediterranean, with its philosophers, merchants, and travelers who spread its legends and passed down its lore, that shaped our collective imagination and nurtured our ideas and aesthetics [. . .] This symposium is a new opportunity for the two sides of the Mediterranean to draw closer together through dialogue. [. . .]"

Address by UNESCO Director-General Audrey Azoulay, at the tenth RIMM, 2020.

DOSSIER

UNESCO, THE PERFORMING ARTS AND LE MONDIAL DU THÉÂTRE FESTIVAL OF AMATEUR THEATER IN MONACO

"Theatre is one of mankind's oldest art forms. Its history merges with the origins of language itself and its various forms of expression reflect our cultural diversity. [...] Arts education is key to forming generations capable of reinventing the world they inherit. It supports the vitality of cultural identities by emphasizing their links with other cultures and thus contributes to the building of a common heritage."

Audrey Azoulay, UNESCO Director-General, on the occasion of the seventieth anniversary of the International Theater Institute, March 27, 2018.

The International Theater Institute (ITI) was established in 1948, three years after UNESCO came into existence, on the initiative of Sir Julian Huxley, first Director-General of the Organization, and British playwright John Boynton Priestley (1894-1984). Dedicated to the performing arts, ITI aimed to raise the status of the artists and promote the use of the performing arts as a vehicle for mutual understanding and peace. Since 1962, March 27 has marked World Theater Day, an event created by ITI and UNESCO to promote theater in all its forms. To safeguard the diversity of those cultural expressions, the UNESCO committee has inscribed many of them on the World Heritage List, among them Nogaku Theater (Japan, 2008) and Khon masked dance drama (Thailand, 2018).

Here again, the dialogue between Monaco, land of Prince Florestan I (1785-1856) and UNESCO is clearly evident. Since the staging of Marcel Pagnol's play *Jazz* at the Grand Théâtre de Monte-Carlo on December 6, 1926, the performing arts have been flourishing in Monaco. Its many theater companies—the Studio de Monaco, Compagnie Florestan, Les Farfadets—have the pick of several venues, including the Théâtre Princesse Grace, Théâtre des Variétés, Théâtre des Muses and Fort Antoine. World Theater Day is celebrated each year by the Department of Cultural Affairs and the National Commission for UNESCO.

The pinnacle of the partnership between Monaco and UNESCO is however, the Mondial du Théâtre Quadrennial, also known as the World Festival of Amateur Theater, launched by the Studio de Monaco Theater Company in 1957. The festival is an offshoot of the International Amateur Theater Association (IATA, established 1952) and placed under the high patronage of the Prince of Monaco and its four founders, Guy and Max Brousse, René Cellario and Jean Ratti. Last held in 2021, the festival has notched up seventeen editions and as many new productions in the course of its sixty-plus years of existence, playing host to symposiums and workshops on confrontation, exchange and teaching—three core themes of interest to the general public and professionals alike. In 1994 the festival welcomed at least twenty-four theater troupes (compared to just twelve in 1957), fully realizing its mission as a hub for encounters, collaboration and education through theater. As a model of everything the IATA stands for, the festival naturally attracted the attention of UNESCO, which has supported it since the outset, notably by covering the travel costs of every theater company invited to participate since the 1970s.

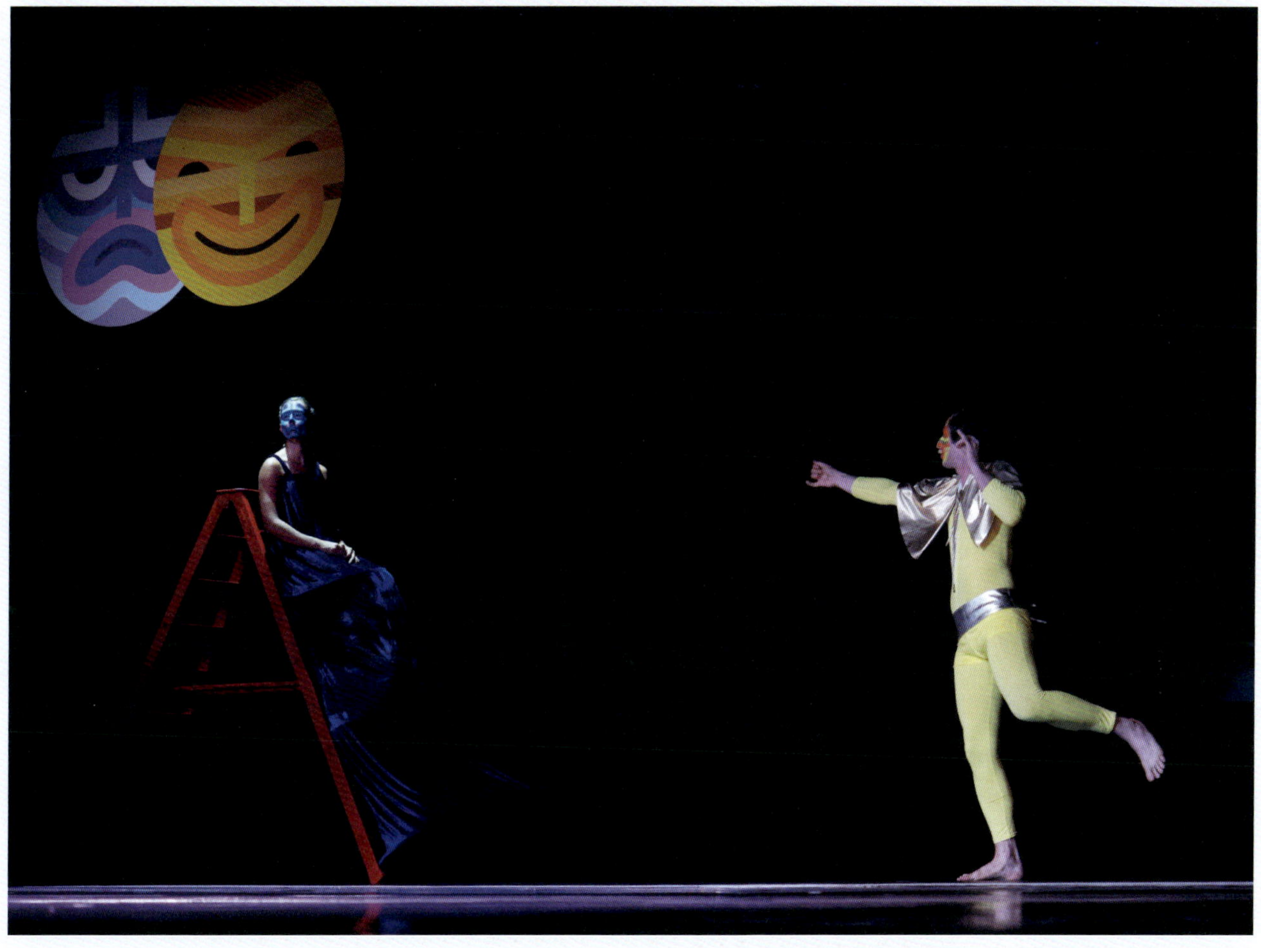

Homepage of the Mondial du Théâtre website. The next event will take place on August 20-27, 2025.

"Monaco, December 16, 1980
Dear Director-General:

In 1977 and 1979, you had the goodness to accept the requests presented by the Government of the Principality, under the UNESCO Participation Program in the Activities of Member States for 1977-78 and 1979-80, in support of the Sixth World Amateur Theater Festival, and the symposium on 'Promoting Human Rights Education Through Children's Literature.'

UNESCO's financial support ensured the success of both events, most notably by making it possible for African theater companies to participate in the World Amateur Theater Festival for the very first time.

Turning now to the seventh edition of this Festival, which is scheduled to take place in Monaco from August 28 to September 6, 1981. The Government of the Principality wishes, on the one hand, to broaden the festival's cultural purview, using the process set in motion for the sixth edition thanks to the presence of representatives from emerging economies, and on the other hand to intensify the dialogue between artists and specialists of different nationalities, cultures, and disciplines."

Letter from André Saint-Mleux, Minister of State of Monaco, to UNESCO Director-General, Amadou-Mahtar M'Bow.

"The month of August will see the Mondial du Théâtre back in action for its seventeenth edition. Every four years, the festival provides a forum for amateur theater companies eager to share their vision of the theater and explore different cultures from around the world. On August 17-22, starting at 6:00 PM, three different theater groups per night will take the stage at the Théâtre des Variétés and the Théâtre Princesse Grace. Admission is free and all are welcome. 'The selection process is really quite simple and based on a joint decision of the International Amateur Theater Association (IATA) and the Monaco organizing committee. We're looking to combine a high level of artistic talent with cultural and geographical representation, aiming for the most international line-up possible but evenly divided between participants from North and South America, Africa, Asia, Europe and Oceania,' says festival director Patrice Cellario. This year there were fifteen successful candidates out of nearly ninety applicants, plus another four added as a precaution by the IATA following the initial selection—a wise decision in the current health crisis. Patrice Cellario explains: 'Four of our original selections, from Japan, Iran, Russia and the United Kingdom, dropped out and had to be replaced. The UK was the last to cry off so just as well we had a Cuban theater company standing by. So this year's line-up will feature performers from Argentina, Belgium, Cuba, Spain, the USA, Finland, France, Italy, Hungary, Lithuania, Morocco, Portugal, the Central African Republic, Slovenia and Slovakia.'"

Art and culture—theater lovers home in on the Principality. *La Gazette de Monaco*, July 24, 2021.

Poster for the 17th World Festival of Amateur Theater, or the Mondial du Théâtre, Monaco, 2021.

DOSSIER

HERITAGE, MONACO AND UNESCO

"With the inclusion of nineteen traditional cultural expressions on the World Heritage List, the first Proclamation of Masterpieces of the Oral and Intangible Heritage of Humanity, in May 2001, made it possible to launch the preliminary process for the official recognition of forms of cultural expression of outstanding value, while sensitizing the governments and the groups concerned to the value of that heritage, and to the importance of handing it down intact and making it better known."

Koichiro Matsuura, UNESCO Director-General, *The Intangible Cultural Heritage: UNESCO'S Role and Priority Fields of Action*, Rio de Janeiro, Brazil, January 22, 2002.

While the preservation of world heritage is not UNESCO's sole preoccupation, it is certainly the best known. This first became apparent on March 8, 1960, when Vittorino Veronese (1910-1986) launched his appeal for global solidarity to save the monuments of Nubia under threat from the building of Egypt's Aswan Dam. His call for action led to the adoption in 1972 of the Convention Concerning the Protection of World Cultural and Natural Heritage, a landmark international treaty connecting environmental protection with cultural heritage conservation. It was initially ratified by twenty State Parties and came into effect in 1975. Monaco added its signature in 1978. At the time of writing, the World Heritage List comprised 1,199 cultural, natural or mixed properties in need of safeguarding, with new properties being added at least every two years. The first marine site won inclusion in 1982, with forty-nine more added since then. In the late twentieth century, a new "intangible cultural heritage" category was defined, recognizing that cultural heritage does not end at monuments and collections of objects. A new convention followed, signed in 2003, for the safeguarding of "practices, representations, expressions, knowledge, and skills—as well as the instruments, objects, artefacts and cultural spaces associated therewith." Effective as from 2006 and ratified by Monaco in 2007, the List of Intangible Cultural Heritage stood at the time of writing at 730 intangible assets.

The Principality of Monaco is not represented on the UNESCO World Heritage List, tangible or intangible, but remains no less committed to its success. In 2018, for instance, it partnered with France and Italy to nominate the cross-border area known as the "Mediterranean Alps" for inclusion on the World Heritage List. Like each State Party to the 1972 Convention, Monaco committed to protecting its own national heritage when it added its signature in 1978. The States Parties are also encouraged to "integrate the protection of [cultural and natural] heritage into comprehensive planning programmes;" to provide historic sites and monuments with appropriate services and personnel; and to conduct research in conservation and take whatever measures are necessary to make cultural heritage an integral part of everyday life. Embodying these objectives, the Rainier III Sculpture Trail (2023) features more than 200 artworks just waiting to be discovered in the gardens, streets and squares of Monaco City. It enjoys the support of the Heritage Institute, under the aegis of the Department of Cultural Affairs, most notably within the framework of the European Culture Days held every year since 1996. Another fine example of the Principality's attention to heritage is the sustainable restoration of the magnificent Renaissance frescoes uncovered in 2015 in the Prince's Palace—a discovery that places the Principality at the heart of world art history. Then there is the role of the different archival repositories: the Archives du Palais Princier (archives of the Prince's palace), the Audiovisual Institute, the Fonds Patrimonial de la Médiathèque de Monaco (Heritage collection of the Monaco Media Library) and the Mission de Préfiguration des Archives Nationales (national archives preparatory mission). All of these bodies play a crucial role in preserving and shedding light on documentary heritage—the memory of a country and a people, certainly, but also the legacy of humankind. Monaco attaches equal importance to the valorization of its intangible heritage, most notably in the realm of religious practice: the feast days of Sainte Dévote, patron saint of Monaco and Corsica, Saint Jean the Baptist, Saint Nicholas and Saint Roman; the processions to mark Good Friday, the Feast of Corpus Christi and the *Fête du Vœu* (feast of the Immaculate Conception); and the Christmastide tradition of the *Pan de Natale*.

We should note too, that alongside French as the official language, there exists the traditional language of *Munegascu: a lenga d'i nostri avi*, ("tongue of our ancestors") that has its roots in Genoese but evolved after Monaco freed itself from tutelage and opened up to its neighbors. In 1924, a local group eager to preserve their native tongue founded what would become the National Committee for Monegasque Traditions and embarked on the task of consigning to paper what had hitherto been a strictly spoken language. Its chief exponent was Louis Notari, who is remembered as the "father of Monegasque literature" for his authorship of the very first work in *Munegascu, La Légende de Sainte Dévote* (1927). A grammar and dictionaries would follow in due course, with lessons in *Munegascu* becoming available from 1972 onward under the impetus of Monegasque writer and presbyter Georges Franzi (1914-1997), and made compulsory in local schools in 1976. Another landmark date, 2015, marked the foundation of the Association des Sites Historiques Grimaldi de Monaco (Grimaldi association of historic sites), bringing together those former French and Italian fiefdoms that share a history with present-day Monaco.

Turning now to Monaco's contribution to world heritage as a UNESCO member, this began with joining the appeal to save the monuments of Nubia and the creation of two committees: an honorary committee featuring Princess Grace; and an international action committee featuring Monaco's former Minister of State, Jacques Rueff. Having ratified all the relevant conventions, Monaco committed to safeguarding imperiled sites in general, and projects compatible with its own scientific and cultural approaches in particular. In 2014 therefore, following on from the "First Nomads of Upper Asia" exhibition the year before, the Principality committed funds for the preservation and sustainable management of the Shoroon Bumbagar site on Mount Maikhan, Mongolia. The Principality these days is particularly sensitive to the plight of imperiled cultural heritage and in a spirit of international cooperation works with international bodies such as the ALIPH Foundation, ICCROM and, of course, UNESCO. Mention may be made here of the funding agreement signed in September 2022 between the Principality and the ALIPH Foundation, committing to protect the cultural assets of Odessa's two museums from the ravages of the Russo-Ukraine war. Marine sites, particularly in the Arctic, are another major area of concern for this country steeped in the legacy of pioneering oceanographer, Prince Albert I. In 2017, coinciding with the launch of the Explorations of Monaco aimed at raising awareness about ocean protection, the Principality and UNESCO signed a strategic partnership aimed at strengthening the activities of the World Heritage Marine program.

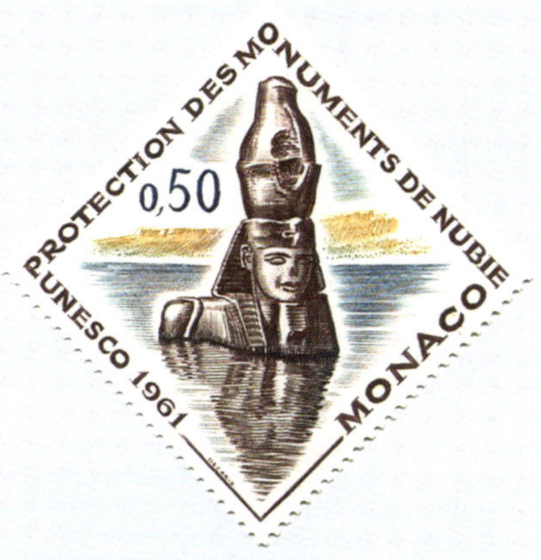

"These monuments, whose loss may be tragically near, do not belong solely to the countries who hold them in trust. The whole world has the right to see them endure. They are part of a common heritage which comprises Socrates' message and the Ajanta frescoes, the walls of Uxmal and Beethoven's symphonies. Treasures of universal value are entitled to universal protection. When a thing of beauty, whose loveliness increases rather than diminishes by being shared, is lost, then all men alike are the losers."

Vittorino Veronese, Appeal by UNESCO Director-General, to save the treasures of Nubia, *UNESCO Courier*, May 1960.

"Protection of the Monuments of Nubia" stamp, UNESCO-Monaco, 1961.

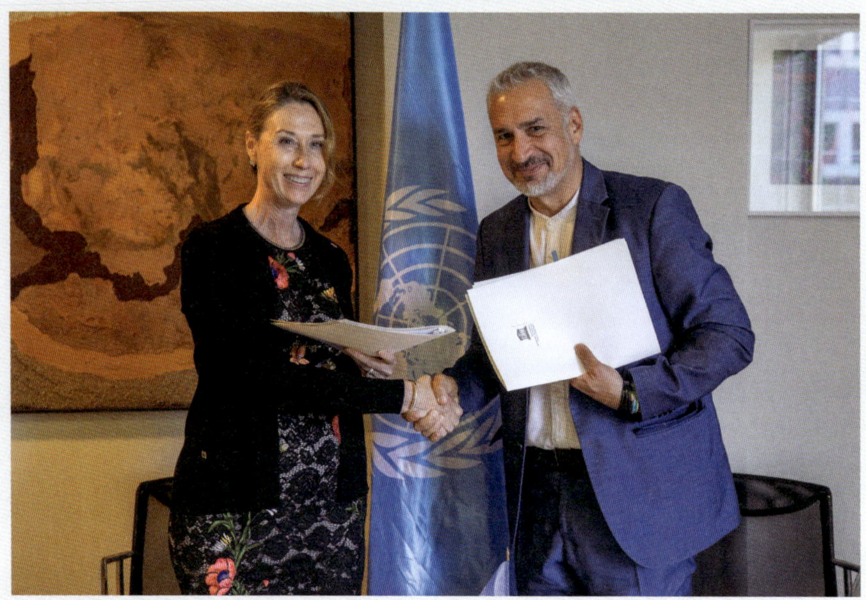

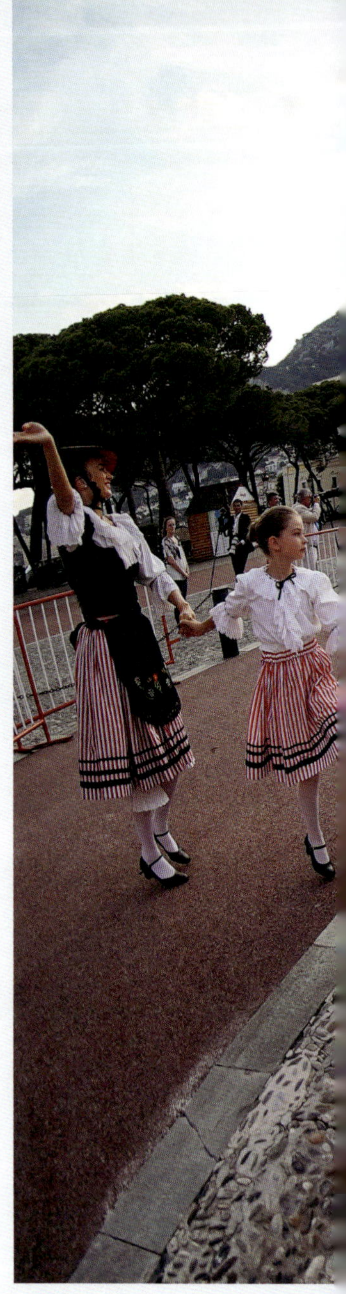

ABOVE On May 17, 2022, the Principality of Monaco and UNESCO signed a new three-year partnership aimed at strengthening scientific research at marine sites on the UNESCO World Heritage List and paving the way for the use of carbon credits to help finance conservation efforts at the sites.

OPPOSITE PAGE The Saint-Jean festival of fire and light, Place du Palais, Monaco, 2023. On the evening of June 23, after a religious ceremony in the chapel of the Palace of Monaco, the *batafoegu* (bonfire) is lit. The La Palladienne group provides the evening entertainment.

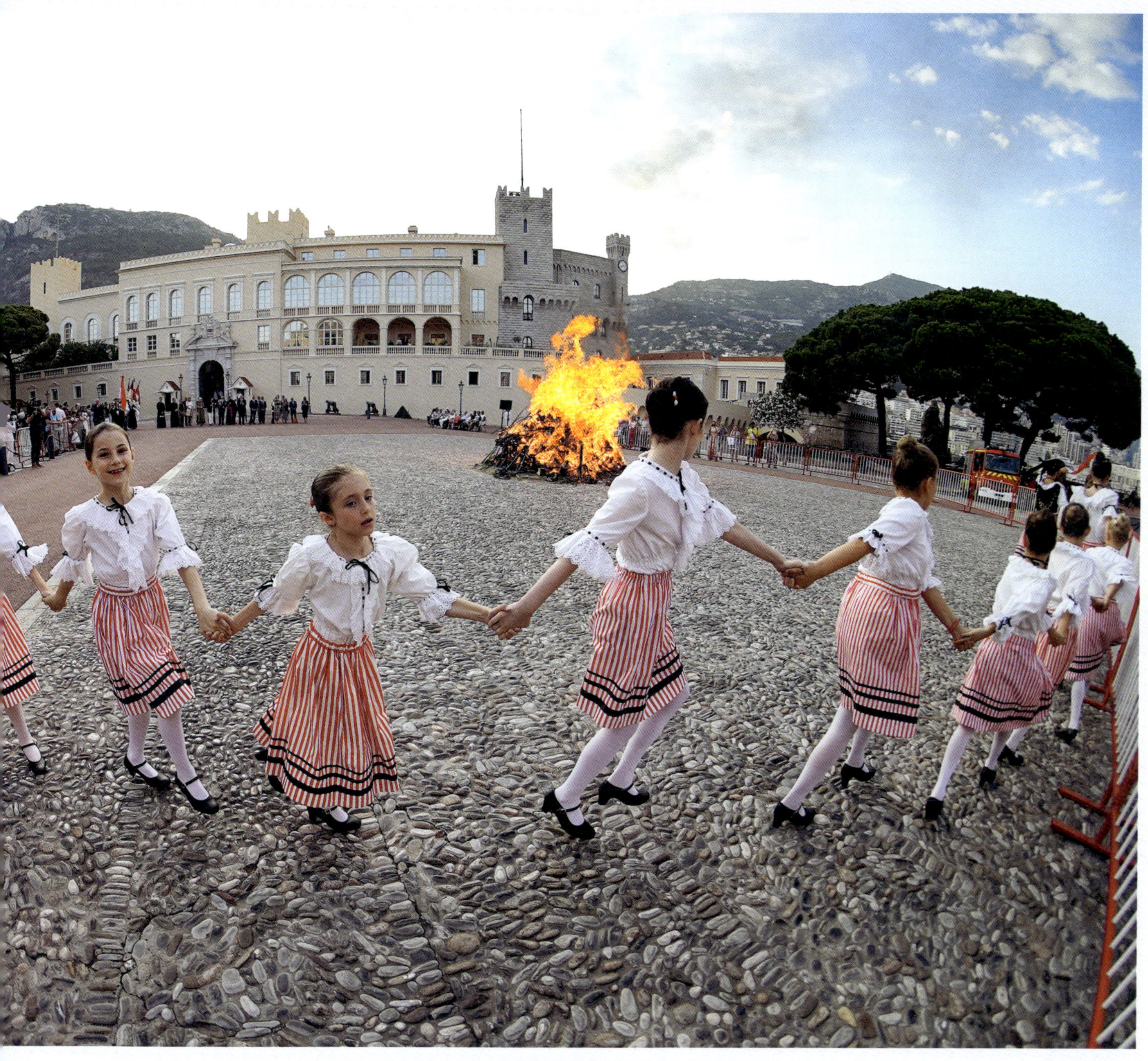

GREAT VOICES

CULTURE—SAVE, PROTECT, RAISE AWARENESS—FROM THE UNIVERSAL TO THE LOCAL

"Intangible heritage is a living fabric from which our history is built. It is not merely culture itself, but the crucible of culture."

Koïchiro Matsuura, Address by UNESCO Director-General, on the occasion of the international meeting on "the intangible cultural heritage: UNESCO's role and priority fields of action" Rio de Janeiro, Brazil, January 22, 2002.

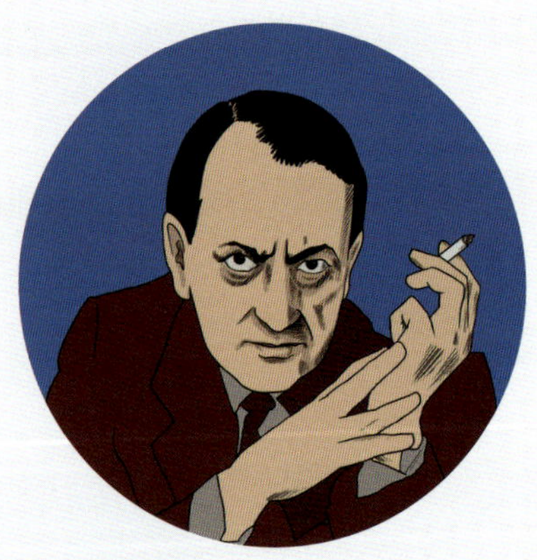

ANDRÉ MALRAUX

"If UNESCO is trying to rescue the monuments of Nubia, it is because these are in imminent danger; it goes without saying that it would try to save other great ruins in Angkor or Nara, for instance if they were similarly threatened. On behalf of man's artistic heritage, you are appealing to the world's conscience as others have been doing, this week, for the victims of the Agadir earthquake. 'May we never have to choose,' you said just now, 'between porphyry statues and living men!' Yours is the first attempt to deploy, in a rescue operation, on behalf of statues, the immense resources usually harnessed in the service of men. And this is perhaps because for us the survival of statues has become an expression of life. At the moment when our civilization divines a mysterious transcendence in art and one of the still-obscure sources of its unity, at the moment when we are bringing into a single, family relationship the masterpieces of so many civilizations which knew nothing of or even hated each other, you are proposing an action which brings all men together to defy the forces of dissolution. Your appeal is historic, not because it proposes to save the temples of Nubia, but because through it the first-world civilization publicly proclaims the world's art as its indivisible heritage. In days when the West believed its cultural heritage had its source in Athens, it could nonetheless look on with equanimity while the Acropolis crumbled away."

Speech delivered in Paris by André Malraux on March 8, 1960, in response to UNESCO's appeal "To save the monuments of Upper Egypt."

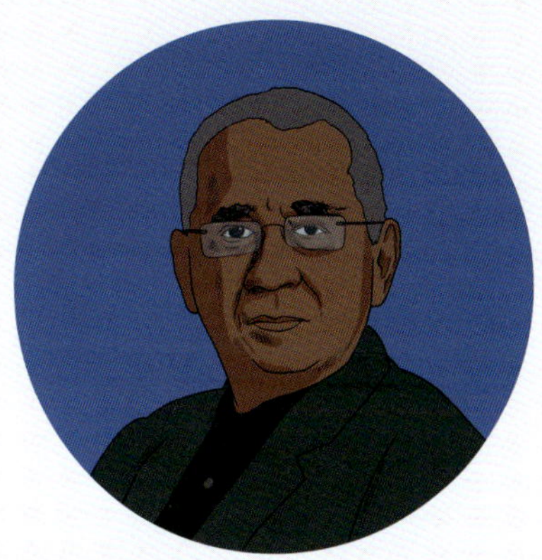

HENRI LOPES

"I think of Amadou Hampâté Bâ and his elders—our living archives. Scholar, sage and holy man into the bargain, Amadou Hampâté Bâ was the living embodiment of the centuries-old values bequeathed him by his native Mali. He was also a model of multi-belonging, open-mindedness, curiosity and tolerance. Born into an animist background, he adopted the Muslim faith and married a European. Every new persuasion, whether religious or philosophical, came to embed itself in his core being, never to displace his cultural heritage. Amadou Hampâté Bâ celebrated and practiced intercultural marriage. Though he never actually wrote about it, cultural diversity was what it was all about *avant la lettre*.

"His address to the international community was in fact a cry for help. It was a plea for a new approach to historical research. Let us remember that until the 1960s historians relied solely on literary and archaeological sources, clearly forgetting that the sacred texts of Judaism, Christianity and Islam were originally transcripts of oral histories. What, if not the ancestors of our African griots, were the bards of ancient Greece that served as the inspiration for Homer's *The Iliad* and *The Odyssey*? And what if not the rewriting of memory was the *Chanson de Roland* sung by trouvères and troubadours at the courts of kings and great princes?

"That the words of Amadou Hampâté Bâ resonated with the international community of the 1960s is evident from UNESCO's response: the preparation and drafting of *The General History of Africa*, a work of pivotal scientific value that has served as the basis for the development of school curricula and history manuals throughout our continent. One of UNESCO's most ambitious projects, *The General History of Africa* has helped to change the way the world sees African civilizations, and the way Africans see themselves. Because let us not forget that the roots of the slave trade, like the roots of colonization, lay in the unflattering conceptions of Africa itself and the people who lived there [. . .] Now that we have regained our place within the international community, we can take a serene view of the manner in which Europe first made contact with Africa."

Henri Lopes, writer, politician, and Congolese diplomat, Ambassador of the Republic of Congo to France, speaking at the high-level panel on the occasion of the tenth anniversary of the Universal Declaration on Cultural Diversity, Paris, November 2, 2011. Source: UNESCO Digital Library.

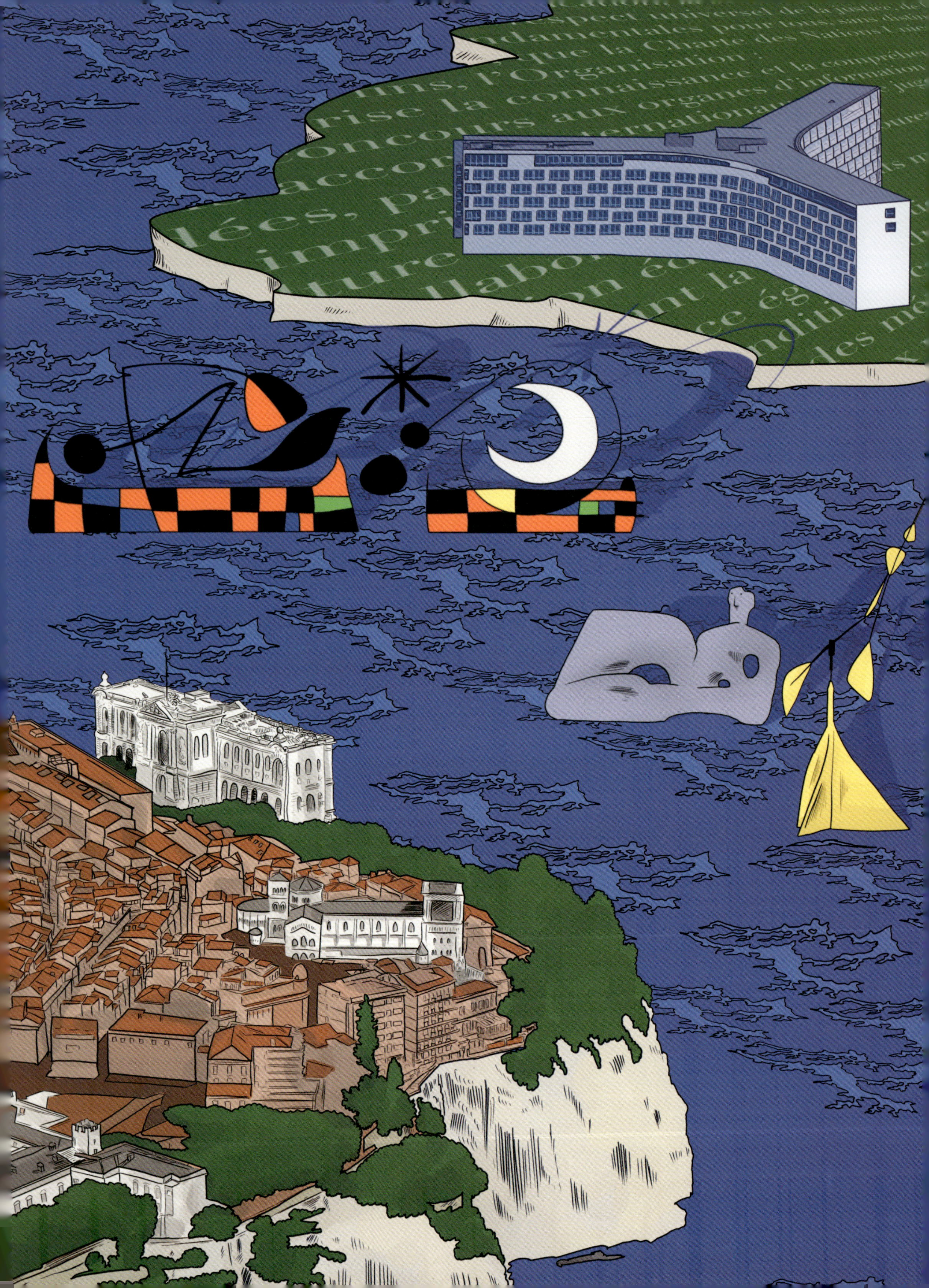

respect universel de la justice
pour tous, sans
que la Charte des Nations
l'Organisation :
la connaissance et la
aux organes d'information

A LIVING CONNECTION

THE PRINCELY FAMILY AND THE UNESCO DIRECTORS-GENERAL

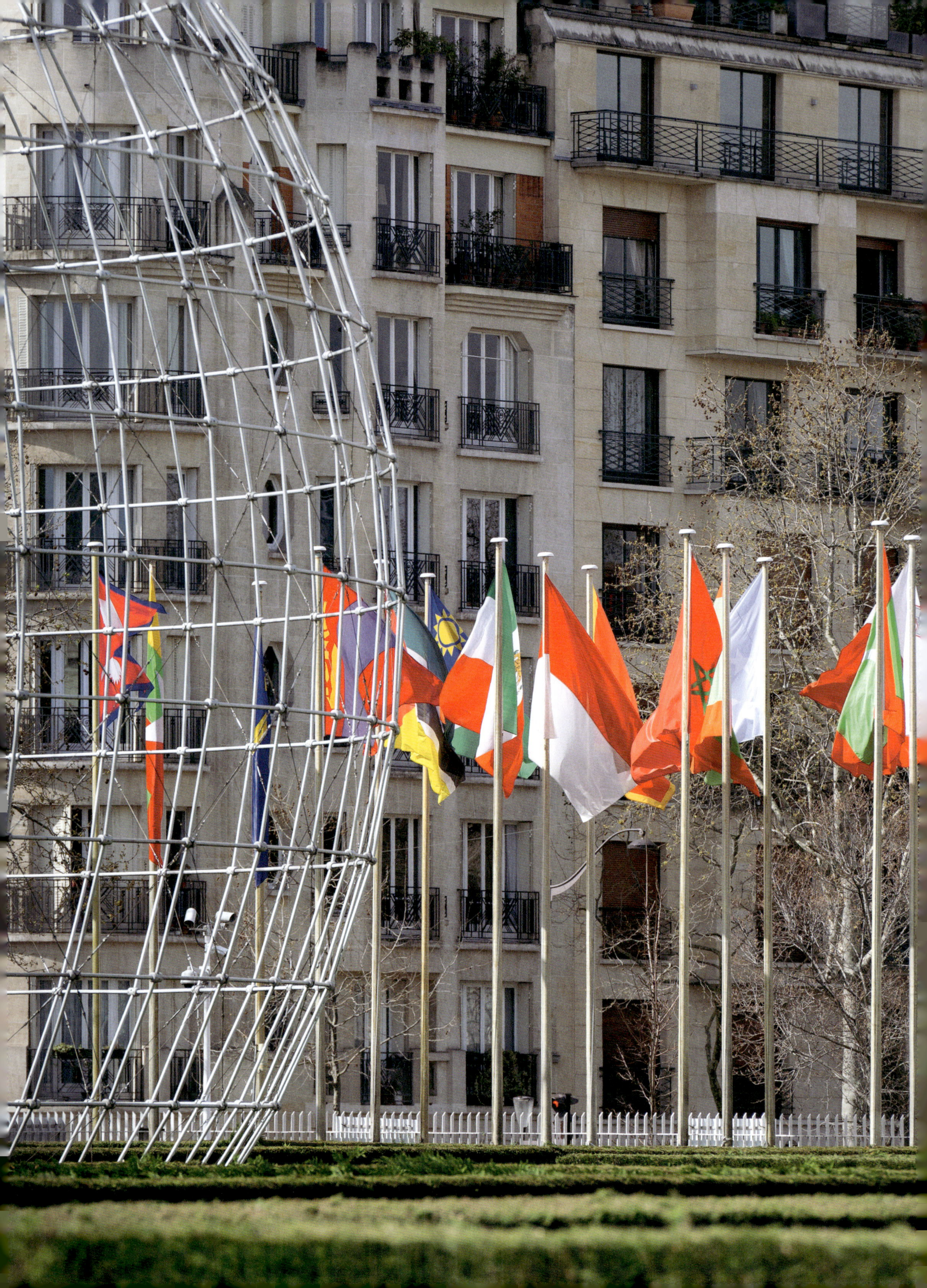

The relationship between UNESCO and the Principality, beyond the programs, commissions, and projects pursued by the different entities, is quite as informal as it is formal, bringing together in the decades that have elapsed since 1949 the members of the Princely Family and the UNESCO Directors-General. This is the story of a relationship driven by opportunity—a relationship that has deepened and evolved over time, too richly complex for us to do anything more here than give the main points, and as it were dip into the story.

The UNESCO Directors-General are senior international officials elected for a four-year term, renewable once, who shall neither seek nor accept instructions from any government or other institution. They visit member states in an official capacity or to inaugurate events supported by UNESCO.

The first Director-General was Julian Huxley (1946-1948), who like Prince Albert I had made expeditions to Spitzbergen and expressed his interest in Monaco's candidacy. His successor, Jaime Torres Bodet (1948-1952), was delighted by Monaco's admission and addressed his congratulations to the Government of the Principality. Jean Thomas, the first person to hold the position of Deputy Director-General of UNESCO, traveled to Monaco in 1957, representing the then Director-General Luther Evans (1953-1958). Two years later, Vittorino Veronese (1958-1961) visited the Principality to inaugurate the IAEA International Conference on Radioactive Waste Management, which was held in Monaco in November 1959 under the auspices of UNESCO.

René Maheu, the emblematic Director-General (1961-1974) described by French historian Chloé Maurel as embodying "the success of UNESCO," made a meticulously planned official visit to Monaco in 1967, a testament to his interest in the Principality. He returned the following year for the opening of the fifth regional conference of European National Commissions for UNESCO.

The dialogue between UNESCO and the Principality has been ongoing ever since, with events in Paris and Monaco alike attracting support from UNESCO Directors-General,

"We all feel that the conference opening this morning will enjoy extremely favorable working conditions in this hospitable Principality, which, in the words of its Sovereign, "hates nothing but hatred itself."

René Maheu, opening address to the Fifth Regional Conference of European National Commissions for UNESCO, June 24, 1968.

The Symbolic Globe, Erik Reitzel, a spherical structure made of 10,000 aluminum rods, assembled in six days by delegates at the Copenhagen Summit (1995) in a show of solidarity.

“You are all aware of my keen interest in UNESCO, and my unshakeable conviction that we must direct our efforts to the maintenance and further development of our relations with this international body. The understanding shown toward us by Mr. Maheu must be for us the most precious form of encouragement.”

Letter from Prince Rainier III to Paul Demange, Minister of State, August 21, 1968.

including Amadou-Mahtar M’Bow (1974-1987), Federico Mayor (1987-1999), Koïchiro Matsuura (1999-2009), Irina Bokova (2009-2017), and the current Director-General, Audrey Azoulay. All of them sit on the Board of Directors of the Prince Pierre Foundation, established in 1966. Audrey Azoulay notably participated in the International Monaco and Mediterranean Meetings in 2020, and the Foundations Dialogue, held by the Prince Albert II of Monaco Foundation in 2023 in the framework of the United Nations Decade of Ocean Science for Sustainable Development.

The Princely Family is in turn firmly engaged with UNESCO and its principles. Health, human rights, environmental protection, sustainable resource management, the fight against poverty and exclusion—the House of Grimaldi makes it a duty to advocate for these causes.

We must begin, of course, by mentioning Prince Pierre, an outstanding figure in the Monaco landscape and wholly committed to UNESCO. A champion of culture, the Prince was a long-standing presence at UNESCO as President of the National Commission and Head of the Permanent Delegation of the Principality of Monaco to UNESCO in the period 1951-1964. Prince Rainier III, whose coming to power in 1949 coincided with his country’s admission to UNESCO, paid several visits to the Organization’s headquarters in Paris. The first took place within a few months of the opening of the new headquarters on the Place de Fontenoy: a private visit on October 22, 1959, but no doubt the most symbolic to judge from the photographs taken of the event. Shown around by Vittorino Veronese, the Prince and Princess Grace were invited to appreciate the modern architectural style of Bernard Zehrfuss, Marcel Breuer and Pier Luigi Novi, together with the beauty of the gardens and the many works of art. The values of the Organization are upheld today by their Serene Highnesses Prince Albert II and Princess Caroline, UNESCO Goodwill Ambassador since December 2, 2003, Princess Stéphanie, chairwoman of the Fight Aids Monaco NGO, which actively engages with UNAIDS, and Princess Charlène, who promotes sport and campaigns for drowning prevention through her namesake foundation.

Prince Albert II at UNESCO in 2015 for the organization’s 70th anniversary.

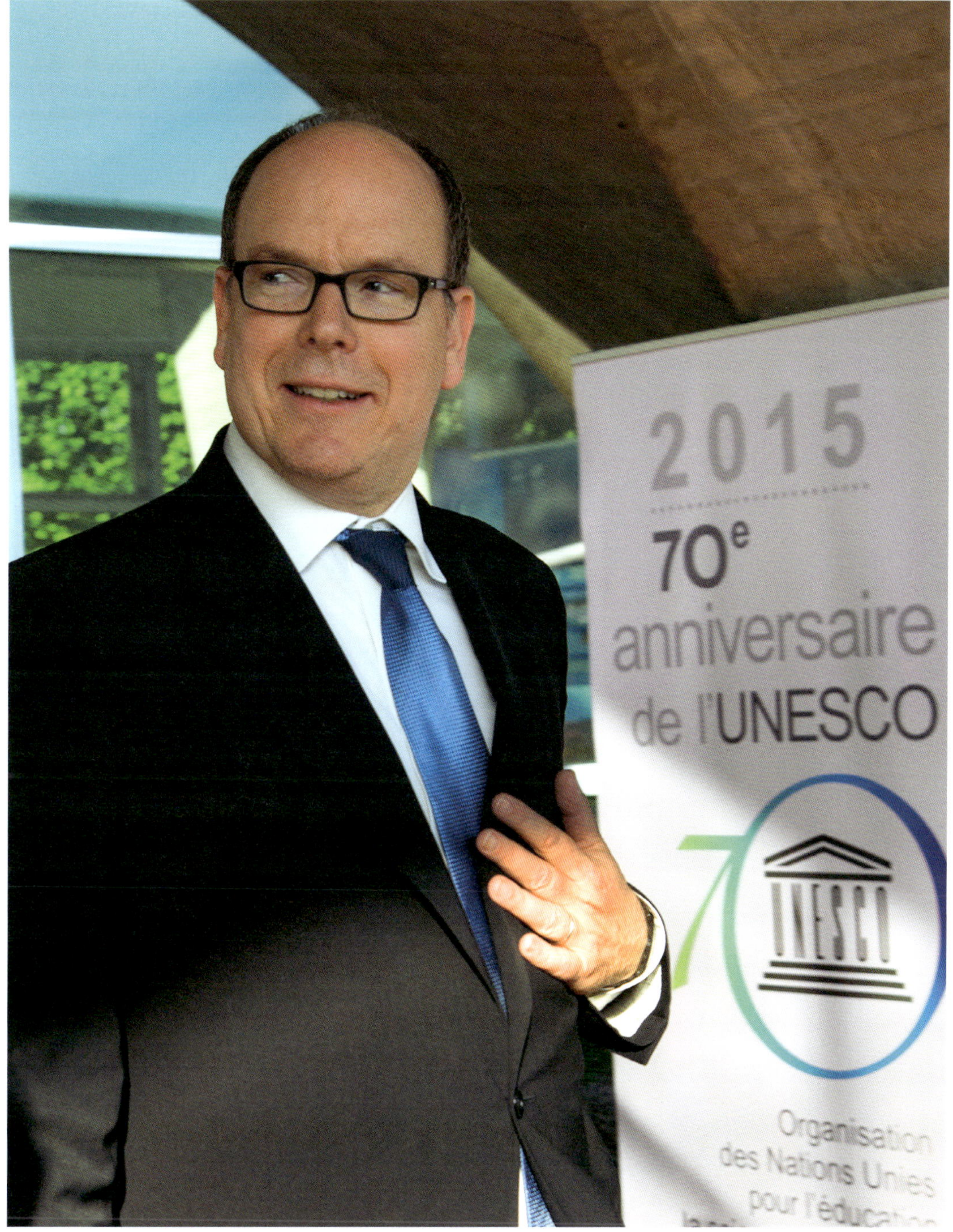
2015
70e
anniversaire
de l'UNESCO
UNESCO
Organisation
des Nations Unies
pour l'éducation

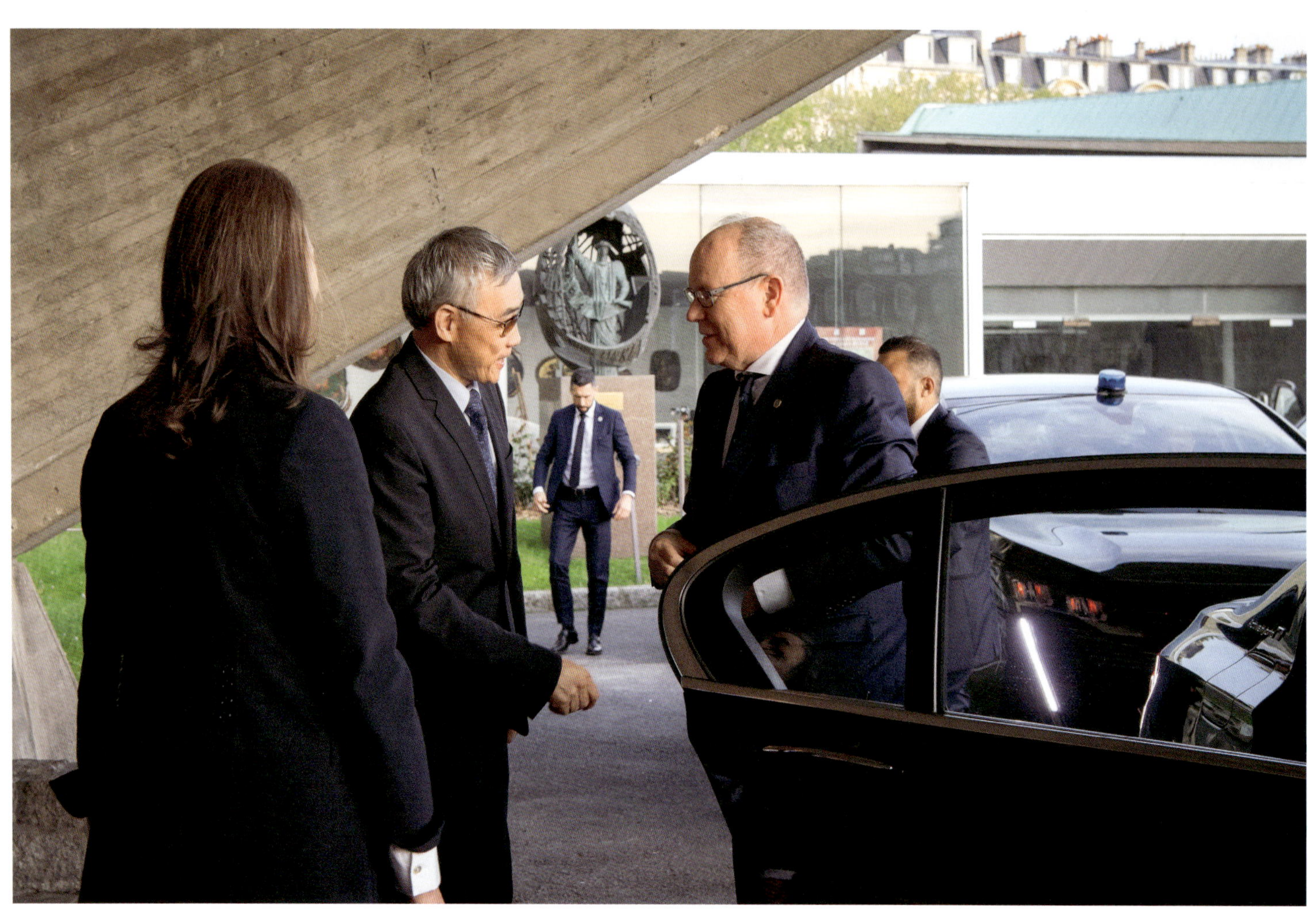

Arrival of Prince Albert II, welcomed by Xing Qu, Deputy Director-General of UNESCO, on April 11, 2024 to celebrate the 75th anniversary of the Principality's accession to UNESCO, with a dinner designed, prepared and served by pupils at the Lycée Rainier III to ambassadors from member states.

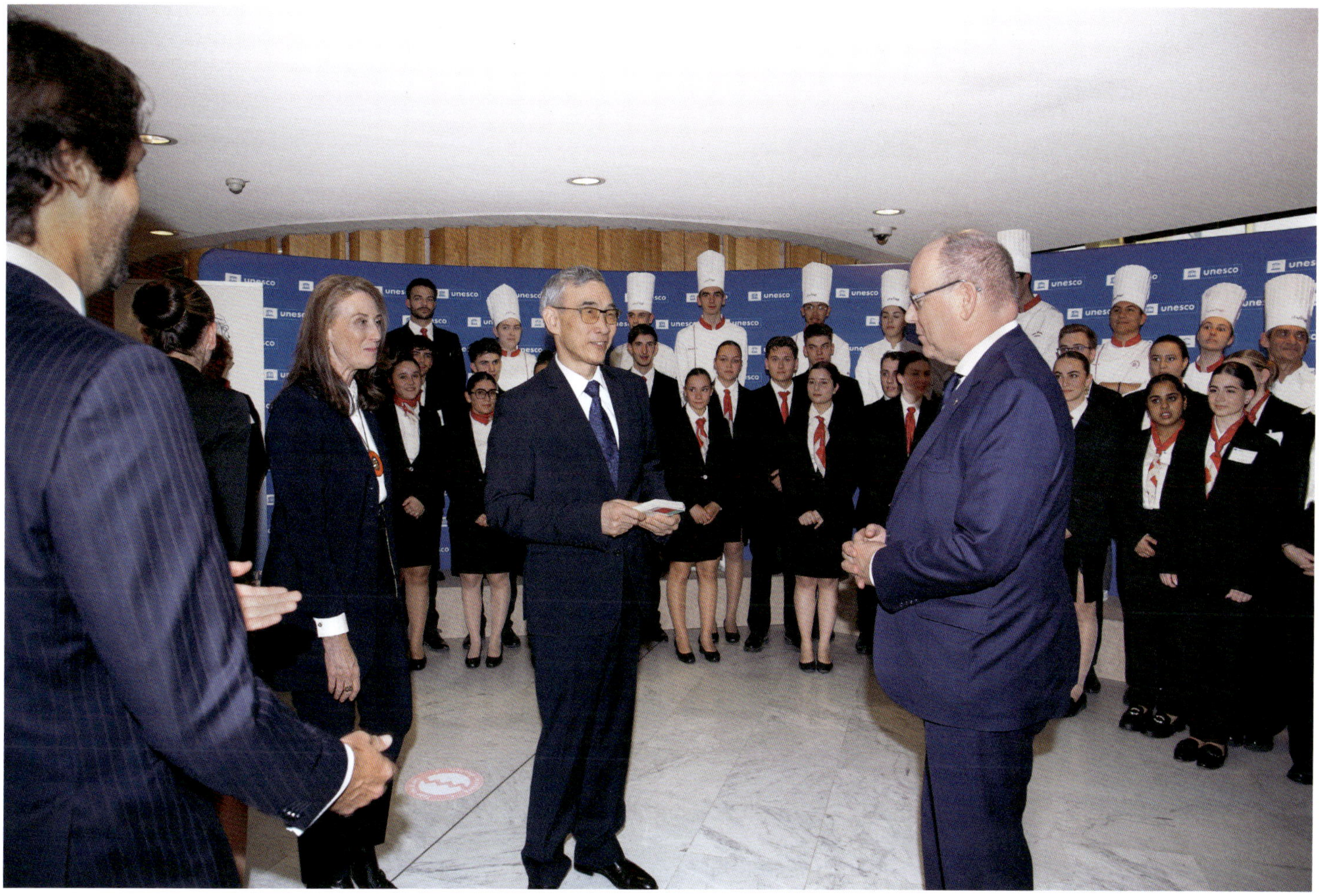

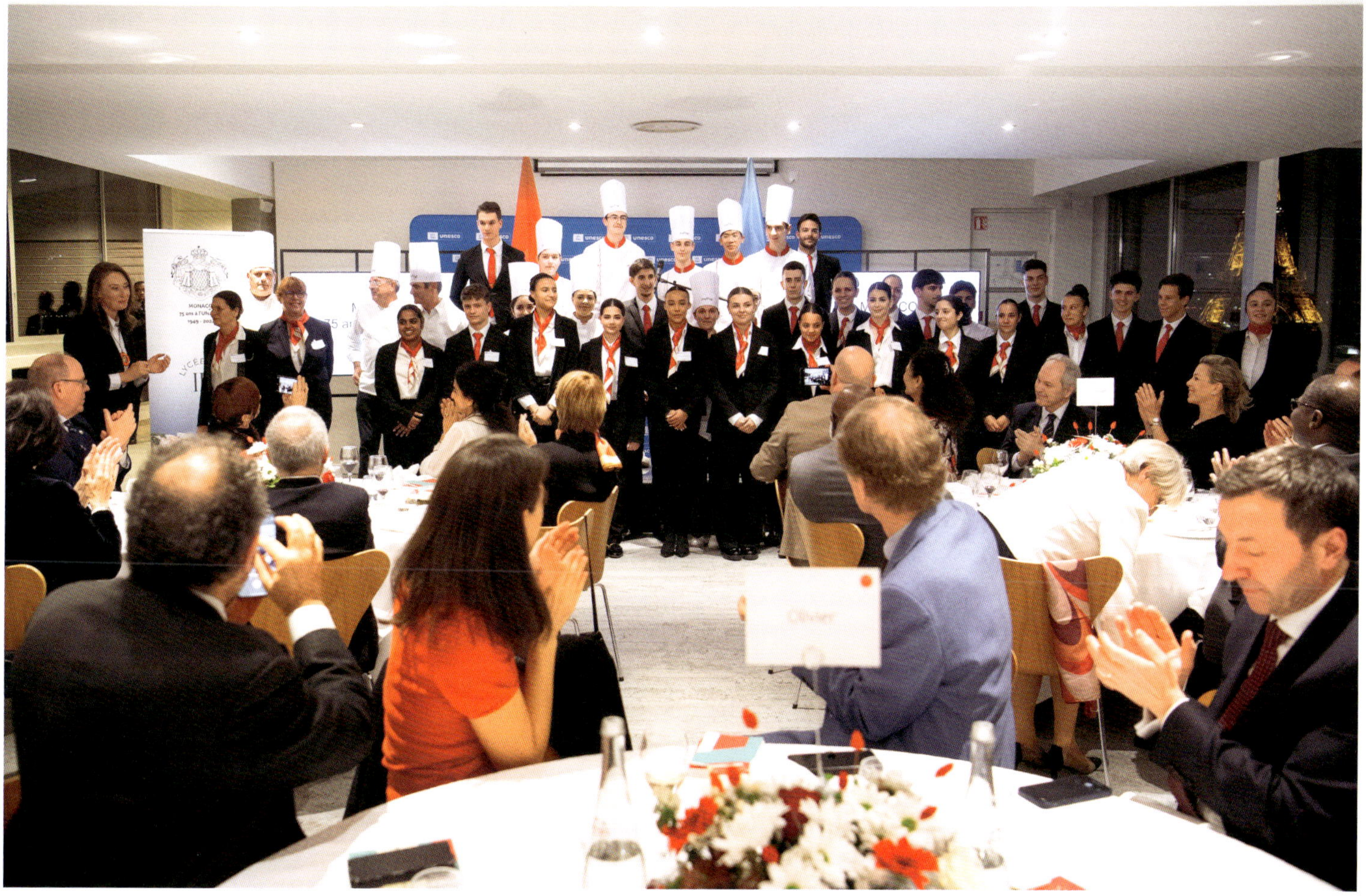

DOSSIER

RENÉ MAHEU, A DIRECTOR-GENERAL IN MONACO

"You are growing up in a period of technological miracles. Your generation will reach the stars, but it is Man that I should like you, above all, to reach, to respect and cherish, in yourselves and in others."

René Maheu, *À tous les jeunes du monde* ("to all young people twenty years old"): a message from René Maheu, Director-General of UNESCO for the New Year 1966, *Le Courrier de l'Unesco*, XVIII, 1, 1965, p. 36.

French intellectual René Maheu (1905-1975) was a professor *agrégé* of philosophy and a former graduate student of the French Ecole Normale Supérieure (ENS). He joined UNESCO in 1947 and made it his career, serving as Director-General from 1962 to 1974, the while radiating a humanism and energy that propelled the Organization forward. His leadership marked UNESCO's golden age, a testament to a man who as historian Chloé Maurel said, even "identified with UNESCO." He was the first Director-General to visit Monaco, preceded in 1957 by his fellow ENS student Jean Thomas, who represented UNESCO as Deputy Director.

The deep ties between René Maheu and Monaco were demonstrated in various ways. In 1966, for example, he agreed to join the Board of Directors of the Prince Pierre of Monaco Foundation. The following year he made his first official visit to Monaco, staying there from May 15 to 18 and noting "the interest shown by the authorities in the Organization's activities, the exciting scientific activities and the wealth of cultural events." In 1968, he returned to Monaco for the Fifth Regional Conference of National Commissions for UNESCO (held June 24-28), delivering several speeches that testified, most notably in a year marked by student-led uprisings, to his preoccupation with the challenges facing young people. He later addressed letters to the Monegasque dignitaries he encountered on that occasion, thanking them for their welcome. Equally noteworthy as an intellectual, in 1973 he delivered a lecture to the Prince Pierre of Monaco Foundation, followed a week later by Armand Lunel (1892-1977), an *agrégé* in philosophy like Mr. Maheu and an honorary teacher at the Lycée Albert Premier and member of the first Monegasque National Commission for UNESCO. That the two men were bonded together in humanism seems likely even if there is no documentary evidence.

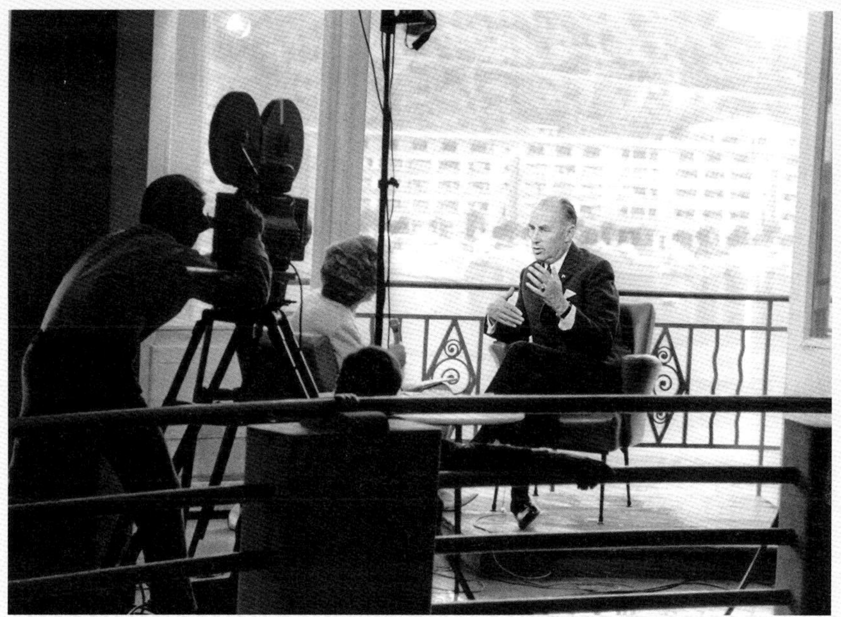

"I have the honor and very pleasant duty of conveying to His Serene Highness and to the Government and National Commission of Monaco the gratitude of the Organization for the generous hospitality which has made it possible for the European National Commissions for UNESCO to meet here today in order to examine together a number of important questions which concern us all. We all feel that the conference opening this morning will enjoy extremely favorable working conditions in this hospitable Principality, which, in the words of its Sovereign, 'hates nothing but hatred itself.' For despite the appeal of so much that is beautiful and of such pleasant surroundings, we have work to do, as a glance at the draft agenda you have before you will show."

René Maheu, opening address to the Fifth Regional Conference of European National Commissions for UNESCO, June 24, 1968.

René Maheu, interviewed in Monaco, June 1968. Photo from a report on the fifth regional conference of European national commissions for UNESCO, with René Maheu interviewed by Radio-Télé-Monte-Carlo on the theme of youth.

DOSSIER

PRINCE RAINIER III AND UNESCO

Prince Rainier III enjoyed a fruitful relationship with UNESCO and its various Directors-General throughout his nearly fifty-six-year reign, which commenced in May 1949, shortly before the Principality's admission to UNESCO, and ended with his death in 2005. In 1959, just a few months after the opening of the Maison de l'Unesco (UNESCO Headquarters, Paris), he and Princess Grace were given a guided tour of the new premises by Vittorino Veronese, a landmark visit that paved the way for the Principality's increasing participation in the activities of UNESCO, and subsequent admission to the United Nations in 1993. For Prince Rainier III, this was pivotal to his policy of raising his country's global visibility.

"You are all aware of my keen interest in UNESCO, and that I remain convinced of the necessity to direct our efforts towards maintaining and developing our relations with this international body. The understanding shown us by Mr. Maheu is most certainly for us the most precious form of encouragement."

Letter from Prince Rainier III to Paul Demange, Minister of State, August 21, 1968.

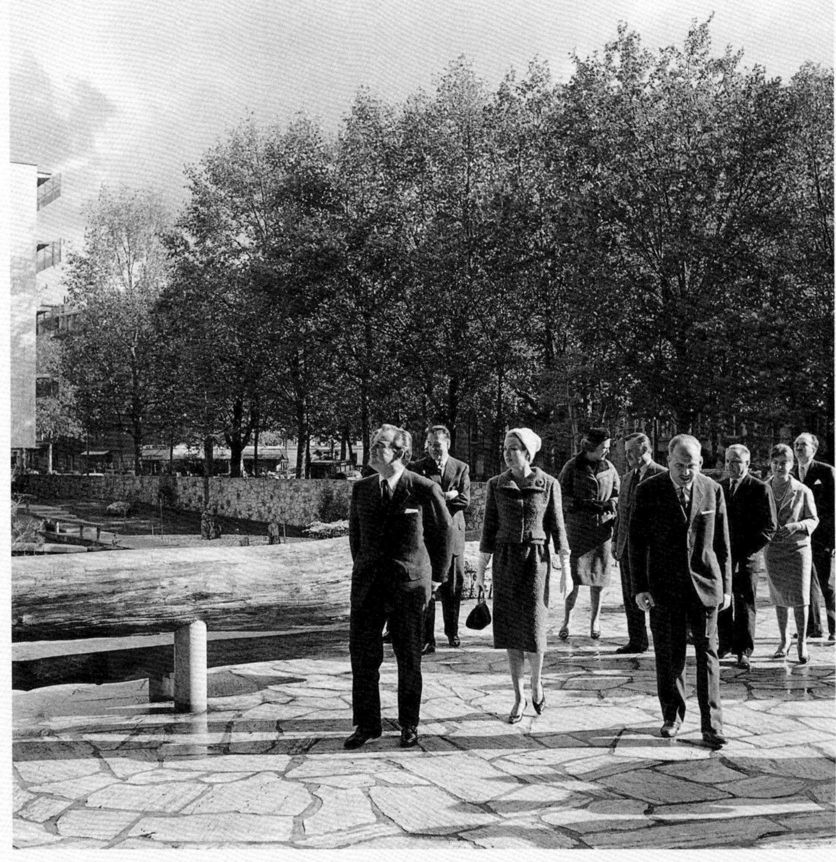

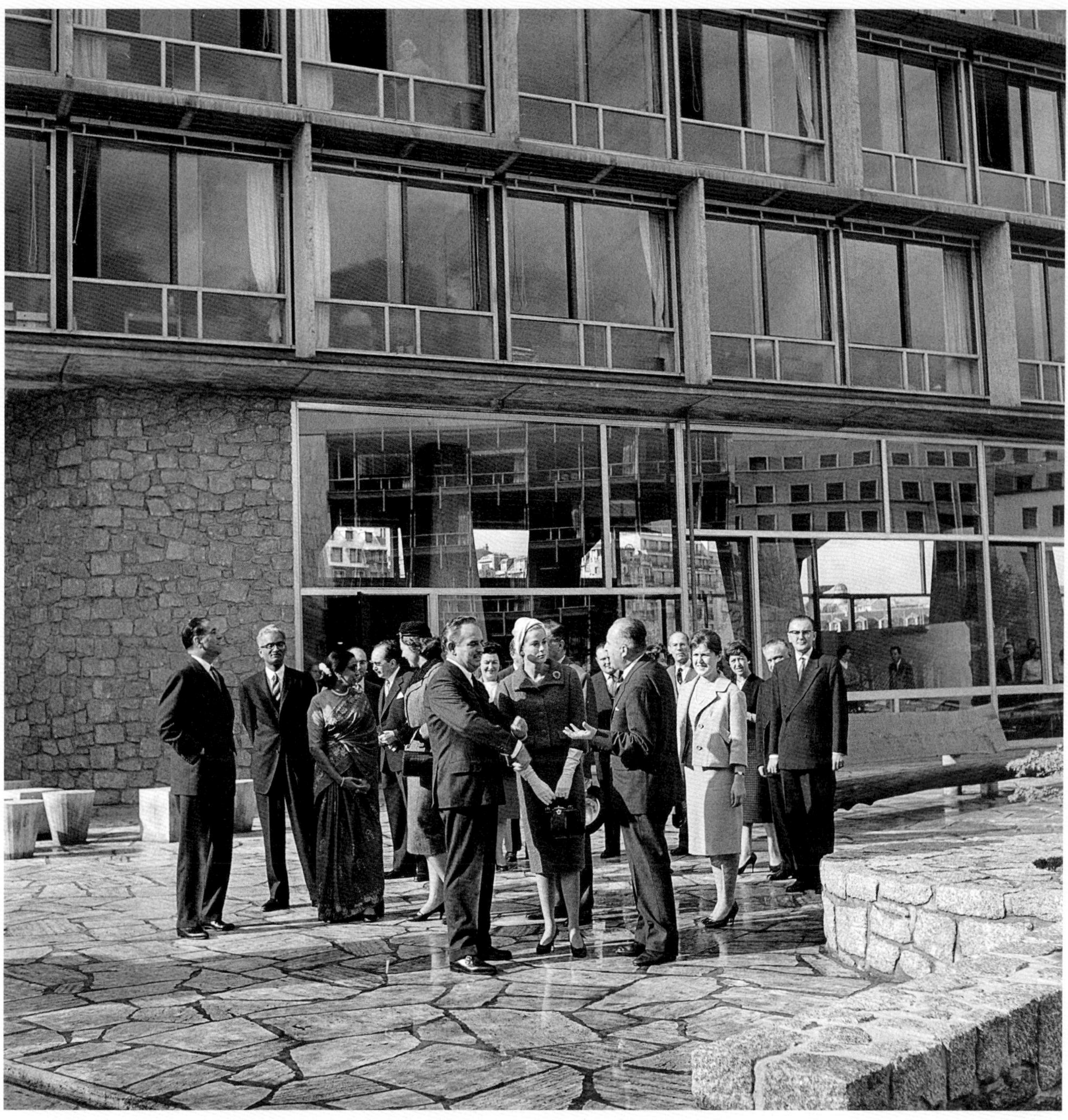

Prince Rainier and Princess Grace, October 22, 1959, with Vittorino Veronese, Director-General, in front of the main building of the new UNESCO headquarters, Place de Fontenoy, Paris.

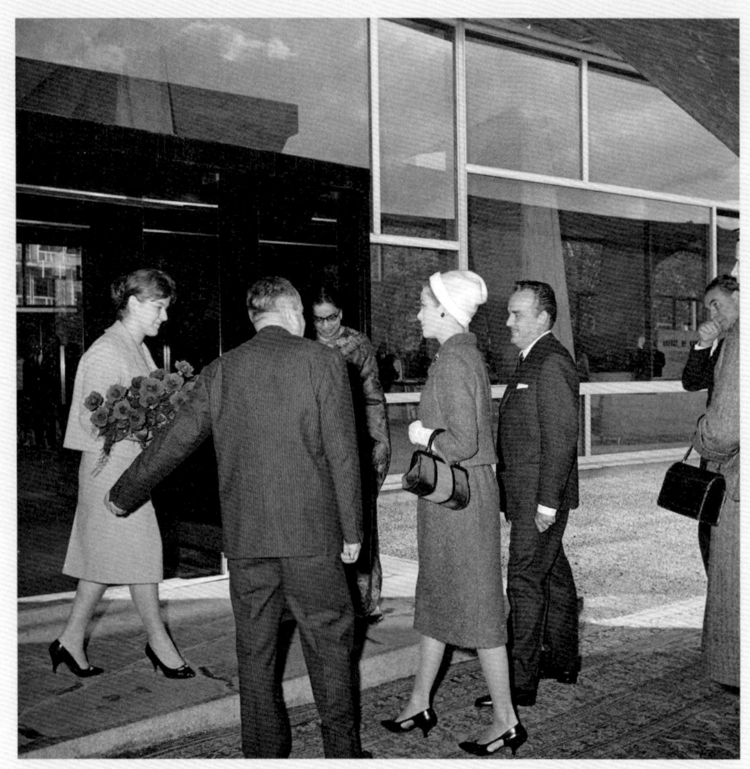

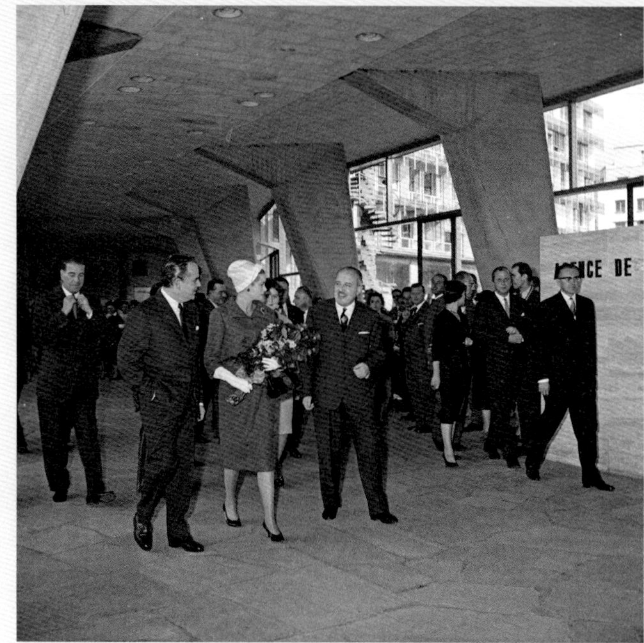

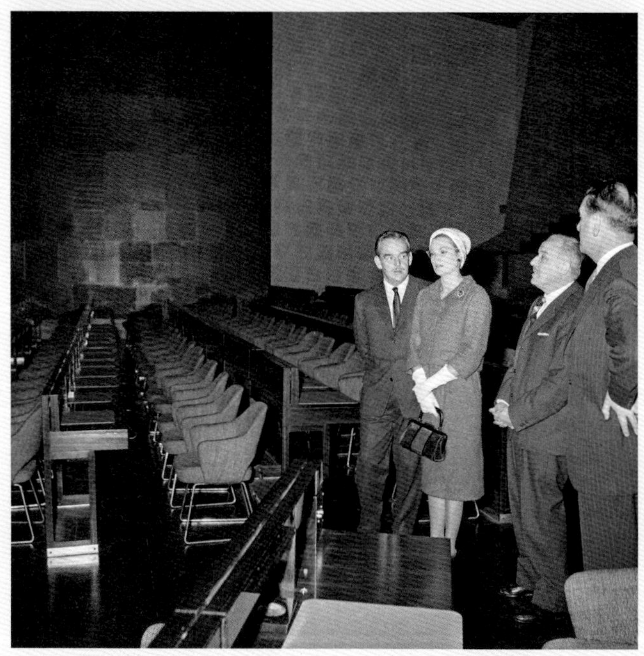

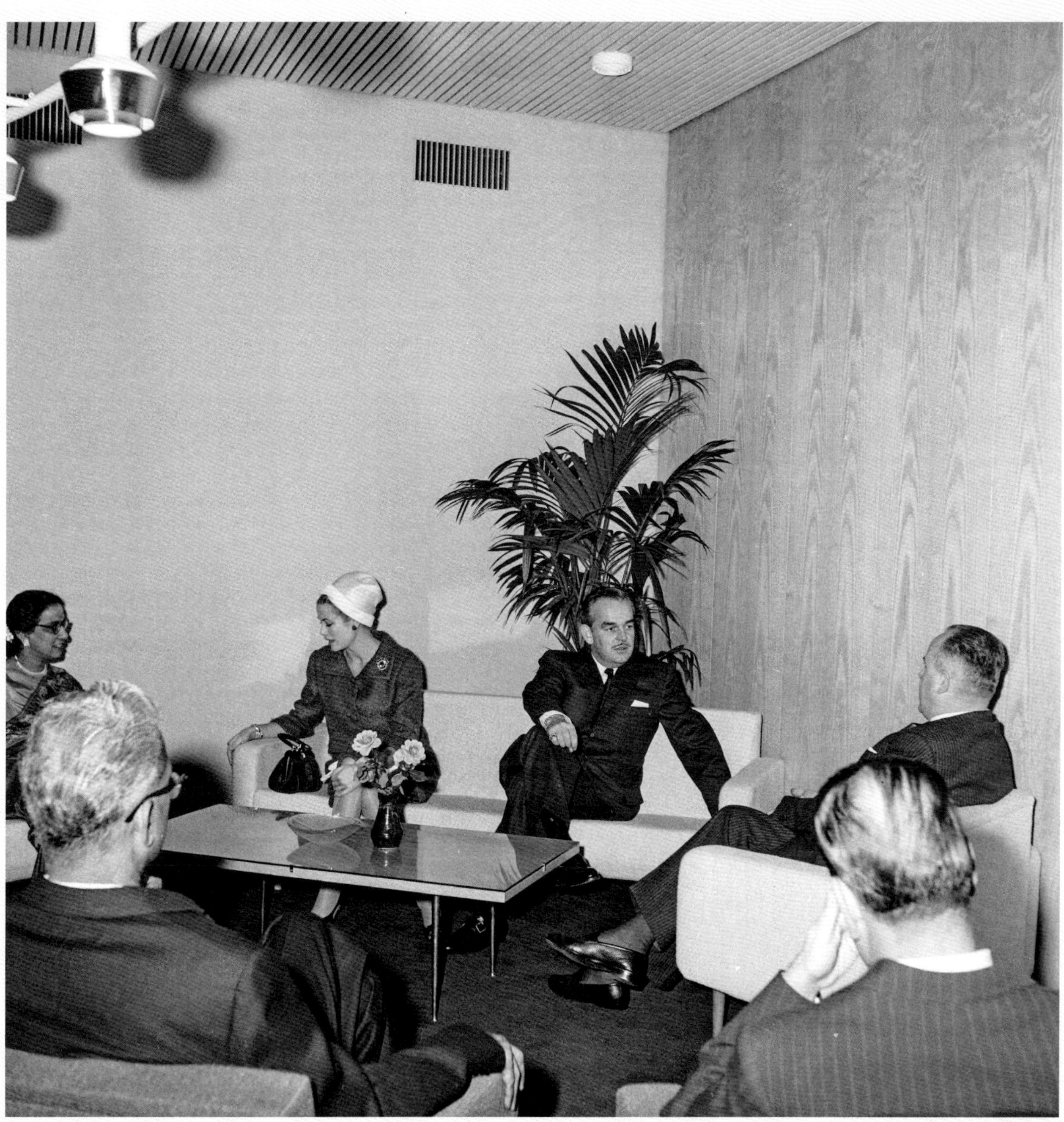

Prince Rainier and Princess Grace, October 22, 1959, with Vittorino Veronese, Director-General, visit the interior of the secretariat building (passing through the lobby) and the rooms of the conference building, Place de Fontenoy, Paris.

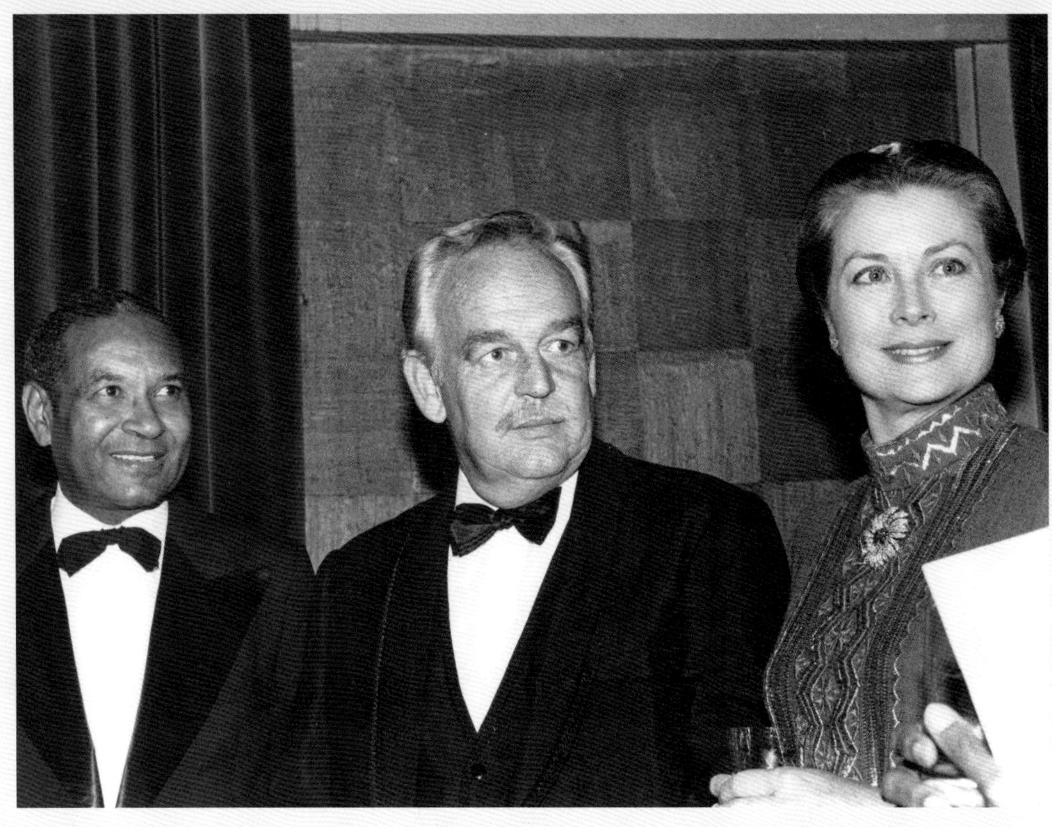

Prince Rainier III, Princess Grace of Monaco and Amadou-Mahtar M'Bow, Director-General, at the Théâtre des Champs-Élysées in Paris on October 15, 1976, for a gala concert celebrating the 30th anniversary of UNESCO.

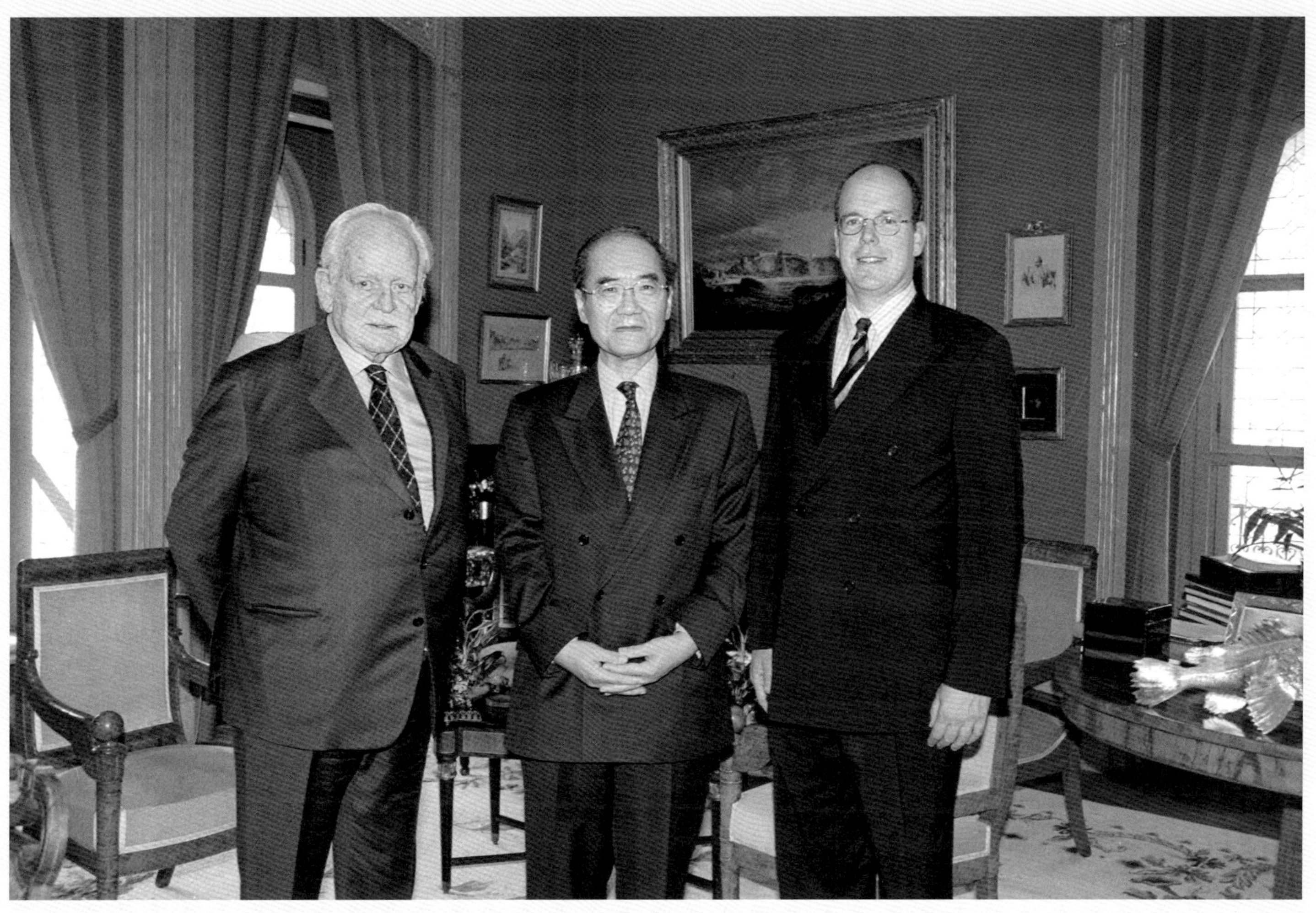

Prince Rainier, Director-General Koichiro Matsuura, and Hereditary Prince Albert in Monaco, ceremonial office of the Palace of Monaco, April 18, 2003.

DOSSIER

THE PRINCELY FAMILY AND UNESCO

The Princely Family's commitment to UNESCO's programs is a testament to the strength of their ever-evolving relationship and is plainly visible in the areas championed by both partners in support of the Organization's core values.

The connection between H.S.H. Prince Albert II and UNESCO has been forged over many years and as many visits to UNESCO, dating back to his days as Crown Prince of Monaco. Since his accession to the throne in 2005, he has pursued and reinforced the Principality's contribution to UNESCO's programs and missions, backed Monaco's admission to the Executive Council (2010-2013), and supported UNESCO in difficult times. His commitment to local and global environmental conservation has a particular resonance with UNESCO's programs to protect maritime heritage, ocean ecosystems and biodiversity in general. The Prince always attends UNESCO for the celebrations of World Oceans. To boost international cooperation in marine research, which lies at the heart of the activities of the Prince Pierre Foundation, the United Nations has designated the years 2021-2030 as the Decade of Ocean Science for Sustainable Development. The Prince is naturally present on other occasions, among them UNESCO anniversaries, tributes and commemorative events that increase the Principality's renown. Needless to say, he was in Paris on April 12, 2024, to celebrate Monaco's seventy-five years of UNESCO membership. With the Olympics upon us at the time of writing, it seems appropriate to mention the Prince's personal commitment to sport, whether the major events staged on home ground or the activities of the International Olympic Committee. It is a commitment the Prince shares with his wife H.S.H. Princess Charlene, founder in 2012 of the Princess Charlène of Monaco Foundation. A nonprofit organization for women and children in difficulty, the Foundation promotes the values of sport, education, and drowning prevention through two sporting disciplines: rugby and swimming. The Princess' commitment is inspired by her experience as a professional swimmer: in 2000 Charlène Wittstock represented South Africa at the Sydney Olympic Games. These days the Foundation runs several programs, delivering swimming lessons, water safety courses, and sport activities designed to help children blossom. Its objectives echo the principles espoused by UNESCO, which considers access to physical education and sport as a "fundamental right" and "tool for inclusion," noting that "physical education is an essential entry point for children to learn life skills," (Declaration of Berlin, UNESCO, 2013).

Her Serene Highness the Princess of Hanover was just a child when she first visited UNESCO headquarters in Paris, accompanied by her parents. It was the first of many visits for this granddaughter of foremost UNESCO figure, Prince Pierre, who as Chairwoman of AMADE (the World Association of Children's Friends) actively pursues his legacy through her commitment to two causes in particular: education and child protection. Appointed a UNESCO Goodwill Ambassador in 2003, Princess Caroline has been building on their relationship ever since, regularly attending workshops and meetings to reaffirm her commitment to education. Most recently, in 2022, she took part in the third International Day to Protect Education from Attack, highlighting the urgent need for action to protect the right to education in the face of conflict, violence, and destruction.

As her sister, Princess Stéphanie, is only too aware, health crises pose another threat to our increasingly fragile world, one she strives to address as Chairwoman of Fight Aids Monaco and a UNAIDS Goodwill Ambassador. Speaking on behalf of the Princely Family and its preoccupation with world health, at a UNAIDS meeting held from June 8-10, 2021, titled *Ending Inequalities and Getting on Track to End AIDS by 2030*, she called for stronger health systems, drawing lessons from the concomitant COVID-19 pandemic and AIDS epidemic. As Chairwoman of the Prince Rainier Commemoration Committee, on June 19, 2023, centenary of the birth of her father, she and the Sovereign Prince were present at the celebrations to mark the thirtieth anniversary of Monaco's admission to the United Nations (May 28, 1993), held at UN headquarters in New York.

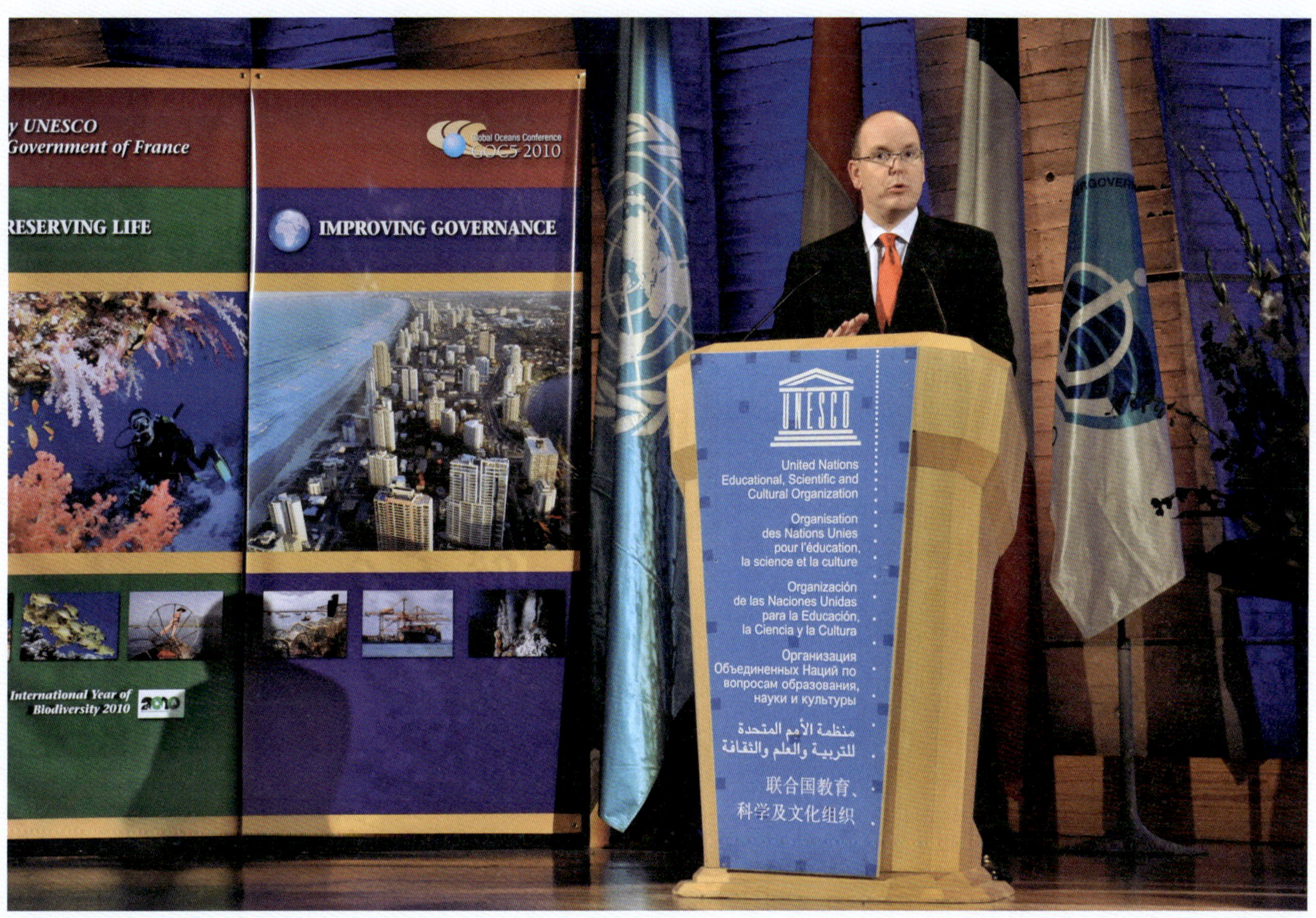

H.S.H. Prince Albert II at the "Global Ocean" conference at UNESCO, May 4, 2010, the fifth global conference on oceans, coasts and islands.

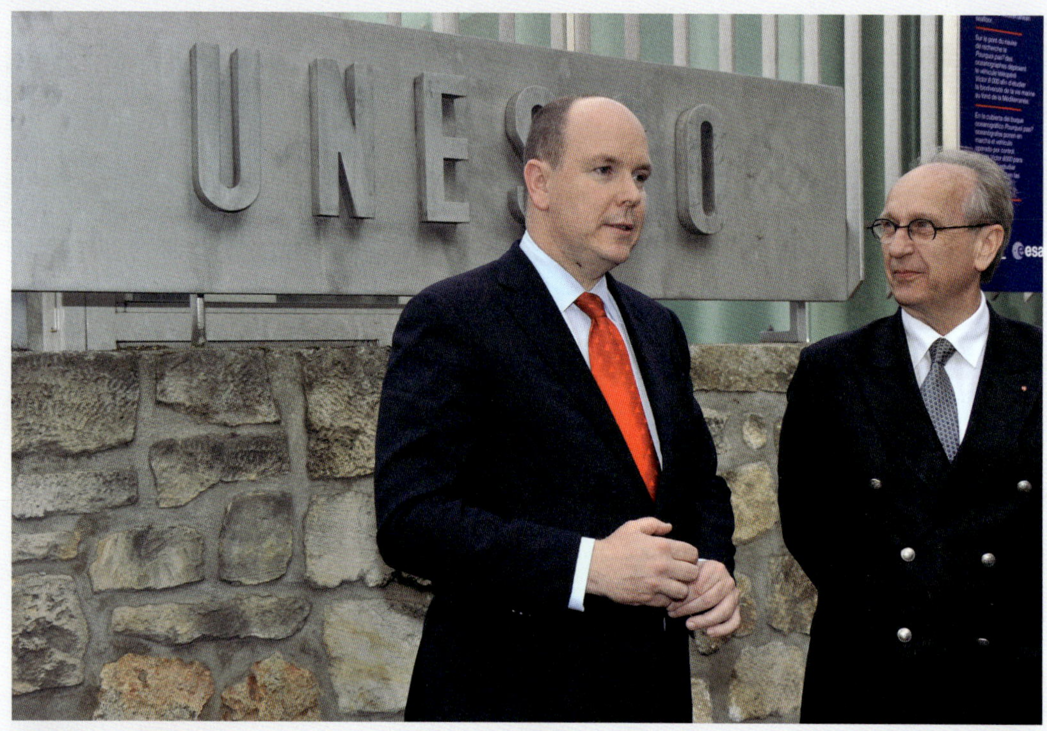

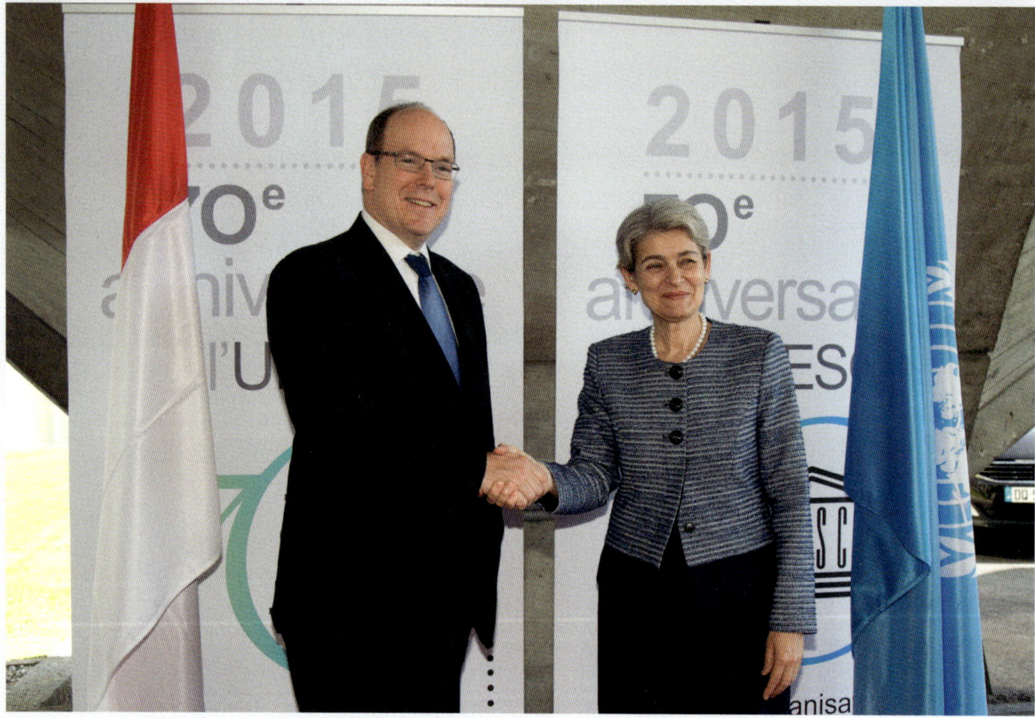

TOP "Global Ocean" conference at UNESCO, May 4, 2010. H.S.H. Prince Albert II with Monegasque UNESCO expert Michel Boisson, oceanographer.

BOTTOM H.S.H. Prince Albert II and Irina Bokova, Director-General, at UNESCO for World Oceans Day, 2015.

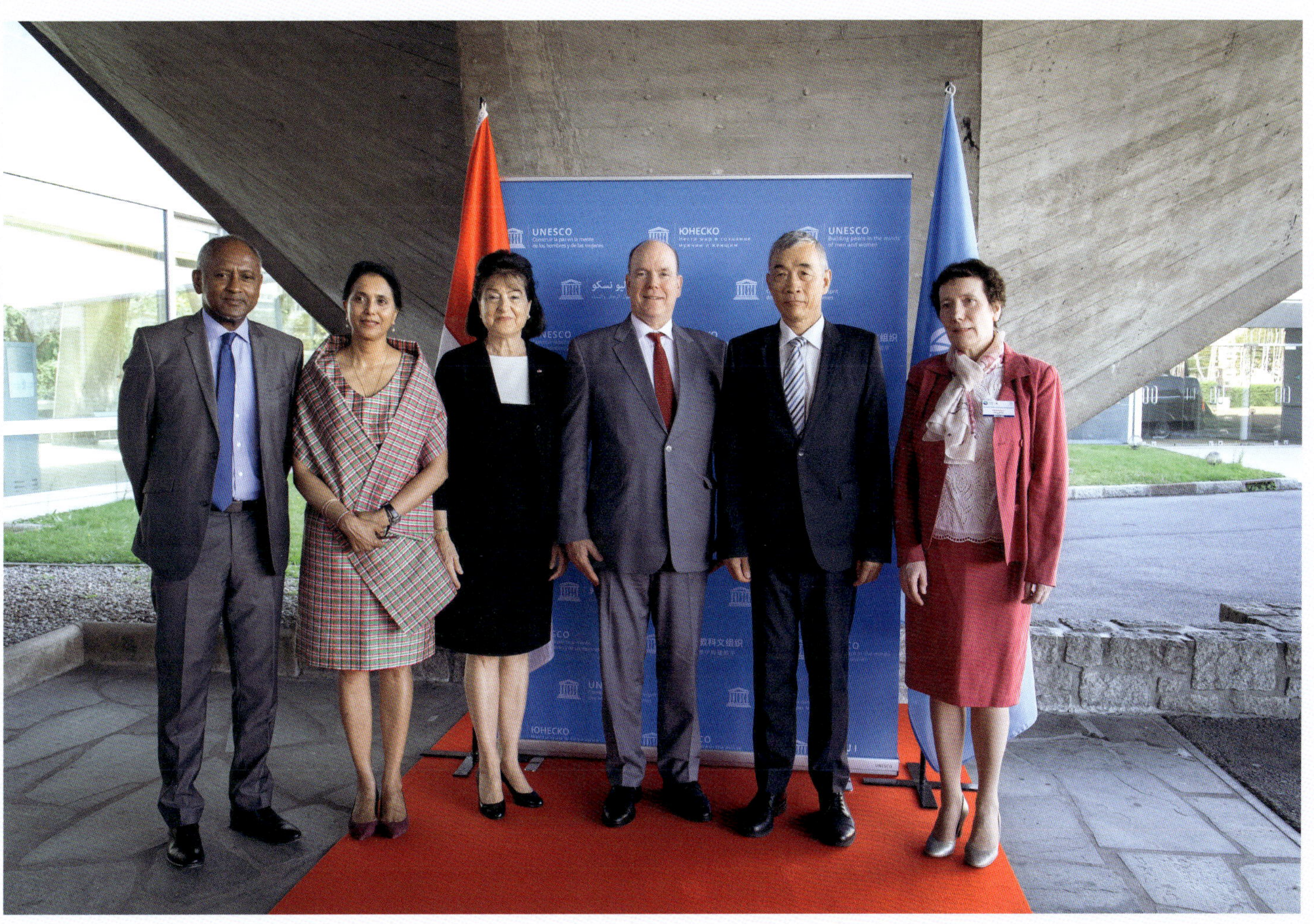

H.S.H. Prince Albert II with, on his left, Deputy Director-General Xing Qu, and on his right, Her Excellency Yvette Lambin-Berti, Ambassador of Monaco, at UNESCO headquarters, on July 28, 2019, on the occasion of the 100th anniversary of the International Union of Geodesy and Geophysics, receives a distinction for his exceptional contribution to raising awareness of the effects of climate change, promoting biodiversity and oceanographic research.

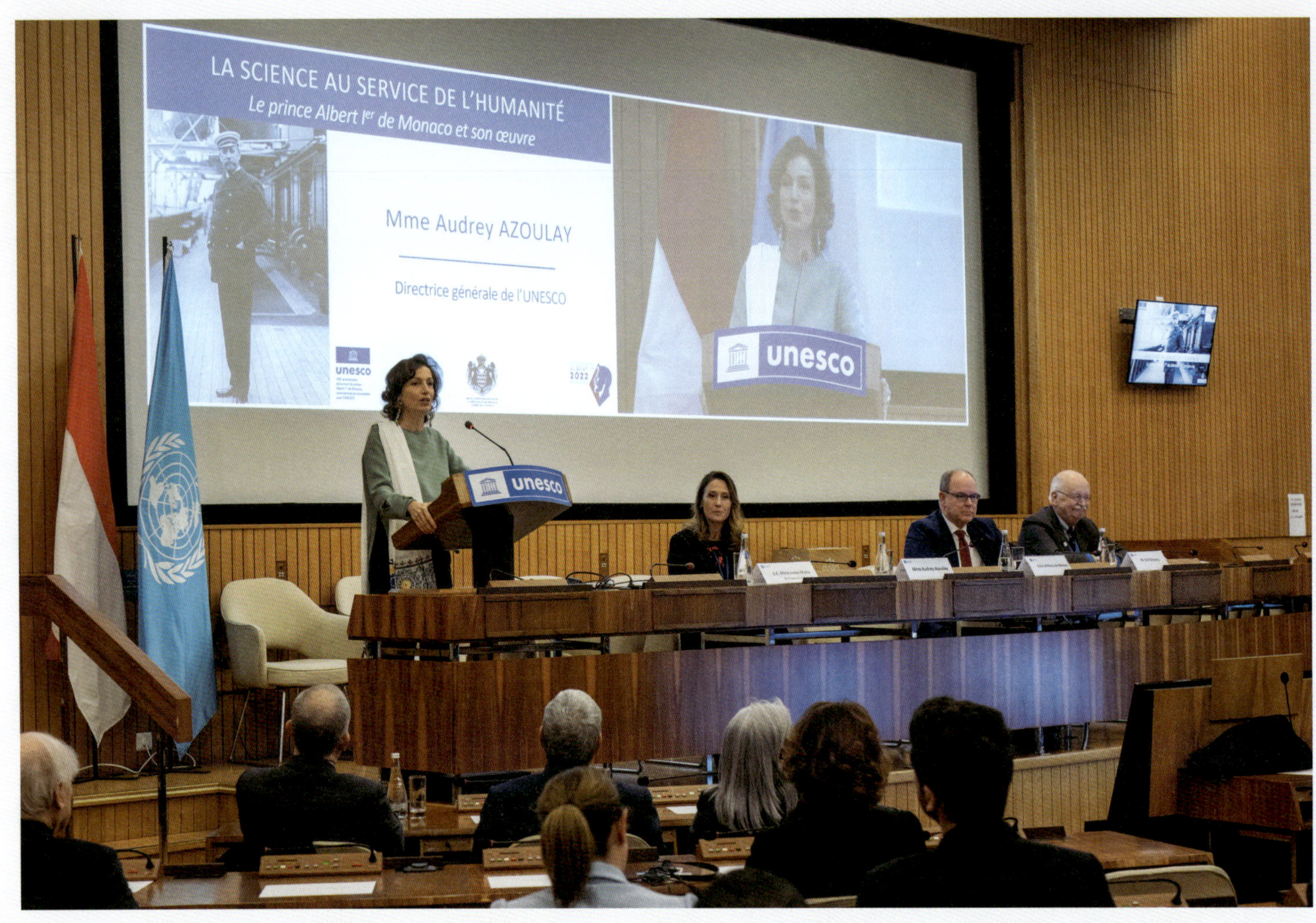

Speech by Audrey Azoulay on December 7, 2002 at the Erik Orsenna conference at UNESCO on the occasion of the commemoration of the centenary of the death of Prince Albert I, in the presence of H.S.H. Prince Albert II.

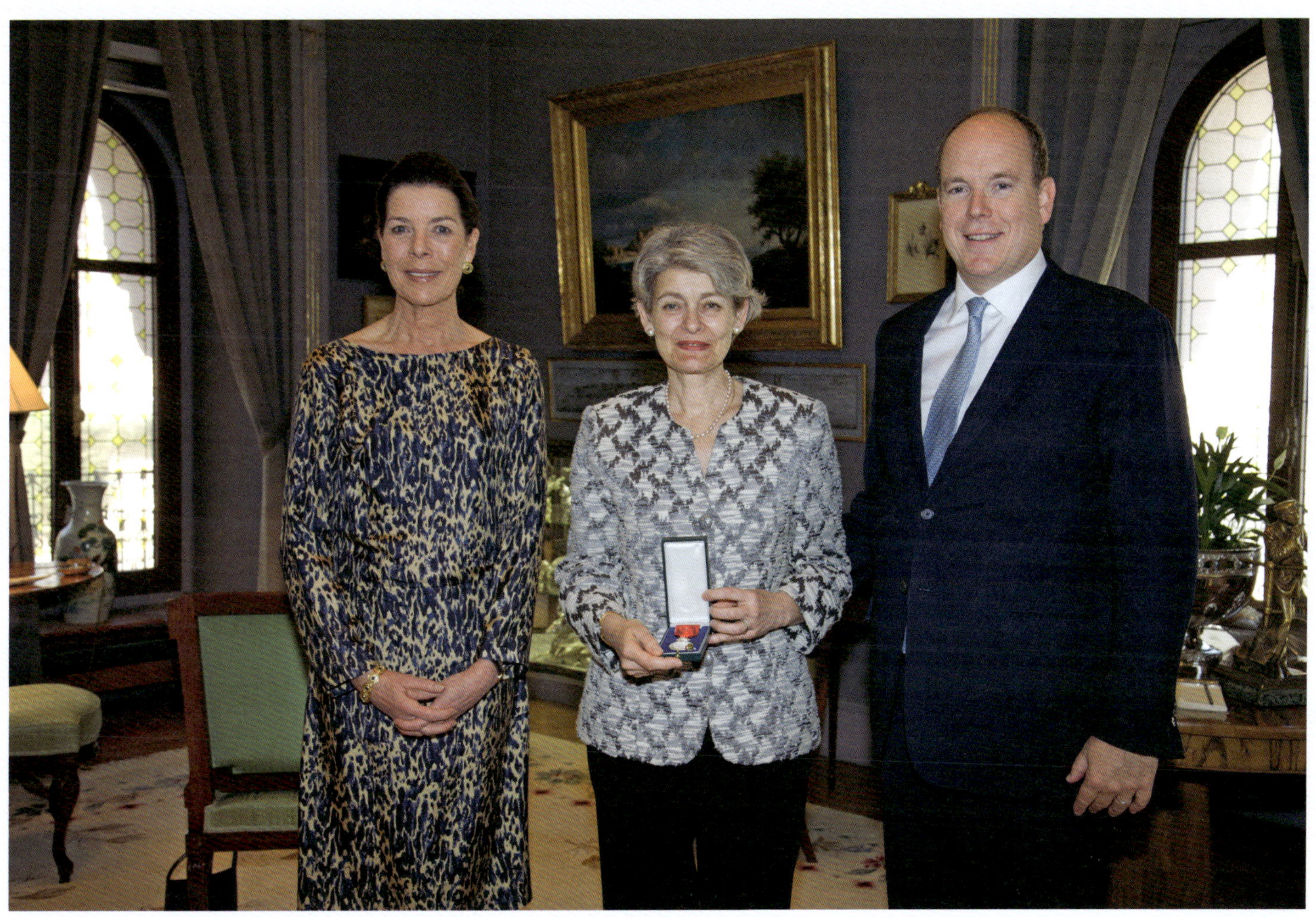

H.S.H. Prince Albert II and H.R.H. Princess of Hanover, at the award ceremony for Irina Bokova, Director-General, appointed an Officer of the Order of Cultural Merit, ceremonial office, Palace of Monaco, March 2013.

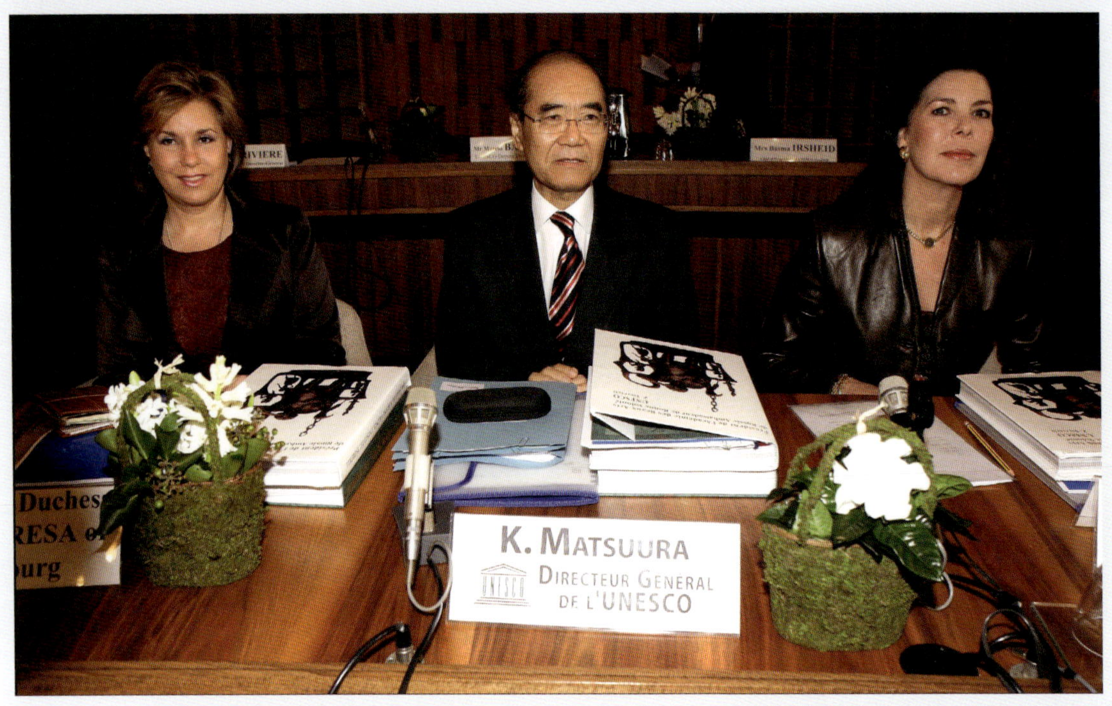

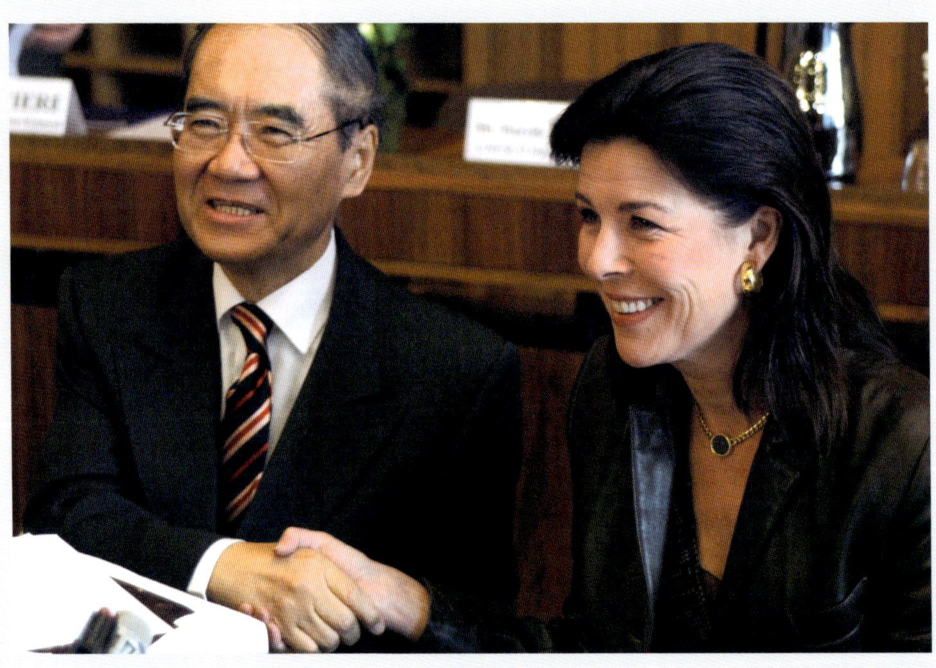

H.R.H. Princess of Hanover and Koichiro Matsuura at the UNESCO headquarters in Paris in 2006 to celebrate the 60th anniversary of the organization.

"Your Royal Highness, it is with great pleasure and honor that I welcome you this evening to UNESCO Headquarters, together with all the dignitaries gathered here on the occasion of your nomination as a UNESCO Goodwill Ambassador. On being so designated, you join other eminent persons who have agreed to spread, through their professional activities and personal charisma, the ideals and messages of UNESCO in the areas of education, science, culture and communication. In welcoming you here to UNESCO, Madame, I welcome not only one of Monaco's foremost personalities but also the Chairwoman of the World Association of Children's Friends (AMADE), whose mission is to protect the life and physical and moral integrity of children everywhere. As Director of the Princess Grace of Monaco Foundation, you also secure significant financial support for children hospitalized in French public hospitals, in particular at the Necker and Robert Debré hospitals Paris. All your efforts testify to your deep compassion for suffering children, and to your commitment to values that we share and strive daily to uphold. [. . .] The education of women and girls being clearly essential for development, there is good reason to pay special attention to the impoverishment of women in the world's poorest countries. Your contribution, Your Highness, will make a significant difference in terms of improving their lot and that of their daughters. My recent visit to the Principality of Monaco, where I was so warmly received by your father, Prince Rainier, together with my visit to the offices of your brother, Crown Prince Albert, was an opportunity to strengthen the already close ties forged over the years between the Principality and UNESCO. The Principality is an important partner of UNESCO, most notably in the field of bioethics."

Address by Koïchiro Matsuura on the occasion of the nomination of Her Serene Highness the Princess of Hanover as UNESCO Goodwill Ambassador, December 2, 2003.

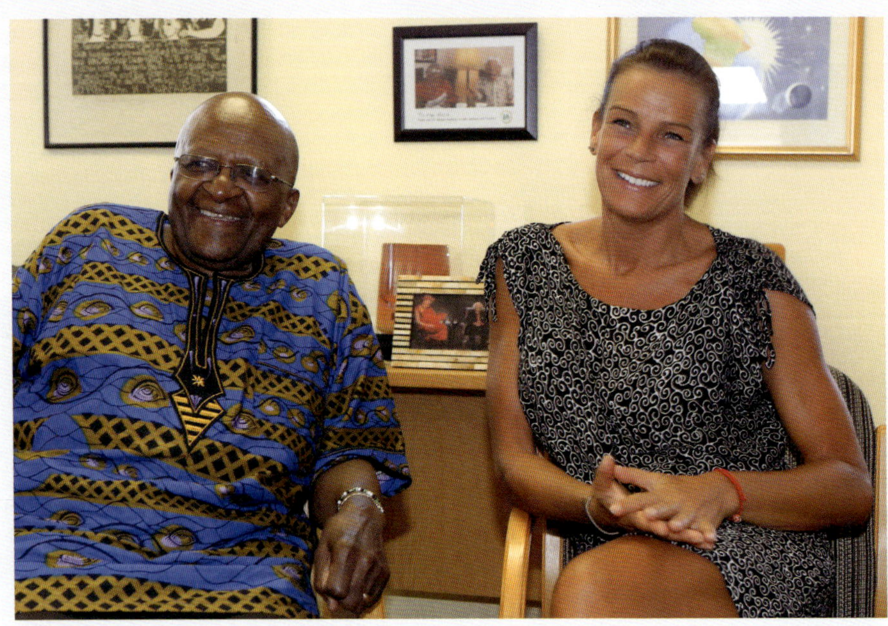

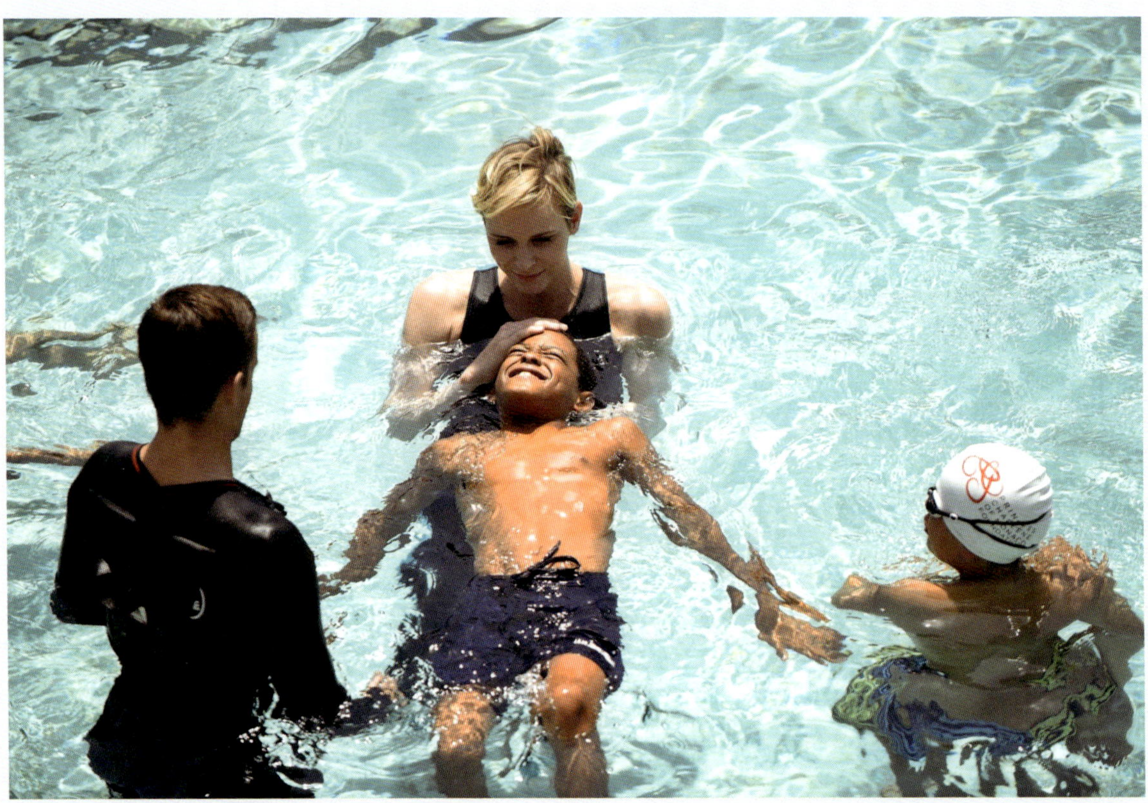

TOP H.S.H. Princess Stéphanie with Archbishop Desmond Tutu, December 5-9, 2012 in Cape Town, Republic of South Africa, as part of her role as UNAIDS Goodwill Ambassador and President of Fight Aids Monaco.

BOTTOM Princess Charlène and her foundation are committed to giving children the best opportunities, to showing them the way through education in the values of sport and solidarity, and to reducing the number of drowning deaths worldwide.

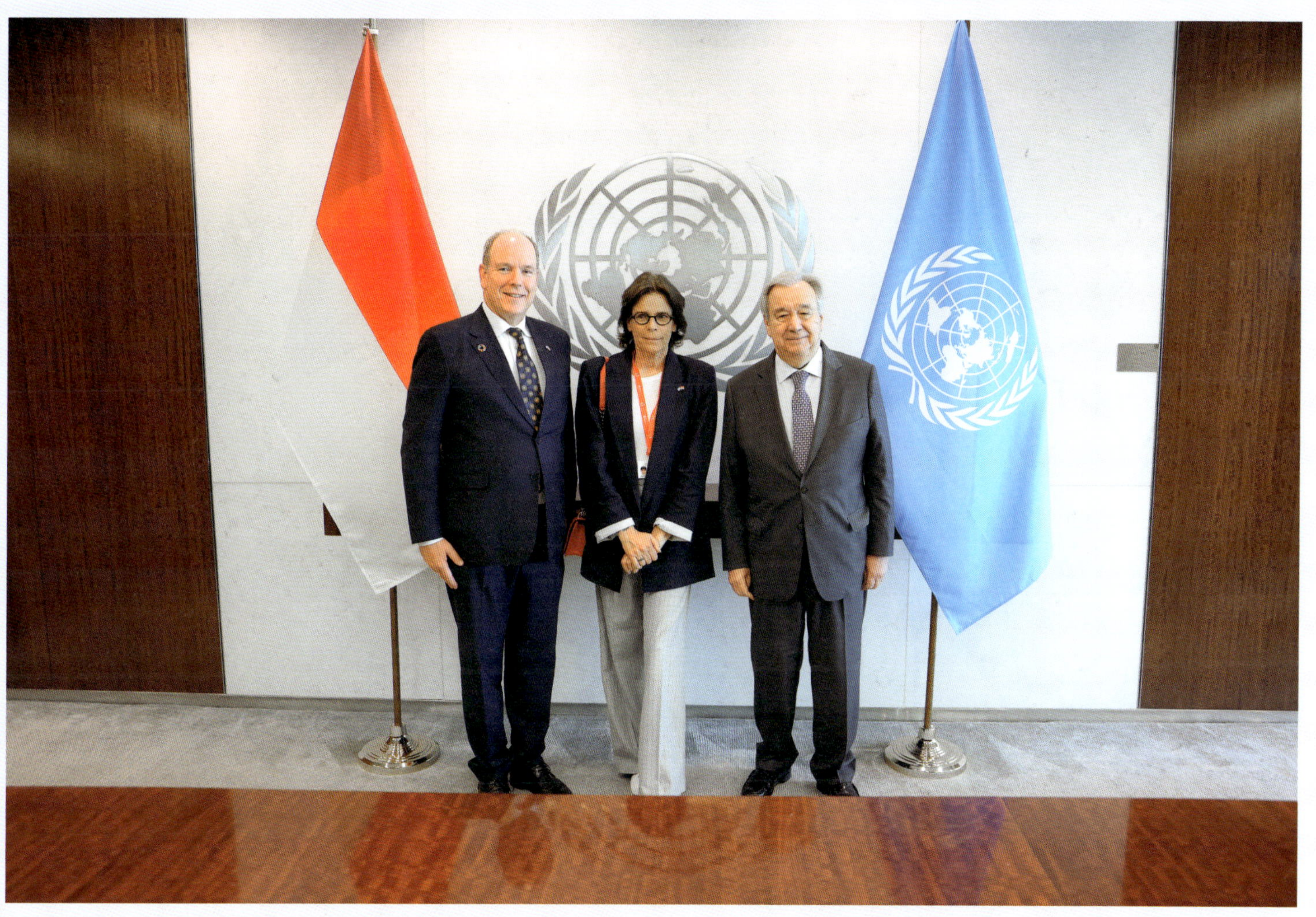

H.S.H. Prince Albert II, H.S.H. Princess Stéphanie of Monaco, and UN Secretary-General António Guterres, in June 2023, at the celebration of the 30th anniversary of Monaco's admission to the UN, as part of the commemoration of the centenary of the birth of Prince Rainier III.

MEMORIES OF UNESCO FIGURES

JACQUES BOISSON
JEAN PASTORELLI
YVETTE LAMBIN-BERTI
ANNE-MARIE BOISBOUVIER
DOMINIQUE NOTARI

WE WANTED TO GIVE MONEGASQUE FIGURES WHO HAVE PLAYED AN IMPORTANT ROLE IN THE ORGANIZATION A CHANCE TO MAKE THEIR OWN VOICES HEARD. EACH OF THEM, IN THEIR OWN WAY AND AT THEIR OWN TIME, HAS WOVEN THE THREADS OF THE CLOSE TIES AND MUTUAL TRUST THAT MAKE UP THIS HISTORIC TAPESTRY. WE WOULD LIKE TO THANK THEM FOR SHARING THEIR RECOLLECTIONS WITH US.

JACQUES BOISSON

Born on January 8, 1940, Jacques Boisson, a graduate of the Institute of Political Studies in Aix-en-Provence and a Doctor of Law, has been Honorary Secretary of State since February 5, 2022, when Yvette Lambin-Berti, former Ambassador Extraordinary and Plenipotentiary of the Principality to UNESCO, took over the post. The lifelong commitment of this great public servant is emblematic of the Principality's involvement in international institutions. His many honors, which include Officer of the Legion of Honor and Grand Officer of the Orders of Saint Charles and Grimaldi, are recognition of his "remarkable diplomatic career" to quote the statement issued by the Prince after the last session of Boisson's career. He served as representative to the United Nations in New York, then to the Council of Europe, and as ambassador to Spain and France. But what is of more interest to us here are his contributions to the preeminent international organization—the first to demonstrate the Principality's commitment to multilateralism—that is UNESCO.

To shed light on his actions and the defining moments of his career, we spoke to Boisson himself, who was kind enough to welcome us into his home. He answered our questions enthusiastically, supplementing his words with various written notes that bear witness to the richness of his political and emotional memory.

Mr. Boisson, could you tell us about your early days at UNESCO as a civil servant and later as Deputy Permanent Delegate?

I was a United Nations international civil servant at UNESCO from 1968 to 1983. My vocation was almost certainly inspired by my meeting with René Maheu (1905-1975), former professor of philosophy, senior French civil servant, and Director-General of UNESCO (1962-1974) during his official visit to Monaco on May 16 and 17, 1967, at the invitation of Prince Rainier III. When I joined the organization less than a year later, the international context was particularly lively, with student protests, decolonization, the Cold War, and development issues giving my early work a special flavor. I arrived at the Place de Fontenoy in April and entered the UNESCO headquarters—dedicated to peace and understanding among peoples—with four other newly appointed young colleagues: one American, one Chinese from Formosa, one Filipino, and one Dominican. "Paris was calm, like the calm before the storm," if you will forgive me for quoting the memoire I published a few years ago under the title *Petite chronique d'un diplomate monégasque*.

I started off in the field of education, one of UNESCO's three main areas of action and the most important at the time, more specifically in the equal access to education department, where I was responsible for compiling and writing a summary of the reports written by the States Parties to the UNESCO Convention against Discrimination in Education. This synopsis work, presented at the General Conference sessions to review the progress and efforts of its members in fulfilling their commitments, was a complex but informative exercise, both academically and diplomatically. It was important to be considerate of states while taking into account their realities and difficulties, especially in the case of developing countries still recovering from colonialism.

I was then transferred to the department of adult literacy and learning, still within the education division. Here, I was responsible for evaluating experimental functional literacy projects based on the principles of critical consciousness developed by the Brazilian intellectual Paulo Freire (1921-1997), who at the time was known for his books on pedagogy and his efforts to develop literacy among the most disadvantaged. I was still unfamiliar with the field, but soon became fascinated by its creativity and innovative nature. This ambitious program, financed by a special fund of the UNDP (United Nations Development Program), was directed by Mr. Bellasène, who represented Algeria and was appreciated as much for his personal qualities as for his teaching skills. Thanks to his advice and protection, I quickly found my feet and became acquainted with projects on all five continents, mainly in Africa, Latin America and Asia. My direct supervisor was a brilliant intellectual of Indian origin—while names often fade from our memories, the power of their ideas remains—who used my work to produce the evaluation documents prepared by our experts in the field in French and Spanish. This meant total and loyal cooperation from the word go. It was a very enriching time for a young Monegasque who, from his vantage point in Paris, discovered a hitherto unknown world whose richness and diversity were a constant revelation.

It was the early 1970s and Mr. Maheu, keen to build on the achievements of his mandate, had the idea of creating a new human rights coordination unit within his cabinet, as the topic was becoming politically indispensable.

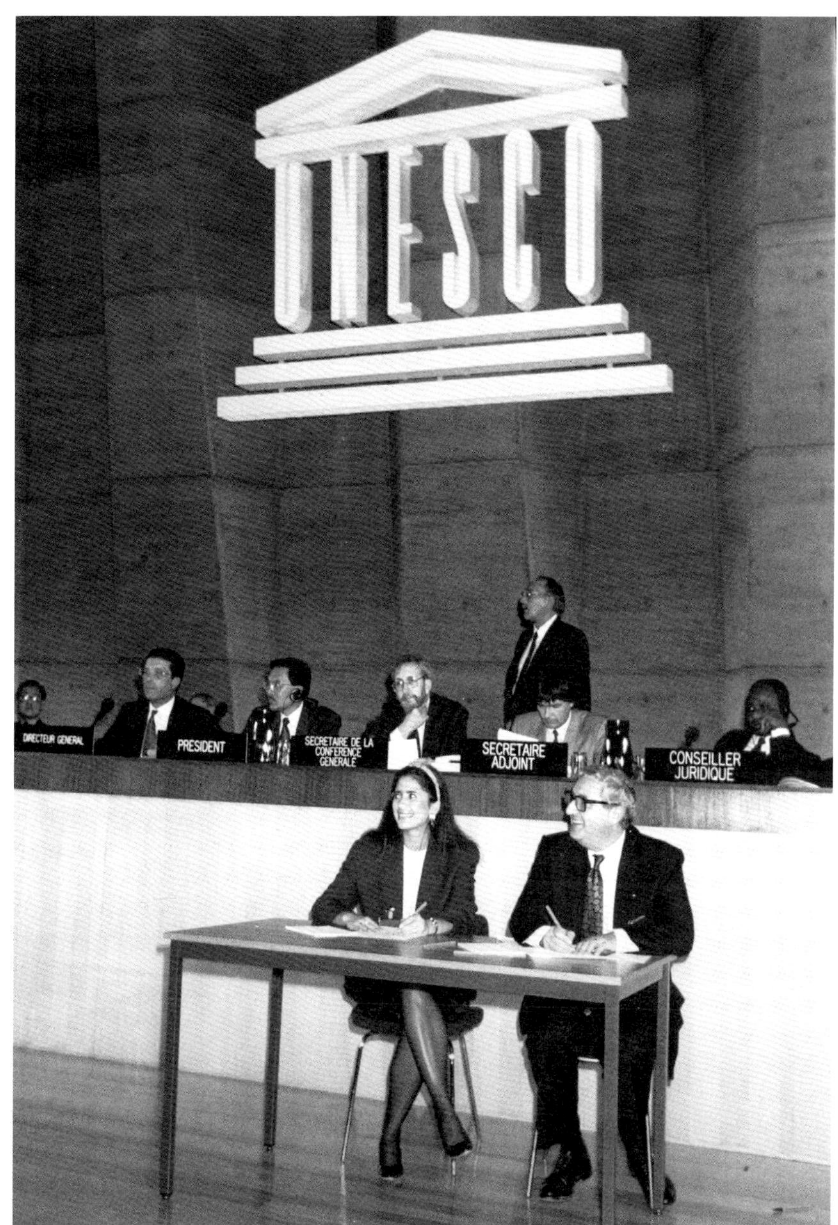

Jacques Boisson, Deputy Permanent Delegate of Monaco to UNESCO (1984-1993), assessor at a secret ballot vote during a session of the UNESCO General Conference. In the background, on the left, is Federico Mayor, UNESCO Director-General, at the presidential podium.

To lead the unit, he appointed Marie-Pierre de Cossé-Brissac (1925-), a graduate of the Ecole Normale Supérieure and a specialist in philosophy, then married to Herzog, the conqueror of Annapurna and former French Secretary of State for Youth and Sports (1958-1966). Initially head of the UNESCO philosophy division in 1969, she led the Human Rights Coordination Unit from May 1, 1973, and sought the assistance of a legal expert to support her in this role. She chose me.

As a result, I found myself in the cabinet of the organization's Director-General, tasked with inventing and implementing a focus area, reporting to a *grande dame*. With the attentive support of the head of the cabinet, Mr. Coueyteau, I devised an ambitious program. It aimed, on the one hand, to promote human rights within UNESCO's sphere of competence and, on the other, to improve the knowledge and practice of these rights by promoting access to education, science, and culture for as many people as possible. To my great surprise, this program was accepted by Mrs. Herzog, the Director-General, and ultimately, without reservation, by the General Conference of UNESCO.

The program was never actually implemented as René Maheu was not

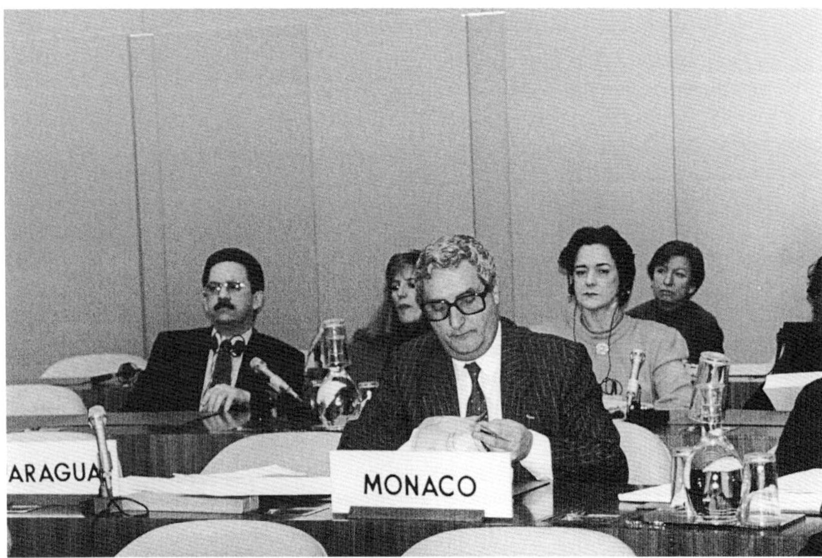

Jacques Boisson, Deputy Permanent Delegate of Monaco to UNESCO (1984-1993), at the Monaco headquarters, preparing to address one of the UNESCO General Conference commissions.

re-elected and was replaced in 1974 by the Deputy Director-General, Amadou-Mahtar M'Bow (1921-), former Senegalese Minister of Education (1966-1968) and Culture (1968-1970), who became the first African director of a United Nations agency: UNESCO (1974-1987). One of his first decisions was to dissolve the Human Rights Coordination Unit and create a Division of Human Rights and Peace within the Human and Social Sciences Sector.

As a result, I was transferred to this new unit and given the role of Program Officer for research and promotion of human rights and the fight against racism, racial discrimination, and apartheid at university level.

I threw myself into this new challenge with great enthusiasm.

The program had to be designed and implemented in a short period of time.

Its development was first overseen by Karel Vasak (1929-2015), a French-Czech university professor and international civil servant for the Council of Europe and a former student of René Cassin (1887-1976) in Strasbourg, then later by Pierre de Senarclens (1942), professor of international relations at the University of Lausanne. It was a wonderful experience that would shape my commitment, stimulate my thinking and, when I became a Monegasque diplomat, help me to be a worthy representative of my country, with useful experience in multilateral diplomacy and knowledge of humanity and peoples.

What were the main focuses of your work at the time?

The main topics and themes of my work were primarily university research and teaching. The scientific research carried out, in a constant renewal of intent, aimed first of all to demonstrate the universality of the principles and fundamental values of human rights, even though they have taken different forms and expressions in most traditions and religions.

I organized a symposium at the UNESCO office in Bangkok, Thailand, that brought together religious leaders and representatives from the world's major denominations: Christians, Muslims, Jews, and Asian religions—including Shinto priests who had never left Japan before—and it was an exemplary intellectual success. I also had the chance to work with historians and specialists in the oral traditions of African and Native American communities in Lomé (Togo), Saint-Louis (Senegal), and San José (Costa Rica). Declarations, conclusions, and recommendations illustrated and perpetuated the results of this work. As part of this program, new human rights concepts were explored, such as the right to a healthy and balanced environment and the right to peace and security. A comparative study of human rights and the rights of peoples, as well as reflection on the violation of human rights by private powers, have paved the way for certain dogmatic developments in these fields. This work has been the subject of publications by UNESCO or by the relevant universities and institutions to which I have contributed. They include, among others: *Les droits de l'homme dans la ville* (Human rights in urban areas—UNESCO Publishing, 1981), *Violation des droits de l'homme : quel recours, quelle résistance ?* (Violations of human rights: possible rights of recourse and forms of resistance—meeting in Freetown, Sierra Leone, UNESCO, 1981), *Droits de Solidarité et droits des peuples* (Solidarity rights and rights of peoples—international symposium in San Marino, 1982; address by Jacques Boisson, representative of the Director-General).

The international protection of human rights was another topic we covered, and was the subject of classes and conferences, mainly in university settings. As early as the 1970s, the specific issue of women's rights was a major concern of the organization. For example, I worked on preparations for the International Women's Year world conference held in Mexico City from June 19 to July 2, 1975, which resulted in the formulation of a global plan of action, including a set of guidelines for the advancement of women and the protection of their rights.

The fight against racism, racial discrimination, and apartheid has also been the subject of significant research and dissemination work, some of it quite original and enlightening. It is important to remember that this was a major commitment by UNESCO, which in 1949 launched a global program to combat racism based on the work of Claude Lévi-Strauss, among others. In 1950, the Declaration on Race was published, stating that there is no scientific basis or justification for racism. However, this sort of battle must be fought continually and its principles tirelessly reasserted. I am thinking, for example, of the symposium at the University of Athens to examine pseudo-scientific theories invoked to justify racism and racial discrimination. It ended with the Declaration of Athens on April 3, 1981, signed by Tahar Ben Jelloun and Albert Jacquard, among others, which concluded that "the latest anthropological discoveries confirm the unity of the human species" and that "one is never justified in proceeding from observation of a difference to the affirmation of a superiority-inferiority relationship."

Topics such as "race and history" and "race and culture" have also been the subject of regular reflection and discussion, such as the meeting of experts in Quebec chaired by Aimé Césaire.

The subject of peace has allowed me to publish two particularly interesting collective works, the first of which is entitled *Consensus and Peace* and the second *Polémologie, recherches sur la paix, irénologie* (Polemology, peace studies, irenology), in which I proudly cite the International Institute for Peace—now the Chapelle de la Paix—created in 1903 by Albert I, Prince of Monaco (1848-1922) to promote and disseminate his pacifist and internationalist ideas by encouraging arbitration between great powers, particularly France and Germany.

A collective publication on the new challenges of international law, edited, coordinated, and published by UNESCO, gave me the opportunity to meet and collaborate with Boutros Boutros-Ghali (1922-2016), then professor of international law and Dean of the Faculty of Law in Cairo, and later Secretary-General of the UN (1992-1996). A few years later, in 1993, I had the honor of presenting him with my credentials as Ambassador Extraordinary and Plenipotentiary of the Principality of Monaco to the UN. We were delighted to see each other again, and for many years we worked in close and friendly cooperation.

Your work undoubtedly took a political turn at times and provided you with enriching encounters.

Yes, you are right to remind me that, as part of my work, I regularly represented the Director-General of UNESCO at United Nations bodies such as the Commission on Human Rights, now the Human Rights Council, and the Sub-Commission on Prevention of Discrimination and Protection of Minorities, which met every year in Geneva, Switzerland, at the United Nations Office in the former League of Nations building. In particular, I had the opportunity to meet Kofi Annan (1938-2018). At the time, the future Secretary-General of the United Nations (1997-2006) was in charge of communications. Whenever I met him in New York, there was a certain affinity between us: the same affinity, as he liked to recall, that united the members of the Association of Former United Nations Civil Servants.

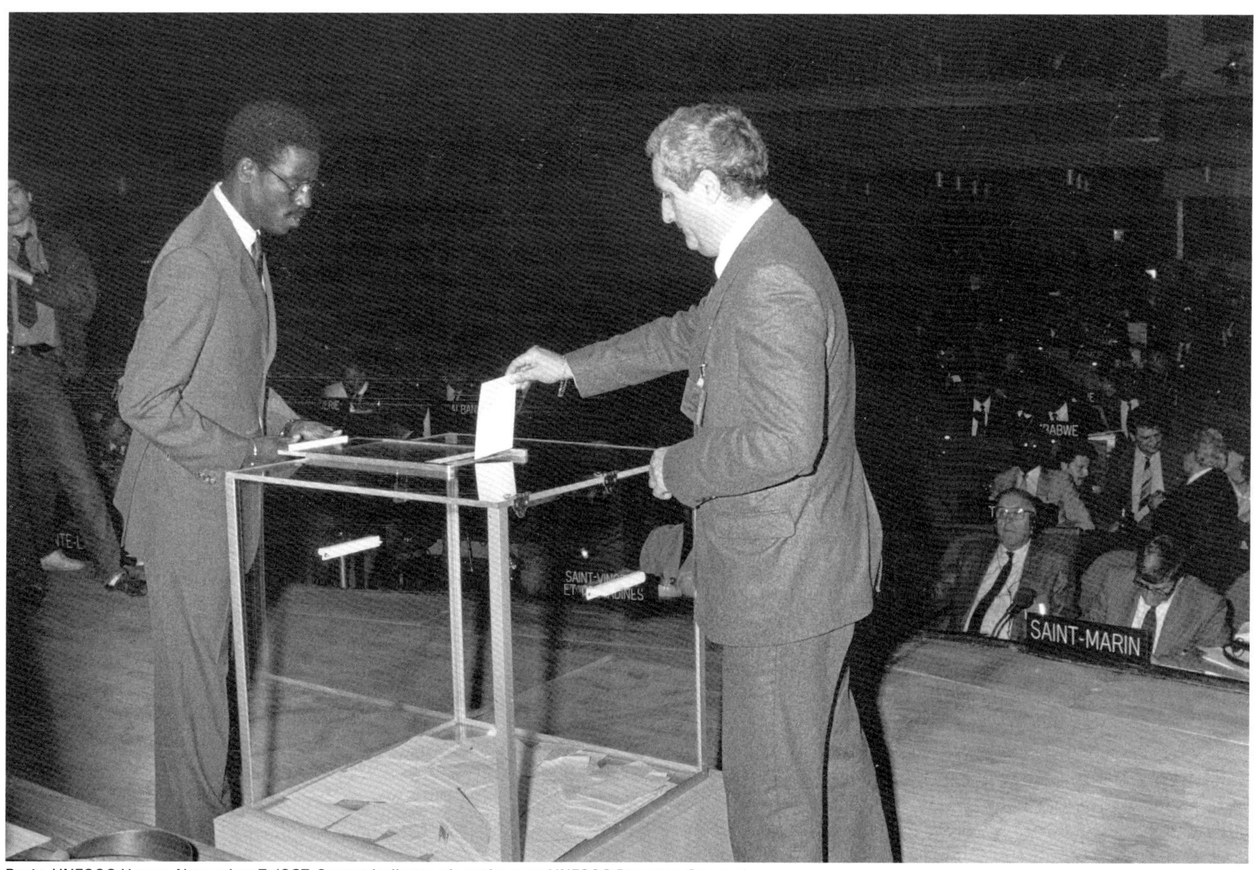

Paris, UNESCO House, November 7, 1987. Secret ballot to elect the new UNESCO Director-General. Jacques Boisson is on the right.

I regularly reported to these UN bodies on UNESCO's activities and actions in these fields, while proposing joint initiatives, which often led me to participate in United Nations meetings and conferences, such as the one in Nicaragua on humanitarian law in times of civil conflict.

At the Saami Institute for Education in Karasjok, Norway, I myself organized a meeting between indigenous and nomadic Saami peoples from northern Sweden, Norway, Finland, Canada, and the Kola Peninsula, then part of the Soviet Union.

Our objective was to highlight and preserve the way of life and traditions—including predominantly animist religious traditions—of these Lapland peoples. We then tried to implement long-term protection and preservation measures with the countries concerned.

I also had the honor of officially representing the Director-General of UNESCO in some extraordinary and sad circumstances. As a Monegasque, my presence at the funeral of Princess Grace in Monaco, after her death on September 14, 1982, was the most emotional of such occasions.

Finally, it must be emphasized that the involvement of Monegasque civil servants in the UNESCO Secretariat has greatly contributed to the establishment and enrichment of effective and constructive cooperation between Monaco and UNESCO. In light of this, I would like to mention the contributions of two other individuals.

First, Anne Willing Grinda, assistant to Prince Pierre de Polignac (1895-1964) on the Monegasque National Commission, brought to UNESCO her knowledge and practical experience of the workings, aspirations, and requirements of national commissions. Next, Dominique Khan Notari, with her considerable financial expertise, has contributed her knowledge to the complex management of the organization's budgetary resources, made up of both foreign and local currencies.

On a personal level, I believe that my experience at UNESCO gave me a pertinent and effective understanding of my diplomatic roles in the service of my country and, in particular, at UNESCO, the role of Deputy Permanent Delegate in 1984, then Permanent Delegate in 2007-2008. This role was a natural continuation of my work as Ambassador Extraordinary and Plenipotentiary of the Principality to the United Nations from 1993 to 2003 and then to the Council of Europe from 2004 to 2006.

I still follow these subjects, which are as topical as ever, with the same interest, in both form and substance. I was delighted to learn that for World Philosophy Day in 2018, UNESCO held an international symposium in Fez entitled "Religions, Identities, Practices, and Plural Perspectives", which explored the homogenization of lifestyles and the plurality of worldviews in the age of globalization—a fruitful line of inquiry that is an extension of the one I have pursued throughout my career.

JEAN PASTORELLI

Jean Pastorelli, born in 1942 and a Commander of the Order of Saint Charles, is a leading Monegasque politician who has served as Minister of Finance and Economy (1988-1995) and Minister of Foreign Affairs and Cooperation (2007-2008). He has also held a number of diplomatic posts at a pivotal time for multilateralism, reflecting the Principality's fresh impetus in international institutions. He was kind enough to share his impressions and to take stock of his work.

I represented my country at UNESCO for two terms: the first, from 1995 to 2003, as Permanent Delegate of the Principality to international organizations, and the second, from 2008 to 2009, as Permanent Representative of the Principality to UNESCO, at the same time as my tenure as Ambassador to France. These two missions, carried out in different international contexts, followed the same fundamental guideline: to assert the Principality's influence and place in the international community in accordance with the policy established by Prince Rainier III and continued by H.S.H. sovereign Prince Albert II. My first assignment came just two years after the Principality's admission to the UN in 1993: an important moment that finally put Monaco on the world map after joining UNESCO in 1949.

My first Permanent Representative post had a broad mandate at the time that I held it, encompassing several international organizations. Although most of them did not require a sustained presence and constant action, they did call for active participation in the main debates. It was in this context that I successfully led the election of Monaco to the presidency of Eutelsat, the French intergovernmental organization tasked with managing the satellite broadcasting of television channels and radio stations, and, at the same time, to the presidency of Intelsat, the intergovernmental consortium based in Luxembourg City and Washington.

My second assignment, which focused on the activities of UNESCO, struck me as very interesting in terms of the structure and scope of its mission, particularly given the number of member states, which, it was said at the time, was greater than that of the UN.

The range of UNESCO's activities is extremely broad, and the work carried out is more or less compatible with the Principality's scope. When it comes to education, we can hold our heads high in comparison to other states, such is the quality of our primary and secondary education. The same can be said of culture: need I remind you of the wealth and influence of the Opera, the Orchestra, the Ballet companies, the Prince Pierre Foundation, the Princess

Grace theater, the Audiovisual Institute, or the Grimaldi Forum? It is no secret that science is the Principality's main asset, having attracted the attention of international observers since the very beginning. Need I mention the work of Prince Albert I, a pioneer in oceanography, magnificently represented by the Museum, the Mediterranean Science Commission (CIESM), and the Scientific Center of Monaco, later created by Prince Rainier. Our sovereign continues to pursue these initiatives today, as demonstrated by the creation of the Prince Albert II of Monaco Foundation in 2006. Not to mention the Principality's contribution to the human sciences, prehistory, and archaeology, particularly the Museum of Prehistoric Anthropology, also founded by Prince Albert I.

The government's proposed direction was first and foremost to ensure a more constant presence at the organization's many and varied meetings by prioritizing new themes in line with the values defended by Monaco, particularly anything related to ethical issues:

Bioethics, a priority for UNESCO in the wake of the Universal Declaration on the Human Genome and Human Rights, unanimously adopted at the 29th General Conference in 1997, was the subject of a symposium held in Monaco on April 28 to 30, 2000, entitled "Bioethics and the Rights of the Child". Organized by AMADE and UNESCO and chaired by the President of AMADE, it culminated in the adoption of a Monaco Declaration on Bioethics and the Rights of the Child.

Information ethics, with the organization of various symposia on information ethics and information rights.

The work of the UNESCO International Oceanographic Commission, created in 1960 and which the Principality joined in 1961. The IOC provides the member states of the United Nations with an essential mechanism for cooperation in the study of the oceans, in which Monaco is particularly involved by virtue of its history. The Managing Director of the Oceanographic Museum represents Monaco.

Monaco's links with the organization are also symbolically manifested in the toponymy of the territory, with the inauguration of the UNESCO garden overlooking the terraces of Fontvieille, and in the presence of the Cathedral Boys' Choir at the opening of a General Assembly.

At the same time, the Monegasque delegation was also active on a number of dossiers proposing new conventions to member states. The signing of the Convention for the Safeguarding of the Intangible Cultural Heritage—hindered by the processes of globalization and social change—at the 32nd session of the General Conference in Paris in 2003 is symbolic of this period. The Permanent Delegation also monitored the implementation of the cultural diversity project championed by the European states of Electoral Group 1, to which Monaco belongs. The debates were marked by a reception held at the Élysée for all the member states, a moment that is etched on my memory, where the French President reiterated in no uncertain terms the need to finalize the convention. The latter came into being in 2005 when the Convention on the Protection and Promotion of the Diversity of Cultural Expressions was signed in Paris.

To underline the results of these monitoring efforts and in-depth work, in 2002 the Government of Monaco proposed that the sovereign nominate the Principality for the UNESCO Executive Board elections to be held at the end of summer 2003. The Prince approved the proposal and the election campaign began.

At UNESCO at the time, the campaign was conducted on two levels:

The first was the electoral group to which a state belongs, which is determined primarily by its geographic location. Monaco belongs to Group 1: "Western European states and others", and had served on the secretariat for many years. The number of representatives from each group (now fixed at nine) varied according to the year and circumstances, and the number of candidates could exceed the number of positions to be filled. If there were more candidates than positions, a decision would be made at the second level by the General Assembly. In other words, there was competition within the group from the outset to achieve a "clean slate". The list was said to be "optimal" when the number of candidates was equal to the number of seats available to an electoral group. This situation was achieved through negotiations within the electoral groups.

Monaco faced two difficulties at this point. Some members of the group believed that only the most important states should be elected to represent the group and ensure robust governance within the organization; and within the group, some members were linked by larger political or economic cooperations.

The Principality therefore had to campaign within the group for equal treatment of all states in international organizations, based on the principle of one state, one vote. More than one hundred and twenty ambassadors and permanent representatives were contacted to draw attention to the attributes of Monaco's candidacy and the possibility of electing "small states".

Despite our best efforts, the campaign was suspended after a major political event: the return of the United States of America to UNESCO. The United States withdrew in 1984 under President Ronald Reagan, citing the perceived ineffectiveness and budgetary excesses of the organization, as well as disagreements over its political orientation. In the aftermath of the attacks on September 11, 2001, the world's foremost power, eager to rebuild international cooperation in all fields, decided in 2003 to rejoin UNESCO, bringing with it its political weight and a significant portion of its funding.

This implied a guaranteed spot on the Executive Board, and Group 1 responded by presenting a "clean slate". Given the importance of the issue, Monaco and three other states withdrew their candidacy. In informing the Chair of Group 1 of the Principality's withdrawal, the Monegasque delegation stated that it might renew its candidacy for future assemblies and that it hoped for the firm support of the group as compensation for this act. In the end, Monaco submitted a new candidacy in 2008, when I was completing my second term as the Principality's Permanent Representative to UNESCO.

A memorandum was prepared regarding Monaco's candidacy for a seat on the Executive Board for 2010-13. This memorandum began by recalling that since joining the organization in 1949, the Principality had always demonstrated its attachment to the objectives and ideals of UNESCO. The creation of an International Institute for Peace in Monaco in 1903 to promote pacifist propaganda and international arbitration was undoubtedly the best expression of this.

The memorandum also recalled the personal involvement of members of the Princely Family in these decisive actions. H.S.H. Prince Albert II, first as Hereditary Prince and then with great determination as Sovereign since 2005, has strived to promote the need to defend the environment. Examples of this include the 2008 symposium on ocean acidification with the participation of the International Oceanographic Commission; the 2009 Experts' Meeting on Sustainable Development of the Arctic; and the Prince Albert II Foundation's contribution to the Fund for the Protection of the World Cultural and Natural Heritage of Outstanding Universal Value, known as the World Heritage Fund. Meanwhile, H.R.H. The Princess of Hanover, was appointed a UNESCO Goodwill Ambassador on December 2, 2003 by the Director-General of UNESCO, Koichiro Matsuura, in recognition of her personal commitment to the protection of children and families and of her contribution to the promotion of UNESCO's programs for the education of girls and women. She is also involved in literacy programs for women and girls in Africa. This memorandum setting out the arguments for Monaco's candidacy was delivered and commented on personally by more than one hundred and twenty ambassadors and permanent representatives.

When Group 1 members were contacted, they were reminded of the precedent set in 2003, when Monaco withdrew its candidacy in order not to undermine the cohesion of the group. Other groups were also contacted, with a particular focus on countries that are influential because of their importance or reputation. The situation in Group 1 was completely different from 2003. There were four candidates and three positions to be filled. The additional candidate withdrew in the summer of 2009, resulting in a "clean slate" and Monaco's election to the Executive Board. All that remained were the results of the General Conference elections, which took place on October 14, 2009. Monaco received the most votes of any elected state.

This marked the beginning of a new chapter in which Monaco's involvement in UNESCO's activities would be strengthened and my successors would be able to develop the missions and renew the projects undertaken.

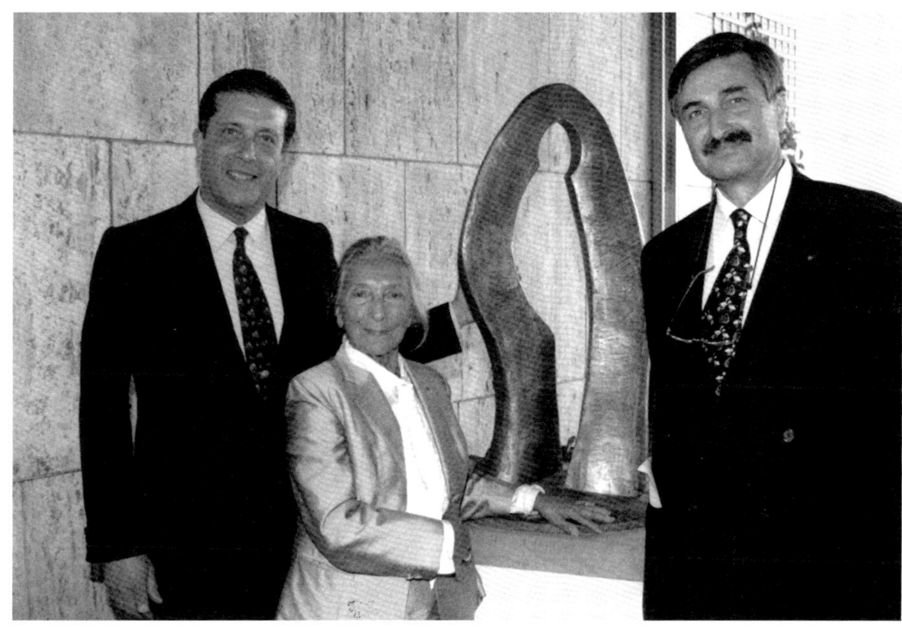

Federico Mayor, Director-General; Monegasque artist Emma de Sigaldi and His Excellency Jean Pastorelli, Ambassador of Monaco, at UNESCO, June 1998.

YVETTE LAMBIN-BERTI

Yvette Lambin-Berti, Secretary of State to H.S.H. Prince Albert II since February 5, 2022, was a Permanent Delegate and Ambassador to UNESCO for twelve years. Since April 1994, she has also been General Secretary of the Monegasque Olympic Committee.

You were the first ambassador to be appointed exclusively to UNESCO when the Principality joined the Executive Board in 2009. What did that moment represent for Monaco?

After the campaign led efficiently by my predecessor, on October 14, 2009, the Principality was elected by a very large majority to the Executive Board for a four-year term (2010-13), during which time we sat with the 57 other members. The Executive Board is one of UNESCO's three constitutional bodies, along with the General Conference and the Secretariat, and is, in a sense, UNESCO's board of directors. Its responsibilities include preparing the agenda for the General Conference and reviewing the organization's work plan and the corresponding budget estimates. This was the first time that Monaco had been elected to the Executive Committee and, in a way, it was a demonstration of full recognition by the other member states. We took it as a sign of trust, while being fully aware of the responsibility we had been given. The privilege of serving the organization required a great deal of dedication and a large team.

Moreover, it coincided with a special moment: the 35th session marked an undeniable turning point in the organization's leadership policy with the election of Irina Bokova as Director-General. A diplomat, member of parliament, and coordinator of relations between her country, Bulgaria, and the European Union, she was the first woman and the first representative from Central Europe to hold this prestigious position.

What do you consider to be the most memorable moments of Ms. Bokova's mandates?

Ms. Bokova had to deal with two major events: the election of Palestine as a member of the organization and its financial consequences (the loss of about 23% of the budget with the withdrawal of the United States of America).

The first was one of those moments that could rightly be called "historic". On November 31, 2011, the General Conference chose to recognize Palestine as a full member, with 107 votes in favor, 14 opposed, and 52 abstention.

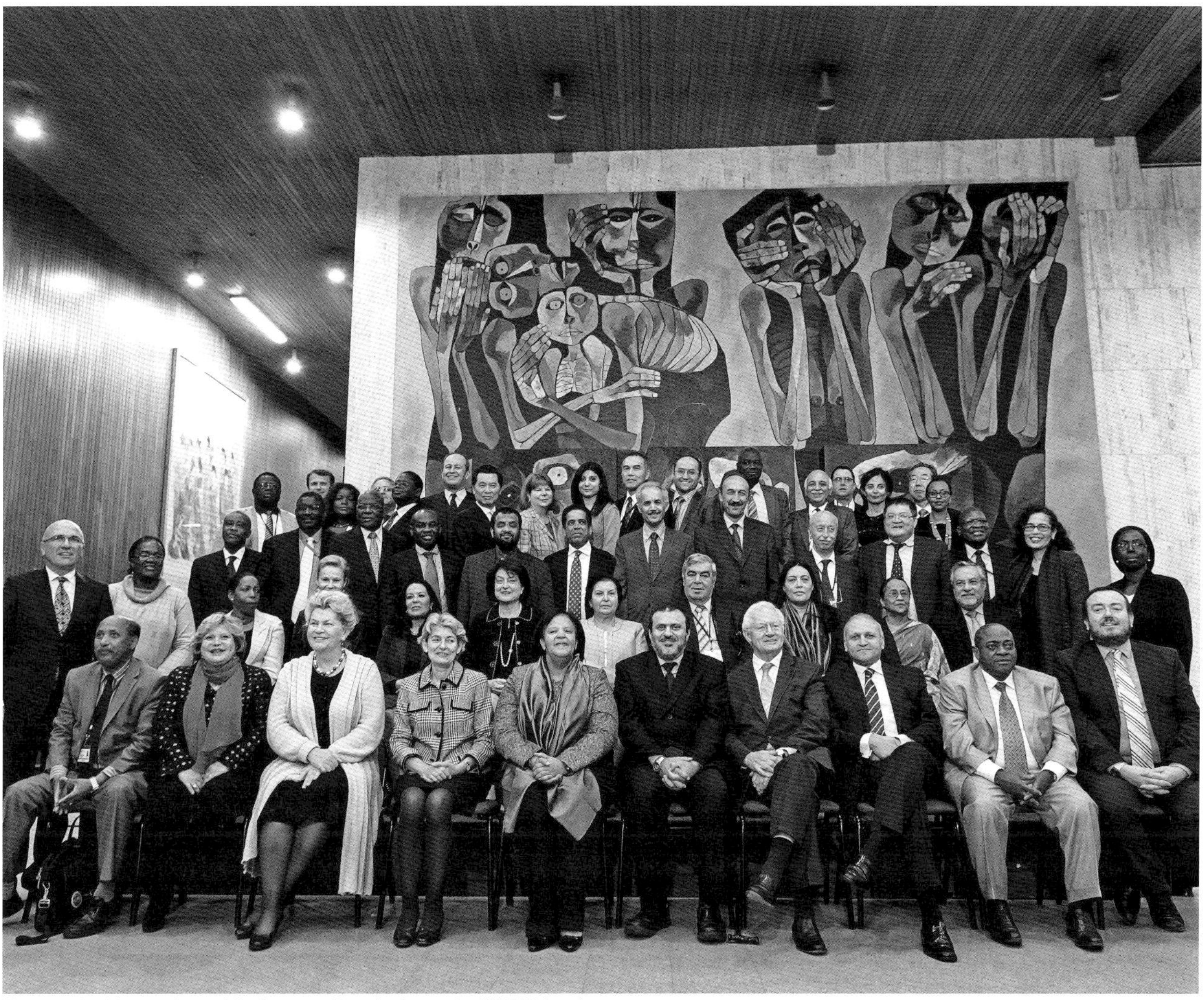

Photograph of the members of the Executive Board, taken at the UNESCO headquarters, with Irina Bokova, Director-General of the organization, October 2013.

Everyone immediately realized the symbolic dimension and the consequences that this would have. The Executive Board played a key role. It had to review financial commitments, cut back on certain programs, and set operational priorities. On its own scale, the Principality contributed in two ways: by supporting these major restructuring efforts (notably through emergency funds) and by contributing to the ad hoc think tanks that were set up. The organization's modes of governance had to be rethought, and that involved a lot of work on cross-functional programs. In particular, we were involved in the analysis of external audits, debates on the prioritization of programs, and all questions relating to staff reductions. UNESCO's wealth lies in the quality of its staff, and cutting programs—for lack of budget, as has been the case in the past—often means losing top-quality experts. And we had to deal with all of that as a matter of urgency.

In addition, the Director-General did her utmost to highlight matters such as equality, the priority given to the education of girls, the link between heritage and sustainable development, and, of course, the continent of Africa. This was crystallized in the concept of "new humanism", developed in 2010 and affirmed in 2015 on the occasion of the organization's 70th anniversary. In summary, I would say that UNESCO's peace diplomacy is not only "soft power", but also "smart power".

"In the twenty-first century, globalization is no longer about 'contacts' but 'sharing'. The global human community has become more self-aware. It has developed closer ties; time and space have contracted. Different peoples are increasingly in contact with one another, cultures entwine, and identities intermingle. All countries are actors in a single globalization process in which all must be able to participate. In this context, building a human community requires surely more than fostering mutual tolerance, respect or understanding, as societies separate from one another [...] History—even recent history—shows that it is easier to declare the existence of a community than to build one. Whole continents have been *de facto* excluded from this community we aspire to—Africa in particular [...]. Our drive must be for a new solidarity, to reintegrate all countries in the universal community. This project may seem utopian, but recent history has also demonstrated the dynamic strength of the desire for unity. I belong to a generation that lived in a divided Europe, split asunder by a wall, and that was able to draw lessons from the past in order to stand together as a continent. In 2000, the United Nations Millennium Declaration setting out the Millennium Development Goals marked a vital step in asserting the common will of all states. Taking its lead from UNESCO, the recent Summit on the Millennium Development Goals held in New York in September 2010 acknowledged the pivotal role of culture and education in attaining those goals—in reducing poverty and in achieving sustainable development. We must seize this opportunity and not give in to the forces of skepticism. We must remember Pico della Mirandola's message to believe in the potential of a free humanity, of the free individual who can be more than a plaything of circumstances."

Irina Bokova, *A New Humanism for the 21st century*, 2010, UNESCO, ERI.2010/WS/1.

More specifically, what were the Principality's concrete commitments?

Of course, it is difficult to sum up twelve years of such diverse activities. Generally speaking, thanks to fruitful exchanges with the other delegations, we gained an understanding of the areas in which Monaco could offer its expertise or support. There are therefore a number of themes, which are of course in line with the main objectives of the Monegasque government, where our contribution is now expected.

One example is our commitments and contributions to the Intergovernmental Oceanic Commission. These projects are sometimes very concrete and of immediate benefit, such as our contribution to the sea-level observing network and the coordination of activities in the Caribbean (GLOSS program). H.S.H. Prince Albert II has also worked tirelessly, visiting UNESCO on multiple occasions to speak about the oceans in 2010 and 2015. We have been very well received every time and it is important to present the work of his foundation, which seeks to protect the planet and promote sustainable development at local and global levels, by protecting marine and terrestrial biodiversity, conserving water, and fighting desertification. The Sovereign Prince's commitments in these areas are now well known and recognized, enabling us to launch highly targeted projects. For example, the "Bourses de Monaco" scholarships have enabled young researchers from developing countries (Guinea, Côte d'Ivoire,

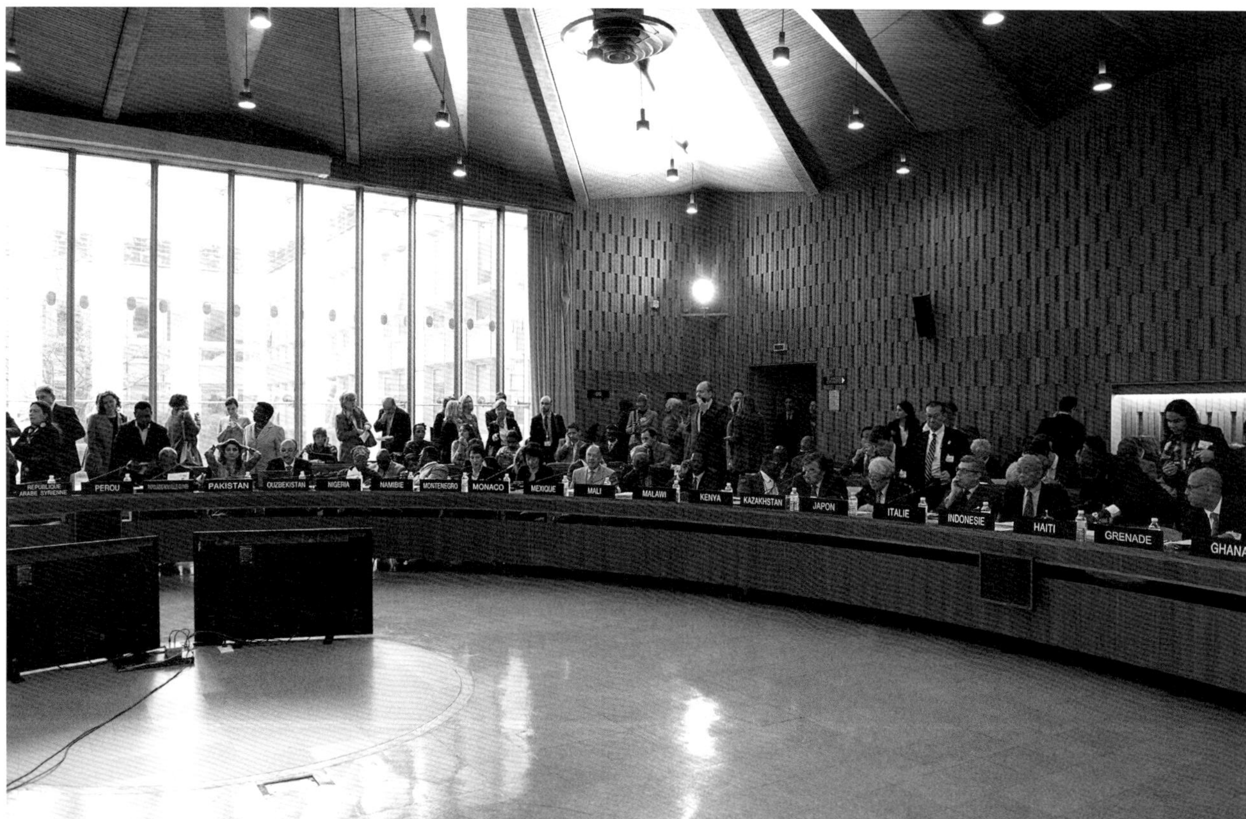

The Executive Board room where Monaco sat, October 2013.

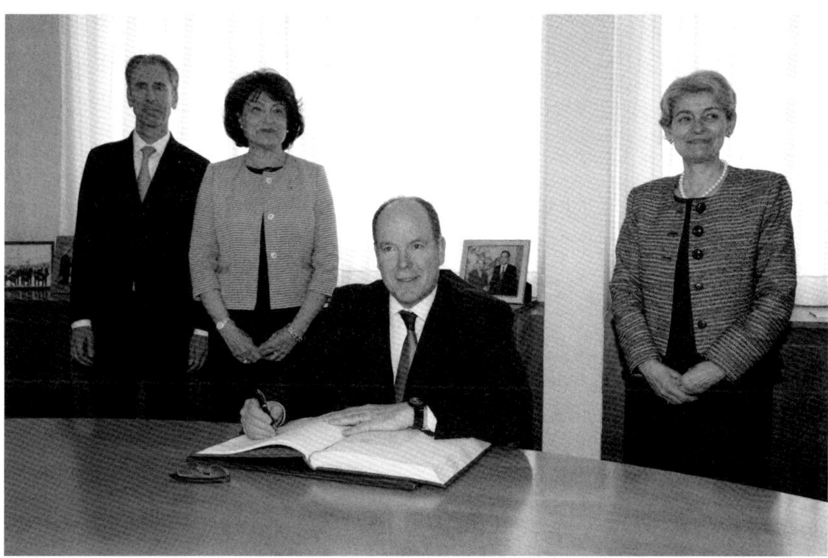

From left to right Gilles Tonelli, Government Counsellor-Minister for External Relations and Cooperation, Yvette Lambin-Berti, Ambassador of Monaco, H.S.H. Prince Albert II, Irina Bokova, Director-General of UNESCO, for the signing of a book on World Ocean Day in Paris in 2015.

Burkina Faso, Morocco, Tunisia, Senegal, and Algeria) to finance their higher education in the field of biodiversity. Another more surprising example is our long-standing partnership with Mongolia in training to combat the illicit trafficking of cultural goods. This resulted in a magnificent exhibition at the Monaco Museum of Anthropology in 2013 entitled "First nomads of Upper Asia, journey into the heart of the steppes" (see photo), to coincide with the 191st session of the Executive Board.

I must also mention our interest—and that of H.R.H. The Princess of Hanover—in the priority of Africa, particularly regarding the education of girls and young women. Since 1995, 180 million more girls have enrolled in primary and secondary education: an undeniable success for UNESCO! However, discrimination still persists, as the current Director-General, Ms. Azoulay, rightly reminds us: "We all know that education is the cornerstone of equality—and the education of girls and women is the first step towards a more gender-equal world." I am firmly convinced of this. For example, we helped build the capacity of educators in schools and institutes in Burkina Faso, with an initial program in 2010-13. And on the topic of education, let me remind you that on November 28, 2012, the Principality became a party to the Convention against Discrimination in Education.

I must also mention one of UNESCO's best-known domains, and rightly so: world heritage. The November 1972 Convention laid the foundations for this collective protection of cultural and natural heritage of universal value, and UNESCO is committed to identifying cultural and natural sites of outstanding interest to the common heritage of humanity. In particular, we have had a very acute experience of the question of protecting tangible and intangible heritage, with the debates on Timbuktu from 2012 onwards, concerning the safeguarding of mausoleums and manuscripts, with, as we know, the major involvement of France in this matter. The delegation follows the passionate debates on the classification of sites and the safeguarding of intangible heritage, as well as the perverse effects resulting from them, in particular the consequences of tourism. We have also begun to think about what might be considered intangible heritage in Monaco. It is a long process and more complex than you might think!

My main impression of those years was that the Principality gained greater recognition thanks to the Executive Board. We consolidated this progress by signing a framework agreement in 2015 that goes beyond our statutory contributions. The Director-General at the time welcomed the Principality's continued commitment to supporting UNESCO's activities, stressing that the "framework agreement will lead to a more coherent content and a more strategic direction for our cooperation."

This has enabled us to forge close links with other delegations, particularly within Group 1, but also outside it. There has been a great deal of all-important yet intangible work, involving meetings, discussions and recognition of what we can do together, sometimes urgently.

What I have noticed is that the vitality of the organization lies in its ability to rethink its own principles in light of what tomorrow will be or what our today already is: bioethics, information societies, debates on artificial intelligence, the various historical and ethical horizons that coexist. The never-ending debates about pluralism, diversity, and a "broader universal" that have been going on since UNESCO's inception are no longer a matter for specialists and intellectuals, but are the very fabric of our societies. In this sense, UNESCO occupies a very special place among UN agencies, and is of great value to the Principality.

ANNE-MARIE BOISBOUVIER

Before being appointed Ambassador and Permanent Delegate of the Principality of Monaco to UNESCO in 2021, Anne-Marie Boisbouvier was a member of the Prince's cabinet. On December 15, 2022, she received the insignia of Knight of the National Order of the Legion of Honor in the presence of H.S.H. Sovereign Prince Albert II and the most important figures of the Principality. Anne-Marie Boisbouvier is also Knight of the Ordre National du Mérite, a Knight of the Order of Saint Charles, and a Commander of the Equestrian Order of Saint Agatha (San Marino).

What work does the permanent delegation of the Principality of Monaco to UNESCO do?

As a form of diplomatic representation, the Monegasque delegation to UNESCO helps define the strategic directions of the organization and ensures that they are properly implemented. It is responsible for maintaining and developing cooperation between UNESCO and the Principality in the fields of culture, heritage, education, science, and information.

The delegation also represents the Principality in its regional group—Group 1, made up of member states from Western Europe (before the collapse of the USSR) and North America, with Canada and now the United States of America since the country's return in July 2023—and in the various groups of which it is a member, such as the Group of Francophone Ambassadors of UNESCO (GAFU), for example.

It also works in concert with the Monegasque National Commission for UNESCO, which acts as a consultative, liaison and information body, mobilizing and coordinating partnerships with civil society and Monegasque stakeholders in this field.

What are the main challenges facing UNESCO today?

Since the re-election of UNESCO Director-General Audrey Azoulay in 2021, the context has been marked by the COVID-19 pandemic and the follow-up to decisions. I would also like to mention the launch of the Global Education Coalition in 2020, and the Transforming Education Summit in New York in 2022, which put education at the top of the global political agenda.

In the field of culture, our work aims to make the cultural sector more resilient and anchored in sustainable development perspectives, by combating the vulnerability of professionals in the sector and by protecting the status of artists. At Mondiacult, the UNESCO World Conference on Cultural Policies and Sustainable Development, held in Mexico City in September 2022, culture was recognized as a 'global public good'.

However, the current context is above all marked by complex geopolitical challenges and multiple crises: Russia's ongoing aggression against Ukraine; the alarming situation in Afghanistan with widespread discrimination against girls and violations of women's fundamental rights in education, the workplace and public spaces; the ongoing conflicts between Armenia and Azerbaijan; and the situation in Israel. Increasingly, we have also had to take natural disasters into account.

In all of these respects, UNESCO's role and missions remain just as relevant as ever in order to 'act now for future peace.' Examples of measures implemented by UNESCO include the opening of UNESCO offices (known as field offices) in various countries, such as in Kabul, Afghanistan, where UNESCO is the only organization still to have a presence in the country, and the more recent creation of a UNESCO Antenna in Kyiv, Ukraine. The launch of actions as part of the Heritage Emergency Fund is also a good example. As a result, 31 projects were launched in 23 countries in 2022 in response to emergencies such as those on Easter Island (Chile), in Madagascar and Afghanistan, and following the floods in Pakistan. Support for Ukraine is also one of the priorities of the Heritage Emergency Fund, and work has also been ongoing in Lebanon and Iraq for several years as part of the 'LiBeirut' and 'Revive the Spirit of Mosul' projects, to which the Principality has contributed.

Another current challenge for UNESCO is to prepare for the issues of the future: first, the adoption of the UNESCO Recommendation on Open Science. Particularly relevant to global scientific cooperation around the COVID-19 pandemic, the agreement between member states promotes equality among scientists and the sharing of the results of their discoveries so that populations and policymakers can benefit from scientific progress; and second, the adoption of the first-ever global recommendation on the ethics of artificial intelligence. It is worth noting that AI is an issue in many fields including culture, where there is an urgent need to create a legal and ethical framework, in particular to protect the work of artists.

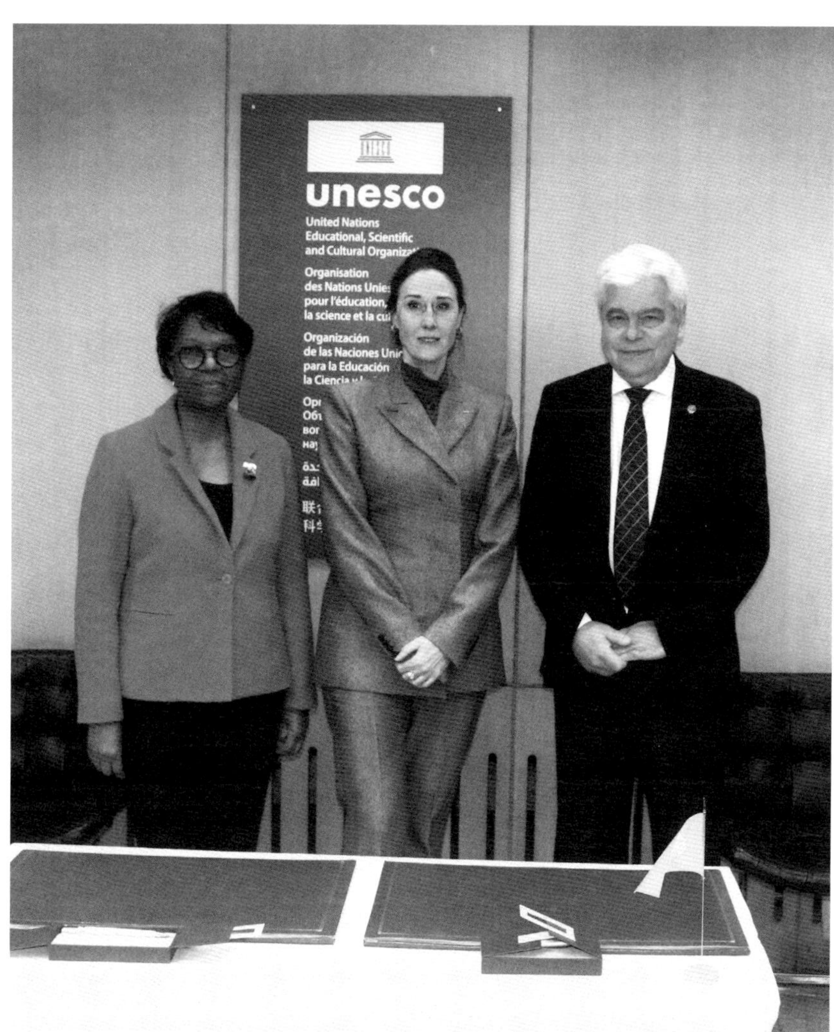

Her Excellency Anne-Marie Boisbouvier, Ambassador of Monaco to UNESCO, at the "signing of a partnership with UNESCO to celebrate the heritage of Prince Albert I", Paris, UNESCO headquarters, December 5, 2022. With Noëline Raondry Rakotoarisoa, representing the UNESCO Assistant Director-General for Natural Sciences, and Vladimir Ryabinin, Executive Secretary of the IOC and Assistant Director-General of UNESCO.

How does the Principality of Monaco fit into this picture?

A member of UNESCO since July 6, 1949, Monaco has always been committed to the values of the organization. The Principality has been involved in the life and activities of this United Nations agency around the world from the outset.

In October 2009, sixty years since its accession, Monaco was elected to the Executive Board by a large and almost unprecedented majority. Its four-year mandate came to an end in November 2013.

In 2015, a cooperation framework agreement between UNESCO and the government of Monaco was signed for the period of 2014-2017. This framework agreement was renewed for two additional four-year periods in 2018 and 2022. Monaco also closely follows the many conferences, intergovernmental bodies and formal group meetings held as part of UNESCO's mandate.

In addition, the Principality has participated in various declarations made by UNESCO and other international bodies condemning Russian aggression in Ukraine since the spring of 2022. In particular, the Principality of Monaco has supported UNESCO by contributing to the emergency fund set up for Ukraine and has backed decisions relating to the preservation of education, culture, information and the protection of journalists.

The Principality of Monaco is also involved with UNESCO through the commitment of H.R.H. The Princess of Hanover as a UNESCO Goodwill Ambassador for the education of girls and young women.

In particular, I recall how she was invited by Her Highness Sheikha Moza bint Nasser, UNESCO Special Envoy for Basic and Higher Education, to participate in the celebration at UNESCO Headquarters in Paris of the third International Day to Protect Education from Attack, on September 9, 2022, and the meetings she had with other UNESCO Ambassadors dedicated to education, such as H.R.H. Grand Duchess Maria Teresa of Luxembourg.

Furthermore, the delegation is committed to promoting the Principality of Monaco at UNESCO in relation to the organization's various themes.

On December 7, 2022, UNESCO held a conference with Erik Orsenna of the Académie Française in partnership with the Albert I Committee, in the presence of H.S.H. Prince Albert II of Monaco and Audrey Azoulay, entitled: 'Science in the service of humanity. Prince Albert I of Monaco and his work', as part of the commemorations organized in 2022 for the 100th anniversary of the death of Prince Albert I of Monaco. It should be noted that the 41st session of the UNESCO General Conference in November 2021 approved the inclusion of this anniversary in the calendar of celebrations for 2022-2023.

On December 12, 2023, this time in association with the Monaco Museum of Prehistoric Anthropology, a tribute was paid to Professor Yves Coppens, French paleontologist and President of the International Scientific Committee of the Monaco Museum of Prehistoric Anthropology, who died in June 2022.

Finally, various events will be held throughout 2024 to celebrate the 75th anniversary of the Principality of Monaco at UNESCO in the organization's three fields: education, science and culture.

I am sure that the Paris 2024 Olympic Games will also serve as a reminder that sport is one of the strengths of the Principality of Monaco.

What are Monaco's priorities at UNESCO?

Monaco is taking part in the Ocean Decade, notably through the commitment of H.S.H. Prince Albert II as a patron of the Alliance and his ambitions for this decade. The government of Monaco has supported the United Nations Decade of Ocean Science for Sustainable Development (2021-2030) since its inception. Its implementation is being overseen by the UNESCO Intergovernmental Oceanographic Commission (IOC). The delegation has an excellent and long-standing relationship with this commission, whose work it supports and promotes. Since the commission does not have a dedicated budget for this project, an alliance has been formed to catalyze support for the Decade by mobilizing targeted resources, networking, and drawing on the influence of its members. H.S.H. Prince Albert II has been a patron of the Alliance since its creation, and his foundation is a member.

Since taking up my post, I have both witnessed and communicated the Sovereign's commitment to this Decade. In particular, the Prince attended the United Nations Ocean Conference in Lisbon in June 2022, where he sat on the Alliance's High Level Panel. The Prince Albert II of Monaco Foundation is also involved in the IOC's activities in this field, notably through a partnership agreement signed on November 17, 2021. As a member of the Decade Alliance, it also participates in the Ocean Decade Foundations Dialogue, which brings together philanthropic organizations that support the oceans. The third Foundations Dialogue was held in Monaco in June 2023 at the invitation of the Prince Albert II Foundation. Audrey Azoulay made a special trip for this occasion, underlining the importance of this matter and, of course, the good relationship between H.S.H. The Sovereign Prince and the Director-General of UNESCO.

More recently, to demonstrate Monaco's excellence and pioneering role in this specific scientific field, I spoke at the opening of an event celebrating the 120th anniversary of the General Bathymetric Chart of the Oceans (GEBCO), organized by its creators: the IHO and the IOC-UNESCO.

We also support the IOC's Global Sea Level Observing System project (GLOSS) and more specifically, the tsunami warning system.

Monaco also contributes by providing financial support to young scientists working toward the Decade's objectives. This was made possible by the 'Man and the Biosphere' program (MAB) in June 2022, which awards research grants via its Young Scientists Award. Since 1989, this program has benefited more than 300 young scientists, 45% of them women, from over 100 countries. Their research specifically focuses on biosphere reserves. As more than 200 of the 738 biosphere reserves include marine, coastal and island areas, the Principality of Monaco made a proposal to strengthen the link between this program and the Ocean Decade.

I thought that this proposal was an ideal way of bringing interdisciplinarity to life within UNESCO: supporting young people through a scientific biodiversity program focusing on knowledge of the oceans. Our Portuguese colleague, Antonio Abreu, who represented our regional group on the Council Bureau, gave us his immediate support and ensured that the item was included at the MAB Council meeting.

I would also like to point out that the Principality of Monaco has contributed financially to the Heritage Emergency Fund since its creation in 2015. To take our commitment to the next level and to renew our confidence with regard to conflict situations, we increased our voluntary contribution in 2022 and maintained it in 2023.

Monaco is also active on the following fronts: the Fund of the Intergovernmental Committee for Promoting the Return of Cultural Property to its Countries of Origin or its Restitution in case of Illicit Appropriation; human capacity-building in the Secretariat of the Fund of the Convention for the Safeguarding of Intangible Cultural Heritage; Convention Concerning the Protection of World Cultural and Natural Heritage; Convention on the Protection and Promotion of the Diversity of Cultural Expressions; and support for the UNESCO World Heritage Marine Programme as part of the collaboration with Monaco Explorations.

This collaboration began in 2017, when Monaco Explorations was established. The UNESCO World Heritage Marine Programme sites are emblematic of the World Heritage Convention for which UNESCO is renowned, particularly among the general public. The cooperation helps promote and highlight Monaco Explorations' missions when they take place at Marine Heritage sites. The two bodies work hand in hand toward the same goal of preservation, for which knowledge is a prerequisite, since we can only protect what we know. The first phase of this agreement was coming to an end when I took up my position, and I could see that the collaboration had strengthened both Monaco Explorations and the World Heritage Marine Programme. Our many ties to UNESCO often focus on a single horizon: the ocean.

Our work to promote the education and schooling of vulnerable children, particularly girls, is also worth mentioning. It is important to have international data for the work carried out by UNESCO and to ensure the continued support of the Principality of Monaco for the education sector, particularly in relation to the commitment of H.R.H. The Princess of Hanover as a Goodwill Ambassador and the activities she carries out with AMADE. The delegation has therefore focused on contributing to the Global Education Monitoring (GEM) report.

The Principality is also active in the following fields: the Holocaust Remembrance Fund and International Holocaust Remembrance Day.

As you know, Monaco advocates for the power of sport as a vehicle for peace and development, and believes it has a key role to play in achieving the UN's Sustainable Development Goals by 2030. Since 2019, the Monegasque government has contributed to the study of doping in sport by financially supporting university research. This support takes the form of the UNESCO Chair in Doping Studies and Analysis of Anti-Doping Policies, which is awarded to a second-year Master's student. As such, the delegation makes financial contributions to the work of experts in physical education and sport and to the Fund of the International Convention against Doping in Sport.

Finally, I would like to mention a commitment that has always been essential to us: the representation of the Principality of Monaco within the francophone group of UNESCO (GAFU) and the promotion of the French-speaking world within UNESCO.

While French remains one of the two languages used at UNESCO out of the five official languages of the United Nations, transcripts of debates are often produced only in English due to a lack of translation resources. This is particularly the case for the IOC, and more specifically for the Decade of Ocean Science. However, the impact of its activities requires that all the documents produced for the Decade be translated into French. Monaco therefore lent its support to two texts: the declaration of the Alliance and Foundations for the Lisbon conference, and the Ocean Decade Africa Roadmap.

Furthermore, the Principality of Monaco has participated in various declarations made by the francophone group of UNESCO (GAFU), in particular on the implementation of the 2005 Convention on the Protection and Promotion of the Diversity of Cultural Expressions, at the ninth conference of the parties to this convention, held from June 6 to 8, 2023.

Finally, we are involved in the activities organized by this group, notably the celebrations surrounding International Francophonie Day on March 20, which will have a special resonance after the inauguration of the Cité Internationale de la Langue Française at the Château de Villers-Cotterêts on October 30, 2023.

DOMINIQUE NOTARI

Dominique Notari was born in 1953 and holds a degree in economics from the University of Paris II (1974), a diploma from Sciences-Po Paris (1976) and a postgraduate diploma in development economics from the University of Paris I (1976). She left to continue her studies in the United States for two years, where she graduated from the Master of International Affairs program at Johns Hopkins University in Washington D.C. (1978). After working at a private bank in Paris for four years at the start of her career, Ms. Notari was appointed to UNESCO in April 1983. She was Assistant Administrator and then Administrator in the Treasury Department of the Financial Management Bureau. In 1992, Ms. Notari was promoted to Head of the Treasury Department, and in 1994, she became Assistant Financial Controller and Treasurer. In 2012, she was appointed by Irina Bokova as Director of the Middle Office Unit of the Treasury Section (BFM/TRS), which monitors UNESCO's investment policy, financial market risks, bank accounts and electronic banking tools.

What were your responsibilities within the organization?

My job was a technical one. My background in finance led me to oversee the management of projects and the organization of funds for various missions, and to analyze calls for tender for major projects. It also involved me visiting the offices responsible for implementing projects in Africa, Asia and Latin America. In this way, I was able to see how effectively these missions carried out the projects approved by the governing bodies.

What projects did you work on?

We didn't decide on the content, but looked at the viability and feasibility from a financial point of view. However, I remember certain files quite well. I had the opportunity to work on projects in the national parks of the Congo designed to protect endangered species, especially great apes. The aim was to transport materials and vehicles to help with logistics in the field. I also recall the project to reinstall the Obelisk of Axum, a symbol of identity, in Ethiopia.

Do you have any personal memories of places or people?

Of course! I remember arriving at the Place de Fontenoy in 1983 as a young civil servant, impressed by the beauty of the place and the magnitude of the task before me. Amadou-Mahtar M'Bow was Director-General of the organization at the time. I spent my first months at UNESCO with Jacques Boisson, who was finishing his term. I also clearly remember the consequences of the withdrawal of the United States in 1984, a few months after my arrival. I was then able to follow the history of the organization and to work under several different Directors-General. I was at UNESCO for 30 years, until 2013, where I ended up as a director and where I spent most of my fulfilling professional career. I am proud to have served, along with Anne Willings-Grinda and Jacques Boisson, as an international civil servant at UNESCO.

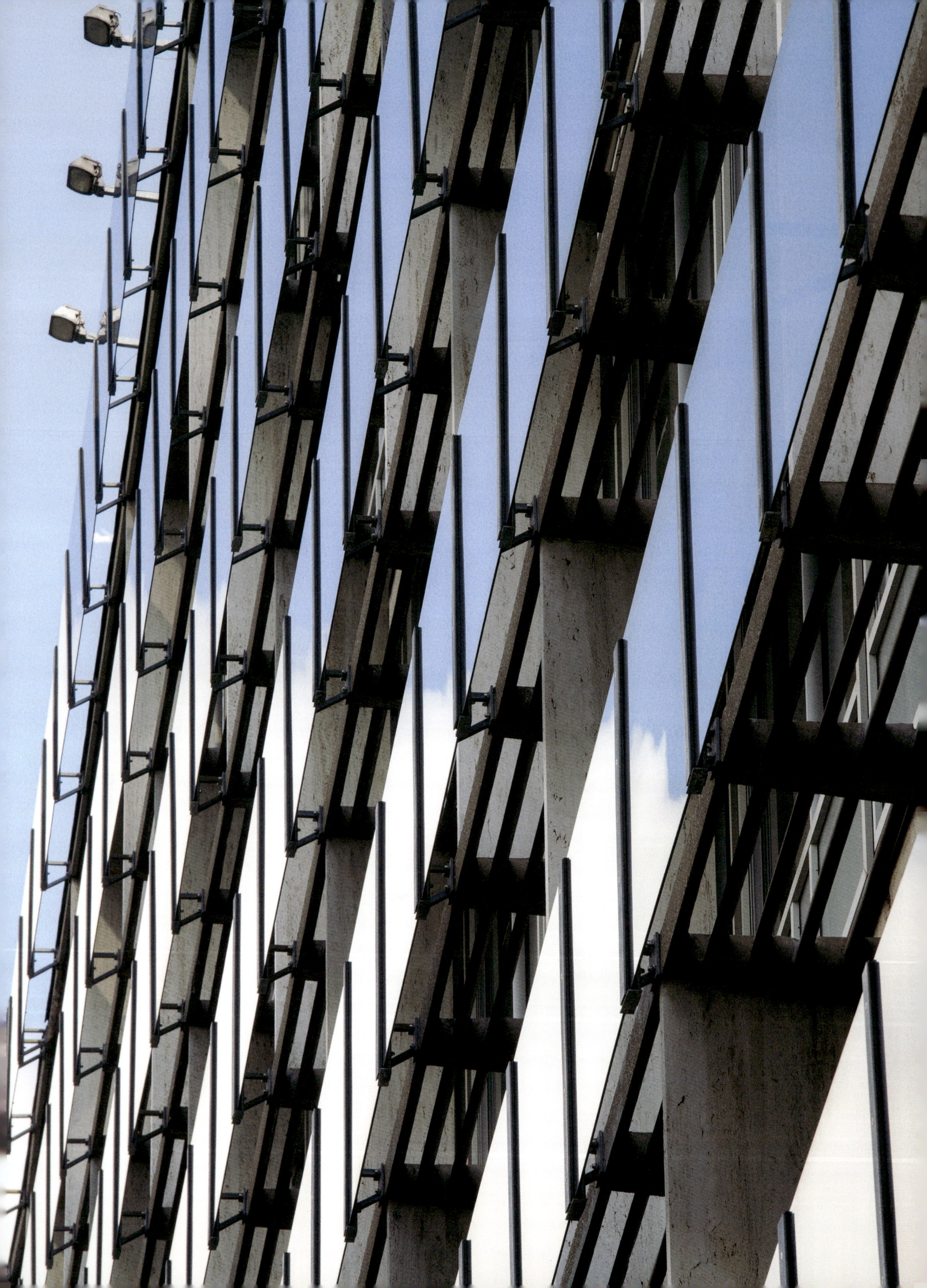

CONCLUSION

"We are a civilization which knows how to make war, but no longer knows how to make peace," wrote the Italian historian Guglielmo Ferrero (1871-1942) in 1931. Such was the monumental task taken on by UNESCO in the aftermath of World War II. Such was the mission it led over the years, without ever pursuing those utopian ideas liable to "sanction, in the name of peace, any form of [human] exploitation," to quote Claude Lefort (1924-2010), writing in the *UNESCO Courier*, 1986. At the end of the twentieth century, UNESCO Director-General Federico Mayor revived the dialogue of civilizations and revitalized the underlying principle by promoting a "culture of peace," where peace means not only the end of armed conflict but also a way of life. As current events never cease to remind us, our sovereign strength, so to speak, lies in peace. It was to achieve peace that UNESCO mustered the muscle and the will of its Member States, a goal that naturally struck a chord with the Principality of Monaco, "[a country] that is enemy to none, with an unshakeable and deep-rooted desire for peaceful understanding between peoples" (Rainier III de Monaco, 1959).

Within just a few decades, Monaco, its successive delegations and UNESCO crafted a shared narrative that served as the bedrock for mutual understanding and trust. Theirs is a relationship spanning seventy-five years and as many new beginnings.

The world of 1949 has so little in common with our present-day world that UNESCO has had to rethink the path forward at every turn. New debates around new issues arising from science and technology; how to harness artificial intelligence; and the urgent need for renewed multilateralism to protect people and the planet or face the consequences ... Every new challenge for UNESCO is a challenge to Monaco's deep-rooted convictions—a reminder to take the pulse of the world, follow its inclinations and put the means at its disposal at the service of its commitments.

Without claiming to be exhaustive, this book is an attempt to convey those inclinations and commitments. Because it is precisely in this patient accumulation of papers, programs and negotiations, these shared legacies and human endeavors, that we may grasp the embodiment of UNESCO's unwavering faith in humanity. A faith that Ivorian philosopher and novelist, Tanella Boni (1954-), one of Africa's foremost women writers, summed up beautifully in *Letters to Future Generations*: "We will have the horizon at our feet, the most beautiful foundation stone for a dwelling place. But this is just a dream, isn't it? You can, without risk of making a mistake, devote time to this dream." This is a dream for the whole of humanity but most especially the oppressed and destitute. And it is a dream shared by UNESCO that has made Africa a global priority for its 2022-2029 programs; and by the World Association of Children's Friends, presided over by H.S.H. Caroline Princess of Hanover, which supports programs to advance women's empowerment and provide schooling for children throughout the African continent. Today more than ever, as Albert Camus used to say: "truth needs to be built, like love and like intelligence; this is the stance we must take at a time when we are being choked by lies, with our backs to the wall." The stance we must take together.

OPPOSITE PAGE Detail of the facade of the UNESCO building, with its characteristic sunshades.

FOLLOWING PAGES The 1,700 m² Japanese garden at the foot of the UNESCO buildings offers a peaceful and meditative space in Paris: *The Peace Fountain* (December 1957) by Isamu Noguchi (1904-1988) completes the composition. It creates a dialogue with the works in the UNESCO Garden in Monaco.

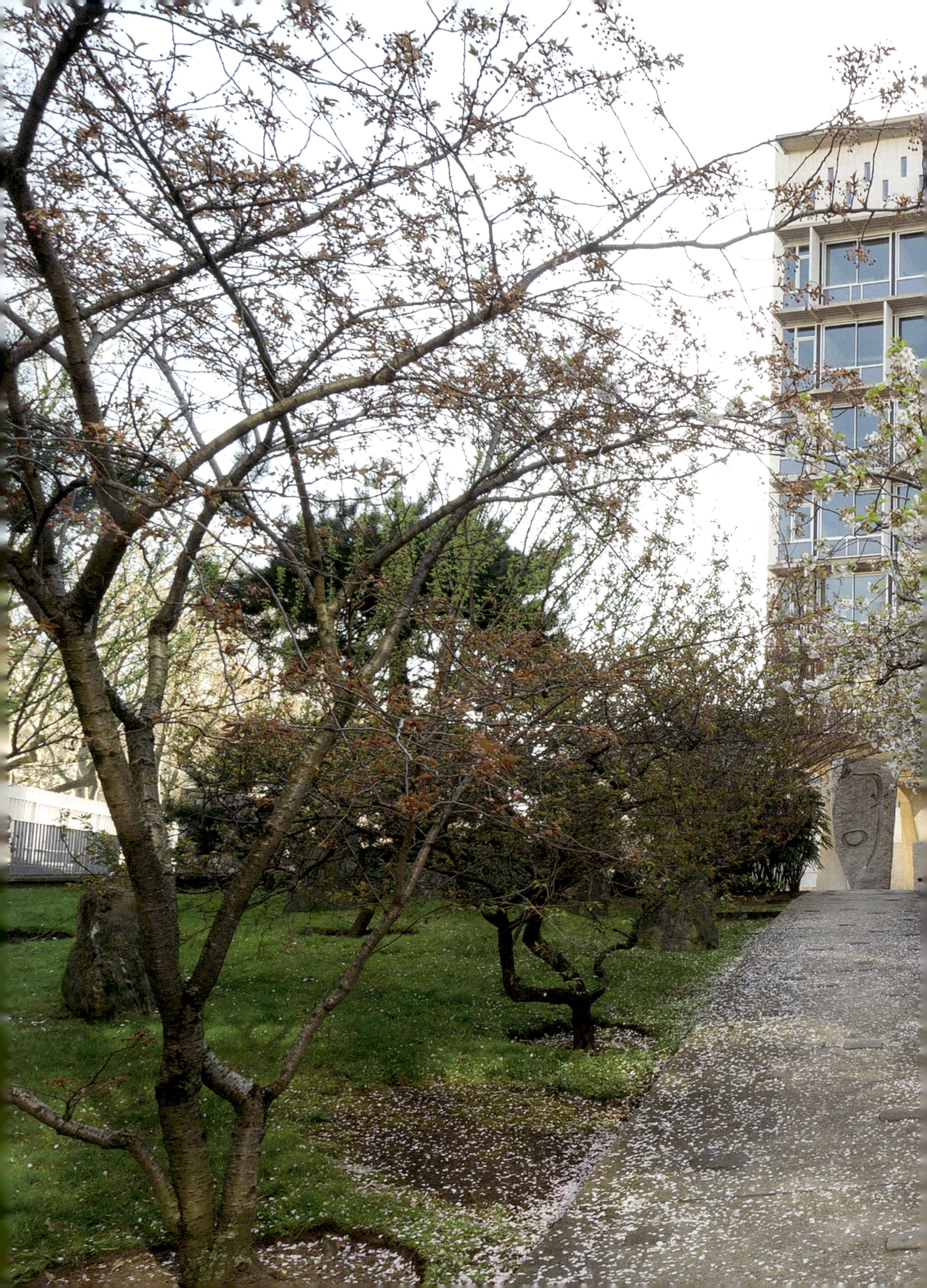

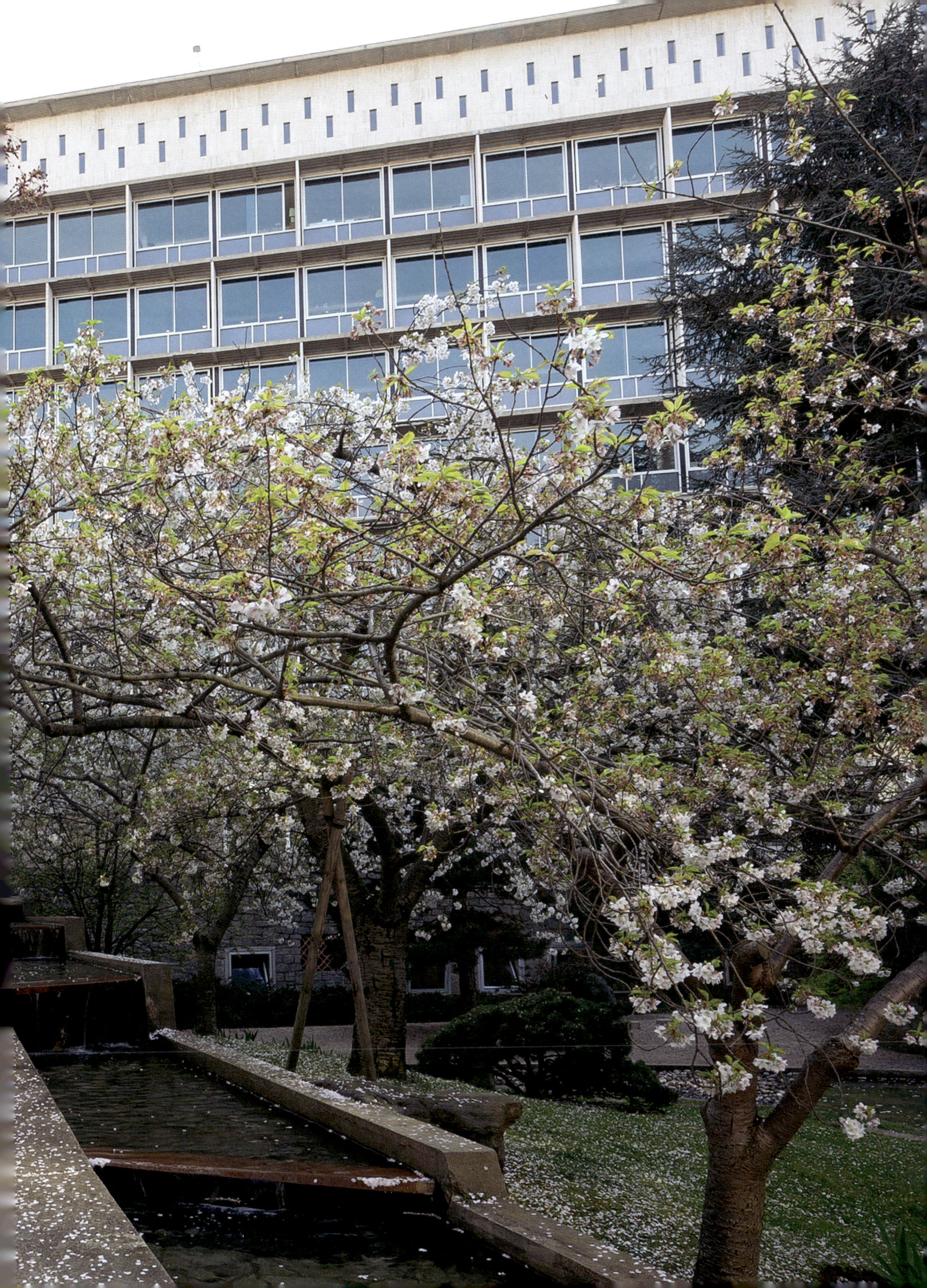

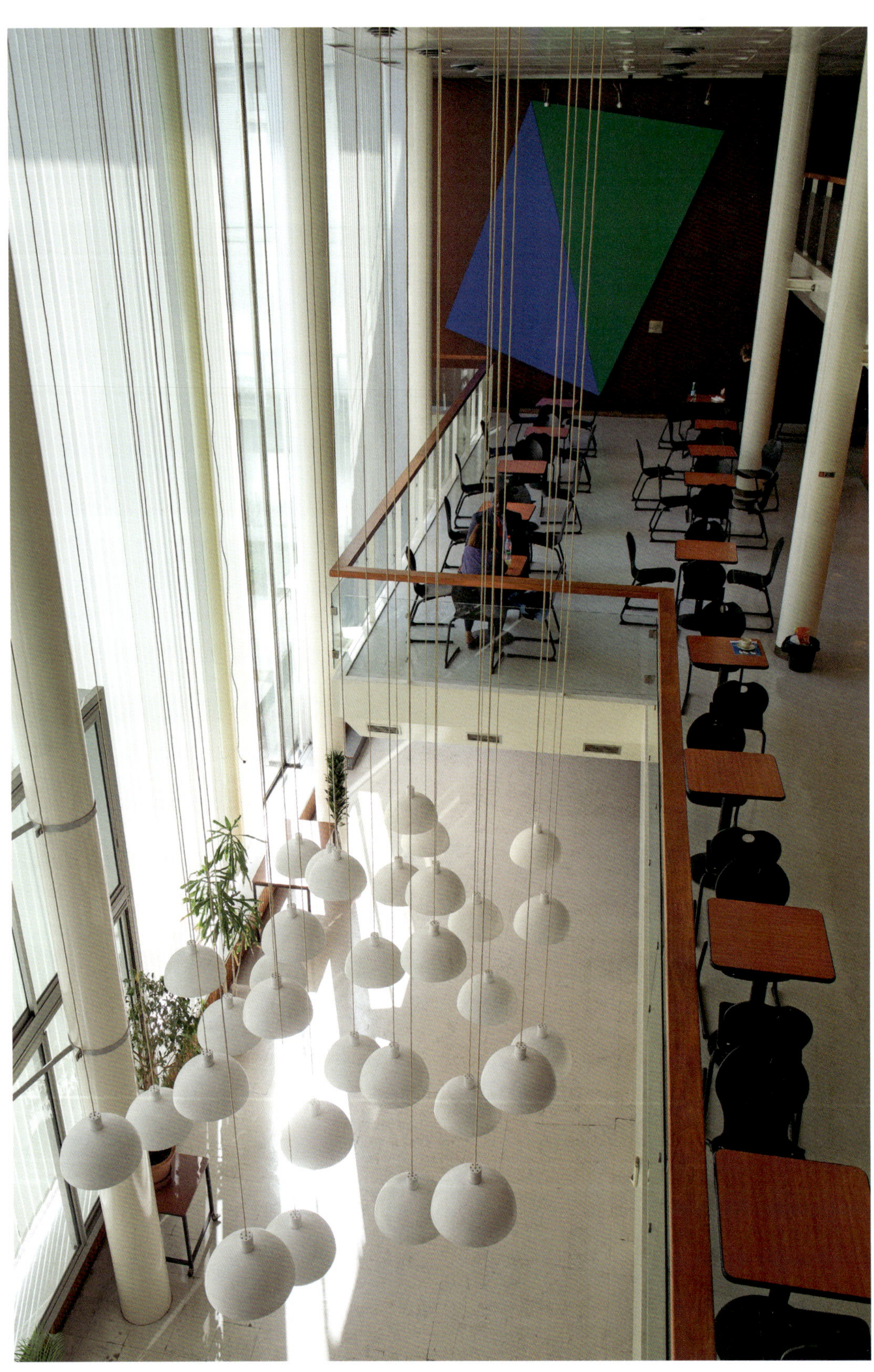

Bar and lounges in a single space on three floors, characterized by their spatial fluidity and glass walls. The suspended light fixtures and the work of abstract painter Ellsworth Kelly (1923-2015) on the back wall complete the modern feel of the space. *Blue Green*, 1969. Acrylic on canvas, two joined panels (Commissioned by UNESCO).

BIBLIOGRAPHY

«60 ans d'histoire de l'UNESCO.» *Actes du colloque international, Paris, 16-18 November 2005.* Paris: UNESCO, 2007.

«Albert Diato, céramiste et peintre.» *Catalogue de l'exposition organisée par la direction des Affaires culturelles de Monaco, Quai Antoine Ier*, Monaco, 2013.

Actes du premier congrès d'histoire de l'océanographie 1966. *Bulletin de l'Institut océanographique*, special issue 2, 1968.

Allemand, Denis, and Philippe Mondielli. *Monaco et la mer.* Nice: Gilletta, 2024.

Aron, Raymond. *Paix et guerre entre les nations.* Paris: Calmann-Lévy, 1984.

Boisson, Jacques. «Une initiative novatrice à l'Unesco.» *Le Monde diplomatique*, February 1984, p. 16.

Bon, Dominique. «Deux érudits monégasques entre Provence et Ligurie : Louis Notari (1879-1961) et Louis Canis (1891-1973).» *Provence historique, Provence terre d'érudition*, no. 266 (2019): 445-463.

Calcagno, Robert, Denis Allemand, and Bernard Fautrier. *Corail. Un trésor à préserver.* Paris: Glénat, 2020.

Carpine-Lancre, Jacqueline, and Thomas Fouilleron. «Les pionniers des sciences à Monaco.» In *Centre Scientifique de Monaco 1960-2010. 50 ans de recherche*, 10-19. Monaco: Centre Scientifique de Monaco, 2010.

Conil Lacoste, Michel. *Chronique d'un grand dessein : UNESCO, 1946-1993 ; les hommes, les événements, les accomplissements.* Paris: UNESCO, 1994.

Dans l'esprit des hommes: UNESCO, 1946-1971. Paris: UNESCO, 1972.

Delors, Jacques. *L'éducation : un trésor est caché dedans.* Paris: Odile Jacob, 1996.

Desmoulins, Christine. *Le siège de l'Unesco.* Paris: Éditions du Patrimoine, coll. "Regards," 2017.

Despret, Vinciane. "To Combat Species Decline We Need Passions of Joy." Interview by Agnès Bardon. *UNESCO Courier*, December 2022.

Droit, Roger-Pol. *Humanity in the Making: Overview of the Intellectual History of UNESCO, 1945-2005.* Paris: UNESCO 2005.

Fouilleron, Thomas. *Histoire de Monaco.* Monaco: DENJS, 2010.

Gabriel, Gabrielli. *Per Carrugi : l'histoire illustrée des rues de la Principauté de Monaco.* Nice: Taurus, 2000.

Lévi-Strauss, Claude. *Race and History.* Paris: UNESCO, 1952, 1958.

Lévi-Strauss, Claude. *A World on the Wane.* New York: Criterion Books, 1961.

Maheu, René. *La civilisation de l'universel.* Paris: Robert Laffont, 1966.

Maritain, Jacques. *L'Homme et l'État.* Paris: PUF, 1953.

Matsuura, Koïchiro. "Ethics and Science." In *Institutional Issues Involving Ethics and Justice*, developed under the auspices of UNESCO, Oxford: Eolss Publishers, 2005.

Mayor, Federico. "Culture of Peace." In *Institutional Issues Involving Ethics and Justice*, developed under the auspices of UNESCO, Oxford: Eolss Publishers, 2005.

Morin, Edgar. *Les sept savoirs nécessaires à l'éducation du futur.* Paris: UNESCO, 1999.

Mylonas, Dennis. *La genèse de l'UNESCO : la Conférence des ministres alliés de l'éducation (1942-1945).* Brussels: Bruylant, 1976.

Novaretti, Béatrice, and Dominique Bon. *Üntra nui e cun vui : deux siècles de fêtes et de traditions à Monaco.* Monaco: Mairie de Monaco, 2017.

Pol-Droit, Roger, and Federico Mayor, eds. *Letters to Future Generation.* Paris: UNESCO, 1999.

Renoliet, Jean-Jacques. *L'UNESCO oubliée : La Société des Nations et la coopération intellectuelle (1919-1946).* Paris: Publications de la Sorbonne, 1999.

Thomas, Jean. *U.N.E.S.C.O.* Paris: Gallimard, 1962.

Winter, Jay. *Dreams of Peace and Freedom. Utopian Moments in the Twentieth Century.* New Haven: Yale University Press, 2006.

Violations des droits de l'homme : quel recours, quelle résistance? Paris: UNESCO, 1983.

JEAN-PHILIPPE VINCI

is a Doctor of Philosophy and a former student of the École Pratique des Hautes Études and Sciences Po Paris, where he worked as a lecturer. He has led several missions with the Delegation of Monaco to UNESCO and the Council of Europe and has been teaching philosophy at the Lycée Albert I in Monaco since 1996. He sits on the Board of Directors of the Prince Pierre Foundation and the Management Committee of the Théâtre Princesse Grace. On July 1, 2024, he was appointed Director of the Department of Education, Youth, and Sports.

STÉPHANE LAMOTTE

is a Doctor of History who teaches at the Lycée Albert I. He is the coordinator of cultural activities at the Department of Education, Youth, and Sports, and the officer responsible for commemorative projects at the Monaco Heritage Institute. He is an associate researcher and lecturer at the CMMC of the Université Côte d'Azur, and served as the secretary of the Albert I Commemoration Committee–2022. He is also the secretary-general of the Alliance Française de Monaco and a member of the editorial committee of the *Annales Monégasques*.

ACKNOWLEDGMENTS

Our gratitude goes first to H.S.H. Prince Albert II and H.R.H. Princess Caroline of Hanover. We also extend our thanks to UNESCO Director-General Audrey Azoulay for her contribution to the prefaces of this book.

We sincerely thank H.E. Anne-Marie Boisbouvier for her trust and support, and warmly thank the ambassadors representing the Principality at important moments in UNESCO's history: H.E. Yvette Lambi-Berti, H.E. Jacques Boisson, and H.E. Jean Pastorelli for their contributions to the editorial committee and their testimonies.

Special thanks to H.E. Jacques Boisson, who received us at his home and shared his documentation and experience as an international official of the Organization. We also thank Dominique Notari for kindly sharing her memories with us.

Thanks to Sophie Vatrican, Counselor at the Princely Cabinet, and to Thomas Fouilleron, Director of the Archives and Library of the Princely Palace, who encouraged this project.

Thanks to the managers of the various archives and heritage funds who allowed us access to the documents presented here. First and foremost, thanks to Eng Sengsavang at the UNESCO archives in Paris, for her kind support in assisting with research and document reproduction. Thanks also to Michaël Bloche (Mission de Préfiguration des Archives Nationales) and Virginie Raimbert (Head of Department at SCADA). Thanks to Vincent Vatrican (Director of the Audiovisual Institute of Monaco), Béatrice Novaretti (Media Library Curator), Alain Bottaro (Regional Fund), and Céline Enrici (Archives of the DREC).

Thanks to Jean-Charles Curau for his support as Secretary-General of the Prince Pierre Foundation and President of SOGEDA.

Thanks to Valérie Bruell-Melchior, Ambassador of Monaco to France; Robert Calcagno, Chief Executive Officer of the Oceanographic Museum; Françoise Gamerdinger, Director of Cultural Affairs; and Olivier Wenden, Vice-President of the Prince Albert II Foundation.

We wish to thank everyone who shared their expertise or documentation: Denis Allemand, Élisabeth Baltzinger, Dominique Bon, Michaël Bloche, Béatrice Cellario, Milène Escarras, Thomas Fouilleron, Jérôme Froissart, Hélène Onoforo Sanaia, Céline Vacquier, Elena Rossoni-Notter, Marie-Aimée Tirole, Geneviève Vatrican, and Vincent Vatrican.

We also thank our collaborators: Damien MacDonald, who enriched the book with his drawings and added the desired touch of modernity, and Jean-Baptiste Leroux for his photographs in Paris, at UNESCO headquarters, and in Monaco.

Thanks to the members of Monaco's delegation to UNESCO: Monique Atangana, Alexandra Bevilacqua, Séverine Dusaintpère (Deputy Permanent Delegate), and Agatha Korczak (First Secretary).

Additional thanks to Christel Alix, Xavier Archimbault, Fabrice Blanchi, Thomas Blanchy, Julien Burle, Pierre Cellario, David Coradini, Rémi Garoscio, Pascal Granero, Frederika Giorcelli, Pierre-Antoine Gérard, Xavier Prache, Élodie Roger-Clément, Christian Roti, and Marie Ygonin.

Thank you to Pauline Dubuisson, Clara Kouyoumdjian, Virginie Mahieux, and Corinne Schmidt of Éditions de La Martinière for their assistance in the design work, and to Flo Brutton for the English translation.

And we must not forget our close friends and family who accompanied us throughout this project—you know who you are.

TRANSLATION OF THE ILLUSTRATIONS FEATURED ON PAGES 22 AND 28

MONACO'S ACCESSION TO UNESCO AFFIRMATION AND RECOGNITION

Monaco's admission to UNESCO happened over the course of the first four General Conferences. The Organization was born in November 1945, in London, with the adoption of the UNESCO Constitution.

The first UNESCO General Conference took place in November 1946, at the Sorbonne in Paris, where Julian Huxley was elected Director-General. In attendance as a guest of the French delegation was philosophy student René Bocca who wrote a report declaring the Principality's interest in joining UNESCO.

Monaco submitted its candidature in anticipation of the second General Conference, to be held in November–December, 1947. As it turned out, this did not leave enough time to examine the dossier and set up the voting procedure.

The vote in Monaco's favor came exactly a year later, at the third General Conference in Beirut. James Torres Bodet, UNESCO's new Director-General, sent the Princely Government a telegram of congratulations.

Monaco officially joined UNESCO on July 6, 1949, as Prince Rainier ascended the throne. In November that year, it attended its first meeting as a full-fledged UNESCO member: the UNESCO General Conference, fourth session, held in Paris.

Jacques Rueff, Minister of State, was head of the Monaco delegation in 1949 and 1950, followed in 1951 by Prince Pierre, who also presided over the newly established National Commission.

SHARED PRINCIPLES OF EDUCATION, SCIENCE, CULTURE AND INFORMATION

The protection and development of children lies at the heart of the commitments undertaken by H.S.H. the Princess of Hanover and the association she chairs, AMADE, most notably in Africa, in line with UNESCO's development and educational policies.

The ocean occupies a central place in our lives. Yet the ocean depths remain largely unexplored. Discovering the ocean, harnessing its power in favor of the climate and biodiversity, is a vocal priority for the Princes of Monaco and UNESCO alike.

Theater, the art of speech, protects cultures, and brings them together, helping to build a common heritage through shared encounters. Monaco has voiced its enthusiasm openly ever since it first trod the boards at UNESCO.

ADDITIONAL CAPTIONS

COVER Prince Rainier, Princess Grace and Vittorino Veronese, Director-General, at UNESCO, based on a photograph of the princely couple's visit on October 22, 1959.

PAGES 4-5 The Y-shaped UNESCO main building, which houses the Secretariat. In the foreground are the flags of the member states, including the red and white flag of Monaco in the center, with *The Symbolic Globe* in the background.

PAGES 6-7 *The Symbolic Globe*, a metal structure by Danish engineer Erik Reitzel (1941-2012). Created in 1995, first in Copenhagen for the UN summit for social development, then installed at UNESCO, the globe evokes the logo of the United Nations and symbolizes UNESCO's aspirations to promote cooperation.

PAGES 8-9 Concrete canopy in the shape of a cornette wimple, designed by Italian engineer Pier Luigi Nervi (1891-1979) to cover the entrance to the secretariat building.

PAGES 10-11 View of the Plenary Hall. Supported by two sloping walls and six central posts, the roof is formed of twelve juxtaposed V-shaped beams.

FOLLOWING PAGES Like the Eiffel Tower in the 19th century, which can be seen from inside the UNESCO building, and later the Pompidou Center, the plans for this modern palace of peace were highly contested at the time.

CREDITS

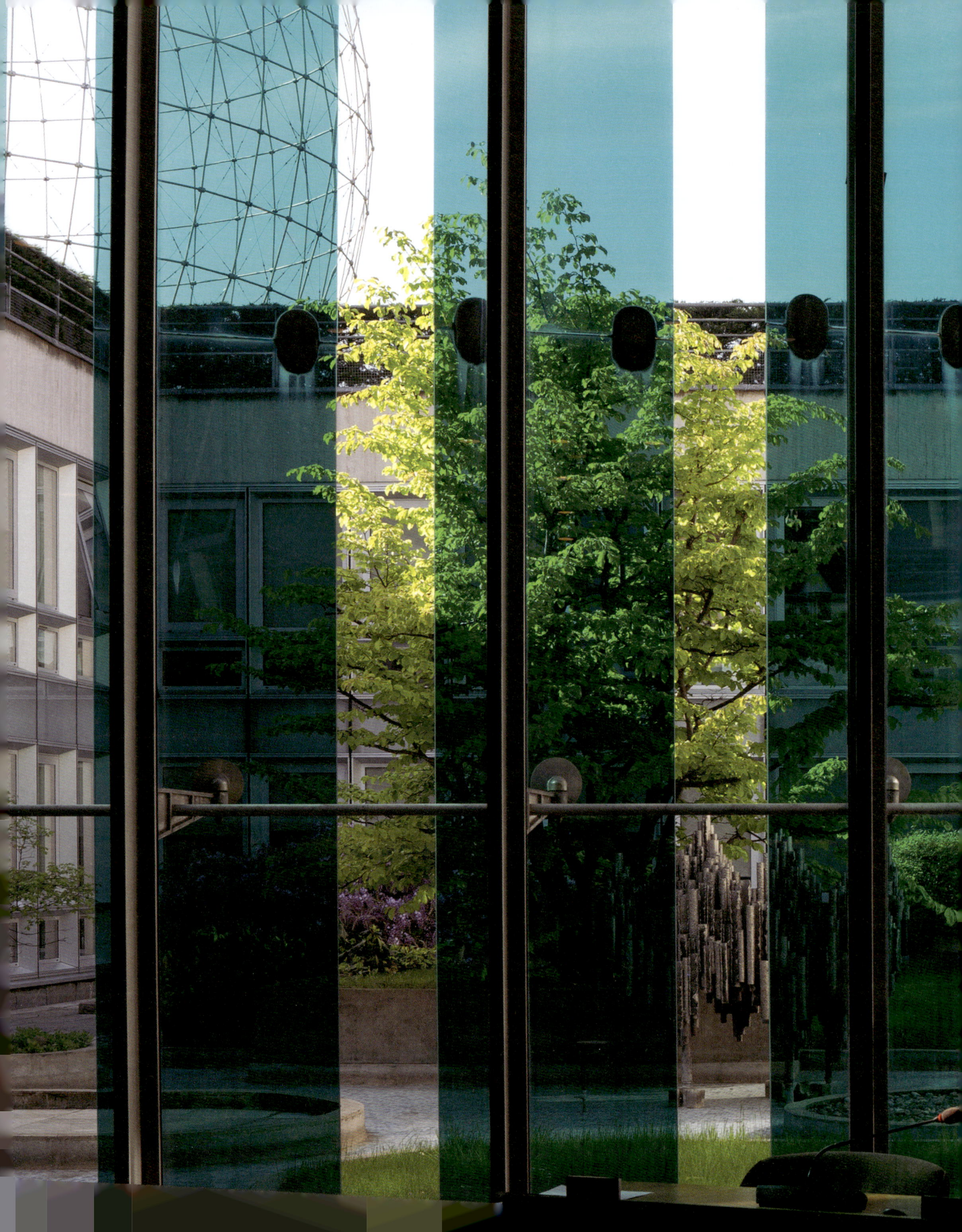

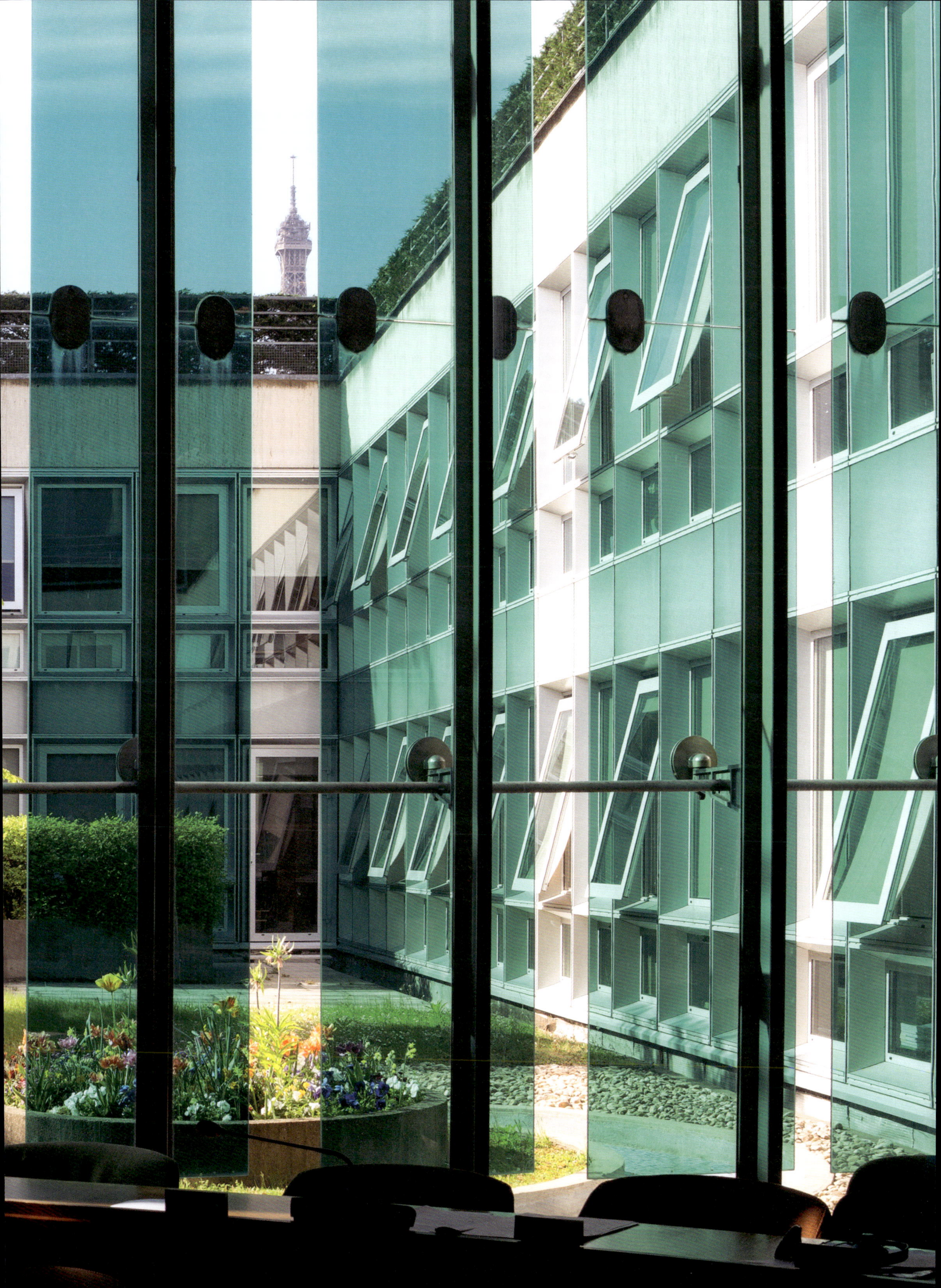

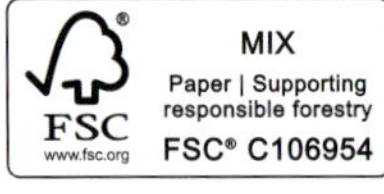

Editorial: Virginie Mahieux
and Pauline Dubuisson
assisted by Clara Kouyoumdjian

Graphic design: Élisabeth Welter

Editorial Partnership: Corinne Schmidt

Illustrations: Damien MacDonald (front and back cover, pages 22, 82, 83, 85, 86, 87, 88, 137, 149, 164, 165 and 166)

Translation from French: Florence Brutton (introduction, chapters 1 to 3) and Acolad (captions, chapter 4)

Proofreading: Acolad

10 9 8 7 6 5 4 3 2 1 Abrams books are available at special discounts when purchased in quantity for premiums and promotions as well as fundraising or educational use. Special editions can also be created to specification.

For details, contact specialsales@abramsbooks.com or the address below.

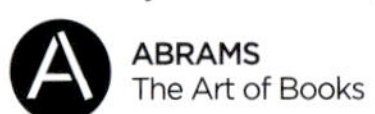

Photoengraving: Quadrilaser

Printed and bound in Slovenia
in September 2024
Legal deposit: November 2024

ISBN: 979-1-4197-8079-0

195 Broadway
New York, NY 10007
abramsbooks.com

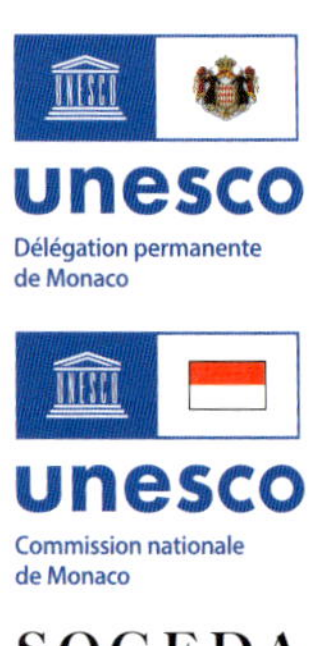